Natural Resource Conservation:

AN ECOLOGICAL APPROACH

Oliver S. Owen   Department of Biology,
Wisconsin State University, Eau Claire

THE MACMILLAN COMPANY, NEW YORK
COLLIER-MACMILLAN LIMITED, LONDON

The Macmillan Company
866 Third Avenue, New York, New York 10022

Collier-Macmillan Canada, Ltd., Toronto, Ontario

Library of Congress catalog card number: 74-119125

Second Printing, 1971

Natural Resource Conservation:

AN ECOLOGICAL APPROACH

Preface

While a member of the biological sciences staff of the General College, University of Minnesota, I taught natural resource conservation to general education classes with an aggregate annual enrollment of over 350 students. This course was not designed for students specializing in conservation or biology, but served as a cultural enrichment course for students of other disciplines. The major objectives of the course were (1) to develop an appreciation of the role natural resources have played in promoting our vitality and economic well-being, (2) to provide insights into the techniques and policies by which these resources can be intelligently managed and utilized, and (3) to foster a sense of the urgency for halting resource abuse and the deterioration of environmental quality. In conjunction with this course, I searched for a suitable text which would emphasize the biological (ecological) approach, have single authorship so as to ensure integration around a central theme, and be written in an informal yet stimulating style. Such a book was difficult to find. After struggling with several unsatisfactory texts, I finally decided to write a book myself.

I am indebted to a host of colleagues, students, and friends who have assisted in many diverse capacities. It will be difficult to include them all in my acknowledgments. I am deeply grateful to those professors who gave generously of their valuable time to read the manuscript critically, especially to Dr. Douglas G. Alexander, Chico State College; Dr. Richard J. Hartesveldt, San Jose State College; Dr. P. Victor Peterson, Jr., California State College at Hayward; and Dr. C. David Vanicek, Sacramento State College. I also wish to thank Dr. Hartesveldt for permission to employ his resource classification scheme.

My brother, Earl W. Owen, has been a continuous source of advice, for which I am deeply appreciative. Dr. Arnold Bakken, Dr. Terry Balding, and Dr. John Gerberich, Department of Biology, Wisconsin State University–Eau Claire, assisted the author. I wish to thank Judith A. Kneer for her diligence and competence in typing the major part of the manuscript; thanks are also due Gerald B. Kneer for much industrious proofreading. Mrs. Rodney G. Hanson also served as manuscript typist.

Photographs were secured from several sources, including the U.S. Department of Agriculture, the U.S. Bureau of Reclamation, the U.S. Fish and Wildlife Service, the U.S. Bureau of Commercial Fisheries, the U.S. Public Health Service, the Wisconsin State Historical Society, the Wisconsin Department of Natural Resources, and the conservation departments of California, New York, and several other states. I am grateful to the several students of the Art Department of WSU–Eau Claire for aiding in the preparation of illustrations. I have appreciated the patience of Mr. William Eastman and Mr. Peter O'Brien of The Macmillan Company's editorial staff with my numerous shortcomings in manuscript preparation.

I shall always be indebted to my former teacher, Aldo Leopold, late Professor of Game Management and Wildlife Ecology at the University of Wisconsin; not only was he a pioneer in the application of ecological principles to the management of game populations, but he expounded a philosophy of land ethics which still serves as a guidepost for man's delicate relationships with his environment.

Finally, and above all, I wish to thank my wife, Carol; without her constant encouragement, patience, and sympathetic understanding during five years of book "widowhood," even my earliest writing attempts would have been abortive.

O. S. O.

Dedication

To my wife,
Carol
and our children
Tom, Tim, and Stephanie

May they never be denied the privilege
of hiking through a forest wilderness,
of stalking deer, or listening to the
dusk-chant of a whippoorwill.

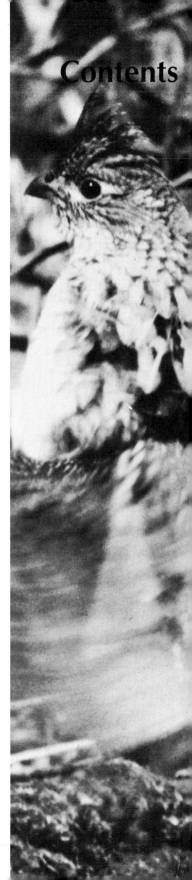

Contents

Introduction

America in Crisis

America is on the sharp edge of crisis. She is degrading her natural environment. She prides herself on conquering outer space, yet after two centuries she still does not know how to manage her "inner" space here on earth. This environmental dilemma is the result of four major factors: rapid population increase, pollution, excessive consumption of resources, and the gradual deterioration of a land ethic.

Population Increase. Demographers inform us that the population of the United States will surge upward from the present 200 million of 1970 to 245 million by 1980 and 330 million by 2000. This is equivalent to a compound interest rate of 1.5 per cent per year. The population increase clouds the entire environmental picture and, in a sense, is the underlying cause of our present crisis.

Unless America's population surge is restrained within the very near future, even the most soundly conceived and efficiently implemented conservation practices will be to no avail. An increase in people means an increase in all types of environmental pollution. It means accelerated depletion of natural resources, most of which are already in short

1

supply or of deteriorating quality. It means that greater numbers of people, living in overcrowded conditions, will make increasing demands on wilderness and recreation areas to "get away from it all." With each upward surge of human population, there will be a corresponding surge in the urgency and complexity of our conservation task. As Robert Heilbroner writes, ". . . the most fearsome reality of all [is] a population that is still increasing like an uncontrollable cancer on the surface of the globe. I know of no more sobering statistic in this regard than that between [1970] and 1980 the number of women in the most fertile age brackets, eighteen to thirty-two, will double."

Pollution. America, the world's most affluent nation, has also become the most effluent. We are degrading our environment with an ever-increasing variety and volume of contaminants. We are polluting lakes and streams with raw sewage, industrial wastes, radioactive materials, heat, detergents, agricultural fertilizers, and pesticides. We are releasing so many toxic materials into our immediate habitat that Rachel Carson, celebrated author of *Silent Spring,* has identified our era as the "Age of Poisons" (2). Our uncontrolled and indiscriminate use of pesticides has contaminated the entire food chain, so that all animals, including man, are affected. For example, you, the reader, have perhaps 7 parts per million of DDT in your tissues this very moment. The long-term effects of such concentrations on humans are unknown. However, laboratory studies on experimental animals have shown that a concentration of 7 parts per million of DDT may have deleterious effects on heart and liver functions, and higher concentrations may interfere with reproductive processes, generate harmful mutations, and induce cancers. Many gases—including carbon monoxide, carbon dioxide, sulfur dioxide, nitrous oxide, and benzopyrenes—most of which are known to cause or contribute to respiratory ailments, are constantly being spewed into the atmosphere.

Americans have become the litter champions of the world. Many tourists seeking refuge from urban ugliness find beer cans on Mount Rainier and banana peels along the Appalachian Trail. The old farm of Robert Frost, memorialized in his poem "West-running Brook," is now buried under rusting automobiles (8).

Once quiet urban neighborhoods have succumbed to a noise barrage mounted by an ever-proliferating number of motor bikes, automobiles, air hammers, trucks, and so on.

Consumption of Materials. As early as 1952 the President's Materials Policy Commission noted that although the United

States had only 10 per cent of the population of the non-Communist world, it consumed 50 per cent of the total non-Communist consumption in raw materials (3). Furthermore, during the brief period since World War I (1918), Americans have consumed more of most materials than was consumed by all mankind in his previous history on earth. In his *Resources and the American Dream,* Samuel H. Ordway has suggested that many demands made on resources by the American consumer are excessive and do not contribute to human happiness in any substantial way (3). Americans are the most overfed, overhoused, overclothed, overmobilized, and overentertained people on earth. Our tremendous consumption of cars, summer homes, color television sets, dishwashers, air conditioners, golf carts, motorized lawn mowers, swimming pools, speed boats, water skis, and so on, certainly does not stem from need. We drive heavier and bigger automobiles than mere transportation requires. For the sake of a quick "pickup" we use high-octane gasoline and spew thousands of tons of irreplaceable lead into the atmosphere. As Harvard's John Galbraith states, "part of our food production . . . contributes not to nutrition but obesity, part of our tobacco contributes not to comfort but to carcinoma . . . part of our clothing . . . is designed not to cover nakedness but to suggest it" (3).

Figure 1–1   As a result of the expanding population, even our wilderness is becoming defiled. Note the debris removed from Blue Star Spring, Yellowstone National Park.

The high rate of consumption is, at least in part, a direct response of the people to an artificial stimulus developed with consummate skill by the want-creating industry—advertising—which is a multibillion-dollar business. On the other hand if Americans should suddenly decrease consumption of goods, the result would be economic chaos. However, there is no doubt that the high consumer demands of our affluent society have adversely affected the quality of our environment, either by using scarce resources unwisely or by increasing pollution.

It is highly questionable whether the gross national product or the sales volume of motor cars or color television sets is a valid measure of human happiness in America. In our hectic scramble for the good life, most of us have lost it. Perhaps we should heed the counsel given by Stewart Udall in *The Quiet Crisis,* "If you want inner peace, find it in solitude, not speed, and if you would find yourself, look to the land from which you came and to which you go" (8).

Deterioration of Our Land Ethic. It is a curious paradox that at the same time that we have built up our standard of living we have permitted our standard of environment to deteriorate. As Aldo Leopold, eloquent spokesman for environmental quality, states in *Sand County Almanac,* "We abuse land because we regard it as a commodity belonging to us. When we see land as a community to which we belong, we may begin to use it with love and respect" (6). In 1870 three fourths of all Americans were either farmers or members of small rural communities. They had a daily acquaintance with the age-old interrelatedness of all aspects of the environment and the living things it supports. Today, however, most Americans are urban dwellers; they are·sealed off from the land of their origin by their own constructions. There are many urbanites today who have never breathed the fragrance of spring-plowed earth, heard the drumming of a grouse, or seen the white water of rushing rapids. They have severed their connection with the land. This separation has eroded urban man's respect for the land, if it has not actually made him contemptuous of it. His aesthetic sense has degenerated to the point where he prefers the roar of a hot-rod to the call of a thrush.

History of the Conservation Movement

From time to time, early in our nation's history, men with vision like George Washington, Thomas Jefferson, Patrick Henry, Jared Elliot, and George Perkins Marsh would express their concern over resource depletion and despoliation. The greatest advances in conservation, however, have been made in this century. They have occurred in three "waves"—the first (1900–1910) under the dynamic and forceful leadership of Theodore Roosevelt and Gifford Pinchot, the second (1930's) under the aegis of Franklin D. Roosevelt, the third wave, which is yet cresting, was spearheaded by the late John F. Kennedy and has persisted under the administrations of Lyndon B. Johnson and Richard M. Nixon.

The First Wave. President Theodore Roosevelt's decision to call the White House Conference of 1908 was greatly influenced by a number of important events in the several preceding decades: the enactment of several laws which regulated the manner in which the public lands (public domain) should be disposed of (including various mining laws and the Homestead Act of 1862); the deep concern of the American Association for the Advancement of Science over the exploitation and depletion of timber in the Great Lakes states, a concern which was formally presented to Congress in 1870 and again in 1890; a study of arid lands by Major J. W. Powell in the 1870's which was instrumental in the inclusion of an irrigation section in the U.S. Geological Survey; a 1907 report by the Inland Waterways Commission, headed by Gifford Pinchot, which pointed out that the use and control of water would have an impact on other resources, such as timber, soil, wildlife, and minerals (1). In addition to these factors, there was growing apprehension in 1908 that resource mismanagement might have tragic future consequences if America's rapidly growing population reached the 200 million projected for 1950.

Invited to the White House Conference on Natural Resources were governors, congressional leaders, scientists, informed sportsmen, and foreign experts. The meeting was unique in American history. As a result of the conference a fifty-man National Conservation Commission was formed composed of scientists, statesmen, and businessmen, under the inspirational leadership of Gifford Pinchot. This commission even-

Figure 1–2 President Theodore Roosevelt, outdoorsman, big-game hunter, and conservationist, at Yosemite National Park. [U.S. Department of Agriculture]

tually completed the nation's first comprehensive natural resource inventory. The White House Conference also indirectly resulted in the formation of forty-one state conservation agencies (many of which are vigorous today) by concerned governors (1, 4).

President Roosevelt employed the natural resource inventory as a basis for withdrawing 200 million acres of public lands from further settlement and entry (making it impossible for private interests to acquire them), with an eye to converting them into permanent public "reserves." Under Roosevelt 148 million acres were added to the National Forests and 180 million acres of coal lands in the western states and Alaska and 5 million acres of phosphate-bearing lands were withdrawn from the public domain. In addition, 1.5 million acres of watershed were reserved to ensure that future development of their water-power potential would be in the public interest (1).

The Second Wave. Franklin D. Roosevelt is a notable example of the right man in the right place at the right time. When F.D.R. assumed office there was urgent need for an imaginative program in job creation (4). Franklin Roosevelt's administration not only created employment, but in the process resolved numerous resource problems as well.

Under the Public Works Administration (PWA), created in 1933, many natural resource development programs were completed with the aid of such federal agencies as the Bureau of Reclamation and the Corps of Engineers. One program initiated by the PWA in 1934 was the Prairie States Forestry Project. Its goal was the establishment of shelterbelts of trees and shrubs along the 100th meridian from the Texan Panhandle to the Canadian border of North Dakota. This project did much to eliminate the destructive effects of wind (1).

The National Resources Board, appointed by F.D.R., completed the nation's second comprehensive natural resource inventory in 1934. In its report not only did the board cite resource problems, but it described proper remedial measures. Through the efforts of this agency, as well as those of the Natural Resource Committee, which superseded it in 1935, there developed a gradual acceptance of the need to plan for future resource requirements on the basis of current resources. Most of the states also established resource planning agencies as a result of the impetus provided by the National Resources Committee.

The Civilian Conservation Corps (CCC), which functioned from 1933 to 1949, profitably engaged almost 2.5 million young men. Much of its work involved conservation projects. At its peak the Corps was organized into 2,652 camps, each with a 200-man capacity, many located in national parks and forests. The forest workers constructed fire lanes, removed fire hazards, fought forest fires, fought pests, and planted millions of trees. The park workers constructed bridges, improved access roads, and built nature trails. In addition, the Corps made lake and stream improvements and participated in flood-control projects, not only on federal lands but even on areas under county or state jurisdiction. The CCC program made outstanding contributions to the conservation of the human resource, for it resulted not only in improved health, skills, and self-respect of the enrollees, but also in decreased delinquency (1, 4).

In 1933 Roosevelt established the Soil Erosion Service in the Department of the Interior. It was superseded in 1935 by the Soil Conservation Service within the Department of Agriculture. The time was ripe for such action. The frequent occurrence of "black blizzards" over the Dust Bowl of the Great Plains bore eloquent testimony of the condition of our soils. Not only has the SCS conducted soil conservation demonstrations to show farmers the techniques and importance of erosion control, but it has been actively engaged in basic research (4).

The establishment of the TVA in 1933 was a bold experiment, unique in conservation history, to integrate the resource development (water, soils, forests, wildlife) of an entire river basin. Although highly controversial, it has received international acclaim, and has served as a model for similar projects in India and other foreign countries (4).

In 1936 President Roosevelt convened the first North American Wildlife and Resources Conference. Attended by specialists in wildlife management, interested sportsmen, and government officials, it had as its objectives (1) a survey of the wildlife resource, (2) a statement of conservation problems, and (3) techniques and policies by means of which these problems might be resolved. This conference convenes annually to this day.

Through the Wildlife Restoration Act of 1937 the states were given financial assistance in the acquisition and development of suitable lands (grassland for prairie chickens, marshland for waterfowl, and so on) for wildlife.

During World War II and the Korean War all the nation's attention and energies were focused on military victory, even at the cost of resource depletion. In the early 1950's the nation enjoyed unprecedented prosperity. It was exceedingly difficult for an affluent society to generate much enthusiasm for conservation, despite continued resource despoliation. To the man on the street, and to many congressmen, the questions of water and air pollution, soil erosion, pesticides, threatened extinction of wildlife and forest mismanagement lacked immediacy. Anyway, America's "scientific and technological know-how," which had swept her to victory on the world's battlefields, would neatly and effectively provide the remedies.

The Third Wave. The third wave of the conservation effort was initiated by the brilliant leadership of John F. Kennedy, who assumed the Presidency in 1961. Kennedy convened a White House Conference in 1962 which was attended by 500 of the nation's leading conservationists. The status of America's resources was reviewed. The main features of Kennedy's natural resource program included preservation of wilderness areas, development of marine resources, reservation of remaining shorelines for public use, expansion of outdoor recreation opportunities, enhancement of freshwater supplies by desalinization, aid to metropolitan areas in solving space problems, formulation of plans for the development of the water resources of all river basins, vigorous action against all forms of pollution, encouragement of scientists and technologists to develop suitable substitutes for resource in short supply, and organization of the Youth Conservation Corps to provide the manpower required to implement much of his program (1).

The impetus given to the conservation movement by Kennedy was sustained after his assassination by his successor, Lyndon B. Johnson. During February of 1965, President Johnson stressed to Congress the urgency of preventing further environmental deterioration and restoring the environment as much as possible to its original state. Many of the bills signed by Johnson were concerned with the upgrading of human resources, control of air and water pollution, preservation of wilderness areas, and environmental beautification. The development of outdoor recreation opportunities for a burgeoning population with unparalleled mobility, leisure, and economic status was also an immediate concern. Conservation's cause was advanced by the following acts, many of which will be discussed in detail in later chapters:

1. *Pollution control*
   - 1964   Clean Air Act
   - 1965   Water Quality Act
   - 1965   Dingell-Newberger Bill
     (supporting pesticide research)
   - 1966   Water Pollution Control Act
   - 1966   Clean Water Restoration Act
   - 1967   Air Quality Act
2. *Parks, recreation, and wilderness areas*
   - 1964   National Wilderness Act

1964 Land and Water Conservation Fund Act
1965 National Recreation Areas Bill
1965 Legislation promoting scenic highways
1965 Legislation which compensated farmers for retiring land for recreational use
1966 Bills establishing:
　　　Cape Lookout (N.C.) National Seashore
　　　Indiana Dunes National Lakeshore
　　　Pictured Rocks (Mich.) National Lakeshore
　　　Guadalupe (Texas) National Park
　　　Bighorn Canyon (Mont. and Wy.) National Recreation area
1966 Legislation curbing construction of highways which would defile scenic areas
1968 Bills establishing:
　　　Redwood (Calif.) National Park
　　　North Cascades (Wash.) National Park
　　　Biscayne (Fla.) National Monument
　　　National Trails System
1968 Wild and Scenic Rivers Act
1968 Added Great Swamp (N.J.) to the National Wilderness Preservation system
3. *Human resources*
1964 Anti-poverty Act (This act provided for a Job Corps composed of indigent young people reminiscent of FDR's CCC, many of the activities being conservation-oriented.)

When President Richard M. Nixon succeeded Johnson in 1969, he appointed Alaska's Walter Hickel as Secretary of the Interior. His appointment was initially regarded with skepticism by many natural resource specialists. However, Hickel quickly allayed doubt as to his qualifications by his forthright and effective handling of the massive oil pollution debacle off the California coast, which had been caused by faulty drilling operations. Conservationists in attendance at the 1969 North American Wildlife and Natural Resources Conference were further heartened upon hearing Hickel's pronouncement that the "goal of achieving environmental quality . . . is worthy of being the *principal* objective of the *new* Department of the Interior."

Conservation Defined

The word *conservation* is derived from two Latin words—*con,* meaning "together," and *servare,* meaning to "keep" or "guard." Literally, therefore, conservation means "to keep together." The word was coined by Gifford Pinchot shortly after the White House Conference of 1908 (7). He conceived of the term after noting the title of "conservares" given to British officials entrusted with the administration and protection of natural resources in India. Professor Harold M. Rose of the University of Wisconsin at Milwaukee defines conservation as "the optimum allocation of natural, human, and cultural resources in the scheme of national development, whereby maximum economic and social security will be assured" (7). In a special message to Congress in 1962 President John F. Kennedy interpreted conservation as "the wise use of our natural environment: it is, in the final analysis, the highest form of national thrift—the prevention of waste and despoilment while preserving, improving and renewing the quality and usefulness of all our resources."

Natural Resource Classification

Any portion of our natural environment—such as soil, water, rangeland, forest, wildlife, minerals, or human populations—that man can utilize to promote his welfare may be identified as a *natural resource.* Natural resources vary greatly in quantity, mutability, and reusability. Because the best type of management for a given resource depends upon these characteristics, the following classification scheme is presented:

I. *Inexhaustible*
  A. *Immutable.* Seemingly incapable of much adverse change through man's activities.
    1. *Atomic energy.* Vast quantities of fissionable materials available in granitic rocks.
    2. *Wind power.* The result of climatic conditions.
    3. *Precipitation.* An unlimited supply. Man, however, will very likely alter the distribution pattern in the future. Weather modification.
    4. *Water power of tides.* Resulting from sun–moon–earth relationships.
  B. *Misusable.* Little danger of complete exhaustion, but when improperly used their resource quality may be impaired.
    1. *Solar power.* The total amount received by growing plants has been reduced by air pollution caused by man.
    2. *Atmosphere.* Local and world-wide pollution because of smoke, exhaust fumes, nuclear fall-out, and so on.
    3. *Waters of oceans, lakes, and streams.* All currently being polluted at increasing rates as a result of human activity.
    4. *Water power of flowing streams.* The reaction of water to gravity.

5. *Scenery in its broadest sense.* Aesthetic values subject to impairment by human activities. Examples: Mt. Rainier, Blue Ridge Mountains, Oregon and Maine coastlines, Grand Canyon.

II. *Exhaustible*

A. *Maintainable.* Those resources in which permanency is dependent upon method of use by man.

1. *Renewable.* The living (biotic) or dynamic resources whose perpetual harvest is dependent upon proper planning and management by man. Improper use results in impairment or exhaustion with adverse socioeconomic consequences for man.

a. *Water in place.* The quantity and quality of water in specific places of use: streams, lakes, subterranean sources.

b. *Soil fertility.* The ability of soil to produce plant substance desirable to man. Renewing soil fertility takes time and money.

c. *Products of the land.* Those resources grown in or dependent on the soil.

(1) *Agricultural products.* Vegetables, grains, fruits, fibers, and so on.

(2) *Forests.* Source of timber and wood pulp.

(3) *Forage land.* Sustains herds of cattle, sheep, and goats for the production of meat, milk, leather, and wool.

(4) *Wild animals.* Deer, wolves, eagles, bluebirds, bullfrogs, spotted salamanders, sphinx moths, fireflies, and so on.

d. *Products of lakes, streams, and impoundments.* Freshwater fish: black bass, lake trout, catfish.

c. *Products of the ocean.* Marine fish: herring, tuna. Marine mammals: porpoises, gray whales, Pribilof fur seals.

f. *Human powers.* Physical and spiritual.

2. *Nonrenewable.* Once gone there is no hope of replacement.

a. *Species of wildlife.* The passenger pigeon, great auk, and Carolina paroquet have become extinct. They represented the end products of perhaps a million years of evolution.

b. *Specimen wilderness.* Within several human lifespans wilderness values cannot be restored even with the most dedicated program.

B. *Nonmaintainable.* The mineral resources. Total quantity is static. Mineral resources are regarded as wasting assets. When destroyed or consumptively used, they cannot be replaced.

1. *Reusable.* Minerals whose consumptive usage is small. Salvage or reuse potentialities are high.

a. *Gem minerals.* Rubies, emeralds, and so on.

b. *Nonconsumptively used metals.* Gold, platinum, and silver; some iron, copper, and aluminum. These metals can be extracted and reworked into new products: jewelry, silverware, vases, and so on.

2. *Nonreusable.* Those minerals with a high or total consumptive use. Exhaustion is a certainty.

   a. *Fossil fuels.* When consumed, gases (potential pollutants), heat, and water are released.
   b. *Most nonmetallic minerals.* Glass sand, gypsum, salt, and so on.
   c. *Consumptively used metals.* Lead in high-octane gasoline and in paint, zinc in galvanized iron, tin in toothpaste containers, iron in cans, and so on.

Fundamental Principles of Conservation

Harmony between man's resource requirements and the resource base depends upon basic conservation principles, several of which follow. An understanding of these principles is basic to an appreciation of the conservation policy in America today. Although briefly mentioned at this time, they will form the basis of much discussion in later chapters.

1. SENSE OF INDIVIDUAL RESPONSIBILITY. Responsibility and privilege go hand in hand. The privilege of being a citizen of the world's greatest democracy is predicated upon responsibility—to government, to our fellow man, and to the natural resources upon which we depend. The history of the United States has been inexorably intertwined with the manner in which Americans have used or abused their natural resources. The farmer who employs excessive amounts of pesticides, the camper who forgets to extinguish his campfire, the trigger-happy "sportsman" who uses robins as targets to test his marksmanship, the snowmobilist who shears off tomorrow's timber, all defile not only their own resource heritage, but more important, the heritage which belongs to all Americans.

2. ROLE OF GOVERNMENTS. Our nation's resources are so extensive and the problems associated with their intelligent utilization are so complex that it is imperative that their ultimate control be a function of local, state, and federal governments rather than of private interests. State and federal governments, in particular, have at their disposal the know-how of sophisticated specialists—agronomists, hydrologists, geologists, range managers, foresters, ichthyologists, fisheries biologists, ornithologists, mammalogists, wildlife biologists, oceanographers, human ecologists, urban planners, and experts in the areas of pollution control and recreation develop-

ment. Moreover, government agencies are funded for research and the implementation of research-based programs. Consequently, they are in a position to get a wide view of a given resource problem and to appraise its possible consequences. An example might be gauging the affect of unsound logging practices on the quality or abundance of other resources.

3. MULTIPLE USE OF A GIVEN RESOURCE. A cardinal conservation goal is to "insure the greatest good for the most people over the long run." Because most resources have multiple functions, the realization of this objective involves delicate and knowledgeable management. For example, a major river may have multiple values: for the swimmer it serves as a refreshing sanctuary from summer heat; for the angler it is the habitat of game fish; for the hunter it provides breeding sites for mallards and teal; for the canoeist it presents a challenge to his skills; for the manufacturer it is an artery for the inexpensive transport of fuel and raw materials and a channel for the discharge of industrial wastes; for the farmer it is a water source for livestock and irrigation systems; for all in the area it may be harnessed to provide inexpensive electricity. It is apparent that the river cannot be all things to all people. Not all of the potential values of a great river can be realized concurrently at the same site. Thus, the interest of the duck hunter in productive waterfowl nesting grounds might conflict with the farmer's interest in irrigation water. Similarly, the interests of anglers and industrialists might be incompatible. The construction of a power dam would effectively block the progress of both canoeists and migratory salmon. Obviously, such conflicting interests might never be resolved. It is for this reason that local, state, and federal governments have enacted legislation to regulate resource utilization in such a manner as to serve best the interests of current and future generations. As we shall see in later chapters, such legislative control is not invariably successful.

4. INVENTORIES AND PROJECTIONS OF RESOURCE USE. In their scholarly survey of future resource needs, Landsberg, Fischman, and Fisher project America's requirements to the year 2000 (5). They estimate that required cropland will increase from the 1960 figure of 368 million acres to 418 million acres by 2000, an increase of 13.5 per cent. As a result of our population growth the requisite production of paper and paperboard will zoom from 34 million short tons (1960) to 134 million short tons by 2000, an increase of 294 per cent. In 1960 many Americans sought relief from the tensions of their crowded world and paid 93 millions visits to 14 million acres of national forests. By 2000 our burgeoning population will require an expanded national

forest system of 57 million acres, a 307 per cent increase, in order to accommodate the expected 2,010 million visits. In 1964 New York City and other metropolitan centers along the Atlantic Coast were plagued with an acute water shortage, which may be only an indication of future water problems. Water depletion from municipal use will increase 130 per cent, from 6.9 billion gallons per day (bgd) consumed in 1960 to 15.9 bgd by the year 2000. By 2000 the American people will consume 194 million tons of iron and steel, compared to only 72 million tons in 1960, an increase of 169 per cent. Fuel (electricity, coal, oil, gas) consumption will expand 142 per cent from the 3.84 quadrillion British thermal units (btu) used in 1960, to 9.32 quadrillion btu by 2000. The final projection for land requirements is the most startling. The total land area in the conterminous United States is 1,904 million acres. In 1960 America's total land requirements for all uses (cropland, rangeland, forests, recreation areas, urban land, transportation, wildlife refuges, and reservoirs) was 1,815 million acres, leaving only 89 million residual acres. However, by 2000, projected land requirements will increase 7.6 per cent to 1,954 million acres, a figure which will exceed by 50 million acres our nation's total land area (5). It is apparent that intelligent resource management is predicated upon periodic resource base inventories that are both accurate and comprehensive, such as was initiated during the administration of Teddy Roosevelt. Without such an integrated inventory-projection policy, unexpected future shortages might upset the nation's economy and cause extensive personal suffering.

5. Interlocking Resource Relationships. Over 100 years ago George Perkins Marsh observed how men had abused agricultural lands in Europe and Asia and how this abuse ultimately resulted in the deterioration of the national economy and well-being. After returning to the United States he expounded the concept that man cannot degrade one part of his environment without simultaneously affecting other parts (8). In other words, natural human environment, although infinitely complex and varied, is a dynamic, organic whole, and therefore cannot be properly investigated by studying it in isolation. Today resource specialists know that Marsh was correct. For example, the removal of a block of Douglas fir, seemingly simple and conclusive in itself, may have far-reaching effects on other resources such as wildlife, fish, soil, water, rangeland, and even atmosphere and climate. The study of such interrelationships between organisms and their environment is known as *ecology*. Aldo Leopold, late professor of game management at the University of Wisconsin, was a leading and eloquent ex-

ponent of the application of ecological concepts to conservation problems. He had the discernment of a great scientist, as is evident in his description of the dynamic interplay of forces involved in the development of mature grassland soil:

The black prairie was built by the prairie plants, a hundred distinctive species of grasses, herbs and shrubs; by the prairie fungi, insects and bacteria; by the prairie mammals and birds, all interlocked in one humming community of cooperations and competitions—one biota. This biota, through ten thousand years of living and dying, burning and growing, preying and fleeing, freezing and thawing, built that dark and bloody ground we call prairie (6).

BIBLIOGRAPHY

1. Allen, Shirley W., and Justin W. Leonard. *Conserving Natural Resources.* New York: McGraw-Hill Book Co., 1966, 432 pp.
2. Carson, Rachel. *Silent Spring.* Boston: Houghton Mifflin Co., 1962.
3. Galbraith, John Kenneth. "How Much Should a Country Consume?" in Henry Jarrett (ed.), *Perspectives on Conservation: Essays on America's Natural Resources.* Baltimore: The Johns Hopkins Press, 1958.
4. Highsmith, Richard M., Jr., J. Granville Jensen, and Robert D. Rudd. *Conservation in the United States.* Chicago: Rand McNally and Co., 1962.
5. Landsberg, Hans H., Leonard L. Fischman, and Joseph L. Fisher. *Resources in America's Future.* Baltimore: The Johns Hopkins Press, 1962.
6. Leopold, Aldo. *A Sand County Almanac.* New York: Oxford University Press, 1966, 269 pp.
7. Smith, Guy-Harold (ed.). *Conservation of Natural Resources.* New York: John Wiley & Sons, Inc., 1958, 474 pp.
8. Udall, Stewart L. *The Quiet Crisis.* New York: Holt, Rinehart and Winston, 1963.

2 Ecological Concepts

An understanding of certain basic ecological concepts will aid in developing an appreciation of not only the problems facing the conservationist, but also the techniques, policies, and regulations by which these problems might be resolved. Among the basic concepts considered in this chapter are photosynthesis, organizational levels, elemental cycles, food chains, laws of thermodynamics, food webs, ecological pyramids (numbers, biomass and energy), tolerance ranges, population growth curves, and mechanisms regulating populations.

Photosynthesis

Photosynthesis may be defined as the "process by which solar energy is utilized in the conversion of carbon dioxide and water into sugar." With a few minor exceptions this process can occur only in the presence of a green pigment chlorophyll, found in plants, which serves as a catalyst for the reaction. An over-all equation for photosynthesis is

$$6\,CO_2 + 6\,H_2O + \text{solar energy} \rightarrow \\ C_6H_{12}O_6 + 6\,O_2 + \text{chemical energy}$$

In a sense, the solar energy is "trapped" by chlorophyll and channeled into sugar molecules

16

in the form of chemical energy. The preceding equation is slightly misleading in that it suggests that the carbon dioxide (CO_2) combines directly with water (H_2O) to form sugar ($C_6H_{12}O_6$). In actuality, however, there are two major phases to the reaction: First, in a process called *photolysis* the solar energy is employed to split the water molecules into hydrogen and oxygen, the latter gas escaping from the plant as a by-product. Second, in a process called *carbon dioxide fixation* the carbon dioxide combines with hydrogen to form sugar. The world's green plants fix 550 billion tons of carbon dioxide annually.

The preceding description of photosynthesis is a gross simplification of an extremely complicated process that involves at least twenty-five individual steps and that is currently the subject of intensive research. Some of the released oxygen may be utilized directly by the plant or may be diffused from the leaf through minute pores (stomata) into the atmosphere, where it becomes available to other organisms. It has been estimated that if all photosynthesis ceased today, the atmospheric supply of oxygen would be exhausted in 2,000 years, at which time, of course, all living things would have perished. There is considerable concern among some ecologists, such as Dr. Lamont Cole of Cornell University, that the progressive contamination of the marine environment with pesticides and industrial wastes may ultimately impair the photosynthetic activity of marine algae, which currently are responsible for 70 per cent of the world's photosynthetic activity, and result in increasingly reduced quantities of atmospheric oxygen. Except for a few simple organisms such as bacteria, which can secure energy by oxidizing inorganic compounds containing sulfur or iron, every living organism is dependent on photosynthesis for survival.

Levels of Organization

As anyone who has ever taken a course in biology knows, one of the outstanding characteristics of any living organism is its organization. In ascending order of complexity the organization levels are the following: atom, molecule, cell, tissue, organ, organ system, and organism. Although the ecologist is certainly concerned with each of these levels, most of his attention is usually focused on the supraorganismal levels—the population, community, and ecological system, or *ecosystem* (9). (Fig. 2–1)

POPULATION. When the layman employs the term *population* he is invariably concerned with numbers of human beings in a given locality. However, the ecologist extends the

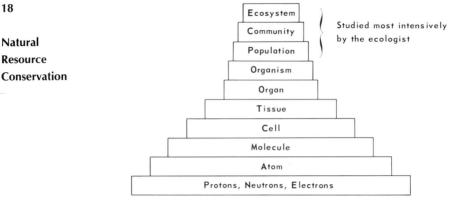

Figure 2–1 Levels of organization. Units become less numerous but of increasing complexity when considered in a base–apex progression.

term to include any organism, human or nonhuman. Thus, he may speak of populations of white pine, black bass, or deer.

COMMUNITY. The layman employs the word *community* in reference to a town or city. The ecologist, on the other hand, would define a *community* as the "total of all living organisms occupying a given locality." He might refer to the community of a woodlot, prairie, marsh, or even a rotting log or drop of pond water. The community of your backyard might embrace many thousands of individual organisms representing a great assemblage of species, from soil bacteria and earthworms to thrushes and oaks.

ECOSYSTEM. The environment of any organism is combined of both living (biotic) and chemicophysical components such as water, gases, salts, animal excreta (urine and feces), wind, heat, cold, solar and nuclear energy. An ecological system, or *ecosystem,* may be defined as any portion of the biosphere in which there is a well-ordered flow of energy and materials between organisms and their environment. Although Tansley, who coined the term, restricted its application primarily to the *community* level, in recent years the concept has been extended to the levels of *population* and *organism.* Major emphasis is on the cycling of elements; the transfer, utilization, and dissipation of energy; and the rates at which these processes occur. The characteristic features of any ecosystem—whether lake, marsh, prairie, spruce forest, or city—are established and perpetuated by regulatory processes such as growth, reproduction, behavior patterns, physiological adaptations, mortality factors, and mass movements such as immigration, emigration, and migration.

Although it is convenient to consider ecosystems as separate entities, they are isolated only on the pages of ecology text-books. In the actual world there is frequently some movement from one ecosystem to another, whether immediately adjacent or thousands of miles distant. Thus, topsoil may be blown from an Oklahoma wheat field to the Atlantic ocean or it may be washed by spring rains into a nearby stream. Snow geese may migrate from the Canadian tundra to a Louisiana rice field. Phosphorus originating in deep marine sediments may eventually be transferred to terrestrial ecosystems as guano deposits by means of the algae–crustacean–fish–cormorant food chain.

As we shall see in later chapters most measures applied by the conservationist involve ecosystem manipulation. Thus, prevention of winter kill of fish (resulting from oxygen-depleted water) might involve removal of snow cover from an ice-bound lake. This permits sunlight to penetrate the ice and become available to submerged aquatic plants for photosynthesis. The resultant increase in dissolved oxygen could prevent massive fish mortality. In this relatively simple example are interactions between such nonliving components as water, solar energy, and oxygen and the biotic components represented by aquatic plants, fish, and man.

Principles of Ecology

The Elemental Cycle. Roughly ninety-two elements occur naturally in the universe; of these about thirty-five to forty are required by living organisms. These elements are continuously passing from the nonliving environment into the bodies of living organisms and back into the inanimate world in "circular" patterns known as *elemental cycles* (7, 9, 10).

THE NITROGEN CYCLE. Nitrogen, which forms about 3 per cent (by weight) of protoplasm, is an essential component of many important compounds such as chlorophyll, hemo-globin, insulin, and DNA (deoxyribose nucleic acid), the hered-ity-determining molecule. Let us trace nitrogen from corn to man. Although, like man, corn is unable to utilize atmospheric nitrogen, it is able to use it as a component of soluble nitrates occurring in the soil. Corn absorbs these salts through its roots. Eventually, through a series of chemical reactions, the nitrogen is incorporated in the protein molecules distinctive to corn. When consumed by man these proteins are converted into amino acids by digestive enzymes and are built up into pro-teins characteristic of man. (Fig. 2–2)

The complex nitrogenous compounds occurring in animal

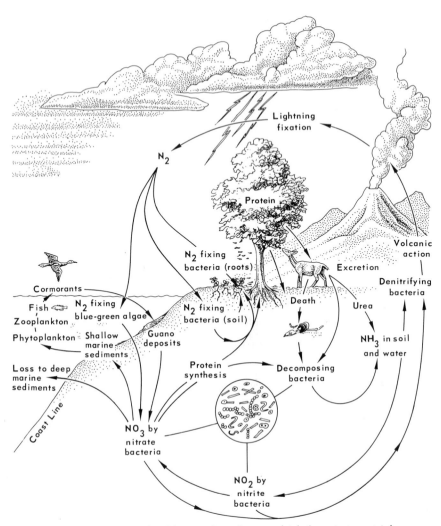

Figure 2–2 Nitrogen cycle. Observe that nitrates which form in terrestrial ecosystems may be lost to marine ecosystems by water transport to deep ocean sediments. However, land-based nitrates washed into shallow sediments may eventually be returned to the terrestrial ecosystem via the phytoplankton–zooplankton–fish–cormorant food chain. [Adapted from Robert L. Smith, *Ecology and Field Biology* (New York: Harper & Row, 1966). Used by permission of the publishers.]

excreta and dead plants and animals may be decomposed by the bacteria of decay into relatively simple ammonia (NH_3) compounds by a process called *ammonification.* The *nitrite bacteria,* which include *Nitrosomonas,* then convert the ammonia compounds into nitrite salts. A third bacterial group, the *nitrate* bacteria, which include *Nitrobacter,* transform the nitrites into nitrate salts, such as potassium nitrate (KNO_3) or calcium nitrate [$Ca (NO_3)_2$]. The conversion of ammonia compounds into nitrites is called *nitrification*. One "turn" of the nitrogen cycle would be completed when a plant absorbs soluble nitrates from the soil (7, 9, 10).

Certain kinds of soil bacteria, known as *denitrifying bacteria*, may break down ammonia compounds, nitrites and nitrates, and utilize the energy released to sustain their vital processes; in the process they release gaseous nitrogen as a by-product. This process, by means of which gaseous nitrogen is temporarily removed from the cycle and thereby is made unavailable for plant or animal life, is known as *denitrification*. It is characteristic of oxygen-depleted soils. However, when soils are well aerated, these same bacteria ordinarily oxidize carbohydrates for their energy needs. It is apparent, therefore, that a farmer can to some degree maintain soil fertility by diligent tillage, for in this manner denitrification is retarded (7, 9, 10).

Despite its abundance, gaseous nitrogen cannot be utilized directly by most organisms. By what means, then, is it "fixed," or brought into circulation? Nitrogen gas may be fixed by electrical discharges in the atmosphere, such as those during a thunderstorm. Volcanic eruptions represent a minor source of fixed nitrogen. However, by far the most important source is nitrogen fixation by soil and water-dwelling bacteria.

Figure 2–3 Nitrogen-fixing legume. Root system of black-eyed peas taken from a Texas farm. Note the nodules. Nitrogen-fixing bacteria are abundant in the black clay soil of this farm because peas have been grown in rotation for the past forty years. [Soil Conservation Service, U.S. Department of Agriculture]

The Food Chain. A food chain may be defined as the transfer of energy and nutrients through a succession of organisms via repeated processes of eating and being eaten. Man forms the terminal link of many food chains. Two representative chains would be corn–pheasant–fox, and spruce–budworm–warbler. In each case the initial "link" is a green plant, or *producer,* which produces chemical energy in a form (glucose) available to succeeding consumer (animal) links. Over 270 billion tons of sugar are produced by green plants annually, most of it (70 per cent) by marine algae, lesser amounts by terrestrial and freshwater vegetation. However, because plants are only about 1 per cent efficient in converting it, and because both cow and man are only about 15 per cent efficient, in the chain grass–cow–man only about 0.02 per cent of the original supply of solar energy is eventually utilized by man. It is apparent that the second law of thermodynamics imposes a limit on the length of food chains, very few having more than five links (9). In the chain clover–grasshopper–frog–snake–hawk, as might operate in a meadow community, the hawk uses only 0.0004 per cent of the incident solar energy. In densely populated countries such as Japan, where there is only 5 per cent as much arable land per capita as in the United States, it is no accident that human food chains generally have only *two* links, in which man has replaced the herbivorous cow, sheep, or pig. Thus, a typical Japanese food chain might be represented in the following way:

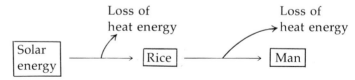

Although Americans currently still live in a land of "milk and honey" (and steaks), and habitually overeat, the time may well come, as a result of our burgeoning population (expected to reach 300 million by 2000), when we will be faced with an ecological ultimatum, either shorten our food chains or tighten our belts. Of course it is much more satisfying to feast on pork chops or T-bones, but the second law of thermodynamics may yet impose the somber transition to algae cakes and alfalfa soup (9).

FOOD WEBS. A food web may be defined as an interconnected series of food chains. In actuality a food chain virtually never exists as an isolated entity, except in an ecology textbook. Consider the food chain corn–pig–man, for example. A pig eats other foods beside corn—such as rats, mice, insects, grubs, earthworms, baby chicks, grass, weeds, and garbage. Similarly,

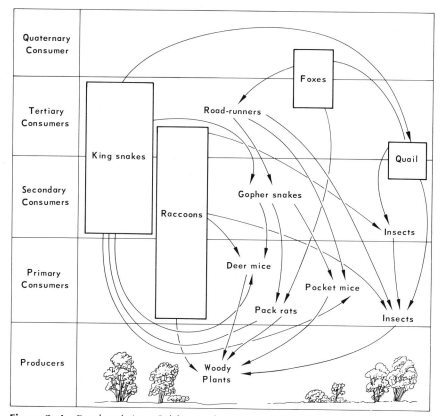

Figure 2–4 Food web in a California chaparral. All the consumers either directly or indirectly depend on the woody shrub "producers." Foxes, quail, and king snakes occupy two trophic levels. Raccoons occupy three. Gopher snakes will occasionally assume the role of scavenger as well as predator. [Adapted from Arthur S. Boughey, *Ecology of Populations* (New York: The Macmillan Company, 1968).]

in addition to pork, a man consumes everything from artichokes to zwieback, from kippered herring to pheasant under glass. In nature, therefore, food chains exist primarily as separate strands of an interwoven food web (9). A typical food web operating in the chaparral community of California is represented in Figure 2-4.

Ecological Pyramids

THE PYRAMID OF NUMBERS. In a *predator* food chain the numbers of individuals are greatest at the producer level, less at the herbivore level, and smallest at the level of the carnivore. This concept is known as the *pyramid of numbers*, first advanced in 1927 by the eminent British ecologist Charles Elton. Figure 2-5 illustrates the pyramid of numbers actually recorded in an

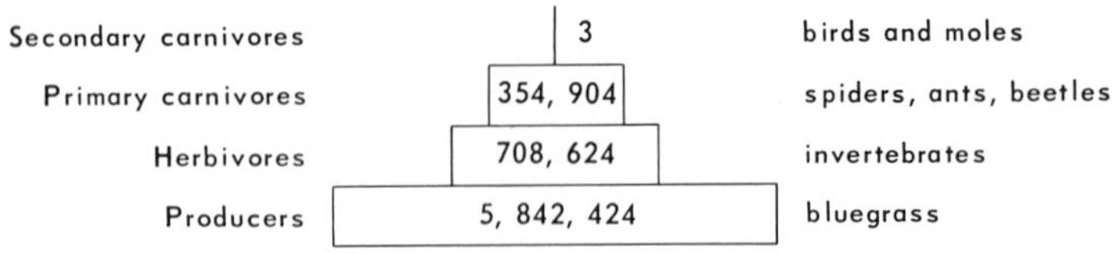

Secondary carnivores	3	birds and moles
Primary carnivores	354, 904	spiders, ants, beetles
Herbivores	708, 624	invertebrates
Producers	5, 842, 424	bluegrass

Figure 2–5 Pyramid of numbers occuring in a 1-acre plot of blue grass. Organisms are arranged according to trophic levels. [Adapted from Eugene P. Odum, *Fundamentals of Ecology,* (Philadelphia: W. B. Saunders Co., 1953). Plant data from Francis C. Evans and Stanley A. Cain, "Preliminary Studies on the Vegetation of an Old Field Community in Southeastern Michigan," *Contribution of the Laboratory of Vertebrate Biology, University of Michigan,* **51**, University of Michigan Press, Ann Arbor, 1952, 1–17 pp. Animal data from G. N. Wolcott, "An Animal Census of Two Pastures and a Meadow in Northern New York," *Ecol. Mono.,* **7** (1937), 1–90 pp.]

acre of bluegrass. Both the numerical and size relationships of organisms in food chains involving *parasites,* however, are *inverted.* This is apparent in the chain dog–flea–protozoan, or in the corn–nematode–bacteria chain, where both protozoans and bacteria are hyperparasites of the parasitic fleas and nematodes. Because numbers pyramids do not provide an accurate picture of either the biomass or energy relationships between trophic levels, they are of somewhat limited value.

THE PYRAMID OF BIOMASS. The ecologist refers to the weight of living substance (protoplasm) in an organism, a population, or a community as its "biological mass," or *biomass.* In a typical food chain ending in a predator, such as sagebrush–antelope–cougar, there is a progressive reduction in total biomass for each successive trophic level, a reduction necessitated by the second law of thermodynamics. (Fig. 2–6)

THE PYRAMID OF ENERGY. The physicist defines energy as the capacity to do work. All organisms require energy for their life processes. Animals require energy for the ingestion, digestion of food, for the conversion of food into protoplasm, for the synthesis of hormones and enzymes, for the circulation of blood, for the maintenance of body temperature, and for respiration, excretion, and locomotion. Plants require energy to carry on photosynthesis, to synthesize growth hormones and leaf pigments, to produce flowers and seeds. All organisms require energy for growth and reproduction. Unlike elements, energy is not cyclical, but is continuously being dissipated from ecosystems and hence must be continuously replenished by means of the incident solar energy. (Fig. 2–7)

Primary production refers to the total amount of sugar produced by photosynthesis; in the world as a whole it amounts to

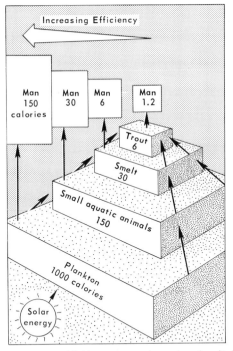

Figure 2–6 Energy pyramid. If man were the only other link in the plankton–man food chain, more than 100 times the energy would be available to him than as the terminal link of the plankton–aquatic animal–smelt–trout–man food chain. [Adapted from Robert B. Platt and George K. Reid. *Bioscience.* (New York: Reinhold Publishing Corp., 1967). After Lamont C. Cole, "The Ecosphere," *Sci. Amer.,* **198**, 1958.]

270 billion tons annually. The ecologist frequently refers to the primary production of a lake, meadow, woodlot, or some other ecosystem. All living organisms carry on *respiration,* a process by means of which glucose (and other organic compounds) is oxidized; the generalized equation is

$$C_6H_{12}O_6 + 6\,O_2 \rightarrow 6\,CO_2 + 6\,H_2O + energy$$

Because plants must respire, ecologists distinguish between *gross production,* which is the *total* amount of energy captured by the plant, and *net production,* the energy which remains after respiration (7).

This net production may be consumed by herbivores. Unlike plants, animals are able to secure energy only by the consumption of energy-bearing food. The total energy ingested by an animal is referred to as its gross energy intake (I). Not all of this I can be converted into protoplasm, but will be used to maintain life functions and to produce heat. Energy used thus by an animal is called respiratory energy (R). The net production by a consumer equals $I - R$. A given trophic level among consumers may lose some net production in the form of voided wastes or as the result of animal mortality. Net production may be visibly manifested in growth or reproduction, or it may be channeled into the next higher trophic level by the act of predation. The ingested food energy (I) which may be eventually eliminated in the excreta is known as excretory energy (E). *Assimilated energy* at any consumer level equals $I - E$. Animals of a given trophic level may die nonpredatory deaths (D) or predatory deaths (P). Frequently when a prey is eaten by a predator, much food is wasted; for example, portions of the body may be uneaten. Such wasted energy is designated by the letter W. Total biomass in a population at a given trophic level may increase, decrease, or remain constant, depending upon the opposing influences of net production and predation. When net production is greater, biomass increases; when the influence of predation is greater, biomass decreases. When both net production and predation are of equal effect, biomass remains constant. To show the fate of energy intake (I) at a given trophic level, the following equation may be employed:

$$I = E + R + D + W + P$$

Of considerable interest to ecologists and all others interested in conservation is the efficiency with which a particular trophic level utilizes gross energy intake. Plant communities generally utilize only a small percentage of the available solar radiation, some of which is reflected or transmitted by the plant surface or reflected or absorbed by ground or water surfaces not covered with vegetation. Gross primary productivity rates for short grass plains and deserts are less than 0.5 gram per square meter per day; for prairie, forest and freshwater communities it ranges from 0.5 to 5 grams per square meter per day. Evergreen forests, estuaries, and coral reefs may yield up to 20 grams per square meter per day (9).

Animals derive energy not only from producers (P) but also from transformers (T), such as fungi, bacteria, detritus feeders, and saprovores, all of which secure their energy from inanimate organic material that accumulates as a result of D, W, and E. In some ecosystems W is relatively high. Thus, adult African lions utilize only 50 per cent of the 44 pounds of prey killed daily; the remainder of the kill sustains considerable numbers of scavengers. Nonpredatory deaths of bluegills in a small Indiana lake amounted to 64 per cent of the protein content of the *standing crop* during the year, but only 29 per cent of the *total protein turnover*. It is exceedingly difficult to secure accurate energy transfer data for entire ecosystems. In a study of

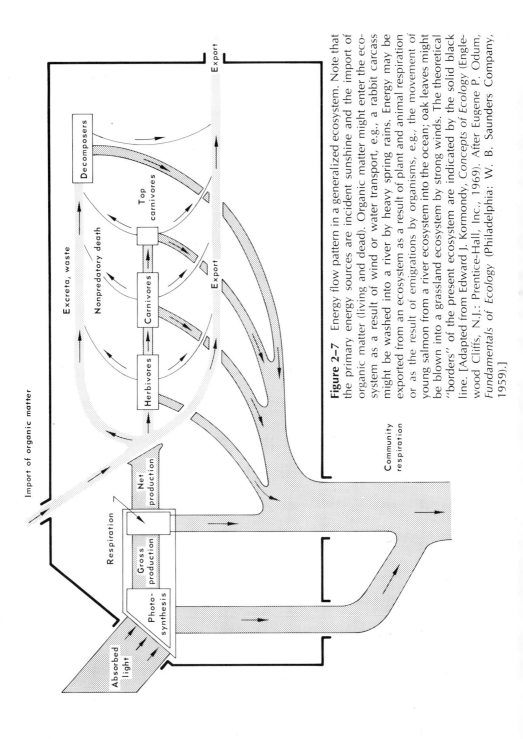

Figure 2-7 Energy flow pattern in a generalized ecosystem. Note that the primary energy sources are incident sunshine and the import of organic matter (living and dead). Organic matter might enter the ecosystem as a result of wind or water transport, e.g., a rabbit carcass might be washed into a river by heavy spring rains. Energy may be exported from an ecosystem as a result of plant and animal respiration or as the result of emigrations by organisms, e.g., the movement of young salmon from a river ecosystem into the ocean; oak leaves might be blown into a grassland ecosystem by strong winds. The theoretical "borders" of the present ecosystem are indicated by the solid black line. [Adapted from Edward J. Kormondy, *Concepts of Ecology* (Englewood Cliffs, N.J.: Prentice-Hall, Inc., 1969). After Eugene P. Odum, *Fundamentals of Ecology* (Philadelphia: W. B. Saunders Company, 1959).]

27

lake ecosystems Lindemann found that there existed a progressive increase in the percentage of gross energy intake channeled to the next higher trophic level by predation (8). In his analysis of a terrestrial food chain (plants–mice–weasels) Golley found a progressive increase in the percentage of respiratory loss at each higher trophic level (4).

Range of Tolerance. In the physical and biotic environment of any organism are factors which can restrict growth, interfere with reproductive success, and even cause death. They are called *limiting factors*. The concept of limiting factors was first introduced in 1840 when a German biochemist, Justus Liebig, noted that the growth of plants was frequently limited by deficiencies of certain elements occurring naturally in the soil, such as zinc, cobalt, manganese, and copper. These elements have become known as "trace elements" because most living plants

Figure 2–8 Law of tolerance. A species population attains a peak under optimal environmental conditions. As such environmental factors as oxygen, carbon dioxide, water, temperature, etc., become less favorable, the population gradually decreases. Although organisms might survive temporarily in a marginal habitat (zone of physiological stress) they would eventually lose out in competition with better-adapted species. [Adapted from Robert L. Smith, *Ecology and Field Biology* (New York: Harper & Row, Publishers, 1966). Used by permission of the publishers.]

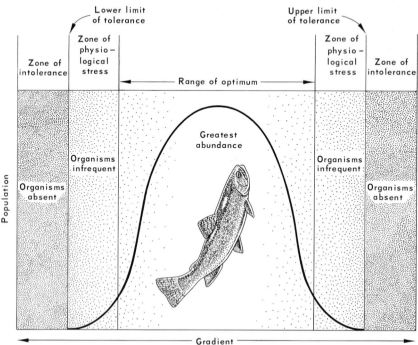

and animals require them in extremely minute quantities (9). For example, a variation in the concentration of zinc in the soil amounting to one part in 200 million may mean the difference between a sick or healthy plant.

Victor Shelford, a pioneer in plant ecology, has shown that organisms may be equally limited by *too much* of a certain environmental factor. For example, a cabbage growing in your backyard vegetable patch requires a minimal amount of soil moisture for vigorous growth, because water is basic to the photosynthetic process. Conversely, if that same cabbage were submerged by spring flood waters, the diffusion of carbon dioxide into the leaves would be so greatly reduced the cabbage would fail to survive. For each organism, therefore, there exists a specific tolerance range for any essential environmental factor below or above which the organism's activity is adversely affected. Note that in Figure 2-8 populations are highest in the optimum range and then gradually taper off (in the familiar bell-shaped curve) to low densities in the zones of physiological stress. Beyond the stress regions are the zones of intolerance in which the values of the factor (water, temperature, soil elements, are so extreme that continued survival is impossible (7, 9, 10). Thus the limits of temperature tolerance for the developing eggs of the brook trout (a denizen of cold, clear, gravel bottom streams in the Northeastern states) are 0 degrees C. and 12 degrees C., with an optimum of 4 degrees C. (9). As Kendeigh has pointed out, a species distribution is limited more by conditions of physiological stress than by the actual *limits* of tolerance themselves, for "death verges on the limits of toleration, and the existence of the species would be seriously jeopardized if it were too frequently exposed to these extreme conditions" (7).

The Sigmoid Population Growth Curve. The population of any organism will be the result of the interaction of the two antagonistic forces of the environmental resistance (ER) and the biotic potential (BP), with the BP tending to "push" the population upward and the ER tending to push it down. It is apparent, then, that the increase, decrease, or stability of a given population depends on the values of ER and BP. When the BP is greater than ER, the population rises. Conversely, when the ER is greater than the BP, the population declines. When both values are the same, the population attains a stability in the form of a dynamic equilibrium (1, 7, 9, 10).

Whenever a species becomes established in a new habitat with good carrying capacity, its population will show a characteristic S-shaped, or sigmoid, growth curve. Such a curve

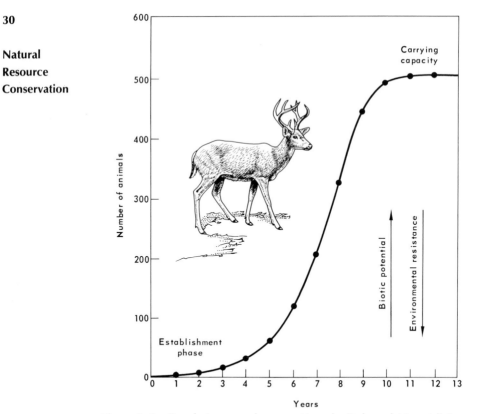

Figure 2–9 Population growth curve. Note the S-shaped (sigmoid) form. The antagonistic influences of the biotic potential and environmental resistance are indicated by arrows. This curve shows the population increase of deer introduced into a new environment with a 500-animal carrying capacity. [Adapted from Raymond F. Dasmann, *Environmental Conservation* (New York: John Wiley & Sons, Inc., 1959).]

usually has four phases, known in chronological sequence as (1) the establishment phase, (2) the explosive (or logarithmic phase), (3) the deceleration phase, and (4) the dynamic equilibrium phase. Once the population has reached the equilibrium phase, no further substantial population surges are possible, for at this point in its growth the population has attained the so-called *carrying capacity* of the habitat. In other words, it has reached the maximum population that the habitat will support under prevailing conditions. (Fig. 2–9)

A number of exotics introduced into the United States from abroad—such as the English sparrow, European starling, and German carp—have followed sigmoid growth curves. Although introduced with good intentions (the sparrow was brought over from Europe to control insect pests), many exotics have destroyed wildlife habitat, disseminated disease, or aggressively competed with more valuable wildlife species for food, cover, and breeding sites.

Einarson describes the population growth of pheasants on Protection Island, off the west coast of Washington, after an initial 1937 stocking of two cocks and six hens. Careful censuses were made yearly from 1937 until 1942, when the study was abruptly halted by World War II. Servicemen stationed on the island promptly applied rather intensive "environmental resistance." Up to this time, however, the birds had closely followed the sigmoid growth curve and had increased to 1,898 birds, a 230-fold increase over the original population (2).

A given crop of corn, bluegills, or deer may be periodically harvested to give a *yield*. One of the most important problems facing scientists in the fields of forestry, wildlife management, agriculture, livestock ranching, and fisheries is how to secure the maximum sustained yield or optimum yield from a given resource. In these cases man is interested in harvesting net production for his economic gain instead of permitting it to die nonpredatory deaths, or to be consumed by herbivores or carnivores. If the yield is greater than net production, it may so greatly reduce a given population as to depress its reproductive potential. On the other hand, if the harvest is less than the net production, the resource is not being managed for maximum economic return. Moreover, when population density rises, the density-dependent factors of competition, disease, and predators affect the yield adversely. There is a point in the growth curve of any species where productivity is highest. This is between the accelerating and inhibiting phases of the curve. Research has revealed that in most species this point is attained when the population is roughly 50 per cent of the asymptote (7).

Population Regulation by Density-Independent Factors. Populations of organisms are controlled by both density-dependent and density-independent factors. The influence of density-independent factors is constant regardless of density and characteristically causes sharp population fluctuations. Heat, cold, drought, floods, blizzards, and hailstorms are obviously all density independent. Hail can decimate a field of young wheat or curtail reproduction in fruit trees. Hurricanes and tornadoes can level vast acreages of valuable spruce and pine. Heavy rains in late spring may sharply limit the hatching success of game birds. A severe spell of cold weather along the Texas coast in January, 1940, inflicted considerable fish mortality; the percentage decline in the catch of flounders, a fish highly vulnerable to cold, was 92.6 per cent at Laguna Madre, 93.6 per cent at

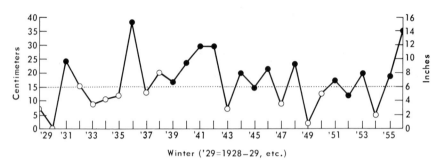

Figure 2–10 Importance of snow depth as a density-independent factor in the regulation of partridge populations in southwestern Finland. Because the partridge is primarily a ground-dwelling herbivore, a dense snow cover could either cause death directly from starvation or indirectly contribute to increased mortality from disease. Graph shows fluctuations of snow level above and below the critical 6-inch depth. Partridge populations the ensuing autumn are shown as having either increased (open circles) or decreased (solid circles). [Adapted from Lawrie Siivonen "The Correlation Between the Fluctuations of Partridge and European Hare Populations and the Climatic Conditions of Winters in Southwest Finland During the Last Thirty Years," *Papers on Game Research,* Helsinki, **17** (1956), 1–30 pp.]

Matagorda, and 95.4 per cent at Aransas, despite considerable variation in size of the original flounder population in these three regions (5). Siltation may smother salmon eggs. Pesticide-contaminated food supplies may cause direct mortality among songbirds or may impair their reproductive success. Robin populations in certain DDT-sprayed areas in Wisconsin were reduced by 69 to 98 per cent. Drought may so reduce water levels in a marsh as to increase muskrat vulnerability to fox predation. Many human activities are density independent with respect to their affect on wildlife. Thus, marsh drainage has severely depleted waterfowl populations. The heated efflu-ent from power plants have either killed game fish or caused them to migrate. The passenger pigeon's extinction was caused in part by the removal of its deciduous forest breeding habitat by the farmer and logger. Some human influences, however, have resulted in population increments rather than decrements. For example, house sparrow populations have flourished be-cause of the abundance of suitable nesting sites and food (waste grain and manure), associated with human settlement. The removal of forests in the eastern United States has per-mitted the eastward extension of such species associated with grassland habitats as the coyote and horned lark. (Fig. 2–10)

Population Regulation by Density-Dependent Factors. Den-sity-dependent factors operate within the limits imposed by density-independent factors. Biotic factors are frequently den-sity dependent. They tend to keep a population in dynamic equilibrium with the environment (7, 9, 10). Just as a governor on a car engine prevents the car from going too fast, so these factors prevent populations from increasing to a level which might result in massive death from starvation or disease. Conversely, when populations decrease below carrying capacity, the declining influence of the density-dependent factors eventually result in a gradual population build-up.

When the number of oaks on an acre increases, competition for sunlight, soil nutrients, and moisture increases proportionately. Individuals with less extensive root systems may die as a consequence of nutrient and moisture deficiencies. Stunted individuals may die because their sunlight is intercepted by taller trees.

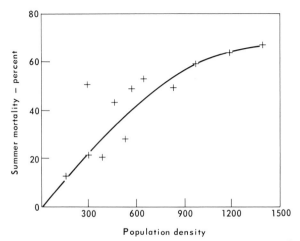

Figure 2–11 Density-dependent mortality in a Wisconsin quail population. As population density increased, there was a corresponding increase in competition for mates, food, water, cover, and territory. Crosses indicate the percentage of the quail population incurring mortality during late summer and fall. Note that the per cent mortality increased with population density, being roughly 12 per cent for a population of 150 and over 60 per cent for a population of 1,400. [Adapted from Eugene P. Odum, *Fundamentals of Ecology* Philadelphia: W. B. Saunders Company, 1959). Data from Paul L. Errington, "Some Contributions of a Fifteen-Year Local Study of the Northern Bobwhite to a Knowledge of Population Phenomena," *Ecol. Mono.*, **15**, 1–34 pp.]

Among animals it is apparent that when food, water, cover, nesting sites, breeding dens, and space are in limited supply, any population increase will intensify competition. Inevitably, this competition will have adverse effects on the physically unfit. Even if they do not incur direct mortality because of fighting, they may be required to disperse to a marginal habitat where death from malnutrition or predation may await them. When the density of pink salmon in impoundments becomes excessive, not only are fewer eggs released, but many are destroyed because of the inordinate stirring of gravel. It has been suggested that lowered fecundity of birds at high densities results from reduced food availability and increased fighting. Sometimes "shock disease," resulting from the stresses associated with crowding and fighting, operates as a density-dependent factor. For example, a herd of four to five Sika deer, introduced in 1916 on 280-acre James Island in Chesapeake Bay, increased to a peak of almost 300, at which point the density was roughly one per acre. Three years later 60 per cent of the herd died, presumably from stress-induced "shock disease."

When population densities are high, predatory mortality tends to increase, not only because individual predators may kill more prey than they require to satisfy their food requirements but because there may be an influx of predators to the area of high prey density and because inferior prey are crowded out to marginal habitat. An intensive study by Paul Errington of horned owl predation on winter populations of bobwhite in Wisconsin and Iowa from 1930 to 1935 showed a definite correlation between prey density and predation intensity as expressed in the percentage of owl pellets containing feathers and bones of quail (3).

The percentage of diseased or parasitized organisms in a population increases with population density, presumably as a result of the increased possibilities of transmission. With his monotypic agriculture and silviculture (large plots planted to a single crop species) man has unwittingly increased the possibilities for the infection of his crops with parasites and disease organisms. The population-limiting effects of wheat rust, corn smut, and Dutch elm disease are widely known. Oak wilt is caused by a fungus that is transmitted from tree to tree either by root grafts or beetles—the greater the concentration of oaks, the easier the transmission. The incidence of infectious diseases in man increases with population density, as is well substantiated by the massive mortality caused by the influenza virus among our soldiers during World War I. Infectious disease is an important controlling factor only during the occurrence of epidemics or epizootics. Because the causative organisms of infectious disease (viruses, protozoa, bacteria) may be transmitted by contact, by ingestion of contaminated food, and by animal agents (*vectors*), it is readily apparent that their influence is directly proportional to host density. In certain colonial sea birds the nest-building instinct is not activated until population density has increased to a critical minimal level. It has been suggested that this factor may have contributed to the extinction of the heath hen and passenger pigeon.

Although we have segregated population-regulating mechanisms into two groups, density independent and density dependent, it is actually exceedingly difficult to distinguish one from the other in the field, because a given organism's density at a given moment is the result of a combination of both density-independent and density-dependent factors acting concurrently.

Biological Succession. Biological succession is the replacement of one community of organisms (plant or animal) by another in an orderly and predictable manner. In a plant succession the plants of each successional stage (grass, shrub, tree) cause changes in incident sunlight, wind velocity, and temperature, as well as in the structure, depth, moisture, and fertility of the soil. These changes result in the replacement of the original stage by another better adapted to the modified environment (7, 9, 10).

EXAMPLE: A PRIMARY SUCCESSION. A succession which develops in an area not previously occupied by a community is known as a *primary succession*. It may become established on a jagged outcrop of granite, on a lava-covered slope, on rubble left in the wake of a landslide, or perhaps on the slag heaps of an open-pit mine.

We shall trace a primary succession as might occur on a rocky substratum in the deciduous forest region of the Eastern United States. The initial stage is called the *pioneer community*. Plants of this stage are adapted to withstand great extremes of temperature and moisture. A typical pioneer plant which might become established on a bare, windswept rocky outcrop might be the *crustose lichen,* whose wind-dispersed reproductive bodies, called *spores,* may be blown into the area. The crustose lichens form a grayish-green crust on the rocks. Although the substratum itself may be dry, the lichen spores nevertheless will develop if adequate atmospheric moisture is available. Once established, lichens begin to modify their immediate localized environment, or *microhabitat.* Weak carbonic acid (H_2CO_3) begins to corrode the underlying rock. Adjoining plants form a trap in which particles, of wind-blown sand, dust, and organic debris begin to accumulate. When an occasional lichen dies, bacteria and small fungi effect its decay. The resultant organic material and the excreta of minute lichen-eating insects which have invaded the microhabitat enrich the relatively sterile soil which has accumulated. This soil now acts as a sponge, rapidly absorbing water which falls as dew or rain. Once sufficient soil has accumulated, mosses and ferns may become established, also by means of wind-distributed spores. Ferns eventually shade out the lichens and replace them in the succession. The soil becomes further enriched with the decay of fern fronds each autumn. Eventually, as the decades pass, windblown pine seeds may fall in the area. They may have originated in some hilltop pine forest or may have been brought by seed-eating birds, such as the pine siskin or red crossbill. The young, sun-tolerant pine seedlings in turn compete successfully with the ferns and eventually replace them in the succession.

As the seasons pass, gray squirrels may temporarily enter the area to bury acorns brought in from a neighboring oak stand, or acorns may be accidentally dropped by a wandering raccoon or by a blue jay during a flight over the young pines. The acorns germinate readily in the relatively fertile soil which has been developing for centuries, since the beginning of the succession. Young oak seedlings, which are vulnerable to direct sunlight, develop successfully in the reduced light under the pine canopy. As an occasional pine dies, its position in the community will be usurped by an oak. Ultimately an oak forest, with its characteristic complement of plants and animals, will become established as the stable terminal climax of the succession. Thus, the bare, windswept rock outcrop is eventually replaced after several centuries by the moist, shadowed interior of a deciduous forest.

Although we have emphasized the succession of *plant communities* because vegetational changes are more basic and conspicuous, it should be emphasized that a succession of *animal* communities occurs also. The occurrence of a given animal species within a community is dependent upon such factors as food, water, cover, breeding sites, humidity, and temperature, all of which change with the plant succession. Thus, Johnston and Odum, in a study of the breeding bird populations of a *secondary succession* developing from abandoned fields in the Georgia Piedmont region, found marked differences in the various stages (6). Some of their data is summarized in Figure 2-12. In this succession the field sparrow, towhee, and cardinal play important roles in seed dispersal. The seeds of some plants actually germinate better after having passed through a bird's digestive tract, apparently because its digestive juices dissolve the seed coat.

Mammalian communities show a similar change in species composition and density with the progress of the succession. Thus, in the Johnston and Odum study meadow mice representative of the grass stage were replaced by cotton mice and golden mice in later forested stages. Similarly, cottontails and

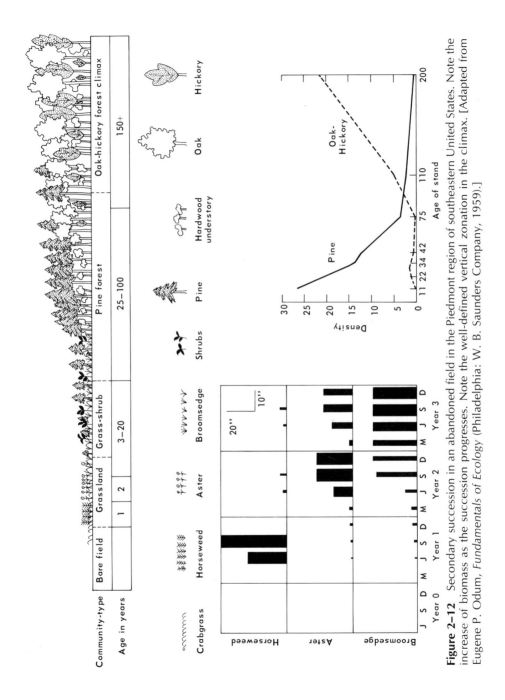

Figure 2-12 Secondary succession in an abandoned field in the Piedmont region of southeastern United States. Note the increase of biomass as the succession progresses. Note the well-defined vertical zonation in the climax. [Adapted from Eugene P. Odum, *Fundamentals of Ecology* (Philadelphia: W. B. Saunders Company, 1959).]

grass snakes of the grass stage were succeeded by oak–hickory representatives, such as the opossum, raccoon, and squirrel. An aquatic succession is illustrated in Fig. 2–13.

The Biomes. Anyone who has driven from New England to California is acutely aware of the marked landscape changes— from evergreen stands in Maine to beech–maple forests in Ohio, from the windswept Kansas prairie to the Arizona desert. Each of these distinctive areas represents a different *biome.* (A biome may be defined as the largest terrestrial community that can be easily recognized by a biologist; it is the biological expression of the interaction of climate, soil, water, and organisms [9].) Although the name of the biome is usually based on its climax vegetation, it should be emphasized that it is composed of both plant and animal components and that it embraces *developmental communities* leading to the climax community, as well as the climax itself. Thus, in northern Minnesota early successional stages of birch–aspen, as well as climax spruce–fir would be included in the *northern coniferous forest* biome, or *taiga.* We shall examine the distribution, physical features, and biota of certain North American biomes discussed in a conservation context later in this book.

TUNDRA. The tundra, which embraces about 20 million square miles, extends around the globe in the northern latitudes between the belt of perpetual ice and snow to the north and the timberline to the south. The ecology of the tundra, because of its relative simplicity, is better understood than that of other biomes. During June and July the far northern tundra near the Arctic Circle is the celebrated land of the midnight sun. Conversely, in January the sun remains below the horizon throughout the diurnal cycle. Annual precipitation is less than 10 inches, most of which occurs as summer or autumn rain. Snowfall is scant. Mean monthly temperatures range from −30°F in winter to plus 55 degrees F. in summer. The upper level of the permanently frozen soil (or *permafrost*) occurs at a depth of 6 to 18 inches. In spring and summer the thawed-out ground is characteristically soggy. Because of poor drainage and low evaporation rate and despite light precipitation, the accumulating melt waters of late spring form thousands of tiny lakes. Characteristic producers are mosses, sedges, grasses, reindeer lichen, and dwarf willows up to 100 years old. Representative animals of the tundra include the caribou, musk ox, collared lemming, willow ptarmigan, snowy owl, and golden plover (7, 9, 10).

BOREAL FOREST. The boreal forest, or *taiga,* is that part of the coniferous forest biome which forms an extensive east–west

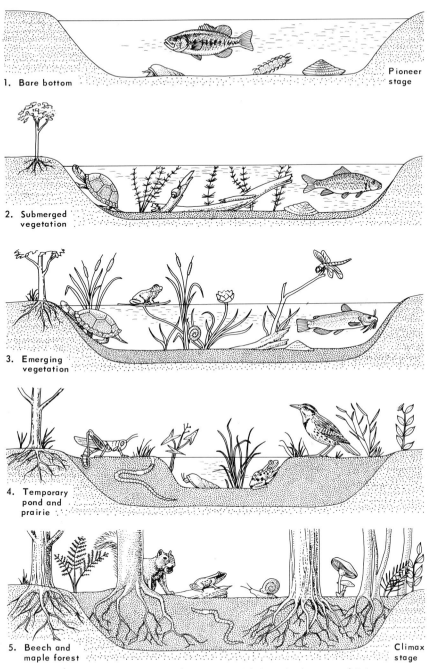

1. Bare bottom — Pioneer stage

2. Submerged vegetation

3. Emerging vegetation

4. Temporary pond and prairie

5. Beech and maple forest — Climax stage

Figure 2–13 Aquatic succession beginning with bare bottom pond (pioneer community) and terminating in beech–maple forest (climax). This type of succession is thought to be typical of many ponds in the Midwest. Note the gradual accumulation of humus (shown in solid black). [Adapted from R. and M. Buchsbaum, *Basic Ecology* (Pittsburgh, Penn.: Boxwood Press, 1957).]

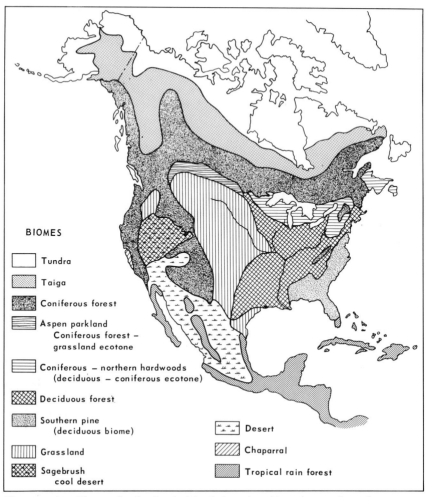

BIOMES

- [ ] Tundra
- [ ] Taiga
- [ ] Coniferous forest
- [ ] Aspen parkland
  Coniferous forest –
  grassland ecotone
- [ ] Coniferous – northern hardwoods
  (deciduous – coniferous ecotone)
- [ ] Deciduous forest
- [ ] Southern pine
  (deciduous biome)
- [ ] Grassland
- [ ] Sagebrush
  cool desert
- [ ] Desert
- [ ] Chaparral
- [ ] Tropical rain forest

Figure 2–14 Biome distribution in North America. Note the southward extension of the coniferous forest biome in the mountains. Within the United States, tropical rain forest occurs only in Florida. See text for comments on other biomes. [Adapted from Robert L. Smith, *Ecology and Field Biology* (New York: Harper & Row, 1966). Used by permission of the publishers.]

belt immediately south of the Arctic tundra and ranges south-ward into the northern United States from Washington to Maine. Characteristic *physical features* include annual rainfall of from 15 to 40 inches, average annual temperatures of from 20°F in the winter to more than 70°F in the summer, and a 150-day growing season. Dominant climax vegetation includes black spruce, white spruce, balsam fir, and tamarack. White birch and quaking aspen are representative of the earlier suc-cessional stages. Moose, snowshoe hare, and lynx are repre-sentative animals (7, 9, 10).

DECIDUOUS FOREST. The deciduous forest biome attains its greatest development east of the Mississippi immediately south of the coniferous forest. Fingers of deciduous forest extend westward into the prairie country along major watercourses, in response to localized increases in soil moisture. Annual precipitation ranges from 30 to 60 inches. Average January temperatures vary from 10°F in the north to 60 degrees F. in the south; average July temperatures range from 70 degrees F. in the north to 80 degrees F. in the south. The growing season (frost-free period) ranges from five months in the north to ten months in the south. The deciduous forest is divisible into several major associations, among which are maple–basswood, beech–maple, oak–chestnut, and oak–hickory. Representative consumers include the red-eyed vireo, ovenbird, deer mouse, gray squirrel, opossum, and white-tailed deer.

GRASSLAND, OR PRAIRIE. The major grasslands of the United States occur in two regions: the Great Plains, a vast area extending from the eastern slopes of the Rockies to the Mississippi River, and the more moist portions of the Great Basin lying between the Sierras on the west and the Rockies on the east. In north temperate latitudes, grasslands apparently represent the vegetational expression of an average annual precipitation which is excessive (over 10 inches) for development of desert vegetation, and inadequate (under 30 inches) for development of forest. Winter blizzards and summer drought may be severe. There is evidence that devastating fires periodically have burned the prairie. Dominant vegetation includes the big bluestem, little bluestem, buffalo grass, and grama grass. The horned lark and burrowing owl are characteristic birds. Dominant mammals include the prong-horned antelope, badger, whitetail jackrabbit, coyote, and pocket gopher.

Figure 2–15 Resident of the grassland biome. The black-tailed prairie dog at the edge of its crater-like burrow entrance. The levee not only serves as a lookout post but prevents flash-flooding of burrow. Washington, D.C., Zoo. [Soil Conservation Service, U.S. Department of Agriculture]

DESERT. American deserts are located in the hotter, drier portions of the Great Basin and in parts of California, New Mexico, Arizona, Texas, Nevada, Idaho, Utah, and Oregon. Deserts occur primarily to the leeward of prominent mountain ranges, such as the Sierra Nevada and the Rocky Mountains. The prevailing warm, humid air masses from the Pacific Ocean gradually cool as they move up windward slopes and release their moisture as rain or snow. The region to leeward of the mountains lies in the "rain shadow," where precipitation is minimal. A desert type of community generally results in those areas getting less than 10 inches of annual precipitation. Rainfall, moreover, may not be uniformly distributed, but may fall periodically in the form of cloudbursts that cause flash floods and soil-eroding run-off. An extremely high evaporation rate aggravates the severe moisture problem. For example, the water which theoretically could evaporate from a given land acre in one year may be *thirty* times the actual amount received as precipitation. Summer temperatures range from about 50°F at night to about 120°F during the day. Desert floor temperature reaches 145 degrees F. in summer.

Only organisms which have evolved specialized structural, physiological, and behavioral adaptations to extreme heat and aridity can survive in the desert. Characteristic producers are prickly pear cactus, suaharo cactus, greasewood, creosote bush, and mesquite. Plant adaptations for desert survival include either extremely shallow or extremely deep root systems; uniformly and widely dispersed plant distribution patterns (to ensure an adequate supply of moisture for the individual plant); succulent water-storage tissues; abbreviated life-spans, which permits plants to take advantage of short wet periods (some plants complete their entire life cycle in eight weeks); and waxy leaf coverings and recessed stomata, to minimize water loss from evapo-transpiration.

Conspicuous among desert animals are the western diamondback rattlesnake, Gila monster, greater roadrunner, Gila woodpecker, white-winged dove. Gambel's quail, black-tailed jackrabbit, antelope jackrabbit, kangaroo rat, pocket mouse, kit fox, collared peccary, and ringtail. Desert adaptations among animals include waxy (insects), scaled (reptiles), and armorlike (armadillo) body coverings that are impervious to water; the excretion of solid nitrogenous wastes (uric acid crystals); the ability to utilize metabolic water to the exclusion of ingested water (pocket mouse, kangaroo rat); the ability to obtain water from the blood and tissue fluids of prey; and the development of burrowing (kangaroo rat) and nocturnal behavior (ringtail, armadillo, and diamondback) (7, 9, 10).

BIBLIOGRAPHY

1. Dasmann, Raymond F. *Environmental Conservation.* New York: John Wiley & Sons, Inc., 1959, 307 pp.
2. Einarsen, A. S. "Some Factors Affecting Ring-necked Pheasant Population Density." *Murrelet,* **26** (1945), 39–44.
3. Errington, Paul L. "What Is the Meaning of Predation?" *Smiths: Report for 1936,* (1937), 243–252.
4. Golley, F. B. "Energy Dynamics of a Food Chain of an Old Field Community." *Ecol. Mono.,* **30** (1960), 187–206.
5. Gunter, Gordon. "Death of Fishes due to Cold on the Texas Coast." *Ecol.,* **22** (January 1940), 203–208.
6. Johnston, David W., and Eugene P. Odum. "Breeding Bird Populations in Relation to Plant Succession on the Piedmont of Georgia." *Ecol.,* **37** (1956), 50–62.
7. Kendeigh, S. Charles. *Animal Ecology.* Englewood Cliffs, N.J.: Prentice-Hall, Inc., 1961, 468 pp.
8. Lindemann, Raymond L. "The Trophic-Dynamic Aspect of Ecology." *Ecol.,* **23** (1942), 399–418.
9. Odum, Eugene P. *Fundamentals of Ecology.* Philadelphia: W. B. Saunders Co., 1959, 546 pp.
10. Smith, Robert L. *Ecology and Field Biology.* New York: Harper & Row, Publishers, 1966, 686 pp.

3 Nature of Soils

"In the sweat of thy face shalt thou eat bread, till thou return unto the ground, for out of it wast thou taken: for dust thou art, and unto dust shalt thou return." This passage from the Biblical story of creation (Genesis 3:19), written by Moses over 3,000 years ago, can be well appreciated by the soil scientist and ecologist of today. As we have learned in our discussion of food chains and pyramids, it is in the soil that all higher terrestrial plants have their roots and from which they absorb life-sustaining moisture and nutrients. Man, in turn, feeds directly upon these plants, upon plant-eating animals, or upon carnivores which prey on herbivores. Thus, virtually all terrestrial life ultimately derives from the dust of the earth. And when man eventually dies, the soil-derived elements in his body will be restored to the earth by the process of bacterial decay.

The average city-dweller equates soil with dirt, but to the farmer, soil is the essence of survival. His economic well-being is inextricably linked with the quality of his land. It may mean the difference between a squalid four-room shack and a comfortable ranch house, between an old-model car and a new one, or between an eighth-grade and a university education for his children. As of 1959, there were 3,703,894 individual farms in America embracing somewhat over 1 billion acres of land. The total value of both farm land and buildings was estimated at $130 billion (15).

Empires and nations, like individuals, are dependent on the soil. As a nation's soil resources are fertile and abundant, in like measure will that state have vigor and stability. When this resource is exhausted, because of mounting demands of a swelling population or long mismanagement, the nation's survival is in jeopardy. Some authorities believe that the decline and fall of the mighty Roman Empire may be attributed as much to the deterioration of soils in the Roman "granary" of North Africa as to political corruption and the invader's prowess. Throughout the annals of recorded human history, soil has been valued highly and has been as attractive a war prize as armaments, buildings, industries, or slaves. During the long search for fertile soil, hitherto peaceable, responsible empires have turned into militant aggressors.

Soil Formation

The development of a mature soil is a complex phenomenon involving the interaction of physical, chemical, and biological processes. The time required depends not only on the intensity of these processes but on the nature of the parent rock. Authorities estimate that the development of 1 inch of topsoil derived from hard rock like basalt or granite may require from 200 to 1200 years. However, soft rocks—such as volcanic ash, sand dunes, river sediments, and shale—may develop into mature vegetation-supporting soil within a few decades. The major processes in soil formation are *physical, chemical,* and *biological.*

Physical Processes

HEATING AND COOLING. Rapid heating and cooling may induce differential contraction and expansion which eventually causes rocks to scale, split, and shatter. This process assumes a particularly prominent role in the arid climates of the desert biome, where the diurnal cycle, especially during summer, may be marked by violent shifts in temperature. Thus, at noon the hot floor of the Arizona desert may register 145 degrees F. and by midnight may have dropped to 65 degrees F.

THAWING AND FREEZING. This process is characteristic of temperate latitudes where there is relatively abundant rainfall. During a winter thaw, rivulets of water from melted snow and ice gradually infiltrate the pores and cracks of surface rock. During a subsequent freeze, the water expands with considerable force, causing rock to flake and fragment.

GLACIAL ACTIVITY. During the Pleistocene Period (1,000,-
000 to 10,000 B.C.), four massive glacial advances moved south-
westward from Canada into the northeastern states as far as
Ohio, Indiana, Illinois, and Iowa. During these movements so
much ocean water was "locked up" in glacial ice that the ocean
level dropped about 250 feet. The massive, dome-shaped glaciers acted like gigantic files, shearing off hilltops and mountain
peaks, gouging out depressions, and pulverizing large boulders.
Their under surface collected rocks, gravel, sand, silt, and clay.
Consequently, when the ice finally melted, a mantle of glacial
drift remained which served as fresh parent material for the
development of future soils. Glaciation has generally enhanced
the value of soils for agriculture by increasing soil fertility and
by leveling the terrain in a way which renders it susceptible to
modern cultivation techniques.

OCEAN WAVES AND RIVER CURRENTS. Ocean waves are
powerful rockgrinders. Boulders are dashed about in the raging
surf like so many marbles, many of them being chipped and
broken in the process. Rivers also play an important role in
soil building. Pebbles of a stream bed may be worn smooth by

Figure 3–1 Geologic erosion. Note the glacial striations on this rock
formation in Wyoming. The boulder in the foreground has been smoothed
and rounded by moving glaciers, one of the physical processes involved
in soil formation. [U.S. Forest Service]

the scouring action of the current. Each stream carries in suspension a load of sand, silt, and clay. Much of this material may ultimately be transported to the ocean at the river's mouth to form a delta. The Mississippi River alone discharges roughly 700 million tons of sediment into the Gulf of Mexico each year. When the major rivers of the world—such as the Mississippi, Nile, and Amazon—periodically overflow their banks, a nutrient-rich load of sediment is deposited along the river bottoms. This special type of soil, called *alluvial soil,* is said to support almost one third of the world's agriculture.

WIND ACTION. The blasting effect of billions of minute, wind-blown sand grains inexorably wears smooth even the roughest boulders. Many of the smoothly rounded outcrops in our arid Southwest have been fashioned by wind erosion. The tiny rock particles may be transported for many miles before settling and becoming part of the soil.

Chemical Processes. Chemical processes of soil formation frequently occur simultaneously with the physical processes. Chemical activity usually causes minerals to lose their sheen

Figure 3–2 Infrared aerial view of the Missisquoi River watershed, Vermont. The delta of the river, formed by water transport of thousands of tons of silt, is visible in the foreground. [Soil Conservation Service, U.S. Department of Agriculture]

and become porous and soft. Among the principle chemical processes involved in soil formation are *hydrolysis, oxidation, and solution.*

HYDROLYSIS. Derived from the Greek, *hydrolysis* literally means "the process of breaking down or disintegrating with water." Hydrolysis is a type of chemical reaction with water which results in mineral decomposition and the formation of an hydroxide. For example, the mineral orthoclase ($KAlSi_3O_8$) reacts with water to form acid silicate clay ($HAlSi_3O_8$) and potassium hydroxide (KOH).

OXIDATION. Because oxidation involves the combination of oxygen with a mineral, it occurs most intensively at the upper surface of rock. It is a characteristic weathering process in iron-bearing deposits. Ferrous oxide (FeO), for example, may be oxidized to form ferric oxide or hematite (Fe_2O_3). As a result of oxidation, the iron-containing rock is more easily disintegrated.

SOLUTION. The solution of minerals occurs prominently in limestone rock. Here the percolating water, bearing dissolved carbon dioxide, gradually eats away the substratum to form minute pores, channels, and crevices. Chemically speaking, the calcitic limestone ($CaCO_3$) is converted to calcium bicarbonate $Ca(HCO_3)_2$ which, in turn, ionizes. The dissolved materials may be transported a considerable distance before precipitating out and eventually contributing to the formation of soil. Under certain conditions huge subterranean chambers are formed, such as Mammoth Cave of Kentucky or New Mexico's Carlsbad Caverns. These caverns are the products of limestone solution occurring over many centuries and their multicolored stalagmites and stalactites form labyrinths of awesome beauty.

Biological Processes. The development of a mature soil is also dependent on the activity of a great number and diversity of organisms. The all-important bacteria influence soil structure, aeration, moisture content, and fertility in many ways which will be discussed later in this chapter. Lichens and mosses that have become established on a rocky substratum may trap wind-blown organic debris—such as plant fibers, seeds, dead insects, excrement, and on on—to a depth sufficient to form a film over the rock's surface. They may also secrete a very dilute carbonic acid (H_2CO_3) which slowly dissolves the rock, thus accelerating its ultimate incorporation into a mature soil. Finally, upon their death, the lichens and mosses will decompose and eventually enrich the soil with their constituent elements. Rock may be splintered by the actively growing roots of trees. Rooted vegetation absorbs nutrient salts from lower levels and deposits them at the soil surface when it dies. Through the centuries, the hoofs of antelope, buffalo, mountain sheep, deer, and livestock have gradually fragmented and pulverized underlying rock. The burrowing activities of earthworms, millipedes, digger wasps, beetle larvae, bull snakes, burrowing owls, pocket gophers, and ground squirrels promote soil aeration and facilitate water passage. Soil fertility is enhanced by animal excrement, especially that of earthworms, arthropods, birds, and mammals. The droppings (guano) of dense breeding colonies of cormorants on the Chincha Islands off the west coast of Peru at one time accumulated to a depth of over 100 feet. Rich in phosphates and nitrates, it was harvested by the Peruvian government and sold as fertilizer, thus eventually enriching distant soils.

Soil Properties

The major properties of soils are *texture, structure, atmospheric content, moisture content,* and *biotic composition.* An understanding of the nature of these characteristics is an essential prerequisite to the study of soil profiles, soil types, soil productivity, and soil management.

Texture. By *texture* is meant the *size* of the individual mineral particles as well as the *proportion* in which they occur. For convenience and efficiency in the study of mineral particles, the USDA has classified soil particles as gravel, sand, silt, and clay, depending upon size. It should be emphasized that these textural classes are relatively stable. Despite the dynamic nature of soil, despite the continuous physical, chemical, and biological activities which are continuously transforming it, and regardless of the soil management activities of the farmer, gravel will not change to sand, or silt to clay, within the average human life-span.

GRAVEL. Soil particles which are over 1 millimeter in diameter are classified as gravel.

SAND. Particles of sand range from 0.05 to 1 millimeter in diameter. This textural class shows very little plasticity or cohesiveness, as is well known to anyone who has tried to build a sand castle. Because the spaces (macropores) between the individual sand particles are quite large, sand is usually well aerated and has good drainage. Because it is composed of quartz (SiO_2), however, which is chemically inactive, it will yield very few nutrients for crop growth.

SILT. The individual particles of silt are microscopic in size (0.002 to 0.05 millimeters). Silt shows a slight tendency to become plastic and sticky when wet. Because silt, like sand, is composed primarily of quartz (SiO_2), its nutrient-supplying ability is poor. When unmixed with other soil texture classes, it is agriculturally unproductive.

CLAY. The individual clay particles are so minute (less than 0.002 millimeters) that they are not even visible with an ordinary microscope. The plasticity and cohesiveness of moistened clay permit it to be fashioned into pots, bowls, and vases. Because of this stickiness when wet, clay soils are worked only with difficulty and are therefore called heavy soils, in contrast to the easily worked light soils that are composed primarily of sand. The more plastic clay becomes, the more likely it is to "puddle," that is, to undergo reduction in pore space and incur reduced permeability to air and water. When clay soils dry out, the individual particles contract so as to form hard clods.

The total amount of air space in clay is somewhat greater than in sand. Because much of this air space is represented by extremely minute pores (micropores), however, the actual rate of water percolation and air movement through clay is much slower than it is through sand. Water in the micropores is held so tenaciously that it is unavailable for most plant root systems. Moreover, because young plant rootlets do not readily penetrate poorly oxygenated clay, soil composed exclusively of clay is quite unproductive. The dominant minerals in clay are kaolinite, mica, and montmorillonite.

Because of its electrical properties clay serves as an important reservoir of plant food. Because the surfaces of the microscopic clay particles are negatively charged, they are able to adsorb many positively charged soil elements, such as calcium, magnesium, potassium, phosphorus, zinc, and copper. Clay frequently retains these nutrients despite the leaching tendencies of percolating water.

LOAM. Very few agricultural soils are composed exclusively of one textural class; usually they represent a mixture in which all four of the major classes (gravel, sand, silt, and clay) are represented in varying proportions. The most desirable soil from an agricultural standpoint is *loam,* which represents a mixture of heavy and light soil materials in the following proportions: sand, 30 to 50 per cent; silt, 30 to 50 per cent; and clay, 0 to 20 per cent. In the best loams the most desirable qualities of sand and clay are combined and their adverse characteristics are precluded.

Soil Structure. We may define soil structure as the arrangement or grouping of its primary particles (gravel, sand, silt, and clay) into *granules,* or *aggregates.*

Figure 3–3 Soil structure. Profiles of soil taken near Newkirk, Oklahoma. Soil sample at left was under poor land treatment, soil at right under excellent cropping system. Poor treatment is reflected in poor structure and low organic matter; good treatment has resulted in good structure and high organic content. [Soil Conservation Service, U.S. Department of Agriculture]

The aeration, moisture content, fertility, and erosion resistance of a soil are all to some degree dependent upon its structure. Plowing, cultivation, liming, and manuring may improve the soil's productivity primarily by changing its structure. Other factors affecting soil structure include alternate freezing and thawing, drying and wetting, penetration by plant roots, burrowing activity of animals, addition of slimy secretions from soil animals, and decomposition of plant and animal residues in the soil.

GOOD STRUCTURE. A good soil structure (that is, one which promotes crop or timber production) has a spongy or crumbly quality. It has an abundance of pores through which life-sustaining oxygen diffuses and through which water can move to the root systems of crop plants. Soil with good structure feels resilient and springy under foot. Such soil is resistant to the erosive effects of wind, rain, and run-off water. Farmers can effectively promote good soil structure by the addition of organic matter, either by manuring, or by plowing under cover crops and crop residues (stubble).

POOR STRUCTURE. A soil with poor structure has a minimum of pore spaces, or "chambers," for air and water, because of the closely packed soil particles. Moreover, the individual soil particles tend to break up or fall apart. It has little resiliency. Because water infiltration is greatly reduced, in arid regions irrigation water may not penetrate to satisfactory depths for crop production. In humid areas, however, poorly structured soils produce drainage problems in low-lying sites, whereas on uplands they may result in severe water run-off and erosion. Although most virgin soils in the grassland and deciduous forest biomes of America originally had good structure, many decades of intensive farming, involving the use of increasingly heavy plowing, cultivating, and harvesting equipment, gradually brought about their deterioration.

Atmospheric Content. Only about 50 per cent of soil volume is actually represented by solid materials such as minerals, plant and animal bodies, and organic residues. The remaining 50 per cent is represented by pore spaces (*macropores* and *micropores*) which occur between the individual soil particles and/or aggregates. When soil is extremely dry because of a protracted drought, these spaces are filled with air. When soil is waterlogged after a violent thunderstorm, they may be filled with water.

In a sense, one can consider soil as continuously inhaling and exhaling. *Oxygen,* which is present in greater concentration in the atmosphere than in the earth, diffuses into the soil pores, whereas *carbon dioxide,* which may approach a concentration of 10 per cent in soil spaces, continuously moves from soil into the atmosphere, where the concentration is about 0.03 per cent. The importance of soil oxygen for plant growth is well demonstrated in apple trees, which require a concentration of 3 per cent merely to survive, of 5 to 10 per cent for elongation of existing roots, and of 12 per cent before new roots will develop. When soil is poorly aerated, the nitrogen-fixing activity of *Rhizobium* (root-nodule bacteria) and *Azotobacter* (free-living form) are adversely affected, thus impairing soil fertility. Moreover, an oxygen-deficient soil curtails the development of crop roots, may cause root deformities, and may severely restrict their role in water and nutrient absorption.

Moisture Content. Water serves several important plant functions. It is essential for photosynthesis and the conversion of starch to sugar. It enables plants to maintain an effective shape or position for reception of incident sunlight by maintaining their turgidity. Water is the solvent medium by which minerals are transported upward to the leaves and sugar is transported downward to the roots. Finally, it is an essential protoplasmic constituent, contributing 85 to 90 per cent of the weight of actively growing organs such as buds, rootlets, and flowers.

CLASSIFICATION OF SOIL MOISTURE. Soil may be classified in relation to its water content as being *saturated*, at *field capacity*, or at the *permanent wilting point*.

Saturated Soil. Soil is said to be saturated when the air in all the micropores and macropores has become replaced with water. This may occur after low-lying fields have been flooded following a severe thunderstorm or excessive irrigation.

Field Capacity. Field capacity refers to the amount of water which remains after the excess has drained away from soil which has become water saturated. Soil particles retain this water with a tension of one-third atmosphere (13).

Permanent Wilting Point. Vigorously growing crops continuously remove soil moisture. As soil moisture is reduced, a critical point is reached when the "pull" of the plant roots for water is not sufficient to prevent permanent wilting. This point is known as the *permanent wilting point*. This amount of water is retained by the soil particles with a tension of fifteen atmospheres. Unless the soil water is replenished, the plant will eventually die.

Because of the limited oxygen available, soil water between field capacity and saturation may not be utilized by common upland crops; it is available, however, to water-loving plants such as rice. Water utilization in most crops is restricted to the moisture range between wilting point and field capacity.

Biotic Composition. Soil is composed of more than just inanimate rock and air and water; it is very much alive and represents the world's largest zoo and botanical garden rolled into one. Were we to take a single grain of fertile topsoil and examine it under a microscope, we would find it swarming with minute organisms. These creatures play a basic role in determining the soil's chemistry, air and water relationship, and fertility.

We shall describe the activities of the major groups of soil plants (bacteria, ray fungi, fungi, and algae) and soil animals (protozoa, nematodes, insects, and earthworms) in building and transforming the soil.

BACTERIA. The top foot of an acre of fertile soil may contain 1,000 pounds of bacterial biomass (5). In a very real sense, bacteria burn up the organic content of the soil. On a hot day in July, the bacteria of one acre burn carbon at a rate equivalent to burning 1.6 pounds of soft coal hourly and generating up to 1 horsepower of energy (1). The energy thus liberated from the organic material is then used in converting soil nutrients into a form available to crops.

Soil bacteria normally do not occur as isolated cells but are found in clumplike, matlike, or filamentous colonies around individual soil particles (5). Bacterial populations, which may form up to 0.03 per cent of the weight of top soil (2), are concentrated in the upper layers of soil, where oxygen and bacterial food in the form of plant debris are abundant. The roots and root hairs of plants are frequently completely enclosed in a bacterial film. The soil in the immediate vicinity of root systems (known as the *rhizosphere*) may be from ten to fifty times more dense with bacteria than other soil (5).

ACTINOMYCETES. Structurally, the actinomycetes occupy an intermediate position between bacteria and the fungi. They are similar to fungi in that they bear branched mycelia. Because of their body form, they have been called ray fungi or thread bacteria. Up to 20 million of these organisms may occur in 1 gram of dry soil. Their aggregate weight in an acre furrow-slice may be as high as 600 pounds. Their habitat appears to be moist, neutral to slightly acid, well-aerated soils possessing an ample quantity of organic matter. The musty odor from old grain and straw is due mainly to actinomycetes (5). The great majority of ray fungi are beneficial, because they decompose organic debris, especially cellulose, and recycle elements which may be utilized by crops (5). Almost 500 antibiotics have been isolated from the actinomycetes, including streptomycin, aureomycin, neomycin, and terramycin. A few parasitic forms may be highly destructive to crops.

FUNGI AND MOLDS. The fungi and molds, like the bacteria and actinomycetes, lack chlorophyll and hence cannot carry on photosynthesis. They secure their energy and carbon from organic residues.

All of us are familiar with the cottony bread mold or the various gray, black, white, and green molds which flourish on decaying fruit and fruit perserves. The larger forest fungi, like the toadstools, puffballs, and mushrooms, are also well known. Very few of us are aware, however, of the mold and fungi of soils, many of the 200 species of which are of microscopic size. There may be 1 million fungi in 1 gram of dry soil, and their per acre biomass may reach 1,200 pounds. Four common soil genera are *Aspergillus, Mucor, Trichoderma,* and *Penecillium.*

Molds occur prominently in the acid soils of deciduous and coniferous forests. Because most soil bacteria are intolerant of acid conditions, the decay and rot of leaf litter is primarily effected by fungi and molds, with some assistance from millipedes, mites, and springtails. Fungi are most effective decomposers and break down even such complex leaf litter compounds as cellulose and lignin with their digestive enzymes. Up to 50 per cent of the decomposed plant debris may then be channeled into the living substance of the soil molds. Molds are unable to thrive in boggy soils because of the limited oxygen available; the resultant accumulation of organic residues is eventually converted to *peat* (5).

Various forest fungi also perform a useful function by entering into a mutualistic relationship with the root systems of trees. This interrelationship is called a *mycorrhiza*, a term meaning "fungus-root" (5). The branching root systems (*mycelia*) of the fungus may form a layer over the tree's root surface or may even penetrate its root cells. The fungus-bearing roots of the tree apparently have greater nutrient-absorbing ability than roots not so associated (5). The nutritive function, although not completely understood, may be due to the fact that fungus-bearing roots may have 200 times the absorptive area of non-mycorrhizal roots (5). Suitable mycorrhiza frequently must be inoculated into soils of forest nurseries established to raise seedlings of trees not native to the region.

SOIL ALGAE. Soil algae are simple plants and are usually unicellular and microscopic. In addition to bearing chlorophyll, some may possess blue, golden, brown, or red pigments. The major groups are the blue, the blue-green, the yellow-green, and the diatoms. Occasionally, after heavy rainstorms the red algae populations will increase greatly, causing light-colored soil to turn a faint crimson color (5). Because algae are chlorophyll-bearing organisms, they must live near the soil's surface, where there is sufficient sunshine for photosynthesis. After the application of commercial fertilizers the soil may turn green, because of the increased amount of green algae. Algae densities up to 800,000 organisms per gram of dry soil have been estimated in samples from Utah. By the release of oxygen, soil algae may aid in soil aeration. Algae may serve as food for other soil organisms. In some areas, such as in grasslands, where blue-green algae are populous, they may serve an important nitrogen-fixing function. The sustained fertility of the Asiatic rice paddies, even after centuries of use, has been partially attributed to this role of the blue-green algae.

SOIL ANIMALS.   In addition to these teeming populations of microflora, the soil community also includes a zoological garden of almost infinite variety, ranging in size from the microscopic, unicellular *protozoa* to relatively large burrowing mammals, such as the pocket gopher and mole.

Protozoa.   There are over 250 species of soil-dwelling protozoa. Several million protozoa may occur in a teaspoonful of fertile soil (5). Their total biomass may approach 200 pounds per acre-foot. Protozoans are primarily restricted to the upper soil layers where suitable food and soil oxygen are abundant. Although most soil protozoa subsist on preformed organic and inorganic substrates, a few apparently ingest other protozoans, algae, and bacteria. It has been suggested, therefore, that if large numbers of nitrogen-fixing bacteria were consumed, their protozoan predators may in this way indirectly limit soil fertility.

Nematodes.   Nematodes are nonsegmented worms which range from the microscopic to over a foot long. Because of their slender shape they have been called eel worms or horse hair worms. Up to 45 billion of these threadlike worms may occur in an acre furrow-slice; fifty may occur in a grain of dry soil. They may be classified as omnivores, predators, and parasites. The omnivores feed primarily on decaying organic matter; the predators prey on earthworms, other nematodes, protozoa, and bacteria; and the parasites infest plant roots. In the South the parasitic forms have severely damaged vegetable crops. On Long Island, New York, the Golden Nematode *(Heterodera Rostochiensis)* is injurious to potato production.

Insects.   Insects form a most interesting component of the soil community. Included among the thousands of species are the larvae of the seventeen-year locust, mound-building ants, beetle larvae, burrow-digging wasps, and the diminutive springtails. Springtails are primitive wingless forms that are able to propel themselves in a series of "jumps" by means of a specialized abdominal appendage. Many insects swarm in the leaf litter of the forest, ingesting and partially digesting the leaf fragments, converting them into a form more readily decomposed by the activity of soil fungi and bacteria. All soil-dwelling insects contribute to the porosity, drainage, and aeration of the soil by their burrowing activities. According to Clark, up to eighty-four cicada emergence holes (by means of which the larvae leave their subterranean haunts to assume an arboreal life as a winged adult) have been counted in a single square foot of ground (7).

Earthworms. In the topsoil of well-manured agricultural land, the population density of the earthworm may reach 1 million per acre. The per-acre biomass, up to 1,100 pounds, may exceed the total biomass of all other soil animals combined. Earthworms prefer soil that is well drained, rich in decomposing organic matter, well supplied with calcium, and with a pH above 4.5. Good drainage prevents flooding of their burrows; decomposing organic debris serves as food.

Earthworms literally eat their way through the soil, sucking in dirt, manure, plant fragments, seeds, insect eggs and larvae, and numerous minute animals, dead and alive, through their mouth with their muscular, suctionlike pharynx. This activity is most prominent in the upper 6 inches of topsoil. After thoroughly grinding this material in the gizzard and digesting it, residues are ejected through the anus in the form of *casts.* There can be as much as 8 tons per acre of these spherical casts in a cultivated field. A study of arable land in Connecticut showed that earthworm casts contained 366 per cent more nitrogen, 644 per cent more phosphorus, and 1,109 per cent more potassium than surrounding soil. By their burrowing activity, earthworms promote soil aeration and drainage and facilitate downward growth of plant roots. With their nutrient-rich casts and nitrogen-containing excretions, they increase soil fertility. Earthworms may bring to the surface up to 18 tons an acre per year. Soil which has been worked over by earthworms usually has a characteristic granular structure.

Soil Profile

When one looks at the exposed face of a road cut or the wall of a rock quarry, it is apparent that it is organized into horizontally arranged layers, or *horizons.* Each of these horizons is distinct with regard to thickness, color, texture, and chemical composition. This cross-sectional view of the various horizons is known as the *soil profile.* Each profile is the expression of a specific combination of soil formation factors, including parent rock, soil age, topography, climate, and organisms.

The major layers from the ground surface downward to bedrock are designated as horizons A (topsoil), B (subsoil), C (parent material), and D (bedrock) (9). These horizons will not all be equally distinct in the different soil types. In fact, in immature soils, where weathering has not fully progressed, some horizons may be missing, whereas in certain soils laid down by water-borne sediment, known as *alluvial soils,* or in soils that have been thoroughly mixed by the burrowing activity of mammals, the stratified pattern may be lacking completely.

The profile of a typical soil is the product of the interaction of climate, vegetation, temperature, rainfall, and soil organisms on parent rock materials operating for many thousands of years. The soil profile, therefore, tells us a great deal about soil history. It represents a kind of soil autobiography by which we can learn much about its origin and development. From the practical standpoint the soil profile is of great economic importance, for it can tell the agronomist immediately whether the soil is best suited for agricultural crops, for rangeland, for timber, or for wildlife habitat and recreation. (Fig. 3–4)

Soil Horizons. Let us examine the basic characteristics of a hypothetical composite soil profile, beginning with the uppermost horizon and moving downward to bedrock. (See Figure 3–6.)

A HORIZON. Mankind is dependent upon the thin envelope of topsoil which covers much of the earth. In America its thickness ranges from 1 to 2 inches on the slopes of the Rockies to almost 2 feet in Iowa corn country. It is from the topsoil, or A horizon, that crop roots absorb vital water. It is within this stratum also that soil organisms abound. Subhorizons within the A horizon can be recognized from top to bottom as follows:

A_{00}. The A_{00} horizon is composed of loosely arrayed organic debris. It perhaps is most conspicuous in the temperate deciduous forest, where it is represented by leaf litter, fallen twigs, fruits, nuts, and animal excrement. By the end of autumn this material may form an aggregate weight of up to 1 ton per acre. This layer is usually missing in prairie soils.

A_0. The A_0 horizon is a layer of organic material in various stages of decomposition and is sometimes known as *humus*. Most of the decay is affected by fungi. This layer is again most conspicuous in forest soils, of course, and virtually absent in prairie soils.

A_1. The A_1 horizon is characteristically a dark-colored layer in which organic material has become thoroughly mixed with soil minerals.

A_2. The A_2 subhorizon is a light-colored mineral layer that is very characteristic of true *podzol* soils, developing under coniferous or deciduous forests. In a sense, it represents a layer of "impoverishment" because of the excessive leaching of soluble soil nutrients by water and organic acids percolating downward from the upper horizons. It is poorly developed or lacking in *chernozemic* soils.

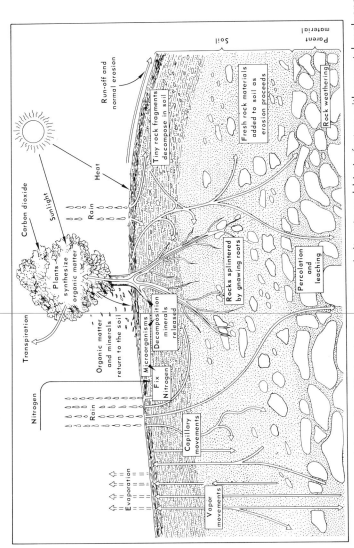

Figure 3–4 Development of the soil profile by the interaction of climatic and biotic factors with parental rock and physiographic features. Rainfall is an essential source of water for photosynthesis and for life maintenance in all organisms (bacteria, fungi, earthworms, grass, trees, etc.) involved in soil development. In combination with land topography, precipitation determines the rate and extent of normal (accelerated) erosion. Although some topsoil is continuously being subjected to natural (slow) erosion, this is partially offset by the addition of fresh rock-derived materials to the soil body. [Adapted from George L. Clarke, *Elements of Ecology* (New York: John Wiley & Sons, Inc., 1954. After Charles E. Kellogg, *The Soils That Support Us* (New York: The Macmillan Company, 1941).]

B Horizon. The B horizon, commonly called the *subsoil,* is a "zone of accumulation" into which silicates, clays, iron and aluminum compounds, and organic matter are carried by percolating waters from the A horizon. In true podzol soils this layer is conspicuously reddish-brown. It is in this horizon that the dense, impermeable *hardpan* of the podzol soil and the claypan of other soil types develop.

C Horizon. The C horizon is composed of the unconsolidated, weathered parent material from which the mineral component of the A and B horizons will ultimately be derived. About 97 per cent of the parent materials in the United States were transported to their present sites by ice, water, wind, and gravity. This parent material will in part determine soil texture and the rate of water absorption and release. Moreover, it will influence the soil's acidity or alkalinity. Thus, if parent material is granitic, soil will mature slowly and tend to be acid; conversely, where limestone represents the parent material, the soil will develop rapidly and remain alkaline even in humid climates which would otherwise promote an acid soil. Granitic soils are usually less productive than limestone soils.

D Horizon. The D horizon consists of the unweathered bedrock formed by geological processes such as sedimentation and volcanic activity.

Major Soil Groups

The U.S. Department of Agriculture, with the assistance of the various state agricultural experiment stations, has mapped more than 14,000 *soil types* over 500 million acres. Soil types are designated by locality and texture. In a 1,100-square-mile region near Merced, California, at least 290 soil types have been distinguished. Soil types are assembled into about twenty *soil groups.* For our purposes it will be necessary only to identify and describe a few major soil groups—true podzols, gray-brown podzols, red-yellow podzols, prairie soils, chernozems, chestnut-and-brown soils, and the desert soils. (Fig. 3–5)

Podzol Soils

Podzolization. Podzolization occurs in a cool, humid climate under forest vegetation. The litter of forest leaves, fruits, and branches decomposes, largely because of fungal activity, to produce a dark brown, extremely acid humus. Percolating water and organic acids carry soluble carbonate and sulphate salts, as well as aluminum and iron compounds,

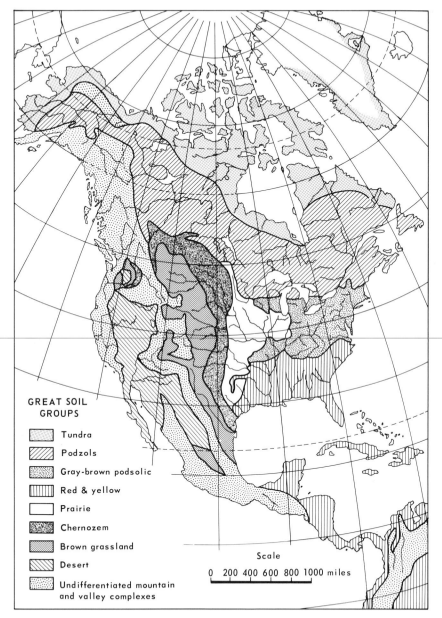

GREAT SOIL GROUPS

- Tundra
- Podzols
- Gray-brown podsolic
- Red & yellow
- Prairie
- Chernozem
- Brown grassland
- Desert
- Undifferentiated mountain and valley complexes

Scale

0   200 400 600 800 1000 miles

Figure 3–5 Major soil groups of North America. [Adapted from Raymond F. Dasmann, *Environmental Conservation* (New York: John Wiley & Sons, Inc., 1968). After Vernon C. Finch and G. T. Trewartha, *Elements of Geography, Physical and Cultural* (New York: McGraw-Hill Book Co., 1942) and C. E. Kelley in *Soils* and *Man* (Washington, D.C.: U.S. Department of Agriculture, 1938).]

downward from the A to the B horizon. This leaching causes the A_2 horizon to assume a gray, ashlike appearance. (The term *podzol* is derived from two Russian words, *pod,* which means *under,* and *zola,* which means *ash.*) The B_2 horizon, on the other hand, because of the addition of iron compounds and organic materials, assumes a distinctive coffee-brown color. (Fig. 3–6)

Figure 3–6 Profile of podzol soil. Note the accumulation of a dense mat of spruce and pine needle litter. The gray color of the thin layer of topsoil contrasts sharply with the dark-brown B horizon. Soluble calcium, potassium, and nitrate salts are leached by the abundant rainfall (over 30 inches annually) beyond the zone of plant root availability down to the C horizon. Although this figure is representative of podzols, considerable variation is possible because of regional differences in climate and parental materials. [Adapted from George L. Clarke, *Elements of Ecology* (New York: John Wiley & Sons, Inc., 1954).]

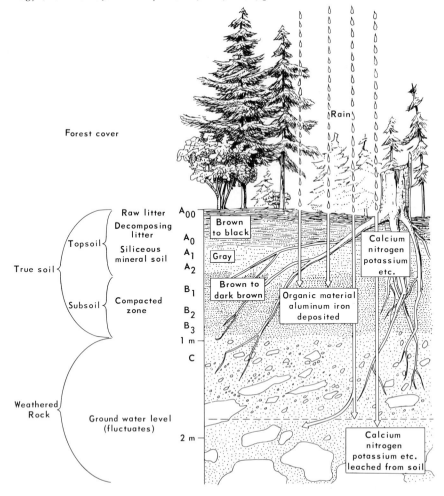

TRUE PODZOLS. The classic example of podzolization occurs in the true podzol soils. These soils develop under the coniferous forests of the northern Lake States, in the uplands of New England, and at high elevations in the Western mountains. Because these soils are inherently infertile, they can best be utilized for timber production, wildlife habitat, and scenic wilderness. Many an enterprising farming venture based on tilling the podzol soils of northern Michigan and Wisconsin in the early part of this century ultimately failed because of the relatively short growing season and the extremely acid and infertile soil. Unless true podzol soil is heavily limed and fertilized, it depreciates rapidly. This is corroborated by many an abandoned farm home now being swallowed up by encroaching second-growth forest. An outstanding exception to the general failure of true podzols as agriculturally productive soils is the famous potato-growing area in Aroostook County, Maine, where intensive fertilization is practiced.

GRAY-BROWN PODZOLS. The gray-brown podzols, which derive their name from the A_2 horizon, occur just south of the true podzols in Minnesota, Wisconsin, Illinois, Michigan, Indiana, Ohio, New York, Pennsylvania, and all the New England states. Less intensively podzolized than the true podzols, the gray-brown have developed under a deciduous forest cover. The extensive leaf litter derived from herbs, shrubs, and trees, sometimes amounting to a ton per acre annually, decomposes much more readily and releases more calcium than the hard mat of needles that forms under coniferous forests. As a result, the gray-brown podzols are less acid and more fertile than the true podzols. These are the soils on which America's pioneer farmers heavily depended. Although the original fertility of such soils is quickly depleted, rainfall and climate are normally benign. Therefore, when proper soil conservation practices are maintained, a great spectrum of agricultural activity can be supported, from the raising of grains, tobacco, potatoes, and fruit to the development of lush pastures for beef and dairy cattle.

RED-YELLOW PODZOLS. The red-yellow group, named after the color of the iron compounds in the subsoil, occupies an extensive area embracing thousands of square miles in the Southeastern United States, ranging southward from Pennsylvania and New Jersey and eastward from Missouri, Oklahoma, and Texas. The virgin soils developed under a mixture of coniferous and deciduous cover. Because of the high average temperatures and the abundant rainfall, the accumulated leaf litter is so rapidly decomposed by the activity of swarming fungi and bacteria that only a thin 1- to 3-inch humus-impregnated layer can develop. Much of the area occupied by these soils is hilly and subject to excessive erosion. Forests are much more extensive than in the gray-brown podzol regions to the north. Although the soil is inherently infertile, the land is amenable to the plow and cultivator, and with proper techniques of erosion control, green manuring, and fertilization, the soils can be reasonably productive. Crops in the red-yellow podzols ranges from cotton, corn, tobacco, peanuts, and soybeans to pasture for beef and dairy cattle.

Prairie Soils.   The prairie soils are sometimes called *brunizems,* a term which means "brown earth," because of the dark brown color of the topsoil. The typical prairie soil forms a vast north-south belt extending from the western margin of the forests westward to about the 100th meridian, and from southern Minnesota in the north to northern Oklahoma in the south. In Iowa and Illinois these soils develop under an annual rainfall of at least 30 inches. The prairie soils, which developed originally under tall grass prairie vegetation, are inherently fertile. The organic content in the A_1 horizon is exceptionally abundant, because it is largely derived from the extensive, dense fibrous root systems of prairie grasses which have rapidly *decomposed in the soil* by the activities of numerous bacteria and fungi. (Loss of organic material resulting from erosion by run-off waters, such as occurs in forest soils deriving organic matter from the *on-surface* accumulation of litter, is minimized.) The A horizon in some rich prairie soils may be 1 to 2 feet thick and has a characteristic dark brown color. The grass cover tends to impart a highly desirable granular structure to the topsoil, which promotes aeration and water absorption. These soils are extremely fertile and support the vast corn belt of the Midwest as well as enormous acreages of wheat and cotton in more southerly regions.

Chernozem Soils.   *Chernozem* is the Russian word for *black earth.* It refers to the extremely fertile, blackish-brown topsoil which may accumulate to a depth of 3 to 4 feet. Developing primarily under mixed-grass prairie, the chernozems extend in a north–south belt 150 miles wide in the Great Plains from the western edge of the tall grass prairie to the eastern margin of the short grass prairie. *Calcification* of the subsoil resulting from leaching of soluble calcium carbonate from above is a dominant characteristic. However, because of an annual rainfall of only 15 to 25 inches, which is usually in the form of brief summer thunder showers, leaching does not carry the calcium through to the C horizon. It is instead deposited in the lower subsoil, where it precipitates out and forms a grayish or yellowish band. The topsoil of the chernozem, characterized by rich organic and nutrient mineral content as well as a highly desirable granular

Figure 3–7 Profile of chernozem soil. The black color of the 2-foot thick A horizon contrasts with the light color of the 1-foot thick B horizon. Note that because of the light rainfall (10 to 30 inches annually) the soluble mineral salts (except for lime which accumulates at the base of the B horizon) are not leached extensively from the A horizon but are available to plants. Observe the extensive mesh of root systems in the A horizon. Upon plant death the *in situ* decomposition of the root systems releases nutrients which become immediately available for future plant generations. Loss of these nutrients by erosion is obviously minimal. The actual dimensions of the chernozem horizons illustrated are typical but may vary considerably depending on regional differences in parental material and climate. [Adapted from George L. Clarke, *Elements of Ecology* (New York: John Wiley & Sons, Inc., 1954).]

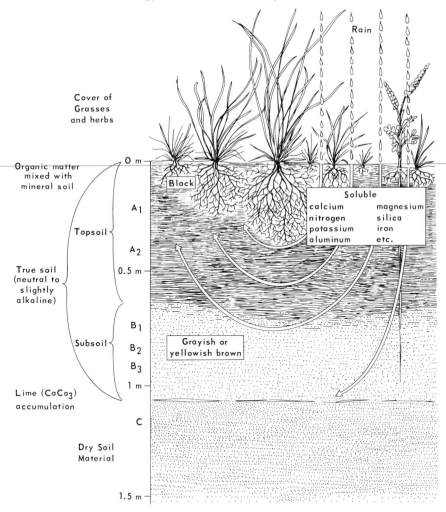

structure, is intrinsically more fertile than any other soil type in the United States. The relatively undependable and low annual rainfall limits its productivity, however. During wet years bumper crops are commonplace, but during years of excessive heat and drought, crop failures may be extensive. Major northern crops produced in these soils are high-quality corn, wheat, barley, oats, and rye. Sorghum is a prominent southern crop.

Chestnut and Brown Soils. The chestnut and brown soils extend in roughly two parallel belts (the chestnut belt just east of the brown soil belt) from Montana and North Dakota south to Texas. They occupy the area between the chernozems to the east and the foothills of the Rockies to the west. A restricted region of chestnut soils occurs in eastern Washington and northern Oregon; brown soils are also found extensively in the Great Basin as a transition between the chestnut and desert soils. Named after the color of their topsoils, the chestnut and brown soils are the principal soils of the arid and semiarid Great Plains. Before encroachment of the white man's civilization, these soils supported teeming herds of antelope and buffalo. Partly because of the limited annual precipitation of 10 to 15 inches, the plant community over these soils is characterized by short grasses, such as grama grass and buffalo grass. The topsoil contains less organic matter than that in the chernozems. Although calcification occurs, because of the scant rainfall the calcified layer in the subsoil is quite close to the surface. It occupies the 2- to 4-foot level and the 1- to 2-foot level in the chestnut and brown soils, respectively. Because of minimal leaching, the soils are rich in mineral nutrients. Nevertheless, it is a hazardous practice to farm these soils when they are not properly irrigated. Intensive grain-cropping and overgrazing of these soils precipitated the destructive dust storms of the 1930's. Although when properly irrigated the chestnut soils are highly productive of grain crops, most of them should probably be used exclusively for rangeland.

The Desert Soils. The desert soils occur in the desert biome, where the annual rainfall averages from about 3 to 12 inches. Desert soils occur extensively in southern and eastern California, southeastern Oregon, Nevada, southern Idaho, southwestern Arizona, western Utah, western Wyoming, southern New Mexico, and western Texas. Vegetation consists to a large degree of specialized drought-adapted plants, called *xerophytes,* such as sagebrush, creosote bush, ocatillo, mesquite, shadscale, and cactus. Because these desert plants are widely spaced, with

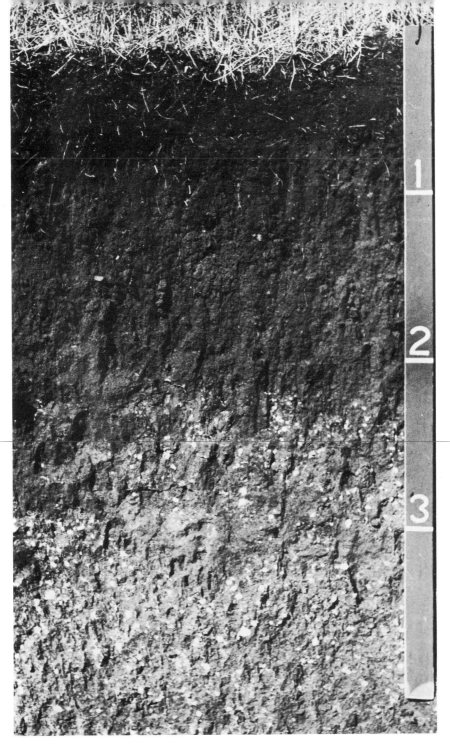

Figure 3–8 Profile of chernozem soil formed from glacial till in South Dakota. Note thick, dark A horizon and the whitish flecks (calcium deposits) in the B horizon. Scale is calibrated in feet. [Soil Conservation Service, U.S. Department of Agriculture]

extensive areas of bare soil between them, water and wind erosion may be severe and may leave a layer of stones called the *desert pavement.* There is a relatively small component of organic matter in the thin band of topsoil. However, because leaching is minimal, the nutrient content of the soil is relatively high. With proper soil management and effective irrigation, certain desert areas, such as the Imperial Valley of California, can produce a variety of valuable crops. Generally, however, desert soils can best serve as rangelands. The rangeland value can be greatly enhanced by such management practices as artificial reseeding, deferred grazing, eradication of water-absorbing weeds, and selective breeding of heat- and drought-resistant livestock.

BIBLIOGRAPHY

1. Allen, Shirley W., and Justin W. Leonard. *Conserving Natural Resources.* New York: McGraw-Hill Book Co., 1966, 432 pp.
2. Bear, Firman E. *Chemistry of the Soil.* New York: Reinhold Publishing Corp., 1964, 515 pp.
3. Bennett, Hugh Hammond. *Soil Conservation.* New York: McGraw-Hill Book Co., 1939, 993 pp.
4. _____ *Elements of Soil Conservation.* New York: McGraw-Hill Book Co., 1955, 360 pp.
5. Dale, Tom, and V. G. Carter. *Topsoil and Civilization.* Norman: University of Oklahoma Press, 1955, 270 pp.
6. Dasmann, Raymond F. *Environmental Conservation.* New York: John Wiley & Sons, Inc., 1959, 307 pp.
7. Clark, Francis E. "Living Organisms in the Soil," *Soils: The 1957 Yearbook of Agriculture.* Washington, D.C.: U.S. Department of Agriculture, 1957, 157–165.
8. Fuller, Harry J., and Oswald Tippo. *College Botany.* New York: Holt, Rinehart and Winston, Inc., 1954, 993 pp.
9. Jenny, Hans. "Soil as a Natural Resource," in Martin R. Huberty and Warren L. Flock (eds.), *Natural Resources.* New York: McGraw-Hill Book Co., 1959.
10. Kellog, Charles E. *The Soils That Support Us.* New York: The Macmillan Co., 1941.
11. Lyon, T. Lyttleton, and Harry O. Buckman. *The Nature and Property of Soils.* New York: The Macmillan Co., 1941.
12. Smith, Guy-Harold (ed.). *Conservation of Natural Resources.* New York: John Wiley & Sons, Inc., 1958, 474 pp.
13. Taylor, Sterling A. "Use of Moisture by Plants," *Soils: The Yearbook of Agriculture.* Washington, D.C.: U.S. Department of Agriculture, 1957.
14. U.S. Department of Agriculture. *Land: The Yearbook of Agriculture.* Washington, D.C., 1958.
15. _____ *Agricultural Statistics.* Washington, D.C., 1965.
16. Waksman, Selman A. *Soil Microbiology.* New York: John Wiley & Sons, Inc., 1952, 356 pp.
17. Wheeler, Margaret F., and Wesley A. Volk. *Basic Microbiology.* New York: John Wiley & Sons, Inc., 1964, 356 pp.

Depletion and Restoration of Soils

4

History of Land Abuse Abroad

When we study the history of land use among the ancient civilizations of Asia, Africa, and Mediterranean Europe, we find an appalling misuse of what was orginally a valuable, life-giving resource. At one time the soil in these areas supported a flourishing agricultural economy. Villages grew into great, prosperous cities. Empires flourished and became powerful. But gradually, as the land was mistreated and erosion took its toll, these proud empires withered and fell. Populations starved or dispersed. Where once there were magnificent cities, there now remains nothing but desolation, eloquent testimony to the massive soil abuse wrought by man.

Mesopotamia. The word *Mesopotamia* ("between the rivers") refers to the location of this semiarid land between two rivers, the Tigris and the Euphrates. The source of these rivers is in a region of more abundant rainfall in the mountains to the north. Mesopotamia is the Biblical "land of milk and honey" and presumably was the site of the Garden of Eden described in Genesis. This is the land of Noah, Abraham and Isaac, the Ark, and the Tower of Babel. It plays a fundamental part in the Jewish, Christian, and Moslem faiths.

69

Mesopotamia may have contributed more to the advancement of civilization and culture than any other region of similar size. Here, in the alluvial flood plains between the two rivers, agriculture was born about 7,000 years ago (26). The oldest known writings of man (dating from 3,000 years before Christ), concerning a plague of crop-devouring locusts, originated from the lower delta of the Tigris and Euphrates (32). This land, properly called the cradle of European agriculture, was, and is today, arid. The thriving agricultural economy, on which a succession of eleven empires was based, depended on irrigation waters channeled from the Tigris and Euphrates by an intricate system of canals built at least 4,500 years before Christ (9, 26). According to some authorities it was possible for these people to irrigate 21,000 of the 35,000 square miles of flood plain. Flooding was a hazard; to protect their fields from floods the Chaldeans restrained the rivers with massive dikes, some of which were over 100 feet thick (32). Food surpluses raised on the fertile land freed millions of people from the necessity of farming, so that they could work in industry, science, and trade. Out of this system emerged a civilization with paved streets, a code of laws, mathematics, astronomy, cuneiform writing, and the calendar.

Because of heavy grazing pressure exerted by large flocks of sheep and goats, because of deforestation, and because of intensive cropping of steep slopes, the Armenian uplands, in which the Tigris and Euphrates had their source, were gradually seriously eroded by water (10). The rivers were red with soil washed from the hills. The accumulated sediment removed from the clogged canals over the centuries now forms huge mounds 50 feet high. The silt load carried by these rivers has filled the Persian gulf to a point 180 miles from where they originally emptied into it. The vital irrigation canals, continuously plagued with loads of sediment, were kept open only by constant vigilance and backbreaking labor, supplied either by slaves numbering up to 10,000 or by prisoners of war (32). As early as 3000 B.C , the Code of Hammurabi provided punishment for anyone who neglected his responsibility in keeping the canals free of sediment (32). As long as they were open, agriculture prospered and the orchards and fields produced bounteous crops. Periodically, however, because of either revolution or invasion by barbaric tribes, the irrigation canals were left unattended and gradually deteriorated beyond repair. The *coup de grâce* was delivered to the irrigation system by conquering hordes of Mongols and Tartars around 1200–1300 A.D.

It should be emphasized that the problem that this land experienced in centuries past and that it continues to have even today is not due to lack of fertile soil (26); it is due to the enormity of an engineering task made compulsory by land abuse at the highland headwaters of the Tigris and Euphrates. When the Mesopotamian agricultural economy was flourishing, it may have supported a population of close to 25 million people (26). Today, in sharp contrast, the population of all Iraq (the modern state that includes the lands of ancient Mesopotamia) is a mere 4 million. The once proud capital of Babylon, at one time the most powerful city on earth, now lies buried under windblown desert sands

North Africa—City of Timgad. When the Roman Empire was at its zenith, most of the land bordering the Mediterranean, including North Africa, was in its domain. The grain grown in North Africa was shipped to Rome to feed its citizens and armies. Timgad was a showpiece community established by the Romans in North Africa in the first century A.D. (26). It was a magnificent town laid out in a symmetrical pattern. Its architectural, engineering, and artistic developments were the marvel of the age. It had a large municipal aqueduct which

Figure 4–1 Ancient Roman city of Timgad, northern Africa. Man is standing beside a base stone of an olive oil press, evidence of olive tree culture in the region (January, 1939). [Soil Conservation Service, U.S. Department of Agriculture]

brought water to the people from a great spring three miles away; a public library; a sculpture-adorned forum and seventeen great Roman baths complete with mosaic tile (26). There were also olive presses and a huge theater with a capacity of over 2,500 people (26). The virgin vegetation on the undulating hills around the town had apparently been a grassland with a scattering of trees. Through the ages, tangled roots of grasses had "sewn" the top layer of soil in place, secure from erosive effects of wind and rain. The agriculturists of Timgad converted these lands into farms and olive orchards. The agricultural economy, apparently based on sound soil management techniques, flourished for many centuries. Then, in the seventh century A.D., disaster came to Timgad in the form of hordes of nomadic invaders (26). The people of Timgad presumably were either dispersed, enslaved, or butchered. The invaders substituted a crude, soil-abusing pastoral culture for Timgad's prosperous crop and orchard culture. The surrounding hills were subjected to intensive overgrazing by great numbers of sheep and goats. Huge dust storms clouded the horizon and descended upon the town. As centuries passed, load after load of wind-blown soil gradually buried Timgad. Only a portion of an arch and three slender columns projected above the shifting dunes. Finally, in 1912, Timgad, lost to mankind for 1,200 years, was rediscovered by a team of French archaeologists. Three decades of excavation work revealed the past magnificence of this once proud African outpost of Roman culture (26).

History of Land Abuse in America

Now let us find out what America's record is with regard to the use and abuse of the land. When the first white settler set foot on our shores, he found spread before him a land of almost incredible natural wealth. Dense forests cloaked the rolling hills in one vast mantle of green. Except for an occasional fire triggered by a lightning storm, forest destruction was virtually nonexistent. For untold centuries, autumn after autumn, the leaf fall blanketed the forest floor, decomposed, and eventually became incorporated into the soil. The excretions and bodies of many generations of woodland animals also contributed to the ultimate fertility of the primeval soil.

It is true that 10 million North American Indians had occupied the continent for many generations before the white man, perhaps for 10,000 years. But the impact of the Indian culture on the resource wealth was negligible. The Indians had no cattle or horses that could overgraze and expose the rich soil; they had no plow for upturning the soil, no axe for cutting huge swaths into the forest. Although they did practice a light, shifting type of agriculture, for the most part they survived by hunting and fishing; by collecting berries, fruits, nuts, eggs, and tubers; and by relocating their villages periodically to ensure access to prime hunting grounds (26).

As Angus McDonald states in his paper "Early American Soil Conservationists," "the felling of the first tree by colonists in the New World, though never mentioned by historians, was an act of great significance (28). It marked the beginning of the most rapid rate of wasteful land use in the history of the world." The colonist who felled that first tree most certainly never dreamed that his act would someday, three centuries later, be described in this way, nor probably would he have cared if he had known. We can only conjecture his purpose for chopping it down. Was it to provide fuel to keep himself and his wife comfortable against the severe New England cold? Was he trying to blaze a trail through the forest? Was he in quest of logs for a cabin or stockade? Posterity shall never know. We do know now, however, that with the felling of that first tree, soil in the immediate area of the stump was a little less protected against the action of water and wind.

As the colonists hacked and chopped and plowed their way westward into the vast wilderness which seemed to engulf them, their immediate thoughts were on how to survive in a strange, wild, and potentially hostile land (41). Later, as settlements were established, a considerable amount of timber was cut and burned to supply the potash markets of Europe (40). In New England, timber was gradually needed for the infant shipbuilding industry which was destined to reach greater proportions than that of even maritime England (29).

Clearings were made in the forest in which the settler could sow amid the half-charred stumps. He planted corn in hills in the fashion of the Indian, many of whose agricultural and hunting practices he learned to adopt. The colonist cultivated the corn hills with crude hoes. Plows were almost nonexistent. (Plymouth, Massachusetts, for example, had no plow for its first twelve years of establishment.) A typical list of equipment owned by the prosperous colonial farmer included hoes, carts, dung fork, flail, grub axe, harrows, hay knife, pickax, pitchfork, scythe, shovel, wheelbarrows, and plow (7). The first American farmer used ancient methods of planting and harvesting grain which were reminiscent of those used in Palestine 3,000 years before. If he was fortunate, he perhaps had a few cattle, horses, or pigs which he grazed at the edge of the clearing. He planted and raised the same crops year after year on the same patch of ground.

Although the first settlers did not come to the Chesapeake Bay region till 1607, and the Puritans did not land at Plymouth Rock until 1620, already by 1685 some of the settlers along the eastern seaboard noticed that corn did not grow as high as it once did and that the ears were getting much smaller. A subtle but definite change in the soil color from dark brown to light brown or gray accompanied the reduction in crop abundance. Settlers also began to notice that after a heavy spring thunder shower, tiny rivulets, yellow and brown with mud, streamed down slopes and cut ominous rills in the topsoil. By the early 1700's, many farms were dissected with ugly gullies. Flood damage noticeably increased. Eventually the topsoil, once primed with fertility accumulated through the ages, either deteriorated because of the intense one-crop farming or was washed away. Settler after settler, weary with the losing battle for agricultural survival, well aware of the seemingly unlimited bounty of fertile land "out West," pulled up stakes, chopped down a little more of the forest, grubbed out a few more stumps, uprooted a few more shrubs, built another cabin and gradually carved out a new farm at the forest margin. But what about the land he had abandoned? Records show that in the populous areas along the Massachusetts coast, soil depletion and deterioration was so widespread that almost all the farmland was abandoned by 1800. The enormity of land abandonment in the New England area when fertile land was publicized in the Middle West may be inferred from the fact that a million acres less land were cultivated in Massachusetts in 1935 than in 1810. Acre after acre was exhausted. Farm after farm was abandoned throughout thousands of square miles of early America. Why stay on and struggle to improve the land when there were unlimited amounts further west? Hall quotes from an anonymous "letter to the editor" written in 1831, "The scratching farmer's cares and anxieties are only relieved by his land washing away. As that goes down the river, he goes over the mountains" (15). Who is to be blamed for this profligate waste? With our wonderful hindsight, it is easy for us, living in the twentieth century (when our population is rapidly increasing and every acre is precious), to criticize these courageous pioneers as "land-hungry squanderers of a vital resource." We must remember, however, that if we twentieth-century critics were to move three centuries backward in time and place ourselves in precisely the same cultural, social, and economic setting, we would have responded in exactly the same way. How could one foresee then that in only three centuries the seemingly unlimited forest would in many areas be leveled; that teeming millions of Americans from Miami to Seattle, and from Boston to San

Francisco, would tax the productivity of every last ounce of arable soil?

This rapid soil deterioration was in part the result of applying traditional European farming methods to the soils of colonial America. These practices were usable on the heavy clay soils of western Europe, where rainfall was more regular and less violent. However, the relatively light, friable forest soils of eastern America were washed away by spring thunderstorms, especially on the steeper slopes. In the late eighteenth century, George Washington wrote to a friend concerning his land at Mount Vernon, "A husbandman's wish would not lay the farms more level than they are; and yet some of the fields . . . are washed into gullies" (15).

In the South, soil exhaustion first occurred in the Tidewater Region, because of intensive tobacco cropping; then, as a result of one-crop cotton farming, soil exhaustion occurred in the Piedmont Region and westward into eastern Texas. Cotton and tobacco are both clean-tilled row crops which provided little vegetative protection to the erosion-vulnerable Southern soils. Today erosion has taken a greater toll in our southeastern states than anywhere else in America.

Guided by the philosophy of Thomas Jefferson, the federal government's official policy in disposing of the public domain west of the Mississippi was to use it as a catalyst in the settlement and development of this sparsely populated region (40). With the passage of the Homestead Act in 1862, the federal government gave the farmer or rancher title to 160 acres of land, provided the land was received in good faith and was occupied for at least five years. This act put the farmer or rancher in the curious position of finding it cheaper to acquire new land than to struggle to build up the fertility of his worn-out, sterile land. In order to secure title to the land under this act, the homesteaders were virtually compelled to break up the virgin prairie sod, whether or not they actually wished to do so.

Impetus was given to the westward spread of American agriculture by the invention of McCormick's reaper in 1831 and of the self-scoring steel plow in 1837. (The heavy prairie soils were inclined to stick to the old type of iron plow.)

The history of the farmers' and ranchers' relation to the soil of the Great Plains, and the dust storms that were in part caused by their activities, will be discussed later. With the passage of the Homestead Act in 1862, large tracts of public land were rapidly converted into privately owned holdings. In fact, during the period from 1860 to 1910 (in which the number of ranches and farms increased from 2 million to over 6 million), about 234 million acres of land passed from public to private ownership.

Figure 4–2 Cyrus H. McCormick's first reaper in action (phototype of original). The light farm equipment of the nineteenth century had only a negligible effect on the soil structure. [U.S. Department of Agriculture]

In this half century, the farm increase was threefold the number which became established during the previous two centuries (1660–1860). The cattle industry boomed in the arid plains from the eastern foothills of the Rockies to the 95th parallel, from the Rio Grande to the Manitoba border. Livestock assumed the ecological role which for centuries had been filled by antelope and buffalo. About 1885, waves of homesteading farmers crossed the Mississippi and took title to land parcels under the Homestead Act. Because of the mushrooming population, there was great pressure on ranchers and farmers for meat and grain. Eager for quick economic gain, many ranchers crowded too many cattle on too small a range for too long a time. As a result, the native grasses, originally lush and vigorous, began to deteriorate, especially during years of drought. The farmers, on their part, sliced deep into the virgin prairie sod with their new self-scoring steel plows, turned up the dark soil, and exposed it to the burning prairie sun. In this upturned earth, which only a few decades before trembled under the pounding hoofs of migratory bison herds, farmers planted wheat in the North and cotton in the South.

Twenty inches of precipitation annually is considered marginal for crop production. The arid and semiarid Great Plains frequently have less. During periods of severe drought, precipitation may be considerably less than 5 inches annually. Meteorologists inform us that throughout history, even before the white man's coming, the Great Plains experienced alternating cycles of drought and adequate rainfall. However, although major drought appears to have recurred at roughly thirty-five-year intervals, the precise time of its occurrence has not been predictable.

Drought visited the Great Plains in 1890 and again in 1910. During each dry spell, crops withered and died. Farms and ranches were abandoned only to be reoccupied during the ensuing years of adequate rainfall. Then came 1914 and World War I; America committed her soldiers and her resources to the Allied cause in 1916.

With American, British, and French soldiers in need of food and with wheat prices at an all-time high of $2 a bushel, the sharp steel of American plows staged yet another assault on the prairie. Exploitation and abuse of our soil resource reached a new peak. Forty million additional acres of American prairie grasses were plowed up. These were grasses that had been adapted by age-old evolutionary processes to survive strong winds, heat, and drought. This grassland community which had maintained an ecological equilibrium with its environment for many centuries was now uprooted. Our doughboys were fed and the Allies won the war. The "emergency force" of wheat farmers had done a superb job of feeding the men in the trenches (and of abusing our prairie soils). Following the war this "farmer army" did not pull out its forces eastward to more humid zones, but continued raising wheat on the same prairie acres year after year.

Then came the Big Drought. For five years, from 1926 to 1931, there was hardly enough rain to settle the dust. On the ranches the buffalo grass and other prairie grasses lost their vigor and withered. Overstocked pastures were clipped to ground level by scrawny cattle. Much livestock was mercifully slaughtered. Droughts had visited the plains before. So had wind storms. But never before in the history of the North American prairie was the land more vulnerable to their combined assault. Gone were the profusely branching root systems of the buffalo grass, the grama grass, the big blue stem and the little blue stem which had originally kept the rich brown soil firmly in place. Gone was the decomposing organic material which had aided in building up stable soil aggregates and the soil cover of grass mat and sagebrush. On the ranches soil structure deteriorated under the concerted pounding given it by millions of cattle.

On the wheat and cotton farms, soil structure broke down under the abuse inflicted by the huge machinery used in plowing, cultivating and harvesting. The stage was set for the "black blizzards."

The Dust Bowl. In the spring of 1934 and again in 1935, winds of gale velocities swept over the Great Plains. In western Kansas and Oklahoma, as well as in the neighboring parts of Texas, Colorado, and Nebraska, the wind whirled minute particles of clay and silt far upward into the prairie sky (29). Brown dust clouds up to 7,000 feet thick filled the air with an upper edge almost two miles high (30). One storm of May 11, 1934, lifted 300 million tons of fertile soil into the air. (This roughly equals the total soil tonnage scooped from Central America to form the Panama Canal.) In many areas, the wilted wheat was uprooted and blown into the air. In the Amarillo, Texas area during March and April of 1935, fifteen wind storms raged for twenty-four hours; four lasted over fifty-five hours (25).

Dust from Oklahoma prairies came to rest on the deck of a steamer 200 miles out in the Atlantic. Dust sifted into the plush offices of Wall Street and smudged the luxury apartments of Park Avenue. When it rained in the blow area, the drops would

Figure 4–3 Dust storm approaching Springfield, Colorado, on May 21, 1937. This storm reached the city limits at exactly 4:47 P.M. Total darkness lasted about one-half hour. [U.S. Department of Agriculture]

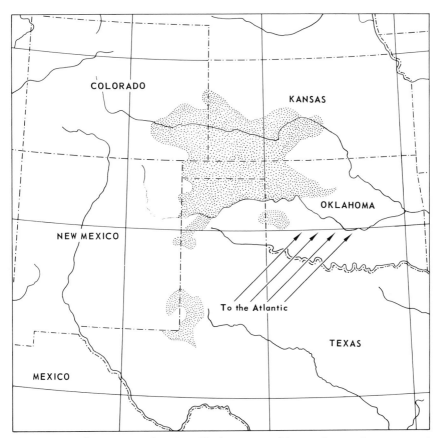

Figure 4–4 The Dust Bowl region. Black areas on this map incurred severe wind erosion during the 1930's. Topsoil was blown as far as the Atlantic Ocean. Over a million farm-acres lost 2 to 12 inches of topsoil. [Adapted from Raymond F. Dasman, *Environmental Conservation* (New York: John Wiley & Sons, Inc., 1968). After Soil Conservation Service map.]

sometimes come down as dilute mud. In Washington, D.C., mud splattered buildings of the Department of Agriculture, a rude reminder of the problem facing it and the nation. A thousand miles westward, harried housewives stuffed water-soaked newspapers into window cracks to no avail. The dust sifted into kitchens, forming a thin film on pots and pans and fresh-baked bread. Blinded by swirling dust clouds, ranchers got lost in their own backyards. Motorists pulled off to the side of the highways. Hundreds of airplanes were grounded. Trains were stalled by huge drifts. Hospital nurses placed wet cloths on patients' faces to ease their breathing. In Colorado's Baca County (March, 1935), forty-eight relief workers contracted "dust pneumonia," four of whom died. Five youngsters belonging to a New Mexico mother smothered to death in their cribs (13).

Figure 4–5 Dust storm in Prowers County, Colorado, approaching at velocity of 30 miles per hour. It lasted from 4:15 P.M. to 7:00 P.M. [Soil Conservation Service, U.S. Department of Agriculture]

Figure 4–6 Abandoned Oklahoma farmstead, showing the disastrous results of wind erosion. [U.S. Department of Agriculture]

When the winds finally subsided, ranchers and farmers wearily emerged to survey the desolation. Two to 12 inches of fertile clay and silt soils had been carried to the Atlantic seaboard. The coarser sand, too heavy to be air-borne, bounced across the land, sheared off young wheat, and finally accumulated as dunes to the leeward of homes and barns. Heavily mortgaged power machinery became shrouded in sand.

The dust storms of the 1930's inflicted both social and economic suffering. Yet a few ranchers and farmers were philosophical about their misfortunes and could even crack jokes about the birds flying backward "to keep the sand out of their eyes," and about the prairie dogs "digging burrows 100 feet in the air!" However, for most dust-bowl victims, the dusters were not very funny. Many were virtually penniless. The 300 million tons of topsoil removed in a single storm on May 11, 1934, represents the equivalent of taking 3,000 farms of 100 acres each out of crop production. Dust-bowl relief up until 1940 alone cost American taxpayers over $1 billion. Seven million dollars (more than was paid for all Alaska) was pumped into a single Colorado county alone (13). The only recourse for many of these ill-fated farmers was to find a new way of life. They piled their belongings into rickety cars and trucks and moved out—some to the Pacific coast, some to the big industrial cities of the Midwest and East. However, our nation was still in the throes of a depression, and many an emigrating family found nothing but frustration, bitterness, and suffering at the end of the road.

The first data on erosion losses were obtained at the Agricultural Experimental Station at Spur, Texas, beginning in 1926. Gradually, with congressional authorization and appropriation, this program was greatly expanded to a national scale. With encouragement from the National Resources Board and then Secretary of the Interior Harold L. Ickes, the newly formed Soil Erosion Service, under the leadership of H. H. Bennett, conducted a Reconnaissance Erosion Survey in 1934. Completed in only two months by a team of 115 erosion specialists, it was unique, not

Figure 4–7 Hugh Hammond Bennett, first director of the Soil Conservation Service. [Soil Conservation Service, U.S. Department of Agriculture]

only because it was the first national survey, but because kinds of erosion as well as degree of severity were classified. The survey revealed that formerly productive agricultural land had to be abandoned in the Southeast, South, and central Southwestern regions of the United States because of severe sheet erosion. Of the 322 million acres that were affected by wind erosion, most were located in the Great Plains from southwest Texas northward to the Dakotas. Within this zone, 9 million acres were destroyed and 80 million acres were seriously damaged. Twenty-five to 75 per cent of the topsoil was depleted from a total area of 663 million acres. There was extensive gullying, and in 90 per cent of the cases it was associated with sheet erosion. Severe gullying occurred on 337 million acres. As late as 1942, total annual erosion damage inflicted on the American people amounted to $3.8 billion, or an annual loss of $20 for every man, woman, and child in the United States.

People learn slowly. Incomprehensible as it may seem, the chronicle we have described of miscalculation, of greed mixed with patriotism, of unfounded optimism in a sudden wheat "bonanza," and of dust and disaster, was duplicated only a few years later in the context of World War II. Favored with above average moisture, crops were abundant and our troops were fed. But after the war, the farmers continued to cultivate

Figure 4–8   Water erosion caused the severe gullies on this North Carolina farm. [U.S. Department of Agriculture]

drought-vulnerable lands. Over 14 million acres were being cultivated in 1955 that should have been kept in sod. Wind and drought again visited the plains. The Soil Conservation Service estimated that between 10 and 15 million acres of land were damaged, and between 1 and 5 million acres of crops were destroyed annually during the "black duster" period of 1954–1957. Fortunately, however, because of the generally high level of national prosperity which prevailed at this time and because of the fewer operators on the land (as a result of consolidations), human privation was not as severe as it was in the 1930's.

Conservationists of Early America. From the preceding discussion it may appear that no one in early America really appreciated the importance of soil as the "cradle" of life for both man and country, or that this "cradle" was gradually breaking down because of mistreatment and wear. This is not true. There were intelligent, farsighted men in all stages of our country's development who were greatly concerned about our profligate treatment of the land and who vigorously attempted to arouse a complacent nation.

The first book on American agricultural problems was written by Jared Eliot (1685–1763) of Killingsworth, Connecticut. He was unusually versatile. As a country doctor he took care of his countrymen's physical ills; as a minister he alleviated their spiritual distress; and as America's first distinguished conservationist he tried to prescribe treatment for their sick farmlands. During horseback visits to rural patients, he made keen observations of agricultural practices. He conducted experiments on soil erosion, sedimentation water, and soil texture. In 1748 he published the first of a series of essays which culminated in the first book on American agriculture. Among his recommendations to farmers were the following:

1. Swamplands should be drained to enhance their agricultural value.
2. Since soil washing is a constant hazard on hillside croplands, great care must be taken when farming such sites.
3. Planting of red clover would aid in soil building.
4. Soil fertility could be restored with the help of animal or plant manure.

Today, we would hardly consider these measures revolutionary, even though we would concede their effectiveness. However, we must remember that Jared Eliot advanced these proposals at a time when soil conservation was about as far removed from public concern as were rockets to the moon.

Every American schoolboy knows that George Washington is

venerated as the "Father of our Country," the hero of Valley Forge, and the first President of the United States. However, very few Americans realize that Washington was a staunch advocate of proper soil practice. His land-use philosophy is well documented in his comments on the soil-depleting practices of early colonists: "The aim of the farmers in this country, *if they can be called farmers,* is not to make the most of the land which is . . . cheap . . . , but the most of the labor, which is dear (expensive); the consequences of which have been, much ground has been scratched over and not cultivated or improved as it ought to have been." Again, referring to his own Mount Vernon estate, Washington wrote the following lines to a friend, "some of the fields are washed into gullies from which all of them have not yet recovered" (15).

Thomas Jefferson and Patrick Henry were also concerned with erosion problems. Jefferson wrote in 1871 that the "fields were no sooner cleared than washed" (15), and Patrick Henry considered soil so vital to America's growth that he once stated: "Since the achievement of our independence, he is the greatest patriot who stops the most gullies." Intermittently, throughout our nation's history, men with vision have warned landowners, but to no avail.

Nature of Soil Erosion

We have observed the manner in which Americans have abused their soil, almost from the day the Pilgrims set foot on it at Plymouth Rock. During the three-century history of soil abuse in the United States, erosion has played a predominant role. Let us now focus our attention on this insidious process and find out what today's soil conservationists are doing not only to arrest erosion, but to rehabilitate the soil.

Definition. The word *erosion* is derived from the Latin word *erodere,* meaning "to gnaw out." Erosion may be defined as the process by which rock fragments and soil are detached from their original site, transported, and then eventually deposited at some new locality. The agent of erosion may be wind, water, waves, glaciers, soil slip, or other rock particles.

Geological Erosion or Natural Erosion. Geological erosion is a process that has occurred at an extremely slow rate ever since the earth was formed 4 to 5 billion years ago. In fact, the mountains, valleys, plains, canyons, and deltas on the earth's surface were sculptured by water and wind erosion working through vast periods of time. The Appalachian Mountains were at one time as tall and rugged as the Rocky Mountains; but since their formation 200 million years ago, at the beginning of the Mesozoic Period, they have been gradually worn down by erosive forces. Were it not for geological erosion, New Orleans would be resting on the bottom of the Gulf of Mexico, for the delta on which it is built was formed by deposition of soil transported by the Mississippi River from sites as much as 1,000 miles away. The Grand Canyon originated as a shallow channel 100 million years ago. It was ultimately scoured to its awesome 1-mile depth by the churning waters of the Colorado.

Accelerated Erosion.   Geological erosion, then, has continued to operate at a slow, deliberate pace for millions of years. However, with man's appearance on the world scene, a species intruded which could "reshape" the natural environment. Because of his activities an *artificial* type of erosion began, which has operated at a much faster rate than natural erosion. It is with this *accelerated erosion* that the conservationist is primarily concerned.

Figure 4–9   The Grand Canyon of the Colorado River, Arizona, as seen from the north rim, a colossal example of the effects of geologic erosion operating for millenia. [Soil Conservation Service, U.S. Department of Agriculture]

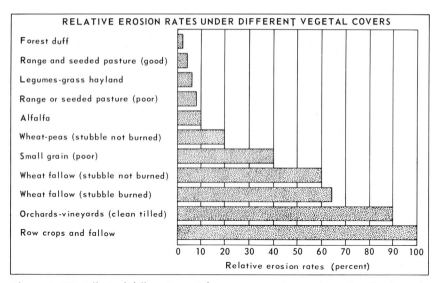

RELATIVE EROSION RATES UNDER DIFFERENT VEGETAL COVERS

Forest duff
Range and seeded pasture (good)
Legumes-grass hayland
Range or seeded pasture (poor)
Alfalfa
Wheat-peas (stubble not burned)
Small grain (poor)
Wheat fallow (stubble not burned)
Wheat fallow (stubble burned)
Orchards-vineyards (clean tilled)
Row crops and fallow

0   10   20   30   40   50   60   70   80   90   100
Relative erosion rates (percent)

Figure 4–10   Effect of different vegetal covers on water erosion rates. Erosion rate from land covered by row crops equals 100 per cent. Soil erosion losses under forest duff is only 3 per cent the loss under row crops. Range in good condition is almost twice as effective as poor range in retarding erosion. Observe the erosion vulnerability of clean-tilled orchards. Flash floods sweeping through California orchards have repeatedly wreaked a heavy loss in topsoil. [Adapted from Ruben L. Parson, *Conserving American Resources* (Englewood Cliffs, N.J.: Prentice-Hall, Inc., 1956). After *Journal of the American Water Works Association, 41,* 10 (October, 1949.)]

Factors Determining Rate of Erosion.   The intensity of erosion depends upon the interaction of a number of factors, including (a) *volume and intensity of precipitation,* (b) *topography of the terrain,* (c) *kind of vegetational cover,* and (d) *soil type* (27).

Volume and Intensity of Precipitation.   Annual precipitation in the United States ranges from virtually nothing in some parts of Death Valley, California, to 140 inches in Washington state. Such pronounced differences in rainfall will be expressed in part by differential erosion rates. However, even more important is the seasonal rainfall pattern.

A town in Florida once experienced a deluge of 24 inches of rain in only twenty-four hours! The ensuing soil loss, resulting from run-off waters, must have been severe. On the other hand, were this 24-inch rainfall the result of daily 1-inch drizzles occurring over a period of twenty-four consecutive days, the erosion threat would have been negligible, simply because the soil would have had sufficient time in which to absorb the water. Surprisingly, even in the arid deserts of Nevada and Arizona, where annual rainfall averages 5 inches, excessive erosion occurs because the entire annual precipitation material-

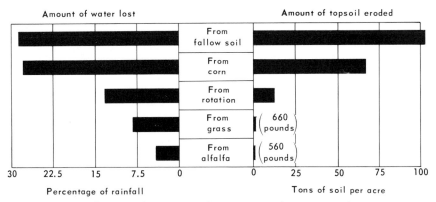

Amount of water lost   Amount of topsoil eroded

Figure 4–11 Influence of vegetational cover on soil erosion and water run-off. Data from research conducted by the Soil Conservation Service at Bethany, Missouri, on Shelby loam on land with an 8 per cent slope. Average annual rainfall in the area is 40 inches. [From *Conserving Natural Resources* by Allen and Leonard. Copyright © 1966 by McGraw-Hill, Inc. Used by permission of McGraw-Hill Book Company.]

izes in the form of a few torrential cloudbursts. As a result, the desert floor is dissected with canyons gouged out by run-off waters.

Topography of the Terrain. It would be expected that intensity of water run-off and soil erosion would be partially dependent on the relative slope of the terrain. Steepness of slope is indicated in terms of percentages. Thus, a 10 per cent slope would be one which drops 10 feet over a horizontal distance of 100 feet. Research conducted by soil scientists has shown the effect of slopes on soil and water losses on farms planted to row crops, crops in which the land is exposed between the rows (5). In each of two studies cited by Bennett on similar soils, a roughly 100 per cent increase in slope resulted in an approximately 300 per cent increase in soil loss caused by erosion. In a third study, a 116 per cent increase in slope (from 3.7 to 8) resulted in a 348 per cent increase (from 19.7 tons to 68.8 tons) in soil loss (5).

Kind of Vegetational Cover. In the foothills of the southern Appalachians, Cecil sandy clay loam is a representative erodible soil. Pronounced differences in soil loss occur under varying types of vegetational cover. Bare soil erodes 2.5 times more rapidly than land planted to cotton, more than 4,000 times as rapidly as grass-covered land, and almost 32,000 times more quickly than land covered with virgin forests (5).

Type of Soil. The structure of a soil can be improved by plowing under a crop of clover or alfalfa (*green manuring*) or simply by adding decaying organic material, such as leaves or

Figure 4–12 Only 1 inch of rain caused this erosion on a burned-over slope in California's Los Padres National Forest. [U.S. Department of Agriculture]

barnyard manure. Studies in Iowa have shown the effect of manuring corn croplands. Lands manured with 16, 8, and 0 tons per acre incurred soil losses of roughly 4, 9, and 22 tons per acre, respectively (5). Soil loss from nonmanured land was over five times that from heavily manured soil. The addition of organic material apparently improved the soil's water-absorbing ability. This trait, in turn, would be expressed in a more dense, vigorous growth of corn. The vegetative mantle thus established would further protect the soil. The developing corn root systems would also penetrate more vigorously between the individual soil particles and tend to bind them in place.

Soil Erosion Control

We shall discuss some of the major land management practices by means of which excessive soil erosion may be controlled. These practices include *contour farming, strip cropping, terracing, gully reclamation,* and establishment of *shelter belts.*

Contour Farming. Contour farming may be defined as plowing, seeding, cultivating, and harvesting *across* the slope, rather than *with* it. It was practiced by Thomas Jefferson, who wrote in 1813, "We now plow horizontally, following the curvature of the hills. . . . Every furrow thus acts as a reservoir to . . . retain the waters . . . scarcely an ounce of soil is now carried off." Jefferson, however, was an exception. In the early days of American agriculture, the farmer who could plow the straightest furrows (usually up and down slopes) was considered a master plowsman and was praised by his neighbors.

An experiment conducted on a Texas cotton field with a 3 to 5 per cent slope revealed that average annual water run-off from a noncontoured plot was 4.6 inches, whereas that for a contoured plot was 65.3 per cent less, or 1.6 inches.

Figure 4–13 Bell County, Texas. The pattern of farm conservation is reflected in the fields of this Texas farmer, who uses contour farming to reduce rain water run-off and its erosive effects on soil. The different shades are caused by different crops (strip cropping) and the pattern conforms to the contours of his fields, with the highest elevation where the smaller rings are. Besides slowing water so that it can soak into the soil better, such measures reduce siltation, the most common cause of water pollution in the United States, according to the U.S. Department of Agriculture. [Soil Conservation Service, U.S. Department of Agriculture]

Strip Cropping. On land with a decided slope, planting crops on contour strips will be an effective erosion deterrent. For effective control the width of the contour strip should vary inversely with the length of the slope. When viewed from a distance, the farmland appears as a series of slender, curving belts of color. A wide-row cultivated crop—such as corn, cotton, tobacco, or potatoes—and a cover crop of hay or legumes are alternated along the contours. Strip cropping is combined frequently with crop rotation, so that a strip planted to a soil-depleting, erosion-facilitating corn crop one year will be sown to a soil-enriching and protecting strip of legumes the next.

Terracing. Terracing has been practiced by man for centuries. It was used by the Incas of Peru and by the ancient Chinese. These civilizations, plagued with relatively dense populations and a modicum of arable land, were forced to till extremely steep slopes, even mountainsides, in order to prevent extensive hunger. The flat, steplike bench terraces that these ancient agriculturists constructed, however, are not amenable to today's farming methods. The modern terrace may be defined as an embankment of earth constructed across a slope in such a way

Figure 4–14 Contour strip cropping on a Washara County, Wisconsin, farm characterized by silt loam with a 4 per cent slope. [Soil Conservation Service, U.S. Department of Agriculture]

Figure 4–15 A system of parallel level terraces has controlled sheet erosion on this farm near Templeton, Iowa. Slope is 5 to 11 per cent. [Soil Conservation Service, U.S. Department of Agriculture]

as to control water runoff and minimize erosion. To be effective, terraces must check water flow before it attains sufficient velocity (3 feet per second) to loosen and transport soil.

Gully Reclamation. Gullies are danger signals that indicate land is eroding rapidly and may become a wasteland unless erosion is promptly controlled. Some gullies work their way up a slope at the rate of 15 feet a year. If relatively small, a gully may be plowed in and then seeded to a quick-growing "nurse" crop of barley, oats, or wheat. In this way, erosion will be checked until sod can become established. In cases of severe gullying, small check dams of manure and straw constructed at 20-foot intervals may be effective, because silt will collect behind the dams and gradually fill in the channel. Dams may be constructed of brush or stakes held secure with a woven wire netting. Earthen, stone, and even concrete dams may be built at intervals along the gully. Once dams have been constructed and water run-off has been restrained, soil may be stabilized by planting rapidly growing shrubs, vines, and trees. Willows are effective. Not only does such pioneer vegetation forestall future erosion, but it obliterates the ugliness of gaping gullies and provides food, cover, and breeding sites for wildlife.

Figure 4–16A (*Before*) Gully erosion on a Minnesota farm. It was scalped and then planted with protective vegetation, primarily locust trees. [Soil Conservation Service, U.S. Department of Agriculture]

Figure 4–16B (*After*) Five growing seasons later the locusts averaged 15 feet in height, and not only served to control erosion but provided wildlife cover and beautified the landscape. [Soil Conservation Service, U.S. Department of Agriculture]

Shelter Belts. In 1935 the federal government, in a strenuous attempt to prevent future dust bowls, launched a shelter belt system which extended across the Great Plains from North Dakota south to Texas. The impetus provided by this project has resulted in thousands of miles of tree belts whose green checkerboard patterns have added color and variety to an otherwise monotonous prairie landscape. In the cooler north and central plains, a typical shelter belt would consist of one to five rows of trees planted on the western margin of the farm in a north–south line, to intercept winter's prevailing westerly winds. Conifers such as red cedar, spruce, and pine provide the best year-round protection. For the southern plains, drought-resistant trees such as Scotch pine, Austrian pine, Chinese elm, and thornless honey locust are desirable (14). Soil blowing can be retarded even further by planting a few rows of corn or a belt of grain between the rows of trees. As indicated in Figure 4–19, an adequately designed shelter belt of adequate height and thickness may reduce a wind velocity of 30 miles per hour to only 8 miles per hour to leeward. The beneficial influence may extend 175 feet to windward and 1,500 feet to leeward of

Figure 4–17 This North Dakota farm is well protected from wind and snow by a 17-year-old windbreak of conifers, fruit trees, and shrubs. [Soil Conservation Service, U.S. Department of Agriculture]

Figure 4–18 Ten-row shelter belt and farmstead windbreak in Osborne County, Kansas. It consists of Russian olive, red cedar, ponderosa pine, bun oak, hackberry, green ash, honey locust, Chinese elm, and osage orange planted at 8-foot intervals. The belt is 160 rods long, part of it on contour. [Soil Conservation Service, U.S. Department of Agriculture]

the trees (1). Although windbreaks occupy valuable land which otherwise could be used for crop production, are relatively slow to grow, and must be fenced from livestock until well established, the accrued benefits far outweigh these minor disadvantages (18). To determine the value of windbreaks, 331 South Dakota farmers were asked in 1955 to provide information concerning their crop yields after shelter belts were established on their lands. Over 88 per cent indicated that yields had increased measurably (14). (Fig. 4–19)

Soil Conservation Service

The "black blizzards" of the 1930's may have had one redeeming feature: they alerted a hitherto apathetic nation more forcefully to the plight of her soil resources than a thousand urgent speeches could have done.

The federal government finally faced up to the soil erosion problem. In 1933 it established the Soil Erosion Service, with H. H. Bennett, long a crusader for a national program of soil

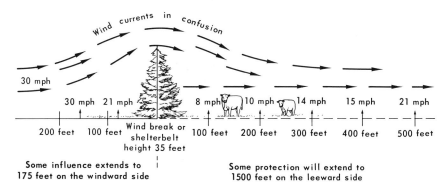

Figure 4–19 Influence of a shelter belt on wind velocity. [Adapted from the Kansas State Board of Agriculture]

erosion control, as its director (18). In 1934 the Soil Erosion Service (SES) set up forty-one soil and water conservation demonstration projects. The labor force for these projects was supplied by Civilian Conservation Corps workers drawn from about fifty camps (18). The projects impressed Congress so forcefully that it established the Soil Conservation Service (SCS) in 1935. The major function of the SCS has been to provide technical assistance to farmers and ranchers so that they utilize each acre of land according to its capability, with methods that are consistent with the needs of the soil as well as those of the landowner. A cardinal feature of the SCS program has been to focus the professional assistance of agronomists, agricultural engineers, botanists, zoologists, ecologists, hydrologists, foresters, and soil scientists on the problem of appropriate land use. The knowledge our scientists and technologists have accumulated to date, relative to the nature, productivity, development, replenishment, erodability, and abuse of soils, has enabled the SCS to set up, with the cooperation of state and county agencies, a national land capability inventory of a general nature, as well as a detailed land capability inventory for farmers and members participating in SCS programs.

Land Capability Classes

The SCS recognizes eight land capability classes, designated on individual farm maps by Roman numerals I–VIII. Classes I–IV may be cultivated. Classes V–VII are best suited for grazing or forestry. Class VIII is suited primarily for wildlife or recreation (10). A brief description of each class follows.

Class I (Light Green). Few or no limitations on cultivation. Suitable for intensive production of row crops. Level terrain, deep fertile soil, and good drainage. Little or no regard for danger of soil loss. Soils friable, easily worked. Usually most productive. Representative crops: cotton, soybeans, corn, and grains. Manuring (animal and green) and inorganic fertilizer periodically required. (Very good land.)

Class II (Yellow). Suitable for permanent cultivation with minor conservation practices. Slight slope renders it slightly susceptible to erosion. Some of this land may require drainage or irrigation. May be slightly stony. Contouring and cover cropping may be required. (Good land.)

Class III (Red). May be cultivated but requires intensive conservation practices, such as strip cropping and terracing, as well as fertilization, cover crops, and crop rotation. (Moderately good land.)

Class IV (Blue). Very intensive conservation practices required if cultivated, and then only once in five to six years. May be steeper than Class III, more difficult to drain, more susceptible to erosion. Unsuited for row crops of the type required to dry in the spring; best suited for permanent vegetation (hay, pasture, and orchards or vineyards if protected by cover crops, such as wheat and vetch, which prevent erosion). (Fairly good land.)

Class V (Dark Green). Nearly level. Not suitable for cultivation; best suited for grazing or woodland. Limited for crop use because stony or wet. Not subject to erosion even if cover removed.

Class VI (Orange). Not arable. Best suited for grazing or woodland. Moderately steep slopes. Vulnerable to water and wind erosion. Shallow, stony, or alkaline soils. Protective measures needed.

Class VII (Brown). Not arable. Severe restrictions if used for grazing or woodland. Woodland use recommended in humid areas. Highly susceptible to erosion if not grazed with extreme care. Very steep slopes; shallow, stony, or draughty soils. Excessive erosion or severe alkali.

Class VIII (Purple). Not arable. Not suited for grazing or woodland use. Extremely rough, high, stony, or barren land; or swamps and marshes that cannot be drained. May be used for wildlife, recreation, or protection of water supply.

Soil Conservation Service Farm Program

The administrative and operative unit of the Soil Conservation Service program is the SCS district, which is organized and run by farmers and ranchers. Each district is staffed with a professional conservationist and several aides who work directly with the farmer on his land. These technicians have had training in many related areas and represent, ideally, a soil scientist, hydrologist, land appraiser, botanist, zoologist, agronomist, chemist, forester, game manager, and agricultural engineer all wrapped up in one superindividual. Any farmer located within the Soil Conservation Service district may request assistance in setting up and maintaining sound conservation practices in the management of his farm. Participation in the SCS program is purely voluntary. By July 1, 1964, 2,971 SCS districts had been organized (18), embracing roughly 5 million farms and 96 per cent of the nation's farm and ranch land.

**Depletion and
Restoration
of Soils**

Figure 4–20 A conservationist and a soil scientist examine an alfalfa stand at Maple Lake, Minnesota, for insect damage and phosphate–potash deficiency. The land is class III with 7 per cent slope. The corn will make 80 to 85 bushels per acre. [U.S. Department of Agriculture]

In the event that a farmer requests technical assistance from his SCS district, four principal steps are followed in executing the conservation program for his farm.

First, the technician and the farmer make an intensive acre-by-acre survey of the farm. On the basis of such criteria, including slope, fertility, stoniness, drainage, topsoil thickness, and susceptibility to erosion, the technician maps out each parcel of land on the basis of its capability. Each plot is ascribed a capability symbol in the form of a Roman numeral or color. This capability map is then superimposed on an aerial photograph.

Second, the farmer draws up a farm plan with assistance from the technician. This plan involves decisions on how each acre will be used and how it will be improved and protected. In other words, shall a given acre be used for crops, pasture, forests, or wilderness area? Usually alternative uses and treatments are considered. Some changes, of course, will not be made simply because they are impractical. The farmer would not move his barn, for example, just because the soil underneath is good for growing corn. In addition to the type of soil, such factors as farm size, amount of rainfall, potential market for crops, and the farmer's age and skills all enter into his ultimate choice concerning the use of his land.

Third, the treatment and uses called for in the plan are actually *applied* to the farm by the farmer, with assistance from one or more technicians. Although much of this application can be completed by the farmer himself, he may find it helpful to enlist the aid of the conservation technicians in connection with such techniques as terracing, contour plowing, strip cropping, establishment of farm ponds, gully control, shelter belting, proper use of cover crops in erosion control, use of legumes in fertility improvement, development of hedgerows as wildlife habitat, and selective cutting involved in the periodic harvest of his wood lot.

The final and most important phase of the program is its *maintenance* from year to year with the assistance of conservation technicians. As time passes, agricultural geneticists might develop a new strain of rust-resistant wheat or a tick-resistant breed of cattle; a plant may be introduced from the Orient or from South America which is more effective in fixing nitrogen than are native legumes; a new subspecies of bluegill may be discovered which thrives in farm ponds, or perhaps a new method of tilling wetlands will be available. These new developments then can gradually be incorporated into the over-all conservation program.

The SCS program has shown considerable stability despite

minor variations from year to year. Each year roughly 3 per cent of our nation's farms are involved in about 100,000 basic conservation plans formulated by the SCS. Typically, contour farming practices under SCS technical aid are newly applied to about 3 to 5 million acres annually; the same amount of range and pasture acreage is seeded. Roughly 4 million acres of land are newly cover cropped. Each year, 50,000 to 75,000 new farm ponds are constructed, and 40,000 to 50,000 new terraces are built. Moreover, under the SCS farm program, smaller acreages of land are improved for irrigation, are drained, or are planted to trees. Roughly 5 per cent of the cropland is annually covered by newly applied SCS-directed practices.

A Look at a Conservation Farm Plan. Let us see how the land of a 96 acre cotton farm in the southern Piedmont area was utilized before and after a conservation farm plan was put into operation (24). Original land use on this farm is indicated in Figure 4–22. This farmer had two mules, two milk cows, four hogs, and fifty hens. Limited pasture meant he had to depend on harvested crops for most of his feed. This farm had a tractor and tractor-drawn plow, disc-harrow, and combine. Mules and mule-drawn equipment were used in planting and cultivating the cotton and corn.

After an acre-by-acre survey was made of the farm, a land capability map was made (Figure 4–21). The subclass symbol E indicates that the entire acreage had a potential erosion problem. The inspection of the farm also revealed that the cropland was not properly terraced. An inadequate water-disposal system for terrace outlets resulted in severe erosion in part of the field. Soils were moderately to severely acid. Supplies of available nitrogen phosphate and potash were low. Among the

Figure 4–21 Land capability map of a southern Piedmont cotton farm as established by the Soil Conservation Service, U.S. Department of Agriculture. [From E. L. Langsford, Charles P. Butler, C. W. Crickman, and Trimble R. Hedges, "Three Farming Systems," in *Soils: The 1957 Yearbook of Agriculture* (Washington, D.C.: U.S. Department of Agriculture).]

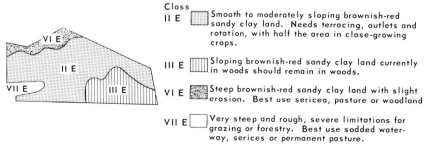

Class

II E Smooth to moderately sloping brownish-red sandy clay land. Needs terracing, outlets and rotation, with half the area in close-growing crops.

III E Sloping brownish-red sandy clay land currently in woods should remain in woods.

VI E Steep brownish-red sandy clay land with slight erosion. Best use sericea, pasture or woodland

VII E Very steep and rough, severe limitations for grazing or forestry. Best use sodded water-way, serices or permanent pasture.

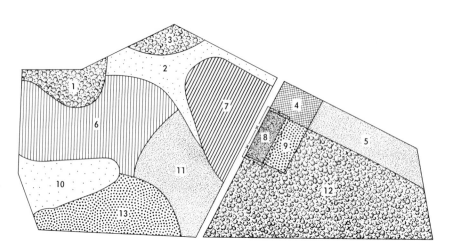

Field number	Acres	Use	Conservation Need
1	2.5		
3	1.5	Woods	Thin and cull, cut annually for sustained yields
12	22.0		
4	2.0	Farmstead	
5	5.0	Cotton	
11	8.0		Build up broad base terraces
7	9.0	Corn	Rotation that would not have row crops on same land more than 2-years in succession.
9	2.0	Wheat	
13	7.0		Apply lime and fertilizer according to needs.
6	25.0	Oats	
2	5.0	Idle cropland	Establish permanent sod crop — grass or Sericea, lime and fertilizer.
10	5.0		
8	2.0	Bermuda pasture	Lime and fertilizer

Figure 4–22 Map showing actual land use on a southern Piedmont cotton farm in 1955. [From E. L. Langsford, Charles P. Butler, C. W. Crickman, and Trimble R. Hedges, "Three Farming Systems," *Soils: The 1957 Yearbook of Agriculture* (Washington, D.C.: U.S. Department of Agriculture).]

land management practices recommended for the farm were the following:

1. Constructing broad-based terraces on cropland.
2. Establishing permanent sod crops in terrace outlets and nearby idle areas that have been badly eroded.
3. Initiating a rotation plan in which two years of row crops are alternated with two years of small grain.
4. Interspersing small grain with lespedeza.
5. Applying limestone to neutralize soil acidity.
6. Accelerating use of fertilizers to enhance crop yields.

Changes from the operation were needed to enable the farmer to take advantage of the modified soil management practices. These changes included the following:

1. Purchasing a tractor-drawn cultivator and planter.
2. Increasing the number of livestock.
3. Providing more forage.
4. Increasing grazing acreage by the erection of more fencing.
5. Using hybrid corn and improved varieties of other crops.
6. Improving wooded acres, culling undesirable trees, and making annual cuttings on a sustained yield basis (24).

Figure 4–23 Map showing recommended land use and land management practices for a southern Piedmont cotton farm. [From E. L. Langsford, Charles P. Butler, C. W. Crickman, and Trimble R. Hedges, "Three Farming Systems," in *Soils: The 1957 Yearbook of Agriculture* (Washington, D.C.: U.S. Department of Agriculture).]

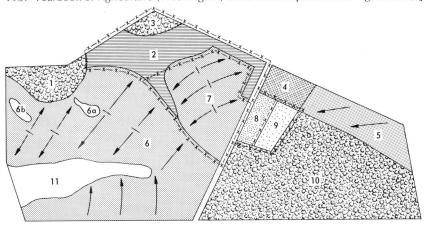

Field number	Acres	Recommended Use	Recommended Land Management
1	2.5		
3	1.5	Woods	Thin and cull, cut annually for sustained yields
10	22.0		
2	5.0	Coastal Bermuda and Crimson Clover	Construct fence; lime and fertilizer as determined by soil analysis
8	2.0	Common Bermuda and Crimson Clover	Lime and fertilizer
9	2.0	Fescue and Ladino Clover	Construct fence; lime and fertilizer as determined by soil analysis
4	2.0	Farmstead	
6a	.5		
6b	.5	Sericea Lespedeza	Establish permanent sod; lime and fertilizer.
11	5.0		
6	39.0	Rotation cropland	Build up terraces, establish 4–year rotation of small grain with row crops
7	9.0	Rotation cropland	Fence to permit grazing small grain, build up terraces, lime and fertilizer as needed.
5	5.0	Rotation cropland	Build up terraces, establish 4-year rotation of small grain with row crops, lime and fertilizer as needed.

After intensive study of the land capability map (Figure 4–21) for the farm in relation to the 1955 land use map (Figure 4–22) soil conservation experts advised a shift from the 1955 cotton–small grain organization to either cotton–small grain–beef cattle (organization A) or small grain–beef cattle (organization B). The estimated income and expenses for the 1955 and alternate organizations are indicated in Table 4–1. The net annual cash receipts for farm alternative A ($3,505) would be 86.2 per cent greater, and those from alternative B ($2,505) would be 31.0 per cent greater than the $1,882 net cash receipts estimated for the 1955 organization.

Table 4–1.* ESTIMATED INCOME AND EXPENSES ON A REPRESENTATIVE FAMILY-SIZE FARM IN THE PIEDMONT AREA FOR 1955, AND ALTERNATIVE ORGANIZATIONS BASED ON 1955 PRICES.

Item	1955	Alternative Organizations	
		A	B
	(cotton–small) grain	(cotton–small) (grain–beef) (cattle)	(small grain) (beef cattle)
Cash receipts			
Crop sales	$2,864	$4,118	$3,083
Livestock and			
product sales	584	1,478	1,478
Forest products sales		91	91
Custom machine work	100	100	100
Total receipts	$3,548	$5,787	$4,752
Cash expenses			
Crop	$1,002	$1,468	$1,239
Livestock	106	130	130
Tractor expense	169	291	319
Machinery expense	91	118	145
Feed purchases	131	85	219
Building repair	75	92	97
Fence repair	10	16	16
Insurance and taxes	82	82	82
Total expenses	$1,666	$2,282	$2,247
Net cash receipts	$1,882	$3,505	$2,505

* Source: E. L. Langsford, Charles P. Butler, C. W. Crickman, and Trimble R. Hedges, "Three Farming Systems," *Soils: The 1957 Yearbook of Agriculture*, Washington, D.C.: U.S. Department of Agriculture, 1957.

Agricultural Conservation Program

The Agricultural Conservation Program (ACP), established in 1936, provides financial aid to farmers who adopt approved soil conservation measures. The money is distributed by local farmer committees after technical approval of the SCS. In 1961 over 1.2 million participating farms, representing 24 per cent of all farms for that year, were awarded $208 million. During the first quarter century (1936–1961) of its operation, ACP subsidized measures for the initial establishment of cover (contour farming, strip cropping, liming, tree planting) were established on 568 million acres. During this same period, the cover of 461 million acres was either improved or protected by such practices as deferred grazing (to promote natural reseeding), tree stand improvement, provision of livestock watering facilities (wells, springs, pipelines), and weed control.

As a result of the integrated functions of the Soil Conservation Service and the Agricultural Conservation Program, our nation's croplands are in substantially better condition than they were in 1934, when the Reconnaissance Erosion Survey was made. According to the Conservation Needs Inventory conducted in 1958 under the leadership of the SCS, in addition to the Class I land not requiring conservation measures, roughly one third of our cropland had received adequate treatment by 1958; no further conservation treatment was required by almost one half of our forested land and one fourth of our rangeland. According to Held and Clawson, although firm data are lacking, we may guess that roughly 40 per cent of the soil conservation job existing in the early 1930's has now been completed (16).

Depletion of Soil Nutrients by Cropping

Before the white man came to North America, this vast continent was populated by 10 million native Indians, considerably fewer people than inhabit the Chicago area today. Although these Indians raised a few crops (corn, pumpkins, beans, squash, and potatoes), for the most part they depended on hunting, fishing, and the gathering of berries, fruits, and nuts. The extensive biomes of prairies, deciduous forest, and coniferous forest were modified very little by human activity. Generation after generation of big blue stem grass, oak, hickory, beach, maple, spruce, fir, and pine lived and died. During their lifespan these plants absorbed large quantities of life-sustaining nutrients from the soil, channeling them into billions of tons of wood, bark, leaves, flowers, roots, and seeds. Eventually, however, when these organisms died, their body nutrients were restored to the soil from which they originated. Soil fertility was also replenished by excreta and decaying carcasses of millions of birds and mammals.

Then came the white man's agriculture, which replaced forest and prairie vegetation with corn, wheat, cabbage, beans, and potatoes. As a result, the normal cycling of soil elements was greatly retarded. For example, a 100-bushel corn crop extracts 78 pounds of soil nitrogen, 36 pounds of phosphoric oxide, 26 pounds of potassium oxide, 25 pounds of calcium, and 18 pounds of magnesium. A 15-ton cabbage harvest absorbs 40 pounds of sulfur (22). One hundred forty-three pounds of nitrogen are removed by a 7-ton potato crop. The uptake of soil nutrients accounts for 10 per cent of a crop's total dry weight (11). Where once they were cycled, many soil nutrients now move down a one-way street—first being channeled into plant or animal crops, then into human digestive tracts and biomass, and then finally as human excrement, being flushed by sewage systems into rivers, lakes, and oceans. (This may also cause enrichment [eutrophication] of lake waters and contribute to undesirable "blooms" of algae.) Livestock manure may have returned soil nutrients in some regions, especially prior to the farm tractor, but it was not sufficient to halt the trend toward soil impoverishment. As Bear so eloquently states, "in many areas of the United States, the land has been turned into a nearly lifeless organic medium that must be nursed along like an invalid at the threshold of death" (3).

Depletion of Soil Nutrients by Erosion

Along with land cropping, the processes of accelerated erosion (which shortsightedness, ignorance, and greed precipitated) have also extracted a heavy toll on soil fertility. Bennett describes the fertility-depleting effects of a 1937 dust storm which originated in the Texas–Oklahoma panhandle and moved northeastward into Canada. Soils laid down on snow-covered land in Iowa were compared with samples from a dune near Dalhart, Texas. Analyses revealed that soil blown into Iowa contained *ten* times as much organic matter, *nine* times as much nitrogen, and *nineteen* times as much phosphoric acid as the dune material which accumulated near the storm's origin (5). Theoretically, it might be conceivable that Iowa farmers would benefit from this nutrient "windfall" by growing bumper corn crops on transplanted Texas soil. Unfortunately, however, much wind-blown topsoil accumulates in residential or industrial areas, and some nutrient-rich soil may be blown out to sea and be lost forever.

Water erosion has also taken its toll of productive soil. Thus, the Mississippi River alone annually discharges 730 million tons of soil into the Gulf of Mexico (1). Each year the combined agents of wind and water deprive America's future generations of crops, livestock, wildlife, and men of nearly 3 billion tons of potentially valuable soil.

Nature of Soil Nutrients

Of the roughly 100 elements naturally occurring in nature, about seventeen are required by plants and about nineteen are required by animals (including man), for health, growth, and reproduction. Four of these essential elements—carbon, hydrogen, oxygen, and nitrogen—derived from air and water, form roughly 96 per cent (by weight) of the fresh plant body. When a plant or animal is burned, these elements are driven off in gaseous form; the solid ash left behind includes the soil-derived mineral elements. The ash forms roughly 5 per cent of the dry weight of a plant and 10 to 15 per cent of the dry weight of man. Boron, which is essential to some plants, is not required by animals. Conversely, iodine and fluorine, valuable to animals, are not essential to plants. Mineral nutrients that are utilized by organisms in large quantities are usually classified as *macronutrients;* those required in only minute amounts are called *micronutrients.* Plant growth may be retarded not only when an element is not present in proper amounts in the soil, but also when it is in a form not readily usable by the plant or when it is not in proper balance with other soil nutrients.

Macronutrients. The macronutrients essential for plants include carbon, hydrogen, oxygen, nitrogen, phosphorous, sulfur, potassium, and calcium (8). Nitrogen is required by plants for the synthesis of protein, nucleoprotein, amino acids, and enzymes. It is essential for the processes of growth, seed production, respiration, and photosynthesis (2). Over every acre of land there are 34,500 tons of gaseous nitrogen (unavailable to plants) (2). According to the former Bureau of Chemistry and Soils, the highest nitrogen content occurs in a podzol soil in Massachusetts, and the lowest in a red and yellow soil in South Carolina. Because carbon, hydrogen, and oxygen are usually abundantly present in air or water, they do not ordinarily represent limiting factors for plant development, except in case of drought (although carbon, hydrogen, and oxygen form 94 to 99.5 per cent of plant protoplasm, only 0.5 to 6 per cent is soil derived), unusually cold weather, or plant disease. As R. L. Cook has pointed out, it should be remembered that many of the symptoms employed as indicators of nutrient-inadequate soil (unusual leaf color, stuntedness, abnormal shape of leaf and stem, leaf and root deterioration) may also be symptoms of parasitic diseases caused by bacteria, fungi, nematodes, or insects (8).

Micronutrients. Micronutrients essential to plants include iron, boron, copper, manganese, zinc, molybdenum, and chlorine (8). The amounts required by crops are exceedingly small. A clover field requires only *1 ounce of molybdenum per acre* (39). Boron requirements are met with one part boron in 1 million parts water, whereas molybdenum requirements are met with one part molybdenum in 1 billion parts water (8). Seven tons of Maine potatoes possessed only 0.2 pound of boron as compared with 143 pounds of nitrogen. Zinc may form only 0.0004 per cent of some plant leaves (37) and is a limiting factor for potatoes in northwestern Minnesota and for sweet corn, peas, and sugar beets in southeastern Wisconsin.

Plants absorb silicon, aluminum, and titanium, which are of no presently known use to either plants or animals. Iodine, fluorine, sodium, and cobalt, which have no apparent plant function but are indispensable to animals, are also taken from the soil (3).

Restoration of Soil Fertility

We shall describe the following methods of restoring soil fertility: animal manuring, green manuring, use of legumes, application of organic and inorganic fertilizers, and crop rotation.

Use of Organic Fertilizers

USE OF ANIMAL MANURE. By animal manure is meant the dung and urine of all farm animals such as horses, cattle, swine, sheep, and goats, as well as poultry. Animal manure benefits the soil by improving soil structure, increasing organic and nitrogen content, and stimulating growth and reproduction of soil bacteria and fungi.

In 1748 colonial farmers were already advised by Jared Eliot that liberal applications of animal manure would increase soil fertility. The manure tonnage annually produced per thousand pounds live weight of farm animal amounts to 15, 13, and 9 tons for the pig, cow, and horse, respectively. Seventy-five per cent of a ton of cow manure is water; the remaining 500 pounds of organic material contains 10 pounds of nitrogen, 5 pounds of phosphoric acid (P_2O_5), and 10 pounds of potash (K_2O). A corn-fed dairy cow returns to the soil (in excrement) 75 per cent of the nitrogen, 80 per cent of the phosphoric acid, and 90 per cent of the potash obtained from her feed. Precautions must be

Figure 4–24 Green manuring. Hairy vetch (a legume) being plowed under at a farm near Storey, Oklahoma, prior to planting a cotton crop. [Soil Conservation Service, U.S. Department of Agriculture]

exercised. Manure which is lying exposed to weather before being spread on the land may lose half of its nutrients through the leaching action of rain. Because legumes and grasses respond well to mineral fertilizers, farm manures should be saved for such rotation crops as corn, cotton, tobacco, cabbage, and potatoes (27). The application of 5 tons of manure per acre in Michigan yielded 46 bushels of corn per acre in contrast to the 35-bushel per yield of nonmanured land, a 31.4 per cent increase. Irrigated alfalfa in Washington responded to a 6-ton per acre manure application with a 1,000-pound per acre yield increase.

Animal manure improves soil structure. It causes the particles in loose sandy soils to bind together so that water retention is increased. The organic matter makes sticky clay soils more granular and porous, thus promoting both ease of tillage and aeration. Animal manure benefits the soil by increasing the organic content of the soil, improving soil structure, stimulating growth and reproduction in bacteria and fungi, and increasing the soil's nitrogen content.

Use of Green Manure. The process of turning under green crops to improve soil productivity is known as *green manuring*. Its effects on soil are similar to those of animal manure. With the latter becoming more scarce as farms become more mechanized, green manure has assumed an especially significant role.

USE OF LEGUMES. On the average, an acre of agricultural land probably loses 60 to 70 pounds of nitrogen yearly in the form of crops which have been harvested, as well as 20 to 25 pounds because of soil erosion. Thus, roughly 80 to 95 pounds of nitrogen per acre will be required annually to prevent a deficit. This can be done with legumes.

Several species can be utilized, including alfalfa, red clover, sweet clover, cowpeas, soybeans, lespedeza, vetch, and crotalaria. The nitrogen fixed by the nodule bacteria is added to the soil and becomes available to the next crop in the rotation. The actual amount of nitrogen fixed varies with the species of host plant, as well as with the number of virulent bacteria of the proper species available in the soil. In a ten-year experiment at Ithaca, New York, Lyon and Bizzel found the relative fixation ability as follows (27), taking alfalfa as 100:

Alfalfa	100
Sweet clover	67
Red clover	56
Soybeans	42
Field beans	23
Field peas	19

Although all nodule bacteria belong to the genus *Rhizobium,* a given species is compatible for only certain legumes. Thus, *Rhizobium melilote* effectively inoculates alfalfa and sweet clovers, whereas *Rhizobium trifolii* is compatible for white Ladino, red, alsike, and crimson clovers. If the legume to be used is native to the area, the correct bacteria usually have already been established. However, inoculation of the legume seed with the compatible bacteria at planting time may be necessary when an exotic legume is employed or when the appropriate bacterial population does not survive during the interval between crops. Seed stores generally have packaged inoculants containing nitrogen-fixing bacteria available for purchase by the farmer. Use of the inoculant ensures that the legume will acquire the proper nodule bacteria early in its development.

OTHER SOURCES. A variety of organic fertilizers may be derived from plant and animal residues. Sources include dried blood, animal wastes obtained from slaughterhouses, steam-treated garbage, dried and ground human sewage, sludge, dried fish scraps from cannery waste, and ground cottonseed meal. Even though most countries utilize human waste to increase soil fertility, this practice has been largely disdained in the United States. In recent years a few sewage disposal plants have prepared commercial fertilizer from sewage sludge.

An interesting source of organic fertilizer is represented by the excrement of wild birds and bats. Fish-eating cormorants have maintained dense breeding colonies on the rockbound Chincha Islands off the coast of Peru. Over the centuries, the guano of these birds has hardened and accumulated to a depth of over 100 feet. For many years these deposits, rich in both nitrogen and phosphorus, were "mined" and shipped all over the world, including the United States, as a form of fertilizer.

Use of Inorganic Fertilizers

NITROGEN FERTILIZERS. Nitrogen forms up to 0.3 per cent by weight of dark brown prairie topsoil—a total of 4,000 pounds per acre (1). A study by Dickson and Crocker showed that the amount of nitrogen in virgin pine forest soils of known age on the slopes of Mount Shasta, California, gradually increased with soil maturity. A steady state, however, was attained after 500 years when nitrogen content leveled off at 4,148 pounds per acre. However, once such virgin soil is subjected to intensive cropping or severe erosion, this initially abundant nitrogen content may be rapidly depleted.

The greatest single inorganic source of nitrogen currently used in American agriculture is a synthetic ammonia process in which nitrogen and hydrogen is combined under pressure in the presence of a catalyst. The nitrogen may be in the form of ammonia and ammonium salts or in the form of urea and nitrates derived from the ammonia. The direct application of anhydrous ammonia to soil was proved feasible in 1947 at the Mississippi Agricultural Experiment Station. Its use has increased more rapidly than that of any other fertilizer. In 1956 the total capacity of fifty-odd anhydrous ammonia factories in the United States was about 4.1 million tons (2).

PHOSPHORUS FERTILIZERS. The principal source of phosphorus fertilizer today is superphosphate. This material (which normally has 16 to 20 per cent available P_2O_5) is synthesized by treating raw phosphate rock with sulfuric acid. One hundred pounds of superphosphate contains about 8, 12, and 18 pounds of phosphorus, sulfur, and calcium, respectively (27).

POTASSIUM FERTILIZERS. For many years prior to World War I the largest single source of potassium fertilizer was located in the Stassfurt deposits of Germany located between the Elbe River and the Harz Mountains. In some regions these beds attained a thickness of 150 feet. During World War I this source was denied to American farmers; after a vigorous search, rich deposits were discovered in the United States. Potassium is rather generously distributed in American soils, forming about 2 per cent by weight of the topsoil, or roughly 40,000 pounds of potash (K_2O) per acre (1). Potassium chloride (KCl), potassium sulfate (K_2SO_4), and potassium nitrate (KNO_3) are all in extensive use today. Because all these salts are readily soluble in water, they are considered an immediately available source of potassium for agricultural crops.

COMPLETE FERTILIZERS. A complete fertilizer is a mixture (in varying ratios) of nitrogen, phosphorus, and potassium fertilizers. It must carry on the container a printed guarantee as to its component nutrients. Such a guarantee is usually stated in percentages. Thus, a 5–10–5 mixture contains 5 per cent total nitrogen, 10 per cent available phosphoric acid, and 5 per cent water-soluble potash. In utilizing inorganic fertilizers, the farmer not only must provide a crop with the total nutrients required for proper growth, but must provide them at the proper time. The same crop may require more of a given element at one time than another. Thus, corn requires the largest amount of potassium from June 20 to July 20, whereas its greatest nitrogen and phosphorus demands occur from July 20 to August 19.

DISADVANTAGES. The inorganic fertilizers, however, are not an unmixed blessing, for their continued use may result in subtle adverse changes of soil structure and contribute to water pollution problems. These disadvantages have been described by Barry Commoner, noted ecologist: "Another example of new problems created by what seem to be technological achievements is provided by modern agricultural technology, which is largely based on replacing the dwindling natural supply of plant nutrients in the soil by the massive use of inorganic fertilizers, especially nitrogen. These fertilizers greatly increase immediate crop yields; but at the same time, the impoverishment of soil organic matter, by altering the physical character of the soil (especially its porosity to oxygen), sharply reduces the efficiency with which the added fertilizer is taken up by the crop. As a result, unused nitrogen fertilizer drains out of the soil into rivers and lakes, where it joins with the nitrate imposed on the water by the effluent of sewage treatment plants, causing overgrowths of green plants and the resultant organic pollution. The drainage of nitrogen from fertilizer has already destroyed the self-purifying capability of nearly every river in Illinois. . . . In the Midwest and California, fertilizer drainage has raised the nitrate level of drinking water supplies

above the safe limit recommended by public health authorities."

Crop Rotation.   Effective crop rotation technique may simultaneously promote soil fertility and minimize erosion. A typical
three-year rotation pattern might involve a wide-row, cultivated soil-depleting crop (corn, tobacco, cotton) the first year;
a narrow-row, noncultivated soil-depleting crop of wheat,
barley, or oats the second year; and a dense, noncultivated
cover crop (grasses, legumes) the third year. The grass–legume
crop of the terminal rotation year would cover the soil with an
almost continuous shield of leaves and stems, which would
receive the full impact of rainfall and minimize erosion. Moreover, the nitrogen-fixing bacteria of the legume nodules would
"fix" about 200 pounds of nitrogen per acre. When properly
practiced, crop rotation would do much either to build up
impoverished soils or to maintain fertility of good soils.

Interaction of Soil Nutrients

The relationship of available soil nutrients to crop vitality
is extremely complex. Many questions remain unanswered.
For example, the interactions of soil elements may be either
beneficial or destructive to the crop. Consider a beneficial interaction. Dean describes a field experiment testing the effect of
fertilizer on oat production at the Iowa Agricultural Experiment
Station (11). When nitrogen fertilizer was employed exclusively, the resultant oat production was 20 bushels per acre;
when phosphorus fertilizer was used exclusively, oat yield
was 28 bushels per acre; but when nitrogen phosphorus fertilizers were employed together on the same soil, resultant oat
harvest was 54 bushels per acre (11). Apparently nitrogen and
phosphorus in combination resulted in greater yields than
could be explained by a purely additive effect. Obviously,
therefore, as far as oats is concerned, soil deficient in either
nitrogen or phosphorus can be rendered more productive when
the deficiency is remedied by fertilization. Now consider a
detrimental interaction. If a given soil is adequate in common
minerals such as calcium, phosphorus, and potassium, any
attempt to increase yield with fertilizer may actually impair the
crop's nutritive quality. In other words, soil can be overfer-
tilized (17). Thus, an excess of calcium in the soil, although
harmless per se, may indirectly result in *chlorosis* (lack of chlorophyll) because it reduces availability of zinc, iron, or manganese.

A research project conducted recently by the Missouri
Agricultural Experiment Station showed that by merely changing the ratio of calcium to potassium, the vegetative bulk of

soybeans was increased by 25 per cent. According to the University of Missouri's William Albrecht, most agriculturists would be elated over these results. On closer examination, however, this same soybean crop, which appeared so vigorous and robust, actually incurred a 25 per cent reduction in protein, a 50 per cent reduction in phosphorus, and a 66 per cent reduction in calcium (17).

Soil Nutrients and Human Health

Some authorities have been concerned that both agronomists and farmers are so preoccupied with crop yield that the crop's nutritional value is inadvertently being ignored. Quantity is being confused with quality. As A. G. Norman of the University of Michigan states, "High yields are not . . . synonymous with a high content of nutrient elements. . . . Crops from well fertilized plots may have a lower content of some (health) essential elements than those from poorly yielding plots, the addition of a fertilizer may cause a reduction in content of some of the other nutrient elements . . ." (17).

Despite remarkable accomplishments in nutritional research within the last few decades, we frankly are not able to pinpoint all the nutrients in vegetables and grains that are essential to human health. As Herber states, "We do not even know how many vitamins there are or which ones are essential" (17). An ear of corn, an orange, or cabbage may appear attractive and wholesome, and may even be delicious. However, if certain health-essential constituents are lacking, man may well incur serious nutritional inadequacies were he to subsist extensively on food grown in soil "doctored up" with a few inorganic commercial fertilizers in the interests of crop volume rather than human health.

Projected Cropland Requirements

From the preceding discussion it is apparent that science and technology have improved attitudes toward the importance and vulnerability of our land resource (especially during the immediate aftermath of the Dust Bowl calamities) and have been instrumental in soil rehabilitation. With the Soil Conservation Service leading the way, wind and water erosion has been retarded and soil structure and fertility have been restored on millions of acres. As a direct result America has been more than able to fill domestic food and fiber requirements. We even have food surpluses which can be shipped to hungry millions abroad. But what of the future, when there will be many more stomachs to fill? For example, as of 1962 the number of people was increasing at the rate of one every eleven seconds, five every minute, 325 every hour, 8,000 every day, 56,000 every week, and 3 million every year. America's projected crop and land requirements for 2000 would seem to give cause for concern. For example, our cropland needs for cotton will increase from 15 million (1960) to 20 million acres (2000), soybean cropland requirements will increase from 23 million acres (1960) to 44 million acres (2000), and land requirements for hay will zoom from 67 million acres (1960) to 118 million acres. For our ten most important crops (including grains, wheat, cotton, soybeans, and hay) over-all requirements will rise from the 319 million acres of 1960 to 378 million acres by 2000, a 12.2 per cent increase, leaving America with a *6-million-acre cropland deficit.*

As a result of our rapid population increase, and shifting dietary standards, demand for cattle and calves (live-weight) will increase from 28.6 billion pounds (1960) to 69.8 billion pounds (2000); demand for hogs will rise from the 1960 figure of 20 billion pounds to 44.3 billion pounds by 2000; egg consumption will jump from 62 billion (1960) to 119 billion by 2000. These human consumer demands obviously rest upon a producer food chain base of livestock feed plants, which in turn will require an increased cropland acreage. How can the impending dilemma posed by the cropland deficit be handled? Probably not by actual acreage increases. After all, virtually all suitable acreage is already being utilized. According to Landsberg, Fischman, and Fisher, in their *Resources in America's Future,* and other leading economists this deficit can be made up principally by increased yields from the existing acreage (23).

There are several methods for increasing our crop yields. First, more intensive use may be made of soil additives. Field trials in Nebraska in the 1950's showed that the optimal rate of fertilizer application would be 130 to 150 pounds per acre and could result in a 250 per cent yield increase to 120 bushels per acre. Nevertheless, as of 1954 only 27 per cent of Nebraska cropland was fertilized and at an average rate of only 42 pounds per acre, at least 66 per cent below the optimal rate. Even today (1970) much of our cropland remains unfertilized. Second, yields can be increased by the use of drought-, disease-, insect-, and wind-resistant crop varieties that are currently being developed by plant geneticists. For example, the use of hybrid corn has virtually doubled corn production in Wisconsin and Iowa in recent years. Third, crop production patterns can be modified to increase yields. A good case in point is the recent translocation of considerable cotton production from the Gulf

States to California, where average per acre yield in 1960 was 981 pounds, 101 per cent higher than the 486 per acre yield in Mississippi and 158 per cent above the Texas yield of 379 per acre. Fourth, yields can be increased by the judicious employment of pesticides to reduce production losses caused by insects, diseases and weeds. Fifth, a revolutionary technology theoretically could result in the mass production of yeast and algae which might be utilized as both human and livestock food; crop residues, such as corn cobs and stubble, might eventually be used as a source of livestock feeds, thus releasing a considerable acreage for production of crops directly usable by man. And sixth, increased per acre yields might result from more efficient farm operations made possible by consolidations. Within the past half century American agriculture has experienced dramatic changes in ownership and farm size. For example, in 1920 there were 6,488,000 farms averaging 148 acres in size. By 1966, however, consolidations had absorbed 3 million of these farms, resulting in a 119 per cent increase in average farm size to 325 acres. Moreover, it is predicted that average farm size will rise to 1,100 acres by 2000. Partly because larger farms permit more effective use of modern agricultural machinery, productivity per acre has jumped 7.7 per cent per year since the 1950's. If average farm size increases to the 1,100 acres predicted for the year 2000, land use shifts could be made that would be more consistent with land capabilities; that is, more Class I land could be utilized for crop production, with a resultant release of Class IV land (hilly, stony) for forest and pasture.

BIBLIOGRAPHY

1. Allen, Shirley W., and Justin W. Leonard. *Conserving Natural Resources.* New York: McGraw-Hill Book Co., 1966, 432 pp.
2. Allison, Franklin E. "Nitrogen and Soil Fertility," *Soil: The Yearbook of Agriculture.* Washington, D.C.: U.S. Department of Agriculture, 1957.
3. Bear, Firman E. *Earth: The Stuff of Life.* Norman: University of Oklahoma Press, 1962.
4. _____ *Chemistry of the Soil.* New York: Reinhold Publishing Corp., 1964, 515 pp.
5. Bennett, Hugh Hammond. *Elements of Soil Conservation.* New York: McGraw-Hill Book Co., 1955, 360 pp.
6. Blakely, J., J. Coyle, and J. G. Steele. "Erosion on Cultivated Land," *Soil: The Yearbook of Agriculture.* Washington, D.C.: U.S. Department of Agriculture, 1957.
7. Clark, William R. *Farms and Farmers.* Boston: L. C. Page and Co., 1945, 346 pp.

8. Cook, R. L. *Soil Management for Conservation and Production.* New York: John Wiley & Sons, Inc., 1962.

9. Dale, Tom, and Vernon G. Carter. *Topsoil and Civilization.* Norman: University of Oklahoma Press, 1955, 270 pp.

10. Dasmann, Raymond F. *Environmental Conservation.* New York: John Wiley & Sons, Inc., 1959, 307 pp.

11. Dean, L. A. "Plant Nutrition and Soil Fertility," *Soils: The Yearbook of Agriculture.* Washington, D.C.: U.S. Department of Agriculture, 1957.

12. Donahue, Roy L. *Soils: An Introduction to Soils and Plant Growth.* Englewood Cliffs, N.J.: Prentice-Hall, Inc., 1965, 363 pp.

13. Eddy, Don. "Up from the Dust," *Reader's Digest,* 37 (1940), 20–22.

14. George, Ernest J., Ralph A. Read, E. W. Johnson, and A. E. Ferber. "Shelterbelts and Windbreaks," *Soils: The Yearbook of Agriculture.* Washington, D.C.: U.S. Department of Agriculture, 1957.

15. Hall, A. R. "Early Erosion Control Practices in Virginia," Miscellaneous Publication No. 252. Washington, D.C.: U.S. Department of Agriculture, 1938.

16. Held, Burnell R., and Marion Clawson. *Soil Conservation in Perspective.* Baltimore: The Johns Hopkins Press, 1965, 344 pp.

17. Herber, Lewis. *Our Synthetic Environment.* New York: Alfred A. Knopf, 1962.

18. Highsmith, Richard M., Jr., J. Granville Jensen, and Robert D. Rudd. *Conservation in the United States.* Chicago: Rand McNally and Co., 1962, 322 pp.

19. Hill, W. L. "The Need for Fertilizers," *Farmer's World: The Yearbook of Agriculture.* Washington, D.C.: U.S. Department of Agriculture, 1964.

20. Holmes, R. S., and J. C. Brown. "Iron and Soil Fertility," *Soils: The Yearbook of Agriculture.* Washington, D.C.: U.S. Department of Agriculture, 1957.

21. Jacks, G. V., and R. O. Whyte. *Vanishing Lands: A World Survey of Soil Erosion.* New York: Doubleday & Co., 1939.

22. Jordan, Howard V., and H. M. Reisenauer. "Sulfur and Soil Fertility," *Soils: The Yearbook of Agriculture.* Washington, D.C.: U.S. Department of Agriculture, 1957.

23. Landsberg, Hans H., Leonard L. Fischman, and Joseph L. Fisher. *Resources in America's Future.* Baltimore: The Johns Hopkins Press, 1962.

24. Langsford, E. L., Charles P. Butler, C. W. Crickman, and Trimble R. Hedges. "Three Farming Systems," *Soils: The Yearbook of Agriculture.* Washington, D.C.: U.S. Department of Agriculture, 1957.

25. Leighton, M. M. "Geology of Soil Drifting on the Great Plains," *Scient. Month.,* 47, 22–23.

26. Lowdermilk, W. C. "Conquest of the Land Through 7,000 Years," *Agri. Info. Bull. No. 99.* Washington, D.C.: Soil Conservation Service. U.S. Department of Agriculture, 1953.

27. Lyon, T. Lyttleton, and Harry O. Buckman. *The Nature and Property of Soils.* New York: The Macmillan Co., 1937.

28. McDonald, Angus. "Early American Soil Conservationists," Miscellaneous Publication No. 1449. Washington, D.C.: U.S. Department of Agriculture, 1941.

29. Mickey, Karl B. *Man and the Soil.* Chicago: International Harvester Co., 1945.

30. *Newsweek,* 5, 13 (March 30, 1935), 5–6.

31. Olsen, Sterling R., and Maurice Fried. "Soil Phosphorus and Fertility," *Soils: The Yearbook of Agriculture.* Washington, D.C.: U.S. Department of Agriculture, 1957.
32. Olson, L. "Erosion: A Heritage from the Past," *Agricultural History,* **13** (1939), 161–170.
33. Pfeiffer, Ehrenfried. *The Earth's Face and Human Destiny.* Emmaus, Pa: Rodale Press, 1947.
34. Reitemeier, R. F. "Soil Potassium and Fertility," *Soils: The Yearbook of Agriculture.* Washington, D.C.: U.S. Department of Agriculture, 1957.
35. Rockie, William A. "Soil Conservation," in Guy-Harold Smith (ed.), *Conservation of Natural Resources.* New York: John Wiley & Sons, Inc., 1965.
36. Sears, Paul E. "Floods and Dust Storms," *Science,* **83,** 9.
37. Seatz, Lloyd, and J. J. Jurinak. "Zinc and Soil Fertility," *Soils: The Yearbook of Agriculture.* Washington, D.C.: U.S. Department of Agriculture, 1957.
38. Smith, Guy-Harold (ed.). *Conservation of Natural Resources.* New York: John Wiley & Sons, Inc., 1965.
39. Stout, P. R., and C. M. Johnson. "Trace Elements," *Soils: The Yearbook of Agriculture.* Washington, D.C.: U.S. Department of Agriculture, 1957.
40. Taylor, Sterling A. "Use of Moisture by Plants," *Soils: The Yearbook of Agriculture.* Washington, D.C.: U.S. Department of Agriculture, 1957.
41. U.S. Department of Agriculture. "Early American Soil Conservationists." Miscellaneous Publication No. 1449. Washington, D.C.: U.S. Department of Agriculture, 1941, 1–2.
42. _____ "Agricultural Land Resources," *Agri. Info. Bull. No. 263.* Washington, D.C.: U.S. Department of Agriculture, 1962.
43. Van Slyke, L. L. *Fertilizers and Crop Production.* New York: Orange Judd Publishing Co., Inc., 1932.

Water

5

The noted Greek philosopher Plato (427–347 B.C.) recognized that the earth's rivers were fed by rain and that water moved in a continuous ocean–land–ocean cycle. This knowledge, however, gradually was lost and during the Dark Ages, hundreds of years after Plato, the bizarre notion was advanced that water flowed magically in a never-ending stream from the center of the earth (17). Today we know that water moves from ocean to air to land to ocean in a pattern known as the *hydrologic cycle.*

The Hydrologic Cycle

Although fluctuations in rate of water movement may occur in certain segments of the cycle, the total water volume involved has remained constant for millions of years. The cycle is powered by solar energy, the *daily* input being greater than all the energy utilized by man since the dawn of civilization. In actuality, water is not continuously moving. It may be temporarily stored (for centuries) either within the earth's crust, on the earth's surface, or in the atmosphere. At any instant, only 0.005 per cent of the total water supply is moving through the cycle (16). Familiarity with the hydrologic cycle is basic to an appreciation of the nature and

117

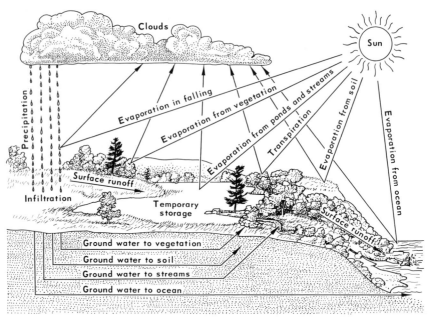

Figure 5–1 The hydrologic cycle. [Adapted from Raymond F. Dasmann, *Environmental Conservation* (New York: John Wiley & Sons, Inc., 1968).]

complexity of the serious water conservation problems confronting America today. (Fig. 5–1)

Ocean. We shall trace the major pathways of the hydrologic cycle, beginning with the oceans, which cover 70 per cent of the earth's surface with salt water up to seven miles deep. The oceans contain 97.2 per cent of the world's total water supply, over 317 million cubic miles (1 quadrillion acre-feet). (An acre-foot is the volume of water covering an acre to a depth of 1 foot.) If the earth were a perfectly smooth sphere, the ocean water would be sufficient to submerge the entire globe to a depth of 800 feet. As water molecules at the ocean's surface warm up as a result of incident solar radiation, they gradually rise into the atmosphere as a gas in a process called *evaporation*. It is estimated that more than 83,700 cubic miles of fresh water are evaporated from the world's salty oceans annually. Were the oceans not constantly refilled, the oceans would drop by 39 inches yearly (16). This atmospheric moisture forms a blanket around the earth which retards heat loss by radiation. Without this water vapor mantle, the earth would have a temperature of −300 degrees F. (6).

Precipitation. As the water vapor rises, it gradually cools, condenses, and forms clouds. Of the 83,700 cubic miles evaporated from the ocean, 71,000 cubic miles return to the ocean as precipitation; only 9,000 fall on land (18). The atmosphere holds a constant volume of less than one-hundred-thousandth (3,100 cubic miles) of the total water supply (16). This atmospheric moisture represents latent energy originally derived from the sun which is released through storms. An ordinary thunderstorm, of which more than 10,000 occur annually, releases more energy than a 120-kiloton nuclear bomb (18). Moisture-laden clouds may be carried inland over coastal areas, such as the Gulf or Pacific coasts, and finally, when cooling off sufficiently (as when they pass upward over the slope of a mountain or when they meet a cold air mass), may release water as rain, snow, hail, or sleet. The average daily precipitation in the United States amounts to 4,300 billion gallons. Our nation's average annual rainfall would be sufficient to cover the entire country (if it were perfectly level) to a depth of 30 inches. Twenty-four thousand cubic miles of water falls on the world's land surface yearly, enough to submerge Texas to a depth of 475 feet. In the United States, unfortunately, rainfall is very unevenly distributed, both in time and space. Annual rainfall on Mt. Waialeale, Hawaii, is 460 inches, whereas fifteen

Figure 5–2 N. Tongass National Forest, Alaska. Glaciers represent a phase of the hydrologic cycle and are powerful agents of geological erosion. This is a view of Mendenhall Glacier. Many of the lakes in the Northeastern states are glacial in origin. [U.S. Forest Service]

miles away it is only 18 inches; this is the result of topographic disruption of wind flow (16). Death Valley receives only 1.7 inches annually, whereas the western slope of the Cascades receives 140 to 150 inches each year (16). A certain town in Florida has been deluged with 24 inches of rain in a single day, yet Bagdad, California, once received only 4 inches in five years.

Bodies of Organisms. Plants absorb soil water through their root systems. Animals get their water by direct absorption through their body surface (amphibians), by drinking (many birds and mammals), or through the plant tissues (herbivores) and animal tissues (insectivores, carnivores) that they consume. In aggregate only 0.003 per cent of our fresh water supply is represented by hydrated plants and animals (1).

Evaporation and Transpiration. Of the 30 inches of annual rainfall, about 21 inches passes back into the atmosphere by evaporation and transpiration. More evaporation and transpiration occur in forested areas than elsewhere (26). Evaporation may take place directly from the surface of wet vegetation, moist soil, lakes and streams or from the bodies of animals and their excreta. Transpiration is the evaporation which occurs through the stomata of plant leaves. An acre of corn may transpire 4,000 gallons in a single day (17), 500,000 gallons in a single growing season. One mature oak tree may transpire 100 gallons per day, almost 40,000 gallons in a year (16). A 1-inch rainfall would be required to restore the water lost by one acre of mature oak trees by transpiration during a twenty-five-day period. Many plants transpire more than 2,000 grams of water for each gram of dry matter synthesized (7). The water which passes back into the atmosphere by evapotranspiration cannot be manipulated or controlled by man. Nevertheless, this water has served man well in sustaining forest, rangeland, residential lawn, and multimillion-dollar crop harvests.

Surface and Ground Water. About 9 inches of the 30 inches of annual rainfall in the United States either contributes to the formation of numerous ponds, lakes, and streams, from which it inexorably flows toward the ocean, or else percolates as *ground water* downward into the pores and channels of the earth's crust. It is this component of the annual precipitation that is of direct concern to the conservationist, for it is only this supply which yields to human control and manipulation and may be used for domestic, industrial, and agricultural purposes.

Even though river channels hold only 0.0001 per cent of the

world's water supply, stream flow is the most obvious method by which water returns to the ocean. Even during ancient times people had a fairly good understanding of river–ocean relationships. Thus, we read in Ecclesiastes 1:7, "All the rivers run into the sea: yet, the sea is not full; unto the place from whence the rivers come, thither they return again." Water flow in the 3.25 million miles of river channels in the United States (16) amounts to an average 1,200 billion gallons a day. It may be represented by a tiny mountain stream or a great river like the Mississippi, which drains an area of 1.2 million square miles and flows 1,200 miles across mid-America to the Gulf. Measurement of stream flow volume is done by more than 6,000 gauging stations operated by the U.S. Geological Survey (11). Surface water, in the form of streams, ponds, and lakes, satisfies about 80 per cent of man's water requirements.

Instead of forming run-off or surface ponds and streams, some of the rainfall and snow melt is absorbed by the soil. In the topsoil and subsoil horizons it is withdrawn by a myriad of plant root systems, transported upward through stems and trunks to countless trillions of chloroplasts which use it as raw material for photosynthesis. (Technically, only the hydrogen is so utilized, whereas the oxygen component of the molecule is diffused into the atmosphere.) Vast amounts of water move downward past the root zone, C and D horizons, into huge porous layers of sandstone, limestone, and shale. Ninety-seven per cent of the world's supply of fresh water (2 million cubic miles) is retained in such water-bearing rock formations known as *aquifers* (16). Occurring up to depths of one mile, they may hold more fresh water than all the world's lakes (including the Great Lakes) combined. When in danger of being depleted, they may be recharged artificially by means of injection wells, by spreading water over the land's surface, or by the use of water pits (11). Our total groundwater supply is equivalent to ten years of precipitation. Moreover, the groundwater of the United States in the upper one-half mile is equivalent to all the water which will run off into the oceans over the next century. This subterranean water may flow at varying rates of a few feet to several miles per year. It may take groundwater 135 years to move one mile laterally through sand (18). Occasionally groundwater may add to stream flow. Eventually, however, it discharges into the ocean to complete one turn of the hydrologic cycle.

The upper level of water-saturated ground, which is known as the *water table*, may coincide with the ground surface, forming marshes or springs, or may be situated at a depth of one mile or more. After heavy precipitation the water table rises;

during drought or intensive use by man it may subside. In some regions along the Gulf Coastal Plain, the water table lies so close to the surface that conventional 6-foot grave excavations tend to fill with water and above-ground burial is necessary.

Water Use

How many times and in how many ways have you made use of water today? From moment to moment, from hour to hour, this remarkable combination of hydrogen and oxygen is serving as an indispensable component of our ecosystem. We use it to wash everything from a ten ton truck to a baby's ear. We use it to extinguish fires and clean city streets, to flush sewage and to power industry. It is the basic raw material for numberless products emerging from our factories.

It takes 14 gallons of water to make one pound of sugar, 30 gallons for a pound of nails. Almost 200 gallons go into the manufacture of a pound of rayon yarn, and one gallon is required to manufacture a small woolen blanket. Seven hundred seventy gallons are required to refine a barrel of petroleum, 65,000 gallons to manufacture an automobile, 500,000 gallons to launch an ICBM rocket (21). One cup of water was needed to make the page you are reading. We employ our rivers and lakes to transport over 100 billion ton-miles of commercial freight each year. Water is the indispensable medium for sporting thrills enjoyed by millions of duck hunters, canoeists, and anglers. We take water into our bodies in a thousand disguises, from buttermilk to beef stew. We use it to irrigate everything from a backyard garden to a desert wilderness.

Man requires water for survival. The development and utilization of water resources have challenged man's resourcefulness and ingenuity for millenia. More than 4,000 years ago, Hammurabi, King of Babylon, boasted that he made the desert bloom after bringing water to it. Long before Christ's birth the people of Egypt, Greece, and Rome had developed well-designed water supply systems. Jacob's Well, so frequently mentioned in Biblical accounts, was hewn through a slab of solid rock to a depth of over 100 feet and is apparently still in use today. The Romans obtained 300 million gallons per day from fourteen huge aqueducts which, laid end to end, would have formed a pipeline over 1,300 miles long. Ruins of these aqueducts may be seen today. According to some authorities, the ultimate collapse of the Roman Empire was caused as much by the eventual deterioration of the water distribution system as by internal corruption or the might of the barbarian invaders. The importance of water to a nation's well-being has been emphasized recently by the chronic Arab-Israeli dispute over water rights to the Jordan River.

Water and Protoplasm (18).   Man could live two months without food but would die in less than a week without water. The body of the average human adult contains 50 quarts (100 pounds). Although the body is 65 per cent water (by weight), the percentage for specific organs varies. It is 2 per cent for tooth enamel, 22 per cent for bone, 75 per cent for brain and muscle, and 83 per cent for kidneys. Water has many functions in the human body. It serves as a solvent which promotes chemical activity. It serves as a transportation medium for nutrients, hormones, enzymes, minerals, nitrogenous wastes, and respiratory gases. It has a thermoregulatory function. The average adult loses 2.5 quarts daily—1.5 quarts by the excretion of urine, 1 pint by perspiration, and 1 pint by expiration. One and one-half quarts are replaced by drinking and the other quart by food ingestion. Death would result were man to lose more than 12 per cent of his body's water content. Most organisms, regardless of body size, food habits or habitat, from the Amoeba to the blue whale, have a high water content. Even the desert-dwelling kangaroo rat is 65 per cent water. The subterranean earthworm is 80 per cent water, the marine jellyfish 95 per cent. Plants are no exception; the water content for corn, grains, and tomatoes is 70 per cent, 87 per cent, and 95 per cent, respectively (16).

Water Problems

Drought.   The *Encyclopedia Americana* defines *drought* as a "period of severe atmospheric dryness and lack of rainfall of sufficient duration to cause widespread damage to crops, extinction of livestock and other economic hardships." Thus defined, a drought always involves financial setbacks, both to the individual and to the nation. According to the U.S. Weather Bureau, a drought exists whenever rainfall for a period of twenty-one days or longer is only 30 per cent of the average for the time and place. The more severe droughts in the United States have been characterized by diminution of stream flow and reduction in groundwater levels; heavy mortality for aquatic wildlife, such as fish and waterfowl; extensive destruction of range, pasture, and farm crops; dessicated topsoil, highly vulnerable to erosion; malnourished, disease-susceptible livestock; high incidence of forest fires; extreme discomfiture for man; and soaring food prices.

The most probable season for drought is summer, when water requirements of both wild and cultivated vegetation are greatest because of the high rates of photosynthesis and transpiration. Although twentieth-century man has contributed to many of his environmental ills by short-sightedness, greed, ignorance, apathy, or gross mismanagement of his ecosystem, we may exonerate him of virtually all responsibility for droughts. They have occurred with surprising frequency in the United States for over 1,000 years. Long before the Weather Bureau began keeping records, drought data were recorded by living tree trunks. Because a trunk lays down relatively wide annual xylem rings during periods of normal moisture and narrow rings during drought, by careful study of ring patterns in ancient trees it is possible to reconstruct the moisture conditions of past ages. In this way we have learned that protracted droughts occurred in the American Southwest roughly during the periods 700–720, 1070–1100, 1275–1300, and 1570–1600 A.D. Droughts are not rhythmic in the sense that we can predict that Syracuse, New York, or Atlanta, Georgia, will have a severe drought in 1985 or 2000. Rather, U.S. Weather Bureau records over the past century reveal that dry years alternate with wet years in an irregular pattern. The Great Plains from Texas to Montana, which include the arid part of the grassland biome, average about thirty-five consecutive drought days each year, and 75 to 100 successive days of drought once in ten years. Up to 120 consecutive rainless days have been recorded for the southern Great Plains, or Dust Bowl region.

DELAWARE RIVER BASIN DROUGHT OF 1961–1965. Twenty-two million people, 13 per cent of the nation's population (31), in New York, New Jersey, and Delaware depend on water drained by the Delaware River and its tributaries from a 12,000-square-mile watershed. The 400-mile-long Delaware was explored by Henry Hudson in 1609. It has its source in the Catskills, 1,800 feet above sea level. Coursing in a tortuous pattern past wooded slope and farm valley, it flows past Trenton and finally empties into the Atlantic at Delaware Bay. Its waters facilitate the prosperity of many adjacent communities, including Wilmington (Delaware), Camden, Trenton, and Philadelphia. Both Philadelphia and New York City utilize the water resources of the Delaware River Basin, either for drinking, industry, or the numerous water-using tasks of day-to-day living. Water shortages have frequently occurred in this region. In 1664 the Dutch governor of New Amsterdam (New York City) was forced to capitulate to the British because his men had run out of drinking water. In 1881 water was so scarce in New York

City that firemen dynamited fires instead of extinguishing them

with water. From 1961 to 1965 this region experienced the most
devastating drought in the entire history of the Northeast, with
the water deficit affecting 300,000 square miles.

What was the cause of this most recent drought? According
to some weather people, the 1961–1965 drought can be blamed
on a shift in the pattern of certain cold Canadian air masses.
They did not move far enough south into the New England
region to cause the warm humid air moving northward from
the Gulf Coast to release its moisture. Instead, the two air
masses converged over the North Atlantic, where precipitation
finally occurred.

As a result of the Canadian air mass shift, the mountain
streams of upstate New York were reduced to a trickle. Famous
trout streams, almost legendary among fishermen, were waterless. Resorts closed in midsummer. In 1963, because of the threat
of forest fires, Governor Scranton of Pennsylvania caused con-
sternation among thousands of would-be deer hunters by closing his state's forests for the hunting season. Wild game of
many species suffered heavy mortality as a result of vanishing
food supplies and protective cover. The hunting and fishing
vacation lands of 30 million people were so adversely affected
that the resort industry alone suffered an annual loss of many
millions of dollars.

A tribe of Pueblo Indians, assembled in Hershey, Pennsylvania, for a powwow, staged an elaborate "rain dance" ritual
in a half-humorous, half-serious attempt to coax a few drops of
moisture from the sullen clouds. A more modern band of "rain-
makers" substituted dry ice and silver iodide crystals for paint
and ceremony in a generally fruitless effort to "manufacture"
the needed rainfall.

The green lawns of residential areas turned brown. Flowers
wilted and died. Some trees defoliated two months prematurely.

At the governor's mansion in Albany, New York, Nelson
Rockefeller was aware that the water level in Alcove Reservoir,
the city's chief water reserve, had decreased from 12 billion
gallons to 4.5 billion gallons, an all-time low. Near Woodbourne,
New York, Neversink Reservoir was in danger of getting a new
name, for its water level rapidly sank to 50 per cent of capacity.

As of 1965, New York State's reservoir system, based upon
detailed studies of ninety years of weather history, had a total
capacity of 572 billion gallons, equivalent to a fifteen-month
water reserve. From the study, it had been determined that the
largest drought to be expected would last two years. However,
the Delaware River Basin drought lasted four years. By August,
1965, reservoir water had dropped to 212 billion gallons. If the

drought had continued, the reservoirs would have been empty by January, 1966.

New York City, with its 7 million people, relies heavily on the Delaware River flow to augment its municipal reservoir supply. But by late October, 1965, the Delaware was at its lowest ebb in fifty-three years. George Washington would scarcely have recognized this shrunken rivulet as the boisterous stream he once crossed. According to a 1954 decision of the U.S. Supreme Court, the City of New York had the right to withdraw 490 million gallons a day directly from the Delaware for its own use. In return, however, it was to release enough water into the river from the reservoirs, during periods of low stream flow, to ensure that salt would not back up from the ocean. In a desperate (though illegal) attempt to conserve the dwindling reservoir waters, New York discontinued releasing water into the Delaware. As a result, saltwater intrusion, advancing at a rate of one-half mile a day, corroded expensive industrial equipment, contaminated the underground aquifers of water-thirsty Camden, and became a threat to Philadelphia.

As the drought persisted, New York City eventually launched an intensive water conservation campaign. A blimp cruised over Times Square with a "Save Water" banner. Skyscraper office buildings turned off their air conditioning. Waitresses still greeted customers with the usual warm smile, but without the usual cold glass of water, now available only by special request, a device which might have conserved 12 million gallons daily. Whenever possible, the fire department used treated water from the harbor to extinguish fires. As a result of this all-out drive to conserve water, per capita water consumption in the greatest water-consuming city on earth was reduced almost 17 per cent, from 154 gallons to 125 gallons.

One positive feature of the drought is that millions of Americans have at last been awakened from their traditional complacency regarding the intelligent use of their primary natural resource. It is easy for those living in areas with abundant normal rainfall (the Northeast has 40 to 50 inches yearly) to be lulled into the belief that a severe drought will never come. Americans have always waited until their natural resources (whether topsoil, rangeland, forest, or passenger pigeon) have been reduced to a precarious state before they become aroused to constructive action.

But they are aroused now. From the wealthy industrialist whose expensive machines were reduced to worthless, corroded hulks as a result of saltwater contaminants, to the housewife who drew mud-colored water from the faucet, most Americans are united in their determination never again to allow themselves or their children to experience the discomfort and apprehension associated with a severe water insufficiency. Public arousal has prodded legislators on local, state, and federal levels into action. As *The New York Times* reported on December 20, 1965, "This change in sentiment has galvanized developmental projects and reforms that will involve governmental and private expenditures in the years immediately ahead, totaling possibly several times a year's national budget of one hundred billion dollars."

Plans for the Future. Water conservation experts who have studied the Delaware River region's water problem feel that significant increments to the usable water resources of the area can be made if pollution abatement is effected on the Hudson River; groundwater resources in the New Jersey Pine Barrens are developed; the water reservoir system in upstate New York is expanded; and evaporation suppressants are employed on the reservoirs.

ANTIPOLLUTION DRIVE. The Hudson River discharges millions of gallons of water daily. Unfortunately, however, the water is not nearly as potable as Henry Hudson found it when he explored this great waterway in 1609. After three centuries of use and abuse, its waters have become badly polluted. It was therefore an historic occasion to conservationists when, in a firm demonstration of civic responsibility, the people of New York in 1965 voted for Governor Rockefeller's $100 billion bond issue for water resource development. A substantial portion of the funds will be used in building a series of sewage disposal and water treatment plants along the Hudson and other waterways. Once pollution of these streams has abated, millions of gallons could be withdrawn daily. After effective removal of impurities at the treatment plants, the water would be available for both domestic and industrial use, thus alleviating much of the demand on currently overtaxed sources of supply.

GROUNDWATER RESOURCES DEVELOPMENT IN THE NEW JERSEY PINE BARRENS. The pine barrens, a desolate wasteland of sand and scrub pine (even though of considerable ecological interest) embrace roughly 2,000 square miles in the sparsely populated coastal plain of southern New Jersey. According to the U.S. Geological Survey, enormous quantities of fresh water are stored here in sand gravel aquifers. Some of these reservoirs are estimated to be almost 6,000 feet thick. If only 25 per cent of the annual water yield (run-off) in this region is recovered, up to 500 million gallons of pure water would be available daily for Philadelphia and New York.

EXPANSION OF THE WATER RESERVOIR SYSTEM.   There was no good excuse for the sinking of Neversink Reservoir or the critically low water levels in other reservoirs. The Delaware River Basin receives almost 10 trillion gallons of rainfall (44 inches) yearly, of which 4.7 trillion gallons (21 inches) are run-off and therefore theoretically available for man's use. According to the U.S. Geological Survey, the combined storage capacity of the ten major reservoirs of the Delaware River Basin (as of 1959) was only 1.4 million acre-feet, only a small fraction of the surface water storage potential. Moreover, the watershed area feeding these ten reservoirs was only 1,840 square miles, a mere 15 per cent of the basin. Even during drought the *minimum* daily water discharge from the basin is *five times* the maximum rate of consumptive use (as of 1955). Even moderate development of the dam and reservoir system in strategic sites such as the Lehigh River at Bethlehem, Pennsylvania, and the Neversink River at Oakland Valley, New York, would provide more than sufficient water to meet even the demands of the population projected for 1975.

In August, 1966, Professor Robert D. Gerard of Columbia University proposed the construction of a dam across Long Island Sound, which would convert the Sound into the largest reservoir in the United States and the tenth largest in the world, with a capacity of 41.8 million acre-feet (Lake Mead's capacity is 29.8 million acre-feet) (12). Within the scope of current technology, the impounded water would be equivalent to twelve times the city's present requirement of 1.25 billion gallons per day. This project could be completed without the loss of a single land acre. The reservoir volume of 41.8 million acre-feet would be three times the aggregate volume of the entire reservoir complex serving New York City at the present time. According to Gerard, other benefits accruing from the project would be the recharging of southern Long Island aquifers, where the water table has receded over 18 feet in fifty years and where there is serious saltwater intrusion; the diversion of water now transported to New York City by deep subterranean aqueducts to other water-short regions; attractive prospects for a pollution-free sport fishing activity; and elimation of the necessity for installing water meters, by which New York City might save at least $100 million (12).

Shortly after Gerard's proposal, New York University's Alistair W. McCrone proposed the less expensive alternative of constructing a dam across the Hudson River just north of Manhattan. Because the Hudson has a normal discharge of 33,000 cubic feet per second, the resulting reservoir would have an immense capacity. It would result in many of the benefits

Figure 5–3 Aerial view of California farm inundated by December flood. [California Department of Water Resources]

proposed by Gerard for the Long Island reservoir scheme and would have the advantage of being close to the city's present water supply tunnel system (20).

Floods. Not only is man plagued by water scarcity, he also is beset with the equally serious problem of too much water from violent rainstorms and floods. Throughout his history man has suffered from the destruction of floods. (Fig 5–4)

In 1811, for example, the "Beautiful Blue Danube" was neither blue nor beautiful when it swept over its banks, inundated large sections of Poland and Austria, washed away twenty-four villages, and drowned 2,000 soldiers. In 1877 the Hwang Ho River of China destroyed 300 villages, left 2 million homeless, and took the lives of 7 million people.

The greatest flood frequency in the United States ranges from February in the Southeast to June in the Northwest (11). Floods have inundated the Mississippi River Valley about once every three years. In 1861 the Sacramento River swept 700 people to their death. In 1889 a dam burst along the rain-swollen Conemaugh River at Johnstown, Pennsylvania, releasing a torrent which caused $10 million damage and took over 2,000 lives. Hurricane-spawned floodwaters moved through Galveston, Texas in 1900, devastated 3,000 buildings, and left 6,000 dead. The Mississippi flood of 1936–1937 extended for 1,000 miles through seven states, drove over 1 million people from their homes, injured 800,000 people, took 500 lives, and caused $200 million worth of property damage. The long-continued flooding of the Columbia lowlands inflicted $100 million damage during the summer of 1942. According to the Army Corps of Engineers, in August, 1955, Hurricane Diane caused $1.6 billion damage along the Atlantic Coast from North Carolina to Maine (25).

Paradoxically, however, in some parts of the world, man's very survival may be dependent on floods. Thus, the flourishing agricultural economy of Egypt has been sustained for millenia by the recurrent flooding of the Nile. Each inundation was eagerly awaited by flood plain farmers, for when the Nile finally receded, it left behind a deposit of extremely fertile topsoil carried from its upstream watershed. So important were these floods to ancient Egypt that the early Egyptian priests kept accurate records of their occurrence.

THE UPPER MISSISSIPPI FLOOD OF 1965. According to the U.S. Army Corps of Engineers, an unusual combination of factors involving excessive rainfall, massive snow melt, and frozen ground set the stage for a "once-in-a-century" flood in the Upper Mississippi River Valley. Late summer rainfall, which was above normal in the St. Paul–Minneapolis region in 1964, caused water-saturated soil conditions at the time of the initial autumn freeze. As a result, the ground was frozen solid to a considerable depth. Then came the snow. The 73 inches which fell in the Minneapolis region was 25 inches above the average for a single winter season. The partial snow melt of early March, followed by severe cold, resulted in a 4-inch ice cover. Finally, the combination of mild April weather (of 1965) and heavy rainstorms (5 inches fell in one area in twenty-four hours) contributed to flood conditions. Swollen with spring run-off waters, the Mississippi River surged over its banks from Minneapolis south to its junction with the Missouri at Hannibal, Missouri. Thousands of acres of winter wheat were devastated. It submerged 90,000 acres of cropland in Illinois alone. The Milwaukee Road's crack streamliner "The Hiawatha" was forced to halt its Minneapolis–Milwaukee run for the first time in history. Merchandise in river-front shops was damaged. At Hannibal, a few resolute shop owners hung out "business as usual" signs, even though much of Main Street was open to motor boat traffic only. At Mankato State College in Minnesota, hundreds of student volunteers erected a sand-bag barrier to restrain the floodwaters. When the sand gave out at Savage, Minnesota, resourceful volunteers filled their bags with wheat. Despite such emergency measures, the rising waters drove 40,000 people from their homes. After a helicopter survey of the

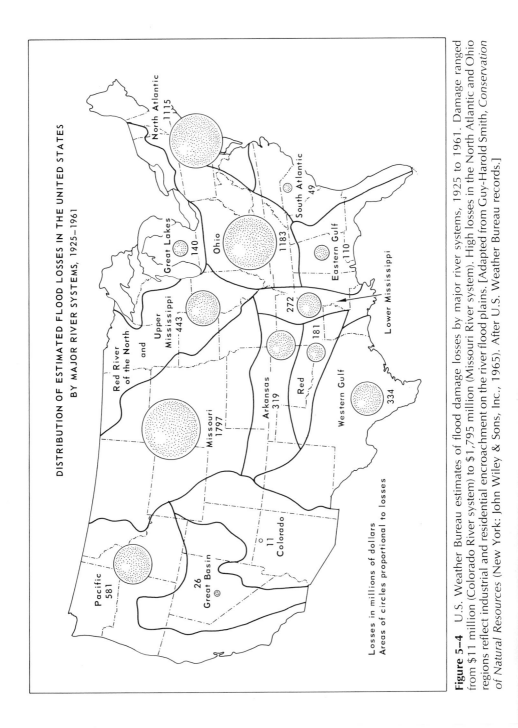

Figure 5–4 U.S. Weather Bureau estimates of flood damage losses by major river systems, 1925 to 1961. Damage ranged from $11 million (Colorado River system) to $1,795 million (Missouri River system). High losses in the North Atlantic and Ohio regions reflect industrial and residential encroachment on the river flood plains. [Adapted from Guy-Harold Smith, *Conservation of Natural Resources* (New York: John Wiley & Sons, Inc., 1965). After U.S. Weather Bureau records.]

stricken area, President Johnson gave this terse, three-word summary of his impressions, "It was terrible." Eventually the waters receded. A thick, smelly deposit of brownish ooze covered the exterior and interior of many river-front homes. Thousands of fish were stranded in stagnant backwaters. The official toll taken by the greatest flood in Upper Mississippi River history read sixteen drowned, 330 injured, and $140 million in property damage.

Flood Control. Although man cannot prevent all floods, he can prevent some of the lesser ones and can restrict the magnitude and destructiveness of others. Flood-control measures include protection of the watershed, measurement of snow pack to predict flood conditions, levees, dredging operations, dams, and prevention of human encroachment on flood plains.

PROTECTION OF THE WATERSHED. A watershed may be defined as the area drained by a single water course. It may range from less than 1,000 acres to more than 1 million. The largest watersheds, such as those of the Ohio, Missouri, Colorado, or Mississippi rivers, are known as drainage basins. All watersheds, large or small, have the basic function of converting

Figure 5–5 Flood damage in Harrison, Arkansas, caused by the storm of May 7, 1961. Four lives were lost. Damage was estimated at $5,278,000. [*Harrison Daily Times*]

precipitation into stream flow (13). Even during a light shower, 0.1 inch of rainfall would be "converted" by a 1-acre watershed into 11.3 tons of stream flow,whereas a watershed of 1 square mile would convert it into 1.74 million gallons of stream flow.

Any type of vegetational cover on the watershed will impede flow velocity, and hence will be of value in flood and erosion control, which is well illustrated by the following incident. On December 31, 1933, merry celebrations ushering in the New Year at LaCrescenta, California, were abruptly ended when floodwaters rushed down from the adjacent hillsides of the San Gabriel Mountains, inflicting $5 million in damage and killing thirty citizens. When flood-control experts investigated the watershed above LaCrescenta, they discovered that the flood-waters originated from a 7-square-mile area in the San Gabriel Mountains which had been burned over only a short time before. The unburned watershed, with its vegetational "sponge" of chaparral, herbs, and grasses, served to restrain the down-hill rush of run-off waters; peak flows were roughly 5 per cent of those of the burned area. Whether it is California chaparral, alfalfa in Alabama, or woodlands in Wisconsin, any type of vegetational cover is to some degree useful in restraining floods.

Figure 5–6 Flooded residential area in a Wisconsin town, on the banks of the Mississippi River. Note sandbagging. [Wisconsin Department of Natural Resources]

Figure 5–7 Brush fire working down Bear Canyon in the Los Padres National Forest, California. Once vegetation is destroyed, the burn area becomes susceptible to soil erosion, and flash floods in the lowlands become more frequent. [U.S. Forest Service]

Recently, Congress enacted the Watershed Protection and Flood Prevention Act, usually referred to as the "Small Watershed Act." The small-watershed program is administered by the USDA's Soil Conservation Service. Protection of large watersheds is primarily the concern of the Bureau of Reclamation, the U.S. Army Corps of Engineers, or the Tennessee Valley Authority (TVA). Although the primary objective of the Act is flood control, it is operated under a multiple-purpose concept, and where possible it embraces problems of erosion, water supply, wildlife management, and recreation. According to the USDA, 8,000 (61.5 per cent) of the 13,000 small watersheds (of less than 250,000 acres) in this country have flood and erosion problems (30). Ralph C. Wilson (28) describes a typical small-watershed project in the Ozark Mountain foothills of Lawrence County, Arkansas. An annual loss of $60,000 had been inflicted by the rampaging waters of Flat Creek. In addition to causing crop, road, and building damage, the floodwaters interrupted school, local industry, and the mail. Drainage canals became choked with sediment washed from the gullied slopes. Through the Soil Conservation District of Lawrence County, the farmers

134

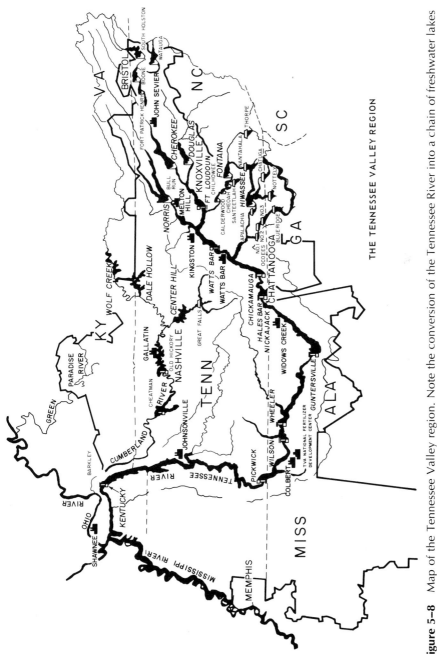

Figure 5-8 Map of the Tennessee Valley region. Note the conversion of the Tennessee River into a chain of freshwater lakes by the construction of multiple dams by the TVA. The accomplishments of the TVA in integrating the natural, economic and human resources of the valley have been widely acclaimed and have served as a blueprint for similar projects abroad. Note that the area served by the municipal and cooperative distributors of TVA power extends far beyond the Tennessee state border into Kentucky, Virginia, North Carolina, South Carolina, Georgia, Alabama, and Mississippi. Over 65 per cent of the electrical power produced in the TVA project is generated by steam plants. [Map from the Tennessee Valley Authority.]

cosponsored the Flat Creek watershed project with the Arkansas Game and Fish Commission. The program initiated a number of standard soil conservation measures. Gullies were reclaimed, and six small dam–reservoir systems were established, including 645-acre Lake Charles. As a result, not only has the flood problem been resolved, but erosion has been checked and fishing, swimming, and boating facilities have been created.

MEASUREMENT OF SNOW PACK TO PREDICT FLOOD CONDITIONS. In recent years the U.S. Geological Service has employed snow surveyors to make measurements of the area and depth of the snow pack at more than 1,000 snow courses in the western mountains. Equipped with snowshoes, skis, and snowmobiles, these hardy men compile data which can be useful in flood prediction. For example, several years ago a survey predicted that the imminent spring snow melt would crest the Kootenai River at 35.5 feet, sufficient to cause extensive flooding at Bonner's Ferry, Idaho. Alerted by this forewarning, federal troops evacuated all residents and reinforced the dikes. On May 21, the river did indeed crest at 35.5 feet as predicted. However, flood damage was minimized and not one life was lost.

LEVEES. Levees are dikes constructed of earth, stone, or mortar that are built at varying distances from the river margin in an effort to protect valuable residential, industrial, and agricultural property from floodwaters. Levees along the Arkansas, Red, White, and Ouachita rivers have given a measure of protection to more than 2 million acres of fertile alluvial land. In the last 150 years a mammoth system of over 3,500 levees and dikes has been constructed along the lower Mississippi River. Levee systems occasionally create special problems. For example, after a protracted rainfall, the drainage of diked lowlands requires pumping the water up over the levees back into the main channel.

DREDGING OPERATIONS. Because of the huge soil deposits that are washed into a stream from the surrounding watershed, the channel tends to accumulate sediment, which increases the probability of a flood. Because of the force of the current of a river or stream, a portion of the bank may crumble and be washed into the stream. Thomson King describes such a bank cave-in near Point Pleasant, Missouri, where the Mississippi River eroded a strip of bank 10 miles long and 2 miles wide and carried soil, trees, and homes downstream. The enormity of this problem can be appreciated when we realize that the Mississippi River, for example, transports roughly 2 million tons of silt daily. To cope with this situation (as well as to deepen channels for navigation), our major river channels are periodically dredged by the United States Army Corps of Engineers.

The importance of periodic dredging is emphasized by the 1852 Yellow River catastrophe in China. As the channel of this river became choked with silt, levees were built higher and higher, until the Yellow River was flowing above the roof tops. Inevitably, a massive surge of floodwaters crumbled the retaining walls and drowned 2 million people.

DAMS. Dams have been used by man since long before the Christian era. The ancients checked the surging waters of the Euphrates and Nile with massive barriers of earth and masonry. The ruins of numerous concrete dams erected by the Romans many centuries ago in northern Africa and Italy may still be observed.

Even though there have been serious criticisms because of their expense and siltation-abbreviated life-span, the United States has committed itself to a vast program of superdam construction. As of late 1966 the Bureau of Reclamation alone had constructed 248 dams, with an impoundment capacity of 129.5 million acre-feet. As of 1960 the United States had 1,300 large

Figure 5–9 Snow surveyors viewing Ward Creek, a tributary to Lake Tahoe. [Soil Conservation Service, U.S. Department of Agriculture]

reservoirs, which occupied an estimated area of 11 million acres. By the year 2000, 10 million additional acres of land will be covered by reservoir waters.

Are these dams effective in flood control? According to Brigadier General W. P. Leber, Ohio River Division Army Engineer, the Ohio River flood of March, 1964, would have caused additional damage of $290 million had it not been for the coordinated system of thirty flood-control reservoirs, plus sixty-two flood walls and levees. He stated that flood crests were reduced by up to 10.5 feet by these flood-control facilities. The water retained by the Shasta dam and others in northern California aids in the prevention of flash floods which formerly harassed the region. Partial flood control is also effected by such dams as the Santee in South Carolina, the Grand Coulee on the Columbia, and the Hoover on the Colorado. In 1965 Los Angeles County, which had experienced repeated floods from rain-swollen rivers, established a coordinated complex of control structures costing nearly $600 million. It involves sixty headwater dams in the mountains, fourteen retention reservoirs in the Los Angeles and San Gabriel Rivers, and six major flood-control dams. This system has proved to be very successful in protecting 325 million acres from flooding.

Cost. The mammoth downstream dams have been con-structed largely by the U.S. Army Corps of Engineers, the Bureau of Reclamation, and the TVA. They are extremely ex-pensive and the costs, running into many millions of dollars, would be prohibitive if it were not for the fact that these dams, in addition to providing flood control, also generate hydro-power, improve navigation, provide irrigation waters, and establish recreational facilities. It should be pointed out, how-ever, that for effective flood control there must be frequent "drawdowns", so that the reservoir capacity is great enough to accommodate floodwaters. Such drawdowns will adversely affect both the hydropower generators and recreational func-tions of the dam (23). Big dams have other negative features, in addition to cost. The reservoir which forms behind the dam may inundate thousands of acres of once fertile agricultural land. In coastal regions the blocking of stream flow may result in saltwater intrusion. Big dams may abuse natural beauty. Thus, the magnificence of the Rainbow Bridge National Monu-ment in northern Arizona is being jeopardized by the encroach-ment of the Colorado River's Glen Canyon Dam reservoir. Some big-dam critics maintain that several smaller dams on headwater tributaries would be equally effective in flood con-trol and would be considerably less expensive than one big dam downstream. Thus, Peterson (24) has compared a large

Figure 5-10 Night view of switchyard at Glen Canyon Dam on the Colorado River, near Page, Arizona. [Bureau of Reclamation, U.S. Department of the Interior]

mainstream reservoir plan with an alternate plan for smaller headwaters reservoirs proposed for the same watershed. The single large mainstream dam would cost $6 million and would have 52,000 acre-feet of flood storage. The fourteen smaller headwaters dams would have 59,100 acre-feet of flood storage and would cost only $1.9 million.

Siltation Problem. Another drawback associated with the construction of big dams is the speed with which their reservoirs are filled with sediment. The huge Lake Mead Reservoir behind Hoover Dam is filling at a rate of 137,000 acre-feet of silt per year, sufficient to destroy the operation of this multimillion dollar structure in less than 250 years. Many of our nation's lesser reservoirs have a life expectancy of less than fifty years. California's Mono Reservoir, which was theoretically designed to provide a permanent water source for Santa Barbara, filled up with sediment within two decades. In addition, biological succession proceeded so rapidly that a thicket of shrubs and saplings became firmly established. For all practical purposes, Mono Reservoir is dead, and buried.

Reservoir Evaporation Losses. Evaporation losses from reservoirs in hot, arid regions, where winds are prevalent, can be considerable. Lake Mead, for example, loses 893 million gallons daily. The top 7 feet of the lake are evaporated annually. The evaporation problem is not applicable to detention reservoirs which are waterless except during flood time. However, because loss is roughly proportional to water area exposed, more water would be lost from several small shallow reservoirs than from a single deep reservoir, even though the capacity of the latter was equivalent A study of Wyoming's Cheyenne River basin has shown that evaporation losses from numerous small stockwater ponds reduced average annual run-off from the basin by more than 30 per cent. About 6 million acre-feet are lost annually from 1,250 large western reservoirs and the loss from all water bodies (lakes, ponds, and reservoirs) in the West amounts to 24 million acre-feet, sufficient to supply all the domestic needs of 50 million people. Although such losses are reduced on small reservoirs in the West with roofs and floating covers, and may be reduced by almost 20 per cent with a monomolecular film of hexadecanol, they still are quite substantial.

The Pollution Problem. The Potomac River was once a beautiful stream. Originating in the Appalachians of West Virginia, its cool waters cut their way through the Blue Ridge Mountains in a spectacular 1,000-foot water gap, then play over a series of falls, some of them up to 35 feet high, before flowing past our nation's capitol and emptying into Chesapeake Bay. Many early explorers used the Potomac as a water pathway into the interior. One called the Potomac "the sweetest and greatest river I have seene." Mount Vernon, the home of George Washington, a mansion of great dignity and beauty, with its white columns and lush green lawns, overlooks the Potomac from a high bluff. Arlington National Cemetery, with its thousands of white tombs and crosses, is not far from the Potomac's shores. This great river, over 358 miles long and draining a basin of roughly 14,000 square miles, is closely associated with events important in American history. Many great battles of the Civil War were fought near its banks and along tributary streams.

But the river has changed. Once a thing of beauty, it is now an "open sewer." Once a delight to the eye, it is now offensive; its waters smell of decomposing garbage and human excrement and are stained with discharge from industrial plants. President Johnson remarked to Congress on October 2, 1965, "Two hundred years ago George Washington used to stand on his lawn down here at Mount Vernon and look on a river that was clean and sweet and pure. In our own century, President Theodore Roosevelt used to go swimming in the Potomac. But today the Potomac is a river of decaying sewage and rotten algae. Today all the swimmers are gone. They have been driven from its banks."

The history of the pollution of the Potomac is similar to that of many other American rivers and streams.

CATEGORIES OF POLLUTION. *Water pollution* may be defined as "any unreasonable contamination of water which lessens its value to man." The problem of water pollution was recognized by Hippocrates (450 B.C.), who suggested filtration and boiling as remedial measures. The substances which pollute the waters of America can be classified into the following eight categories: *sewage, infectious agents, nutrients, synthetic organic chemicals* (such as household detergents and pesticides), *inorganic chemicals, sediments, radioactive materials, and heat.*

Figure 5–11 A sign of the times. Throughout America swimming beaches have been closed due to pollution, as was this lake front beach at Hammond, Indiana. July 1, 1962. (*Hammond Times*)

Figure 5-12 Sewage runs into Rapid Creek at Rapid City, South Dakota, through this culvert. Many thousands of gallons of untreated sewage daily by-passed the Rapid City Sewage Treatment Plant and emptied into this stream. November 25, 1962. [*Rapid City Daily Journal*]

Sewage. A recent survey revealed that raw sewage from 11 million people living in 1,342 communities is being discharged into streams and lakes with no treatment whatsoever and that 17 million people in 1,337 communities require either new or enlarged sewage systems (16). It would take at least $30 billion to develop effective municipal sewage facilities to accommodate the current population of our country.

As we learned earlier, bacteria serve man and all of life as the recycling agents of essential elements, such as nitrogen and phosphorus, which otherwise would be locked into organic compounds. As soon as sewage is discharged into a stream, the solids settle to the bottom and are immediately acted upon by stream bacteria. However, this bacterial activity consumes oxygen dissolved in the water. (To promote decomposition of sewage, some disposal plants add oxygen during sewage treatment.) As the sewage load increases, the stream oxygen level decreases. The oxygen required by a given load of organic waste is known as its biological oxygen demand, or BOD. Degree of pollution can be recognized and measured by the BOD test, in which a sample of sewage-contaminated water is incubated for five days at 20 degrees C., and the amount of oxygen consumed is determined by comparing the amounts present before and after incubation (23).

All aquatic life is dependent upon oxygen for survival. Organisms have different oxygen-tolerance limits. An adult game fish, such as a black bass, requires a minimum of 4 parts per million of dissolved oxygen. In badly polluted waters the oxygen level may drop considerably below 4 ppm. As a result, aquatic vertebrates either will die or will emigrate from the discharge area. Undesirable forms, such as *Tubifex* worms and insect larvae, will become dominant (26). Sewage water also shows increased levels of carbon dioxide and foul-smelling hydrogen sulfide gas (26). The net effect of sewage pollution in a stream, therefore, is to impair its recreational and aesthetic value severely. Even with efficient waste treatment methods, which America obviously does not have, by 1980 our organic wasteloads (domestic plus industrial) will be *sufficient to consume all the dissolved oxygen in the dry weather flow of our nation's twenty-two river basins.*

In order to reduce domestic sewage pollution, scientists have urged the installation of small units by homeowners which could segregate solid from liquid waste; these wastes would then be carried to separate treatment plants where they could be more effectively processed. Other experts have suggested that human sewage might be channeled into the ocean by lengthy pipelines extending far beyond the coastal regions.

Figure 5–13 Sewage treatment plant at Oyster Bay, New York. [New York Conservation Department]

Infectious Agents. By the term *infectious agents* is meant organisms, such as protozoa, bacteria, and viruses which can live inside or on the human body as parasites and cause disease. The causative organisms of cholera, amoebic dysentery, polio, typhoid fever, and infectious hepatitis are capable of transmission by sewage discharge and stream flow for many miles from their point of origin. One cup of water randomly taken from the Connecticut River near Hartford recently contained twenty-six different species of infectious bacteria which typically occur in human fecal matter (32). Infectious organisms may have their origin in the wastes discharged from hospitals, private homes, and even slaughterhouses. They may be unsuspectingly taken into the human body via contaminated drinking water. The nineteenth-century cholera epidemic in London was caused by cholera germs originating from a single sewage-contaminated well. In this modern era of ultra sanitation and ultrasterilization, one takes germ-free tapwater for granted. However, there are public water systems in this country today contaminated with injurious microorganisms which can cause chills, fever, pain, nausea, malaise, paralysis, and even death.

Recently, Kabler surveyed the research on this problem for the span of time from 1922 to 1959. In this survey domestic sewage wastes were analyzed for infectious organisms before and after sewage was exposed to various treatment processes. To his surprise, almost all infectious bacteria, fungi, and viruses occurring in the untreated sewage also could be identified in the treated samples, although their numbers were reduced. Among the organisms which passed through the treatment processes were the bacteria of typhoid, paratyphoid, cholera, salmonellosis, tuberculosis, anthrax, and tetanus. All viruses, including the polio virus, and such parasitic worms as hookworm, roundworm, and tapeworm were present.

In 1916 and 1924, two major typhoid epidemics along the Atlantic Coast were traced to contaminated clams and oysters. Fifteen hundred people were infected; 150 people died in the 1924 epidemic. After the 1924 outbreak the shellfish companies formed a compact with the Public Health Service whereby interstate health controls and standards were established (32). In the early 1960's some youngsters were playing along the Hudson River into which 400 million gallons of human sewage are discharged daily. They ate a watermelon which they found floating in the river. Later, eight of these children contracted typhoid fever. From May to July 1965, 18,000 of the 130,000 residents of Riverside, California, were stricken with fever, diarrhea, and vomiting. Three died. The causative organism was *Salmonella typhimurium,* a bacterium related to the typhoid organism. Chlorination of the municipal water supplies brought the epidemic under control. In each of the preceding cases, the disease could be traced to sewage-contaminated waters.

Over 166 strains of viruses were discovered by Kelly and Sanderson in treated sewage as recently as 1957. Many kinds of disease-causing viruses have been found in sewage even after chlorination, a process expressly designed to destroy microscopic agents of infection. From time to time we all complain of vague pains, headache, and stiffness. Sometimes we go to a doctor for diagnosis, only to have him say, "You probably have some kind of virus." Where did the virus come from? It is quite possible, as Dr. John A. Zapf, Jr., told a recent national conference on water pollution, that "water may be implicated in viral diseases as yet not recognized."

One well-known virus which may be lethal to man is infectious hepatitis. From 1844 to 1956 there were at least six outbreaks of water-borne infectious hepatitis in the United States. Another extensive outbreak of this disease occurred in 1961 in New York and New Jersey. During an ensuing investigation, it was revealed that each disease victim had eaten clams harvested from Raritan Bay, off the Jersey coast. The clams had taken the virus into their bodies during the process of filtering food from the sewage-contaminated waters (32).

Nutrients. Nutrients represent an important limiting factor for all plants, whether they are agricultural plants important to man as a food source, or aquatic algae and weeds growing in some stream. All other things being equal, the more nutrients available—such as the nitrogen, phosphorus, and potassium found in sewage, agricultural, and industrial wastes —the faster and more luxuriantly plants will grow. Aquatic vegetation has become an increasing nuisance in 190,000 miles of drainage canals, 170,000 miles of irrigation canals, and in 42 million acres of inland freshwater ponds, lakes, and streams (excluding the Great Lakes) (28). Bountiful growth of crop plants, of course, from man's perhaps narrow and selfish point of view, is desirable; but the almost explosive growth of aquatic vegetation may sometimes pose a problem. Dense blooms of algae may cause the death of bottom-dwelling rooted plants by intercepting sunlight. These growths may obstruct areas otherwise desirable for swimming and boating. They may impart a foul taste to the water that is costly or impossible to remove by water purification systems. Furthermore, when the lush growth eventually dies in late summer, the ensuing decomposition releases hydrogen sulfide gas, which not only discolors lead paints and tarnishes silverware, but has the odor of rotten eggs. Property values decline because of this. Lake Washington, near Seattle, and Wisconsin's Rock River are good examples of water defiled by nutrient pollution. Lake Erie has been polluted by years of run-off from fertilized fields along its shore.

Where do these nutrients originate? They have three main sources: agricultural fertilizers, domestic sewage, and industrial wastes. As our nation's farmers strive to feed a rapidly increasing human population, they inadvertently also feed population explosions of water weeds. Thus, the amount of agricultural fertilizer used in the United States increased from 6 million tons in 1935 to 25 million tons in 1960, and was close to 30 million tons as of 1967. Eventually these nutrients are washed into streams by run-off waters and trigger the biological chain of events described. The nitrogen and phosphorus contained in human sewage have a comparable effect. The rapid increase in water milfoil, sea lettuce, and plankton in the lower Potomac below Washington, D.C., is probably the result of the 45 tons of nitrogen and phosphorus compounds being discharged into the river daily. In 1965 there were 100,000 acres of Eurasian water milfoil in Maryland alone, a 100 per cent increase since 1961 (28).

Early in 1970, Donald E. Wilkinson, Secretary of the Wisconsin Department of Agriculture, emphasized the gravity of fertilizer pollution and suggested that the use of high phosphate and nitrate fertilizers by Wisconsin farmers may be restricted in the near future to "alleviate the algae problems in our waters," even though the fertilizer curb would reduce crop production for a time.

The gravity of the water problem caused by livestock excrement, particularly in the Midwest, is emphasized by Washington University's environmentalist Barry Commoner:

"A livestock animal produces much more waste than human beings, and the waste produced by domestic animals in the United States is about ten times that produced by the human population. Much of this waste production is confined to feed lots—in 1966 more than ten million cattle were maintained in feedlots before slaughter, an increase of 66 per cent over the preceding eight years. This represents about one half of the total U.S. cattle population. Because of the development of feedlot techniques—much of it in the Midwest—the United States is confronted with a huge waste disposal problem, one considerably greater than the human sewage we are attempting to handle with grossly inadequate treatment. The result is predictable—massive, still unresolved, pollution problems exist, especially in the surface waters of the Midwest." (10).

Because there is no prospect of a substantial reduction in the tonnage of domestic sewage and agricultural fertilizer entering our water courses, and because the use of toxic chemicals as control agents on aquatic vegetation is expensive and may be harmful to fish, some form of "biological" control may have to be found. Currently, research is being conducted to determine the feasibility of using insects, snails, and disease organisms in controlling growth of aquatic weeds and plankton (28). It may be some time, however, before such methods may be employed extensively and with safety. As of 1966 a number of herbicides which were effective for controlling water weeds were found to be harmless to fish, birds, and mammals and had a low level of acute oral toxicity for man. Plankton algae can be controlled by copper sulfate at a concentration of 0.1 to 0.5 part per million by weight; a concentration of 1 part per million by weight will kill filamentous algae. Although trout are killed at these concentrations, there is no deleterious effect on bluegill or bass. Sodium arsenite is violently toxic to warm-blooded vertebrates, including man. Nevertheless, it has been extensively employed (under rigid state regulations) to eradicate submerged weeds. Its use is either discouraged or prohibited in many states. In restricted areas of high recreational value, filamentous algae and submerged weeds may be controlled by shading the lake bottom with a black plastic sheet for a three week period early in the growing season. In this way photosynthesis will be terminated and result in plant death (28).

Synthetic Organic Chemicals. Since World War II, the old-fashioned soaps have gradually been replaced in America by synthetic detergents available in a bewildering array of brand names. Soaps were readily decomposed by bacterial activity (that is, they were *biodegradable*) shortly after their discharge into municipal sewage lines or suburban cesspools. However, the most widely used synthetic detergents, the alkyl-benzene-sulfonate (ABS) type, up to very recently were non-biodegradable, had high foam stability, and remained intact sometimes for years.

Occasionally, detergents would clog water-treatment plants and percolate into groundwater aquifers, thus contaminating community water supplies. At Kearney, Nebraska, ABS detergents moved 4,000 feet in fourteen months before contaminating a private well. A recent survey by Dr. Walton, now at the University of Minnesota, revealed that 50 per cent of the private wells in the Minneapolis–St. Paul area were contaminated with ABS detergents. If the concentration of the ABS detergent is 0.75 part per million or more, it will actually foam when drawn

Figure 5–14 Sandy Run Creek in Montgomery County, Pennsylvania, forms foamy clouds because of its heavy detergent load. [U.S. Department of Agriculture]

from the tap. Fish growth has been impaired by less than 2 parts per million of ABS.

Under mounting pressure from an indignant public and scathing indictments from congressmen, the detergent industry ultimately switched from alkyl benzene sulfonate to linear alkylate sulfonate, which is more amenable to the decomposing action of bacteria. This $1.2 billion a year business, which in 1969 was producing five billion pounds of phosphate, is faced with yet another formula revision. In December 1969, Representative Henry Reuss, of Wisconsin, told the House Subcommittee on Conservation and Natural Resources that the detergent industry was the principle cause of accelerated eutrophication. The percentage of phosphate occurring in seventeen leading brands in 1969 ranged from 21.6 per cent (Fab) to 43.7 per cent (Axion). A bill introduced by Reuss would make the manufacture or import of phosphate containing detergents illegal after June 30, 1971. Although sewage treatment plants could be built that would remove phosphate from the waste effluent their construction would impose a formidable burden on the taxpayer. At the hearings of Reuss' Subcommittee, Carl Klein, Assistant Secretary of the Interior, announced that a $100,000 study of possible phosphate substitutes had been launched.

Inorganic Chemicals. Industry's water use is increasing daily. It increased from 77 billion gallons per day in 1950 to 140 billion gallons per day in 1960. Estimated use for 1980 is 363 billion gallons per day and for 2000 is 662 billion gallons per day. Water is industry's most important raw material. It is used as a solvent, as a cleansing agent, as a mineral extractant, as a coolant, as a waste-removal agent, and so on.

The chemical industry is an important pollution source. Rate of pollution has kept pace with this industry's growth, which is one of the most rapidly growing industries in America. By 1963 total sales had increased 500 per cent since 1939, and by 1975 they are expected to have increased 1,000 per cent. Sales of synthetic organic compounds have zoomed. Thus, plastics sales increased from 20 million pounds in 1928 to 6 billion pounds in 1961, synthetic rubber increased from zero in 1928 to over 2 billion pounds in 1961, nylon (and other noncellulose fibers) increased from zero in 1928 to 800 million pounds in 1961.

Industrial pollution of water is much in evidence. Dyes from a factory stain a Mississippi tributary green. A creamy discharge from a Michigan paper mill forms a curd which accumulates along the shore. Oily scums spread over the Rouge River near Dearborne, Michigan. The Merrimack River bubbles with nauseating gases. Water from a Minnesota iron mine stains a trout stream. Partly because of industrial pollution the Niagara Falls emanate foul odors. Parts of the Missouri run red with slaughterhouse blood. Because thousands of industrial plants are employing the Mississippi River as an "open sewer," conservationists have renamed it the "Colon of mid-America." There is certainly little resemblance between its clear, sparkling headwaters at Lake Itasca (Minnesota) and the foul-smelling broth of domestic and industrial waste which spews into the Gulf at New Orleans.

Industrial wastes are destructive in many ways. Some have a high BOD, some have foul odors, some impart an ugly appearance to a stream, some are toxic to aquatic life, some curtail photosynthesis, and of course all industrial wastes help render the stream water unfit for human use.

Organic wastes with a high BOD include the peelings and cores from fruit- and vegetable-processing plants; the excrement, blood, and discarded tissues from slaughterhouses; distillery residues; the hair and fleckings from tanneries; and the sulfite liquors of paper and pulp mills. As of 1966 seven paper and pulp mills discharged 210 million gallons of sulfite waste liquor into Puget Sound. In terms of BOD, this was equal to the domestic sewage from a population of 8.4 million people,

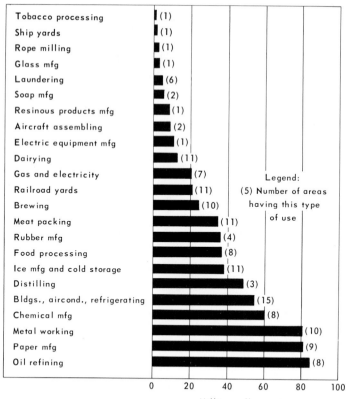

Figure 5–15 Industrial use of ground water in the United States. Based on a sample of twenty urban areas. (Water from municipal systems is not included.) [From *Conserving Natural Resources* by Allen and Leonard. Copyright © 1966 by McGraw-Hill, Inc. Used by permission of McGraw-Hill Book Company.]

which is remarkable when one considers that the entire state of Washington has a population of only 2.8 million (32).

Industrial pollutants may be severely toxic to aquatic vertebrates. Some wastes that are harmless alone may be lethal in combination with other contaminants. Heavy metal salts are an example. Thus, 8 parts per million of zinc or 2 parts per million of copper alone will not be injurious to game fish; however, 0.1 part of the two combined will eradicate the fish. Spectacular fish kills have been caused in this way (26).

The effective treatment of industrial wastes, in particular those from chemical industries, is exceedingly complex and in many cases methods of treatment are unknown. Thanks to the Water Pollution Control Act of 1965, which now provides more muscle than was ever before to bring industrial offenders in line, a number of plants are studying possible methods of

Figure 5–16 Biologists examining fish destroyed by cheese factory wastes discharged into stream near Loganville (Sauk County), Wisconsin. [Wisconsin Conservation Department]

either reducing the amount of discharged waste or at least rendering it less toxic before release. They are finally beginning to accept the principle elucidated by the federal Water Pollution Control Administration that pollution control is part of the expense involved in operating their plants. Some industries have effectively reduced pollution by converting their waste into commercially valuable by-products. Thus, the sugar beet industry has found a market for dessicated pulp and other former wastes. One company received a gross return on a single by-product that amounted to one tenth of the payment received for the beets. Tanneries have similarly discovered that hair and fleckings have value and that their reclamation reduces the putrescence of a stream.

In 1965 an American–Canadian International Joint Commission reported that pollution in the Rainy River at International Falls, Minnesota, was a menace to health. It further stated that this pollution was largely caused by the effluent from a large paper and pulp plant located on the river's shore. Twelve years of dealing with this plant by the Minnesota Water Pollution Control Commission produced no improvement in the situation. In 1966, however, a company spokesman stated that several studies were being launched to abate pollution. One of them involved a "dry-barking" process in which the bark from poplar and aspen trees is removed without water. Other projects included a mill that would reduce the sulfite liquors so characteristic of pulp mill wastes.

Recently, the Kimberly-Clark Corporation planned to construct a giant pulp and paper mill in northern California. However, a state statute required that the effluent discharged into the Sacramento River have no poisonous effect on newly hatched salmon and steelhead trout. These fish are an important wildlife resource which attract anglers to California from all over the United States. The problem was finally solved after many technical difficulties, with the construction of a $2 million waste-purifying plant capable of treating 12 million gallons of mill waste daily.

Wastes from food-processing plants pose a special problem. The effluent, containing suspended inedible plant fibers, is rich in organic content and has an extremely high BOD. One of the most successful techniques for removal of this type of waste has been developed at Seabrook, New Jersey, where wastes are sprinkled on the floor of a forest. Some areas of the forest have received up to 4,000 inches of water in four years, with no apparent reduction in infiltration capacity.

On the other hand, some of the waste-disposal schemes that industry has proposed are not well conceived. For example, to dispose of acid waters resulting from a steel-cleaning process one company planned to drill a well 4/5-mile deep into an 1,800-foot stratum of porous sandstone. This is similar to sweeping pollution under the rug. It may be a stopgap answer for our generation, but the final effective solution is simply being postponed for our descendants who may require the use of these contaminated aquifers in the next century.

Sediments. Every day the American people lose about $1 million as a result of silt-polluted water. Silt inflicts damage on our public water supplies, on our reservoirs, and on hydropower plants. It clogs up the irrigation canals of the Western farmer and impedes the progress of coal and ore barges along the Mississippi River. Beds of aquatic vegetation on Lake Erie that were once important breeding grounds for fish have literally been smothered by river silt as a result of poor land-use methods in the watershed. Suspended clay particles cloud the water to such a degree that submerged aquatic plants (*Chara, Potamogeton,* and *Elodea*) and floating phytoplankton die because of their inability to photosynthesize organic food. Cessation of photosynthesis in turn reduces the oxygen level in the water and results in extensive mortality of game fish and invertebrate food organisms.

Over 2,000 billion gallons of silt-polluted water must be filtered annually so that one can draw a glass of water that is clear rather than the color of diluted mud. Over 3,000 reservoirs in the United States provide water for roughly 25 per cent of our population. However, the reduced reservoir capacity caused by their rapid siltation is equivalent to the daily water requirements of 250,000 people.

Maximum daily concentrations of silt of up to 130,000 parts per million have been recorded in the turbulent waters of the Colorado River at Grand Canyon, and up to 270,000 parts per million have been recorded in certain muddy Iowan streams. This represents the work primarily of accelerated erosion. In some areas up to 9,000 tons of soil per square mile per year are washed downstream. According to the Soil Conservation Service, which recently made a survey of 157 watersheds, 70 per cent of the silt is attributable to sheet erosion, 10 per cent to gully erosion. Each year our streams wash 1 billion tons of silt into the Atlantic, Pacific, and Gulf of Mexico. If this silt load had a volume of about 1 cubic foot per 100 pounds, it would be more than adequate to cover the entire city of Washington D.C., with a blanket of mud. It is apparent that the best way to control siltation is to employ sound land-use practices—such as contour farming, cover and strip cropping, and gully reclamation—on the watersheds.

Radioactive Materials. Such elements as uranium and radium possess highly unstable atomic nuclei. This disintegration results in radiation emissions which may be highly injurious, and even lethal, to man. Such elements are said to be radioactive. Once the mushroom-shaped cloud has dissipated following a nuclear blast, radioactive dust may circle the globe, at altitudes of 10,000 feet or more, several times before being washed to the earth by rain. With each new nuclear weapon test, more of these materials are released into the environment. Eventually some of the radioactive material, such as strontium 90 (which can cause bone cancer), percolates down through the soil into our groundwater reservoirs or is carried by run-off waters into streams and rivers. In either case, public water supplies may be contaminated. Radioactive rain 200 times higher than the standard set as safe for drinking, fell in the San Francisco Bay region following nuclear bomb tests. The construction of a number of large nuclear reactors and the increasing use of radioactive materials in medical research represent other potential contamination sources. Radioactive cobalt, for example, has been widely used in cancer therapy in recent years.

Low-level radioactive waste is commonly removed by diluting it in water. An Atomic Energy Commission report in 1957 indicated that 9 billion gallons of liquid waste being discharged annually, primarily into large rivers, the sea, and the soil, have 2 million curies of radioactivity. How diluted must these wastes be? Let us suppose, for example, that a radioactive waste solution is discharged from a nuclear-reactor research center and that the 1 ppm concentration of strontium 90 gives off 0.002 curie per milliliter. This may seem quite dilute. However, this concentration of strontium 90 is *2.5 billion times* the maximal concentration permitted by the National Committee on Radiation Protection. Each teaspoon of this contaminated solution would have to be diluted with about 2.5 million gallons of water before its release into a river would be permitted. The crucial problem is that minute amounts of water-borne strontium may accumulate to extremely high concentration levels in living tissue. For example, the level of radiostrontium 90 in the skeleton of a perch living in water contaminated by seeps from an adjacent liquid atomic waste disposal area was 3,000 times greater than that of the lake water (25).

In 1956 the Oak Ridge National Laboratory reported that reduction of radioactivity to safe limits by water-treatment processes would not be effective unless initial radioactivity levels are somewhat lower than 1.0 microcurie per milliliter (11). Although biological agents such as bacteria can decompose organic wastes, the only agent capable of "destroying" radioactive material is time itself. Given enough time, all of the unstable nuclei of the element will decay. However, it would be theoretically possible for some radioactive materials to remain in underground aquifers for over 1,000 years before the potentially harmful emissions finally ceased.

Heat. Roughly 66 per cent of all water used in industry is for cooling purposes. One petrochemical plant uses 160,000 gallons of water per minute to cool its products. Most electrical power plants withdraw considerable quantities of water from nearby streams, circulate it through heated equipment, and return the warmed water to its stream source. Because electrical power production is expected to double in the next decade, heat pollution of our water courses will increase proportionately, unless remedial measures are taken. Power navigation and dam impoundments are additional sources of heat pollution.

Heat pollution is undesirable for several reasons. Warm water does not have the same oxygen-holding capacity as cold water. Therefore, such game fish as black bass, trout, and walleyes, which require a minimal oxygen concentration of about

4 ppm, would either have to emigrate from the polluted area or die in large numbers. Eventually, the polluted stretch of stream would be invaded by less desirable warm-water fish such as carp and bullheads. The decreased oxygen saturation level of warmed water would also impair the ability of aerobic bacteria to oxidize accumulated organic wastes discharged from domestic and industrial sewer lines. The net result could be an unsightly, foul-smelling river.

Various solutions to the heat problem have been proposed; some are already in practice. Several industries have installed cooling towers, where the heated effluent water can cool. Other plants have employed air rather than water as a coolant. Thus, an air-cooled carbon-black plant in Texas uses only 0.25 gallon water per pound of carbon black manufactured, whereas water-cooled plants use up to 14 gallons per pound. One state institute is investigating the possible role of artificially generated turbulence in providing rapid mixing of the heated water once it is discharged into the stream.

Although artificially heated water is generally considered deleterious to aquatic ecosystems, it may have certain limited redeeming features. Thus, in the Northern states, the warmed-up water downstream from power plants may serve as an ice-free wintering area for waterfowl, or may permit northward range extensions of fish. In 1969 the Water and Electric Board of Eugene, Oregon, announced the results of an experiment in which the warm water discharged from a paper mill was sprayed on fruit trees and prevented frost damage. Experimenters plan to distribute the heated water through subterranean pipes to determine whether the resultant soil temperature increase would permit an extended growing season and allow double harvests of certain crops.

ENFORCEMENT OF POLLUTION LAWS. In his State of the Union message to Congress in January, 1970, President Nixon proclaimed "Clean air, clean water, open spaces—these should once again be the birthright of every American. . . . If we act now, they can be. . . ." He vowed that pollution standards would be more strict and more stringently enforced. A direct result of the federal government's firmed-up posture against water polluters were the criminal charges filed by the U.S. Attorney General's office against seven industrial firms in New York City and New Jersey, for contaminating the tributary waters of New York harbor. Among the concerns named for discharging oil and waste into the harbor were: E. I duPont de Nemours and Co., Texaco, Inc., Central Railroad of New Jersey, and the General Aniline and Film Corporation. They were prosecuted under a law enacted in 1868. Upon conviction the violators are subject to a $2500 fine for each offense. Affirming the stricter attitude of the federal government toward pollution, U.S. Attorney Frederick B. Lacey proclaimed: "Our rivers can no longer be used as a dump for garbage and waste. Water pollution is a serious health hazard and a threat to our environment." In a further demonstration of the stringent new policy, Attorney General John N. Mitchell announced that thirteen Chicago area firms (including International Harvester, Pure Oil Company and Proctor and Gamble Co.) were being charged with water pollution. After an intensive investigation by the U.S. Corps of Army Engineers, they were being accused of discharging such wastes as soybean oil, solvent, cyanide, grease, gasoline, ground limestone, fuel oil, suspended solids, and kerosene into Chicago area rivers, some of which empty into Lake Michigan. The litigation is an expression of the Federal Water Pollution Control Administration's efforts to arrest pollution of Lake Michigan. According to U.S. Attorney Thomas A. Foran, the action is "only the first step" in a "new program to enforce vigorously the federal criminal law against pollution."

Despite mounting public opinion against the environmental degradation caused by pollutants from industrial sources, many concerns still drag their feet. This attitude was prevalent at a conference of businessmen and government officials convened by the Federal Water Pollution Control Administration in late 1969. A representative from International Harvester maintained: "Industry can spend nothing (on pollution abatement) it does not first earn in profits." In a similar vein a U.S. Steel official voiced his opposition "to treatment for treatment's sake."

In order to prod industry into more effective pollution control, Senator Proxmire of Wisconsin suggested, early in 1970, that legislation be enacted which would compel industry to pay "by the pound" for their discharged pollutants. Total annual revenue from this source would amount to $1.5 billion. In an address at Memphis State University March 4, 1970, economist Walter W. Heller, professor at the University of Minnesota and former adviser to President John F. Kennedy, contended that industry must pay for the use of water and air just as it pays for raw materials, machinery and labor. According to Heller: "This is good sound economics and sound social policy. . . . It has to be done by tough national regulations and penalties, regulations that treat all competitors alike. Giving special tax incentives and rewards to those who install pollution-abatement facilities is the wrong road to take. . . . It imposes the costs on the public . . . , instead of on the users of the product where they belong."

In any event effective water pollution control programs,

whether instituted by federal, state or municipal governments or by private industry, will be expensive. Experts are largely agreed that adequate control of water pollution on a nation-wide basis will cost a minimum of $30 billion during the five year period 1970–1975. Ultimately, of course, the consumer will finance any industrial projects by paying higher prices for goods, while the taxpayer will support governmental programs. Considering the resultant environmental gains, however, the costs per capita would be minimal. It has been estimated, for example, that a mere 25¢ per month increase in most consumers' electric bills would finance the annual $700 million dollar expense to curb industrial and power plant pollution.

New Sources of Water. It is apparent that as our population continues to increase, as more and more sewage must be diluted and transported, as Americans acquire more leisure time for recreational use of water resources, as more water-using gadgets—such as garbage grinders, automatic washers, and air conditioning units—proliferate, the per capita water use in this country will inevitably increase. The per capita average daily use of water, which was only 600 gallons in 1900, increased to 1,500 gallons in 1960 and is expected to be 2,300 gallons by 1980 and 2,700 gallons by 2000. The United States Public Health Service has estimated that the total municipal water use was only 21 billion gallons per day in 1960, but estimated that needs will rise to 29 billion gallons per day by 1980, and to 43 billion gallons per day by 2000.

Where will this additional water come from? Not from the skies. Total annual rainfall in the United States has remained fairly constant for many centuries, except for occasional wet and dry spells, and probably will remain so for many centuries to come. Possible methods for alleviating the impending water shortage problem include *reclamation of sewage water, development of groundwater sources, use of asphalt pavements to catch and retain rainfall in desert areas, the development of giant water wells formed by nuclear explosions, the desalination of seawater, eradication of phreatophytes, forest removal, rain making, and the transfer of surplus water supplies from Canada to water-deficient areas in the United States.*

RECLAMATION OF SEWAGE WATER. Although it might seem repugnant to utilize treated sewage water, sewage effluent is 99 per cent water, and when the 1 per cent of pollutant is removed, the final water product may be purer than the original substance (21). The Advanced Waste Treatment Research Program was recently launched by the U.S. Public Health Service to explore and develop effective methods of processing sewage waste water for direct and deliberate use. Its major objectives are twofold, first, to separate pollutants from the water and dispose of them harmlessly, and second, to recover the purified water product. Thus, in one process both the problem of sewage pollution and of water shortage would be solved. Several conversion processes have recently been investigated. The most promising processes in an operation treating 10 to 20 million gallons per day, together with the estimated cost of purifying 1,000 gallons, follow: foam separation process (2¢), coagulation-solids removal (4¢ to 8¢), adsorption (14¢ to 18¢), electrodialysis (40¢ to 50¢). Pilot plants have been established at Washington, D.C., Lebanon, Ohio, and three California sites (16). These laboratory-scale operations probably could become engineering realities by 1976.

Processed sewage water is already being utilized for a variety of functions. The Bethlehem Steel plant at Baltimore, Maryland, employs 150 million gallons of sewage effluent daily for steel-cooling purposes (16). Golf greens are sprinkled with it in San Francisco, Las Vegas, and Santa Fe, New Mexico. Treated sewage water is used to irrigate crops in the San Antonio area (21), and ornamental shrubs along highways in San Bernardino, California, are watered with it (2). For many years the Pennsylvania State University discharged sewage effluent directly into a stream. In 1962, however, it distributed the treated sewage water to nearby croplands and woods. Within three years multiple benefits were derived. Not only was crop production increased 300 per cent, but crops showed an increased protein content. Moreover, the annual lowering of the water table was reduced from 75 feet to just a few feet; tree growth was accelerated; and forest-dwelling wildlife benefited (21).

As a result of its location in a semiarid region, Los Angeles has been plagued with a perennial water shortage problem. The city daily discharges 600 million gallons of sewage water into the Pacific Ocean. Reclamation of this water would be considerably more economical than seawater desalination. The big problem besetting water engineers, however, has been the elimination of virus-contaminants which might be disseminated throughout the city and cause epidemics. Recently, Professor Albert Bush of the University of California at Los Angeles devised a method of virus removal which would permit the reclamation of 50 per cent (300 million gallons per day) of the Los Angeles sewage waters. The reclaimed water could theoretically be used against brush fires, for irrigation, or for swimming and boating.

Los Angeles daily discharges 17 million gallons of processed sewage water over "spreading beds" at the edge of town.

Eventually, this water seeps into aquifers which supply the town's wells. This water is of higher quality than water piped 200 miles from the Colorado River. Treated sewage water has also been employed in southern California to form a barrier to saltwater intrusion. By the early 1960's, water-table levels had been dropping steadily in the coastal region, in some areas to a point 25 feet below sea level (2). As a result, saltwater encroachment progressed at the rate of one mile per year. To check this intrusion, a freshwater wall was erected by injecting sewage water into a series of coastal wells (2).

DEVELOPMENT OF GROUNDWATER RESOURCES. Ground water forms 97 per cent of the world's freshwater supplies. In the forty-eight contiguous states there are 53,000 cubic miles of fresh water in the aquifers located in the upper half-mile of the earth's crust (28). This is 100 times the volume in the total run-off in all of our nation's water courses. Almost any 20-foot well in New England will deliver 2 to 5 gallons per minute; 50-foot wells near Miami frequently yield 1,000 to 1,500 gallons per minute.

However, most of the wells in the United States are at present too shallow and yield less than 400 gallons daily. In an effort to alleviate the impending water deficit, aquifers will be tapped to depths of 500 to 2,000 feet. Utilization of the increased supplies must be carefully planned from the long-range economic viewpoint. In some situations the proper decision may be to "mine" the water until the supply is exhausted; in other cases it may be better to draw the water on a sustained-yield basis (25).

The U.S. Geological Survey has embarked on at least fifty computer studies of surface and groundwater resources as part of a nation-wide project to determine America's future water needs. Intensive efforts are being made to locate and develop new aquifers. Location determinations can be made by charting the earth's varying electrical sensitivity, by seismographs (25), by sampling cores taken during well drilling (11), by the study of geological features at the surface, and by aerial photography to determine the nature of groundwater sources at or near the surface (24). Hydrologists are also employing radioactive tracer techniques to determine the pattern and rate of aquifer water flow. Such data will enable them to predict how withdrawal from one site will affect water tables at other points. These studies are already yielding results. Water-rich strata have been located in the southern California and Arizona region, which should markedly enhance the agricultural potential of this notoriously water-deficient area. Another was found at Salisbury, Maryland (29). A recent aquifer discovery under glacial

Passaic Lake in northern New Jersey is capable of yielding 30 million gallons daily (29). After a hurricane had disrupted conventional water supplies, a 2,000-foot well shaft drilled under brackish Lake Pontchartrain in Louisiana provided emergency water for washing and drinking (29).

USE OF ASPHALT COATINGS IN DESERT REGIONS. Many desert plants possess remarkably flattened root systems which lie just a few inches below the desert floor, which permits utilization of rainfall before it vaporizes. Recently, the U.S. Geological Survey developed a "human adaptation" that might be equally efficient in securing rainfall in desert regions. The technique involves coating the desert floor with water-impervious asphalt. Collected rainfall could be channeled into large water-holding pits from which it could be drawn off periodically either for irrigation or to raise the water table. On an experimental nine-acre asphalt-coated area near White Sands, New Mexico, 60 per cent of the rain water was salvaged, compared to 3 per cent on a control plot. The Survey estimates that up to 130,000 gallons of rainwater would be available from each asphalt-coated acre. Based on an annual precipitation of 15 inches, a six- by nine-mile area would collect over 8 billion gallons yearly, sufficient to meet all the water requirements of 100,000 people (29).

GIANT WATER WELLS FORMED BY NUCLEAR EXPLOSIONS. The nuclear bomb, cause of so much human suffering and mental anguish, may at last be utilized to promote man's welfare. Although research is still just beginning, Dr. A. M. Piper, research scientist with the Water Resources Division of the U.S. Geological Survey, Menlo Park, California, believes that subterranean nuclear bomb detonations might be used in the construction of huge water wells. For example, a 100-kiloton bomb (equivalent to 100,000 tons of TNT) exploded roughly one-third mile below the surface will form a rubble chimney about one-quarter mile high, with a diameter of 140 yards. Such a well would have a storage volume of 30 million gallons and groundwater flow into the well would be 500 times as great as for a drilled well of equivalent depth. Unfortunately, whether such wells can be employed in complete safety is not yet known.

DESALINATION OF SEAWATER. "Water, water everywhere, nor any drop to drink" wailed the sailor in the *Rhyme of the Ancient Mariner*. It is a curious paradox that 70 per cent of the earth's surface is covered by oceans, in some places up to 6 miles deep, yet a water shortage harasses man from New York to New Delhi. Deeply concerned with this dilemma, in 1952 Congress authorized a research and development program for the im-

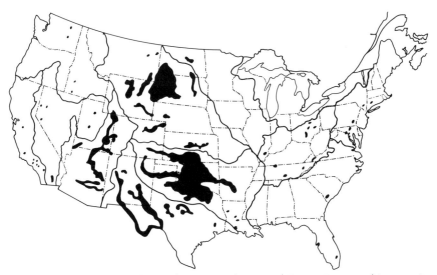

Figure 5–17 Regions of brackish water in the United States. Because this water is not potable, it must be desalinated. This map was based on a survey by the Office of Saline Water, U.S. Department of the Interior. [From *Conserving Natural Resources* by Allen and Leonard. Copyright © 1966 by McGraw-Hill, Inc. Used by permission of McGraw-Hill Book Company.]

provement of desalination processes. Various types of desalination plants have been constructed, including flash distillation, solar distillation, freezing, electrodialysis, and nuclear power. Coalinga, California, was the first city in the United States to provide a community supply of fresh water by desalination. Electrodialytic methods there reduce the mineral salt content of the well water from 2,200 to 300–350 parts per million and yield 28,000 gallons daily (2). Webster, South Dakota, which initiated operation of an electrodialytic plant in October, 1961, has a capacity of 250,000 gallons per day and reduces salinity from 1,800 to less than 275 parts per million (2). At Port Mansfield, Texas, where saltwater intrusion from the Gulf of Mexico contaminates artesian well sources, an $827,000 plant was dedicated in December, 1965, with a 250,000-gallon capacity (32). Although electrodialytic conversion is suitable primarily for smaller communities because of limited capacity, it could be profitably employed in at least 1,000 American communities where water sources are at least 1 per cent salt (31).

Flash Distillation. The federal government established a flash distillation plant in Freeport, Texas, which utilizes water from the Gulf Coast. The water is superheated to 250 degrees F., vaporizes, condenses in cool coils, and is conveyed to storage

161

tanks. The resultant product, which is produced at the rate of 1 million gallons per day, tastes so flat that salt must be added to enhance palatability. Some authorities predict that by 1986 huge flash distillation plants with capacities of 500 million gallons per day will be constructed in critically water-short urban areas.

The multistage flash distillation plant which was constructed at San Diego, California, in 1962 has received considerable publicity. This plant can convert 1 million gallons per day at a cost of 97¢ per 1,000 gallons. It provided San Diego with 1.33 per cent of its water supply (2). In 1963, when Castro threatened to choke off the water supply used by American marines at the Guantanamo Naval Base, the San Diego plant was dismantled and shipped to Cuba to ensure a continuing source of fresh water.

Solar Distillation. In addition to conducting its own research in solar distillation, the federal government is heavily subsidizing investigations at universities and institutes. The University of California, Franklin Institute (Philadelphia), Massachusetts Institute of Technology, New Mexico Highlands University, New York University, and the University of Wisconsin have all been involved in solar distillation research. The seawater conversion Solar Research Station set up at Daytona Beach, Florida, in 1958 pumps seawater from the mouth of the Halifax River. This water, which has a salinity of 35,000 parts per million, is channeled into a glass-roofed basin to a depth of 7 to 12 inches. The water absorbs solar energy, vaporizes, and condenses on the glass roof from which it is collected. This station also has two stills with plastic roofs. The total yield of the three stills is 500 gallons of fresh water daily. When there is adequate sunshine, roughly 1 pound of fresh water is secured per square foot of basin surface per day.

Nuclear-Fired Plants. In 1964 the federal government published a report in which it proposed the construction of mammoth nuclear-powered plants which would not only provide fresh water but would also yield electrical power. One of these plants would be capable of producing 620 million gallons per day, enough water to supply the needs of a major city. However, the water would cost 25¢ per 1,000 gallons even before delivery. Householders would have to pay perhaps 40¢ per 1,000 gallons for delivery to their homes. More recently a plant has been proposed for southern California which will produce 150 million gallons per day at a cost of 22¢ to 30¢ per 1,000 gallons, but will provide the Los Angeles region with 1.8 million kilowatts of electricity.

This program, however, has certain drawbacks. According to
Professor John C. Maxwell, Department of Geological Engineering, Princeton University, these plants would inevitably produce enormous quantities of heat, concentrated brine, and
radioactive wastes. If not properly dissipated, the warmed-up
ocean waters near the plant might trigger such a "bloom" of
marine plants that a thick green algal "soup" could some day
smother the California coast. Moreover, the radioactive waste,
which remains potentially injurious for up to 1,000 years,
would have to be contained in some manner which would remove its threat to human survival.

ERADICATION OF PHREATOPHYTES. Phreatophytes are undesirable plants that occur primarily in the arid Southwest.
They absorb and transpire exceptionally large volumes of
water, roughly 50 to 100 per cent more than agricultural
crops (25). Among the most important phreatophytes, which
cover about 16 million acres (25), are salt cedar, cottonwood,
willow, greasewood, rabbitbrush, cattail, and tule. The salt
cedar, whose roots extend down to the water table, inflicts a
20-trillion-gallon water loss in a 900,000 square mile area of
western United States (18). Hydrologists of the U.S. Geological
Service determine the volume of water loss with delicate mois-
ture-sensitive infrared film that is exposed while flying at low
altitudes over a given salt cedar stand (16). The data are then
radioed back to a computer on the ground (16).

Herbicides have superseded mechanical control methods because of superior effectiveness and lower cost ($25 to $43 per
mile) (25). One to 6 million acre-feet of water can be saved
annually, according to the Senate Select Committee on National
Water Resources, if the phreatophytes are properly controlled. This salvaged water could be pumped into irrigation
systems (2).

FOREST REMOVAL. It has been estimated that the daily
domestic requirements of 100,000 people can be satisfied with
12 million gallons of water. Were this water spread over a 10-
square-mile watershed, it would form a layer only 0.1 inch deep.
However, in a single day, the root systems of a growing stand
of timber (on that same 10-square-mile watershed) could absorb
twice this amount of water. It is apparent, therefore, that as
water demands increase, responsible officials must eventually
determine whether a given watershed acreage is more valuable
for water collection and storage than for timber, wildlife habitat,
scenic beauty, or some other function. It could well be that timber, with its high water requirements, should be replaced with
grass or some other vegetation with lesser water needs. Water-

shed research in humid West Virginia and North Carolina has shown that clear cutting has produced maximal annual increments of 12 to 16 inches, or 326,000 to 434,000 gallons per acre. Increases were smaller in partial cuttings. In North Carolina the clear cutting of oak stands growing in deep soil resulted the following year in sufficient increment per square mile to supply the needs of 6,800 people (13).

However, such techniques will not be invariably successful. It depends upon the individual climate, topography, forest, and soil. For example, the thinning of lodgepole pine stands in the Rockies of Colorado did not substantially increase over-all yield (13).

RAIN MAKING. Rain making is a novel approach to increasing man's water supplies. One technique involves seeding clouds with crystals of dry ice and silver iodide, with the hope that these crystals will serve as condensation nuclei around which moisture droplets will collect until a drop of rain is formed (25). In 1957 a presidential Advisory Committee on Weather Control concluded that although seeding had no clearly defined influence in increasing precipitation in nonmountainous areas, seeding of winter storm clouds in the mountainous Western states resulted in a 10 to 15 per cent increase in rainfall. However, because of the high cost of rain-making ventures, the employment of this technique is perhaps ill advised except under emergency conditions of water shortage. One drawback is the lack of control over the volume and distribution of induced precipitation. For example, a late July rainfall might benefit the corn farmer but might be damaging to cut alfalfa awaiting the bailer (11). Increased rainfall may improve forage for cattle, but may be deleterious to fruit orchards. According to the U.S. Geological Survey, rain making probably could be used to greatest advantage in the West, where increased mountain snowfall can be used to boost water supplies for valley ranches during the ensuing arid summer. The potential of cloud-seeding for increasing water supplies is under continuing study at the National Center for Atmospheric Research, which was established at Denver, Colorado, in 1961 (2).

TRANSFER OF SURPLUS WATER. Several Southwestern states, such as Nevada, Utah, New Mexico, and Arizona, have an average annual rainfall of about 10 inches, but otherwise have relatively good agricultural potential. On the other hand, British Columbia and the Yukon Territory in western Canada receive an abundance of pure, clear water from such great rivers as the Peace, Fraser, Yukon, and Athabaska, but western Canada has rugged terrain, sterile soil, and an abbreviated growing season. Much of this water, which largely originated in melting snow fields and glaciers, is currently flowing unused into the Pacific and Arctic Oceans. In order to resolve this dilemma, the late Donald M. Baker, former water-planning engineer for Los Angeles County (32), with the support of a private engineering firm, proposed a boldly imaginative plan for channeling the superabundant Canadian water to the water-deficient regions of the United States and Mexico. The 500-mile-long Rocky Mountain Trench, extending from northern British Columbia to Montana, would be employed as a gigantic collecting reservoir. This water would be pumped 2,500 feet upward over mountain barriers and would eventually be distributed by a complex series of pumps, canals, siphons, and tunnels. If this project materializes, the juice from California grapefruits or Arizona sugar beets may well have originated in snowflakes drifting down a Yukon mountainside 2,500 miles away.

It is estimated that the NAWAPA project would require thirty years to complete and would cost about $100 billion. It would supply abundant water to seven Canadian provinces, thirty-three of the United States, and three states in northern Mexico (32). Total irrigation water provided would be 142 million acre feet—25 million for Canada, 97 million for the United States, and 20 million for Mexico. (Mexico would receive eight times as much water from NAWAPA as Egypt will eventually derive from her giant Aswan Dam project.) The new water supplies would bring an additional 41 million arid acres under crop production at a cost of under 1¢ per 1,000 gallons. In addition, 40 million acre-feet of water would be channeled annually into the Great Lakes to stabilize their water level and alleviate the serious pollution problems caused by shore-based industries. Furthermore, almost 37 million acre-feet would be available for industrial uses at a cost of only 3¢ per 1,000 gallons. Electrical power generated at Niagara Falls could be increased by 50 per cent. Thirty-eight million additional kilowatts of power would be available to northern United States and Alaska, 30 million to Canada, and 2 million to Mexico. The increased annual national income from agriculture, livestock, mining, and manufacturing industries would be $30 billion for both the United States and Mexico, and $9 billion for Canada (32).

The NAWAPA project is still in the hypothetical stage. It has many diplomatic, economic, legal, engineering, and social problems. One problem would be the translocation of nearly 60,000 people now residing in future reservoir sites. A more difficult problem might be the reluctance of Canada to participate. Because the water shortage is primarily an American concern, because the Great Lakes pollution originates mostly in

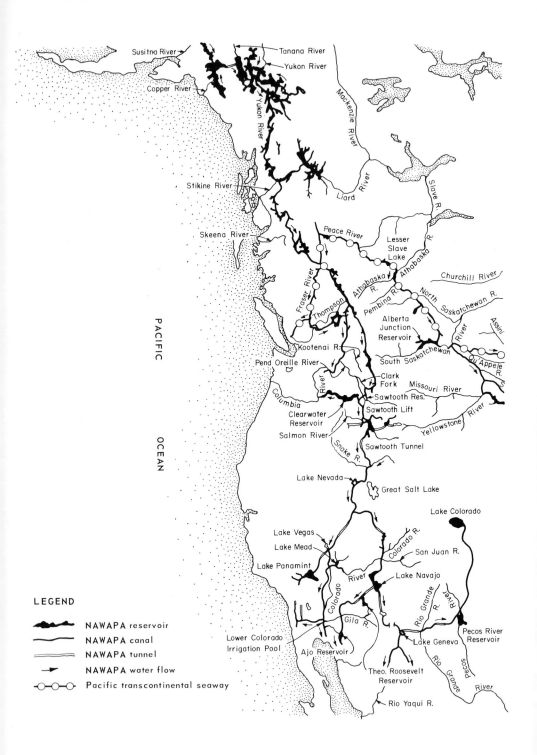

LEGEND

NAWAPA reservoir
NAWAPA canal
NAWAPA tunnel
NAWAPA water flow
Pacific transcontinental seaway

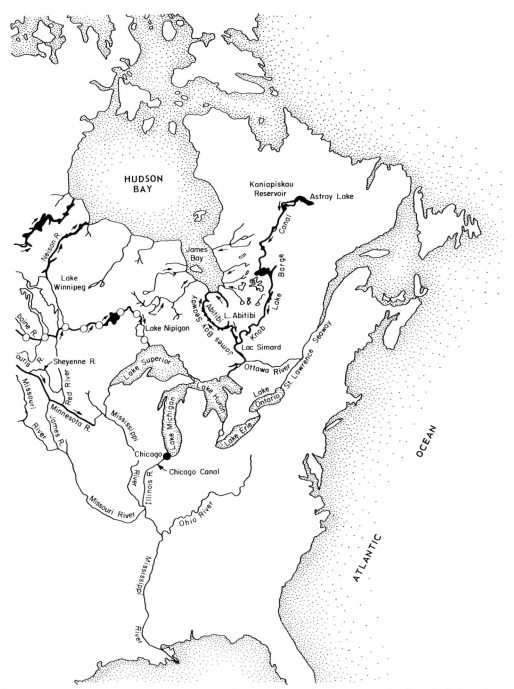

Figure 5–18 Water sources, reservoirs, canals, tunnels, and flow pattern in the North American Water and Power Alliance Plan. [Adapted from Guy-Harold Smith, *Conservation of Natural Resources* (New York: John Wiley & Sons, Inc., 1965).]

America, and because most of the water appropriated in the NAWAPA project would belong to Canada, her attitude can be appreciated. Some Canadians view the NAWAPA project with skepticism because they feel Canada's future development may ultimately depend on the use of this water. Despite the apparent difficulties attending its execution, NAWAPA represents the type of imaginative planning that is essential if we are to ensure abundant high-quality water supplies for North Americans in the twenty-first century.

Irrigation

New England and other normally humid regions of the United States have experienced intermittent drought, but an extensive area of the desert biome and the more arid portion of the grassland biome are characterized by more or less permanent drought. Here, through long eons of interaction with the environment, animal residents have evolved moisture-securing and moisture-conserving adaptations which have promoted their survival. Modern man, however, a relative new-comer to this austere region, has not had to depend on long evolutionary processes to "adapt" to the environment. Instead, with the aid of his mental powers, he has "shaped" the environment to fit his own design. The most significant and dramatic example of man's habitat-shaping talents in this region is modern irrigation.

History of Irrigation. Perhaps the first use of transported water in arid land farming in what is now the United States was made in 700 A.D. by Indians living in the valleys of the Salt and Gila rivers of Arizona (4). Employing crude digging tools, they were able to construct 125 miles of canals sufficient to irrigate 140,000 acres of food plots (4). By 1400 A.D., these early agriculturists, known as the Hohokam ("Those who have gone"), mysteriously disappeared along with their irrigation economy (4). In the seventeenth century, under the influence of Spanish priests, irrigation systems were established in California and Texas adjacent to Catholic missions. In 1847 the Mormons of Utah, faced with possible starvation during the ensuing winter, channeled water from City Creek to their parched potato and grain fields.

Irrigation has emancipated thousands of arid climate farmers from an extremely precarious economic existence. Irrigation provides them with production insurance. Instead of putting everything into one crop, which might be totally destroyed by storms, drought or disease, irrigation permits several crops a

Figure 5–19 Central Valley, California. Aerial view of the Contra Costa irrigation canal. Mount Diablo is on the horizon.

year. Moreover, it allows a more diversified agriculture. The irrigation farmer raises everything from apples, sugar, and beef in Washington and Oregon to grapefruit, dates, and celery in California. The Central Valley of California, receiving irrigation water from the reservoir behind Shasta Dam in northern California, produces 80 per cent of the country's grapes, 33 per cent of its fruit, and 25 per cent of its vegetables. It produces 220 different crops (18). In 1963 American farmers were irrigating 33 million of the country's 75 million acres amenable to profitable irrigation. Population projections indicate that by the year 2000 America should be irrigating 55 million acres, or 73.3 per cent, of the irrigable acreage, to satisfy our nation's food requirements (32).

Irrigated Area. Most of the land west of the 97th meridian (which extends from North Dakota through eastern Texas) receives less than 20 inches of rainfall annually. Because corn requires 29 inches, cotton 31 inches, oranges 32 inches, rice 36 inches, and alfalfa up to 52 inches of rainfall per year, it is obvious that successful production of these crops would be impossible without irrigation. About 6 per cent of our nation's cropland is irrigated (2). Although the seventeen Western states have only one fifth of the country's population, they use 52 per cent of the water consumed in the United States, 90 per cent of which is used for irrigation (10). In 1963, when 90 per cent of the irrigated acres in the United States was located in the seventeen Western states and Hawaii, the top five irrigated crops were pasture, alfalfa, cotton, sorghum, and corn. The "Big Four" in irrigation, as of 1960, were California (25 per cent of the total acreage), Texas (12 per cent), Colorado (10 per cent), and Idaho (10 per cent). During the period between 1950 and 1965, cotton production from irrigated lands in California, Arizona, and New Mexico nearly doubled from 1.639 million to nearly 3 million bales annually (32). Although irrigation is less extensive east of the Mississippi, where groundwater provides 62 per cent of the irrigation requirements, many a breakfast in Chicago or Baltimore has depended on irrigation-grown oranges from Florida or rice from Arkansas. Supplemental irrigation is employed for North Carolina tobacco and for dairy pasture and truck crops between Washington, D.C., and Boston (25). Irrigation in the thirty-one Eastern states increased more than 600 per cent from 0.4 million acres in 1939 to 2.6 million acres in 1963.

Dams and Irrigation. When Theodore Roosevelt signed the Reclamation Act of 1902, the federal government, through the Bureau of Reclamation, assumed responsibility for conserving, developing, distributing, and most effectively utilizing the limited water resources of the arid West. This objective has been implemented in part by the imaginative construction of a series of dams and reservoirs. (During the first decade of the Bureau's existence, over 97 per cent of its program was irrigation-oriented (29).) The first dam constructed, appropriately named the Roosevelt Dam, was constructed on the Salt River near Globe, Arizona, in 1911. The largest dam constructed is the Hoover Dam, on the Colorado River. The Colorado drains almost one thirteenth of the United States. In order to control the river, prevent flooding, and provide irrigation water and cheap electrical power for thousands of farmers in the arid Southwest, the Bureau constructed this 6.5-million-ton concrete dam.

Figure 5–20 Scenic view of Flaming Gorge Dam on the Colorado River from a point along transmission line road about 1 mile from dam. [Bureau of Reclamation, U.S. Department of the Interior]

Standing as high (726 feet) as a sixty-story skyscraper, the Hoover Dam contains enough concrete to form a two-lane highway from Chicago to San Francisco. The impounded water forms Lake Mead, the largest man-made lake in the world. One hundred nineteen miles long, it has an area of 246 square miles. Its storage capacity of nearly 30 million acre-feet would be adequate to meet all the water requirements of New York City's 7 million residents for twenty years.

Although, as a result of increasing urbanization, Bureau of Reclamation projects have recently become geared to domestic and industrial functions, about one third of all impounded water is still used in irrigation. In fiscal 1966, the Bureau achieved the greatest construction record in its sixty-four-year history, completing eleven dams with an aggregate storage capacity of 2.8 million acre-feet of water (29). In addition, the Bureau completed 733 miles of canals, pipelines, and laterals for effective distribution of impounded water to farmlands, towns, and industries located many miles from reservoir sites (29). At the end of 1966, seventeen additional dams were being constructed with a combined impoundment capacity of 5 million acre-feet, and 248 Reclamation dams had been completed that were capable of impounding 129.5 million acre-feet of water, sufficient to cover New York State to a depth of 4 feet (29).

In 1966 the Bureau laid the first sixty-two miles of the giant Westlands Water District System in California which eventually will provide irrigation water for 500,000 acres of cropland. Under a $157 million contract with the District, the cost of construction will gradually be repaid by water-using irrigationists. The water will be transported to the District from northern California by facilities of the Bureau's Central Valley Project.

Irrigation Methods. Irrigation water is either pumped or delivered by gravity flow through the main irrigation pipe line or irrigation canal to "laterals," which transport the water to individual farms. The laterals frequently follow fence lines and field borders. Up to 750,000 gallons of water may be needed to irrigate a single acre. Irrigation is an extremely complex and exacting operation which demands a high degree of planning, field preparation, and technical skill. Although irrigation is costly, the long growing seasons which permit several crops a year and the high market value of the cash crops make it economically feasible. Major methods of irrigation are *sheet* irrigation, *furrow* irrigation, *sprinkler* irrigation, and *subirrigation*.

SHEET IRRIGATION. The sheet method of irrigation, frequently used for hay, grain, and pasture crops, is employed on

Figure 5–21 Delta, Colorado. Irrigating a field planted to sugar beets with siphon tubes drawing water from a concrete head ditch. [Bureau of Reclamation, U.S. Department of Interior]

land which has a slight grade. The topsoil must be carefully prepared beforehand. The water, which is drawn from laterals at the upper end of the slope, gradually flows downgrade as a "sheet." Soil erosion and leaching of nutrient salts are problems associated with this method.

FURROW IRRIGATION. In the furrow method, water may be withdrawn from the laterals by means of siphon tubes or gates in the ditch bank and transported directly into the furrows between crop rows. It is used primarily for row crops such as corn, cabbage, and sugar beets and for orchards and vineyards. Where irrigation is common, it may be employed on alfalfa. Erosion problems can be alleviated by contouring the furrows.

SPRINKLER IRRIGATION. Sprinkler irrigation, extensively used in the East, involves costly equipment and is restricted primarily to crops of high cash value. Evaporation losses may be considerable. Considerable water pressure is necessary. Sprinklers may be either stationary or rotary. Up to 1 inch of water may be applied hourly. The "big gun," one of the more recently developed rotary types, is powered by propane gas and propels a stream of water half the length of a football field. The advantages of this method are multiple, including

Figure 5–22   San Joaquin Valley, California. Aerial view of sprinklers in Belridge Irrigation District. [California Department of Water Resources]

effective regulation of water flow, erosion control, and reduction of the weed problem (25).

SUBIRRIGATION.   With subirrigation, water is introduced below the ground surface. Requisite conditions include level land; a porous, water-pervious soil stratum just below the surface to promote vertical and horizontal water flow; an impervious layer below the pervious one, to retard soil loss by seepage; and a relatively high water table. Because of these prerequisite conditions, subirrigation can be used effectively in only a few regions, such as the Everglades of Florida and parts of California's Central Valley (25).

Irrigation Problems

WATER LOSS DURING TRANSIT.   Some irrigated fields receive their water from reservoirs or streams located hundreds of miles away. The fruit-raising Central Valley of California, for example, gets its water from the Colorado River, 300 miles to the east. During transit considerable amounts of water are lost. According to the United States Department of Agriculture, only 1 of every 4 gallons drawn for irrigation is actually absorbed by crop root systems. The remaining 3 gallons are lost to evaporation, to water-absorbing weeds, or to ground seepage. Seepage losses through unlined, porous dirt canals may amount to 10 per cent per mile, so that reduction to a negligible volume would occur after only ten miles of transit. Such loss can be minimized by lining canals with water-impervious materials, such as wax coatings or plastic and butyl-rubber membranes. Asphalt and "shotcrete" (cement mortar applied under air pressure) have also proved valuable in reducing seepage.

DEPLETION OF GROUND WATER. Sources of irrigation water vary greatly among the seventeen Western states. Although the Mountain states (Montana, Wyoming, Colorado, and Idaho) receive over 80 per cent of their irrigation water from surface sources (reservoirs, farm ponds, and rivers), many areas in the High Plains secure over 75 per cent of their water supplies from ground sources. In west Texas, much irrigation water is derived from wells. In 1946 there were only 2,000 wells in the entire South Plains region of west Texas (32). By 1966 the number had

Figure 5–23 Construction of irrigation canal. Note plastic lining to prevent water loss during transit. Earth has been placed on the plastic for temporary protection against wind ballooning. [Soil Conservation Service, U.S. Department of Agriculture]

increased fifteenfold, to 30,000. West Texas grows 25 per cent of our nation's cotton with this well water (32).

In one part of Arizona, overdraft of ground water lowered the water table by 400 feet, resulting in the loss of 320,000 acres of cropland because of the prohibitive cost of irrigation. Irrigation-induced lowering of water tables has also occurred in California's San Joaquin Valley, where the groundwater overdraft in the Arvin-Edison Water Storage District is nearly 65 million gallons (200,000 acre-feet) annually (29). In coastal areas such overdraft may result in salt water intrusion.

CONSUMPTIVE USE OF WATER. Some conservationists criticize irrigation in the semiarid West as a profligate use of water. From their viewpoint, irrigation-based crop production is not needed to satisfy America's food requirements. Farmers annually draw four times as much water for irrigation as is used by municipalities. Irrigationists use 60 per cent as much water as our nation's industries. Moreover, although almost 97 per cent of the water drawn for municipal or industrial use may largely be used again (in some cases only after proper treat-

Figure 5–24 A 4,000 gallon per minute irrigation well near Carlton, Colorado. The concrete-lined ditch is designed to carry 20 cubic feet per second. [U.S. Department of Agriculture]

ment), much irrigation water is *consumed* and cannot be reused. Over 60 per cent of all irrigation water is lost by transpiration, evaporation, and seepage during transit. In the opinion of these conservationists, a higher standard of living might be possible for more people if water currently consumed by irrigation were diverted to industrial and municipal use.

The Imperial Valley Story. The story of the Imperial Valley is one of America's greatest success stories in irrigation. The Imperial Valley, which is 110 miles long and 50 miles wide, lies in the Colorado Desert in southern California, just east of Los Angeles, with San Diego in its southwest corner. In prehistoric times this area was submerged by salt water from the Gulf of California. Gradually, however, it was built up with millions of tons of fertile soil released by overflow of the Colorado River during its flow to the sea. At the turn of the century this valley was a hot desert wasteland. Annual rainfall, which is almost immediately vaporized because of hot, drying winds, is a paltry 1.5 to 3 inches, hardly enough to settle the dust. The Imperial Valley, however, is wasteland no more. Where once there were lizards and cacti, there now flourish fruit and vegetable farms from which lettuce, tomatoes, watermelons, sugar beets, onions, asparagus, oranges, and dates are shipped to all parts of the United States. This has been made possible by the 1940 completion of the 200-foot-wide All-American Canal, which conveys water from the Colorado River eighty miles away to a half-million acres of fertile Valley soil. The potential of this area for crop production had always been there. There was an abundance of sunshine and a long growing season (up to ten cuttings of alfalfa have been made). The limiting factor was water, and that was overcome with imagination, resourcefulness, and engineering skill.

BIBLIOGRAPHY

1. Ackerman, Edward A., and George O. G. Lof. *Technology in American Water Development.* Baltimore: The Johns Hopkins Press, 1959.
2. Allen, Shirley W., and Justin W. Leonard. *Conserving Natural Resources.* New York: McGraw-Hill Book Co., 1966, 432 pp.
3. Atomic Energy Commission, Division Reactor Development. "Status Report on Handling and Disposal of Radioactive Wastes in the AEC Program," *U.S. AEC Report,* **742** (1957), 1–41.
4. Barnes, Kenneth K. "Water Makes the Desert Bloom," *Outdoors USA: The Yearbook of Agriculture.* Washington, D.C.: U.S. Department of Agriculture, 1967, 125–130 pp.
5. Bradley, C. "Human Water Needs and Water Use in America," *Science,* **138** (1962), 489.
6. Cheyney, E. G., and T. Schantz-Hansen. *This Is Our Land.* St. Paul: Webb Publishing Co., 1950.
7. Clarke, George L. *Elements of Ecology.* New York: John Wiley & Sons, Inc., 1954, 534 pp.

8. Clawson, Marion, R. Burnell Held, and Charles H. Stoddard. *Land for the Future.* Baltimore: The Johns Hopkins Press, 1960, 570 pp.
9. Colman, E. A. *Vegetation and Watershed Management.* New York: The Ronald Press Co., 1953, 412 pp.
10. Commoner, Barry. "Salvation: It's Possible." *The Progressive,* April, 1970, 12–18.
11. Cunningham, Floyd F. *1001 Questions Answered About Water Resources.* New York: Dodd, Mead, 1967, 258 pp.
12. Gerard, Robert D. "Potential Freshwater Reservoir in the New York Area," *Science* (Aug. 19, 1966), 870–871.
13. Jones, E. Bruce, Richard Lee, and John C. Frey. "Land Management for City Water," *Outdoors USA: The Yearbook of Agriculture.* Washington, D.C.: U.S. Department of Agriculture, 1967.
14. Kendeigh, S. Charles. *Animal Ecology.* Englewood Cliffs, N.J.: Prentice-Hall, Inc., 1961, 468 pp.
15. Leopold, Luna B. *The Flood Control Controversy.* New York: The Ronald Press Co., 1954, 278 pp.
16. _____ *Water.* New York: Time, Inc., 1966, 200 pp.
17. _____ and Walter B. Langbein. *A Primer on Water.* Washington, D.C.: U.S. Department of the Interior, 1960.
18. Lull, Howard W. "How Our Cities Meet Their Water Needs," *Outdoors USA: The Yearbook of Agriculture.* Washington, D.C.: U.S. Department of Agriculture, 1967, 104–109 pp.
19. Lunin, Jesse. "The Constant Fight Against Pollution," *Outdoors USA: The Yearbook of Agriculture.* Washington, D.C.: U.S. Department of Agriculture, 1967, 149–153 pp.
20. McCrone, Alistair W. "Water Proposals for New York," *Science* (Oct. 19, 1966), 215.
21. Mattison, C. W., and Joseph Alvarez. *Man and His Resources in Today's World.* Mankato, Minn.: Creative Educational Society, 1967, 144 pp.
22. Maxwell, John C. "Prospects for Future Water Supply in the United States," *Jour. Amer. Water Works Assoc.,* **57,** 5 (1965).
23. Odum, Eugene P. *Fundamentals of Ecology.* Philadelphia: W. B. Saunders Co., 1959, 546 pp.
24. Peterson, Elmer T. "Insoak Is the Answer," *Land,* **11** (1952), 83–88.
25. Smith, Guy-Harold (ed.). *Conservation of Natural Resources.* New York: John Wiley & Sons, Inc., 1965.
26. Smith, Robert L. *Ecology and Field Biology.* New York: Harper & Row, Publishers, 1966, 686 pp.
27. Soil Conservation Service. *Water Facts.* Washington, D.C.: U.S. Department of Agriculture, 1964.
28. Timmons, F. Leonard. "The Water Weed Nuisance," *Outdoors USA: The Yearbook of Agriculture.* Washington, D.C.: U.S. Department of Agriculture, 1967.
29. U.S. Department of the Interior. *The Third Wave.* Washington, D.C.: U.S. Department of the Interior, 1967.
30. White, Gilbert F. "Flood Plain Safeguards: A Community Concern," *Outdoors USA: The Yearbook of Agriculture.* Washington, D.C.: U.S. Department of Agriculture, 1967, 133–136 pp.
31. Wilson, Ralph C. "Small Watersheds Make A Big Splash," *Outdoors USA: The Yearbook of Agriculture.* Washington, D.C.: U.S. Department of Agriculture, 1967, 110–112 pp.
32. Wright, James Claud. *The Coming Water Famine.* New York: Coward-McCann, 1966, 255 pp.

Rangelands

6

The grasses, which evolved about 200 million years ago, cover 20 per cent of the earth's surface. Grasses are adapted to survive in a great variety of climatic regimes from sea level to mountain top. In the United States alone, grasses, in the form of rangeland, pasture, or meadow, cloak roughly about 1 billion acres. The grass family, called the *Gramineae,* from the Latin word for grass *gramina,* embraces over 6,000 species, over 1,400 of which occur in the continental United States (20). Although grasses may comprise only a small percentage of the plant species in a particular area, the individual grass plants are usually extremely numerous, forming up to 90 per cent of natural prairie vegetation. They range in size from tiny plants less than 1 inch in length to the giant bamboos, over 100 feet tall, whose trunks are used as timber (6).

Importance of Rangelands to Man

Thousands of years before the Christian era, man had learned to cultivate species of the grass family as a food source. The Indo-Chinese culture was based on rice, the Mediterranean culture on wheat, and the culture of early America on maize, or corn.

179

The leaves of grasses, whether big bluestem or blue grama, convert solar energy to a form usable by animals—including jack rabbits, cattle, and men. Carnivorous man secures this energy in the form of veal, beef, mutton, or lamb. On the other hand, grazing herbivores—such as cattle, sheep, and goats—obtain this energy directly by chewing and digesting the grasses. In a very real sense, therefore, the Biblical statement, "All flesh is grass," is true.

The amount of energy trapped by grass plants is considerable. Only 700 acres of grassland (and there are 1 billion acres in the United States) secure from the sunlight during a single day as much energy as is released by a small atomic bomb or 20,000 tons of TNT. One pound of grass has enough energy to keep you walking for one and one-half hours, washing dishes for three hours, or sawing wood for one-half hour.

In 1968 the 109 million beef cattle on farms and ranches in the United States (at $149 per head) were worth $12.6 billion, and the 18.1 million grazing sheep (valued at $19.20 per head) represented a total resource worth $365 million. The cattle and sheep industry in the United States produces about $12 billion worth of meat and other products yearly—roughly 7 per cent of our nation's gross national product. This industry, which dwarfs even the steel and automobile industries, produces over 18 billion pounds of dressed beef yearly (90 pounds for every man, woman, and child in the United States), in addition to 1 billion pounds of veal and 715 million pounds of lamb and mutton.

In 1964 the United States exported over 11 million cattle hides, 3 million sheepskins, and 2 million calf skins. In that same year, over 200 million pounds of shorn wool valued at over $100 million was clipped from 26.4 million lambs and sheep. These were products dependent on grass.

Grass Plant Biology

In order to appreciate certain aspects of rangeland management, we should first briefly examine the anatomy and physiology of a generalized grass plant.

Roots. Unlike the simple *taproot* system of many rangeland weeds consisting of a single main root, the *fibrous root* system of a grass plant has a number of major roots, each of which may have many primary, secondary, and tertiary branches (Fig. 6–1). A plant with a taproot can be easily uprooted with a rather negligible amount of earth clinging to it. Conversely, a grass plant is exceedingly difficult to uproot, and it comes free with a big

Figure 6–1 New Mexico. Comparison of root systems of blue grama (*left*) and a shrub. The dense root system of grama is much more effective in binding soil and preventing erosion. [Soil Conservation Service, U.S. Department of Agriculture]

clump of earth adhering to it. Dr. Dittmer of the University of New Mexico has estimated that the fibrous root system of a 21-inch rye plant may bear 14 million branches, over 300 miles long. He further estimated that 1 cubic inch of soil taken from under a Kentucky blue grass plant may contain up to 2,000 root branches. It is no wonder that grass is the cover par excellence in controlling soil erosion. (Fig. 6–1)

Stems.   The aerial stems of most grasses are hollow and many-jointed. Because they bear a growth zone at the base of each joint, when conditions of moisture and temperature are optimal they may grow rapidly. In addition to aerial stems, many grasses possess horizontal stems, known as *runners* or *stolons* if occurring above ground or as *rhizomes* if underground. When actively growing, the plant sends out these horizontal stems. A bud forms at the tip of each horizontal stem and develops into a new grass plant. This type of reproduction is called *vegetative.* A rhizome may develop into a new plant, even though the parent plant has succumbed to drought or cold or has been consumed by some rangeland herbivore, such as steer or rodent. Although stolons and rhizomes grow only 1 to 2 feet a year, the youngest plant may be located a considerable distance from the original parent. The rhizome, therefore, is a remarkable structure which performs not only the function of plant dispersal and reproduction but permits survival under adverse climatic and biotic environment conditions. Buffalo grass, one of the dominant species of the western short-grass prairie, is frequently able to persist only because of its ability to form rhizomes.

Leaves. The grass leaves that arise at the stem joint are spear-shaped and are arranged in two rows along the stem, each leaf being on the opposite side of the leaf below or above. A unique feature of the leaf is its *basal* rather than *apical* growth zone. Most plants, such as alfalfa, clover, sage, or mesquite, have leaves with apical (toward the leaf tip) growth zones. Were a jack rabbit or steer to clip off such a leaf tip, leaf growth would be terminated, thereby reducing the vigor or the plant, which was dependent on that leaf to manufacture a certain quota of food. But when a leaf tip of rangeland grass is clipped, as long as the basal zone remains intact, the leaf can grow in a short time to its original length. In fact, the grass leaf can be grazed again and again without adverse affects, thus providing a continuous food reservoir for the grazing animal. Range ecologists generally regard the upper 50 per cent of the grass shoot (stem and leaves) as representing a "surplus" which can be safely eaten by livestock or wild herbivores (deer, antelope, elk, and so on) without damaging the plant. The lower 50 per cent, known as the *metabolic reserve,* is required by the plant for survival, for this minimum of photosynthetic equipment is needed to manufacture foods required by the roots. When a range is badly overgrazed, the herbivores "bite" into the metabolic reserve, frequently clipping the grass to the bare ground, causing starvation and death of the root system and rendering that particular locus of rangeland vulnerable to erosion.

Flowers. Grasses are included among the flowering plants. Grass flowers are extremely minute (⅛ to ¼ inch long) and rather nondescript (20). Bright colors usually are associated with pollination by insects, which are attracted by color. Because grass flowers are wind-pollinated, bright colors are not essential. Each flower is enclosed by a dry, papery scale (the *chaff*, which is separated from the grain in wheat).

The male sexual part of a flower, known as the *stamen*, produces thousands of tiny dustlike pollen grains in its pollen sacs. (A single corn plant will produce up to 50 million pollen grains.) The extremely light pollen grains are transported by the wind for considerable distances and have been collected at an altitude of 4,000 feet. Some have been blown from South America across the Gulf of Mexico to Louisiana. The female sexual flower part, known as the *pistil*, produces a somewhat flask-shaped ovary. Although most grass species bear bisexual flowers, a few, such as the corn plant, produce female flowers (ears and silks) at the lower part of the plant and male flowers (tassels) at the top. In buffalo grass, the individual plant is either male or female, bearing only unisexual flowers.

Seed. An embryo is formed when the egg is fertilized by the sperm in the pollen grain. This embryo, together with a food reservoir and an enclosing protective seed coat, composes the *seed.* Seeds may simply drop to the ground at the base of the parent plant and germinate the following spring, thus entering into competition with the parent for sunlight, moisture, and soil nutrients. Some seeds may be dispersed by wind, washed down slopes by run-off waters, or carried away by animals. Some grass seeds have sharp spines which readily adhere to the wool of a sheep, or the hide of a steer or antelope, only to drop off many yards or even miles from the parent plant. Rodents such as pocket mice and kangaroo rats may transport grass seeds to their burrows. A number of grasses have successfully invaded the United States from abroad as seeds. Thus, Kentucky bluegrass, which is considered a top quality forage species, apparently was accidentally introduced from Europe as a grain contaminant by early colonists.

During protracted drought grass seeds may remain dormant near the ground surface for several years. Then, as soil moisture gradually accumulates during a wet year, they may germinate and cause a drab straw-colored rangeland to turn green within a few days.

Origin of the Western Livestock Industry

The initial development of the Western range livestock industry was shaped by Spanish influence early in the sixteenth century. The ancestors of many of our Western range cattle were shipped from Spain to Florida, Cuba, and Mexico. In 1540 (only forty-eight years after Columbus discovered America and fully sixty-seven years before the first English settlement at Jamestown) that bold explorer, Coronado, in his quest of the elusive Seven Cities of Cebola, led a band of adventurers across our

Western prairies. With them went 5,000 sheep, 1,000 horses, and 500 head of cattle (25). The native Indians of Arizona and New Mexico soon acquired some of the Spanish sheep and ponies (which may have escaped from Spanish enclosures and run wild on the plains), grazing them on the semiarid plains all year long in a semiwild state. They were so adept at raising ponies, which they used in hunting antelope and buffalo, that when Lewis and Clark arrived at a small Shoshone Indian village in Idaho in 1805, a herd of 700 Spanish ponies greeted their astonished eyes (25).

Under Spanish guidance the cattle industry became firmly entrenched in Mexico. In an effort to expand the industry, the Mexican government, in 1821, enticed thousands of American settlers to move to Texas by awarding them huge tracts of land. By 1830, 20,000 American settlers had responded to the lure. After the bloody Alamo, the defeat of the Spaniards, and the admittance of Texas to the Union in 1848, the United States government continued a policy of liberal land grants. As a result, the number of cattle in Texas reached 330,000 by 1850, 3.5 million by 1860 (25).

Another focal point of Spanish influence on America's future livestock industry was the California mission, established in the late eighteenth century. In addition to establishing fields of vegetables and lush orchards, the Spanish padres also raised cattle, sheep, and horses. So flourishing were their ranches that by 1834 the twenty-one missions in California maintained 423,000 cattle, 61,600 horses, and 321,500 sheep, goats, and pigs (25).

Barriers to Settlement of the Plains. The westward flow of agricultural settlement from the East halted abruptly when it reached the grassy vistas of the Plains. There were several reasons for this. First, geographers of the time had incorrectly named this region the Great American Desert, suggesting it to be a harsh, barren, arid land of considerable hazard and of minimal value to prospective settlers. Second, the Plains Indians occupied the prairie. Now mounted on Spanish ponies, they represented a formidable barrier to settlement. As Everett E. Edwards so vividly writes, "For 2½ centuries the Plains Indians maintained themselves 'gainst the Spaniards, English, French, Mexicans, Texans and Americans, despite missionaries, whiskey, diseases, gun powder and lead" (9). Third, the vast sea of grass on the western horizon was a completely strange and forbidding habitat for most of the settlers, who had been born and raised on semiforested land east of the Mississippi.

Rapid Settlement of Plains and Expansion of Livestock Industry. However, about this time, several factors set the stage not only for rapid prairie settlement, but also for a phenomenal expansion of the livestock industry. Among these predisposing influences were the following:

1. The natural tall-grass and short-grass plant communities of the plains were well stocked with nutritious livestock foods.
2. The extension of railroad lines into the Plains (Missouri, Kansas, and Nebraska) facilitated mass movements of settlers and livestock.
3. The population boom in the East and North, and the gold-mining industry in Colorado and California provided a ready market for beef, mutton, and wool. (During the Civil War, the Confederate army was fed to a considerable extent on Texas beef.)
4. The federal army exerted continual pressure on the hostile Plains Indian in the post-Civil War period, eventually forcing the surrender of Chief Joseph in the Bear Paw Mountains of Montana in 1877.
5. The buffalo, which at one time formed herds numbering millions of animals, was virtually eradicated as a serious competitor of range cattle for forage. Many of the trains carried buffalo hunters, whose major responsibility was to shoot enough bison to feed construction crews.
6. Invention of barbed wire made available for the first time an inexpensive but effective means of restricting cattle movements so that they would not get lost or mixed up with herds belonging to other ranchers, and so that they could be easily transferred from one pasture to another.
7. The federal government, under the provisions of the Homestead Act, encouraged settlement by offering 160 acres of land to every settler who would in good faith occupy and develop the site for a period of at least five years.
8. Unscrupulous land companies, backed with capital from the East, Scotland, and England, publicized the prairie as a "green gold" paradise, where a settler could grow wealthy almost as fast as a buffalo grass seedling could grow to maturity. A considerable promotional literature had wide circulation. One book, excessive in its claims for the prairie country's economic possibilities, was known as *Brisbane's Beef Bonanza* (25). One chapter of this book, "Millions in Beef," described in detail how an initial investment of $25,000 would yield a net profit of $51,378 in only six years (25). One Iowa farmer traveled a considerable distance to look at a land parcel which was described as having a river flowing through the middle of it. Upon surveying his prospective purchase, he looked in vain for the stream. When he asked the agent about it, the latter replied, "Why the stream is underground. It's flowing right beneath our feet" (15).

Shortly after the termination of the Civil War, market prices for steers in urban centers of the North and East zoomed to $50 per head. At this time Texas had roughly 3.5 million head of cattle. Ranchers began driving thousands of cattle along trails to railroad shipping yards. One of the most famous routes, the Chisholm Trail, began in San Antonio in southern Texas and ended several hundred miles further north at the railroad yards of Abilene, Kansas. Some Texas cattle were trailed north to Canada, after being driven two to three years and having grown up on the move. By 1885 over 5 million head of cattle were herded northward along these trails, to be shipped by rail throughout the United States (24). It was during the trail-drive period (which ended with the advent of barbed wire fences) that some of the most colorful and violent history of the western range was written. This was an era dominated by cowboys, rustlers, horse thieves, and range wars.

The livestock boom really accelerated during the 1880–1885 period. According to Stewart, twenty giant companies were organized in Wyoming alone, involving a capital of over $12 million (26). Similar expansion occurred throughout the Great Plains from Canada to Mexico. Many of the new outfits had 5,000 to 10,000 head of cattle. Near Brownsville, Texas, the celebrated Santa Gertrudis ranch spread over 500,000 acres of prairie. The XIT outfit in the Texas panhandle (which extended twenty-five miles from east to west and 200 miles from north to south) was perhaps the largest cattle ranch on the North American continent (26). As a result of such expansions, the cattle population in the seventeen Western states mushroomed from only 4.6 million head in 1870 to 26.6 million in 1890, nearly a sixfold increase in two decades; sheep increased from 500,000 head in 1850 to 20 million by 1890 (23).

Rangeland Depletion

The cattle industry's phenomenal expansion was responsible for much of the settlement of the West. For this we can thank thousands of courageous, hardworking ranchers and farmers. However, we cannot thank them for the ruthlessness with which they abused a once bounteous grassland resource.

Cattlemen severely depleted the ranges in many areas. Where a given pasture could have supported only twenty-five cattle, many were trying to graze 100. As a result, the big bluestem, the blue grass, and the buffalo grass were gnawed down to the roots. Once the grass plant's metabolic reserve had been eliminated, the vitality of the root system became severely impaired and death was the inevitable result. Many of these nineteenth-century stockmen were so engrossed in numbers of range animals that they disregarded the fact that four head of livestock, sick and scrawny from undernourishment, would not have as much market value as one head in prime condition after grazing on good forage.

We must not be too severe in our criticism, however. These ranchers could not take a course in range management or plant ecology and learn about the principles of plant succession, limiting factors, and range of tolerance.

In 1918, in a desperate attempt to increase our food production during the emergency caused by World War I, our federal forest authorities permitted an additional million animals to graze on forest ranges despite the already overly severe grazing pressure. In addition, much valuable rangeland was ripped up and turned face down by the newly developed "goliath" plows and then was seeded to wheat. Many of these farming enterprises were ill fated. Thus, except for one bumper crop year, the average annual income for a 640-acre wheat farm in western Kansas over a twenty-one-year period was only $35 (3).

Finally, in 1932, the seriousness of the range problem

Figure 6–2 New Mexico. This range during season of best growth barely provides sufficient forage to keep livestock alive. Cattle must cover a large area to get feed. Range deterioration will continue until livestock pressure is relieved. [Soil Conservation Service, U.S. Department of Agriculture]

prompted Congress to request the U.S. Forest Service to make a survey of the over-all range condition. The survey showed conclusively the rangeland productivity had been reduced by 50 per cent. On some Utah ranges, rice grass (a valuable forage species during the critical winter period when most pasture is covered with snow) was reduced almost 90 per cent under the intense grazing pressure (2). The survey further revealed that the removal of extensive grass cover had exposed 80 per cent of the range to erosion of varying degrees of severity (2).

Rangeland Restoration

As a direct consequence of the Forest Service report on the condition of our Western range, Congress enacted the Taylor Grazing Control Act in 1934. This represented the successful culmination of a long struggle on the part of conservationists to place our ailing public rangelands under effective federal control. The act had three major objectives: (1) The checking of deterioration, (2) the institution of projects designed to maintain and improve the range, and (3) the stabilization of the rangeland economy. Although only 80 million acres of rangelands were included in the original provisions, the acreage was increased to 160 million acres by 1959. Since the end of World War II, the administration of these rangelands has been charged to the Bureau of Land Management. The lands included in these grazing districts were, at one time, among the most badly depleted in the nation. Even in 1951, after several years of protection under the Taylor Grazing Control Act, the Bureau of Land Management estimated that 50 per cent of the land was severely eroded and 32 per cent was suffering from moderate erosion; on only 18 per cent was erosion damage slight or nonexistent. The basic organizational and operational unit in the scheme is the grazing district, which is roughly analogous to the soil conservation district. The grazing district is run by a local committee of ranchers in collaboration with representatives of the federal government. As of 1959 these lands were divided into fifty-nine grazing districts (primarily in Utah, Nevada, Arizona, New Mexico, Colorado, Wyoming, Idaho, Montana, Oregon, and California) ranging in size from 3 million to 9 million acres. By 1959, over 7.7 million head of livestock were being grazed in these districts by roughly 17,000 ranchers. Each rancher was charged a fee for the privilege of grazing his animals on these federal lands. The fees as of 1959 were 22¢ for five goats or sheep, 22¢ per head of cattle, and 44¢ per horse. During the 1956–1964 period alone, almost 11.5

million acres of rangeland was reseeded, and 11,835 acres of shelter belts were established within the framework of the grazing district.

Rangeland Regions

In this chapter we are primarily concerned with the rangelands of the seventeen contiguous Western states, which embrace roughly 730 million acres. (It should be emphasized, however, that the pastures of the thirty-one contiguous states east of the Mississippi River actually support more livestock.) Because the Western rangeland has extremely varied soils and climatic regimes, we would expect the plant communities, which are an expression of soil–climate interaction, also to be highly diverse. Although many millions of acres of valuable grazing land occur in forested regions, we shall discuss these important areas in the context of forest conservation (Chapter 7). Some authorities, such as Stoddard and Smith of Utah State, recognize nine regions of range vegetation (26). Here we shall consider only three: tall grass, short grass, and intermountain shrub.

Tall Grass Region. As we recall from our biome discussion, this community is located primarily east of the 100th meridian (which bisects North Dakota and Kansas) and originally formed a band 150 to 500 miles wide extending from Canada to Mexico. Because the chernozem soil occupied by the virgin tall grass community was extremely fertile, only about 20 million (8 per cent) of the original 250 million acres still are in grass; the remainder (92 per cent) has been plowed and converted into productive cropland. The most extensive remnants are now located in North Dakota, Nebraska, Oklahoma, and Kansas. This plant community is well named, for one of its dominants, big bluestem (*Andropogon gerardii*), once attained a height of 12 feet, completely engulfing man and beast in a "sea of grass." In the climax condition, big bluestem and little bluestem (*Andropogon scoparius*) comprise roughly 72 per cent of the vegetation. Under heavy grazing pressure the forage production may decline 90 per cent, from 3,000 pounds to only 300 pounds per acre. According to Stoddard and Smith, one major disadvantage to these grasses is that, as they mature, soluble nutrients in the foliage and stems tend to leach away, so that by winter the grasses are almost worthless as forage (26). (Fig. 6–3)

Short Grass Region. The short grass range extends from the 100th meridian west to the eastern foothills of the Rockies, and

Figure 6–3 San Antonio, Texas. Close-up of big bluestem—a native perennial bunchgrass. March is the optimal planting time. Abundant in true prairie climax. [Soil Conservation Service, U.S. Department of Agriculture]

from the Canadian border south to central Texas and southern New Mexico. Embracing an area of 200 million acres, this region supplies one third of our nation's range beef. The dominant grasses are blue grama (*Bouteloua gracilis*), which produces 50 to 95 per cent of the forage, and buffalo grass (*Buchloe dactyloides*). Both are highly nutritious and extremely attractive to cattle. Because buffalo grass is capable of reproducing by rhizomes as well as by seeds, it has marked ability to survive. When short grass range deteriorates, it is frequently invaded by low-value weed species, such as prickly pear cactus, Russian thistle, and snake weed. Because much of this region has less than 20 inches of rainfall yearly, the sod should never be set to the plow. It was the plowing of this short grass sod by thousands of wheat and cotton farmers, combined with protracted drought, that precipitated the black blizzards of the 1930's.

Intermountain Shrub Region. This vast rangeland, composed primarily of shrubs and half-shrubs, occupies the Great Basin

Figure 6–4 Woodward, Oklahoma. A close-up of buffalo grass—a perennial, highly palatable, drought-resistant species. Thrives on clay and loam soils. Best adapted to regions having 15 to 30 inches of rainfall. Best pasture results from deferred grazing. [Soil Conservation Service, U.S. Department of Agriculture]

from the Cascade and Sierras in the west to the Rockies in the east, and from Canada to Mexico. It includes parts of Oregon, southern Idaho, western Wyoming, northern Arizona, eastern California, western Colorado, and most of Utah and Nevada. Many of the plants have the adaptations of typical *xerophytes* for survival under extremely arid conditions: (1) small leaves with waterproof coverings to minimize moisture loss resulting from transpiration and evaporation, (2) extensive root system, (3) wide spacing, and (4) ability to grow rapidly during wet seasons and to become at least partially dormant during drought. In the relatively cool northern part of this region (Montana and Wyoming) the dominant plant is big sagebrush (*Artemisia tridentata*), which forms extensive acreages of rolling blue-green cover. A typical sagebrush density for Wyoming at an elevation of 6,500 feet is twenty-five to thirty plants per 100 square feet. Five acres of sagebrush range in good condition will support one animal unit for one month. Sagebrush provides forage during spring and fall. In winter, when grasses are blanketed with snow, thousands of sheep and cattle (as well as deer and antelope) feed on the persistent leaves. Other characteristic dominants of the northern shrub region are rabbit brush (*Chrysothamnus nauseosus*), greasewood (*Sarcobatus vermiculatus*), snakeweed (*Gutierrezia sarothrae*), and winter fat (*Eurotia lanata*), which is appropriately named because it is valuable as winter forage.

Classification of Rangelands for Management Purposes

Range Site. A *range site* may be defined as a distinctive kind of rangeland which has a particular potential for producing forage of nutritional value to livestock. This potential depends upon the interplay of soil type and climatic factors such as precipitation, evaporation, wind, and temperature. If the climate remains constant, the vegetation which will ultimately develop at a range site will compose a *climax community*. In an earlier chapter, we defined the climax as the stable terminal community of a biological succession. Once such a climax, or vegetational potential, has been realized at a given range site, it will theoretically remain established indefinitely as long as the environment remains unchanged.

There are many environmental factors—such as overgrazing, excessive rainfall, protracted cold periods, population explosions of herbivores, or ill-considered attempts to convert the range site into a corn, wheat, or cotton field—which may temporarily prevent the range site from realizing its vegetational potential. Drought also may influence the structure of the vegetational community. Thus, a three-year drought in Arizona caused a 43.5 per cent reduction in the density of black grama (*Bouteloua eriopoda*) (23). Sooner or later, however, when sound range management practices are followed, the climax (or subclimax) community ultimately will be restored.

NAMING OF RANGE SITES.   The Soil Conservation Service technicians name each range site in a given area on the basis of permanent features which are readily identified, such as the type of soil, nature of the terrain, climate, and in a very general way, the kind of climax vegetation characteristic of the site. Typical names for range sites might be Clay Lowland, Saline Flats, Wet Meadow, and Sandy Savannah.

DESCRIPTION OF RANGE SITE.   Once the range site has been identified, the Soil Conservation Service prepares a description of the site which is placed in the files of the local grazing district and is then available for reference by interested ranchers. The description includes the name of the range site, location, climate, topographic features, soil characteristics, and nature of the climax vegetation.

Figure 6–5   Near Van Horn, Texas. Rough stony mountain site in desert shrub grassland in fair condition. It is composed primarily of Chino grama, black grama, and sideoats grama. [Soil Conservation Service, U.S. Department of Agriculture]

Range Condition. The term *range condition* may be defined as the current condition of the range site in relation to its theoretical potential. It refers to the health or productivity of the range.

CLASSES. Various criteria are employed as a basis for establishing categories of range condition. Among them are: (1) the species composition of the plant community in terms of the plant succession, (2) the vigor of the plants, (3) the amount of plant residue or mulch on the ground, (4) the condition of the soil, with regard to structure and erodibility, and (5) the number of animal units which can be supported per acre. Four range condition classes are recognized on the basis of these criteria: (1) excellent, (2) good, (3) fair, and (4) poor. (See Figure 6–6.) It must be emphasized that in comparing range conditions, one must always deal with ranges belonging to identical or very similar range sites. It is apparent that a range in the arid sagebrush region of Wyoming may be in "excellent" condition and still be much less productive than a "good" ranch in the semiarid short grass region of Nebraska. We shall now describe the range condition in terms of the preceding criteria.

Composition of the Plant Community. Ranchers frequently classify the various range plants in three categories

Figure 6–6 A lightly grazed pasture consisting of a dense growth of tobosa with some sacaton, on the right of this fence. At the left is overgrazed rangeland where the vegetation has become sparse; there is a growth of worthless soleropogon and some sacaton. [Soil Conservation Service, U.S. Department of Agriculture]

with respect to the dynamics of plant succession: (1) *decreasers,* (2) *increasers,* and (3) *invaders.* Decreasers are highly nutritious, highly palatable members of the climax community which generally decrease under heavy grazing pressure. Representative decreaser species are big bluestem, little bluestem, blue grama, wheat grass, and buffalo grass. Increasers, on the other hand, are generally less palatable but are still highly nutritious climax species which tend to increase (at least temporarily) when a range is heavily grazed. Apparently this increase is the result of reduced competition with the decreasers, whose numbers have lessened. When severe grazing pressure continues over a long period of time, even the increasers begin to decrease, apparently not being able to withstand trampling by hoofs of grazing animals, and are replaced by invaders. The invaders— such as ragweed, cactus, and thistle—may be considered as undesirable weed species, low in nutritional value and not very desirable for grazing animals. Invaders frequently are annual forbs or herbs that thrive best under sunlight intensities much higher than the 1 to 2 per cent of full sunlight occurring under a dense stand of climax grasses. Because their roots are simple *taproots* instead of the dense *fibrous roots* of a typical grass, these invaders are not very effective in binding the soil. A range in excellent condition has a high percentage of decreasers and no invaders. Conversely, a range in poor condition characteristically has a low percentage of high-forage-value decreasers and a relatively large component of low-forage-value invaders. As a result of this forage differential, an excellent range may require only 1 acre per animal unit month, whereas 5 or even 10 acres may be required on poor range.

Plant Vigor. Reduction in plant vigor usually precedes change in the composition of the range plant community. Thus, if decreased vitality of forage species can be detected quickly enough, reduction in size of the herd may allow the range to regain its original vigor by natural processes. Recognition of reduced vitality is based upon plant color (dark green or yellow), number of leaves, seed production, plant size and weight, and ability to reproduce by stolons or rhizomes.

Plant Residue or Mulch. Mulch is herewith defined as dead plant material which accumulates on the ground surface. It represents a very reliable indicator of range condition (23). Mulch represents a link between the forage plants and the organic content of the soil. When mulch decreases in quantity, soil fertility ultimately will decline and the range will deteriorate. Mulch serves to increase the porosity (and hence drainage and aeration) of the soil; it may prevent seed transport by wind and water. The amount of mulch on a range varies with the temperature, moisture, plant composition, grazing pressure, and other conditions. A study by Edmunson of a California range dominated by wild barley (*Hordeum leporinum*) showed 1500 pounds of mulch per acre where forage was considered in excellent condition as compared with only 400 pounds for range in poor condition (24). In humid regions the per-acre weight of mulch on excellent range may reach 0.5 ton and equal the current annual forage production.

Condition of Soil. As might be expected, an excellent range would have a relatively thick layer of fertile, spongy, erosion-resistant soil. Run-off water would be clear and minimal. The soil of a poor range, on the other hand, would characteristically be shallow and infertile. Moreover, because of the considerable area of bare ground and because of the fact that the simple taproots of the annual weeds which invade the poor range are inadequate soil binders, the land is highly susceptible to erosion. Frequently the range is dissected with gullies. Run-off water is brown with silt and is excessive.

Plant Indicators. Any rancher capable of identifying the major plant components of his range could, in this way, determine range condition. Sometimes he only needs to identify a single species. The use of plants as "indicators" of range condition is based upon the ecological concept that a plant is the expression, or product, of its total environment, whether it be soil, moisture, temperature, light, animals, or even other plants. In other words, a given plant represents the effect of a certain environmental cause, and simply by identifying the presence of a particular species of plant, the ranch manager can assume certain characteristics of the environmental cause. It is true that any plant may thus serve as an indicator. However, the best (most precise) indicators would be plants having an extremely narrow *range of tolerance* for certain environmental factors. Some species indicate certain soil types. In southern Arizona, for example, salty soils are indicated by saltgrass (*Distichlis stricta*), alkaline soils by alkali sacaton (*Sporobolus airoides*), and heavy alluvial soils, subject to periodic flooding, are indicated by tobosa (*Hilaria mutica*) (23). Of greater immediate concern to the rancher than soil type is the question of whether his pastures are deteriorating under heavy grazing pressure. Plants whose presence indicate overgrazing include gumweed (*Grindelia squarrosa*), snakeweed (*Gutierrezia sarothrae*), rabbitbrush (*Chrysothamnus*), cactus (*Opuntia*), bullthistle (*Cirsium*), locoweed (*Astragalus*), pigweed (*Amaranthus*), sunflower (*Helianthus*), wild daisy (*Erigeron*), plantain (*Plan-*

tago), goldenrod (*Solidago*), nettle (*Urtica*), tarweed (*Hemizonia kelloggii*), creosote bush (*Larrea divaricata*), and dandelion (*Taraxacum*) (26).

Elements, Soil, Range Plants, and Livestock Health. Of the roughly 100 elements in the physical universe, only about thirty or so actually become incorporated into living substance. This is true not only of man, but of all living members of the range-land community, from blue grama to Black Angus. A steer or antelope secures these elements from range plants; these plants, in turn, obtain their elements from the soil, air, or water. In the final analysis, therefore, the availability of an essential element to a range animal depends, to a large degree, upon its abundance or scarcity in the soil. Proper nutrition of livestock is just as important a facet of range management as pest control, deferred grazing, or artificial reseeding. Here we shall consider the role of phosphorous and cobalt in livestock nutrition, the nature of deficiency symptoms in livestock, and the way in which deficiencies may be relieved.

Phosphorus. Most rangeland soils are to some degree phosphorus deficient. For U.S. soils as a whole, maximal soil deficiencies occur in the coastal area from Texas to Mary-land (12). Even though soil has relatively abundant amounts of phosphorus, if bound up in insoluble compounds (iron, aluminum), it will not be available for plant and (later) animal use. A large percentage of phosphorus derived from range forage is concentrated in bones, hair, wool, and horns. Hum-phrey cites one authority as estimating that six boxcars of fat cattle would contain the equivalent of all the phosphorus con-tained in the upper 6 inches of an acre of soil, and because many cattle have been raised and shipped away from some ranges for almost a century, the loss of soil phosphorus has been con-siderable (12). Phosphorus may also be removed by erosion. Up to 37.75 pounds per acre may be eroded annually from plowed land with no vegetational cover. On the other hand, the loss from land of the same type continuously covered with blue grass is only 0.16 pound per acre.

Phosphorus and calcium are essential for the proper develop-ment of a sturdy skeleton. When both calcium and phosphorus are deficient in an animal, the bones lose their rigidity and are easily broken. The animal loses its normal appetite for food and virtually starves when surrounded by abundance. It develops instead a bizarre appetite for wood, bones, hair, tin cans, and rotting flesh. The deficiency may be remedied by supplying phosphorus in drinking water or by feeding the animal ground bone meal. The soil could also be fertilized with a compound containing phosphorus, so that ultimately the cattle would secure the element through their forage.

Cobalt. For many years Australian ranchers were mystified over the manner in which sheep and cattle, virtually surrounded by lush, knee-high forage, would gradually waste away and starve to death. The cause of the curious malady was not determined until 1935, when researchers discovered that the rangeland soils were deficient in cobalt and that this element was essential to animal health. Cobalt-deficient areas have also been identified in New Hampshire, Massachusetts, New York, Michigan, Wisconsin, North Carolina, and Florida. The cobalt-insufficiency disease, known as "salt sick" in Florida, was the greatest single cause of loss to the cattle industry of that state in 1931. In New Hampshire this disease is known as "Burton-ail," in Michigan as "lake shore disease," and in Massachusetts as "neck-ail." Cobalt deficiency symptoms in cattle are similar to those for phosphorus deficiency.

Researchers have disclosed an important role played by cobalt in animal nutrition. Apparently it forms an essential raw material in the synthesis of vitamin B_{12}, which occurs in the "first stomach," or rumen, of the cow. The vitamin B_{12} is then transported by the bloodstream to the red bone marrow of ribs, sternum, limbs, skull, and vertebrae. Here, in some way not perfectly understood, this vitamin promotes the production of healthy red blood cells. Because several million red blood cells die in the cow's body each second, production of new cells must proceed at the same rate if anemia is to be prevented.

Intensive investigations in Australia have revealed that cobalt content in forage grasses shows a direct correlation with soil content. They also found that the addition of a minute quantity of cobalt chloride, 4 ounces to the acre, was sufficient to maintain a healthy pasture for two years. Cobalt can also be fed directly to sheep and cattle by mixing 0.5 ounce of cobalt chloride with 100 pounds of salt.

It is apparent that soil chemistry is basic to the chemistry of producers grown in that soil, and ultimately to that of livestock. Although slight cobalt and phosphorus deficiencies may not be limiting to range vegetation, the effect on livestock may be lethal. The rancher should make soil chemistry a basic consideration in range management and should realize that it is as important as terrain, rainfall, rangeland pests, composition, and condition of range plants.

Effect of Drought on Range Forage. Drought is perhaps the rancher's greatest environmental problem. He can to some degree control rodents, poisonous plants, brush and weeds, predators, disease-causing insects, and soil chemistry, but there is absolutely nothing he can do (except for cloud seeding) about controlling drought. He can adjust to it, but that is all. Moreover, drought is unpredictable.

DETERIORATION. Through processes of evolution operating through many centuries, Western range plants developed a variety of drought adaptations (described in Chapter 2) which enable them to survive as a species, even though individual plants may succumb.

Nevertheless, a severe drought may effect a drastic deterioration of the range plant community, regardless of severity of grazing pressure. Three examples follow. (1) In the Snake River plains of southern Idaho, the 1934 drought caused an 84 per cent reduction from the range plant cover of 1932, even though livestock had been excluded from the study plot. (2) During a thirteen-year period marked by an aggregate eight years of drought, the black grama (*Bouteloua eriopoda*) cover of an ungrazed plot was reduced 89.1 per cent (26). (3) In western Kansas, the 1934 drought killed 74.8 per cent of plants on study areas which were overgrazed and 64.6 per cent on pastures which were grazed in moderation (4).

RANGE RECOVERY. Once the dry spell has ended, range recovery may be fast or slow, depending upon precipitation. Thus, a lightly grazed Montana pasture required eight years to return to good condition after the 1934–1936 drought.

The close correlation between rainfall and range plant growth was strikingly evident in a study conducted in southwest Utah on the Desert Experimental Range of the U.S. Forest Service. Dry herbage production in October ranged from 95 pounds per acre when total rainfall the preceding year was under 4 inches, to more than 450 pounds per acre when precipitation the preceding year was 10.5 inches. Moreover, the relationship between rainfall and forage weight was so precise that it could be expressed in terms of a mathematical formula. (Fig. 6–7)

Range Management

Range management has been defined by Stoddard and Smith as "the science and art of planning and directing range use so as to obtain the maximum livestock production consistent with conservation of range resources" (26). In the context of range management we shall here consider methods of maintaining the range in good condition, such as varying the grazing pressure, manipulating stock, and using fire and reseeding. We shall consider the selection and development of cattle breeds.

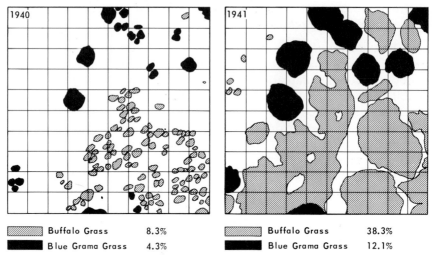

Buffalo Grass	8.3%	
Blue Grama Grass	4.3%	

Buffalo Grass	38.3%	
Blue Grama Grass	12.1%	

Total coverage of quadrat 12.6 per cent and 50.4 per cent.

Figure 6–7 Recovery of drought-depleted range following a period of adequate rainfall. Basal cover of range vegetation near Ness City, Kansas, had been reduced to only 12.6 per cent of the area of a sample meter quadrat by the autumn of 1940. Overgrazing had contributed to the deterioration. However, within one year after the return of adequate rainfall, range grasses responded sufficiently to cover 50.4 per cent of the sample plot. [Adapted from Ruben L. Parsons, *Conserving American Resources* (Englewood Cliffs, N.J.: Prentice-Hall, Inc., 1956). After Albertson and Weaver, *Ecol. Mono.* **14** (January, 1944), 1–29.]

Finally, we shall describe problems posed by rangeland pests and how they can best be controlled.

Shifting Stocking-Level Policy. The rancher must be prepared to make adjustments to the severe drought years which will inevitably occur. Two methods of adjustment may be employed. Firstly, he may employ a shifting stocking-level plan in which grazing pressure is adjusted to forage capacity. Thus, if a pasture which originally supported 100 head is reduced by drought to only 25 per cent of its original carrying capacity, the rancher obviously may run only twenty-five head on that depleted pasture, thus necessitating sale of seventy-five excess head, possibly at very low prices. When a wet year recurs, the pasture may once more support the original 100 head, thus necessitating purchase of seventy-five additional cattle to keep that pasture grazed to capacity. This "shifting-numbers" technique involves many economic problems. Frequently a rancher starts out with good intentions of reducing his herd. However, because of a poor market he retains his full herd even during the height of the drought. The result may be disastrous, not only for the range, because of the combination of drought and overgrazing, but also for the herd, which may incur wholesale malnutrition and even starvation. The sight of gaunt cattle moving lethargically in search of a few sprigs of green grass in a well-trampled field of thistles and cactus is the unpleasant aftermath of such mis-management.

Stable Stocking-Level Plan. Secondly, to adjust to drought a stable stocking-level technique may be followed. Many author-ities advise ranchers in the arid western plains to stock their pastures permanently to only 65 per cent of average capac-ity (26). For example, if 100 head of cattle is average capacity on a given pasture, the rancher would stock only sixty-five head, even though the pasture may be slightly overgrazed during a dry year and somewhat undergrazed during a wet spell. The "surplus" growth of forage during the wet season will by no means be wasted, for the foods manufactured by this green herbage will provide a nutrient reserve which the plant, if a perennial, will draw upon during the next drought.

Stock Manipulation—Water and Salt Distribution. Another range management problem is to ensure a proper herd distri-bution pattern so that livestock will make uniform use of avail-able forage. Because cattle, for example, concentrate in wet meadows and along stream margins and avoid ridges and slopes, part of the range may become severely overgrazed while another part, of equal food value, may be completely ignored. Livestock distribution can be directly controlled with barbed wire fencing and herding, both of which are rather costly. In-direct methods, much less expensive but highly effective, in-volve the strategic distribution of water holes and salt blocks. Because cattle and sheep normally congregate around water sources (one cow requires 10 gallons per day), the salt blocks should be placed roughly 0.5 mile from the nearest water source, preferably on ridges, gentle slopes, or openings in brush or forest, to induce the livestock to frequent areas they normally would avoid.

Salt is essential to the vigorous health of range animals. Sheep, for example, require 0.25 to 0.5 pound per month. Within three weeks after being deprived of salt, cattle develop an unusual craving for it. When salt deprivation continues, the animals show loss of appetite, emaciation, roughening of the coat, extreme weakness, and ultimately complete collapse. In some ranges where the soil is naturally high in phosphate and sulphate salts, livestock may partially satisfy their salt requirements by grazing on salt-absorbing vegetation. An analysis of the leaves and stems of range plants in New Mexico showed the equivalent of about 0.28 per cent salt for saltgrass (*Distichlis*) and 1.83 per cent salt for greasewood (*Sarcobatus*).

Deferred Grazing System. When livestock are allowed to graze in a pasture continuously throughout the grazing season, the more palatable (and usually more nutritious) range plants frequently are so seriously overgrazed that they incur a reduction in vitality and reproductive potential. To remedy this problem, several range management experts advise *deferred grazing* (26). The main features of this system are represented in Figure 6–8. Note that the ranch is divided into three pastures, A, B, and C, and that each of them are deferred for two successive years within a six-year period. During years 1 and 2, forage plants in pasture A are allowed to reach maturity and drop their seeds before livestock are permitted to graze on them late in the season. Even though the grasses become rather dry at this time, they still are highly nutritious. A certain amount of grazing after the seeds have been produced may be advantageous to the pasture, because with their foraging activity cattle not only scatter the grass seed, but by trampling the seeds underfoot thrust them into the ground and enhance germination success. The net result of deferred grazing is the increased size, density, weight, vitality, reproductive potential, and nutritional value of the deferred forage species. Note that

Figure 6–8 Deferred grazing. [Adapted from Ruben L. Parsons, *Conserving American Resources*, (Englewood Cliffs, N.J.: Prentice-Hall, Inc., 1956). After A. W. Sampson, *Range Management*, (New York: John Wiley & Sons, Inc., 1952).]

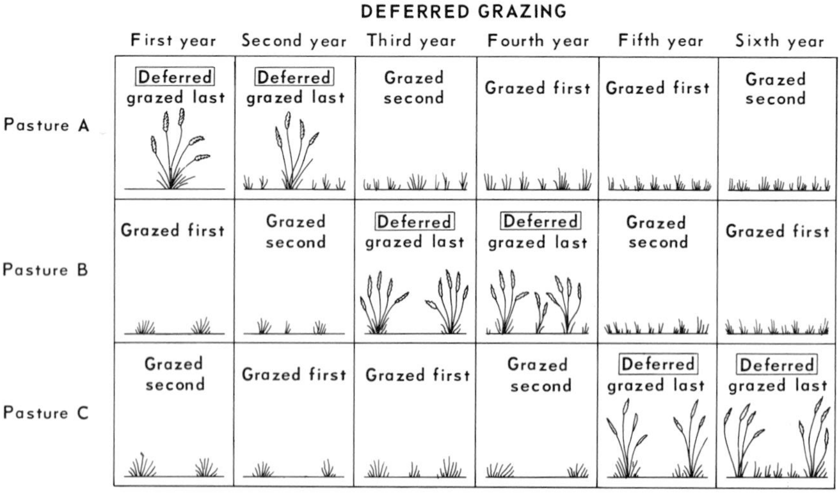

DEFERRED GRAZING

	First year	Second year	Third year	Fourth year	Fifth year	Sixth year
Pasture A	Deferred grazed last	Deferred grazed last	Grazed second	Grazed first	Grazed first	Grazed second
Pasture B	Grazed first	Grazed second	Deferred grazed last	Deferred grazed last	Grazed second	Grazed first
Pasture C	Grazed second	Grazed first	Grazed first	Grazed second	Deferred grazed last	Deferred grazed last

Figure 6–9 Destructive burning of bluestem grass pasture in Kansas. [Soil Conservation Service, U.S. Department of Agriculture]

in Figure 6–8, pasture A is deferred the first and second years, pasture B the third and fourth years, and pasture C the fifth and sixth years. Thus, for this hypothetical ranch all three pastures, within a six-year rotation plan, receive temporary release from grazing pressure.

Use of Fire. In addition to the employment of grazing pressure, a rancher may utilize fire to control the floral composition and growth rate of his pastures. Admittedly controversial, this technique has both positive and negative features. According to Dr. Jack R. Harlan, agronomy professor at Oklahoma Agricultural and Mechanical College, range burning has the following deleterious results: many plants are either destroyed or incur depressed vitality because of food reserve depletion; weed invasion is facilitated; soil erosion is promoted because of loss of vegetational cover; effectiveness of rainfall is reduced because of decreased permeability of the mulch-deprived, sun-baked soil; and much valuable organic nitrogen is destroyed. The positive features of range burning are listed by Harlan as follows: old plants of low forage value are removed; new growth may develop earlier because it is not shaded by old straw and is of greater nutritional value than it would be were the range left unburned. In general, range burning, from the short-term

203

Figure 6–10   Controlling grass fire with portable fire-fighting units on western Oklahoma rangeland. [Soil Conservation Service, U.S. Department of Agriculture]

viewpoint, is probably good for cattle and is favored by cattlemen who are leasing rangeland. However, on a long-term basis, burning is probably deleterious to the range and is usually disparaged by the landowner.

Reseeding of Range.   Through ignorance, greed, or incompetence almost 80 million acres of America's rangelands were virtually destroyed. If these acres are to be restored within the next few decades, they will have to be reseeded by artificial methods. Natural reseeding alone will not accomplish the job fast enough. Although initial grass-planting experiments were conducted as early as 1895, almost all of the 1,500 experimental seedings resulted in failure. Since these early days of frustration, however, much progress has been made. The following material has largely been obtained from the fine paper, "Restoring the Range by Reseeding," by Pearse, Plummer, and Savage which appeared in the 1948 *Yearbook of Agriculture* (18).

METHODS OF RESEEDING RANGE.   *Broadcasting.* Seeds may be broadcasted by hand or airplane. Unless some provision, however, is made for covering them, the project will probably fail. Uncovered seeds may be blown away by strong winds, may succumb to protracted winter cold, may be consumed by birds and jackrabbits, or may be washed away during heavy spring rainstorms. Sometimes ranchers may drive a herd of cattle over the area to trample the seeds into the ground. If seeding is done in recently burned-over timberland, the loose covering of ashes may ensure reseeding success. Similarly, if reseeding is synchronized with autumn leaf fall, the leaf litter may provide sufficient seed cover for successful germination.

Airplane broadcasting, the only feasible method in rough, mountainous areas, can be both inexpensive and effective. Thus, in the fall of 1944, a burn in a Douglas fir and ponderosa pine stand in the Cabinet National Forest of Montana was seeded by airplane at a cost of only $1.20 per acre. Only two years later the burn area was cloaked with a dense stand of timothy, Kentucky blue grass, and orchard grass, which not only gave full erosion protection, but also provided a ton of food per acre for grazing animals. Although much rather sensational publicity has been given to the technique of encasing seeds in pellets of prefertilized mud and broadcasting them from airplanes, this method has almost universally met with failure or poor results, partly because of poor germination.

Figure 6–11 Seeding California rangeland by helicopter. [Soil Conservation Service, U.S. Department of Agriculture]

Drilling. When rangeland is fairly even, not too rocky or brush-covered, the use of a mechanical drill which may plant seeds at a uniform depth is preferable to either hand broadcasting or broadcasting by plane. Row spacing of about 1 foot is desirable on most ranges. The density of seeds planted should be sufficient to make use of the available moisture; too great a density would reduce seedling vigor because of competition for nutrients, light, and moisture; underseeding would permit invasion by weeds.

Selection of Appropriate Species in Reseeding. Not all species of native grasses have the same tolerance for such environmental factors as heat, cold, drought, acid soils, stony soils, infertile soils, trampling, grazing pressure, and parasites. Moreover, because our rangelands extend for almost 1,500 miles from the Canadian border to Mexico, encompassing a great variety of climatic conditions and soil types, for a reseeding operation to be successful species must be adaptable to the specific range site to be reseeded. Thus, cool-season grasses like wheat grasses, fescues, bromes, and bluegrasses would be appropriate for the cool growing season regions of the western intermountain region. On the other hand, in the warm Southwest, where summer temperatures commonly exceed 100 degrees F., warm-season plants like grama grass and buffalo grass are more appropriate. In recent years the U.S. Department of Agriculture has introduced a great number of species from abroad and has grown them on an experimental basis to determine their adaptability to the American range. A few have proved their ability to establish themselves thousands of miles from their origin. Thus, Russian wild rye (from Siberia) grows vigorously in our northern rangelands, being quite resistant to the bitter winter cold; on the other hand, the heat-tolerant Bermuda grass, imported from the semitropics, fares well in the deep South.

VALUE OF RESEEDING. Although we still have a long way to go there is little doubt that by artificial methods of reseeding we shall eventually be able to reclaim most of the 80 million acres of rangeland we once so disgracefully destroyed. Most reseeding can be accomplished for less than $5 per acre; the direct value of increased food supplies may amount to 50¢ per acre annually. In general, ranges which have been properly reseeded will support a greater number of livestock in better condition over a longer period than equivalent ranges which have not been seeded. Many plantings in the West, for example, have been grazed for fifteen successive years and still produce from three to twenty times as much forage as they did prior to seeding. Much greater forage and livestock production was possible in the intermountain region after many acres of big sagebrush were plowed up and seeded to crested wheatgrass. A classic example of how artificial reseeding can improve rangeland is provided by a 500-acre plot in the Fish Lake National Forest in Utah. Before seeding, this area supported a vigorous cover of sagebrush and rabbitbrush which provided forage for only eight head of cattle. However, only three years after it was seeded to wheat grasses and bromes (at a nominal cost of $3.22 per acre) it was able to sustain 100 cattle.

Cattle Breeds. For greatest efficiency in rangeland use, the proper breed of herbivore, in the form of cattle or sheep, is just as important as having the proper type of forage plant. The food chain is only as strong as its weakest link. Without an efficient second link (herbivore), the efficiency of the first link (producer) in converting solar energy to food energy is more or less dissipated.

The Texas longhorn, introduced to the United States by the Spaniards in the sixteenth century, and once grazed by the millions, is now found only in wildlife preserves and zoos. It has been replaced by a large variety of breeds, either imported from abroad or developed on our own western range.

Figure 6–12 Texas longhorn steer on the King Ranch at Kingsville, Texas. [U.S. Department of Agriculture]

HEREFORD. This large, powerfully built breed, its "white face" contrasting handsomely with its red-brown body, is perhaps the favorite of our Western rangelands. Its meat is of high quality. It is able to withstand the severe winter cold. It is unsurpassed in its ability to find enough food to survive even under the adverse conditions of drought and heavy snow. (The rustling ability of Western cattle was severely tested during the winter of 1886–1887, when temperatures dropped to −60 degrees F. and forage was sealed off with snow. Some ranges experienced 90 per cent cattle mortality.) However, when it comes to milk production, the Hereford ranks poorly.

SHORTHORN. Numerically, the shorthorn ranks second to the Hereford on our Western range. When forage is plentiful, its flesh is unexcelled. However, under adverse grazing conditions, as when forage is concealed by snow, the shorthorn might starve where the Hereford might survive. Evenly tempered and easily managed, the shorthorn is the best milk producer among our beef cattle.

ABERDEEN-ANGUS. The handsome, black Aberdeen-Angus is an excellent beef animal. However, because of its nervous temperament it is difficult to herd and to manage in the feed lot.

BRAHMAN. The large, light-colored Brahman, introduced from India about 1849, is ungainly and has long, drooping ears and loose folds of skin hanging from the neck. Although extremely excitable, these excellent rustlers are unsurpassed in their ability to withstand heat, drought, and bloodsucking fleas and ticks. Because certain ticks may transmit the causative organism of Texas cattle fever, a potentially lethal disease, its tick-resistant ability is highly regarded in the South.

SANTA GERTRUDIS. Research geneticists of the U.S. Department of Agriculture and cattlemen themselves are continuously conducting breeding experiments in an effort to develop superior breeds. A cross between two different breeds, known as a *cross breed* or *hybrid,* will sometimes combine the better traits of each parent and lack their undesirable characteristics. One of the most successful hybrids ever developed on American rangelands in recent years is the Santa Gertrudis. This breed was developed by geneticists on the world-famous King Ranch at Kingsville, Texas. It was developed after a series of crossings, the original of which involved a Brahman bull and a shorthorn cow (10). As the King Ranch geneticists hoped, the dark red Santa Gertrudis hybrid combined the beefiness, milk-producing ability, and docility of the shorthorn with the drought, heat, and tick resistance of the Brahman. As a result, the Santa Gertrudis is a breed par excellence for the hot, arid rangelands of the Southwest.

Plant Pests. The rancher is periodically confronted with invasion of his pasturage by woody, low-value shrubs, such as mesquite, sagebrush, juniper, burroweed, creosote bush, and many others. In Texas alone, mesquite and juniper cost the livestock industry $20 million annually (19). Unless effective control methods are established, aggressive spread of these weed species may seriously depress the livestock-carrying capacity of the range. Within the limited scope of this text we shall consider this problem in terms of a single species, the mesquite.

MESQUITE. The mesquite (*Prosopis juliflora*) is a thorny desert shrub, sometimes attaining the form of a tree, with relatively small, leathery leaves. Like all representatives of the pea family (*Leguminosae*), it produces large, pulpy seed pods. The extensive root system in older plants may have a 100-foot circumference and penetrate to a depth of 50 feet.

Figure 6–13 Mesquite covers millions of acres of southern Great Plains rangeland. [U.S. Department of Agriculture]

Of all woody plant invaders of the Southwestern grasslands, mesquite ranks first in terms of distribution, abundance, and aggressive encroachment of rangeland pastures (23). Many plant ecologists believe that for millenia mesquite invasion was prevented by periodic grassland fires probably ignited by lightning strikes or by Plains Indians (as an aid in hunting). Even though grasses were consumed in the conflagration along with mesquite, many grasses can mature and produce seeds within two years, whereas mesquite requires a longer period. As a result of this time differential for maturation and reproduction, were there recurrent fires at intervals of, say, two years, the mesquite would be at a reproductive disadvantage and, therefore, would be prevented from spreading (12). Ecologists also believe that prior to the introduction of domestic grazers, the vigorously growing climax vegetation of the grassland biome, with the aid of deep fibrous root systems, was able to compete successfully with mesquite for sunlight and limited soil moisture. However, when the white man drove off the Indians, introduced cattle and sheep by the millions, and instituted new methods of fire control, the two main factors responsible for confining mesquite were no longer operative (26). The frequently overstocked range herds caused serious pasture deterioration. The deeply and extensively rooted climax species declined and were replaced by increasers, which in turn were replaced by invaders with shallow, simple taproots that were competitively inferior to mesquite (30). The mesquite invasion was facilitated by a curious mutualistic relationship with cattle. The late-summer-maturing mesquite pods, some up to 8 inches long, provide cattle with nutritious food (23). After digesting the pulp, cattle eventually void the seeds with their excrement, frequently a considerable distance from the parent plant. The seeds, still viable and well fertilized, show a surprisingly high germination success (12). Kangaroo rats also play a role. They often facilitate mesquite dispersion when they permit forgotten mesquite seed caches to germinate (26). By such means, the mesquite encroachment has been facilitated until this thorny invader has blighted 50 million acres of Texas prairie alone.

Methods of Control. Mesquite, like other woody, shrubby invaders of the rangeland community, may be controlled more or less successfully by fire, mechanical devices, and chemicals.

FIRE. Dense, mature mesquite stands can be controlled to some degree by flame torches, thus duplicating in the twentieth century the natural type of control which operated for thousands of years before the white man restructured the arid grassland ecosystem. Major disadvantages of this method are that older trees tend to sprout vigorously from the upper branches after the fire (26) and that much valuable grass may be consumed along with the mesquite. Moreover, unless a very hot fire can be obtained sufficient to destroy the mesquite, burning will place the grasses at a competitive disadvantage and aggravate the problem.

GRUBBING AND PLOWING. Grubbing the plants out of the ground or plowing them up are effective control measures (30). However, this is extremely costly, up to $25 per acre (26); the ground is torn up and disturbed by the operation; it is necessary to repeat the operation periodically to remove new seedlings and sprouts; and in the case of plowing, the whole area must be carefully reseeded with nutritive forage grasses (26).

SODIUM ARSENITE. Sodium arsenite when ap-

Figure 6–14 Las Cruces, New Mexico. A spoonful of 25 per cent fenuron pellets will kill a medium-sized mesquite bush. This method, shown at the Jornada Experimental Range, is very effective on bush stands up to 70 per acre. [U.S. Department of Agriculture]

plied directly to a sawed-off stump or to the sapwood exposed by the removal of the bark may be very effective in destroying mesquite (26). Although rather expensive, experiments in Arizona showed that the increased weight gains of livestock feeding on the available food grasses, suddenly released from mesquite competition, may repay the original cost within ten years (19). However, the great toxicity of sodium arsenite to livestock, deer, antelope, elk, and man himself makes it imperative for the rancher to employ this chemical with extreme caution (26).

2, 4–D. The growth and development of plants is regulated by special chemicals called auxins, or growth hormones. The plant is very sensitive to the concentration of these hormones, and too little or too much of the hormone will result in arrested growth and even death. Within the last decade, biochemists have been able to synthesize compounds (2,4–D) (2,4,5–T) which duplicate the characteristics of growth hormones in broad-leafed plants but have no effect on narrow-leafed plants such as grasses. When these chemicals are sprayed in sufficient concentrations on mesquite foliage, "top kills" are easily accomplished. Aerial spraying, being one third as costly as ground spraying, is the method of choice (26).

POISONOUS PLANTS. Each year death from plant poisoning claims 4 per cent of all livestock grazing in our Western ranges. In some years one out of every seven Wyoming sheep die from this cause. At Harper, Oregon, 1,000 out of 1,700 sheep died from greasewood poisoning in 1930. There are over 400 plant species in the United States that are poisonous to livestock.

Because most poisonous plants do not occur in the climax community but have rather the status of "weedy invaders," control can largely be effected simply by the prevention of overgrazing. Moreover, because most poisonous plants are unpalatable to livestock, they normally will be avoided unless they are the only plants available to half-starved animals. Although only 2 ounces of water hemlock root will kill a sheep and only 8 ounces will destroy a cow, most poisonous plants are quite harmless unless large quantities have been ingested.

The white loco and its close relatives (the purple loco and blue loco) are lethal to great numbers of range animals annually. Because they are extremely abundant, widely distributed, and lethal to all range livestock, including horses, cattle, sheep, and goats, some authorities consider them the most destructive of all poisonous plants. Curiously, the white loco is a member of the pea family, Leguminosae, which also includes some of the rancher's most beneficial species, the nitrogen-fixing alfalfa and clover. The white loco, which may bear either white or red flowers, ranges from western Minnesota to Montana in the north, to Arizona and Mexico in the south.

Seriously poisoned animals get the "blind staggers," characterized by loss of weight, erratic gait, inability to see clearly, weakness, extreme nervousness, and crazed behavior. (*Loco* is Spanish for *crazy*.)

Apparently the toxic effects are caused by the element *selenium*, which frequently occurs in the tissues of the locoweed in high concentrations. In fact, the plant is dependent on selenium for maximal growth, so that it may be used as an indicator of selenium-bearing soils. Selenium is distributed widely in the shales of many Western states. South Dakota and Arizona have relatively high concentrations. Even if soil concentrations are negligible, the locoweed can absorb enough to build up high concentrations. In one study one species of loco growing in topsoil having a selenium content of only 20.4 parts per million was able to build up a selenium concentration of 2,590 parts per million in its tissues, a 125-fold increase. In another study *Astragalus bisulcatus* had 4,300 ppm of selenium in its tissues, whereas fifty plants of *Andropogon scoparius* (little bluestem) growing in the same general region averaged only 0.8 parts per million.

Most livestock tend to shun locoweed and other selenium-bearing plants, possibly because of their characteristic garlic-like smell. Therefore, if the range is kept in good condition, locoweed poisoning will be reduced to a minimum.

Animal Pests. Within the rangeland community a number of herbivorous animals such as grasshoppers, jack rabbits, and prairie dogs compete intensively with livestock for forage.

GRASSHOPPERS. Of the 142 species of grasshoppers collected in Western range vegetation, the most destructive and widely distributed are the lesser migratory grasshoppers. During periods of peak abundance they may gather in swarms and migrate several hundred miles. For several years of cool, wet weather, the grasshopper populations may remain small, so that the rancher may barely be aware of their presence. Then comes the year of severe drought, with perhaps only 5 inches instead of the usual 15 inches of rainfall. With environmental factors now at the optimum of the grasshoppers' tolerance range, the populations rapidly increase until it is almost impossible to take a single step through a grama grass pasture without flushing several of them. During a peak year, grasshoppers may so deplete forage that livestock either must move to other pastures or starve. The havoc wrought by hordes of grasshoppers has been eloquently recorded in the Bible (Joel 2:3): "The land is as the Garden of Eden before them, and behind them a desolate wilderness, yea, and nothing shall escape them."

During the drought year of 1937, grasshoppers inflicted an aggregate forage damage of about $66 million in twenty-four states. Morton estimated that in 1936 there were roughly twenty-five grasshoppers per square meter in his Montana rangeland study area and that they consumed or destroyed 67 per cent of the total forage production. He estimated that 3 acres of grasshoppers consumed as much forage as one cow. Infestations may reach three times the density he recorded. J. R. Parker, of the U.S. Department of Agriculture, has estimated that one large adult grasshopper consumes 30 milligrams of vegetation (dry weight) daily, as compared to the cow's daily requirement of 20 pounds. In other words 301,395 "hoppers" would eat as much as one cow (16).

One interesting facet of the grasshopper-rangeland relationship is that these insects are much more populous in overgrazed ranges than in moderately grazed fields. A study in southern Arizona revealed that the insect order Orthoptera (largely represented by grasshoppers) had a population of 180,000 per acre on overgrazed lands compared to only 20,000 per acre on range in average condition—a 9:1 population differential. It may be, therefore, that an effective method of controlling grasshopper plagues is to ensure that the range is not being subjected to excessive grazing pressure.

Investigators for the U.S. Department of Agriculture are continuously searching for an effective biological method of grasshopper control. Thus in 1949 two species of predatory flies belonging to the family Nemistrinidae were discovered in Montana (13). Female flies may lay eggs in crevices of tree trunks or in fence post fissures at the rate of roughly one per second over a fifteen-minute period, until a total of 1,000 have been deposited. Within about ten days, tiny wormlike maggots emerge from the eggs, are borne aloft and whisked away by the wind for a considerable distance, and eventually are dropped among the range grasses. When a squirming maggot comes into contact with a grasshopper, the parasite burrows its way into the host and feeds on its soft, living tissues until the grasshopper succumbs. In some foci of grasshopper infestation, up to 80 per cent of a single species have been victims of predation by nemestrinid flies. Because the female predators are such efficient egg producers and because the minute eggs can be easily transported to regions of grasshopper infestations, nemestrinid flies may someday serve as agents of biological control.

JACK RABBITS.   Under conditions of excessive drought jack rabbits seriously compete with cattle and sheep for high quality forage. On the basis of stomach analyses and appraisal of fenced quadrats, seventy-five antelope jack rabbits consume as much forage as one cow, and fifteen eat enough food to sustain one sheep. During their investigation researchers estimated that the jack rabbit population numbered 7,500 animals on 50,000 acres, or a density of one jack rabbit per seven acres. The aggregate weight of the rabbits was roughly 7 per cent that of the cattle with which they were competing. They concluded that the dense rabbit population was a major *limiting factor* in keeping the rangeland plant community at a low or retrogressive successional stage. The overall effect of the heavy grazing pressure was to prevent re-establishment of highly nutritious decreaser species and to favor intrusion by low-value increasers, as well as invaders such as mesquite, cacti, and weeds.

PRAIRIE DOGS.   In his excellent paper "Rodents, Rabbits and Grasslands," Dr. E. R. Kalmbach, former biologist of the U.S. Fish and Wildlife Service, summarized the major ecological and economic effects of rabbits and pests on the Western range (13). He reported on one four-year study in Arizona where it was found that the Zuni prairie dog consumed 69 per cent of the total annual production of wheatgrass, 83 per cent of the blue grama, and 99 per cent of the dropseed. Of an aggregate 2,252 pounds per acre of these valuable forage species, 1,819 pounds per acre (80 per cent) were consumed by prairie dogs. Moreover, it was found that the food habits of prairie dogs and cattle are virtually identical; any plants consumed by prairie dogs will also be eaten by cattle, and these forage species are eaten in the same sequence of preference. Sometimes, because of their colonial behavior, prairie dogs will completely overgraze their residential pastures and will be forced to emigrate to new food sources or starve.

In the early nineteenth century prairie dog "towns" covered millions of acres. The range of the black-tailed prairie dog alone extended in a broad band from northern Montana and North Dakota south to Texas and New Mexico. Ranchers, however, soon recognized its potential as a serious forage competitor with cattle. After relentless persecution, by trapping, shooting, and poisoning, this interesting little creature has been almost completely eradicated. Only on wildlife preserves are they found in any numbers today.

KANGAROO RATS.   The intriguing pocket-sized kangaroo

rat of the southwestern United States digs extensive burrow systems. During nocturnal foraging, it stuffs its cheek pouches with seeds and deposits them in its burrow, to be utilized later during food scarcity. In one study an average of 3.7 pounds of plant material was discovered in each of twenty-four burrows examined. With a kangaroo rat density of two per acre, this would mean a per acre decrement of 7.4 pounds of forage. In addition, many forage plants suffer from retarded growth because of foliage depredations by kangaroo rats too early in the growing season. These rodents may also be effective passive dispersal agents of undesirable "invader" species such as mesquite. This occurs when caches of mesquite seeds in underground burrows are forgotten and later germinate.

Pest Control

NATURAL CONTROL. Under natural conditions rodent populations are controlled primarily by density-dependent regulative factors such as predation and disease.

Predation. Populations of many rodents fluctuate sharply. Thus, kangaroo rat counts per roadway mile in California ranged from a high of seventy-five in autumn (1936) to a low of two the ensuing spring. When rodent populations peak, heavy losses are inflicted by natural predators such as hawks, owls, badgers, skunks, and snakes. It may be that disease and marginal food supplies render rodents more vulnerable under these conditions.

Disease. Microscopic disease organisms may be just as effective controllers of high-density rodent populations as predatory hawks or snakes. Susceptibility of rodents to disease parasites frequently is directly correlated with the density of the rodent population. It may be that when ranchers attempt to control rodents with poison, they unwittingly increase their ability to survive disease epidemics which might have operated much more efficiently and with less expense.

CONTROL BY RANGE MANAGEMENT. In addition to control by natural agents, pest populations may be reduced by poisoning, trapping, rounding-up, and proper stocking of the range.

Poisoning. One extensively used method of controlling rodents is to place strychnine-poisoned grain near burrow entrances. Jack rabbits may be effectively poisoned in winter when their usual food sources are covered with snow and ice. Under such conditions jack rabbits have been known to travel at least a mile for food.

Roundups. In winter jack rabbits frequently congregate in protected areas where food and shelter are available. At this time dozens of control-conscious ranchers may cooperate in a large-scale roundup yielding several thousand dead rabbits in one day.

Proper Stocking. The rangeland pest, whether grasshopper, jack rabbit, prairie dog, or kangaroo rat, becomes a serious problem only during population peaks, and these peaks usually coincide with rangeland deterioration. It should be emphasized that these pests do not *cause* the initial depletion of pasture. The high pest populations represent *symptoms* rather than causal factors of range deterioration. Kalmbach has compared range abuse to a wound (13). The "wound" was initially inflicted by excessive stocking, and the ensuing rodent build-up merely served to irritate the wound and prevent it from healing properly. Just why a range in good condition (well-stocked with climax plants) should be unsuitable habitat for certain rabbits and rodents has never been fully explained. It may be that the tall vegetation obstructs the vision of these relatively defenseless animals and makes them more vulnerable to predation. In any event most rangeland experts agree that shooting, trapping, and poisoning campaigns are really only stopgap procedures; the best long-term solution to the pest problem seems to be simply a four-strand barbed-wire fence—for keeping excess cattle off the deteriorating range.

Case of the Peccary. The javelina or collared peccary is a favorite game animal among many sportsmen of the Southwest. Up to 4,000 of these snorting rooters of the desert shrub community are taken in a single year. Although their range in the United States is restricted to Texas, southern New Mexico, and southern Arizona, they range southward through Mexico into South America. Because this herbivorous "wild pig" occupies marginal rangeland, on which harassed ranchers strive to support a few head of livestock, it has long been regarded with a jaundiced eye. In years past ranchers have shot these creatures on sight. Because the peccary is gregarious, the kill in certain areas has been high. Concerned by this persecution of an intriguing game animal, wildlife biologists have made thorough studies of its feeding habits. Their findings have completely exonerated the peccary. Neal in Arizona, for example, found that 84.5 per cent of stomach contents analyzed consisted of the roots, stems, and fruit of the relatively worthless prickly pear cactus, whereas nutritive range grasses, preferred by livestock, formed an insignificant 8.6 per cent of the diet. According to Humphrey,

Figure 6–15 Coronado National Forest, Arizona. A peccary shown in its natural habitat. Note gravel pavement of desert floor and the cactus in the background. [U.S. Department of Agriculture]

moreover, it may well be that the peccary has been instrumental in *improving* range condition rather than causing its deterioration (12). In rooting up fleshy weed plants, it not only makes room for preferred grasses but also by stirring the soil unwittingly prepares their seedbed. The case of the javelina points up the need for a critical study of all aspects of an ecological problem before taking impulsive action which may be poorly conceived.

The Predator Problem. Livestock losses of over $1 million are annually inflicted by a variety of livestock predators such as coyotes, cougars, bobcats and bear. Through millenia of pre-Columbian time, there existed large herds of herbivores, such as buffalo, elk, and bison, which satiated the appetites of grassland carnivores. (The cougar is capable of killing ten to twenty deer monthly.) Beginning with the sixteenth-century introductions of Spanish livestock, however, the wild grazers were partially replaced with man's domesticated variety—cattle, sheep, and goats. The native grazers declined in numbers or were displaced westward to semimountainous wilderness retreats. The carnivores persisted, however, (much to the ranchers' vexation), finding domesticated herbivores fully as savory and nutritious, and probably somewhat more vulnerable, than the wild grazers.

Of all rangeland predators, the coyote perhaps poses the most serious problem. This wily, resourceful brush wolf has become a romantic symbol of the Western plains—and a thorn in the side of the rancher. Where the coyote has become numerous, sheep ranchers have waged all-out extermination campaigns— poisoning, trapping, shooting, even pursuing the animal and killing it in its own den. When a rancher destroys a coyote that has been killing, say, ten sheep a year, simple arithmetic might suggest that this rancher will be ten sheep richer each year thereafter. However, it is not quite that simple. For one thing, the coyote feeds on other animals besides sheep. Thus a study of coyote feeding habits revealed livestock (actually killed by coyotes) formed only 14 per cent (by volume) of its diet as compared to the 49.5 per cent represented by range-grass-consuming rabbits and rodents. It is apparent, therefore, that the value of the few sheep saved by destroying a coyote may be considerably less than the value of forage consumed by rodents and rabbits which the coyote would have removed from the rangeland community.

BIBLIOGRAPHY

1. Allen, Shirley W., and Justin W. Leonard. *Conserving Natural Resources.* New York: McGraw-Hill Book Co., 1966, 432 pp.
2. Bennett, John B., F. R. Kenney, and W. R. Chapline. "The Problem: Sub-Humid Areas," *Soils and Men: The Yearbook of Agriculture.* Washington, D.C.: U.S. Department of Agriculture, 1938, 68–76.
3. Carter, Goodrich, Bushrod W. Allin, and C. Warren Thornthwaite. *Migration and Economic Opportunity: The Report of the Study of Population Redistribution.* Philadelphia: University of Pennsylvania Press, 1936, 763 pp.
4. Chapline, W. R. "Grazing on Rangelands," *Grass: The Yearbook of Agriculture.* Washington, D.C.: U.S. Department of Agriculture, 1948, 212–216.
5. _____ and C. K. Cooperrider. "Climate and Grazing," *Climate and Man: The Yearbook of Agriculture.* Washington, D.C.: U.S. Department of Agriculture, 1941, 459–476.
6. Corner, E. J. H. *The Life of Plants.* Cleveland: The World Publishing Co., 1964.
7. Coulter, Merle C., and Howard J. Dittmer. *The Story of the Plant Kingdom.* Chicago: The University of Chicago Press, 1964.
8. Dasmann, Raymond F. *Environmental Conservation.* New York: John Wiley & Sons, 1959, 307 pp.
9. Edwards, Everett E. "The Settlement of Grasslands," *Grass: The Yearbook of Agriculture.* Washington, D.C.: U.S. Department of Agriculture, 1948, 16–25.
10. *Encyclopaedia Brittanica,* Vol. 5. Chicago: William Benton, Publisher, 1968.

11. Fabrizius, Peter. "Grass: Nature's Richest Storehouse," *Science Digest,* **32** (1952), 1–4.
12. Humphrey, Robert R. *Range Ecology.* New York: The Ronald Press Co., 1962.
13. Kalmbach, E. R. "Rodents, Rabbits and Grasslands," *Grass: The Yearbook of Agriculture.* Washington, D.C.: U.S. Department of Agriculture, 1948.
14. Milne, Lorus J., and Margery Milne. *Plant Life.* Englewood Cliffs, N.J.: Prentice-Hall, Inc., 1959.
15. Northen, Henry T. *Introductory Plant Science.* New York: The Ronald Press Co., 1953, 601 pp.
16. Parker, J. R. "Grasshoppers," *Insects: The Yearbook of Agriculture.* Washington. D.C.: U.S. Department of Agriculture, 1952, 595–605.
17. Parson, Ruben L. *Conserving American Resources.* Englewood Cliffs, N.J.: Prentice-Hall, Inc., 1956, 550 pp.
18. Pearse, C. Kenneth, A. Perry Plummer, and D. A. Savage. "Restoring the Range by Reseeding," *Grass: The Yearbook of Agriculture.* Washington, D.C.: U.S. Department of Agriculture, 1948, 227–233.
19. Pechanek, Joseph F., Charles E. Fisher, and Kenneth W. Parker. "How to Control Noxious Plants," *Grass: The Yearbook of Agriculture.* Washington, D.C.: U.S. Department of Agriculture, 1948, 256–260.
20. Platt, Rutherford. *This Green World.* New York: Dodd, Mead, 1943.
21. Price, Raymond, Kenneth W. Parker, and A. C. Hull, Jr. "The Foundation of the Range," *Grass: The Yearbook of Agriculture.* Washington, D.C.: U.S. Department of Agriculture, 1948 553–556.
22. Renner, F. G., and B. W. Allred. *Classifying Rangeland for Conservation Planning, Agriculture Handbook No. 235.* Washington, D.C.: Soil Conservation Service, 1962.
23. Sampson, Arthur W. *Range Management.* New York: John Wiley & Sons, Inc., 1952.
24. Smith, Guy-Harold (ed.). *Conservation of Natural Resources.* New York: John Wiley & Sons, Inc., 1958, 474 pp
25. Stewart, George. "History of Range Use," *The Western Range.* Senate Document No. 199. Washington, D.C., 1936, 119–133.
26. Stoddard, L. A., and A. D. Smith. *Range Management.* New York: McGraw-Hill Book Co., 1955.
27. U.S. Department of Agriculture. *Agricultural Statistics.* Washingtion, D.C.: U.S. Department of Agriculture, 1965.
28. U.S. Forest Service. *The National Grasslands Story.* Washington, D.C.: U.S. Forest Service. 1964.
29. Weaver, J. E. *North American Prairie.* Lincoln, Neb.: Johnsen Publishing Co., 1954.
30. _____ and F. W. Albertson. *Grasslands of the Great Plains.* Lincoln, Neb.: Johnsen Publishing Co., 1956.

Forest Resource

7

Value of Forest Resource

The forest resource is valuable as a refuge of wildlife, for commerce, and for recreation.

Wildlife. In addition to their beauty, our forests provide "board and room" for many forms of wildlife. It is in the forest that herbivores find sustenance and there that predatory carnivores search for prey. In the forest interior wildlife find refuge from the elements, store food supplies, and breed.

Commercial Value. From early colonial days, when the straight, sturdy trunks of New England spruce and pine were fashioned into masts for the Royal Navy, until today, fully three centuries later, American forests have been the source of a variety of products useful to man. Today our forests provide the raw materials for over 5,000 products worth $23 billion annually (3). They support an industry which employs 1.3 million people and has an annual payroll of over $6 billion.

To help maintain the world's highest standard of living America uses more wood per capita than any nation on earth. Each year, every man, woman, and child in the United

221

Figure 7–1 Gun stocks, samples of veneer, and other products derived from walnut. [Forest Service, U.S. Department of Agriculture]

States uses about 204 board feet* of lumber. (Much of this is imported from Scandinavia and Canada.) In 1962 Americans used 37.3 billion board feet, enough to build 3.5 million six-room cottages, or build a 4-foot-wide boardwalk long enough to bridge the distance to the moon at least seventy times. Americans eat, sleep, work, and play in a world of wood. Whether it be tooth picks, telephone poles, photographic film, maple syrup, acetic acid, or cellophane, Americans depend heavily on wood and wood-derived products. Each year Americans use over 0.5 million barrels of turpentine to thin their paints, over 30 million railroad ties to cushion their trains, over 200 million fence posts to fence their lands. Each year, well-fed Americans use over 232,000 tons of napkins, buy over 1 million tons of paper bags, use 2 million tons of newsprint, and purchase 2 million tons of writing paper.

* A board foot is a unit of measurement used in the lumbering industry to refer to a volume of wood 1 foot square and 1 inch thick.

Recreation. Our forests provide sanctuary from the bustle of the modern city. The crowding which characterizes life in the big metropolitan areas of America makes it urgent to escape periodically to the country for the quiet and beauty which can only be found there.

The Tree: A Living Organism

To develop a better appreciation of the importance of our forest resource, the operation of destructive environmental factors, and how the forest can most effectively be managed, we shall briefly examine the anatomy and physiology of a tree.

Roots. Roots have three major functions: anchorage, absorption, and food storage.

ANCHORAGE. The root system of a tree is much more elaborate than most people realize; it forms a complex branching and rebranching arrangement of "living cables" adapted for holding the tree firmly in the soil. An oak tree 37 feet high may have a root system which thrusts downward with rock-splitting

Figure 7–2 "Mountain" of pulp logs at a pulp mill in New York. [New York State Conservation Department]

force to a depth of 14 feet, and may extend radially 60 feet from the base. The roots of a large mesquite, representative of arid soil, penetrate downward to a depth of 75 feet for precious water. On the other hand, hemlock and tamarack, found in coniferous forests, are notoriously shallow rooted. Some authorities believe that the valuable stands of even-aged white pine, which were highly prized by the nineteenth-century lumber industry and which extended from New England west to Minnesota, became established as a subclimax stage after the climax spruce and firs were uprooted by an extensive hurricane.

ABSORPTION. In an earlier section we mentioned that a tiny rye plant only 20 inches high may have a water-absorbing system composed of 14 million root hairs. No one has ever been able to uproot a living 100-foot-tall Douglas fir to count its root hairs, but Platt has suggested that, end to end, they might extend around the globe at the equator. It is through these root hairs that the tree absorbs water, oxygen, and soil nutrients such as nitrate and phosphate salts. The tree's roots may have to absorb 200 pounds of water for every pound of sugar photosynthesized in the canopy.

FOOD STORAGE. Most roots serve as storehouses for surplus foods transferred from the canopy. During periods of stress, when photosynthesis is reduced by drought, cold, or leaf consuming insects (such as gypsy moth larvae and spruce bud worms), the energy-rich starches held in the roots are converted into soluble sugars and transported upward through the trunk to food-deficient organs.

Trunk. The tree trunk is the most valuable tree part to the forest industry. It is primarily from the trunk that wood for construction materials, furniture, plywood, and paper pulp is derived. Proper forest management requires knowledge of the architecture and design of a trunk, its functional organization, the manner and rate of growth, and many other characteristics. (Reference to Figure 7–3 will be helpful in the following discussion.)

OUTER BARK. The outer bark, or "cork," of the tree is composed of dead cells with greatly thickened walls which have become impregnated with waterproofing materials. As the tree trunk grows in diameter, the pressure generated by the trunk's interior causes the bark to break up into a pattern of ridges, scales, or plates which is species characteristic (14). One can often identify the species simply by an examination of the bark's texture, surface pattern, and color. Thus, in the mature shag bark hickory (*Carya ovata*), long, shaggy dark patches tend

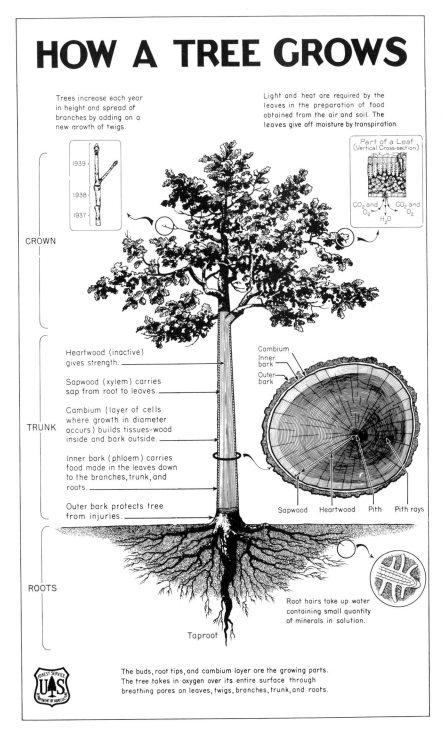

HOW A TREE GROWS

Trees increase each year in height and spread of branches by adding on a new growth of twigs.

Light and heat are required by the leaves in the preparation of food obtained from the air and soil. The leaves give off moisture by transpiration.

1939
1938
1937

Part of a Leaf
(Vertical Cross-section)

CO_2 and O_2 CO_2 and O_2
H_2O

CROWN

Heartwood (inactive) gives strength.

Sapwood (xylem) carries sap from root to leaves.

Cambium (layer of cells where growth in diameter occurs) builds tissues-wood inside and bark outside.

Inner bark (phloem) carries food made in the leaves down to the branches, trunk, and roots.

Outer bark protects tree from injuries.

TRUNK

Cambium
Inner bark
Outer bark

Sapwood   Heartwood   Pith   Pith rays

ROOTS

Root hairs take up water containing small quantity of minerals in solution.

Taproot

The buds, root tips, and cambium layer are the growing parts. The tree takes in oxygen over its entire surface through breathing pores on leaves, twigs, branches, trunk, and roots.

Figure 7–3 The biology of a tree. [U.S. Forest Service]

225

to slough off; in the paper birch (*Betula papyrifera*), on the other hand, the attractive cream-white bark tends to peel off in thin paperlike layers—a characteristic exploited by the Indian in fashioning birch-bark canoes. In addition to "locking" moisture inside the trunk, the outer bark serves as the tree's first line of defense against wood-boring insects, fungous growths, fire, and herbivorous vertebrates, such as rodents, rabbits, and deer (11).

INNER BARK, OR PHLOEM. Just inside the outer bark is a thin sheath of bark composed of elongate *phloem* cells. Arranged end to end in long vertical columns, these cells form pipe lines for the rapid transport of sugar, photosynthesized by the leaves, downward to the roots, either for immediate use or for storage. When their usual food supplies are covered with snow, such herbivorous animals as mice or rabbits may girdle a tree by removing a section of phloem and outer bark all the way around the trunk. Because this effectively cuts off food supplies to the roots, the tree's death is inevitable.

CAMBIUM. The cambium is a delicate sheath of embryonic cells occurring just inside the phloem. These cells continue to reproduce throughout the life of the tree; cells displaced to the outside of the cambium differentiate into phloem, and those forming on the inner cambial surface transform into xylem cells (11). Growth in thickness of the trunk from seedling to patriarch is dependent exclusively on cambial activity.

WOOD. The xylem cells that are continuously proliferated from the cambium may appear in the form of relatively long cylindrical *vessel elements* or as much shorter *tracheids*, which taper at either end. Wood from deciduous trees may have either vessel elements or tracheids; in coniferous woods the vessel elements are lacking (11). Ultimately the vessel elements and tracheids die, lose their protoplasm, and become water-conducting "pipes." Up to 900 gallons of water may be conducted through the xylem of a large oak daily. Because of their thick, rigid walls, the xylem cells form the "skeleton" of the tree, firmly supporting the combined weight of branches, twigs, leaves, flowers, and seeds. Because the woods of most deciduous trees are hard and dense, they are commonly called *hardwoods*. Most coniferous woods, which are relatively soft and porous and which yield much more readily to the saw, are popularly known as *softwoods*. However, these classes are not mutually exclusive, for some "softwood" species, such as hemlock, actually have harder wood than such "hardwood" species as basswood and poplar.

Perhaps you have cut down a tree in your backyard and have examined the stump's cross section. The wood is readily distinguishable into a darker, drier, more dense central core, known as the *heartwood,* and a lighter, moist, more porous layer immediately ensheating it, known as the *sapwood.* Sapwood is composed of dead, hollow xylem cells that actively transport water and soil nutrients. As they get older, these "pipe" cells gradually become so clogged with gums and resins they they lose their conducting function; they then become part of the heartwood. In some species the striking color of the heartwood (as in the case of black walnut, red cedar, and redwood) adds greatly to its value. The heartwood of an overmature tree frequently becomes vulnerable to heart-rot fungus. Such trees quickly become hollow and are completely valueless to the forest industry. On the other hand, such stubs frequently make good breeding dens for opossums, flying squirrels, and raccoons, as well as suitable nesting cavities for owls and woodpeckers; thus, they serve to increase the forest's capacity for wildlife.

AGE DETERMINATION. Xylem cells formed by the cambium during seasons when adequate moisture is available are relatively large in diameter and have thin walls. On the other hand, the xylem formed without adequate moisture usually are small in diameter and have thick walls. In the north temperate zone of the United States, where a wet period alternates with a dry period, the wood is laid down in the form of easily distinguishable concentric *annular* rings. A forester may quite accurately determine the tree's age by counting these rings. However, instead of felling a tree and examining the stump, he uses a device called an increment borer, by means of which he can withdraw a core sample from the trunk (11). With this technique tree longevity may be determined. Birches are old at forty, maples at fifty to seventy-five; but oaks, hickories, and walnuts may live 200 to 300 years. Conifers usually live longer than hardwoods, because their resins render them more resistant to insect and fungus attacks. Some specimens of Douglas fir, ponderosa pine, and Western hemlock along the Pacific Coast are 500 to 1,000 years old. Some California redwoods are more than 3,000 years old. Three bristle cone pines (*Pinus aristata*) growing in the White Mountains along the southern California–Nevada border germinated from seeds produced over 4,000 years ago. They are the oldest living organisms known to science.

Any marked variation in the width of the annular rings may reflect abnormal environmental conditions. Thus, extremely narrow rings may suggest to the forester that the tree's growth

Figure 7–4 Cross-section of a pine trunk. Note the annular rings. [U.S. Department of Agriculture]

Figure 7–5 Large redwoods in Del Norte State Park, California. Interesting light patterns are created by sunlight filtering through dense fog. [U.S. Forest Service]

Figure 7–6 Inyo National Forest, California. This picturesque old bristle-cone pine, locally referred to as "The Old Ranger," still stands despite the harsh environment. Some bristlecone pines are over 4,000 years old. [U.S. Forest Service]

was severely limited during that particular year because of drought, insect attacks, or parasitic fungi. It could also mean that growth was impaired because of intensive competition for sun, moisture, and soil nutrients. Variations in the width of annual rings in ancient redwoods have enabled experts to reconstruct patterns of West Coast climate dating back to 1000 B.C.

Leaves. The anatomy and function of a tree leaf was described in the section on photosynthesis in Chapter 2.

Reproductive Organs in Deciduous Trees. The sexual organs of a tree are found in the flower. In deciduous trees such as the apple, cherry, tulip, catalpa, and magnolia, these flowers may be large and brightly colored, whereas in the elm, willow, cottonwood, birch, and maple they are much reduced in size and inconspicuous. The fragrance and bright colors of the large flowers serve to attract insects which inadvertently become dusted with mature pollen grains during their feeding activities. When such insects fly to another flower these pollen grains may accidentally be transferred to the sticky surface of a pistil, thus effecting pollination. Species with minute, drably colored flowers (such as the willow, aspen, and birch) are usually pollinated by wind or falling rain. The pollen grain eventually develops a pollen tube, which grows down the neck of the pistil toward the ovary, which houses the eggs. After the tip of the pollen tube has dissolved a "sperm" moves through the open end of the tube to unite with an egg and effect fertilization. Eventually the fertilized egg develops into a *seed*. A seed may be defined as the embryo, together with a supply of stored food, which is enclosed by a protective wall or seed coat. The coat protects the embryo against dessication, insects and fungal parasites. Seeds vary in weight from forty per pound in the black walnut (*Juglans nigra*) to 414,000 per pound in the Western red cedar (*Thuja plicata*). Large, heavy seeds may be disseminated by squirrels, birds, or other animals. A robin may digest the pulp of a cherry and then void the pit several miles from the parent tree. Frequently such voided seeds show better germination success than seeds which have not been so "processed." Cottonwood seeds are provided with cottony tufts which facilitate wind transport. Maple seeds are provided with "blades"

Figure 7–7 Staminate and pistillate flowers of the Allegheny chinkapin growing at Silver Springs, Maryland. [U.S. Department of Agriculture]

and revolve like minature propellers as they drop to earth. By such agents of dispersal competition among seedlings for moisture, sunlight, and soil nutrients is reduced to a minimum. Sunlight intensity plays an important role in seedling survival. Climax species, such as sugar maples and basswood, can grow well in shade and are said to be *shade tolerant*. On the other hand, the white oaks, willow, white birch, and quaking aspen, all subclimax species, develop best in full light and die in dense shade. These species are said to be intolerant to shade. We shall see that the cutting method used by the logger depends in part upon whether he proposes to harvest tolerant or intolerant timber species.

Reproductive Organs of Coniferous Trees. The United States derives 75 per cent of its paper pulp from coniferous trees, of which there are 570 species in the world (14). In conifers, flowers are extremely minute and are enclosed between the scales of cones. Unlike flowers of most deciduous trees, which are bi-

Figure 7–8 Staminate flowers of the Eastern white pine. [U.S. Department of Agriculture]

sexual, the flowers produced by conifers are either pollen-producing male flowers or egg-producing female flowers. The pollen cones are usually much smaller than the seed cones. The latter may vary in length from the ½-inch cone of the jack pine to the 20-inch cone of the sugar pine.

In spring and early summer millions of tiny dustlike pollen grains are dispersed by the wind for a distance of a few feet to several miles. Were these pollen grains to fall on concrete highways, rocky outcrops, rooftops, or lakes and streams, they would perish; a very small percentage, however, come to rest, purely by chance, on the female cone of the same tree, or another tree of the same species and thus ultimately effect fertilization and the generation of a winged pineseed. In most pines two years are required for the seed cone to mature. When maturity is attained, at the end of the second summer (11), the scales (which protected the seed during development) open up, releasing large quantities of dry, light seeds, which may be dispersed by wind, such seed-eating birds as grosbeaks and siskins, or even woodland mice and squirrels. Many species of wildlife are dependent upon pine seeds for food. They form almost 70 per cent of the red cross bill's (*Loxia curvirostra*) diet.

Figure 7–9   Leaves and cone of the long-leaf pine collected at Gainesville, Florida. [U.S. Forest Service]

Even the American Indian of the Southwest supplemented his diet with the nutritious and highly edible seeds of the pinyon pine (*Pinus edulis*).

The seed cones of jack pine (*Pinus banksiana*) occasionally may remain tightly closed for several years with the mature, viable seeds within. However, when these cones are heated by a forest fire they open wide releasing seeds in much greater numbers than usual. A recent study in Minnesota has shown that 15,000 jack pine seedlings had sprung up in the ashes of a fire which had warmed the seed cones of only six mature trees. Usually considered highly destructive, fire may actually favor reproduction in the jack pine and other conifers.

History of Exploitation

The Colonist and the Forest. When the first white man arrived in America dense forests covered half the land (3), an area of 950 million acres (7), equivalent to all of Norway, Sweden, Italy, Germany, Spain, and France put together. This forest extended westward to the Appalachian summit and beyond into the uncharted wilderness of mid-America. Historians will never learn the name of the settler whose ax sent the first ill-fated tree crashing earthward, nor will they identify the species of tree, or the place and time of the event. We do know, however, that the death of that first tree initiated the most ruthless and accelerated exploitation of a forest resource this earth has ever witnessed. (Fig. 7–10)

Not all of the timber was squandered. Colonists chopped down trees to provide logs for their cabins and firewood to burn. From the trees they fashioned handles for axes with which to chop down more trees. Showing great resourcefulness, they worked logs into tables and chairs, wagons, fence posts, and bowls. Many a turbulent Appalachian stream was bridged with timbers carved from the forest. Colonists erected wooden stockades around their tiny settlements to deter the savage. Much of the forest resource, however, was destroyed simply to get it out of the way (1). The woods had to be removed to make way for corn hills, squash, beans, pumpkins, and livestock pasture. Moreover, because hostile Indians lurked in the forest, security from attack was in some cases almost directly proportional to the distance between the forest edge and the cabin door. Gradually at first, then faster, the virgin forest yielded to ax and torch.

Depletion of the Softwoods. Early in colonial history the king's foresters reserved the tallest and straightest white pines

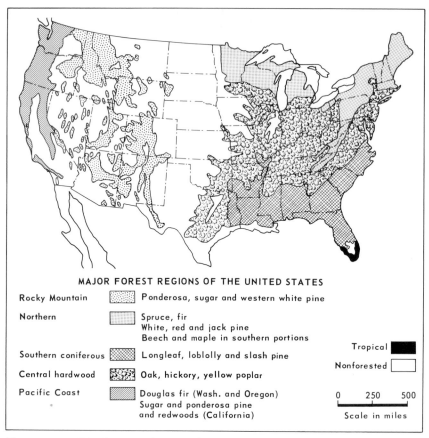

MAJOR FOREST REGIONS OF THE UNITED STATES

Rocky Mountain — Ponderosa, sugar and western white pine

Northern — Spruce, fir
White, red and jack pine
Beech and maple in southern portions

Southern coniferous — Longleaf, loblolly and slash pine

Central hardwood — Oak, hickory, yellow poplar

Pacific Coast — Douglas fir (Wash. and Oregon)
Sugar and ponderosa pine
and redwoods (California)

Tropical

Nonforested

0   250   500
Scale in miles

Figure 7–10 Distribution of major forest types in the United States. [Adapted from Richard M. Highsmith, J. Granville Jensen, and Robert D. Rudd, *Conservation in the United States* (Chicago: Rand McNally & Company, 1962).]

in New England for the British navy by marking them with a "broad arrow." For many decades the position of the British navy as the world's mightiest was in part dependent on its American source of white pine (3). After the Revolutionary War, American logging companies fed white pine into the boat-building industries dotting the north Atlantic coast from Portland to New Bedford. These early logging outfits probably never heard the word *conservation* or the phrase *sustained yield.* For these men a forest had no future, only a present and a past. Why should they worry about tomorrow? There would always be more timber, somewhere. So they "cut out and got out." In their haste, they wasted 25 per cent of the harvest. Many logs were floated downstream to sawmills. When jams formed, logs were blasted loose with dynamite—a crude technique which rendered large numbers of valuable logs worthless (13). During the "cut out" operations, branches, twigs, bark and other "slash" were left on the forest floor. After becoming tinder dry, this material occasionally became ignited and quickly blazed into a full-scale forest fire. The Peshtigo, Wisconsin fire of 1871, which started in this way, destroyed over 1 million acres of forest and claimed 1,500 lives (5).

By 1900 the pine stands of Minnesota and Wisconsin were so badly depleted, that the loggers again were forced to leave. They now split into two groups, one moving to the Pacific Northwest in quest of the Douglas fir, Western hemlock, Western red cedar, and redwood, the other moving to the South for the pines located there. Much of the Southern pine had become established as a stage in the ecological succession which followed the abandonment of soil-depleted tobacco and cotton farms. The lumber interests were so dedicated and efficient in their "cut outs" that by 1940 the once magnificent stands of long-leaf, short-leaf, loblolly, and slash pine were being reduced to remnants (3).

Figure 7-11 Extensive stands of white pine once occurred in Minnesota, Wisconsin, Michigan, and New York. These stumps were left after the last big white pine stand in Michigan was cut at DeWard, 1900–1908. A few of these huge stumps should be preserved. [U.S. Department of Agriculture]

Depletion of the Hardwoods.   As was mentioned, the extensive deciduous forest biome originally embraced a variety of communities ranging from the elm–maple–basswood stands of Minnesota and Wisconsin to the beech–maple forests of Michigan and Ohio, from the oak–chestnut mantling of the Appalachians to the oak–hickory groves of Indiana. Although of considerable potential value, these stands posed a difficult and frustrating harvesting problem to the commercial timber men. For the more desirable species, such as walnut and oak, frequently occurred in *mixed* stands, which included a number of relatively worthless "weed" species, quite unlike the uniform single-species stands of white pine in the North. Instead of being able to "clear-cut," much more laborious "hunt and pick" methods were required. These methods were too slow for ambitious men engaged in a head long "rush to riches." As a result, although commercial loggers did thin out many deciduous forests, and although many a cabinet was fashioned from black walnut, many a chestnut was converted into fence posts, and many a maple did find its way into a parlor floor, the impact of the commercial logger on our original hardwood stands was relatively slight.

Figure 7–12   Waupaca County, Wisconsin. Logging crew and sled load of pine logs. [1890–1910 (?)]. Note old-fashioned saw in center of picture. [State Historical Society of Wisconsin]

Figure 7–13 Train load of huge logs on way to California sawmill. [1910–1920(?)]. [U.S. Department of Agriculture]

Figure 7–14 Allegheny National Forest, Pennsylvania. A 120-acre stand of virgin forest was logged over in the late 1920's. Although the standing trees continue to grow, some of the overmature trees die and fall, so net growth in such stands is often zero. Eventually the fallen trees rot and contribute to the organic content of the soil. [U.S. Forest Service]

If not the lumberman, then what was the factor which reduced our virgin hardwoods to today's pathetic handful of wood lots? For farmers, road and dam builders, and enterprising industrialists, the deciduous forest formed a block to progress. It had to be removed. The retreat of this vast biome, which once extended from the Atlantic to the Mississippi, continues unabated to this day.

U.S. Forest Service

There are four federal bureaus that are charged with the administration and management of our nation's forested areas. They include the Soil Conservation Service, which is concerned with farm-management-associated forests; the Tennessee Valley Authority, charged with timberland management in the vicinity of the numerous dam–reservoir sites along the Tennessee River and its tributaries; and the Fish and Wildlife Service, which is interested in improving forest habitat for game and fish. However, the Forest Service, a bureau of the Department of Agriculture, has the primary responsibility of managing our nation's forests so as to promote "the greatest good for the most people" over the long run. Although the Service has headquarters in Washington, D.C., it is highly decentralized, with ten administrative regions, each of which embraces several states. (Thus, the North Central Region, based in Milwaukee, includes Ohio, Michigan, Indiana, Illinois, Iowa, Wisconsin, Minnesota, Missouri, and North Dakota.) A tropical forestry unit has headquarters in Rio Piedras, Puerto Rico.

The first Chief Forester was Gifford Pinchot, appointed by Theodore Roosevelt in 1905. Pinchot was a zealous crusader for resource conservation and infused the Service with a spirit that persists to this day (5). The Forest Service divides its attention now between three major areas: (1) administration and protection of the national forests; (2) research on forest, watershed, range, and recreation management; on wildlife habitat improvement; on forest product development; and on fire and pest control; and (3) cooperation with the state and private forest owners in the fifty states, Puerto Rico, and the Virgin Islands in promoting sound forest management.

The Forest Service protects and manages 154 national forests and grasslands embracing 182 million acres with 990 billion board feet of timber. Included under its supervision are the grazing lands of 6 million head of livestock and habitat for one third of America's big game animals. In a single year (1968) the Service has extinguished 9,731 fires. It annually grasses about 180,000 acres.

Figure 7–15 Theodore Roosevelt and Gifford Pinchot (to left of Roosevelt) standing at the base of a giant redwood called "Old Grizzly." [U.S. Department of Agriculture]

Forest Management

We shall now consider various aspects of forest management as practiced by the Forest Service, many state forestry departments, and an increasing number of enlightened private owners, with respect to: *sustained yield, block cutting, reforestation,* and *pest and fire control.*

Sustained Yield. Today's lumbermen are a different breed from the "cut-out-and-get-out" loggers of the late nineteenth and early twentieth centuries. After studying German silvicultural techniques, American foresters learned that a forest can be managed in such a way that a modest timber crop may be harvested indefinitely year after year without being depleted if annual decrements are counterbalanced by annual growth increments. This is called the *sustained-yield* concept. (Fig. 7–16)

Annual measurement of a timber crop is somewhat different from measurement of a crop of corn. The latter matures in a single growing season, whereas an aspen may require twenty years and a Douglas fir 100 years to attain a harvestable age.

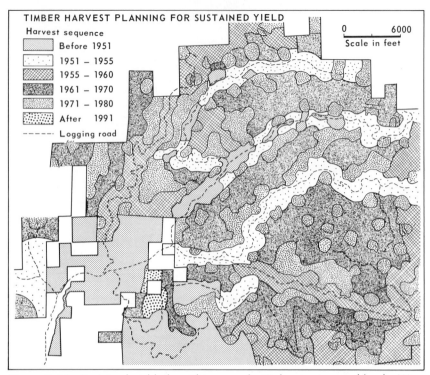

Figure 7–16 Sustained-yield plan. This map of a timber tract owned by the Weyerhaeuser Company demonstrates the type of long-range planning required for successful sustained-yield forestry. Symbols indicate areas which will mature and should be harvested within a given decade. Note the large number of well-distributed logging roads providing fire protection and serving as logging facilities as well. [Adapted from Richard M. Highsmith, J. Granville Jensen, and Robert D. Rudd, *Conservation in the United States* (Chicago: Rand McNally & Company, 1962). Weyerhaeuser Company map.]

To determine the volume of the annual forest crop of a given acreage, the volume lost to destructive agencies is subtracted from the growth for that year. A comprehensive nationwide forest inventory, conducted by the United States Forest Service in 1952, revealed growth rate of Western forests to be about 1 per cent of the growing stock of 273 billion cubic feet. However, because each year about 3.75 billion cubic feet was harvested, our forest stocks incurred an annual decrement of about 1 billion cubic feet. It is encouraging to note that by 1965, because of intensified forest management, for the first time in many decades, timber growth exceeded timber cut, even though much of the growth was not of excellent quality.

Block Cutting. The block-cutting method of timber harvest, which is the standard logging practice in the Northwest in both

240

private and public forests, is employed on even-aged stands composed of only a few species and is applicable only to trees whose seedlings thrive best in full sunlight. The Douglas fir on the Pacific Coast is harvested by this method. Perhaps the most valuable timber species in the world, it has been imported to Europe, where it has proved superior to native species. Some Douglas fir in Washington and Oregon stand over 200 feet high and are over 1,000 years old.

A Douglas fir, unlike a beech or maple, is not a climax tree and is not shade tolerant as a seedling. Therefore, this species would not be amenable to selective cutting, because its seeds would not germinate in the reduced light intensity of the forest floor. Moreover, its place in the forest would rapidly be appropriated by shade-tolerant species. In addition, a 100-foot Douglas fir weighing several tons could not be removed without badly bruising and killing younger growth. With the block-cutting technique an entire patch of evenly aged mature trees, possibly forty acres in area, is removed, leaving an unsightly rectangular "scar" in the midst of the forest. Because a large number of such blocks may be removed, when viewed from the

Figure 7–17 Block cutting of old-growth Douglas fir in the Gifford Pinchot National Forest, Washington. Mt. St. Helens in background. [U.S. Forest Service]

Figure 7–18 The slash in this cut-over area in the Kootenai National Forest, Montana, has been piled in windrows by a bulldozer to reduce the fire hazard. [U.S. Department of Agriculture]

air a block-cut forest resembles a giant green-and-brown checkerboard. In addition to its use on Douglas fir in Oregon and Washington, the block-cutting method has been used effectively in harvesting even-aged stands of Southern pine and subclimax aspen forests in northern Minnesota, Wisconsin, and Michigan.

Let us see now why this method of harvest results in a sustained yield. Suppose that a Wisconsin farmer who owns fifteen acres of aspen woods wishes a yearly harvest of pulpwood logs. He could log off a 1-acre block year after year for fifteen successive years. At the end of this period, if each block removed had been successfully reseeded, he would have fifteen age classes, all one acre in area, ranging from one to fifteen years in age. At the end of this fifteen-year period, he could harvest one acre of fifteen-year-old pulpwood stock, year after year for an indefinite period, as long as he ensures successful reseeding. The length of the cutting cycle or rotation depends upon the species of tree and on its intended commercial use. For aspen and birch, to be used as pulpwood, it varies from ten to thirty

Figure 7–19 Felling a large Western red cedar in the Wenatchee National Forest, Washington. A wedge is employed to start the tree falling. [U.S. Department of Agriculture]

years; on the other hand, the rotation for Douglas fir, to be used as lumber, may be up to 100 years.

The block-cutting technique has one big drawback. Although the timber resource may be most effectively utilized when a patch of forest is logged off, almost all the other uses of the forest may be severely impaired. How much water run-off can be retarded by a bare patch of ground? How many grouse or deer could that patch support? Because of this inherent deficiency, whenever a situation develops where either block cutting or selective cutting may be used to *equal* advantage, selective cutting should be chosen.

Reforestation. The sustained-yield concept dictates that whenever timber is removed, either by block cutting or by selective cutting, the denuded area must be reforested. This may be done by natural or artificial methods. Similarly, any forested land which has been destroyed by fire, insects, disease, hurricanes, or strip-mining activities also should be reforested, even though timber may not be its ultimate primary use.

243

After block cutting a few mature wind-firm trees may be left intact on a ridge within the otherwise logged-off site as a seed source. Scattered by wind and to a lesser degree by birds, rodents, and run-off water, the seeds will eventually become dispersed throughout the denuded area. Natural reseeding, however, is usually not completely adequate. One reason is that some tree species, like loblolly pine, may have only one good seed-producing year out of every two- to five-year period. (In a good year seed production may be ten times that in a poor year.) Another reason is that the dispersed seeds must reach mineral soil to develop properly. Because of these drawbacks, natural reseeding is usually combined with aerial, hand, or machine seeding.

In rugged terrain aerial seeding is the method of choice. Seeds are sown from planes flying slowly just above treetop level. Unfortunately, many aerially sown seeds fall on infertile soil or are consumed by birds and rodents. To minimize loss to animals, the seeds are frequently coated with a toxic deterrent. Except in the case of exceptionally small seeded trees, such as hemlock (*Thuja*) and spruce (*Picea*), rodent eradication is virtually a prerequisite to successful seeding.

If the logged-off site is of even topography, power-driven seeding machines may be advantageously employed, as has

Figure 7–20 One-year-old pine seedling protected by good litter and duff. Still thrifty and vigorous in late September following a dry season. Huntsville, Texas. [Soil Conservation Service, U.S. Department of Agriculture]

Figure 7–21 A sample slash pine plantation in Miden, Louisiana. Trees average 50 feet in height. Every other row is thinned. [Soil Conservation Service, U.S. Department of Agriculture]

been done in the cut-over land of Wisconsin and Michigan. Not only are these machines capable of planting up to 8 acres per day, but simultaneously they fertilize the soil and apply a herbicide to prevent weed encroachment.

In addition to the bird and rodent problem, a major disadvantage to seeding is the high number of first-year seedlings killed by frost, drought, hot weather, insects and autumn leaf fall. As a result, seeding, even by artificial methods, is less effective than planting young trees from plantation stock. In the South and in the Lake States, trees can be planted at a rate of 150 per man-hour. Open fields in the Middle West have been planted with the aid of an ordinary mould-board plow. On flat land, three men, a tractor, and a planting machine can set 1,000 to 2,000 trees per hour.

STRIP-MINE AREAS. Reforestation frequently is required in areas denuded by strip mining. This has been the case in the coal-mining regions of the Appalachians. A few years ago extensive open-pit and shaft mining operations in the anthracite regions of northeastern Pennsylvania left 112,928 acres defaced with barren spoil banks and waste dumps. In 1961, with the cooperation of the Northeastern Forest Experiment Station, the

Pennsylvania Power and Light Company initiated and financed "Operation Trees" in an attempt to rehabilitate the despoiled areas. The company donated $100,000 and furnished 625,000 seedlings of the 100 million eventually required. From 1963 to 1966, 3 million seedlings were planted under the supervision of the Pennsylvania Department of Mines. Moreover, between 1928 and 1966 the U.S. Forest Service planted 6.625 million trees. These plantings were not done in a haphazard manner. Intensive studies were conducted by the Forest Experiment Station to determine the tree species best suited to the extremely acid conditions. Of ten conifers, three hardwoods, and one hybrid poplar clone tested, the European white birch appeared best adapted to the acid sites. Reforestation in this region has not only reduced erosion and minimized acid drainage, but has partially restored the original beauty of the area, and has shown that some spoil banks may have at least a modest timber and wildlife producing potential.

Tree Farms. A tree farm is a private land area used for growing timber for profit. The tree farm movement was started by the Weyerhaeuser Company at Montesand, Washington, in 1941. It is currently sponsored by the American Forest Products Industries, composed of the timber, paper, pulp, and plywood industries and private owners of forestlands. In applying for certification the owner must demonstrate to an inspecting forester that he is employing sound forest management practices, such as sustained yield and effective pest and fire control. When a state tree farm certification committee has approved the forester's report, the tree farm owner is awarded the official roadside tree farm sign as recognition of his achievement. This movement has grown from 8,086 tree farms embracing 39 million acres in 1956, to 29,000 farms covering 66 million acres in the mid-1960's.

Multiple Use. A primary objective of the United States Forest Service is to make the greatest number of forest resources available to the greatest number of Americans. This principle is graphically portrayed in the Multiple Use Tree, the official National Forest symbol, which is enclosed by a ring bearing the legend "National Forests—Lands of Many Uses." The trunk of the tree represents the American people, who benefit from the varied resources of our forests—timber, water, forage, wildlife, and recreation. These five major forest-derived resources are in turn symbolized by the five branches of the multiple-use tree. The single line which is used to inscribe the tree suggests the ecological interactions not only between the resources, but between them and the people who use or abuse them (21).

Multiple-use management of forests looks simple on paper. In actual operation, however, it is an extremely complex ecological problem with a veritable thicket of coalescing cause-and-effect relationships. For example, the Forest Service is frequently forced to utilize a given forest acre primarily for one resource while sacrificing its potential for other values. A given acre of forest cannot be all things to all people. If a given acreage of Douglas fir is to be developed for high-quality timber, then block cutting of this acreage would certainly be a perfectly valid management procedure. However, at the same time, the wholesale removal of a timber block would greatly impair the value of that particular acreage in terms of flood and erosion control, wildlife habitat, and recreation. Sound multiple-use management must weigh the needs of the people, and these vary both in time and place. Thus, timber production may have top priority in the valuable Douglas fir and Western hemlock stands of Washington and Oregon, but in the low-value, second-growth forests of populous New York, where many city-dwellers require occasional doses of "wilderness tonic," recreational values would have high priority.

We shall now briefly examine some examples of how the Forest Service has managed our forests in terms of such uses as flood and erosion control, rangeland, and wildlife habitat.

Figure 7–22 Sullivan–Green State Forest, Indiana. Fishing in a lake created by strip mining. The trees planted along the formerly denuded banks not only enhance the beauty of the region but provide valuable wildlife cover. [U.S. Department of Agriculture]

USE OF FORESTS IN FLOOD AND EROSION CONTROL. Ever since the late nineteenth century many of our Western valley towns situated at the base of steep mountain slopes have been periodically battered by brief but damaging flash floods spawned by sudden summer storms. One hour a valley stream would be placid, the next it might be transformed into a churning torrent, bearing soil, rocks, uptorn shrubs, and debris washed from the slope of a mountain. Surging down the valley, the swollen stream might cause considerable property damage and loss of life.

One of the regions hardest hit by this type of flash flood was Davis County, Utah, at the eastern margin of Great Salt Lake. Harried citizens, beleaguered by recurring disasters, finally asked Congress for federal assistance. In his book *Land, Wood and Water,* the late Senator Robert S. Kerr, of Oklahoma, describes the work of the Forest Service in dealing with the problem (9). Kerr describes how, during their meticulous survey, investigators discovered that much of the flood-triggering run-off originated from areas that had been depleted of their vegetational cover. These denuded parts of the watershed had either been burned over, overgrazed, or plowed up and converted into marginal croplands. In some areas the run-off waters carved gullies 70 feet deep. During one rainy period up to 160 times as much water ran off an abused plot than ran off an undisturbed one. In 1936, with the aid of bulldozers, the gullies were filled in, slopes were contoured, the bare soil was carefully prepared as a seedbed and planted to rapidly growing shrubs and trees. Only eleven years later, in 1945, severe August rainstorms put the rehabilitated water shed to the test. An investigation revealed that fully 93.5 per cent of the rainfall was retained by the newly forested area. Moreover, soil erosion was reduced from the pretreatment figure of 268 cubic feet per acre to a mere trace (9).

USE OF FORESTS AS RANGELAND. Our forests frequently include, in addition to timber, considerable areas of high-quality livestock forage. Thus, of the 186 million acres comprising our National Forests and National Grasslands, 100 million acres (over 53 per cent) provide forage for 6 million cattle and sheep belonging to 19,000 farmers and ranchers. (Most of this is in the West. In the Lake States and Central States most forest grazing occurs on farm woodlots.) Graziers pay fees for the privilege of grazing their livestock in National Forests. In a typical year, grazing fee receipts amount to $3.7 million, of which 25 per cent (about $947,000) is returned to state coffers for the improvement of highways and schools in the counties where the fees were levied (18).

Figure 7–23 The dense litter in this North Carolina forest will absorb spring run-off and aid in the prevention of erosion. [U.S. Forest Service]

Figure 7–24 Sheepherder and two sheep dogs watch over sheep grazing in a high meadow within the Plumas National Forest, California. Some 18,000 sheep graze the summer ranges of the Plumas under paid permit. [U.S. Forest Service]

In 1963 the Forest Service conducted a study on the Front Range in the Rockies to determine what effect the introduction of high-quality exotic forage grasses would have on beef production. Thus, calves were grazed part time on native bunch grass range and than transferred to an adjacent range composed of such exotics as Sherman big bluegrass (*Poa ampla*), crested wheat grass (*Agropyron desertorum*), and Russian wild rye (*Elymus junceus*). When weaned the calves raised on the integrated grazing plan were 17 pounds heavier and worth $4 more per head than calves raised exclusively on native range (18).

Another Forest Service study in the low-timber-value post oak and blackjack oak forests of the Ozark Mountains revealed how these areas can be converted into high-value rangeland. By spraying herbicides to kill the scrubby trees, preparing the forest floor as a seedbed by fertilizing and setting carefully regulated fires, and then seeding heavily with small bluestem and fescue grass, cattle forage per acre could be increased 100 times (17).

During a typical year rangeland improvements made in our National Forests by the Forest Service include reseeding 100,000 acres, applying rodent-control measures on 25,000 acres, checking the growth and spread of undesirable noxious weeds on 162,000 acres, constructing more than 2,000 miles of fence, and developing more than 1,900 livestock-watering sites.

USE OF FORESTS AS WILDLIFE HABITAT. Our nation's 154 national forests and nineteen national grasslands embrace 186 million acres, almost 1 acre for each American. Two thirds of the sportsmen visiting this vast public hunting ground seek big game; the remainder seek upland game and waterfowl. In 1965 the hunters spent 14 million visitor days in the national forests and grasslands and bagged 604,000 big-game animals, 95 per cent of which were deer and elk.

The United States Forest Service attempts to manage our national forests in such a way as to provide the best possible habitat for wildlife. Sometimes best management involves increasing the forest "edge" habitat, frequented by many game animals such as deer, rabbit, and pheasant. Forest edge improvement for game may be integrated with timber harvesting and the construction of fire lanes and logging trails. Because game food and cover are more abundant in seral than in climax stages, retardation of succession by prescribed burning may be beneficial to wildlife. During the fiscal year ending June 30, 1965, the Forest Service seeded and planted game food on 43,156 acres, protected 33,147 acres of key wildlife habitat, and employed regulated burning to improve the wild-game carrying capacity of 44,572 acres (19). We shall briefly describe two game habitat development programs recently initiated by the Forest Service, one for turkeys and the other for deer.

Improvement of Turkey Habitat. In an attempt to improve wild turkey habitat on the Jefferson National Forest in Virginia, a number of clearings were made in the otherwise dense timber and were then heavily seeded with ladino clover and bluegrass. Once these plants had become well established, the turkeys in the region made heavy use of the openings as feeding areas, consuming not only large quantities of grass, clover, and weed seeds, but also insects attracted to the newly introduced vegetation. As a direct response to the modified forest environment, the turkey population increased from twelve birds to 125 birds within a six-year period (17) (20).

Solving the Deer vs. Forest Reproduction Problem. A sizable deer herd generally poses such a browsing menace to young hardwood seedlings that in many situations there are two alternatives, to maintain the deer herd and sacrifice the seedlings, or vice versa. For example, basswood and hemlock have been completely eliminated by deer browsing in certain

Figure 7–25 A logger and a fisherman greet each other along the Santeetlah Creek in North Carolina's Nantahala National Forest. The logger is transporting part of the timber harvested annually from the surrounding watershed, and the angler is anxious to fill his creel. [U.S. Department of Agriculture]

mixed hardwood–hemlock forests of the North, with only sugar maple and red maple being able to survive. In Rocky Mountain National Park mule deer (and elk) have prevented aspen stand establishment. It was of considerable interest, therefore, when Forest Service researchers, working in an Appalachian hardwood stand in North Carolina, discovered at least a local solution to the problem (19). In the study area three years after a heavy cutting had been made, deer showed a rather surprising preference for old stump sprouts to seedlings; they consumed 60 per cent of the sprouts but only 10 per cent of the seedlings (22). Therefore, by cutting down hardwoods of little commercial value, such as weed species, mishapen or fire-scarred trees, the volume of stump sprout food could be deliberately increased to the point where a fairly large deer herd could be sustained while concurrently assuring vigorous regeneration of valuable hardwoods (19).

Pest and Fire Control. The most serious agents of forest destruction are disease and insect pests. Under the authority of the Forest Pest Control Act of 1947, surveys are annually conducted in both private and public forests to permit early detection of pest population increases so that they may be arrested before reaching disastrous levels. In fiscal 1962 Congress appropriated $9.35 million for pest control and an additional $2.995 million for research. (Fig. 7–26)

DISEASES. Forest diseases resulting from parasitic fungi, rusts, mistletoes, viruses, and nematodes cause roughly 45 per cent of the total saw timber destruction. Young seedlings are especially vulnerable to nematode infections. Heart rot fungus (*Polyporus* and *Fomes*) alone is responsible for about 33 per cent of the total forest damage. (This fungus, however, may be beneficial as an important agent in the decay of fallen logs, dead stubs and slash, thus recycling elements and removing flammable debris). The remaining 12 per cent of disease damage may be attributed primarily to white pine blister rust (*Cronartium ribicola*), dwarf mistletoe (*Arceuthobium*), oak wilt (*Chalara quercina*), Dutch elm disease (*Ceratostomella ulmi*), elm phloem necrosis (caused by a virus), and oak wilt (*Certocyster fagacearium*). The most injurious disease pests are exotics, accidentally introduced to the United States, which have suddenly been released from environmental factors that ordinarily keep them in check.

Oak Wilt. The oak wilt fungus is threatening extensive oak forests of the Southern Appalachians and upper Mississippi Valley. The parasite enters the host tree via roots or bark

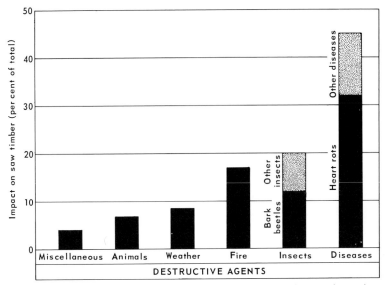

Figure 7–26 Impact of destructive agents on saw timber (indicated in per cent of total impact). [Adapted from Guy-Harold Smith, *Conservation of Natural Resources* (New York: John Wiley & Sons, Inc., 1965). Data from *Timber Resources Review,* U.S. Forest Service.]

wounds. Healthy trees may become infected by root grafts with an adjacent diseased tree or by the disseminating agency of nitidulid beetles (*Glischrochilus* and *Colopterus*) which acquire the fungus while consuming mats of fungus spores just under the bark of diseased trees. Squirrels and possibly birds may also serve as disseminating agents. The fungus spores are transmitted throughout the host by water flowing through xylem tissue. Eventually the fungus clogs the xylem vessels and causes leaf death. Characteristic symptoms include discolored leaves, premature defoliation, and cracked bark (caused by the spore mats).

Chestnut Blight. At the turn of the century, the American chestnut (*Castanea dentata*) was a conspicuous, attractive, and valuable member of the deciduous forest in the Eastern United States; in some areas, such as the Appalachians, it formed over 50 per cent of the stand. Both man and beast found its nuts nutritious and palatable. Tannin, a substance of prime importance in the leather-tanning process, was derived from its bark; from its straight trunk were fashioned durable fence posts and rails. Today, however, only the leafless "skeletons" of these trees remain. You can tramp the Appalachians for weeks without finding a single living mature tree. In New England a few living sprouts from native stumps may be found.

Figure 7-27 These American chestnut trees in the mountains of North Carolina have been killed by the chestnut blight. [U.S. Department of Agriculture]

The near extinction of the once abundant chestnut was caused by a parasitic fungus (*Endothia parasitica*), inadvertently introduced along with nursery stock from China. The parasite was first reported in New York City in 1904. Once established, the fungus spread rapidly, virtually eliminating the chestnut as a commercial species by 1914. After gaining access through a bark wound (possibly caused by fire, insects, or rodents) the fungus invades the cambium and phloem, spreads rapidly, and ultimately plugs the food-conducting phloem tissue, causing the leaves to turn brown and wither. Eventually, when the malnourished roots no longer can absorb soil moisture and nutrients, the tree dies. Trunk and branches swell at foci of infection and form cankers which produce tiny reproductive spores. During dry seasons light spores are formed which are wind disseminated. During wet seasons, heavy, sticky yellowish-brown tendrils of spores ooze from the cankers and adhere to the bodies of bark beetles, squirrels, or bills and feet of woodpeckers. (Up to 1 billion spores have been washed from the feet of one woodpecker.) During migrations woodpeckers may fly twenty miles or more daily, thus serving as superb dispersal agents.

In recent years Oriental chestnuts, which are quite resistant to the blight, have been introduced. Although these trees do well when given solicitous care under nurserylike conditions, they are unable to survive in the wild. Forest geneticists have been crossing the resistant Oriental chestnut with the American chestnut in an attempt to develop a blight-resistant hybrid. If successful, the chestnut may yet again be an important component of our deciduous forests.

White Pine Blister Rust. The blister rust parasite (*Cronartium ribicola*) has primarily infected the white pines of New England and Lake States and the Western white pine and sugar pine of the Pacific Coast. Many of these stately trees, over 200 years old and 150 feet tall, have withstood wind, storm, hail, sub-Arctic cold, drought, fires, and insect attacks only to succumb to this microscopic fungus. The blister rust was introduced accidentally from Germany, first being found in North America at Geneva, New York, in 1906. When new infections were introduced on the West Coast, hope for its eradication was abandoned.

The first signs of the infection, which attacks all five-needle pines, are the yellowish spots which speckle the needles. Within three years the parasite spreads to the branches and main trunk, causing the tree's death when it girdles the inner bark. Numerous minute, orange spores are released during spring and summer from elongated yellowish blisters. When

Figure 7–28 Tree infected by white pine blister rust. [U.S. Department of Agriculture]

wind-borne these spores may be carried 100 miles. Although more than 99 per cent eventually die, a few may alight and germinate on the leaves of domesticated or wild gooseberry or currant (*Ribes*) bushes, which will serve as an alternate host. The infected leaves of the new host present a frost-white appearance. Eventually, after a period of development, a new type of spore is produced, which may be wind-blown for a maximum distance of 1,000 feet. If some of these spores alight upon white pine needles, they will in turn germinate, thus completing the parasite's life cycle.

Eradication of Host. Because the blister rust requires two hosts to complete its life cycle, it can be eradicated simply by depriving the rust of one of them. White pine timber is much more valuable than jam; hence, all gooseberry and currant bushes within a 1,000-foot radius of a white pine stand are destroyed. These thorny shrubs may be grubbed out by hand or bulldozer, burned, or treated with a herbicide. The U.S. Forest Service surveys about 3 million acres in its blister rust control operations and eradicates *Ribes* from about 234,000 acres annually.

Use of Antibiotics. Several antibiotics have been developed recently which have proved effective in blister rust control. One antibiotic, *phytoactin,* has been successfully used on infected western white pine. Another, *cyclohexamide,* has given promising results on parasitized white pine seedlings without having any harmful residual effect on the beneficial root-associated mycorrhizae (19). The U.S. Forest Service treats over 100,000 acres of infected pine with rust-killing antibiotics annually.

Development of Resistant Pines. In recent years Forest Service geneticists have succeeded in developing rust-resistant hybrids. By 1980 a 100-acre seed orchard of resistant hybrids will have developed a mass quantity of seeds suitable for use in planting several hundred thousand acres to rust-resistant pine (17). The extension of this program of "genetic control" may ultimately eliminate the blister rust as a major agent of forest destruction in this country.

INSECTS. Insects account for 20 per cent of all timber destroyed, ranking second only to diseases as a destructive agent. Each year insects ruin 5 billion board feet of timber, roughly equivalent to 10 per cent of our total annual timber harvest. Each tree species has its own unique assemblage of insect pests. An oak tree may be ravaged by over 100 species. No part of a tree's anatomy is spared.

Figure 7–29 A young Western white pine stand in the St. Joe National Forest (Idaho) is being sprayed with the antibiotic fungicide phytoactin to arrest the damage being caused by the white pine blister rust. [U.S. Department of Agriculture]

Timber-valuable pine trees are under insect attack from the top of the terminal shoot down to the roots. Terminals may be killed or deformed by grubs of the white pine weevil (*Pissodes strobi*) or by larvae of the Ponderosa pitch moth (*Dioryctria ponderosae*). The small pine bark aphid (*Pineus strobi*) consumes needles. Leaves may be stripped and skeletonized by the nearly hairless caterpillars of the spruce budworm (*Choristoneura fumiferana*). Sawfly (family *Diprionidae*) larvae cause defoliation. Fresh green pine cones may be attacked by cone beetles (*Conophthorus*); mature dry cones may be attacked by the slender white cone borer larvae of the family *Cerambycidae*. Seeds are susceptible to the mining activities of the minute, legless white larvae of the seed chalcids (*Chalcidae*). Several species of bark beetles (*Dendroctonus*) consume the inner bark. Wood of living and dying trees is ravaged by flat-headed borers (*Buprestidae*); sawed lumber and seasoned wood are devoured by the black-horned pine borer (*Callidium antennatum*). Even the finished wood products may be riddled by soft white and brown termites (*Reticulitermes*) (6).

Gypsy Moth. In 1869 pupae of the gypsy moth were shipped through the mails from France to Medford, Massachusetts, at the request of a young scientist who was conducting silkworm research. Unfortunately, a few of the insects escaped from his laboratory and soon became established in nearby woodlands. Released from the controls exerted by its native European predators, the gypsy moth population rapidly increased. An early writer describes an infestation in an Eastern town as follows: "The street was black with them (caterpillars) . . . they were so thick on the trees that they were stuck together like cold macaroni . . . the foliage was completely stripped from all the trees . . . presenting an awful picture of devastation." Although the larvae prefer oak leaves, they will also consume birch and ash foliage, and when full grown will even eat pine needles. An intensive attack will kill a white pine. Even though defoliation may not kill some trees directly, it may increase their vulnerability to fungus infections, windstorms, and drought.

Currently the gypsy moth is widely distributed throughout 40 million acres of forest in northeastern United States (13). Ever since 1890 federal and state agencies have made strenuous efforts to curb its range extension and check population increases. Descriptions of some of these measures follow:

1. QUARANTINE. The federal government has imposed a quarantine on all materials such as branches, bark, and

Figure 7–30 Leaf-eating caterpillars of the gypsy moth damage hundreds of thousands of dollars worth of forest and shade trees in the Northeastern states annually. They hatch in April from eggs laid the previous year. [U.S. Department of Agriculture]

soil in the infected area. (Unscrupulous individuals have periodically attempted to violate the quarantine. Some have even mailed uncertified evergreen boughs in boxes labeled *laundry*.)

2. DDT SPRAY. In extensive forests the moth can be effectively controlled with DDT sprayed from the air at a 1 pound per acre dosage. Just one load from a C-47 can spray as large an area as a spray truck can cover in four years.

3. PARASITES. A parasitic fly (*Compsilura concinnata*) has been successfully imported from Europe for gypsy moth control. After alighting on a moth larva, the female fly injects her young directly into its body, whereupon they rapidly consume their host's tissues. The United States Forest Service has also successfully employed viral spray as a control (20). It is applied at concentrations of 1 trillion polyhedra virus to 1 gallon of water. A larval moth becomes infected when it feeds on viral-contaminated foliage.

4. USE OF SEX ATTRACTANTS. Shortly after emergence from their pupa cage, the strong-winged male moths are attracted to the weak-flying female by a species-specific chem-

Figure 7–31 Cape Cod, Massachusetts. This is a typical gypsy moth trap picked up in the field. It contains captured gypsy moths lured into the trap by gyplure, a synthetic attractant which confuses male moths into "thinking" a female is inside the trap. Once inside, the moth becomes entangled in a sticky substance and is unable to extricate itself. [U.S. Department of Agriculture]

ical attractant known as *gyptol.* Within the past few years the United States Department of Agriculture researchers have succeeded in synthesizing a chemically related substance, *gyplure,* from a constituent of castor oil. Gyplure has proved equal to gyptol as a sex lure. Under laboratory conditions male moths may be deluded into "mating" with small wood chips impregnated with gyplure. Large numbers of such impregnated chips could be released from airplanes over badly infested areas. Male gypsy moths might be induced to copulate with the chips and squander their sperm, thereby curtailing reproduction (2).

5. STERILIZATION. In 1965 Forest Service researchers sterilized a number of male moths with radioactive cobalt-60 in an attempt to duplicate the screw worm fly eradication success. However, because sterilized males do not compete successfully for females with fertile males, certain refinements in this avenue of control will have to be made (19).

Bark Beetles. Almost 90 per cent of insect-inflicted timber mortality is caused by bark beetles. They destroy roughly 4.5 billion board feet annually. Adult beetles attack a tree by boring through the bark and then tunneling out egg chambers and galleries with their powerful jaws. The tiny grubs which hatch from the eggs consume the phloem and cambium, and if sufficiently numerous (1,000 per large tree) may actually girdle the tree and kill it within a month. The bark beetle group includes a large number of destructive species. The Western pine beetle (*Dendroctonus brevicomis*) killed 25 billion board feet of Ponderosa pine along the Pacific Coast between 1917 and 1943. The mountain pine beetle (*Dendroctonus monticolae*) has killed an aggregate 20 billion board feet of sugar pine, western white pine, and lodgepole pine in California alone. The Black Hills beetle, (*Dendroctonus ponderosae*), which feeds on Ponderosa pine in the Rocky Mountains, destroyed 2.5 billion board feet of timber from 1895 to 1946.

The fluctuating populations of the Engelmann spruce beetle (*Dendroctonus engelmanni*) in the higher elevations of the Rockies form an interesting ecological study. For many years prior to 1942, these beetles were at least partially held in check by predatory insects and birds; woodpeckers were especially well adapted for feeding on them. Woodpeckers have extremely long sticky tongues with which they can probe the beetle galleries and snare their bean-sized prey. Whenever the beetle population increased, an influx of woodpeckers would soon check the incipient build-up, thus keeping the population in dynamic equilibrium. During this pre-1942 period the spruce beetles had concentrated on moisture-deficient trees, or on trees in which the sap flow was not sufficiently vigorous to

Figure 7–32 Englemann spruce bark beetle larvae located just under the bark of a tree in the White River National Forest, Colorado. These beetles have destroyed over 2 billion feet of Engelmann spruce timber on the White River. [U.S. Forest Service]

protect the trees from beetle intrusions. However, in 1942, a violent windstorm uprooted thousands of spruce. The fallen trees formed a food bonanza for the spruce beetles. Because they were protected from woodpeckers by the interlocking branches of the prostrate trunks and probably also as a result of the superabundant food supply, the beetle population increased sharply. They now could more fully realize a reproductive potential in which a single pair could theoretically give rise to 10,000 progeny in a single breeding season. In 1949 a portion of the beetle population drowned in a small lake and drifted ashore, forming a solid drift of beetles 1 foot deep, 6 feet wide, and two miles long (15). The beetle hordes were now so numerous that they successfully attacked even young, vigorously growing trees (heretofore protected by their sap flow), as well as overmature trees and wind-blown timber. Within a six-year period (1940–1946), the spruce beetles had destroyed 20 per cent of the Engelmann spruce in Colorado, a volume of 3 billion board feet—sufficient to provide homes for a city of 2 million people. The rate of timber destruction by beetles in the region was seventy-five times the rate of destruction by fire.

An inexpensive but effective method of controlling bark beetles is to soak the bark of infested trees with a formula of one part DDT to six parts fuel oil, applied to bark with power sprayers at a rate of 7 gallons per tree (15). Another method is to fell infested trees, then peel and burn the bark; the peeled logs may then either be kiln dried, heated to 125 degrees F. for one hour, sun-dried, or scorched with a flame thrower. Egg galleries of standing trees may be cut out with a chisel and the wound painted with pruning paint. In some cases egg galleries may be injected with ethylene dichloride or carbon disulfide. On a long-term basis, perhaps the best method of "control" is to prevent infestations from occurring in the first place. This may be done by sanitation techniques, by burning all potential bark beetle breeding sites such as senile and wind-blown trees, logging accumulated slash and debris, and the stubs of lightning and fire-killed specimens.

FIRE. Even before the white man's coming, North American forests have been consumed by flames. Annual ring sequence studies on giant redwoods indicate these trees have been exposed to fire about once every twenty-five years over the past ten centuries. Early Spanish and French explorers write of traveling through dense clouds of smoke issuing from flaming forests. Every three minutes a forest fire starts somewhere in the United States. During the 1940–1950 period, fires consumed an average of 21.5 million acres of timber yearly, which is the equivalent of sending the entire state of Maine up in smoke (13). From 1955 to 1964, 1,175,664 forest fires, at an average rate of 322 per day, burned 76,000 square miles of forest range and watershed. Although fire may not kill a tree outright, it may cause distorted growth and impair its timber value. Fire annually is responsible for 17 per cent of saw timber destruction from all causes. Because of the better fire-control techniques that have been developed recently, the total acreage of destroyed timber has gradually been reduced. For example, the 125,371 forest fires which broke out in 1968 succeeded in burning only 4.2 million acres, roughly 20 per cent of the 1940–1950 annual average of 21.5 million acres.

MAJOR FIRES. A few of the forest fires which have been destructive of timber, property, and/or human life are listed.

The Miramichi, Michigan, fire of 1825 consumed 3 million acres of coniferous forest.

The Peshtigo, Wisconsin, fire of 1871 killed 1,500 people and devastated 1.25 million acres of timberland.

The Hinckley, Minnesota, fire of 1894 consumed 160,000 forested acres and killed 418 men, women, and children. Many more would have been engulfed by the flames had not a warning been given by Father Lawler, a Catholic priest, who ran down the main street of Hinckley shouting, "Run for your lives." Some of the villagers found safety by crouching up to their armpits in the water of a gravel pit; others escaped by boarding a moving freight train.

The Cloquet, Minnesota, fire of 1918 took a toll of 432 lives, destroyed $30 million worth of timber and property, and advanced to the outskirts of Duluth, Minnesota, before being checked (5).

The Tillamook, Oregon, fire of 1933 ravaged 270,000 acres and destroyed 12 billion board feet of timber (7).

The Bar Harbor, Maine, conflagration of October, 1947, devastated the famed resort area, consumed 400 homes, including many plush estates, and put 3,500 vacationists to flight (14). This was only one of a series of Maine forest fires during October which burned 240,000 acres and caused several million dollars' worth of property and timber damage.

FIRE CLASSES.   Forest fires may be classified as (1) surface, (2) soil, or (3) crown, according to the substratum being consumed.

1. Surface fires.   The surface fire is the most common type. It moves along the forest floor, fed by tinder-dry pine needles, crisp leaf litter, twigs, vines, shrubs, logs, leathery mushrooms, and the leaf-woven homes of ground-nesting birds. Driven by the wind, these fires may burn intensely but are of short duration. An occasional tree will have its bark singed, making it susceptible to insects and fungus growths. The most destructive aspect of the surface fire is that in consuming millions of germinating seeds and seedlings, it destroys the forest of the future. (Fig. 7–33)

2. Soil fires.   Surface fires may develop into soil fires, which consume the humus and peat content of the forest soil immediately underlying the leaf litter. Some penetrate to a depth of 6 feet. Because soil fire fuels rarely dry sufficiently to burn, they are uncommon. Largely deprived of access to oxygen and wind, the soil fire burns slowly but continuously, sometimes for months, issuing a considerable amount of smoke, but little flame. Low-lying smoke clouds from soil fires may form serious traffic hazards. In October, 1966, smoke-blinded motorists speeding along a Wisconsin freeway near Mauston were

Figure 7–33 Santa Rosa County, Florida. Surface fire in second-growth timber. These woods were set on fire by a neighboring landowner to make the grass look greener. However, the effect on grazing will be adverse. [U.S. Department of Agriculture]

involved in a chain-reaction wreck which claimed four lives and destroyed several cars. The tremendous heat generated by soil fires may destroy timber in an insidious, underground attack on their heat-sensitive roots. Soil fires are extremely destructive to the organic content of podzol soil, and hence reduce its water-absorptive role. Moreover, in killing billions of soil fungi and bacteria, the soil fire impairs the soil's role in recycling nitrogen and other essential elements in the forest ecosystem. Soil which nature required centuries to build may be consumed by a soil fire in a matter of hours and be converted into an inert, sterile medium, largely incapable of supporting life.

3. *Crown Fire.* The highly spectacular and destructive crown fire may also originate from a surface fire. The crown may be ignited by wind-blown sparks. Flames from burning litter may find a combustible pathway to the canopy by way of pendant dried moss streamers or via resin flowing down a conifer

Figure 7–34 Ochoco National Forest, Oregon. Forest fire burned approximately 100 acres in August, 1951. [U.S. Department of Agriculture]

Figure 7–35 Payette National Forest, Idaho. The aftermath of a forest fire. All life is destroyed, even the soil organisms. [U.S. Department of Agriculture]

trunk. Heat from a surface fire may ignite dry crown needles. In a strong wind the crown fire may jump from crown to crown with a speed of up to 40 miles per hour. Wind-driven sparks and brands may be carried far in advance of the original fire and ignite "spot" fires, thus making it extremely hazardous for man or beast to remain in the crown fire's path. Jemisen (8) describes a crown fire at Freeman Lake, Idaho, which devastated 20,000 acres within a twelve-and-a-half-hour period. When the fire started the relative humidity was only 10 per cent and the air temperature was 90 degrees F. Although the wind was of only moderate velocity, a 350-acre spot fire was ignited fully 3 miles ahead of the parent blaze. (Fig. 7–34)

Cause of Fires. A study of the causes of forest fires reveals the average American's irresponsibility with regard to forest conservation. Roughly 90 per cent of all forest fires are started by man. Only 10 per cent are triggered by natural causes such as lightning (20).

There is not much that we can do to prevent lightning-caused fires. Even before the Pilgrims settled at Plymouth Rock, destructive fires originated in electrical storms. During the period 1900–1963 over 58 per cent of the 68,400 forest fires that occurred in the Rocky Mountains and along the Pacific Coast were ignited by lightning. In 1901 over 1,100 lightning-originated forest fires occurred in the national forests of Idaho and Montana within a two-week period. Currently research is being conducted on seeding thunder clouds with dry ice in an effort to dissipate the electrical charges causing lightning.

We definitely can do something about 91 per cent of the forest fires which we have ignited ourselves. Many fires are caused by careless people:

- The tourist who deftly flicks a lighted cigarette stub into a bed of dry pine needles, while thinking only about getting to the motel in time for supper.
- The fisherman who is in such a frenzy to "snag those big bass" that he forgets to drown the dying coals of his campfire.
- The brush burner "cleaning up" in the wake of a logging operation who is so intent on the cottage he is building for his family that one of his brush fires gets out of control and flares into a holocaust, consuming enough timber to build a thousand homes.

As John D. Guthrie, former fire inspector for the United States Forest Service has written so well, "To stage a forest fire you need only a few things—a forest, the right atmospheric conditions, and a spark either from a lightning bolt or a match in the hands of a fool or a knave. The formula is simple . . . the larger

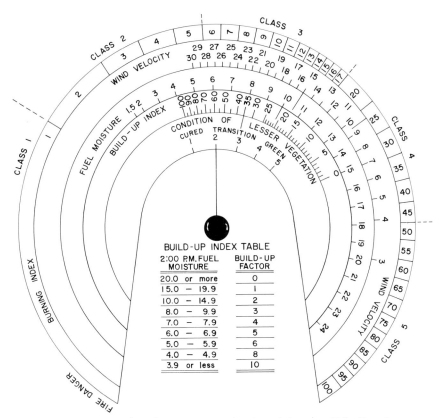

Figure 7–36 Forest fire danger meter developed by the U.S. Forest Service. [U.S. Forest Service]

the forest, the drier the air, the bigger the fool, the bigger the fire you will have."

Firefighting. Even during the first three decades of this century, firefighting was a poorly organized, haphazard operation that relied primarily on hand tools and the ineffectual efforts of bucket brigades. The technique of modern forest fire suppression, however, is an intensively organized, well-coordinated operation which employs the latest technological developments, from infrared scanners to helicopters (16). In 1965, 113,685 forest fires consumed 2.6 million acres of timber. Only 0.12 per cent of the forest land protected with a modern fire suppression system was burned, whereas 4.28 per cent of unprotected timber was destroyed (20). In other words, only 1 acre of protected forest was burned for every 34 acres of unprotected forest. We shall describe fire suppression in sequential order:

Figure 7–37 A fire control worker employs the fire-finder alidade to make a fix on a smoke. Olympic National Forest, Washington. [U.S. Department of Agriculture]

Figure 7–38 Helicopters are employed to scout fires, transport men, and deliver urgently needed supplies to firefighters. [U.S. Forest Service]

Figure 7–39 Smoke jumper of the U.S. Forest Service in action over the Lolo National Forest, Montana. [U.S. Forest Service]

(1) fire detection; (2) dispatching and transport of fighters; and (3) fire suppression.

FIRE DETECTION. Fire detection is frequently made by observers stationed in look-out towers. Most well-forested states have a network of such spotting towers in operation. During seasons of severe fire hazard, this detection work is frequently supplemented with airplane patrols. Once the fire is spotted, the precise position is determined and radioed to the dispatcher.

DISPATCHING AND TRANSPORT. The dispatcher immediately alerts one or more firefighting teams. Over 2,000 fighters have been used in major conflagrations. The fighters rush to the scene of the fire by truck or jeep if roads are accessible. In rugged mountainous country, "smoke jumpers" may parachute into the area of the fire. They are equipped with lightweight parachutes capable of slow descent and provided with steering slots which facilitate pin-point landings. The national forests of mountainous regions in Washington, Oregon, California,

Montana, Idaho, and New Mexico are protected by a corps of 350 United States Forest Service smoke jumpers. Forest fire suppression is most effective at night, when fire intensity is reduced and fighters find the heat less oppressive. To exploit the possibilities of nocturnal fighting, special lights and markers have been developed by the United States Forest Service for reducing hazards attending the night transport of helicopter-borne fighters. With the help of smoke jumpers, many remote blazes which in 1930 might have flamed out of control may now be extinguished within a matter of minutes.

Fire Suppression. The actual suppression or attack pattern employed by fighters varies greatly depending upon the size of fire, terrain, fire class, wind direction, location of roads, availability of water supplies, and relative humidity. We shall describe just a few of the techniques, devices, and materials used in modern forest fire suppression.

Fire Lanes. The fire lane is a 10-foot-wide strip which is plowed up around the periphery of the fire with the aid of special fire plows, bulldozers, and gasoline-powered brush and sapling cutters. In well-managed forests these lanes usually have already been systematically carved out of the forest at regular intervals. Because a fire lane is denuded of all combustible material, it effectively checks the fire's advance.

Back Fires. Occasionally, in an effort to head off an advancing fire, the intervening forest between the fire head and a fire lane may be set on fire. If wind conditions are right, the back fire will burn its way toward the major fire; when both fires meet they will die from lack of fuel. This technique may boomerang if the wind suddenly shifts direction.

Water. Water may be sprayed from a portable back-tank or tank truck. Portable motor pumps may take water from a nearby stream or lake. Some fighter teams have special well-drilling equipment with which they can sink a shallow well shaft within fifteen minutes. In rough country helicopters have laid 1,500 feet of fire hose in less than a minute. Some planes have special water tanks which can skim water from a lake for use in dousing the fire.

Fire-Retardant Chemicals. Fire-retardant chemicals almost three times more effective than water can be sprayed from back-tank and tank truck, or may be dropped on the blaze from a plane in the form of chemical bombs. Huge air tankers with up to 4,000 gallons capacity were first employed in 1956, when 124,000 gallons of fire-retardant chemicals were released on twenty-four fires. A variety of such retardant chemicals as

Figure 7–40 Fire suppression in the Angeles National Forest, California. [U.S. Forest Service]

Figure 7–41 Ozark National Forest, Arkansas, April, 1966. A U.S. Forest Service plane drops a chemical slurry to suppress a fire. [U.S. Department of Agriculture]

viscous water, sodium borate, bentonite clay, and ammonium compounds have been applied to forest fires in recent years.

Aerial Photography. Aerial photographers may take pictures of the fire, develop them in a dark room aboard the plane, and within minutes parachute them down to the firefighters below. The pictures will show the fire boss the over-all pattern and status of the fire. They may suggest to him how best to deploy his men, not only for most effective suppression, but also to prevent possible encirclement by flames.

PRESCRIBED BURNING. Not all forest fires are destructive. Ecologists are generally agreed that a number of our nation's valuable timber stands may be established and maintained because of fire. Examples include the old-growth, even-aged stands of Douglas fir in the Northwest, of red pine in northwestern Minnesota, and of white pine in northwestern Pennsylvania and southwestern New Hampshire. Certain less valuable species, such as pitch pine on sandy soils near the mid-Atlantic Coast and jack pine in the Lake States, are also considered to be "fire types" or "fire climaxes."

Today foresters employ *prescribed burning* to improve quality of timber, livestock forage, and wildlife habitat. Prescribed burning may be defined as surface burning according to a plan in which the utmost precaution is taken in terms of (1) dryness of fuel, (2) wind velocity (3 to 10 miles per hour preferred) and direction, (3) relative humidity, (4) type of fire (head, flank, or back), and (5) composition and combustibility of fuel. The long-term effect on the forest in terms of multiple use receives top priority. Prescribed burning has been employed with considerable success in Southern stands of long-leaf slash pine and more limited success on short-leaf loblolly–hardwood stands. At the Alapaha Experimental Range in Georgia, prescribed burning is conducted only in the afternoon under damp conditions, and the low fire line is usually extinguished by ensuing night dewfall (15). Any pine stand 8 to 15 feet tall may be prescription burned, whereas the highly fire-resistant long-leaf pine (whose terminal bud is protected by a group of long needles) may be burned without ill effect already at the grass stage.

In the long leaf-slash pine stands of the South, prescribed burning may serve (1) to reduce crown fire hazard by removing highly combustible litter, (2) to prepare the forest soil as a seedbed, (3) to increase the growth and quality of livestock forage, (4) to retard a forest succession leading to a low-value scrub oak climax and maintain the high-timber-value pine subclimax, (5) to promote legume establishment and resultant soil enrichment, (6) to increase the amount of soluble mineral ash (phosphorus, potassium) available to the forest flora, (7) to stimulate the activity of soil bacteria, (8) to control brown spot needle blight (*Scirrhia acicola*) of seedling long-leaf pines, and (9) to improve food and cover conditions for wild turkey and quail.

Forest Conservation by Efficient Utilization

During the "cut out and get out" logging operations of the 1890's, lumbermen were interested only in logs. The rest of the tree—stump, limbs, branches, and foliage—was left in the forest as worthless debris which frequently served as tinder for a catastrophic fire. Further waste occurred at the sawmill, where square timbers were fashioned from round logs. Slabs, trimmings, bark, and sawdust were hauled to the refuse dump and burned. Even today, three fourths of a century later, almost 25 per cent of the forest harvest is squandered (8). It is apparent that unless we also practice conservation *after* a tree is finally harvested and removed from the forest, all the solicitous effort devoted to protecting it from destructive diseases, insects, and fires, during the thirty to 100 years *before* the harvest seems futile.

Although we are still much too wasteful of our timber resource, a definite trend toward more efficient utilization is under way. The United States Forest Products Laboratory at Madison, Wisconsin, is the world's largest institution dedicated to the study of the mechanical and chemical properties of wood and how this resource can most effectively be used by man. Whereas early in the timber industry wood had primarily only two uses, as lumber or as fuel, through the efforts of the Forest Products Laboratory and similar research centers, a number of ingenious methods have been developed for utilizing almost every part of the tree, including the bark.

The forest industry has become much more diversified. Whereas in 1890 almost 95 per cent of the forest harvest was converted into lumber, by 1962 only 37.3 billion board feet, or 54 per cent, of the 68 billion board feet of forest products consumed by the American people were fashioned into boards and timbers (1). In the last few years techniques have been developed for making extremely useful products from scrap boards, shavings, wood chips, bark, and sawdust. A few of these technological triumphs follow:

1. The development of superior, *waterproof glues* which can cement together an indefinite number of short boards (originally discarded as scrap) into sturdy *structural beams* of almost unlimited length or thickness (20). (Fig. 7–42)

2. The development of methods for *compressing small particles,* such as wood chips and shavings, into "particle board" or "hardboard" construction materials (20). It is intriguing to reflect that the handsome cabinet for your stereo, or even the walls of the room in which you are sitting this moment at one time may have existed as a nondescript heap of wood scraps.

3. The development of a great variety of *bark-derived products.* Not too long ago bark either was left lying on the forest floor gradually to disintegrate under the multiple assault of weather, insects, and fungi, or bark residues were put to the torch at the sawmill's refuse dump. This lowly bark, which for decades had been considered by the lumberman as an irritating nuisance, has suddenly achieved status in the forest industry. Today modern man comes face-to-face with bark-derived materials almost every way he turns. The successful drilling of an Oklahoma "gusher" may have been possible because of an oil-well-drilling compound derived in part from bark; the leather in your belt, shoes, and wallet may have been tanned with bark-derived *tannin;* your Thanksgiving turkey may have been raised on shredded bark litter. Bark is even the source of *quercitin,* which is used in checking hemorrhaging during surgery (4).

Figure 7–42 Testing the tensile strength of glued-laminated beams, 50 feet long and 31 inches deep, at the U.S. Forest Products Laboratory, Madison, Wisconsin. [U.S. Forest Products Laboratory, U.S. Forest Service]

Meeting Future Timber Demands. Demographers predict that by the year 2000 our population will reach 332 million, roughly a 75 per cent increase over the 1966 figure of 190 million. The nation's demands on its timber resources will increase accordingly. The amount of forest per capita will decrease from the 3 acres of 1958 to 1.75 acres by 2000. In a scholarly survey, *Resources in America's Future,* Landsberg, Fischman, and Fisher (10) review the present status of our nation's resources, future demands, and the methods by which these demands might be met. Much of the following material is derived from this source.

The projected total lumber consumption by 2000 will be 98 billion board feet, a 164 per cent increase above the 1960 figure of 37 billion board feet; by 2000 plywood utilization will be 133 billion square feet, a 504.5 per cent increase above the 22 billion square feet consumed in 1960; pulpwood use will rise 307.4 per cent from the 27 million short tons of 1960 to the 110 million short tons projected for 2000 (10). In aggregate, the over-all projected domestic timber demand for the year 2000 is 29 billion cubic feet, 17 billion cubic feet in excess of the projected annual growth of slightly over 12 billion cubic feet.

These demands may be met in the following ways:

1. *By upgrading and extending forest management in all forests, public and private, large and small.* Where can the greatest gains be made? Primarily on the small, privately owned woodlots. This is true for two principal reasons. First, the small ownerships (under 5,000 acres) embrace 55 per cent of our forest land, comprise one third of our saw timber, and contribute about 40 per cent of our annual timber harvest. Of the 4.5 million small forest ownerships in the United States over 50 per cent are under 30 acres. Yet these small owners, primarily farmers, control twice as much timberland as is included in the entire National Forest System. Second, the small forest owner has until now sadly botched his forest management responsibilities. According to Richard E. McArdle, former chief of the U.S. Forest Service, the small forest owners can meet the projected demand for the year 2000, if they:

   a. Reforest their lands three and one half times more rapidly than they are at present.
   b. Improve the quality of their timber stands at nine times the current rate.
   c. Convert much more rapidly from wasteful cutting to sustained-yield harvesting.
   d. Increase forest protection so that damage by disease, insects, and fire is reduced at least 50 per cent.

Perhaps greater incentives for upgrading forest management among small landowners may be supplied by consolidating several small stands under one management, by providing better insurance against timber losses, by providing reforestation assistance, and by discouraging premature cutting through liberalized tax assessments. Let us hope that the small owners, with encouragement and technical and financial assistance from both federal and state agencies, will shoulder their full forest management responsibility.

2. *By increasing the tempo of harvesting mature Western timber.* Eastern stands, primarily under private ownership, are generally poor-quality, understocked second- or third-growth hardwoods located on small farm woodlots. Because timber growth rates are highest when trees are young and lowest in mature trees, the Eastern forest growth rate is quite high, roughly six times that of Western stands. However, total volume is low because of much commercial forest land which is either poorly stocked or barren. Western forests (including those in coastal Alaska), primarily under public ownership, have almost 50 million acres of old-growth saw timber (that is, timber 10 inches or more in diameter at chest height), over 20 million acres of which is unutilized virgin forest. Because of the high inventory of mature timber, annual growth increments are low. These mature Western stands should be more intensively harvested, together with the upgrading of our Eastern forests (10).

3. *By increasing our forest acreage.* Because our timber deficit by 2000 will be 17 billion cubic feet, and because one forest acre can annually produce only 55 cubic feet of timber, 300 million more forest acres (in addition to the current 484 million acres) would be sufficient to remove the projected deficit. However, it is not realistic to expect such forest extensions. Rather, because of the acute need for more agricultural, urban, and industrial lands, the total forested acreage probably will decrease by 2000 (10).

4. *By more effectively controlling destructive forest agents.* The combined impact (mortality plus impaired growth) of diseases, insects, grazing, fire, and storm is roughly 75 per cent of the annual harvest.

5. *By increasing utilization of wood residues and of weed species.*

6. *By developing superior (faster-growing; better-grained; disease-, insect-, fire-, and drought-resistant) trees through the techniques of grafting and hybridization.*

7. *By increasing use of wood substitutes.* Plastics and aluminum foil might be used in packaging; fiber glass, concrete, bricks, and aluminum might replace construction timber; bagasse from sugar cane could be employed instead of pulp in paper manufacture (10).

8. *By increasing imports.* As of 1963 we were already importing 5 to 6 million tons of newsprint annually, as well as 10 to 15 per cent of our timber consumption. The best we can expect from our Canadian source by 2000 is a fourfold increase of our 1960 imports, or 3 billion cubic feet of softwood annually. This would tax Canadian supplies to the limit. Current imports of hardwood plywood from Japan and the Phillipines may be expanded. In addition, by 2000 the tropical and subtropical hardwood forests of certain developing nations in South America and Africa might be tapped (10).

BIBLIOGRAPHY

1. Allen, Shirley W., and Justin W. Leonard. *Conserving Natural Resources.* New York: McGraw-Hill Book Co., 1966, 432 pp.
2. Carson, Rachel. *Silent Spring.* Boston: Houghton Mifflin Co., 1962.
3. Cheyney, E. G., and T. Schantz-Hansen. *This Is Our Land.* St. Paul: Webb Publishing Co., 1950.
4. Clepper, Henry E., and Arthur B. Meyer. *American Forestry: Six Decades of Growth.* Washington, D.C.: Society of American Foresters, 1960.
5. Dasmann, Raymond F. *Environmental Conservation.* New York: John Wiley & Sons, Inc., 1959, 307 pp.
6. Forbes, R. D. *Forestry Handbook of the Society of American Foresters.* New York: The Ronald Press Co., 1965.
7. Highsmith, Richard M., Jr. *Conservation in the United States.* Chicago: Rand McNally and Co., 1962.
8. Jemisen, G. M. in Ralph C. Hawley and Paul W. Stickel (eds.), *Forest Protection.* New York: John Wiley & Sons, Inc., 1948, 355 pp.
9. Kerr, Robert S. *Land, Wood and Water.* New York: Fleet Publishing Co., 1960, 380 pp.
10. Landsberg, Hans H., Leonard L. Fischman, and Joseph L. Fisher. *Resources in America's Future.* Baltimore: The Johns Hopkins Press, 1962.
11. Northen, Henry T. *Introductory Plant Science.* New York: The Ronald Press, 1953, 601 pp.
12. Odum, Eugene P. *Fundamentals of Ecology.* Philadelphia: W. B. Saunders Co., 1959, 546 pp.
13. Parson, Ruben L. *Conserving American Resources.* Englewood Cliffs, N.J.: Prentice-Hall, Inc., 1956, 550 pp.
14. Smith, Guy-Harold. *Conservation of Natural Resources.* New York: John Wiley & Sons, Inc., 1958, 474 pp.
15. U.S. Department of Agriculture. *Insects: The Yearbook of Agriculture.* Washington, D.C.: U.S. Department of Agriculture, 1952.
16. U.S. Forest Service. *Annual Report, 1962.* Washington, D.C.: G.P.O., 1963.
17. _____ *Annual Report, 1963.* Washington, D.C.: G.P.O., 1964.
18. _____ *Annual Report, 1964.* Washington, D.C.: G.P.O., 1965.
19. _____ *Annual Report, 1965.* Washington, D.C.: G.P.O., 1966.
20. _____ *Forest Fire Statistics.* Washington, D.C.: G.P.O., 1965.
21. _____ *Multiple Use Management.* Washington, D.C.: G.P.O., 1966.

Wildlife

8

America's wildlife resources provide aesthetic, recreational and economic benefits. Often the recreational and economic values are closely related. For example, sport fishing and hunting are big business. Over $1 billion are spent annually by hunters alone. In 1970 the needs of hunting and shooting sportsmen were being supplied by 1,400 manufacturers. Sporting arms and ammunition sales reached $300 million in 1970. The sporting firearms industry has over 20,000 employees and a payroll of more than $100 million. Each year at least $5 million are spent on hunting dogs. America's hunters travel 5 billion miles annually. Whether it be muskellunge fishing in Wisconsin or antelope shooting in Wyoming, the quest of quail in Georgia or pheasant in the Dakotas, sportsmen are attracted from considerable distances to pursue their favorite pastime.

History of Abuse and Depletion

The Bison. It is estimated that up to 60 million bison roamed the North American prairies in the late eighteenth century. An observer, Colonel R. I. Dodge, standing at the summit of Pawnee Rocks in Arkansas, stated that he could

Figure 8–1 Flushing a pheasant on an Indiana hunting preserve. The game-farm-reared birds were released in patches of good wildlife cover such as the sargo in this picture. [Soil Conservation Service, U.S. Department of Agriculture]

see 6 to 10 miles in all directions and the entire panorama was "covered with buffalo, looking at a distance like a compact mass."

For centuries the culture and economy of the Plains Indian were intertwined with the bison. He depended on buffalo meat (pemmican and jerky) as a dietary staple. From sinews he fashioned bowstrings. From bone he wrought tools and ornaments. Hides were used in bedding, garments, and shelters and as "canvases" by Indian artists. The rare albino hides were thought to be capable of healing a variety of ills. Even the dried feces, known as buffalo "chips," provided badly needed fuel.

For many years the prairie grasses, buffalo, and Plains Indians represented the major living components of a balanced ecosystem. The unmounted Indian made slight impact on the buffalo hordes with his lances and arrows. When the herds emigrated to new range, the Indian quickly broke camp and followed, for the herd represented his food, clothing, and shelter.

When the Civil War ended, a ruthless campaign of bison butchery was launched which brought this animal to the brink of extinction. Apparently the United States Army believed that the subjugation of the fierce Plains Indian would be assured

Figure 8–2 Cow buffalo suckling her calf. Note patches of molting hair. Kaibab National Forest, Arizona. [U.S. Forest Service]

once the buffalo was exterminated. It has been estimated that during 1871 and 1872 about 8.5 million buffalo were slaughtered, about one seventh of the peak population. Such butchery was facilitated by the westward extension of several railroads into the prairie country. These railroads employed professional buffalo hunters to provide their crews with food. One hunter, the celebrated Buffalo Bill Cody, sometimes was able to kill 200 "shaggies" in one day. During the winter of 1872–1873 almost 1.5 million hides were shipped via three railroads to eastern markets and sold for $3 per hide. However, less than 1 per cent of the meat was marketed and much of it went to waste. Over 100,000 animals were killed just for their tongue, which was considered a delicacy. Once the tongue had been sliced off, the rest of the carcass was left to rot. "Bone pickers" collected skeletal remains and shipped them by the ton to fertilizer plants in Kansas and Minnesota. Kansas plants paid $4.5 million for bones over a period of thirteen years. The long facial hair was used for stuffing mattresses. A buffalo wool company was even established in the Red River Valley. However, after shipping a few yards of wool cloth to England, this enterprise collapsed. Inevitably the buffalo hordes dwindled to scattered bands. By 1889 only 150 bison survived in the wild; in 1894 the last wild buffalo was shot by a rancher in Parke County, Colorado. Sound management practices have successfully built up the herd in several wildlife refuges from the 250 animals which still survived in captivity.

The Passenger Pigeon. The Passenger pigeon (*Ectopistes migratorius*) was once the most abundant bird on earth. Early in the nineteenth century the renowned ornithologist Alexander Wilson observed a migrating flock which streamed past him for several hours. Wilson estimated the single flock to be one mile wide and 240 miles long and composed of about 2 billion birds. (The population of this flock was roughly ten times the total North American waterfowl population of today.) Yet not one passenger pigeon is left today.

What factors contributed to the passenger pigeon's extinction? Firstly, many potential nest and food trees (beech, maple, oak) were chopped down or burned to make room for farms and settlements. The pigeon fed extensively on beech nuts and acorns; the single flock observed by Wilson could have con-

Figure 8–3 Extinction. When the last living passenger pigeon, Martha, died at the Cincinnati Zoo, on September 14, 1918, a unique organism was removed from the human ecosystem forever. [State Historical Society of Wisconsin]

sumed 17 million bushels per day. Secondly, disease may have taken a severe toll. The breeding birds were susceptible to infectious disease epidemics, because they nested in dense colonies. Schorger reports that in 1871 a concentration of 136 million pigeons nested in an 850-square-mile region in central Wisconsin. Up to 100 nests were built in a single tree. Thirdly, many pigeons may have been destroyed by severe storms during the long migrations between the North American breeding grounds and the Central and South American wintering region. Bent cites a record of an immense flock of young passenger pigeons which descended to the surface of Crooked Lake, Michigan, after becoming bewildered by a dense fog. Thousands drowned and lay a foot deep along the shore for miles. Fourthly, the low biotic potential may have been a factor in their extinction. Although many perching birds, such as robins, lay four to six eggs per clutch and ducks, quail, and pheasants lay eight to twelve eggs, the female pigeon produced only a single egg per nesting. Fifthly, the reduction of the flocks to scattered remnants possibly deprived the birds of the social stimulus requisite for reproduction. Sixthly, the bird's decline was hastened by persecution from market hunters. They slaughtered the birds on their nests. Every imaginable instrument of destruction was employed, including guns, dynamite, clubs, nets, fire, and traps. Over 1,300 densely massed birds were caught in one throw of the net. Pigeons were burned and smoked out of their nesting trees. Migrating flocks were riddled with shot. Over sixteen tons of shot were sold to pigeon hunters in one small Wisconsin village in a single year. Pigeon flesh was considered both a delectable and fashionable dish in the plush restaurants of Chicago, Boston, and New York. Sold for 2¢ per bird, almost 15 million pigeons were shipped from a single nesting area at Petoskey, Michigan, in 1861. The last wild pigeon was shot in 1900. Martha, the last captive survivor, died on September 1, 1914, at the age of twenty-nine, in the Cincinnati Zoo.

Waterfowl. When Captain Howard Stansburg explored the Bear River marshes of Utah in 1849, he was amazed by the immense numbers of waterfowl. "Thousands of acres, as far as the eye could reach seemed literally covered with them." Other explorers used phrases like "clouds of ducks" and "thunderlike sounds" to indicate the waterfowl abundance. The redhead duck (*Nyroca americana*) occurred in dense rafts, several miles long, numbering up to 50,000 birds. Eventually, however, the waterfowl populations dwindled. The decline was due in part to marsh and pothole drainage for agricultural purposes and in

Figure 8–4 Shooting "wild pigeons" in Iowa. Copied from *Leslie's Illustrated Newspaper*, September 21, 1867. Note the gunner firing point-blank into the densely massed birds. Over 100 birds are resting on the base branches of the oak in the background. [State Historical Society of Wisconsin]

part to frontal assaults by market hunters and so-called sportsmen. Live decoys and multiple-gun rigs were employed. One Maryland hunter used a 100-pound gun to slaughter and cripple large numbers of birds with a single shot. Albert M. Day documents some of the early carnage: One "sportsman" killed sixty-four broadbill, ninety-eight black duck, and one gadwall in four hours; a Connecticut hunter bagged 127 birds in one day. During the winter of 1893–1894 over 120,000 mallards were sent to market from Big Lake, Arkansas. One Minnesota market hunter boasted of slaughtering 6,000 ducks in one season. Waterfowl flesh was considered gourmet fare in the metropolitan areas. The Palmer House in Chicago featured a menu which included a dozen species of wild game. In the 1880's wild mallards sold for $3 a dozen, teal for $2, wild geese for $4.50, and canvasbacks for $6 per dozen. Professor William J. Hamilton reports that dead ducks littered the platforms of North Dakota railroad stations in the 1890's; during hot weather it was not uncommon for many carcasses to spoil and be hauled away by the wagon load to the dumping ground.

Other Wildlife.   The fate of upland game, big game and fur-bearers during this period of wildlife carnage was no better. An early trapper-hunter proudly relates killing 1,000 deer, 600 beavers, 500 foxes, 400 fishers, 150 otters, 100 bears, several thousand mink, and tens of thousands of muskrats during his lifetime. In the late nineteenth century bear and deer hung from hooks like beef in the game markets of Chicago. Venison was sold in Minnesota butcher shops at 9¢ per pound; many tons were shipped to Boston to satisfy Eastern epicurean demands.

Today's Endangered Species.   Within the relatively brief time span since the first American settlements were established, many species of wildlife have become extinct; others have had their ranks greatly reduced. Currently the U.S. Fish and Wildlife Service considers at least 60 species of birds and 27 mammals to be in danger of extinction unless a concerted effort is made to preserve them. We shall describe the status of two endangered species—the grizzly bear and whooping crane.

Grizzly Bear.   The grizzly bear (*Ursus horribilis*) is easily distinguished from the much more abundant and widely distributed black bear (*Ursus americanus*) by its grizzled brown fur, shoulder hump, and concave face. Its huge front claws are effectively employed for digging rodent prey from their burrows and for ripping the flesh of a variety of animals, including, on occasion, the colts, calves, and lambs of the rancher. The grizzly originally ranged throughout western North America, from the Arctic to subtropical Mexico and eastward to the grassland biome. Although 11,000 of these magnificent beasts wandered the wilds of Alaska in 1963, only a remnant survives in the United States proper, primarily in the mountainous regions of Wyoming, Montana, Colorado, and Idaho. In California, where it once was relatively abundant, and captured bears were prodded into savage encounters with range bulls, this interesting carnivore was eradicated by 1922. The livestock man has been an important contributing factor to its present endangered status. Many a rancher who has come across the torn carcass of a choice calf has waged an emotion-charged personal program of grizzly eradication, employing poison, traps, bullets, and hounds. Such environmental resistance has proved especially severe because of the bear's limited biotic potential—the female giving birth to single or twin cubs in *alternate* years. Restrictive hunting laws have given the grizzly a measure of protection throughout much of its diminished range. In national wildlife refuges such as Glacier and Yellowstone National Parks, it had been unlawful to kill the grizzly for many years, although the ban was lifted for 1967. Future management for grizzly survival will probably include its removal from livestock areas to mountainous wilderness haunts.

Whooping Crane. The 4-foot whooping crane (*Grus americana*) is the tallest bird on the North American continent. Snow white, except for its scarlet crown and black wing tips, it resembles a flying cross as it passes overhead, with its graceful neck projecting forward and sticklike legs trailing behind. In the early nineteenth century its breeding range extended throughout the grassland biome from the prairie provinces of Canada south through the Dakotas to Iowa. It wintered along the Gulf Coast from Mexico east to Florida. As of 1970, however, it was known to nest only in Wood Buffalo National Park in northern Alberta, Canada, and the wintering area was restricted to the Aransas Wildlife Refuge on the Texas coast. Although very slowly increasing in numbers, only fifty-five wild and eight captive whooping cranes survived as of 1969.

Among the factors which have contributed to the endan-

Figure 8–5 These two adult whooping cranes, photographed on the Aransas National Wildlife Refuge, Texas, represent about 4 per cent of the total world population of the species. [U.S. Fish and Wildlife Service]

gered status of this strikingly handsome bird are the following: appropriation of its prairie nesting habitat by rancher and farmer, intensive shooting, severe storms during migrations, and low biotic potential—only two eggs being laid per clutch.

Avian species which have "flown their last flight" are the great auk of the North Atlantic which became extinct because of intensive hunting by 1844; the Hawaiian rail, extinct by 1893 because of predation by introduced rats; the Carolina parakeet of the Southeastern United States, which became extinct by 1920 because overhunting and the removal of its woodland habitat; and the Molokai thrush of Molokai Island, Hawaii, which passed into oblivion in 1936 due to the destruction of its habitat and the inadvertent introduction of predatory rats and disease organisms.

Wildlife Management and Restoration

Through the years American biologists and legislators have employed a number of techniques for restoring, maintaining, and increasing game populations. They include protective laws, wildlife refuges, predator control, and most recently, habitat development. In addition, several exotic species have been introduced.

Game Laws. Throughout human history there have been a few farsighted citizens aware of the importance of wildlife to man's happiness and welfare and of the ease with which this resource can be depleted, if not exhausted, by the unrestrained human "predator." Thus, as early as 700 B.C., Moses decreed (Deuteronomy 22:6) that although eggs and nestling birds could be taken for food, the adult breeding stock should be spared "that it may go well with you and that you may live long."

Although game was generally abundant during early colonial times, constant hunting of a few species such as the white-tailed deer prompted some states to enact protective laws. Thus, in 1646 Rhode Island established the first closed season on deer, and by 1694 Massachusetts was also protecting this popular game species. In 1708 New York afforded protection to upland game such as the ruffed grouse, wild turkey, and the heath hen. The first law to protect does was enacted by Virginia in 1738; in 1788 this state prohibited the use of hounds in hunting deer. Rhode Island was the first state to enact legislation barring spring shooting of migratory waterfowl. In 1874 the American people became so aroused over the near extermination of the buffalo that Congress was prodded into passing a protective law; unfortunately, it was vetoed by President Grant. The first game bag limit was set by Iowa in 1878. Kansas, Montana, and Texas all barred sale of protected game in 1897.

During most of the nineteenth century, however, protective game laws were poorly enforced. Very few officials were sufficiently courageous to punish the numerous violators. Nevertheless, greater respect for restrictive game legislation developed by 1878 when New Hampshire and California employed game wardens charged with the responsibility of law enforcement. By the turn of the century, thirty-one states employed wardens.

In 1894, just three years before the last wild bison was shot in Colorado, a bison law was passed that made poaching in Yellowstone Park punishable by fine or imprisonment. Several states in the late 1890's tried to protect the vanishing passenger pigeon by enacting appropriate laws. But by the time these laws were passed the buffalo herds had been reduced to remnants, and the pigeon was well on the road to oblivion.

Wildlife Refuges.   The federal wildlife refuge program had its inception with the establishment of the Pelican Island Refuge on the east coast of Florida in 1903. Since this modest beginning, the program has rapidly expanded to include 321 units (as of 1968) embracing 28.6 million acres, an area equivalent to almost the entire state of Pennsylvania. Refuges range in size from the tiny Mille Lacs Refuge consisting of two small islands in a Minnesota lake to the mammoth 8.9-million-acre Arctic National Wildlife Refuge in Alaska. Federal refuges may be placed in three categories: those designed primarily to accommodate waterfowl; those designed to serve big-game animals such as mountain goats, antelope, and deer; and those designed to save endangered species from threatened extinction.

Introduction of Exotics.   Another phase of wildlife development and management involves the introduction of exotic species. They may be brought over to provide game, to serve as predators in controlling some pest, or simply to add color to the native wildlife community. Welty reports that in the late nineteenth century several societies were organized for the explicit purpose of introducing and dispersing exotic species of birds (63). Most of these efforts failed despite an extensive program in which hundreds of thousands of individuals representing over one hundred foreign species were released. Formerly, the Biological Survey, and currently, the U.S. Fish and Wildlife Service, have had the responsibility of permitting or barring such imports. (Several years ago, according to Gustafson et al. (31), a would-be smuggler tried to bring four exotic finches into the country by tying them around his ankles inside his socks!) A few introductions have been successful, notably that of the ring-necked pheasant, which was originally intro-duced to Oregon from Asia in the late nineteenth century. After several additional plantings elsewhere in the United States, it became the most important upland game bird in much of the agricultural Midwest. South Dakota prides itself on being the pheasant capital of America.

Some introductions have had an adverse affect on the native wildlife community. Notable among such unfortunate importa-tions is that of the English sparrow in 1865 and the European starling in 1880. Both of these aggressive and noisy species have appropriated breeding habitat formerly utilized by more attrac-tive and/or melodic native species such as the bluebird, purple martin, and red-headed woodpecker. The Indian mongoose was introduced to Puerto Rico to control rats and itself became a predator on poultry and ground-nesting birds. It is apparent, therefore, that all aspects of the ecology of the proposed exotic must be thoroughly studied before it is released. With such investigations, future harmful introductions will be held to a minimum. Our experience with the ring-necked pheasant is a convincing demonstration that the right exotic in the right habitat may ultimately form an important component of our wildlife resource. In recent years fourteen exotic species of game birds were being reared in twenty-one states with the objective of ultimate release.

Predator Control.   The control of predators assumed a popular and conspicuous role early in wildlife management history. It was only natural for the nimrod, tired and disappointed after tramping the fields in fruitless quest of elusive quail or cotton-tail, to vent his frustration by blaming the hawk or fox. His thesis was based on grade-school arithmetic. If a fox in a certain meadow eats thirty rabbits a year, a rifle bullet through that fox's brain will mean thirty additional cottontails available for hunters. In the past, pressure has been exerted by sportsmen's organizations on state legislators to enact bounty laws resulting in the expenditure of funds which could have been used to greater advantage in the acquisition and development of wild-life habitat. Money paid by a state for bounties may be con-siderable, ranging from $2 for a fox and $15 for a bobcat, to $25 for a coyote and $35 for a timber wolf. Game officials in many states, however, have been re-examining predator control in the last few years. The bounty system has been criticized for several reasons.

The possibility for fraudulent bounty claims is well pointed up in an account related by Gustafson et al. Some years ago, a

Figure 8–6 Red fox pup peers out from behind a rock at Kettle Moraine State Forest, Wisconsin. Predators add interest and sparkle to the out-of-doors, well worth the few rabbits and other small game they may take. [U.S. Department of Agriculture]

Midwestern state had placed a bounty on squirrels. To claim the bounty all that was required was to turn in the squirrel's tail. Some quick-witted youngsters devised a scheme whereby they live-trapped a number of squirrels, cut off their tails, released the animals, and turned in their tails for payment. Because the de-tailed squirrels suffered no reduction in biotic potential, the squirrel population remained at a relatively high level, thus assuring a continuous supply of tails (and bounty payments) for the enterprising youths!

Many accusations against predators are ill founded. A good example is the crow, frequently the recipient of the duck hunter's wrath for destroying nests and making a meal of eggs and ducklings. However, an analysis of crow stomachs in Michigan revealed that two thirds of the diet was composed of beetles, grasshoppers, and other herbivorous insects, all of considerable crop-destroying potential. The barn owl is frequently persecuted by the harried farmer for raiding his chicken yard or by the irate hunter for seizing quail and rabbits. However, a three-year investigation by Michigan state biologists has revealed the misdirection of their control efforts. An examination of 2,200 barn owl pellets (regurgitated masses of indigestible bones and fur) showed absolutely no trace of poultry or game birds. Although 1.07 per cent of the owls' diet was indeed made up of birds, the great majority of them were the pestiferous starlings and English sparrows. Further, over 90 per cent of the mammals represented in the pellets were mice, primarily the meadow mouse, a species capable of inflicting serious crop damage.

Most ecologists consider the predator as forming an essential part of the ecosystem. As Dasmann has pointed out, the number of predators in the apex of a food pyramid is dependent on the number of prey animals at the lower levels, and *not the reverse*.(14). Thus, in an analysis of data provided by Errington's fifteen-year study of Wisconsin quail, Lack showed that the greater the quail population in spring, the heavier the mortality (including predation) the following fall (40). In some cases, paradoxical as it may seem, predators may actually promote the welfare of the prey species by culling the aged, crippled, and disease-ridden individuals from the population. Moreover, predators may serve a useful role in keeping the resilient prey population within the limits imposed by the carrying capacity of its habitat. A lack of predatory pressure might release a population explosion resulting in habitat deterioration and culminating in massive death caused by starvation and disease.

Habitat Development. Currently the best prospect for increasing wildlife populations is to increase the amount and quality of suitable habitat. Many game biologists consider habitat development absolutely indispensable. In other words, even with protective game laws, predator control, exotic introductions, transplantations, and artificial propagation, wildlife populations will nevertheless be in jeopardy if at the same time their habitat is usurped, destroyed, or permitted to deteriorate. Conversely, if an abundance of high-quality wildlife habitat is available, game populations will remain relatively high regardless of the lack of predator control, artificial propagation, introductions, and transplantations.

It is not surprising, therefore, that habitat acquisition and development programs are receiving high priority among many state game divisions, as well as wildlife research units administered by the U.S. Fish and Wildlife Service. We shall describe some of these programs later in conjunction with case studies of deer and waterfowl. At this time, however, it may be well to show what can be done by private landowners.

Because over 85 per cent of the hunting lands in the United States are privately owned or controlled (59), and because it is on the private farms, ranches, and woodlots that most of the grouse, quail, doves, pheasants, and rabbits are produced, the biggest contribution to an abundant and varied game resource (as in the case of forest development) can be made by the private citizen. Fortunately, many of the land practices that are effective in soil and water management may be simultaneously applied toward the goal of wildlife habitat improvement.

STRIP CROPPING. Aldo Leopold has shown that the greatest wildlife populations occur where there is a high degree of *edge,* or interspersion of various habitat types. Edge can be artificially enhanced by strip cropping. For example, a cover crop of alfalfa, which would provide cover and nesting sites, could be alternated with corn or wheat, which would provide food. Strip-cropped land will support about twice as many ground-nesting birds as land planted to a monotype. Almost two thirds of a million acres are strip-cropped annually in the United States (59).

FARM PONDS. The rancher can make livestock watering ponds highly attractive to wildlife by planting a vegetational fringe of grasses, legumes, dogwoods, elder, buttonbush, and willows along the margins to provide food, cover, and breeding sites. A wildlife survey of ninety-one such ponds in Missouri revealed that ten species of mammals and ninety species of birds had established home ranges in the immediate pond area. Fifty-five per cent of these pond margins supported quail, 63 per cent muskrats, 65 per cent mourning doves, and 85 per cent cottontails. In South Dakota 40,000 man-made ponds provided habitat for 141,000 ducks, or an average of 3.5 ducks per pond. About 60,000 such wildlife-adapted farm ponds are being constructed annually in Soil Conservation Districts (59).

"ODD" AREAS. Almost every farmer has "odd" areas on his land which are not suitable for production. They may be rocky knolls, sandy blow-out areas, fence corners, or bogs. They may be fenced off from livestock and planted to wildlife food and cover. Although each individual odd area is minute in size, in aggregate such areas form 10 million acres of wildlife carrying habitat in the United States.

Figure 8–7 Taylor County, West Virginia. Farm ponds beautify the landscape and provide water for livestock, recreation, and fire protection. [U.S. Department of Agriculture]

LIVING FENCES. Before the advent of barbed wire in 1874, ranchers and farmers resorted to other devices for separating woodlot from pasture, or cropland from marsh. In much of the deciduous forest biome split rail fences were used; in rocky New England crude fences were constructed from boulders removed from the path of the plow; and in the Lake States rows of pine stumps were employed. Osage orange was used in Midwestern prairies as a "living fence." None of these fences was as "neat" as the barbed-wire fences that replaced them; nevertheless, they were much more picturesque, and they reserved more land between boulders, trunks, stumps, and zigzagging rails for potential use as wildlife habitat. The barbed-wire fence reserved *nothing* for wildlife. Because the farmer could now plow to within inches of his fences, results for upland game were disastrous.

In recent years game biologists have encouraged landowners to replace barbed-wire fences with living fences composed of native or exotic shrubs (such as the *multiflora* rose), which may provide food, cover, and travel lanes for pheasants, quail, and cottontails. To date, an encouraging 2,000 such fences are being

292

constructed annually (59). When planted at 1-foot intervals, the exotic *multiflora* rose, introduced from Asia, produces a thorny livestock barrier within three to five years. Not only is it attractive, but it provides cover for rodent-destroying skunks and weasels. Song bird density in such a fence, according to an Ohio study by Dambach, is thirty-two times that in open crop fields. Other fence shrubs suitable for game use are bayberry, tartarian honeysuckle, silky cornel, and highbush cranberry.

WOODLOT MANAGEMENT. Eighteen per cent of the land in five Midwestern states is either wooded or in "waste" areas. A woodlot can be a wildlife desert or a paradise depending on how it is managed by the landowner. It should be properly fenced off, to prevent cattle from grazing and trampling herbaceous ground cover which might serve as a suitable bird and mammal habitat. In 1941 a comparative study was made in Ohio of two adjoining woodlots, one grazed and the other protected for ten years from grazing by the erection of a barbed-wire fence. The ungrazed woodlot had 53,000 young trees up to 21 feet tall and the grazed woodlot 1,000 seedlings under 5 inches in height. Nineteen species of birds nested in the ungrazed lot to only eight for the grazed area. Annual avian density averaged

Figure 8–8 The cottontail rabbit, shown here on the alert to possible danger, is perhaps the most valuable game animal in the United States. [Soil Conservation Service, U.S. Department of Agriculture]

1.7 pairs per acre in the fenced grove compared to only 0.4 pairs per acre in the unfenced area. Here and there an occasional brush pile should be strategically placed to serve for rabbits. A good number of hollow stubs should be left standing to serve as potential breeding sites for opossums, raccoons, flying squirrels, woodpeckers, and owls. In Southern stands of long-leaf and loblolly pine, wildlife foods may be provided by planting strips of bicolor lespedeza. Wild grape, bittersweet, Virginia creeper, and blackberry bushes planted at the woodlot margin will enhance its wildlife value. Occasionally the undigested seeds in the droppings of birds which have used brush piles as refuge or roosting sites will germinate and develop into a thicket of vines and berry bushes.

MUSKRAT MARSH MANAGEMENT. The water level of a marsh is important in determining its carrying capacity for muskrats. Smith has pointed out that low water levels may force muskrats to vacate their lodges (which may become highly vulnerable to the red fox) and seek emergency refuge in abandoned woodchuck burrows or even a corn crib (57). When low water levels occur in winter, muskrats are locked out of their food source of succulent aquatics by an icy barrier. They are then forced to wander overland in search of food and become easy prey for mink. If the owner of a muskrat marsh has water

Figure 8–9 Wildlife habitat improvement. Aerial view of Horicon Wildlife Refuge, Wisconsin, showing ditching made to raise carrying capacity for muskrats. [Wisconsin Conservation Department]

sources available such as a nearby stream, well, or pond, he may effectively regulate the water level of the marsh to the muskrats' benefit. If the water level is maintained at 6 inches during summer, such preferred muskrat foods as cattail, bulrush, arrowhead, and burreed will flourish, and red fox depradations will be curbed; then in late autumn the marsh can be flooded to the 2-foot level to prevent a muskrat freeze-out.

HABITAT DEVELOPMENT AND ECOLOGICAL SUCCESSION. In our earlier discussion of ecological succession, we indicated that both plant and animal communities change as the physical environment (available sunlight, moisture, wind velocity, soil fertility) changes. Dasmann (14) has classified a number of game species according to the successional stage of which each is characteristic, as follows: *Climax species:* bighorn sheep, caribou, grizzly bear, musk ox, passenger pigeon. *Midsuccessional species:* antelope, elk, moose, mule deer, pronghorn antelope, ruffed grouse, sage grouse, white-tailed deer. *Low-successional species:* bobwhite quail, doves, hares, rabbits, ring-necked pheasants. From the preceding classification, it is apparent that the game biologist can regulate the abundance of these species by manipulating ecological succession. Thus, he could permit a succession to proceed on its natural course to a climax, or, by employing such artificial devices as controlled burning, controlled flooding, herbicides, plowing, and logging, he could retard the succession or even revert it to the pioneer stage.

Because climax-associated or wilderness species such as caribou, bighorn sheep, and grizzly bear will flourish only in relatively undisturbed climax communities, their survival depends to a large degree on the establishment of state and national refuges. Without such protected islands in the oceans of successional disturbance caused by man, these climax-associated species would face decline and extinction—a fate already met by the passenger pigeon.

Midsuccessional species such as the moose, white-tailed deer, and ruffed grouse, according to Dasmann, must be regarded as purely temporary phenomena, as temporary as the vegetational community on which these herbivores depend for food. In northern Minnesota, for example, moose are not found in the dense, well-shaded spruce-fir climax forest, but in midsuccessional thickets of willow, aspen, and birch. Inevitably, when these thickets are shaded out by climax spruce and fir, the local moose, a highly sedentary species, will gradually decline in numbers and ultimately die out. On the other hand, such devices as logging or controlled burning, may open up a dense climax forest and permit the eventual establishment of sun-tolerant birch and aspen as well as the moose which utilize them as a primary food source. In any event, these midsuccessional species are disturbance-dependent and without the intervention of game biologist, lumberman, or forest fire (ignited by lightning or man), they will vanish.

The low-successional species, such as rabbits, quail, and doves, are greatly dependent on major disturbances of the ecological succession by man. All these species, for example, find food and cover in the weedy pioneer plants which invade an area that has been denuded by human activity. Such vegetation may become established when a cotton or corn field is abandoned or when a fresh road cut becomes exposed to invasion by wind or animal-borne seeds.

In many Southeastern states the natural climax is composed of oak-dominated hardwood stands, a community of inferior timber value and poor carrying capacity for quail. Controlled burnings have been used periodically in this region to hold the succession in a subclimax stage. These fires effectively destroy the heat-vulnerable oak seedlings but promote the establishment and survival of fire-tolerant and timber-valuable long-leaf pine, as well as a great variety of herbs and shrubs which provide top-quality food, cover, and nest sites for quail. Here, then, we have a good example of how succession can be regulated by a single device, controlled burning, to promote the twin objectives of high-value timber and wildlife.

Habitat Requirements of Wildlife

We may consider habitat to be the general environment in which an organism lives—its natural home. The habitat of a wild animal provides certain essentials: shelter, food, water, breeding sites (den, nest, or burrow), and a fairly well-defined area called the *territory* in which an animal has psychological dominance over intruders.

Cover. Cover may serve to protect an animal from adverse weather conditions. Good examples are the dense cedar swamps which protect white-tailed deer herds from winter winds and drifting snow and the leafy canopies of apple trees which shield nestling robins from the heat of the midday sun. Cover may also protect wild animals from predators. Representative of this function is the thicket into which a cottontail plunges when eluding a fox or the marsh grasses which conceal a teal from a hawk. Even water may serve as cover, as for a muskrat or beaver, providing relative security from all land-bound predators, from wolf to man.

Food. On the basis of food habits, vertebrate animals may be classified as herbivores, spermivores, insectivores, frugivores, carnivores, omnivores, and so on. The tendency to eat certain basic food types is inherited but is subject to modification on the basis of experience. There may be considerable variation in food habits within the species, and even in the same individual, depending on such variables as health and age of animal, season, habitat, and food availability. An animal's access to adequate food may be influenced by many factors, including population density, weather, habitat destruction (by fire, flood, or insects), and plant succession.

Because mammals (and presumably birds) must spend 90 per cent of their waking hours searching for food, the importance of food availability is emphasized (13). Occasionally, when a food occurs in superabundant quantities, an animal will exploit this source, even though it is not a usual dietary item. Consider some examples: Even though the green-winged teal's diet is 90 per cent vegetarian, it avidly consumes the maggoty flesh of rotting Pacific salmon. Although the lesser scaup is not

Figure 8–10 Black-capped chickadee feeding from hand. These birds respond so readily to human imitation of their territorial song that they will perch on one's head. [U.S. Department of Agriculture]

normally a scavenger, the stomachs of ducks which had been feeding at the mouth of a sewer were filled with slaughterhouse debris and cow hair (as well as rubber bands and paper). A house wren, usually insectivorous, fed its nestlings large quantities of newly hatched trout from an adjacent hatchery (63). In a study of winter mink diets in Missouri, Korschgen found that volume percentage of fish increased from 11.9 in 1951 to 27.4 in 1953 apparently because low water levels increased the vulnerability of the prey (38). Similarly, during periods of drought or high muskrat population densities, muskrat may become the principal mink food, although at other times it forms only 1 to 2 per cent of the mink diet.

Dietary changes are frequently seasonal in character. Thus, although the red fox consumes mice throughout the year, Hamilton describes the following shifts in its diet: winter—carrion, offal, frozen apples; spring and summer—snakes, turtles, and eggs, an occasional fawn, blackberries and raspberries; autumn —wild cherries, grapes, grasshoppers (33). Welty reports that barn owls near Davis, California, which had subsisted primarily on house and deer mice during spring and summer, shifted to gophers and voles during autumn and winter (63).

Animals that consume a great variety of foods are *euryphagous.* The omnivorous opossum is a classic example. It consumes fruits, blackberries, persimmons, corn, apples, earthworms, insects, frogs, snakes, lizards, newly hatched turtles, bird eggs and young, mice, and even bats. It is apparent that during critical periods when usual foods are scarce, the euryphagous animal is well adapted to survive. Thus, although staple foods for the ring-necked pheasant are corn, sorghum, rye, wheat, barley, soybeans, lesser ragweed, and pigeon grass, Errington found that when its usual foods are covered with ice and snow, the bird shifts to the seeds of bittersweet, sumac, and black locust (23).

A *stenophagous* animal, which maintains a specialized diet, is more vulnerable to starvation when its usual foods are scarce. For example, a spell of freezing weather in late April which causes a dearth of flying insects will frequently result in considerable starvation losses to chimney swifts and purple martins. Similarly, when a parasite caused 90 per cent destruction of eelgrass along the Atlantic coast from 1931 to 1933, the wintering population of brants, which depends on eelgrass almost exclusively, was reduced by 80 per cent (44).

Water. Roughly 65 to 80 per cent of wild animal biomass is composed of water. It serves many functions. It flushes wastes from the body. As a major blood constituent it transports nutri-

Figure 8–11 Wildlife habitat improvement. Chukar partridge (introduced from Asia) attracted by a "guzzler," a recently developed watering device employed in arid regions. [California Department of Fish and Game]

ents, hormones, enzymes, and respiratory gases. Animals can survive for weeks without food but only a few days without water. Although fed dried pears, a water-deprived domestic pigeon died in five days (60). Mourning doves have been known to lose 15 per cent of their body weight when water-deprived for twenty-four hours at 39 degrees C (63). Buffalo herds living in arid Western grasslands traveled many miles to water holes, leaving trails which are visible to this day. Mourning doves may fly up to 30 miles from nesting site to watering place. Dove and quail populations have been increased in the Southwest by the installation of "gallinaceous guzzlers"—devices which collect rainwater (14). Some herbivores (e.g., wild donkeys) may recover up to 25 per cent of water loss in less than two minutes, thus minimizing the predator hazard (15). Birds and mammals may secure their water from dew or may drink it as it drips from foliage and tree trunks after a shower. During the northern winter, when liquid water is scarce, the author has observed English sparrows and starlings eating snow. The versatile Adelie penguin, according to Robert Cushman Murphy, may drink salt water or fresh water as well as eat snow. Many animals living in arid regions satisfy their water requirements by consuming water-containing foods. Desert carnivores, such as the rattlesnake, desert fox, prairie falcon, and bobcat, may secure water from the blood and body fluids of prey. The desert-dwelling grasshopper mouse feeds extensively on insects having a 60 to 85 per cent water content (15). Forty-four per cent of the white-throated wood rat's desert diet consists of cacti and other succulent plants. The kangaroo rat may not require ingested water during its entire life span, because it can make effective use of the metabolic water synthesized within its tissues from the breakdown of fats and proteins (49).

Home Range. Smith defines a home range as "the area over which an animal habitually travels while engaged in its usual activities" (57). Home range may be determined by marking, releasing, and recapturing an animal. Animals may be tracked with geiger counters after having been fed radioactive materials. Dyed foods will result in colored feces; the home range can then be determined on the basis of dropping distribution (15). Birds may be individually marked with colored leg bands or spray paints. Small mammals can have their ears notched or toes clipped. Large mammals (buffalo and elk) can be tattooed or marked with colored plastic collars so that visual identification is possible at a distance.

Herbivores usually have smaller home ranges than carnivores. Animals occupying a deteriorated habitat maintain larger home ranges than those in a good habitat. A few home ranges for herbivorous mammals are as follows: field mouse, 0.5 acre; deer mouse, 0.5 acre (good habitat) or 5 acres (poor habitat) (15); porcupine, 1 kilometer; beaver, under 1 kilometer (12). According to Burt, buck cottontails have a home range of 8 to 20 acres compared to the doe's 3 acres (8). Adams found the buck snowshoe hare's home range was 25.2 acres compared to the female's 18.9 acres (1). In one study 70 per cent of the released muskrats were retaken within 160 feet of original capture (15). Bull moose may have a summer home range of only 100 acres of swamp. After attaching miniature radio transmitters to the bodies of eastern wild turkeys, Ellis and Lewis, with the aid of portable receivers, acquired telemetric data indicating an annual average home range of 1,100 acres for four adult gobblers (20). Although more data are required, the mink appears to occupy a home range embracing 15 to 100 miles of lake or river shoreline.

Kolenosky at al. determined by telemetric methods that the maximum ranges of timber wolves in east-central Ontario were

3.2 kilometers (with ground receivers) and 9.6 kilometers (with receivers in airplanes) (37). Burt, on the other hand, reports that timber wolves have circular runways 20 to 60 miles in diameter.

Territory. Noble defines a territory as "any defended area." Territories are usually defended against individuals of the same species. Nice set up the following classification of avian territories in terms of areas defended: Type A—entire mating, feeding, and breeding area; Type B—mating and nesting area; Type C—mating area; Type D—nest only; Type E—nonbreeding areas such as feeding and roosting sites (47).

Van Tyne and Berger summarize the various functions which avian territorialism might serve: provision of adequate food; a mechanism for establishing and maintaining the pairing bond; regulation of population density (territories are on the average smaller where food is superabundant); reduction of interference with breeding activities (copulation, nest building, incubation); reduction of predation losses (resulting from famil-

Figure 8-12 The male ruffed grouse establishes and maintains its territory by the use of mechanical rather than vocal sounds. Here is a male "drumming" on a half-decayed log with its wings. The sound is reminiscent of the "put-put" of an outboard motorboat. It is employed in courtship as well as in territorial activity. Agassiz National Wildlife Refuge. [Bureau of Sport Fisheries and Wildlife, U.S. Department of the Interior]

iarity with refuge sites as well as from the population dispersion); and reduction of infectious disease transmission (little evidence) (61).

Average territorial areas (in square meters) for certain avian species follow: black-headed gull in England, 0.3; eastern robin in Wisconsin, 1,200; red-winged blackbird in Wisconsin, 3,000; black-capped chickadee in New York, 53,000; great-horned owl in New York, 500,000; and golden eagle in California, 93 million (63). The varying areas here depend partly on function, partly on size of bird. The black-headed gull's territory is concerned with nest defense only, that of the horned owl and golden eagle with defense of mating, nesting, and feeding area.

Territorial behavior is well developed in many species of fish, including the sunfish, bass, sticklebacks, and minnows. Male black bass and sunfish will defend their nests by rushing toward an intruder.

Territoriality is not readily observed in mammals, because many species are nocturnal or fossorial (burrowing). It appears rather poorly defined. Thus Murie has reported two female wolves with litters occupying a den simultaneously in Mount McKinley National Park, Alaska (5). In a study of the prairie

Figure 8–13 The golden eagle, like most carnivorous birds, maintains an extremely large territory—in some cases, up to 93 million square meters. [Wisconsin Conservation Department]

spotted skunk in Iowa, it was found that a den was not the private possession of one skunk, but was co-inhabited by the entire local skunk population. However, according to Burt territoriality occurs in squirrels, beavers, female chipmunks, bull sea lions, muskrats, rabbits, mice, and domestic dogs. There are two fundamental types, defense of nesting site, as represented by the muskrat and beaver, and food store protection, as in the red squirrel which may cache and defend several bushels of green pine cones (8). According to Davis and Golley, the social dominance hierarchies of some mammals serve the functions filled for others by territoriality.

Animal Movements

Large-scale movements of animals serve functions for both the individual and the species. Individuals may secure more favorable food supplies, breeding facilities, climate, or simply more living room. A species may benefit if movements result in establishment in a new habitat where the species may persist in the event formerly occupied habitats are destroyed. Movements may also aid the species by increasing the amount of genetic variability upon which natural selection may operate. Three basic types of movements among vertebrates are dispersal of the young, mass emigration, and migration.

Dispersal of Young. The phenomenon of dispersal occurs in the young of many birds (gulls, herons, egrets, grouse, eagles, owls) and mammals (muskrats, fox squirrel, gray squirrel). In a pine-oak barrens in central Pennsylvania, Chambers and Sharpe found that up to half of the juvenile ruffed grouse emigrated from their nesting areas to all points of the compass, some up to a distance of 7.5 miles (10). Broley reports that young bald eagles banded in Florida moved northward immediately after nesting, some arriving 1,500 miles distant in Maine and Canada by June (7). Van Tyne and Berger postulate that the eagle was a bird of more northern origin whose establishment in Florida may have been relatively recent (61). Therefore, dispersal was adaptive because it enabled eagles to escape the intense heat of the Florida summer. According to Errington up to 40 per cent of a wintering muskrat population may disperse in spring (24). They are primarily young animals who have been ejected by the established, more aggressive adults. Such dispersal apparently is an important mechanism for controlling population densities. Many of the dispersing young move into marginal habitats, where they incur heavy mortality from predation and accidents.

Figure 8–14 Five precocial ruffed grouse young shortly after hatching. [Wisconsin Conservation Department]

Mass Emigration. Mass emigrations frequently occur when a population has peaked because of extremely favorable conditions (food, weather) and then experienced a greatly reduced food supply. Under such conditions the only alternatives to starvation are aestivation, hibernation, or emigration. Emigrations of grosbeaks and crossbills into the northern states from the Canadian taiga result from pine seed crop failure. Crossbills are highly erratic in their movements, in terms of season and direction; even time and place of nesting is apparently determined by the availability of an adequate seed supply. Snowy owl emigrations into the United States from the Canadian tundra are correlated with the population crash of their lemming prey. Ornithologists recorded 13,502 snowy owls during the 1945 to 1946 emigration, which extended as far south as Oregon, Illinois, and Maryland. Twenty-four were observed out over the Atlantic. Some were seen in Bermuda (51).

Latitudinal Migrations. Winter bird densities in the southern latitudes of the United States are high, not only because of the permanent residents but also the many individuals which breed in more northern latitudes. For the most part territorialism is relaxed; many species traveling, feeding, and roosting

304

Figure 8–15 Snowy owl. This predator emigrates from the Arctic tundra to the United States when the lemming is at the trough of its four-year cycle. [Bureau of Sport Fisheries and Wildlife, U.S. Department of the Interior]

in flocks. Food supplies, such as insects, fruits, and seeds, are more readily available than in northern latitudes. In spring, however, the lengthening photoperiod eventually triggers a neuroendocrine mechanism which causes some birds to migrate northward. Presumably the northern habitats have a higher carrying capacity for the migrants and their future broods. In far northern latitudes, during the summer there is more time in one twenty-four-hour cycle for feeding young. For example, in northern Alaska (69 degrees N. lat.) a robin brood was fed twenty-one hours a day by the female parent. Welty has suggested that the exploitation of two different habitats (winter and summer) may ensure a more balanced supply of vitamins and minerals (63).

Altitudinal Migrations. As Kendeigh has pointed out, the conditions of less snow, higher temperatures, and more available food supplies—which latitudinal migrants secure by moving thousands of miles to the south—are secured by altitudinal migrants simply by moving a few miles down the mountain side (36). The elk herds of the Jackson Hole country in Wyoming

Figure 8–16 Big game. Two bull elk with fully grown antlers still in velvet graze in the Gallatin National Forest, Montana. [U.S. Department of Agriculture]

ascend the mountains in spring, keeping pace with the receding snow line, and spend the summer at relatively cool upper levels. Murie noted that only when the first snows covered their food supplies, whether in September or November, did the elk move down to the sagebrush valleys for the winter (45). The bighorn sheep of Idaho make similar migrations (in herds of five to fifty animals), which may be 40 miles long. Altitudinal migrations are characteristic of several birds breeding in the Colorado Rockies. Thus the pine grosbeak, black-capped rosy finch and gray-headed junco all nest at higher altitudes than those at which they winter. Curiously, the blue grouse reverses the usual altitudinal migration; it winters at higher levels than it breeds. Orr has postulated that this arrangement perhaps lessens winter competition with other species for buds and conifer needles (51).

Population Dynamics

Biotic Potential. *Biotic potential* (BP) may be defined as the theoretical maximum population growth rate of a species. Let us take a hypothetical case. Suppose all American robins lived to be ten years old and that each adult female annually fledged eight young. If the robin population started in 1970 with only a single breeding pair, there would be 1,200 million million million robins by 2000—a population so enormous that the earth could accommodate only 1/150,000 of it (63).

According to Dasmann, natality varies with size of clutch or litter produced, the number produced annually, the minimum and maximum breeding age of the individual, sex ratio, mating habits, and population density (14).

Clutch size in birds, which is primarily determined by heredity, varies greatly with the species. One-egg clutches were characteristic of the now extinct great auk and passenger pigeon and may have been a factor in their extinction. Loons, eagles, great horned owls, and whippoorwills lay two-egg clutches; passerines (thrushes, warblers, sparrows, blackbirds) lay four to six eggs per clutch; eight to fifteen egg clutches are representative of ducks, pheasants, quail, and grouse. A hen Hungarian partridge may produce twenty eggs per clutch. Clutch size probably is determined by the maximum number of young a species can adequately nourish.

Geographic variation in clutch size has been observed. Thus clutch size in the European robin varies from 3.5 in the Canary Islands, to 5.8 in Holland and 6.3 in Finland. Larger clutches in more northern latitudes appear correlated with the number of daylight hours (up to twenty-four in the far north) in which food may be gathered for the young (63). According to Wallace,

Figure 8–17 Ruffed grouse nest at base of tree with clutch of eleven eggs. Note oak leaf lining. [Wisconsin Conservation Department]

the number of broods reared by barn owls during the breeding season appears dependent on food availability; several broods may be reared when mouse populations peak, but the owl may not nest at all when mice are scarce.

Because it is exceedingly difficult to find mammalian litters, data are frequently indirectly determined by counting embryos in the uteruses of collected specimens or by counting the placental scars if animals are secured after the breeding season. From litter-size data collated by Davis and Golley, there appears to be an inverse relation between litter size and weight of the adult (15). According to Kendeigh, the number of young per litter are limited by uterine size and the number of the female's mammary glands (36). The average number of embryos found in various species follows: moose, 1.12; black-tailed jack rabbit, 2.3; fox squirrel (Michigan), 3.02; bobcat, 3.2; California vole, 4.3; coyote, 5.54, and muskrat, 7.49. In the widely distributed opossum there is considerable geographic variation in litter size, ranging from 6.5 embryos in Florida to 8.9 in Missouri.

The number of young produced appears to vary with food abundance. Thus Cheatum et al. found that the white-tailed deer in New York averaged 1.7 embryos per season on good range as compared to only 1.1 on deteriorating range (11). In mammals (and birds) excessive population density may curtail reproductive success because of fighting, interference with mating, and generally stressful conditions. Weather may determine litter size; thus Brambell found European rabbits to have a reduced number of pregnancies in the cold spring of 1942 (6). Litter size increases from south to north in voles, rabbits, shrews, deer mice, and tree squirrels but not in fossorial or hibernating species. This may be an adaptation which compensates for the severe winters of northern latitudes.

Longevity. Approximate longevity (in years) observed in some mammals (based primarily on zoo-confined animals) are deer mouse, five and one-half; river otter, eleven; red fox, twelve; gray squirrel, fourteen and one-half; wolf, sixteen and one-half; beaver, nineteen; elk, twenty-two; buffalo, twenty-two and one-half; polar bear, thirty-four (26). Maximum known ages of banded wild birds include: mourning dove, nine; robin and barn owl, ten; woodcock, twelve; crow and red-winged blackbird, fourteen; starling and mallard, sixteen; Canada goose, twenty-three; and herring gull, twenty-eight (27).

Mortality. In actuality, however, very few wild animals ever die from old age. The animal usually dies prematurely as a result of one or a combination of adverse physical and biotic factors known as *environmental resistance* (ER). ER may be represented by predators, human activities, parasites, diseases, starvation, floods, drought, accidents, and so on. Thus on the basis of 5,558 band recoveries it has been shown that 70 per cent of the mourning doves in the Southeastern United States die during their first year of life and 55 per cent during each ensuing year (63). The mean annual adult mortality (percentage) and the mean further life expectancy (years) for different birds follow: royal albatross, 3, 36; herring gull, 30, 2.8; bluejay, 45, 1.7; American robin, 48, 1.6; California quail, 50, 1.5.

Edminster's ruffed grouse study showed only 40 per cent survival in three-month-old birds (18). Only a small percentage of the eggs laid by most avian species actually develop into fledged young. Percentages of eggs fledged for several species follow: field sparrow, 35.7; bluebird, 44.5; American robin, 44.9; mourning dove, 46.6; European starling, 75.1; and house wren, 79.0.

Life Tables. To manage a particular game species effectively, it is essential for the game biologist to determine such population characteristics as the per cent composition and life expectancy of the various age classes. Such data are embodied in a *life table* for the species. Age class structure can be determined in wild populations only if animals of known age have been marked or tagged, or if age criteria are recognizable either in the field or on captured animals.

Age in the deer is gauged primarily on the basis of tooth eruption and wear. In all juvenile rabbits the epiphyseal cartilage of the humerus persists; in adults it has been replaced by bone. The tail feather tips of young ducks, geese, and swans are V-notched or square-ended, whereas in adults they are usually rounded or pointed. Perhaps the most reliable age criterion for waterfowl is the size of the bursa of Fabricius, a blindly ending sac in the dorsal wall of the cloaca. Present only in the immature, it attains its greatest development in birds two to four months old. Fish age can be determined by annular growth rings in the scales. In collecting age (and sex) data, game biologists frequently check hunter game bags or fishermen's creels to enable them to secure a sufficiently large sample.

A life table is a statistical device in which the mortality (and survival) characteristics of the various age groups of a population are given in an organized manner. The Dall mountain sheep (*Ovis d. dalli*) was one of the first big-game animals for which a life table was constructed. Adolph Murie made an intensive study of this species in Mount McKinley National

Park, Alaska. Major mortality factors included predation by timber wolves and bear, and diseases such as necrotic stomatitis and actinomycosis ("big jaw"). Human predation was not a factor because hunting was illegal. Murie collected 829 skulls from the remains of carcasses. On the basis of dental criteria and growth rings on the horns, he was able to determine the age of over 600 animals at time of death. These data were later

Figure 8–18 Dall mountain sheep in Arctic Alaska. [Bureau of Sport Fisheries and Wildlife, U.S. Department of the Interior]

used by Deevey to construct a life table (16). (See Table 8–1.) The table is set up on the basis of an initial cohort of 1,000 individuals. Columns are headed by standard notations. Age of animals in years is represented by column x, l_x refers to the number surviving after a certain number of years, d_x is the number dying during successive time intervals, q_x is the mortality rate during successive intervals with respect to the population at the beginning of the period, and e_x refers to the life expectancy at the end of each age interval. The Dall sheep table indicates that mortality is high during the first year of life (as in most vertebrates). Then mortality lessens gradually, only to increase sharply at about age eight. The table reveals a maximum longevity of fourteen years and an average life span of 7.09 years.

STABLE, IRRUPTIVE, AND CYCLIC POPULATIONS. Aldo Leopold has classified wildlife populations as being either *stable, irruptive,* or *cyclic* (42). Stable populations are characterized by a

Table 8–1. LIFE TABLE FOR THE DALL MOUNTAIN SHEEP (Ovis d. dalli)*†

x	x^1	d_x	l_x	1000 q_x	e_x
Age (Years)	Age as per cent deviation from mean length of life	Number dying in age interval out of 1000 born	Number surviving at beginning of age interval out of 1000 born	Mortality rate per thousand alive at beginning of age interval	Expectation of life, or mean life time left to those attaining age interval (years)
0–0.5	−100	54	1000	54	7.06
0.5–1	−93.0	145	946	153.0	——
1–2	−85.9	12	801	15.0	7.7
2–3	−71.8	13	789	16.5	6.8
3–4	−57.7	12	776	15.5	5.9
4–5	−43.5	30	764	39.3	5.0
5–6	−29.5	46	734	62.6	4.2
6–7	−15.4	48	688	69.9	3.4
7–8	−1.1	69	640	108.0	2.6
8–9	+13.0	132	571	231.0	1.9
9–10	+27.0	187	439	426.0	1.3
10–11	+41.0	156	252	619.0	.9
11–12	+55.0	90	96	937.0	0.6
12–13	+69.0	3	6	500.0	1.2
13–14	+84.0	3	3	1000	0.7

* This table is based on the known age of 608 animals which died before 1937 (both sexes). Average life for these sheep is 7.09 years.
† Table appeared in Edward S. Deevey, Jr., "Life Tables for Natural Populations of Animals," *Quart. Rev. Biol.,* **22** (1947), 283–314.

saw-toothed curve as a result of random increments and decrements. However, from a long-range standpoint, the population remains at a rather constant level. Most wildlife populations become stable once they have reached the asymptote of the sigmoid curve, or, in other words, have reached the carrying capacity of the habitat. Bobwhite quail are representative species having stable populations. In this species population fluctuations are frequently seasonal. Thus, shortly after the young have hatched, populations will be at a peak; in early spring after a severe winter characterized by crusted snow, quail populations will be low. Factors such as disease, predators, climate, cover, and food availability may vary, resulting in slight upward or downward population swings. Even intrapopulation shifts in age and sex ratios may affect population levels.

After fluctuating mildly for many years, some populations, such as those of deer and house mice, may suddenly increase sharply or *irrupt* and then suddenly crash to a very low level. Irruptions are highly erratic and unpredictable. In some cases they occur when there is an unusually favorable climate for reproduction or an unusually abundant, though temporary food supply. Fur return records of the Hudson's Bay Fur Company, Canada, revealed four raccoon irruptions (1867, 1875, 1897, and 1899) during the period 1850–1910. Thus the pelt returns in one three-year period were about 4,000 in 1866, 24,000 in 1867, and 6,000 in 1868. Hall reports a house mouse irruption in California in which an area of exceptionally favorable habitat temporarily supported a density of 80,000 mice per acre. In the arid regions of the Southwestern United States, a year of unusually abundant rainfall may result in irruptions of jack rabbits, quail, and chukar partridges because of the temporarily increased vegetational foods. When rainfall reverts to normal, food supplies diminish and populations subside to their original levels.

Cyclic populations show sharp increases, followed by crashes, at rather regular intervals. To some degree the population peaks and troughs can be predicted. The most thoroughly studied cycles occur at three- to four-year (lemming) or at ten-year (snowshoe hare, lynx, grouse) intervals. The three- to four-year cycle is characteristic of the brown lemming of the North American tundra biome. Other species in which this cycle has been observed include the northern shrike, red-tailed hawk, meadow vole, martin (mammal), and sockeye salmon. The lemming forms the principal food of the arctic fox, red fox, snowy owl, and pomarine jaeger; therefore the populations of these predators varies with that of their lemming prey. Apparently these predators have few alternative prey species on which to feed. Although many snowy owls starve during the winters of lemming population troughs, large numbers will emigrate to the United States, some moving as far south as North Carolina. In his study of brown lemming crashes in northern Alaska, Pitelka found that the peak lemming population overgrazed vegetation which had served as protective cover (53). During the ensuing spring's snow melt, the lemmings therefore became highly vulnerable to predation and their numbers were drastically reduced.

The ten-year cycle is not well understood. It is characteristic of the snowshoe hare, an occupant of the northern coniferous forest or taiga, and has been reported for the muskrat (Iowa), ruffed grouse, sharp-tailed grouse and willow ptarmigan. Also involved in this cycle are quail, partridges, pheasants (in the northern portions of their range), and northern grouse. The Canada lynx, which preys largely on the snowshoe hare, has a ten-year cycle that lags just behind that of the hare. The lynx cycle has been elucidated by Elton and Nicholsen by examination of the Hudson Bay Company's lynx pelt returns (21).

Green and Evans, in a study of snowshoe hare in the area of Lake Alexander, Minnesota, found "shock disease" to have been responsible for the cyclic phenomenon (28). In recent years a number of other workers have implicated "shock disease" in population cycles. The theory is that when populations peak, the increased stress caused by fighting and other physical contacts, in addition to the impaired nutritional value

Figure 8–19 A classic example of a wildlife population cycle. Based on pelt records of the Hudson Bay Company. Note the roughly ten-year interval. [Adapted from Eugene P. Odum, *Fundamentals of Ecology*, (Philadelphia: W. B. Saunders Company, 1959). After D. A. Maclulich, *University of Toronto Studies*, Biological Series No. 43, 1937.]

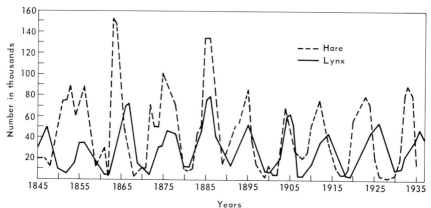

of marginal food supplies, and the greater energy expended in searching for food and cover, results in stimulation of the pituitary gland by way of neural pathways and the hypothalamus. The pituitary is stimulated to produce ACTH, (adrenocorticotrophic hormone) which in turn causes the adrenal gland to increase its secretion of cortins. These hormones then cause a reduction of the reproductive function. Eventually the pituitary-adrenal system becomes exhausted and death ensues.

A number of other theories have been advanced to explain the immediate cause of the nine- to ten-year cycle. They include variations in weather, fluctuations in solar radiation, depletion of food supply, disease, and changes in nutrient levels of plant foods. It may be that several of these in combination are responsible for the cycles. As yet, however, much of the underlying mechanism remains to be defined.

BIBLIOGRAPHY

1. Adams, L. "An Analysis of a Population of Snowshoe Hares in Northwestern Montana," *Ecol. Mono.,* **29** (1959), 141–170.
2. Allen, D. L. *Our Wildlife Legacy.* New York: Funk and Wagnalls Co., 1954.
3. Banfield, A. W. F. "Preliminary Investigation of the Barren Ground Caribou," *Wild. Mgt. Bull.,* Ser. 1, Nos. 10A–B (1954), Department of Northern Affairs and National Resources, Ottawa, 79 and 112 pp.
4. Bellrose, F. C., T. G. Scott, A. S. Hawkins, and J. B. Low. "Sex Ratios and Age Ratios in North American Ducks," *Ill. Nat. Hist. Surv. Bull.,* **27** (1961), 391–474.
5. Bourliere, François. *The Natural History of Mammals.* New York: Alfred A. Knopf, 1956, 364 pp.
6. Brambell, F. W. R. "The Reproduction of the Wild Rabbit (*Oryctolagus cuniculus L.*)," *Proc. Zool. Soc. London,* **114** (1944), 1–45.
7. Broley, Charles L. "Migration and Nesting of Florida Bald Eagles," *Wilson Bulletin,* **59** (1947), 3–20.
8. Burt, William Henry. *Mammals of the Great Lakes Region.* Ann Arbor: The University of Michigan Press, 1957, 246 pp.
9. Cardinell, H. A., and D. W. Hayne. "Corn Injury by Redwings in Michigan," *Tech. Bull. No. 198.* Pp. 1–59. Mich. Agri. Exp. Station, 1945. East Lansing, Mich.
10. Chambers, R. E., and W. M. Sharp. "Movement and Dispersal Within a Population of Ruffed Grouse," *Jour. Wild. Mgt.,* **22** (1958), 231–239.
11. Cheatum, E. L., and C. W. Severinghaus. "Variations in Fertility of White-tailed Deer Related to Range Conditions," *Trans. North Amer. Wild. Conf.,* **15** (1950), 170–189.
12. Clarke, George L. *Elements of Ecology.* New York: John Wiley & Sons, Inc., 1954, 534 pp.
13. Dale, F. M. "The Role of Calcium in Reproduction of the Ring-necked Pheasant," *Jour. Wild. Mgt.,* **19** (1955), 325–331.
14. Dasmann, Raymond F. *Wildlife Biology.* New York: John Wiley & Sons, Inc., 1964, 231 pp.

15. Davis, David E., and Frank B. Golley. *Principles in Mammalogy.* New York: Reinhold Publishing Corp., 1963, 335 pp.

16. Deevey, E. S. "Life Tables for Natural Populations of Animals," *Quart. Rev. Biol.,* **22** (1947), 283–314.

17. Dumont, Philip A. "Refuges and Sanctuaries," in *Birds in Our Lives.* Washington, D.C.: U.S. Fish and Wildlife Service, 1966, 506–523.

18. Edminster, F. C. "The Effect of Predator Control on Ruffed Grouse Populations in New York," *Jour. Wild. Mgt.,* **19** (1939), 325–331.

19. Einarsen, A. S. "Specific Results from Ring-necked Pheasant Studies in the Pacific Northwest," *Trans. North Amer. Wild. Conf.,* **7** (1942), 130–145.

20. Ellis, James E., and John B. Lewis. "Mobility and Annual Range of Wild Turkeys in Missouri," *Jour. Wild. Mgt.,* **31** (1967), 568–581.

21. Elton, Charles, and M. Nicholson. "The Ten-Year Cycle in the Numbers of the Lynx in Canada," *Jour. Anim. Ecol.,* **11** (1942), 215–244.

22. Errington, P. L. "Habitat Requirements of Stream-Dwelling Muskrats," *Trans. North Amer. Wild. Conf.,* **2** (1937), 411–416.

23. ———. "Emergency Values of Some Winter Pheasant Foods," *Trans. Wis. Acad. Sci. Arts and Let.,* **30** (1937), 57–68.

24. ———. "Natural Restocking of Muskrat-Vacant Habitats," *Jour. Wild. Mgt.,* **4** (1940), 173–185.

25. ———. "Predation and Vertebrate Populations," *Quart. Rev. Biol.,* **21** (1946), 144–177, 221–245.

26. Flower, S. S. "Contributions to Our Knowledge of the Duration of Life in Vertebrate Animals. Mammals," *Proc. Zool. Soc. London,* 1931, 145–234.

27. ———. "Further Notes on the Duration of Life in Animals. Part IV. Birds," *Proc. Zool. Soc. London.* Series A, **108** (1938), 195–235.

28. Green, R. C., and C. A. Evans. "Studies on a Population Cycle of Snowshoe Hares in the Lake Alexander Area," *Jour. Wild. Mgt.,* **4** (1940), 220–238, 267–278, 347–358.

29. Greenhalgh, Clifton M. "Food Habits of the California Gull in Utah," *Condor,* **54** (1952), 302–308.

30. Gullion, G. W. "Territorial Behavior of the American Coot," *Condor,* **55** (1953), 169–186.

31. Gustafson, A. F., C. H. Guise, W. J. Hamilton, Jr., and H. Ries. *Conservation in the United States.* Ithaca, N.Y.: Comstock Publishing Co., 1949.

32. Hall, E. Raymond. "An Outbreak of House Mice in Kern County, California," *Univ. Calif. Pub. Zool.,* **30** (1927), 189–203.

33. Hamilton, W. J., Jr. *The Mammals of Eastern United States.* Ithaca, N.Y.: Comstock Publishing Co., 1943, 432 pp.

34. Herman, C. M. "The Blood Protozoa of North American Birds," *Birdbanding,* **15** (1944), 89–112.

35. Karplus, M. "Bird Activity in the Continuous Daylight of Arctic Summer," *Ecol.,* **33** (1952), 129–134.

36. Kendeigh, S. Charles. *Animal Ecology.* Englewood Cliffs, N.J.: Prentice-Hall, Inc., 1961, 468 pp.

37. Kolenosky, George B., and David H. Johnston. "Radio-Tracking Timber Wolves in Ontario," *Ecology and Behavior of the Wolf.* College Park, Md.: Animal Behavior Society, 1966.

38. Laskey, Amelia R. "A Study of Nesting Eastern Bluebirds." *Birdbanding,* **10** (1939), 23–32.

39. Korschgen, Leroy J. "December Food Habits of Mink in Missouri," *Jour. of Mam.,* **39** (1958), 521–527.

40. Lack, D. *The Natural Regulation of Animal Numbers.* Oxford: Clarendon Press, 1954.

41. Layne, James N., and Glen E. Woolfenden. "Gray Squirrels Feeding on Insects in Car Radiators," *Jour. of Mam.,* **39** (1958), 595–596.

42. Leopold, Aldo. *Game Management.* New York: Charles Scribner's Sons, 1933, 481 pp.

43. Mech, L. David. "Telemetry as a Technique in the Study of Predation," *Jour. Wild. Mgt.,* **31** (1967), 492–496.

44. Moffit, J., and C. Cottam. "The Eel-Grass Blight and Its Effect on Brant," *United States Fish and Wildlife Service Leaflet,* 204 (1941), 1–26.

45. Murie, O. J. *The Elk of North America.* Harrisburg, Pa.: The Stackpole Co.

46. Nagel, W. V. "How Big Is a Coon?" *Missouri Conservation,* **4** (1943), 6–7.

47. Nice, Margaret M. "The Role of Territory in Bird Life," *Amer. Mid. Natur.,* **26** (1941), 441–487.

48. ———. "Nesting Success in Altricial Birds." *Auk,* **74** (1957), 305–321.

49. Odum, Eugene P. *Fundamentals of Ecology.* Philadelphia: W. B. Saunders Co., 1959.

50. Olson, Harold. "Beetle Rout in the Rockies," *Aud. Mag.,* **55** (1953), 30–32.

51. Orr, Robert T. *Vertebrate Biology.* Philadelphia: W. B. Saunders Company, 1961, 400 pp.

52. Petrides, George A. "The Determination of Sex and Age Ratios in Fur Animals," *Amer. Mid. Nat.,* **43** (1950), 355–382.

53. Pitelka, F. A. "Population Studies of Lemmings and Lemming Predators in Northern Alaska," *15th Int. Cong. Zool.,* Sect. X, Paper 5 (1959).

54. Rasmussen, D. Irvin. "Hunting – An American Heritage," *Outdoors USA: Yearbook of Agriculture.* Washington, D.C.: U.S. Department of Agriculture, 1967, 62–64,

55. Schorger, A. W. "The Great Wisconsin Passenger Pigeon Nesting of 1871," *Proc. Linn. Soc.,* New York, **48** (1937), 1–26.

56. Seton, Ernest T. *The Arctic Prairies.* New York: Charles Scribner's Sons, 1923, 308 pp.

57. Smith, Robert L. *Ecology and Field Biology.* New York: Harper & Row, Publishers, 1966, 686 pp.

58. Smith, A. G., and H. R. Webster. "Effects of Hail Storms on Waterfowl Population in Alberta, Canada - 1953," *Jour. Wild. Mgt.,* **19** (1955), 368–374.

59. Soil Conservation Service. "More Wildlife Through Soil and Water Conservation," *Bulletin No. 175.* Washington, D.C.: U.S. Department of Agriculture, 1958.

60. Streseman, E., in W. Kuekenthal and T. Krumbach. *Handbuch der Zoologie. Sauropsida; Aves.,* Berlin and Leipzig (1927 to 1934).

61. Van Tyne, Josselyn and Andrew J. Berger. *Fundamentals of Ornithology.* New York: John Wiley & Sons, Inc., 1959.

62. Wallace, George J. *An Introduction to Ornithology.* New York: The Macmillan Co., 1955, 443 pp.

63. Welty, Joel Carl. *The Life of Birds.* Philadelphia: W. B. Saunders Co., 1962, 546 pp.

64. Yocum, C. F. "The Hungarian Partridge (*Perdix perdix* Linn.) in the Palouse Region, Washington," *Ecol. Mono.,* **13** (1943), 167–201.

The Ecology
and Management
of Deer

9

Deer are the most abundant, intensively hunted, thoroughly studied, and widely distributed big-game animals in the United States. The two native species are the white-tailed deer and the mule deer. The white-tail occurs along forest margins, in semiwooded agricultural areas throughout the eastern United States, from Canada to the Mexican border and from the Rockies eastward to the Atlantic. Only in the Great Basin and in California is its absence conspicuous. The mule deer ranges from North Dakota, western South Dakota, northwestern Nebraska, Colorado, New Mexico, and western Texas west to the Pacific Coast (4).

Description. Deer are members of the family Cervidae, which include elk, moose, and caribou. Thirty subspecies of the white-tail occur in North America. The antlers, which are present normally only in the buck deer, are an extremely rapidly growing extension of the frontal bone of the skull. During development, the antlers are invested with "velvet," a covering of skin, richly supplied with nourishing blood vessels. In late fall when these blood vessels constrict, the velvet becomes dry and is rubbed off on a tree trunk until the antlers become completely bare and highly polished.

Figure 9–1 Three-year-old buck white-tailed deer. Note the abundant browse. Fulton County, Georgia. [U.S. Forest Service]

They become brittle and are dropped by midwinter. The weight of the adult buck ranges from 80 pounds in the rare collie-dog-sized key deer of the Florida Keys to the 300-pound buck of the Lake States. The average adult buck and doe in the Lake States weigh 170 and 145 pounds, respectively. Northern bucks stand 3 to 3½ feet tall at the withers but appear much larger.

The mule deer is distinguished from the white-tail primarily by the larger ears, a tail which is either black on top or black-tipped, and antlers in the male which branch equally, instead of having a number of prongs extending from a main beam. When on the run, mule deer display a curious stiff-legged gait, quite unlike the more graceful bounds of the white-tail.

In both species the light summer coat of rust-brown gives way to a dense gray-brown winter coat with the approach of cold weather. The hairs of the winter coat are provided with air-filled spaces which serve to insulate the animal from the cold. In the white-tail the ample tail is held erect at the slightest indication of danger, thus exposing the snow-white undersurface, which apparently serves to signal a warning to nearby asso-

Figure 9-2 Two mule deer bucks at the National Bison Range, Montana. Note black-tipped tail and large ears. [Bureau of Sport Fisheries and Wildlife, U.S. Department of the Interior]

ciates. The sharply edged hoofs of both species are adapted for running over a firm, compact surface at speeds up to 45 miles per hour. When hard pressed by wolves or dogs, deer will lash out with their hoofs in self-defense.

In Minnesota in 1970, over 250,000 big-game hunters (primarily deer hunters) spent more than $20 million. A survey conducted by the U.S. Fish and Wildlife Service in 1955 indicated that 4.4 million big-game hunters (primarily deer hunters) spent about $324 million, an average of $73.38 per hunter. This includes not only money spent on guns and ammunition, but expenditures for other equipment and travel. It is apparent that deer hunting means big business for thousands of American manufacturers and merchants.

Early in the twentieth century, as a result of intensified farming, lumbering, highway and railroad construction, development of industry, establishment of communities, as well as persecution, the white-tail was almost exterminated from much of the original deciduous forest biome. However, it recovered

Figure 9–3 Hunter poses with eight-point white-tail bagged in Iron County, Wisconsin. [Wisconsin Conservation Department]

rapidly during the 1930's and is found today in regions where it had been virtually absent for seventy-five years. Bersing lists several factors that contributed to the mid-1930's build-up of northern deer herds: the provision of food and cover in the second-growth timber that resulted from effective forest protection; better game law enforcement by wardens, which caused the termination of illegal hounding and market hunting; the one-buck law and other restrictive hunting regulations; the control of natural predators; and the establishment of deer refuges (2). The white-tails were formerly rare in the dense, well-shaded climax stages of the coniferous forest biome. They were very uncommon in northeastern Minnesota, where available browse was scarce. It was not until the forests were opened up by logging and fire in the late nineteenth and early twentieth century that deer occurred in this area in appreciable numbers. (Deer prefer "edges," interspersions of vegetational types, rather than solid stands of homogeneous vegetation.) Deer browse now became available in profusion in the form of sprouts germinating from old stumps or shrubs and saplings representing the early stages of post-fire and post-logging succession. Similarly, during the shrub stage coming in five to ten years after a fire, the black-tailed deer herds of northern California's redwood region attained fully twenty times the population levels occurring in the climax forest. By 1920 the white-tail was well established in northeastern Minnesota's Superior National Forest. In some southwestern states white-tails have increased because of the additional food and cover provided by irrigation. The white-tail's population in the United States increased from 3,181,675 to 5,135,040 (an increase of 61 per cent) during the thirteen-year period 1937–1949. By 1963, according to the United States Big Game Inventory, white-tail numbers had increased to 7 million.

Food Habits. The deer's dentition is specialized for cutting and grinding plant materials. Although it lacks both incisors and canines in the upper jaw, it is able to seize twigs, press them between the sharply edged lower incisors and a heavy leatherlike pad on the upper jaw, and then, with a wrenching movement, tear them off the shrub, leaving a ragged browse mark, easily distinguished from the neatly clipped browse marks of rabbits. Tougher bark and stems are ground up with broad, powerful molars. In arid regions of the West, deer populations have been considerably increased by the installation of "guzzlers," which catch and retain rainfall for deer use.

Researchers in Wisconsin and Pennsylvania have found that

Figure 9–4 In studying the population dynamics of a deer herd, it is essential for the game manager to know the age structure of the herd. Relative tooth wear is a good age criterion. The molars of this 8.5-year-old jaw are severely worn. [Wisconsin Conservation Department]

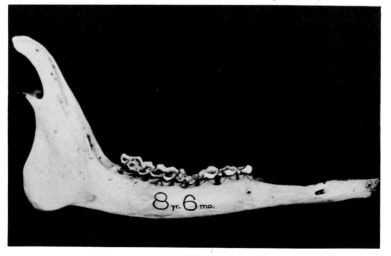

the average adult white-tailed deer requires at least 1 quart of water and 5 pounds of natural browse daily for every 100 pounds of deer. Thus, a 130-pound deer would consume about 6.5 pounds, a 300-pound deer 15 pounds. The amount of browse available in a particular region depends in part on the species composition of the cover. Thus, a study by Dalke in the Missouri Ozarks (in which he clipped all the browse to a height of 5 feet) showed a post oak–blackjack oak community to yield 140 pounds per acre, in contrast to the 111 pounds per acre produced by a black oak–hickory stand. Browse production also depends on the age of the cover. Thus, in thirty-five-year-old hardwood stands in Pennsylvania, seven species produced 35 pounds per acre, only 17.5 per cent that of the 200-pounds-per-acre yield of seven-year-old "brush" stage hardwoods (38). In a plantation of loblolly pine at the Southern Forest Experimental Station in Texas, the available browse in a thirty-year-old stand thinned at ages twenty to twenty-five was related to the degree of thinning: lightly thinned stands produced 154 pounds (oven dry) per acre, compared to the 199-pounds-per-acre yield from heavily thinned stands. In a study of white-tail browsing habits in commercially cut cove hardwood stands in the southern Appalachians, Moore and Johnson concluded that preference was determined more by growth rate and succulence than by plant species (28).

The deer's stomach, which is composed of four compartments (rumen, reticulum, omasum, and abomasum), plays an interesting though passive role in aiding the deer to escape predators. The deer (which feeds primarily during the twilight hours just after sunset and the hours just before sunrise) feeds on the move, munching a bud here, a succulent stem there, and rapidly fills its second compartment (reticulum), which serves as a sort of temporary storage chamber. Here water is added to the food and bacterial fermentation occurs. With the aid of a muscular kneading the food is reduced to a pulpy mass. When satiated, the deer beds down in a dense thicket, regurgitates the mass of food into its mouth and slowly "chews its cud." When thoroughly masticated, the ground-up material is swallowed and eventually passed to the fourth stomach compartment, the abomasum, for the terminal chemical phase of digestion. This feeding behavior pattern has survival value, because the period during which the animal is conspicuous and most vulnerable to predation is reduced to a minimum.

According to Atwood the white-tailed deer consumes 614 species of plants in the United States, including thirteen ferns, thirty-nine conifers, forty-four grasses and sedges, and 484 dicots (37). Not all plants, however, are equally palatable or

nutritious. By examining the degree of browsing on various
plant species and by analyzing stomach contents, Minnesota
researchers have roughly determined food preference ratings
for a number of browse species. These studies suggest that
white cedar, mountain maple, red-osier dogwood, and black
ash sprouts are all important winter white-tail foods and are
avidly consumed when available. On the other hand, red pine,
tamarack, alder, and black spruce are among the poorest winter
deer foods in Minnesota. White cedar is the only native browse
species that could be exclusively eaten by Minnesota deer without their losing weight; conversely, deer have frequently
starved even though their stomachs were filled with balsam fir.
Light, medium, or heavy stocking levels on white-tailed deer
range in eastern Texas may be quickly determined by comparing utilization rates of three palatability classes. Browse preference studies in Wisconsin, where plants were given one of
four preference ratings, showed that deer gave top preference
to the following: ground hemlock, white cedar, hemlock,
mountain ash, red maple, staghorn sumac, alternate-leaved
dogwood, wintergreen, and wild cranberry (9). In a stomach
analysis study of the black-tailed deer in western Washington,
Brent found the six most preferred foods to be trailing blackberry, salal, grasses, red alder, vine maple, and western hemlock.

The nutritional value of a plant to deer depends ultimately
on the availability of certain soil nutrients. Thus, deer dependent on vegetation growing in calcium-deficient soil will be
stunted and will have poorly formed bones and antlers. Pregnant does subsisting on such food will frequently abort their
calcium-requiring embryos. Plant palatability depends on its
protein content, which in turn is dependent on soil nitrate
availability. In the final analysis, a good "crop" of deer (or
other game), like a good crop of corn or wheat, depends on
soil chemistry. French et al. determined that deer require a
7 per cent protein diet merely for maintenance, a 9.5 per cent
protein level for moderate growth, and a 13 per cent protein
level for optimal growth and reproductive performance. Protein
levels in old-growth chaparral range in Lake County, California,
are markedly inferior to shrubland (brush and grass) range,
because they fall below maintenance levels in late fall and early
winter and attain optimal levels only during a brief period in
late April and early May. In the shrubland range, however,
protein levels never fall below maintenance values and are
optimal for six months of the year. This is reflected in reproductive rates for mule deer in the two range types. Thus Taber
reports that peak mule deer populations in California's north-

ern coast range after May fawning were sixty per square mile in chaparral range compared to ninety per square mile in shrubland (36).

Breeding and Reproduction

By mid-August, in the Lake States, a white-tailed buck's antlers are fully developed. The velvet dries and is removed by being rubbed against the ground, rocks, or a tree trunk. The peak of the breeding season occurs in the northern states in mid-November. Once the bucks have polished their antlers and the sex urge is upon them, they will seek out a receptive doe. When two bucks confront each other near a doe an intense struggle may ensue, in which each buck attempts to establish a *moving territory* around the doe. The bucks may charge each other, engage antlers, and attempt to wrestle the rival off balance or gore him. During the struggle the antagonists' hoofs may tear up the ground over a 0.5 acre area. Although serious wounds are rare, occasionally a buck may be disemboweled. If the bucks' antlers interlock and cannot be disengaged, both combatants may die from broken necks or starvation. A buck may run with a doe for about three days. If she is unreceptive, the buck will seek another female. During the breeding season a doe remains in heat for only one day; if she does not mate she will enter heat one month later. Antlers are shed by bucks from mid-December through January. The calcium-rich antlers gradually disintegrate because of weathering and the gnawing activity of rodents.

A doe usually gives birth to a single fawn after her initial pregnancy and to twin fawns thereafter. In a study of mule deer fertility rates in Utah, Robinette et al. found that 84 per cent of yearling deer were pregnant and averaged 1.32 fetuses per doe; two-year-olds, with a pregnancy rate of 99 per cent, averaged 1.77 fetuses per doe (30). Triplets and quadruplets occur but are uncommon. In addition to age, the health of a doe may influence the number of young she produces. Thus, a severe winter which leaves the doe in a malnourished condition may cause her to resorb her embryos. In Vermont an estimated 93 per cent of the mature does over 75 pounds had fawns during a given year (37). However, on Texas range which had been severely overgrazed by livestock, only 42 per cent of the does had young. An experimental dietary study by Verme on a captive white-tail herd in Michigan revealed that productivity of well-fed does was three times that of inadequately nourished animals (38).

Fawns are usually dropped in a thicket where they are well

Figure 9–5 Fawn white-tail from the Nicolet National Forest, Wisconsin. Note the spotted coat. [U.S. Forest Service]

concealed from predators. Although a young fawn might seem quite vulnerable to wolves, coyotes, and wild dogs, protection is afforded by its dappled coat, which causes it to blend with the shifting shadows, and by its almost complete lack of scent.

When mortality factors are minimized, white-tail populations may increase rapidly. Thus, an initial population of six deer (four does and two bucks) which were introduced in 1928 to the 1,200-acre George Reserve in southern Michigan increased to over 160 head after only six years, when controlled hunting was permitted to protect food and cover. The average increase rate for this six-year period was 60 per cent. A Maryland herd of three bucks and three does increased to an estimated 1,000 head from 1926 to 1941. The average annual increase rate for this sixteen-year period was 37.7 per cent. According to David B. Cook under optimal conditions a deer herd could double its population annually (37).

Carrying Capacity of the Range

According to Taylor carrying capacity may be defined as "the maximum number of deer per unit area that can be supported through the year without deterioration of the range" (37). Carrying capacity for deer, as for most wildlife, is primarily dependent on food and cover. After an irruption food and cover may be only a fraction of pre-irruption abundance (37). Dunkeson reports that the failure or abundance of the acorn crop in a range having much oak cover may determine whether or not the herd is in balance with the carrying capacity of the range. Carrying capacities of different ranges may be highly variable. In Michigan the best hardwood stands can winter 640 deer per section; this is three times the winter carrying capacity of the better coniferous ranges. Densities vary from a low of one-half to one deer per section in Indiana to 438 deer per section in the Edwards Plateau of Texas (37).

Environmental Resistance

Among the various environmental factors adversely affecting deer populations are malnutrition, predation, accidents, parasites, and disease.

Figure 9–6   Note how deer have browsed the twigs of this young pine. When deer populations are dense in winter deer yards, damage to pine stands may be severe. [Wisconsin Conservation Department]

Malnutrition. Winter is a critical season for deer survival in the northern states because available food is extremely limited. Much potential food, such as herbs, mosses, fungi, seedlings, low-growing shrubs, and stump sprouts, is frequently covered with snow. Under such conditions the only available plant materials are buds, twigs, and the foliage of shrubs and trees. If the deer population exceeds the carrying capacity of the habitat (as it has in many of the Lake States in the past few decades), deer will consume all the available browse up to the height they can reach when rearing up on their hind legs. As a result, a conspicuous *browse line* will form at a height of 4.5 to 5 feet, a definite warning to the game biologist of deteriorating range. Under these conditions fawn mortality is high, not only because of their restricted "reach," but because the young rank at the bottom of the buck-doe-fawn social hierarchy as observed by Kabat et al. in a Wisconsin deer yard (19). During the winter

Figure 9–7 Severely overbrowsed Wisconsin deer yard. Note the two deer in the background who are rearing up on their hind legs in an effort to browse coniferous foliage. [Wisconsin Conservation Department]

Figure 9–8 Just a small sample of the thousands of white-tailed deer which annually starve during severe winters (with deep snow cover) in Wisconsin, Minnesota, Michigan, New York, and Pennsylvania. [Wisconsin Conservation Department]

of 1955–1956 game wardens in Michigan found large numbers of deer floundering in snow drifts, severely weakened from malnutrition. Over 115,650 deer died that year, at least one third perishing directly from starvation, the remainder from predators and disease which merely finished off the deer after starvation had set the stage.

Emergency feeding of starving deer is not considered sound management by most game biologists. They argue that it permits the survival of deer whose future progeny will exert even greater demands on the available natural browse, thus aggravating the problem. Artificial feeding may facilitate the spread of disease by promoting concentrations of highly susceptible animals. Moreover, it is expensive. During the period 1934–1956 Wisconsin spent over $.5 million on the purchase and distribution of 7,000 tons of artificial feed (2). To feed the Michigan deer herds properly for one winter would cost $800,000 or roughly $16 to $40 per head.

Figure 9–9   Note the dead deer lying on the floor of the car after crashing through the windshield. Several thousand deer are killed by cars annually in Wisconsin. [Wisconsin Conservation Department]

Accidents.   Dahlberg and Guettinger report at least thirteen types of fatal deer accidents in Wisconsin (9). They include death by auto and train, entanglement in browse trees, falling over a cliff, enmirement in muck, drowning, lightning strike, herbicide poisoning, and antler locking while fighting. A speeding convertible can be a more significant mortality factor than a wolf. During 1944–1960 Minnesota game wardens reported that 7,937 (79.39 per cent) of 9,991 deer deaths were caused by motor cars as compared to only 457 (4.57 per cent) fatalities caused by predation. In 1954 cars killed 1,093 Wisconsin deer. Currently an estimated 3,000 deer are killed annually by Minnesota motorists. According to Taber et al. (1958) most accidents to the black-tailed deer of California's chaparral range were experienced by male fawns (36).

Predation.   Among deer predators may be listed wolves, cougars, bobcats, coyotes, and domestic dogs. During 1951–1960 wolves in the wilderness of the Superior National Forest de-

Figure 9–10   Dog kill near Radisson, Wisconsin. Note the slashed throat of this yearling deer. [Wisconsin Conservation Department]

stroyed 1.5 deer per square mile annually. In 1950 wolves killed 6,000 (17 per cent) of the 37,000 deer in the forest. According to Thompson 97 per cent of 435 wolf scats (deposited fecal matter) collected in northern Wisconsin from 1946 to 1948 contained the remains of deer. Despite much contrary opinion wolves do not cull the weak, sickly, crippled, or senile individuals but simply take any deer regardless of sex, age, or physical condition. However, because hunting pressure in the remote backwoods country of the Superior National Forest is extremely light, accounting for only 0.65 deer per square mile, wolf predation serves to regulate a deer herd which in 1961 was on the verge of exceeding the carrying capacity of the range. Since there were only 350 timber wolves in the entire state of Minnesota in 1965, the impact of wolf predation on deer in that state must be negligible.

Although one cougar may kill an estimated fifty or more deer annually, cougars are unimportant as regulators of deer populations because of their scarcity, except in localized areas of Arizona and other parts of the Southwest. King reports seeing a black bear killing a black-tail fawn and consuming the entire carcass (21). Bobcats weighing 25 pounds can kill deer weighing 175 pounds, usually attacking when the latter are lying down.

Deliberate aggressive responses of mule deer does toward bob-cats which have approached fawns have been observed (17). Deer remains were found in only 3.5 per cent of 300 bobcat scats collected in Michigan. Surprisingly, the most serious deer slayer other than man is the dog. Beagles, German shepherds, and airedales have been implicated. Pregnant does and young fawns are especially vulnerable. In March, 1962, dogs killed forty-three deer on the Carlos Avery Game Refuge in Minnesota. Hamilton estimates that during one January dogs killed 1,000 snowbound deer in New York. In summary, over most of the white-tailed deer's range domestic dogs which have gone astray are the most significant predators; except in local situations wild predators are of little consequence. In remote hunting areas where hunting pressure is light, a higher predator population might be advantageous in preventing disastrous irruptions.

PREDATOR CONTROL AND THE KAIBAB DEER IRRUPTION. As mentioned in the chapter on wildlife, predator control may have deleterious effects on the very game species that well-intentioned game biologists are trying to protect. Perhaps the most celebrated of such cases is that involving the mule deer herd in the Kaibab National Forest in the Grand Canyon region of Arizona. For many years a deer population of about 6,000

Figure 9–11 This classic example of a deer irruption occurred in a herd of mule deer on the Kaibab Plateau on the north edge of the Grand Canyon, Arizona. It was caused by an intensive predator removal campaign. Note that repeated warnings of impending disaster were ignored. [Adapted from Edward J. Kormondy, *Concepts of Ecology.* (Englewood Cliffs, N.J.: Prentice-Hall, 1969). After A. S. Leopold, *Wisconsin Conservation Bulletin,* No. 321, 1943.]

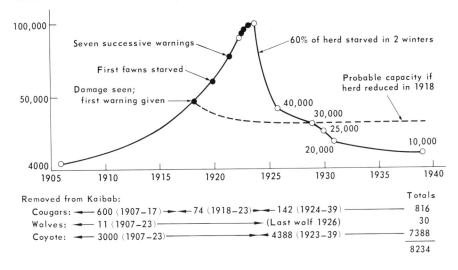

head lived here in dynamic equilibrium with a biotic environment that included a variety of predators, such as the wolf, coyote, cougar, and bear. However, in 1906, the same year the area was proclaimed a national forest by Theodore Roosevelt, an all-out predator control campaign was launched in a naïve attempt to increase the deer herd for the combined benefit of tourists and hunters. All predators were drastically reduced in numbers. The wolf was eradicated. With the ER reduced, the deer population's BP attained full expression, the herd climbing to a peak of 100,000 by 1924, a sixteenfold increase within sixteen years. Unfortunately, however, the herd had increased beyond the carrying capacity of its range. A browse line became well-defined on palatable shrubs and trees, such as aspens and conifers. Herbs were grazed down to the bare ground. Thousands of valuable seedlings, representing the timber of the future, were destroyed. Then came the inevitable "crash." Saved from a quick, sudden death from predators, deer now began to succumb to slow, agonizing death by starvation. Within the six-year period from 1924–1930, 80,000 deer starved, their gaunt, emaciated carcasses bearing eloquent testimony to man's heavy-handed and simple-minded solution to an extremely delicate and complex ecological problem.

Parasites and Disease Organisms. Over forty species of parasites have been found infesting white-tailed deer in the United States. The giant liver flukes, which are 1 to 3 inches long, also parasitize cattle and elk. The only species reported in Wisconsin is *Fascioiloides magna* (9). They adhere to bile ducts in the liver by means of a sucker and receive their nourishment directly from liver tissues and fluids. These flukes do not affect the venison and are harmless to man (9). Infestations show great variation in Minnesota, ranging from 1.1 per cent in the Superior National Forest in 1948 to 68.8 per cent in St. Croix Park in 1952. Although the flukes usually are not harmful, a heavy infestation may kill a deer or at least increase its susceptibility to starvation, traffic accidents, and predation.

The throat bot is the larval stage of the large beelike deer nose fly. The commonest species in Wisconsin is *Oestrus ovis* (9). The adult female deposits eggs or minute maggots near the nostrils of the host. The maggots crawl back into the throat pouches and feed. Fifty-two maggots have been found in a single Wisconsin deer. The parasites overwinter in the deer, emerge from the nostrils in spring, drop to the ground and pupate. In summer the sexually mature adults emerge and mate, completing the life cycle. Although these pests cause deer to sneeze and cough in apparent discomfort, most deer seem to tolerate them without undue harm.

Brucellosis and leptospirosis are both caused by micro-organisms. Heavy infestations are most likely to occur when the deer population is at a peak. Both diseases may cause a pregnant doe to abort her fawns.

Hemorrhagic septicemia is caused by the *Pasteurella* bacterium. Although it primarily afflicts livestock, in the Western states it may cause serious deer mortality. A type of arthritis caused by *Staphylococcus* bacteria has been reported in a five-and-one-half-year-old whitetail. Longhurst et al. report that hoof rot is an important mortality factor for California mule deer (25). It is caused by an anaerobic soil-dwelling bacterium found in the mud of watering places. The concomitance of a peak deer population and drought may result in a considerable mule deer die-off caused by animal concentrations at water holes.

Fluorosis. Karstad reports of fluorosis in the white-tail deer in the vicinity of an industrial complex (20). Fluorides were obtained by deer from both drinking water and vegetation. Fluoride contents of up to 7,125 parts per million were recorded in mandibular bone. These levels were associated with excessive tooth wear and fracture of both jaw bones and teeth.

Management of the Deer Populations

Censusing. Before calculation of the permissible harvest for the ensuing fall hunting season can be made, and before certain management techniques such as habitat changes, predator control, and transplantations can be meaningfully applied, the game manager must determine the approximate size of a deer herd in a given area, as well as its trend. Is the herd increasing or decreasing? If so, at what rate? Is it stable? What was the mortality during a given period? What is the relative browsing pressure on the various vegetational types? These questions can be answered only by some sort of census. Three census techniques applicable to deer are the drive, the fecal pellet count, and the aerial census.

DRIVE CENSUS. In the drive census an area of at least 0.5-mile square is selected and covered by about 100 counters, who move simultaneously along pre-established guide lines that have either been blazed or marked with string. CCC workers made 234 deer drives in the heavily timbered habitat of northern Minnesota from 1935–1939 and counted an average of fifteen deer per square mile. Ruff reports that in the Appalachian region costs were 22¢ per acre on 200–800 acre plots (31).

FECAL PELLET COUNTS. The fecal pellet count is most effective in early spring when fecal pellet groups that have accumulated since the autumn leaf fall may be counted. Random plots about 150 acres in size are employed. On the basis of the number of pellet groups counted and the time during which they accumulated, the game manager can indirectly estimate the number of deer in the area. Thus, the accumulation of 130 pellet groups per acre in 100 days would indicate 0.1 deer per acre or sixty-four deer per square mile (640 acres). As Smith states, the number of pellet groups observed will vary with the sex, age, diet, and health of the animals, as well as the season, rate of decomposition, and nature of the vegetation (33). On good range an average deer may deposit fifteen pellet groups per day, on poor range only thirteen groups. In 1960 at Camp Ripley, Minnesota, 224 plots averaged 5.3 pellet groups, indicating a deer density of almost sixty-four per square mile.

AERIAL CENSUS. An aerial census is made from a plane flying at an altitude of about 300 feet and a speed of 90 miles per hour. Two observers record the number of deer seen along a strip one-quarter mile to either side of the plane. From 1947 to 1953 aerial flights were conducted in northern Minne-

Figure 9–12 Group of twelve deer photographed from plane during an aerial census in the Upper Souris Refuge, Foxholm, North Dakota. [U.S. Fish and Wildlife Service]

sota along 5,582 linear flight miles in which 2,790 square miles of deer habitat were covered. An average of 1.4 deer was observed per square mile. Such aerial censuses may be used to determine over-all population *trends;* they do *not* provide a precise population count. It is very difficult to secure accurate counts in coniferous forest stands or in hardwood stands (oaks) that retain their leaves in winter. Moreover, in the Rockies deer have been known to seek cover as soon as the plane appears.

Trapping. Deer may be effectively trapped with a wooden or aluminum alloy drop trap baited with corn, alfalfa, cedar browse, or some other preferred food. Trapping success increases as range food availability decreases. In a seventy-five-day period the Texas Game, Fish and Oyster Commission caught 1,575 deer. The average cost of trapping one deer in Arkansas was $25 to $32 (37). Recently animals have been anesthetized by shooting them with a dart or hypodermic-injecting device loaded with drugs such as succinyl-choline chloride, flaxedil, and nicotine sulfate (10). Various techniques were employed by Hawkins et al. to capture 507 white-tails in the Crab Orchard Wildlife Refuge in Illinois (18). Methods included corral traps, box traps, Tranimul (an oral sedative), crossbow, longbow, and snares. When deer were susceptible to baiting, trapping was most effective; when natural browse was abundant the bow methods were more effective. Diasepam, a tranquilizer applied to corn, was used by Montgomery et al. to capture twenty-nine Illinois white-tails during the period 1964–1966 (27).

Determination of Movements and Range of Marked Deer. Live-trapped deer may be marked in various ways to permit individual recognition after release. Aluminum ear tags, dyes, and reflecting collars (visible by day and night) have been used. Individual deer may be identified by various color combinations of plastic collars and markers or by some natural deformity such as a misshapen antler. Nylon-base vinyl collars have been used by Hawkins et al. on Illinois white-tails, on which symbols can be seen at 300 yards with 7 × 35 binoculars (18). In Texas deer have been affixed with bells to permit records of nocturnal movements. More recently, deer have been equipped with miniature transistorized radio transmitters by means of a special harness; their movements are then recorded by portable receiving sets. With such techniques data can be secured to answer questions of importance to sound deer management. How long does a deer live? What is its growth rate in wilderness habitat as compared with a semiagricultural environment? How rapidly and how far does a deer disperse from its fawning site? Do deer on overbrowsed ranges disperse more rapidly than deer on good range? Are there sexual differences in mobility? Age differences? What are the dimensions of a deer's home range?

Recapture of marked deer has provided much interesting data. In many cases the home range of the Columbian black-tail is less than 1 square mile in area. The black-tail's attachment to its home range is so strong that an animal will prefer to starve within its own home range rather than sustain itself on an abundance of food available just outside. A small percentage of black-tails, for some unknown reason, will *wander* beyond the home range limits only to return at a later time. A. S. Leopold et al. observed that the Jawbone herd on the western slope of the California Sierras maintained a summer home range of 0.5 to 0.75 mile, whereas the winter home ranges were under half the summer area (24). The home ranges of pregnant does or those with young fawns were considerably smaller than the average. Regardless of size, however, each deer home range contains the essentials of bedding areas, watering sites, food, and cover.

A study by Hahn and Taylor revealed that most white-tailed deer in Texas spend their lives within a radius of 2 miles. After having been transported from their original home range, however, individual Texas bucks have traveled considerable distances to get back to their original locality, one traveling 340 miles in nine months.

During nine winters from 1951–1960 game biologists at Camp Ripley, Minnesota (a mixed deciduous-conifer habitat), captured and marked 478 deer. Most of these animals proved to be highly sedentary, for 168 were retrapped in 1960 at the same point where they were originally captured. Nevertheless, the average dispersal distance for all deer recovered was close to 10 miles.

Transplanting and Stocking. The introduction of deer into an area is defensible only when the range can support them and would otherwise be inaccessible. If a suitable area is already occupied, the high biotic potential of deer will ensure its being stocked to carrying capacity. Transplanting animals to a deer-occupied range which is overbrowsed would not increase the herd but merely add to starvation losses. A notably successful introduction was made in the Blue Mountains of southeastern Washington. From the ten white-tails introduced from northeastern Washington in 1938, the herd grew to at least 250 head by 1956, roughly a twenty-fourfold increase in eigh-

Figure 9–13 Deer trap at the Aransas Wildlife Refuge, Texas. Note sign describing trapping and transplanting of deer. [Bureau of Sport Fisheries and Wildlife, U.S. Department of the Interior]

teen years. In 1965 thirteen mule deer were introduced from northwestern Colorado to Boiling Springs State Park, Oklahoma; in a follow-up survey the same year no live animals were sighted, although two dead deer were found (8). Extensive transplantings conducted throughout the United States have thoroughly mixed the original white-tail subspecies, especially in the South. Herds in northern Georgia have received transplants from Michigan, Wisconsin, Montana, Mississippi, Texas, and Europe.

Cover Improvement. Some habitats within the general range of the white-tail may have an ample supply of good deer food, but may nevertheless be of very low deer carrying capacity because of dearth of cover. The importance of cover as a protection against gales, blizzards, drifting snow, and predators (including man) is very apparent in the grassland biome of eastern South Dakota (now primarily covered with grain fields), where the white-tail congregate in the fingers of forest which extend westward along river bottoms. It is also evident in the white-tail's use of well-sheltered cedar swamps as winter yarding areas in the Lake States. Similarly, white-tails used only 11 per cent of their summer range in a 1,035-acre study area in Pennsylvania, concentrating in coniferous areas at low elevations during severe winters. In 1936 game biologists of the Minnesota Conservation Department and the U.S. Fish and Wildlife Service transplanted large black spruce, balsam fir, and white cedar to provide cover on burned areas. Development of fir and cedar was impaired by heavy browsing, but the black spruce thrived, prividing cover not only for deer, but for ruffed grouse and snowshoe hares. Such areas are checked periodically to determine transplant survival and verify the optimal combination of species, planting pattern, and planting density required for topnotch winter deer cover.

Browse Improvement. Many species of deer food plants are utilized only at an early developmental stage when the more succulent young twigs and stems are at browse level. As these plants mature the basal portions become lignified, tough, and unpalatable, while the preferred portions become unavailable to deer because they have grown out of reach. Game biologists have discovered that the browse value of such plants can be maintained simply by *topping,* or cutting back the old growth. In a study by Ferguson et al. on the winter range of mule deer in southwestern Idaho, tops of bitterbrush were cut off at the 3-foot level. The following year growth was 900 per cent that of controls (14). Krefting et al. conducted a similar study on mountain maple in Minnesota (22). To simulate varying browsing pressures, 20, 40, 60, 80, and 100 per cent of the annual growth was clipped on experimental plants. A high degree of browsing pressure tolerance by mountain maple was indicated in that only one of six mountain maple clumps perished even after nine successive years of 100 per cent clipping. These experimental clippings produced a sustained supply of deer food of which 80 per cent was utilized. In both the Idaho and Minnesota studies cuttings provided an effective management tool for improving deer food supplies.

Deer Exclosures. Game managers frequently question what effect the browsing pressure exerted by a deer herd will have on plant succession. Is the range capable of maintaining itself? Will it deteriorate? The best method for answering these questions is the construction of deer exclosures—fenced-off plots inaccessible to deer but situated within the deer range. After several years the vegetation outside and inside the exclosure may be compared. If the deer herd was excessive, there would be a noticeable absence of young seedlings (such as jack pine) *outside* the exclosure, whereas *inside* there would be a conspicuous abundance. If such a vegetational contrast exists, the deer herd should be reduced, perhaps by liberalizing hunting regulations in the area in an effort to abate the browsing pressure. In recent years, Minnesota has maintained forty-seven deer exclosures scattered throughout the state, embracing a whole spectrum of habitats, from the pioneer community stage following an oak–jack pine burn to the climax community of a maple-basswood forest.

Control of Deer Damage. Deer may be destructive to tree plantations and natural forest reproduction. In Pennsylvania reforestation programs were impossible to complete successfully during peak deer populations (37). Deer have browsed 95 per cent of jack pine reproduction in northern Minnesota. Excessive deer herds in Wisconsin have caused an average of $50,000 damage to national forests alone over a ten-year period (37). Deer damage to young trees was 100 times that caused by fire.

When high populations of deer occur in farming country, depredations on crops and orchards may be considerable. Deer will consume alfalfa, oats, buckwheat, soybeans, and corn.

Figure 9–14 Two- to three-year-old white-tail doe feeding on planted food plot in the Nantahala National Forest, North Carolina. [U.S. Forest Service]

They will make forays into truck gardens and feed on melons, pumpkins, strawberries, carrots, cabbages, celery, peanuts, and potatoes (38). Many buckwheat farms in Pennsylvania have been abandoned because of deer damage. In spring and early summer deer will consume the tender buds of fruit trees; in autumn they may gorge themselves on ripened apples. Big bucks may injure young apple trees in fall while using them as rubbing posts to polish up their antlers. A single deer has destroyed eighty-seven two-year-old orchard trees in three nights. In eastern Maine crop and orchard damage caused by deer amounted to $25,000 to $50,000 annually.

For twenty years, from 1925 to 1945, Minnesota deer herds were closed to hunting and the white-tail population gradually increased—showing a typical species response to decreased ER. By the early 1940's however, Minnesota farmers began to complain of deer damage and resorted to a number of home-made repellents, such as bearskin strips, wolf urine, dried blood, and cow dung. Firecrackers, rockets, and acetylene gas exploders gave only temporary relief. Tall woven wire fences prevent deer invasions but are expensive. Goodrite Z.I.P., a commercial repellent which acts as a lung irritant, has proved effective. Because agricultural depredations by deer are symptomatic of excessive herds, perhaps the best solution is liberalization of hunting regulations in the immediate area of crop damage.

Regulation of the Deer Harvest. One of the primary objectives of deer management is to provide a shootable surplus for the hunter. Several decades ago, when deer were relatively scarce, state legislatures restricted hunting by closing or abbreviating the season, by timing the season so as to ensure an absence of tracking snow, by restricting firearms to shotguns, and by restricting the kill to one per hunter. The doe was afforded special status. The deer herd build-up was further implemented by winter feeding, introductions, predator control, and the establishment of refuges.

In response to these measures, as well as to the great abundance of edge and food available in the wake of extensive fires and logging, the herd increased rapidly—too rapidly. In only thirteen years the white-tail population credited to forty-five states increased from 3,181,675 in 1937 to 5,135,040 in 1949, a gain of 61 per cent. It soon exceeded the range's carrying capacity, browse lines appeared, winter starvation was common, and the range rapidly deteriorated.

Many state game departments advised legislators to reverse the trend by liberalizing hunting regulations. After much prodding from the professional game biologists herd reduction was implemented by opening and extending seasons, timing the season with the occurrence of tracking snow, legalizing the use of rifles, lifting the ban on does, establishing bow seasons, and removing bounties on predators. Access roads were built to facilitate hunter movement to back country.

As of 1970 the overpopulation problem is far from solved. Despite liberalized laws, hunters rarely harvest more than 10 per cent of the herds. One reason is the deer's secretive behavior; the animals rarely emerge from protective cover during daylight hours of the hunting season. Dasmann (1964) reports

Figure 9–15 Annual population fluctuation in a deer herd occupying a range with a carrying capacity of 440 head. Note that even during a closed season the various agents of ER (starvation, parasites, predation, disease, accidents, etc.) will reduce the herd to the carrying capacity of the range. It is apparent that a considerable surplus may be safely harvested by hunters. With or without an open season, the population of the herd by the end of the winter–spring hardship period will be virtually the same. [After Raymond F. Dasmann, *Environmental Conservation* (New York: John Wiley & Sons, Inc., 1968).]

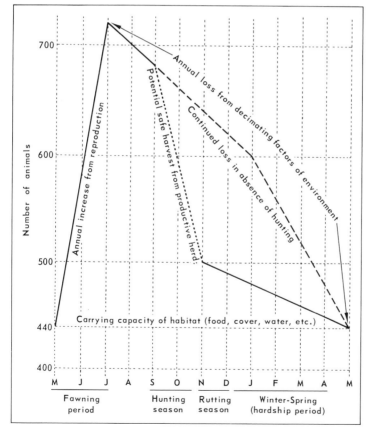

the inability of hunters to *see* a single deer in an area supporting a population density of 100 per square mile (10). A 10 per cent annual harvest is simply not enough to appreciably check herd increase. According to Taylor (1956) "annual removal of deer (by hunting, transfer, or otherwise) should be based on actual yearly increase in numbers as related to available deer foods Usually at least one third of a fall population of deer can be taken, year after year, if both sexes are removed in equal numbers. Ordinarily, the game manager does not need to be concerned either with inbreeding or with an overwide buck-doe ratio." (37).

Deer populations frequently vary from region to region within a single state, being high perhaps in semiwooded agricultural regions and low in climax forests and near urban centers. Therefore, a state may be divided into a number of zones, each with its own set of regulations. (One state has had sixty zones.) In zones where herds are at low levels, the season may be closed completely or may be open to bow hunters only. In overpopulated zones, the season may be opened on bucks, does, and even fawns. In some states game managers are not permitted to practice what they preach, because their technical knowledge in game management is far in advance of a receptive public or political climate. Too often the framers of our hunting laws yield to pressures exerted by hunters, misguided nature lovers, and resort owners, to whom the essence of game management is "more deer." Only when regulations are formulated in accordance with the advice of professionally staffed conservation departments will hunting regulations serve as an effective management tool.

Bibliography

1. Behrend, Donald F., and Robert D. McDowell. "Antler Shedding Among White-tailed Deer in Connecticut," *Jour. Wild. Mgt.*, **31** (1967), 588–590.
2. Bersing, Otis S. *A Century of Wisconsin Deer.* Madison, Wis.: Wisconsin Conservation Department, 1956, 184 pp.
3. Blair, Robert M. "Deer Forage in a Loblolly Pine Plantation," *Jour. Wild. Mgt.*, **31** (1967), 432–437.
4. Burt, William H., and Richard Grossenheider. *A Field Guide to the Mammals.* Cambridge, Mass.: The Riverside Press, 1952, 200 pp.
5. Cahalane, V. H. *Mammals of North America.* New York: The Macmillan Co., 1947.
6. Cheatum, E. L. "Disease in Relation to Winter Mortality of Deer in New York," *Jour. Wild. Mgt.*, **15** (1951), 216–220.
7. Cheatum, E. L., and C. W. Severinghaus. "Variations in Fertility of White-tailed Deer Related to Range Conditions," *Trans. North Amer. Wild. Conf.*, **15** (1950), 170–190.

8. Clark, T. W. "Mammals of Boiling Springs State Park, Woodward County, Oklahoma," *Proc. Okla, Acad. Sci.,* **46** (1966), 36–38.

9. Dahlberg, Burton L., and Ralph C. Guettinger. "The White-tailed Deer in Wisconsin," *Tech. Wild. Bull. No. 14.* Madison, Wis.: Wisconsin Conservation Department, 1956.

10. Dasmann, Raymond F. *Wildlife Biology.* New York: John Wiley & Sons, Inc., 1964, 231 pp.

11. _____ and W. Hines. "Logging, Plant Succession and Black-tailed Deer in the Redwood Region," Mimeographed, Humboldt State College, Aroata, Calif., 13 pp.

12. _____ and R. D. Taber. "Behavior of Columbian Black-tailed Deer with Reference to Population Ecology," *Jour. of Mam.,* **37** (1956), 143–164.

13. Davis, David E., and Frank B. Golley. *Principles in Mammalogy.* New York: Reinhold Publishing Corp., 1963, 335 pp.

14. Ferguson, Robert B., and Joseph V. Basile. "Topping Stimulates Bitterbrush Twig Growth," *Jour. Wild. Mgt.,* **30** (1966), 839–841.

15. French, C. E., L. C. McEwen, N. D. Magruder, R. H. Ingram, and R. W. Swift. "Nutrient Requirements for Growth and Antler Development in the White-tailed Deer," *Jour. Wild. Mgt.,* **20** (1956), 221–232.

16. Hamilton, W. J., Jr. *The Mammals of Eastern United States.* Ithaca, N.Y.: Comstock Publishing Company, Inc., 1943, 432 pp.

17. Hanson, William R. "Aggressive Behavior of Mule Deer Toward Bobcat," *Jour. of Mam.,* **37** (1956), 458.

18. Hawkins, R. E., D. C. Autry, and W. D. Klimstra. "Comparison of Methods Used to Recapture White-tailed Deer," *Jour. Wild. Mgt.,* **31** (1967), 460–464.

19. Kabat, C., N. E. Collias, and R. C. Guettinger. "Some Winter Habits of White-tailed Deer and the Development of Census Methods in the Flag Yard of Northern Wisconsin," *Tech. Wild. Bull. No. 7.* Madison, Wis.: Wisconsin Conservation Department.

20. Karstad, Lars. "Fluorosis in Deer (*Odocoileus virginianus*)," *Bull. Wild. Disease Assoc.,* **3** (1967), 42–46.

21. King, David G. "A Black Bear Kills a Fawn," *Can. Field Nat.,* **81,** 2 (1967), 149–150.

22. Krefting, L. W., M. H. Stenlund, and R. K. Seemel. "Effect of Simulated and Natural Deer Browsing on Mountain Maple, "*Jour. Wild. Mgt.,* **30** (1966), 481–488.

23. Lay, Daniel W. "Deer Range Appraisal in Eastern Texas," *Jour. Wild. Mgt.,* **31** (1967), 426–432.

24. Leopold, A. S., T. Riney, R. McCain, and L. Tevis, Jr. "The Jawbone Deer Herd," *Game Bull. No. 4,* California Division of Fish and Game, (1951) 1–139.

25. Longhurst, W., A. S. Leopold, and R. F. Dasmann. "A Survey of California Deer Herds, Their Ranges and Management Problems," *Game Bull. No. 6,* California Department of Fish and Game, (1952) 136 pp.

26. Martin, F. R., and L. W. Krefting. "The Necedah Refuge Deer Irruption," *Jour. Wild. Mgt.,* **17** (1953), 166–176.

27. Montgomery, G. G., and R. E. Hawkins. "Diazepam Bait for Capture of White-tailed Deer," *Jour. Wild. Mgt.,* **31** (1967), 464–468.

28. Moore, William H., and Frank M. Johnson. "Nature of Deer Browsing on Hardwood Seedlings and Sprouts," *Jour. Wild. Mgt.,* **31,** (1967), 351–353.

29. Orr, Robert T. *Vertebrate Biology*. Philadelphia. W. B. Saunders Co., 1961, 400 pp.

30. Robinette, W. Leslie, J. S. Gashwiler, Dale A. Jones, and Harold S. Crane. "Fertility of Mule Deer in Utah," *Jour. Wild. Mgt.,* **19** (1955), 115–136.

31. Ruff, Frederick J. "The White-tailed Deer on the Pisgah National Game Preserve, North Carolina." Washington, D.C.: Department of Agriculture, 249 pp. (mim.)

32. Sikes, Dennis, Frank A. Hayes, and Annie K. Prestwood. "Staphylococcal Arthritis in a White-tailed Deer (*Odocoileus virginianus*)," *Can. Jour. Comp. Med. and Vet. Sci.,* **32** (1968), 388–391.

33. Smith, Robert L. *Ecology and Field Biology*. New York: Harper & Row, Publishers, 1964, 686 pp.

34. Taber, R. D. "Deer Nutrition and Population Dynamics in the North Coast Range of California," *Trans. North Amer. Wild. Conf.,* **21** (1956), 156–172.

35. _____ and Raymond F. Dasmann. "The Dynamics of Three Natural Populations of the Deer *Odocoileus hemionus columbianus*," *Ecol.,* **38** (1957), 233–246.

36. _____ and Raymond F. Dasmann. "The Black-tailed Deer of the Chaparral," *Game Bull. No. 8,* California Department of Fish and Game, 1958, 161 pp.

37. Taylor, Walter P. (ed.). *The Deer of North America*. Harrisburg, Pa.: The Stackpole Co., 1956, 668 pp.

38. Verme, Louis J. "Influence of Experimental Diets on White-tailed Deer Reproduction," *Trans. 32nd North Amer. Wild. Nat. Res. Conf.* (1967), 405–420.

The Ecology and Management of Waterfowl

10

Life Cycle of the Mallard

To acquire a frame of reference for our discussion of waterfowl ecology and management, it may be well to sketch first the major events in the life cycle of the mallard, the most abundant, popular, delicious and sought-after duck on the North American continent.

Description.   The handsome drake or "greenhead," with its white neck ring, chestnut breast and orange-yellow feet, is readily identified. The hen, like so many female ducks, is a subdued grayish brown, a color which presumably affords the nesting bird a measure of concealment from predators.

The Winter Season.   Although hardy birds can survive the severe cold of northern winters, they require a certain minimum of open water. They winter in the brackish estuaries of southeastern Alaska as well as in the Lake States, where streams are warmed and kept open by power plants. Over a million mallards have been recorded at Christmas on the Fort Randall Reservoir in South Dakota. Winter flocks numbering many thousands occur along the Gulf Coast and in the Mississippi River Valley just south of the east-west barrier of ice-bound waters. Hundreds of thousands congregate in the White River National Wildlife Refuge in Arkansas. A few mallards over-winter in Baja California and central Mexico.

Breeding. In early spring, as soon as the ice cover melts on northern sloughs and potholes, many hundreds of thousands of mallards migrate to their northern breeding grounds. Imme-diately after arrival in the general nesting area, several drakes will ardently pursue a single hen in the so-called courtship flights. Eventually the hen "chooses" one of the pursuing drakes by touching him with her bill. After the hen has selected the nest site (usually in some hayfield or marsh), the drake will establish his territory in the area and drive off encroaching mallard drakes. The nest is lined with dried grasses, broken flags, reeds, down, and the hen's breast feathers. It may be concealed under arching vegetation. Not only are such nests difficult to detect by a hawk or skunk, but also by the game biologist. In wooded country the hen may appropriate an unused hawk's nest (43).

The biotic potential is high, the initial clutch of ten or eleven buffy (or whitish) eggs being followed by second or even third clutches of about eight eggs each, in the event that earlier nest-ings are destroyed by such forms of environmental resistance as spring floods, fire, predators, and the mowing machine.

Figure 10–1 Young mallards just hatching in nest at the Valentine Refuge, Whitewater Lake, Nebraska. [U.S. Fish and Wildlife Service]

Mallard productivity in some regions appears correlated with spring rainfall, being high during wet springs and low during spring droughts. Mayhew's observations in the Sacramento Valley (California) suggest that a high relative humidity and periodic egg wetting are prerequisites for a good hatch (29). As the hen initiates her twenty-eight-day incubation period, the drake forsakes her, eventually moults in late summer, and assumes a dull gray-brown *eclipse* plumage. While in eclipse plumage, the male is flightless and vulnerable to predation, trapping, or corral drives. The drake skulks in the sloughs until recovering its breeding plumage and flight capability in late fall. The precocious ducklings are able to follow the hen almost immediately after hatching.

Food Habits. The omnivorous mallard is a "dabbling" duck, characteristically feeding in shallow water, often tipping to an almost vertical position as it stirs up the bottom ooze, straining out crustaceans, molluscs, algae, and the seeds of aquatic plants. The adults, weighing 2 to 3 pounds, maintain a diet which is 90 per cent vegetable and 10 per cent animal matter. Analysis of 1,578 stomachs from twenty-two states and two Canadian provinces revealed the following consumption percentages: sedges, 22; grasses, 13; smartweeds, 10; pondweeds, 8; duckweeds, 6; and coontail, 6 (28). Lesser amounts of wild celery, water elm, wapato, acorns, and buttonbush seeds were ingested. One mallard stomach contained 2,560 seeds of duckweed, 8,700 of sedge, 28,160 of bulrush, and 35,840 of primrose willow (28). Occasionally, mallards will resort to an oak woods and consume such large quantities of acorns they are temporarily incapable of flight. Molluscs and insects form 6 and 3 per cent, respectively, of the duck's food. The duckling's diet is the reverse of the adult's, consisting of 90 per cent animal material and 10 per cent plant matter. In studies of captive wild mallards, Jordan found that ducks eight and nine weeks old consumed 44 per cent more food than adults (24). The high protein content in the young birds' diet apparently is essential for the rapid growth that will culminate by autumn in an organism capable of migrating over 1,000 miles. (In some species of ducks the fall weight may be fifty times the weight at hatching (42).)

The U.S. Biological Survey and later the U.S. Fish and Wildlife Service have collected stomach analysis data on game ducks since 1901. Analysis of 7,998 ducks of eighteen species collected in 247 localities in the United States and Canada revealed that 73.07 per cent (by volume) of the food consisted of plants (28). The seven most important plant foods were pondweed, 11.04 per cent; bulrush, 6.42 per cent; smartweed, 4.71 per cent;

wigeongrass, 4.27 per cent; muskgrass, 2.48 per cent; wild millet, 2.38 per cent, and wild celery, 2.33 per cent. Animal materials comprised 26.93 per cent of the duck's food, of which molluscs (9.84 per cent) and crustaceans (3.44 per cent) were the most important (28).

Autumn Migration. In the autumn the mallards of the Northern states and Canada congregate in large flocks. They may invade agricultural areas and consume waste grain. Northern mallards linger until the ponds and sloughs become ice-bound in early November, when they begin a spectacular migration known as the "Grand Passage," which will terminate hundreds or even thousands of miles to the south, wherever open water, food, and cover are available. A mallard banded at Green Bay, Wisconsin, November 23, 1930, was shot five days later near Georgetown, South Carolina, over 900 miles away. For some inexplicable reason, the migratory instinct in some mallards may not be activated. Such was the case in Canada in January, 1966, when exasperated wildlife officials employed a mass air lift as a last resort, after the ducks had resisted all other attempts to move them (31). Many mallards are shot before they complete the fall migration, falling to the guns of 3 million duck hunters, deployed on a broad front from the Bear River marshes of Utah

Figure 10–2 Hunter calling ducks in flooded greentree reservoir at Wynne, Arkansas. [Soil Conservation Service, U.S. Department of Agriculture]

to the South Carolina river bottoms, from Wisconsin's corn fields to the farm ponds of Arkansas.

Environmental Resistance

A variety of environmental influences, both biotic and physical, prevent waterfowl from expressing their high biotic potential. Among those discussed below are storms, mudballing, pothole drainage, drought, appropriation of duck habitat for recreational areas, pollution (from industrial, navigational, and pesticidal sources), predators, disease organisms, and habitat impairment by carp.

Storms. During their extensive migrations between breeding and wintering ranges, waterfowl may incur considerable storm mortality. In October, 1935, a severe snowstorm suddenly developed during the peak of the fall migration in northern Minnesota. As the low-flying flocks, composed primarily of lesser scaup, flew over Thief River Falls, they apparently were blinded by street lights and crashed into power lines and buildings. When the storm subsided, the bodies of roughly 4,000 ducks littered the town's streets (26). The Armistice Day blizzard of 1940 was also highly destructive. In addition to claiming the lives of many hunters (forty-nine in Minnesota alone), thousands of exhausted ducks alighted on ponds and became frozen in the ice.

Mudballing. Clay soils may become so sticky after a gentle rain that they adhere to the feet of waterfowl and eventually form *mudballs*. If sufficiently heavy, such mudballs can cause death from exhaustion. Extensive mudballing occurred in the Muleshoe National Wildlife Refuge of Texas during 1945–1946, causing the death of 500 ducks, typical mallard and pintail victims acquiring mud weights of 400 and 750 grams, respectively (34).

Pothole Drainage and Drought. The most productive duck factory on the North American continent is located in the grassland biome of Manitoba, Saskatchewan, Alberta, the Dakotas, western Minnesota, and northwestern Iowa. This region produced 53 per cent of the continent's waterfowl during 1950–1957 (26). The ducks are raised primarily on tiny potholes, 1 or 2 acres in size, where all the basic waterfowl habitat requirements of food, cover, water, and nesting sites are usually met. However, the drainage of considerable pothole acreages for agricultural purpose, some of which, inexplicably, was actually

Figure 10–3 Aerial view of dried-up potholes near Antler, Saskatchewan. These duck breeding grounds are also utilized by beaver. [Bureau of Sport Fisheries and Wildlife, U.S. Department of the Interior]

subsidized by the federal government, has long posed a critical habitat impairment problem. In 1948 the government paid $17,285 to 350 farmers of Day County, South Dakota, to dig 43 miles of drainage canals (9). As a result 1,400 potholes representing 6,285 acres were eliminated as duck nesting areas. During 1949–1950 in Minnesota, North Dakota, and South Dakota 64,000 potholes were destroyed, representing a loss of 188,000 acres of waterfowl habitat (26). In 1955 only 56,000 of the original 150,000 square miles of pothole habitat still remained. In Iowa alone, over the last sixty years, 2.4 million hectares of pothole country has shrunk to 20,000 hectares— a reduction of well over 90 per cent. Severe drought in the 1930's and early 1960's compounded the problem by drying up many potholes which hitherto had escaped drainage. In Canada alone during drought conditions, the number of potholes may be reduced from a wet season peak of 6.7 million to 1.7 million, with corresponding reduction in waterfowl populations (39). It should be mentioned here that much drainage has benefited both agriculture and game, other than waterfowl. Thus the Black Swamp in Wood County, Ohio, which was converted into a profitable agricultural region, now affords some of the best pheasant hunting in the state.

Appropriation of Duck Habitat for Water Sports and Recreation. For many centuries of pre-Columbian time, the weed beds and marshes along the western end of Lake Erie provided optimal habitat for thousands of waterfowl. Today, as a result of a mushrooming human population with increasing amounts of leisure time, the area's waterfowl carrying capacity has been severely impaired. Where once mallards paddled, motorboats churn. The scuba diver has replaced the scaup; the marsh has given way to the marina. Over 3,000 boats are berthed along a 0.5-mile shoreline of Lake St. Clair. They appropriate space once used by waterfowl. During the summer large numbers of motorboats trim the tops of emergent food plants with great efficiency. We would not expect a field of daisies to be capable of reproduction were we to go through them with a power mower; neither can duck food plants survive unless they are permitted to keep their reproductive heads above water to effect pollination. It is apparent that in this confrontation of waterfowl, concerned with survival itself, and man, concerned only with week-end water fun, the interests of man have been served—with catastrophic effect on waterfowl.

Industrial Pollution. Poisonous discharges from river and lakeshore industries, such as paper pulp mills, dye plants, tanning industries, and organic chemical plants, may have a direct toxic effect on waterfowl. The birds may ingest these poisons along with their food with fatal results. Moreover, they may die indirectly, but just as surely, when these toxic discharges kill off the phytoplankton base of their food chains.

Sometimes nature compounds pollution problems in a freakish, unpredictable pattern. A good case is the following story. In November, 1962, the severe cold caused the bursting of an oil distillate tank at Savage, Minnesota. As a result, 1.4 million gallons spewed onto the frozen Minnesota River. At Mankato, a protracted spell of subzero weather caused a 3-million-gallon tank of soybean oil to break open and release its contents likewise to the river. When the March thaw came, the pollutants slowly moved downstream and entered the Mississippi River near St. Paul. The *southward* flowing oil met *northward* moving flocks of ducks along a 30-mile stretch of river below St. Paul. The feathers of thousands of ducks, primarily lesser scaup, became matted with oil. Unable to fly, over 10,000 of the oil-fouled birds died from exposure, exhaustion and starvation. Hundreds of birds were retrieved by rescue teams of wildlife biologists and college students from the University of Minnesota and Mankato State College. The National Guard was called to keep oil from spreading into protected channels. The rescue operations made newspaper headlines. The governor of Minnesota was even pictured in a Minneapolis newspaper holding a bedraggled duck in his arms. For a few brief days the ordinary citizen became keenly aware of the threat which industrial pollution poses for our waterfowl resource.

Oil Pollution. An excess of 100,000 waterfowl are destroyed annually by oil pollution. Oil hazards for marine birds developed about 1925 when oil-burning ships replaced those utilizing coal as fuel (32). Much of this pollution occurs in Atlantic coastal waters. Resolutions to control marine oil pollution proposed at the 1954 International Conference on Pollution of the Sea by Oil were ratified by twenty-eight countries and the United States (22). Nevertheless, as a result of wilfulness, carelessness, and accidents, oil pollution continues. Oil kills ducks by matting their feathers and impairing their insulative function. An oil-soaked area the size of a quarter will kill a murre according to Leslie M. Tuck of the Canadian Wildlife Service in Newfoundland (32). Oil may also prove lethal if ingested accidentally during preening and drinking (30). "Accelerated starvation" may frequently occur when oiled ducks exhibit a greatly increased metabolic rate in conjunction with a retarded food intake (20).

In 1954 oil spillage from a shipwreck off the Canadian coast destroyed 1,500 ducks (22). One quarter million murres, eiders, razorbills, and puffins died off Newfoundland because of jettisoned oil during the winter of 1960. Oil killed 4,000 ducks in Long Island Sound in December, 1960 (30). Another 4,000 ducks, almost 20 per cent of the wintering population in Narragansett Bay, were destroyed by an oil spill in 1961. In 1969 thousands of waterfowl were destroyed off Santa Barbara, California, because of an oil spill resulting from faulty drilling operations. Oil pollution of fresh-water habitats frequently originates in industrial sources. During the spring of 1960 10,000 ducks, primarily canvasbacks aggregating in a restricted area of open water in the Detroit River, were killed by an oil spill (30).

Lead Poisoning. Lead toxemia resulting from the ingestion of spent shot causes an estimated 2 to 3 per cent annual waterfowl loss in the United States, almost equivalent to the combined duck production of North and South Dakota (5). (Nearly 25 per cent of 8,000 waterfowl investigated in southern France contained lead shot.) From 1940 to 1963 over 1,500 Canada geese died in Wisconsin from lead poisoning. The heaviest duck mortality from lead poisoning has occurred along the Mississippi flyway, especially in Louisiana, Illinois, Missouri, Indiana,

Figure 10–4 Oil-soaked duck taken in the Atlantic off the New England coast. [Bureau of Sport Fisheries and Wildlife, U.S. Department of the Interior]

Figure 10–5 Hunter in the act of decreasing the mallard population by one. [State Historical Society of Wisconsin]

and Arkansas (5). Because there are 280 pellets of #6 shot in one shell, and the average hunter requires five shots to kill one duck, he deposits 1,400 pellets on waterfowl habitat for each bird taken. In 1952 goose hunters at Horicon Marsh (Wisconsin) required thirty-six shots to bag one bird. Sixty thousand pellets per acre were counted in the San Joaquin River marshes of California; 118,048 per acre were recorded from the bottom of Wisconsin's Lake Puckaway (5). Species incurring heaviest losses have been the bottom feeders, such as mallards and pintails, which ingest the shot inadvertently along with food and grit. Ducks may confuse shot with the seeds of certain pondweeds. According to a British study, roughly 70 per cent of mallards bearing a single ingested shot will succumb if they persist in a wild seed diet (22). Nevertheless, up to 179 pellets have been recovered from a pintail and 451 from a trumpeter swan (5).

After ingestion chemical reactions within the digestive tract cause the release of soluble lead salts, which may paralyze the gizzard and cause starvation in a month. In acute cases poisoning of the liver, blood, and kidneys may cause death in one to two weeks. Symptoms include extreme emaciation, protruding sternal keel, absence of fat deposits in the body cavity, hypertrophied gall bladder, and characteristically green-stained gizzard lining and vent (5).

Stopgap measures to reduce mortality include covering the pellet-bearing feeding area with fine gravel. Plastic-coated lead pellets have not proved successful in reducing the toxemia (22). Perhaps the best long-term solution to the problem would be the substitution of nontoxic iron alloy for lead shot (5).

Botulism. The prostrate bodies of dead and dying ducks littered the mud flats of a western marsh. Here a mallard feebly fluttered its wings and voided bright green droppings; there a widgeon struggled vainly to lift its head out of the stagnant ooze; a Canada goose was blinded by the yellowish slime which covered its eyes; a blue-winged teal gasped and died. What had happened to these birds? They were the victims of *botulism*, a disease caused by the toxic metabolic wastes of the anaerobic bacterium *Clostridium botulinum*, type C (21). Although most prevalent in the West, it has been recorded from Canada to Mexico, from California to New Jersey. During the summer of 1910 this tiny organism was responsible for millions of waterfowl deaths. In 1929, and again in 1932, an estimated 100,000 to 300,000 waterfowl in the Great Salt Lake (Utah) died from botulism (21). In 1965 botulism claimed the lives of 20,000 birds in Utah's Bear River Migratory Bird Wildlife Refuge.

The optimal environmental conditions for a population build-up of *Clostridium* include (1) exposed stretches of stagnant alkaline flats, (2) an abundance of "trapped" organic matter, such as aquatic vegetation, to serve as food, (3) high water temperatures. These conditions are most likely to occur in late summer during periods of protracted drought. The shallow-feeding dabbling ducks are especially vulnerable because they accidentally ingest the toxic material along with aquatic plants and their invertebrate foods. Apparently, invertebrates serve as a specialized microhabitat for the bacteria where growth and reproduction are favored (21). Once absorbed by the blood stream of the waterfowl, the toxin affects the nervous system, rendering the birds flightless and eventually causing death by respiratory paralysis. At the Bear River Wildlife Refuge many thousands of sick ducks have recovered after receiving antitoxin shots. Such treatment, however, would be prohibitively costly

Figure 10–6 Botulism at the Bear River Migratory Bird Refuge. Biologist picks up sick and dead birds. Sick birds are given antitoxin treatments at the duck hospital. Since the hospital was established, the loss of waterfowl from this disease has dropped off greatly on the refuge. [Bureau of Sport Fisheries and Wildlife, U.S. Department of the Interior]

and time-consuming in the event of a major outbreak. Thus prevention seems to be the answer. Kalmbach and Gunderson have suggested that prevention can be effected by rapidly raising the water level of the marsh or mudflat so that *Clostridium* no longer has optimal conditions for reproduction (25). Such flooding would both lower the water temperature and dilute the toxin. Research is currently being conducted to determine whether botulism cannot be controlled indirectly by reducing the invertebrate populations (21).

Destruction of Waterfowl Habitat by Carp. To many a barefooted youngster armed with canepole and worms, a carp might seem a prize, but to the sophisticated duck hunter, it is a notorious destroyer of waterfowl habitat. Carp can eradicate dense growths of sago pondweed, water milfoil, and coontail, all favored duck foods (33). By means of enclosure experiments, E. W. Threinen and W. T. Helm showed that carp could quickly devastate growths of floating-leaf pondweed. Lake Koshkonong in southern Wisconsin was once almost blanketed with rafts of canvasbacks, which fed on the abundant buds of wild celery

Figure 10–7 Unloading botulism-stricken ducks at the Bear River Migratory Bird Refuge, Utah. They will be given antitoxin shots at the duck hospital. A very high percentage of treated birds recover. [Bureau of Sport Fisheries and Wildlife, U.S. Department of the Interior]

and pondweed nuts. Late in the nineteenth century, however, carp were introduced to Lake Koshkonong. In a brief time the fish uprooted the choice waterfowl food plants, and the thrilling panoramas of rafting "cans" quickly vanished except in memory. Hundreds of waterfowl feeding areas throughout the United States have had similar histories. Moreover, recent food analysis studies have shown that young carp will compete directly with ducklings for protein-rich invertebrates, so essential for growth and development. Scuds and water fleas are preferred by carp under 5 inches; 5- to 11-inch carp prefer aquatic insects (33).

The turbidity caused by carp, which stir up the bottom muds while searching for plant rootstocks and invertebrates, may restrict photosynthesis sufficiently to eliminate certain duck food plants not actually directly killed by the fish. According to Frederick C. Lincoln, this factor was partially responsible for the impaired waterfowl carrying capacity of the Potomac River and the Susquehanna Flats in the late 1940's (27).

Carp are extremely difficult to eradicate. Once under control, however, a given site may rapidly recover its original ability to support waterfowl. This has been demonstrated at the Lake Mattamuskeet Wildlife Refuge (North Carolina), where carp had infiltrated from brackish coastal waters in the 1930's. Because of their deleterious impact on waterfowl, refuge personnel under the direction of W. G. Cahoon launched an intensive carp control campaign in 1945 (10). It included the erection of a barrier to further infiltration and an extended seining operation which netted 2.4 million pounds of carp from 1945 to 1960 (10). Already by 1952 water turbidity was markedly reduced and duck food plants were becoming established on the formerly barren lake bottom. As a result Lake Mattamuskeet once again is a celebrated waterfowl wintering ground, currently being utilized by 60,000 to 80,000 Canada geese, 80,000 to 150,000 ducks and teal, and hundreds of whistling swans annually (10).

Predators. Whether egg embryo, hatchling, or adult, the seventy-plus species of North American waterfowl are vulnerable to predation by fish, reptiles, birds, and mammals. Large muskellunge and northern pike will consume ducklings. During the summer of 1941 Victor Solman estimated that 10 per cent of the duckling crop produced on the Saskatchewan Delta was destroyed by northern pike (17). The remains of scaup, scoters, widgeon, auks, guillemots, cormorants, grebes, and loons, have been found in the stomachs of goosefish from the Gulf of Maine (6). In the Southern states newly hatched mottled duck young may be consumed by blue crabs, garfish, turtles, alligators, snakes, boat-tailed grackles, skunks, opossums, and raccoons. Choate reports that gull predation was largely responsible for nesting losses of the American eider on five islands in Penobscot Bay, Maine (12). Paul L. Errington found duck remains in twenty-four (15.1 per cent) of 158 great horned owl pellets collected in spring from an Iowa marsh (17). During one breeding season mammalian predators destroyed 52 per cent of 333 duck nests in California's Sacramento Valley (2). In 1958 two grizzly bears destroyed the eggs and nestlings of 160 snow geese and 135 brant nests in less than one week. Mink, skunks, raccoons, and foxes destroyed 100 (54 per cent) of 186 nests of the blue-winged teal in northwest Iowa (18).

Cartwright has suggested that crow predation of eggs and ducklings, which usually results in the parent birds renesting at some later date, may actually be beneficial to the prey species (11). His reasoning is that without such disturbance the nesting cycles of all breeding pairs of a given duck species would be synchronized; hence, the birds would be highly vulnerable to the vagaries of weather such as freezing, drought, and heavy rains. However, the predator-induced staggering of nestings (a mallard may renest three times) over a longer season would minimize the severity of such losses (11).

Waterfowl Management

The various aspects of waterfowl management that shall be described include habitat development, banding studies, administrative use of the migratory flyways, population surveys, and the establishment of hunting regulations.

Habitat Development. Waterfowl habitat may be improved by retarding aquatic succession, creating openings in dense marsh vegetation, constructing artificial ponds, and developing artificial nests and nest sites.

RETARDING AQUATIC SUCCESSION. Ecological succession, which was described in an earlier chapter, may proceed in an aquatic as well as terrestrial habitat. Thus, the basin of a lake or pond, once providing excellent food, cover, and nest sites for waterfowl, may with the passage of time become filled with the bodies of decaying plants and animals, as well as with sediment washed in from surrounding hillsides. Eventually the aquatic community will be succeeded by a terrestrial community, which will proceed toward the climax typical of the region, whether it be coniferous forest, deciduous forest, or grassland.

It is apparent that were it allowed to proceed unchecked,

ecological succession would slowly but surely impair and eventually completely destroy the carrying capacity of the site for waterfowl. This insidious trend of succession is retarded in many shallow ponds and potholes on the Great Plains by periodic droughts. In the more humid regions of the deciduous and coniferous forest biomes, drought may be "simulated" by draining the pond at regular intervals of about six years. When water milfoil (a rooted aquatic) begins to dominate the submergent vegetation at the Red Lake Wildlife Refuge in northern Minnesota, it serves as an indicator to the refuge manager that it is time to drain the pond. The exposed pond bottom is then broken up with a disc to eradicate any invading plants such as cattail, phragmites, or willow, which otherwise might secure a roothold. The pond is permitted to remain dry for one year. As a result of the increased aeration and the accelerated bacterial decomposition of organic materials which occurs at this time, a number of essential minerals such as calcium, magnesium, potassium, and nitrates are released in a form which can be absorbed and used by duck food plants. After one year in the bare bottom stage, the pond is reflooded; the mineralized nutrients dissolve to form high concentrations and greatly enhance the pond's nutritional value. Moreover, invading weeds such as golden dock and smartweed may become established on the exposed pond bottom, and when the pond is reflooded they may be available to hungry ducks.

CREATING OPENINGS. Although waterfowl require cover for protection from both weather and predators, they also require channels and openings through which they can paddle or waddle (between nest site and feeding area, between feeding and loafing area,) or which may serve as areas where the birds may secure aquatic food supplies. Such essential openings may be established by the natural agencies of hurricane and lightning-triggered fires or they may be developed by man-directed agencies such as controlled burning, and the use of explosives.

Controlled Burning. Fire may be highly destructive to waterfowl habitat when it consumes a drought-parched marsh. However, when carefully controlled by trained personnel, it may serve as an important agent in habitat improvement. For example, in North Carolina at the Mattamuskeet National Wildlife Refuge, marshes are regularly burned each winter. Not only can openings be created in this way, but in a brief time overwintering geese, hard-pressed for food, will move into the burn to feed on the green shoots which burgeon in the mineral-enriched earth. In Louisiana alone biologists burn nearly a million marsh acres yearly (45).

Use of Explosives. In marshland with a fairly high water table, explosives may be used to good advantages in blasting out potholes. This technique has been used successfully in recent years in South Dakota, Minnesota, Wisconsin, and Michigan. Although dynamite was originally employed, it proved to be rather expensive, and has been widely replaced with ammonium nitrate (AN), which is soaked in fuel oil and then detonated with the aid of a dynamite primer (8). In Minnesota as of 1964, a pothole 35 feet long, 25 feet wide, and 7 feet deep could be blasted out of heavy clay soil at a cost of only $11 (8). Such dynamited potholes retain their usefulness as a waterfowl habitat for decades. In 1962 Strohmeyer evaluated potholes in northwestern Iowa which had been dynamited twenty-one to twenty-two years previously (38). Although on the average they retained only 29 per cent of their original depth, they were nevertheless effective in restricting the development of emergent vegetation. Moreover, waterfowl nests were situated near the potholes.

CONSTRUCTION OF FARM PONDS. Where sloughs and potholes are scarce, waterfowl habitat can be created by the construction of artificial ponds. Between 1936 and 1962, the U.S. Department of Agriculture assisted Soil Conservation District farmers in building 2.2 million ponds; it is estimated that almost 3.5 million will have been completed by 1980 (16). Roughly two thirds of these ponds will be usable by waterfowl, either as nesting, feeding, and loafing areas by resident birds or as rest areas where migrating waterfowl may touch down for a brief respite, before resuming their strenuous journeys (16). The farmer can increase the carrying capacity of his pond by erecting artificial nest boxes for mallards and wood ducks; by dumping piles of rocks or anchoring logs and bales of hay in the open water to serve as preening and sunning areas; by periodically draining the pond to promote the mineralization of organic matter and the release of nutrient elements, which can then be recycled into the waterfowl food chain; and by seeding the pond with choice duck food plants. With the extensive employment of such pond management procedures, the 3.5 million farm ponds of 1980 will provide at least partial use for an estimated 10 million birds (16).

CONSTRUCTION OF ARTIFICIAL NESTS AND NEST SITES. Through eons of time and natural selection, each species of waterfowl has evolved its own unique instinct for nest site selection and nest construction. It would appear almost impertinent, therefore, for man to attempt to improve upon nature by constructing artificial nests and sites for waterfowl. How-

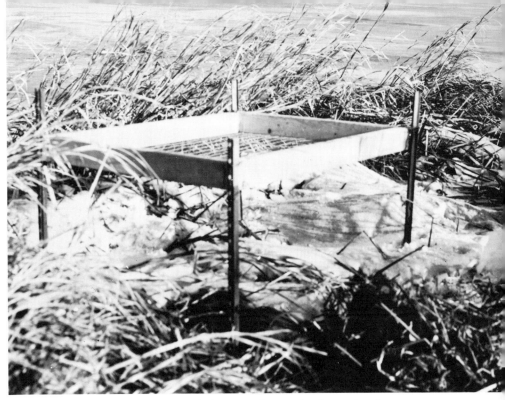

Figure 10–8 These goose nesting platforms at the Sand Lake National Wildlife Refuge increase the carrying capacity of the refuge for these birds. [U.S. Fish and Wildlife Service]

ever, game biologists have done precisely this—and with encouraging success. Moreover, not only do these man-made nests serve the reproductive function as well as natural nests, but they may be even more effective in minimizing the environmental resistance represented by mowing machines, predators, and nest site competitors.

Wood ducks have nested in tree cavities for millenia. Within the past two decades, however, it has been found that this species will readily accept a substitute in the form of a nest box constructed of roofing paper or wood. Two vexing problems, however, attend the use of such boxes. First, the eggs, nestlings, and incubating females are often destroyed by climbing predators. Thus, a seventeen-year study in Illinois of 820 wood duck nesting failures revealed that 51 per cent of the nests were destroyed by fox squirrels, 37 per cent by raccoons, 10 per cent by snakes, and 2 per cent by opossums (4). Such predation can be minimized by affixing a metal collar to the base of the nest box to serve as a predator barrier. The second problem concerns nest box competition from the aggressive and ubiquitous starling. This has been resolved by the use of large entrance holes, the resultant increase of light within the box apparently serving as a deterrent to the starlings which prefer relatively dark cavities (8).

Jones and Leopold report on a third highly unexpected problem which developed along a slough in the Sacramento Valley of California, where the erection of nest boxes over a nine-year period had resulted in a sizable breeding wood duck colony. In later years nest desertion, nesting interference, and compound nesting all resulted as breeding density increased more rapidly than additional boxes could be supplied. Primarily responsible was the deterioration of territorial behavior by nesting pairs. Finally, the production of young became *inversely* proportional to breeding density (23).

At the Patuxent Research Center (Maryland), straw-filled wire baskets have proved particularly successful as nest sites for Canada geese. To reduce predation they are supported at least 1 foot above the water by stakes. At the Blackwater National Wildlife Refuge (Maryland), compound houses have been readily taken over by mallards. These houses have two side-by-side compartments within a single boxlike unit.

Mallards and black ducks usually nest on the ground in hay-fields and marshes. Occasionally, however, they will make use of dead stumps for nesting purposes. At the Montezuma National Wildlife Refuge in New York, Cowardin et al. used artificial structures to increase the number of available woodland nest sites for these species, to the extent that nest densities in timbered areas compared favorably with those of nonwooded habitats (13).

One of the most serious mortality factors for ground-nesting ducks in the southwestern Lake Erie region is the haymower, because mowing of the initial alfalfa crop here coincides with the duck nesting peak. Thus, only 3.3 per cent of 317 waterfowl nests in an alfalfa habitat in 1963 were successful in producing young, mowing machines being responsible for almost 75 per cent of the nest destruction. To offset such losses, biologists constructed a number of cylindrical, open-ended nesting units made of chicken wire and marsh grass. The program was initially set up in 1961; use by ducks gradually increased from 2 per cent (2 of 100) in 1962 to 25.9 per cent (28 of 108) by 1965, when twenty-six mallards, one black duck, and one wood duck raised clutches in the artificial nests. Nesting success in these artificial nests was remarkably high, for example, 71.6 per cent (9 of 11 nests) in 1963.

WATERFOWL REFUGES. Our system of national refuges was launched in 1903 when Theodore Roosevelt established the Pelican Island refuge in Florida's Indian River to protect the rapidly depleting population of brown pelican. From this

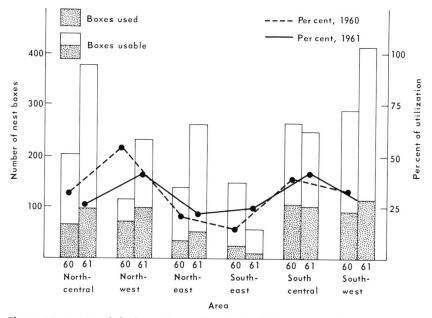

Figure 10–9 Wood duck nest box utilization in Ohio, 1960 and 1961. The Ohio Department of Natural Resources erected nest boxes in an attempt to augment wood duck production. In 1960, 373 of 1,176 (31.7 per cent) were utilized, and 461 of 1,569 (29.4 per cent) were occupied in 1961. [Adapted from R. Kahler Martinson, "Wood Duck Nest Box Utilization," 1961, Kenneth W. Laub (ed.), *Game Research in Ohio,* Vol. 2 (August, 1963).

modest beginning the federal refuge system has grown to 304 refuges covering about 29 million acres. Of these, 229 (77.4 per cent) were primarily established to provide a suitable habitat for waterfowl, either for nesting purposes, as wintering grounds, or as stopover areas for migrants. In 1934 Congress passed the Migratory Bird Hunting Stamp Act, which authorized that funds for the acquisition, maintenance, and development of waterfowl refuges be derived from the sale of "duck stamps." These stamps must be purchased by each waterfowl gunner at the start of the hunting season. From 1937 to 1968 close to 90 million stamps were sold. Our national waterfowl refuges annually provide over 1.25 billion waterfowl-use days. (One waterfowl-use day is one day's use by one duck, coot, swan, or goose.) Our refuges produce over 500,000 ducklings each year. The Tule Lake (California) and Agassiz (Minnesota) refuges each produce 30,000 ducks yearly, and the Malheur (Oregon) refuge produces 40,000 annually (35). Huge concentrations of ducks and geese utilize some of the refuges during the fall migration. For example, in the Klamath Basin Refuge on the California-Oregon border, where considerable acreages of wheat and barley are grown exclusively as waterfowl food, a

Figure 10–10 Waterfowl habitat improvement. The area to the left of the fence was protected from grazing by cattle. Note that food and cover are abundant compared to the grazed area to right of fence. [U.S. Fish and Wildlife Service]

peak of 3.4 million ducks and geese were recorded in 1964. Similarly, during the fall of 1966, up to 147,000 Canada Geese, stopped over at the Horicon National Wildlife Refuge in southern Wisconsin—the greatest concentration of this species ever recorded in the United States (44). In addition to these major refuges, the federal government in recent years has acquired a large number of small wetland areas in the marsh and pothole country of North Dakota, South Dakota, Minnesota, and Nebraska. As of 1965, 10,000 units embracing 66,000 acres in fifty-seven counties had been scheduled for purchase, lease, or easement (15). State governments have also been active in wetland acquisition, funds being derived for this purpose in Wisconsin from a cigarette tax, in South Dakota from non-resident hunting license fees, and in Minnesota by a dollar increase in the fee for small-game licenses (9).

Banding Studies. Waterfowl may be captured for banding purposes by a variety of baited traps. Canada geese are effectively taken with nets which are shot over the baited birds with miniature cannons (Figure 10–11). During the late summer moulting period, when ducks are temporarily flightless, thousands of adults and juveniles may be corraled in huge drives. Recently, tranquilizers have been employed. During the winter

Figure 10–11 Close-up of cannon showing firing mechanism on right and three ropes attached to a heavy metal piston, which when fired carries the net out over the waterfowl. [U.S. Fish and Wildlife Service]

1965–1966, Crider et al. captured 573 Canada geese and five blue geese in Florida with the oral hypnotic alpha-chloralose (14). At dosages of 0.25 gram per cup of bait mortality was only 2.6 per cent.

Scientific bird banding had its inception with the work of a Danish schoolmaster, Mortensen, who marked storks, hawks, and starlings as well as waterfowl. The American Bird Banding Association, which was organized in 1909 at New York City, conducted pioneering banding studies in the United States (26). Since 1920, when bird banding became an official project of the old Biological Survey of the Department of Agriculture, over 11 million birds (of all species in addition to waterfowl) have been leg-banded with serially numbered metal bands. (On June 30, 1940, the Biological Survey was transferred to the Department of Interior and has been consolidated along with the old Bureau of Fisheries into the Fish and Wildlife Service.) Records of the species, age, sex, weight, date, and banding locality are filed in the Bird Banding Laboratory at the Patuxent Wildlife Research Center at Laurel, Maryland. About 5 million waterfowl had been banded by 1967. Each year, primarily in refuge areas, roughly 300,000 ducks, geese, and swans are banded. About 32,000 waterfowl bands are recovered annually. Although most recoveries are made by hunters, a considerable

Figure 10–12   Projected net trap with catch of Canada geese. Sand Lake Refuge, South Dakota. [U.S. Fish and Wildlife Service]

Figure 10–13   Banding Canada goose at the Blackwater National Wildlife Refuge, Cambridge, Maryland. Note band dispenser. Cannon net is in background. [Bureau of Sport Fisheries and Wildlife, U.S. Department of the Interior]

Figure 10–14 Releasing banded duck. Note trap in background. [New York State Conservation Department]

number are also recovered by biologists, bird watchers, and interested amateur naturalists who retrieve bands from birds killed by storms, pollution, predators, and disease.

Analysis of recovery data provides waterfowl biologists with information concerning growth rate, longevity, and hunting pressure, as well as the length, speed and route of migration. From banding studies we know that some snow geese may travel 2,000 miles nonstop from James Bay, Canada, to the Texas coast in two days. Several years ago the Patuxent Wildlife Research Center received a letter from Rodolfo Marino, a pharmacist, who shot a blue-winged teal in a marsh 2 miles from his home in Peru. The serial number on the enclosed band revealed the bird had been banded only six months previously in Saskatchewan, fully 7,000 miles distant. Even more remarkable was the record of a pintail recovered in England only eighteen days after being banded in Labrador. Another pintail, banded in northwestern California, was taken at Baykal Lake, Russia (46). Still another pintail banded in California turned up three months later in New Zealand after a transoceanic flight of over 2,000 miles.

From the practical standpoint of waterfowl management, however, the most significant information accruing from waterfowl banding studies is that most migratory waterfowl breeding in the Northern states and Canada funnel into four rather well-defined flyways on their way to their southern breeding grounds. Known as the Atlantic, Mississippi, Central, and Pacific flyways, they have served as operational units in the formulation and administration of hunting laws by state and federal governments. It should be emphasized, however, that these flyways are not mutually exclusive. Thus, many mallards that nest in the prairie provinces of Canada begin their fall migration by moving southward along the Central Flyway into South Dakota; eventually, however, they swerve southeast-ward, switching to the Mississippi Flyway in Minnesota and continuing along the flyway to their wintering ground. Apparently, these birds do not consult the flyway maps. (Fig. 10–15)

Use of the Flyway as the Administrative Unit. The individual waterfowl flyway serves as the administrative unit in the setting up of hunting regulations. The soundness of this procedure is apparent when we realize that each flyway is unique with respect to population density, migration dates, species composition, and various forms of environmental resistance such as drought, disease epidemics, and hunting pressure. Thus, a liberal bag limit on the black duck may make sense on the Atlantic flyway, where this species is relatively abundant; however, on a flyway where the bird is scarce, such liberality might be disastrous. Again, it could well be that the duck "factories" of Yukon, British Columbia, and Alaska, which feed the Pacific flyway, might be highly productive at the same time that drought and botulism raise havoc in the Manitoba "factory," which normally funnels ducks and geese into the Central and Mississippi flyways. To prescribe identical hunting laws for all four flyways would be a serious mistake under such conditions. Even if populations on two flyways such as the Central and Mississippi were at similar levels, because hunting pressure is much heavier on the Mississippi flyway, uniform regulations for the two would be grossly unsound.

Population Surveys. In 1962 many a Minnesota hunter stared in amazement when the waterfowl hunting regulations were published. For he read that the daily bag limit on the mallard, his "bread-and-butter" duck, had been reduced to a single bird for each day, and moreover, that a closed season had been placed on redheads and canvasbacks. A typical comment might have been, "What's going on anyway? What do those arm-chair 'biologists' in Washington think they're doing?" In actuality, the annual hunting laws are formulated on the basis of a mas-

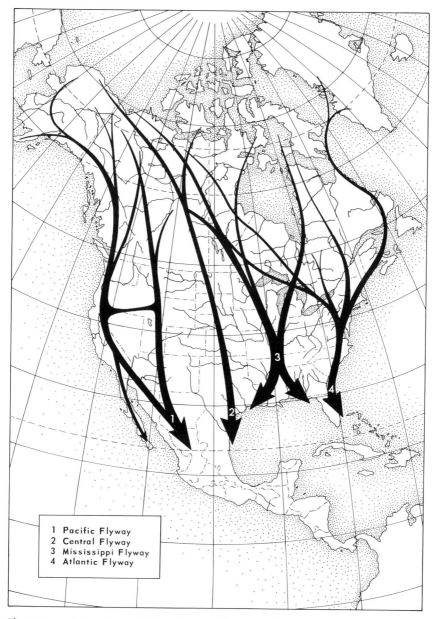

Figure 10–15 Major waterfowl flyways. Recovery data on many thousands of waterfowl have revealed that four major flyways are followed during migration: (1) Pacific, (2) Central, (3) Mississippi, and (4) Atlantic. Note that flyways are not mutually exclusive. For example, ducks reared in Alberta and Saskatchewan might initially move down the Central Flyway and later switch over to the Pacific Flyway to complete their fall migration to wintering grounds in California or Mexico. Species like mallard, baldpate, and scaup might use all four flyways. [Adapted from Robert T. Orr, *Vertebrate Biology,* 2nd ed. (Philadelphia: W. B. Saunders Company, 1961).]

Figure 10–16 Two "sportsmen" at the turn of the century exerted considerable predatory control during a single day of hunting. At least thirty-five birds were shot, most of them mallards. [State Historical Society of Wisconsin]

sive volume of population data secured by means of waterfowl kill surveys, winter surveys, and breeding population and production surveys.

WATERFOWL KILL SURVEYS. After each hunting season the Fish and Wildlife Service mails out questionnaires to a sample of hunters from each of the flyways. In 1958–1959 over 17,000 hunters received questionnaires on the Mississippi flyway alone (41). Although only about 70 per cent of the recipients respond, much valuable information may be secured concerning the relative size of the kill, its species, age, and sex composition, and so on. Thus the 1960 survey revealed that of 9.8 million ducks bagged nation-wide, the heaviest mortality was sustained by the mallard (3 million), the green-winged teal (689,000) and the American widgeon (555,100). The 1963 to 1964 mail survey showed a kill increase over the previous season on all four flyways, with the Mississippi flyway kill of 3.2 million birds representing a 123 per cent increase over the previous year.

WINTER SURVEYS. Although the winter waterfowl population surveys are administered by the Fish and Wildlife

Service, much of the actual field work is conducted by crews of the various state conservation departments. The surveys, which are made by boat, car, and plane, cover all major winter duck concentrations in Canada, the United States (including Alaska) and Mexico (41).

BREEDING POPULATION AND PRODUCTION SURVEYS. Breeding ground surveys, which are conducted in late spring and early summer, determine the relative size of the waterfowl population in comparison to the previous year and also form an index of the number of broods on the water (41). Within the last few years, aerial crews have sampled 2.4 million square miles of the best "duck factories" in North America (41). Since 1946, planes flying at about 100 miles per hour and an elevation of 150 feet have followed identical patterns of transects year after year. Waterfowl are counted to a distance of 0.25 mile on both sides of the transect line. The results of these breeding ground surveys form the basis for predicting whether, let us say, the fall flight of mallards through Wisconsin, or of widgeons through Washington and Oregon, will be heavier, thinner, or about the same as the previous year.

Hunting Regulations and Population Fluctuations. North American waterfowl populations fluctuate from year to year, a population low being only 50 to 75 per cent that of a peak year (19). The waterfowl gunner too often expects a peak year every year, and if hunting falls short of his expectations he is apt to complain about how the state and federal waterfowl biologists have botched their management jobs.

As we have learned, the population of any game animal, including waterfowl, during a given year, is a result of the interaction of both positive and negative factors relating to reproduction, climate, food availability, competitors, parasites, disease organisms, nesting habitat, predation, and other phenomena. Now, if all these factors, both positive (favoring survival) and negative (hampering or preventing survival) were constant, we would expect waterfowl populations to remain constant as well. However, the influences of these environmental factors are highly variable and the waterfowl harvest annually available to the hunter fluctuates accordingly.

Although hunting regulations such as closed seasons, length of season, and bag limits are adjusted according to shifting waterfowl population levels, hunting mortality represents only a small percentage of the total ER. Ludlow Griscom, the noted ornithologist, presents some interesting data (here slightly modified) in support of this thesis (19). Suppose, for example, that in the spring of 1970 the North American duck population

Figure 10–17 End of a good day's hunting. [Bureau of Sport Fisheries and Wildlife, U.S. Department of the Interior]

numbered 125 million. Because each adult female can lay a clutch of ten to sixteen eggs, the biotic potential for 1970 would be 600 million to 1 billion young. However, because only about 125 million birds will again return to the breeding grounds in the spring of 1971, it is apparent that 475 to 875 million birds will have perished in the interim because of ER. Of this ER, the estimated 1970 hunting kill of an estimated 20 million birds represents only about 4 *per cent* of the total annual mortality. This is not to say that hunting pressure regulation is not significant. It becomes extremely important, for example, when nesting success is poor (as from drought). The preceding data do illustrate, however, that despite the most intensive efforts of professional waterfowl biologists, waterfowl populations are bound to fluctuate. Consequently, the hunter should be prepared to accept the occasional low populations along with the occasional high.

BIBLIOGRAPHY

1. Addy, C. Edward. "Atlantic Flyway," *Waterfowl Tomorrow*. Washington, D.C.: U.S. Fish and Wildlife Service, 1964, 167–184.
2. Anderson, A. "A Waterfowl Nesting Study in the Sacramento Valley, California, 1955," *Calif. Fish and Game*, **43** (1957), 71–90.
3. Barry, Thomas W. "Brant, Ross' Goose, and Emperor Goose," *Waterfowl Tomorrow*. Washington, D.C.: U.S. Fish and Wildlife Service, 1964, 145–154.

4. Bellrose, F. C. "Housing for Wood Ducks," *Illinois Natural History Survey,* Circular 45. Urbana, Ill.: Illinois Natural History Survey, 1953.

5. _____ "Spent Shot and Lead Poisoning," *Waterfowl Tomorrow.* Washington, D.C.: U.S. Fish and Wildlife Service, 1964, 479–485.

6. Bigelow, H. B., and W. W. Welsh. "Fishes of the Gulf of Maine," *Bull. U.S. Bureau of Fisheries.* No. 40, Part I (1924), 527.

7. Buller, Raymond J. "Central Flyway," *Waterfowl Tomorrow.* Washington, D.C.: U.S. Fish and Wildlife Service, 1964, 209–232.

8. Burger, George V., and Clark G. Webster. "Instant Nesting Habitat," *Waterfowl Tomorrow.* Washington, D.C.: U.S. Fish and Wildlife Service, 1964, 655–666.

9. Burwell, Robert W., and Lawson G. Sugden. "Potholes—Going, Going . . . ," *Waterfowl Tomorrow.* Washington, D.C.: U.S. Fish and Wildlife Service, 1964, 369–380.

10. Cahoon, W. G. "Commercial Carp Removal at Lake Mattamuskeet, North Carolina," *Jour. Wild. Mgt.,* **17** (1953), 312–317.

11. Cartwright, B. W. "The Crash Decline in Sharp-tailed Grouse and Hungarian Partridge in Western Canada and the Role of the Predator," *Trans. of the 9th North Amer. Wild. Conf.* (1944), 324–329.

12. Choate, Jerry S. "Factors Influencing Nesting Success of Eiders in Penobscot Bay, Maine," *Jour. Wild. Mgt.,* **31** (1967), 769–777.

13. Cowardin, Lewis M., Gerald E. Cummings, and Porter B. Reed. "Stump and Tree Nesting by Mallards and Black Ducks," *Jour. Wild. Mgt.,* **31** (1967), 229–235.

14. Crider, E. Dale, and Jimmie C. McDaniel. "Alpha-chloralose Used to Capture Canada Geese," *Jour. Wild. Mgt.,* **31** (1967), 221–228.

15. Dumont, Philip A. "Refuges and Sanctuaries," in Alfred Stefferud (ed.), *Birds in Our Lives.* Washington, D.C.: U.S. Fish and Wildlife Service, 1966, 561 pp.

16. Edminster, Frank C. "Farm Ponds and Waterfowl," *Waterfowl Tomorrow.* Washington, D.C.: U.S. Fish and Wildlife Service, 1964, 399–408.

17. Errington, Paul L. "Talon and Fang," *Waterfowl Tomorrow.* Washington, D.C.: U.S. Fish and Wildlife Service, 1964, 323–332.

18. Glover, F. A. "Nesting and Production of the Blue-winged Teal (*Anas discors* Linnaeus) in Northwest Iowa," *Jour. Wild. Mgt.,* **20** (1956), 28–46.

19. Griscom, Ludlow. "Waterfowl," in Eugene Connett (ed.), *Duck-shooting Along the Atlantic Tidewater.* New York: William Morrow and Co., Inc., 1947, 308 pp.

20. Hartung, Rolf. "Energy Metabolism in Oil-Covered Ducks," *Jour. Wild. Mgt.,* **31** (1967), 769–777.

21. Jensen, Wayne I., and Cecil S. Williams. "Botulism and Fowl Cholera," *Waterfowl Tomorrow.* Washington, D.C.: U.S. Fish and Wildlife Service, 1964, 333–341.

22. Johnson, Raymond E. "We Are Warned," in Alfred Stefferud (ed.), *Birds in Our Lives.* Washington, D.C.: U.S. Fish and Wildlife Service, 1966, 561 pp.

23. Jones, R. E., and A. S. Leopold. "Nesting Interference in a Dense Population of Wood Ducks," *Jour. Wild. Mgt.,* **31** (1967), 221–228.

24. Jordan, J. S. "Consumption of Cereal Grains by Migratory Waterfowl," *Jour. Wild. Mgt.,* **17** (1953), 304–311.

25. Kalmbach, E. R., and M. G. Gunderson. "Western Duck Sickness: A Form of Botulism," *Tech. Bull. No. 411.* Washington, D.C.: U.S. Department of Agriculture, 1934.

26. Lee, Forrest B., et al. "Waterfowl in Minnesota," *Tech. Bull. No. 7.* St. Paul: Minnesota Department of Conservation, 1964.

27. Lincoln, Frederick C. "The Future of American Waterfowl," in Eugene Connett (ed.), *Duckshooting Along the Atlantic Tidewater.* New York: William Morrow and Co., Inc., 1947, 308 pp.

28. Martin, A. C., and F. M. Uhler, "Food of Game Ducks in the United States and Canada." Research Report No. 30. Washington, D.C.: U.S. Fish and Wildlife Service, 1951. (Reprint of *U.S.D.A. Tech. Bull.,* **634** (1939).)

29. Mayhew, W. W. "Spring Rainfall in Relation to Mallard Production in the Sacramento Valley, California," *Jour. Wild. Mgt.,* **19** (1955), 36–47.

30. McCallum, Gordon E. "Clean Water and Enough of It," *Waterfowl Tomorrow.* Washington, D.C.: U.S. Fish and Wildlife Service, 1964, 471–478.

31. McMahon, Patrick. "Determined Ducks Defy Transportation," *Canadian Audubon,* **29** (1967), 8–10.

32. Milne, Lorus J., and Margery Milne. *The Balance of Nature.* New York: Alfred A. Knopf, 1961, 329 pp.

33. Moyle, John B., and Jerome H. Kuehn. "Carp, a Sometimes Villain," *Waterfowl Tomorrow.* Washington, D.C.: U.S. Fish and Wildlife Service, 1964.

34. O'Neill, E. J. "Waterfowl Grounded at the Muleshoe National Wildlife Refuge, Texas," *Auk,* **64** (1947), 457.

35. Salyer, J. Clark, and Francis G. Gillett. "Federal Refuges," *Waterfowl Tomorrow.* Washington, D.C.: U.S. Fish and Wildlife Service, 1964, 497–508.

36. Schrader, T. A. "Waterfowl and the Potholes of the United States," *The Yearbook of Agriculture.* Washington, D.C.: U.S. Department of Agriculture, 1955, 596–604.

37. Sincock, L. Morton, M. Smith, and John L. Lynch. "Ducks in Dixie," *Waterfowl Tomorrow.* Washington, D.C.: U.S. Fish and Wildlife Service, 1964, 99–106.

38. Strohmeyer, David L., and Leigh H. Fredrickson. "An Evaluation of Dynamited Potholes in Northwest Iowa," *Jour. Wild. Mgt.,* **31** (1967), 525–532.

39. Studholme, Allan T., and Thomas Sterling. "Dredges and Ditches," *Waterfowl Tomorrow.* Washington, D.C.: U.S. Fish and Wildlife Service, 1964, 359–368.

40. Threinen, C. W., and W. T. Helm. "Experiments and Observations Designed to Show Carp Destruction of Aquatic Vegetation," *Jour. Wild. Mgt.,* **18** (1954), 247–251.

41. U.S. Fish and Wildlife Service. "Status Report of Waterfowl," *Special Scientific Report on Wildlife. No. 45.* Washington, D.C.: G.P.O., 1959.

42. Welty, Joel Carl. *The Life of Birds.* Philadelphia: W. B. Saunders Co., 1962, 546 pp.

43. Wetmore, Alexander, et al. *Water, Prey and Game Birds of North America.* Washington, D.C.: National Geographic Society, 1965, 464 pp.

44. *Wisconsin State Journal.* April 22, 1969.

45. Yancey, Richard K. "Matches and Marshes," *Waterfowl Tomorrow.* Washington, D.C.: U.S. Fish and Wildlife Service, 1964, 619–626.

46. Yocum, Charles F. "Pintail Banded in Northwestern California Taken at Baykal Lake, Russia. (*Anas acuta*)," *Condor,* **69** (1967), 205–206.

Freshwater Fisheries 11

In 1965 over 28 million sportsmen devoted 523 million recreation days to pitting their luck and skill against the scaly denizens of our lakes, streams, farm ponds, mountain brooks, and impoundments. They spent almost $3 billion, averaging about $100 per fisherman. Of this sum, 27 per cent was spent on bait and guides, 15 per cent on food and lodging, 14 per cent on transportation, 11 per cent on rods, reels, and other equipment, and 4.5 per cent on licenses and privilege fees. In 1965 the average angler traveled about 800 miles to and from his fishing haunts. Transportation media included motor car, bus, train, airplane, helicopter, mule, and snowmobile. In aggregate, our nation's fishermen, whose numbers increased 36 per cent from 1955 to 1965, traveled 22.7 billion passenger miles.

The Lake Ecosystem

Fish occur in a great variety of freshwater habitats, from rushing mountain streams to sluggish rivers, from tiny farm ponds to large natural lakes. In order to develop an appreciation of the general features of aquatic habitat and to provide some background for our later

375

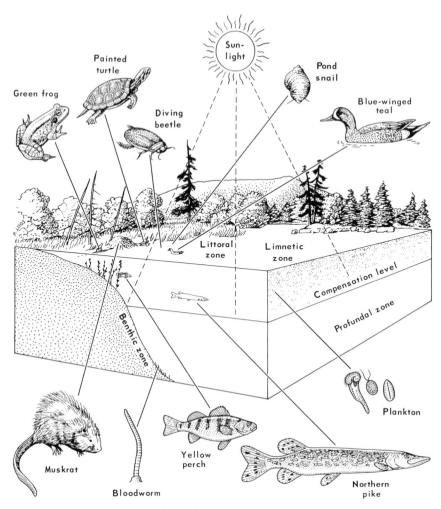

Figure 11-1 Stereo view of a lake ecosystem in midsummer showing littoral, limnetic, and profundal zones. Observe rooted vegetation in the littoral. The level at which there is insufficient sunlight penetration to sustain photosynthesis is known as the compensation level. [Adapted from Robert L. Smith, *Ecology and Field Biology* (New York: Harper & Row, Publishers, 1966). Used by permission of the publishers.]

discussions of fish conservation and management, we shall briefly describe the major features of a lake ecosystem. Ecologists usually recognize three major lake zones, the littoral, limnetic, and profundal.

Littoral Zone. The littoral zone may be defined as the shallow, marginal region of a lake which is characterized by rooted vegetation. The rooted plants usually are arranged in a well-ordered sequence, from shore toward open water, as emergent, floating, and submergent. Representative emergent plants include cattail, bulrush, arrowhead, and sedge.

376

Characteristic floating plants include water lilies and duck-weed. Among typical submergents are *Potamogeton, Chara, Elodea,* and *Vallisneria.* Because sunlight penetrates to the lake bottom, this zone sustains a high level of photosynthetic activity. The swarming, floating microorganisms known as *plankton* frequently impart a faint greenish-brown cast to the water. The term *plankton* means "the wanderers"; it is quite appropriate because these organisms are largely incapable of independent movements through the littoral zone and are passively transported by water currents and wave action. Plankton are divisible into plants (chiefly algae), known as *phytoplankton,* and animals (primarily crustaceans and proto-zoa), known as *zooplankton.* The littoral zone provides suitable food, cover, and/or breeding sites for an abundance and variety of aquatic life including both invertebrates (diving beetles, dragonflies, damsel flies, rotifers, protozoans, crayfish, mussels, snails) and vertebrates (pickerel, sunfish, yellow perch, frogs, salamanders, turtles, rails, grebes, ducks, herons, water shrews, muskrats). Per unit volume of water, the littoral zone produces more biomass than either the limnetic or profundal zones. A small pond may consist entirely of littoral zone; however, a deep lake with an abruptly sloping basin may possess an extremely restricted littoral zone (37).

Limnetic Zone. The limnetic zone may be defined as the region of open water beyond the littoral down to the maximal depth at which there is sufficient sunlight for photosynthesis. This is the depth at which photosynthesis balances respira-tion—known as the *compensation depth.* The light intensity here is about 100 foot-candles or 1 per cent of full sunlight. Although rooted plants are absent, this zone is frequently characterized by a great abundance of phytoplankton, dom-inated by filamentous algae, diatoms, and desmids. In large lakes these phytoplankton may play a much more important role as producers than the more conspicuous rooted plants of the littoral zone. In spring, when nutrients and light are opti-mal, phytoplankton increase rapidly to form *blooms.* The lim-netic zone derives its oxygen content from the photosynthetic activity of phytoplankton and from the atmosphere immediately over the lake surface. The atmospheric source of oxygen be-comes significant primarily when there is some surface dis-turbance of the water caused by wind action, a canoe paddle, or the propeller of a speedboat. Fish are the most characteristic vertebrates. Suspended among the phytoplankton are the zoo-plankton, primarily minute crustaceans (copepods, cladocerans) which form a trophic link between the phytoplankton food base and the higher aquatic animals (37).

Profundal Zone. The profundal zone embraces the area immediately beneath the limnetic zone. It extends downward to the lake bottom. Because of limited penetration of sunlight, green plant life is absent. In north temperate lattitudes where winters are severe, this zone has the warmest water (4 degrees C.) in winter and the coldest water in summer. Large numbers of bacteria and fungi occur in the bottom ooze, sometimes up to 1 billion bacteria per gram. These bacteria are constantly bringing about decomposition of organic matter (plant debris, animal remains, and excreta) that accumulates on the bottom. Eventually these organic sediments are mineralized and the nitrogen and phosphorus is put back into circulation in the form of soluble salts. In winter, because of the reduced metabolism of aquatic life and the greater oxygen-dissolving capacity of colder water, oxygen ordinarily is not an important limiting factor for fish if the ice cover remains clear of snow. In midsummer, however, when the metabolic rates of aquatic organisms are high, the oxygen-dissolving capability of the warm water is relatively low, and the oxygen-demanding processes of bacterial decay are proceeding at high levels, oxygen depletion or *stagnation* of the profundal waters may result in extensive fish mortality, frequently involving desirable game species (37).

Figure 11–2 Midwinter distribution of oxygen and temperature in a lake ecosystem. Note influence on fish distribution. [Adapted from Robert L. Smith, *Ecology and Field Biology* (New York: Harper & Row, Publishers, 1966). Used by permission of the publishers.]

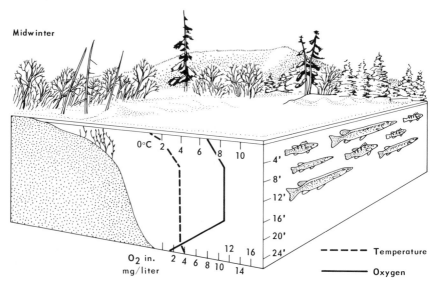

Thermal Stratification. In temperate latitudes lakes show marked seasonal temperature changes. In winter the coldest water forms ice at 0 degrees C. and floats at the surface. The water at increasing depths below the ice is progressively warmer and more dense. The heaviest water at the bottom of the lake has a winter temperature of 4 degrees C. All winter the water remains relatively stable. In spring following the ice melt, the surface water gradually warms up to 4°C. At this point all the water is of uniform temperature and density. Hence the strong spring winds cause considerable stirring, which results in a complete mixing of water, dissolved oxygen, and nutrients from lake surface to lake bottom, a phenomenon known as the *spring overturn.* As spring progresses, however, the surface waters become warmer and lighter than the water at lower levels. As a result the lake becomes *thermally stratified.* The upper stratum, which usually has the highest oxygen concentration and is characterized by a temperature gradient of less than 1 degree C. per meter of depth, is called the *epilimnion* ("upper lake"). The middle layer of the lake, typified by a temperature gradient of more than 1 degree C. per meter, is known as the *thermocline.* The bottom layer of water, like the epilimnion, shows a temperature gradient of less than 1 degree C. per meter and is known as the *hypoliminion* ("bottom lake").

Figure 11–3 Midsummer distribution of oxygen and temperature in a lake ecosystem. Note the stratification. [Adapted from Robert L. Smith, *Ecology and Field Biology* (New York: Harper & Row, Publishers, 1966). Used by permission of the publishers.]

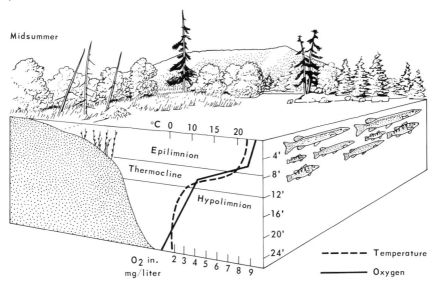

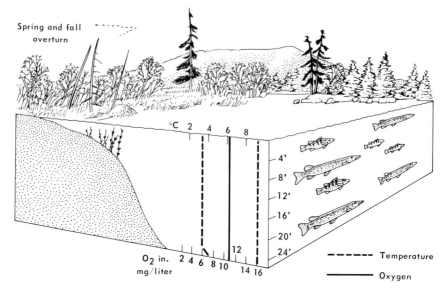

Figure 11-4 Spring and fall overturn in a lake ecosystem. Note that uniformity of temperature and oxygen distribution is expressed in dispersal of fish through much of the lake from surface to bottom. [Adapted from Robert L. Smith, *Ecology and Field Biology* (New York: Harper & Row, Publishers, 1966). Used by permission of the publishers.]

Figure 11-5 Looking down on male large-mouthed black bass guarding its nest. [Wisconsin Conservation Department]

Unless the lake is exceptionally clear so as to permit phyto-planktonic photosynthesis, the hypolimnion in late summer frequently becomes depleted of oxygen because of the *biological oxygen demand* (BOD) of bacterial decomposers, the reduced or nonexistent photosynthetic activity, and the minimal mixing with upper waters as a result of density differences (37).

In autumn the surface waters gradually cool, as a result of conduction, evaporation, and convection. Eventually a point is reached where the lake attains temperature uniformity from top to bottom. Because the water is now also of uniform density, it becomes well mixed by wind and wave action in what is known as the *fall overturn.* Nutrients, dissolved oxygen, and plankton become uniformly distributed. As winter approaches, the lake gets colder until the water attains a uniform temper-ature of 4 degrees C. at which it has maximal density. As the surface cools below 4 degrees C. it becomes lighter. Eventually the surface water may freeze at 0 degrees C. During the winter season in icebound lakes there exists an inverted temperature stratification, with the coldest water (ice) at the surface and the warmest water (4 degrees C.) on the bottom (37).

Biotic Potential of Fish

As with most organisms, freshwater fish have an extremely high reproductive capacity. Thus Dreyer et al. report an average of 6,357 eggs from Lake Superior ciscos (10). Thirteen thousand eggs were found in the ovaries of a brown bullhead only 1 foot long. Lake Michigan alewives produce 11,000 to 22,000 eggs per female. A 3-pound large-mouthed bass carried 40,000 eggs in its ovaries. The large-mouthed bass produces up to 7,000 eggs per pound of fish. Some bass nests in Michigan have had up to 4,000 fry per nest. A 10-pound female northern pike may deposit 100,000 eggs at spawning time. Up to 67,000 eggs have been found in one bluegill. A 35-pound muskellunge may bear 225,000 eggs. A 20-pound female may produce over 2 million eggs. Over 1.25 pounds of eggs were taken from a 12.5-pound Columbia River sturgeon. It is apparent that were it not for the negative effects of the ER, these species would soon choke river channels and lake basins with their aggregate biomass.

Environmental Resistance

Tagging studies have revealed that the environmental resis-tance operating on fish population is fully as impressive as their reproductive capacities, for roughly 70 per cent of a given

Figure 11-6 Dead fish in a bay across Arrowwood Lake, Arrowwood Refuge, Kensal, North Dakota. [U.S. Fish and Wildlife Service]

fish population dies each year. Thus, theoretically, if a million young hatch, 300,000 will survive by the end of the first year, 90,000 by the end of the second, and only *six* by the end of the tenth. In 1939 an analysis was made in Minnesota of 15,000 perch caught in Ottertail Lake. Few were more than one year old. Age class analysis indicated that only 2.8 per cent survived to the second year, and only 1 per cent reached the age of four (12). A similar study on brook trout showed a survival of only 0.6 fish out of every 182,000 eggs laid at the end of five years.

Among the many types of ER encountered by fish, we shall briefly consider pollution (siltation, temperature pollution, industrial pollution, pesticidal pollution) oxygen depletion, rough fish, parasites, predators, and fishing pressure.

Siltation. Many tons of sediment may be discharged into lakes and streams by run-off waters as a result of abusive land practices in their watersheds. If siltation continues unchecked for several decades, a shallow lake may gradually become filled with sediment and be converted into a marsh—a form of aquatic succession. Obviously, such a radical habitat conversion would eliminate all fish life. However, even from a short-term standpoint, siltation may adversely affect fish. Although fish may tolerate turbidities of up to 100,000 parts per million for brief periods, concentrations of 100–200 parts per million may be directly harmful under conditions of chronic exposure. Silt may clog up the gills of fish under extreme situations and cause death by asphyxiation, as occurred in the Pecos River of New Mexico. Sand and gravel spawning beds may be destroyed. Fertilized eggs may be smothered with mud. A study of trout reproduction in Bluewater Creek, Montana, revealed that egg hatching rates were highest, up to 97 per cent, where sedimentation was minimal. The larvae of aquatic insects such as stoneflies and mayflies, which represent favored fish foods, may be eradicated by a blanket of silt. Photosynthetic rates may be depressed by the reduced sunlight penetration resulting from water turbidity, causing diminished concentrations of dissolved oxygen. Here we see yet another example of how proper management of one resource (soil) indirectly enhances another (fish). Effective siltation control can be best accomplished by the proper use of such soil conservation measures as strip cropping, contour plowing, terracing, and cover cropping.

Thermal Pollution. Cold-water habitats which for many years had supported brook and rainbow trout have been desecrated by the removal of bordering thickets and overarching trees. Once such sunlight-intercepting vegetation has been removed, average water temperatures increase and the trout, which generally cannot tolerate water temperatures above 70 degrees F. for any lengthy period, either succumb or emigrate. For most warm-water species, temperatures of 93 degrees F. to 96 degrees F. are critical. Modern steam-generating power plants are important sources of heat pollution. They draw large volumes of water from rivers as coolant for their condensers. One Georgia plant utilizes over 400 million gallons daily. Later the warmed-up water is discharged back into the stream. Cold-water fish may incur severe mortality as a result. Moreover, heated water may destroy their phytoplankton and invertebrate foods. Spawning runs may be blocked by such temperature barriers. Heated water has certain redeeming influences, however. In the Northern states it keeps streams ice free; in the South it permits the threadfin shad, a valuable forage fish, to extend its winter range northward.

Pollution from Industry and Other Sources. Pulp and paper mills, distilleries, vegetable canneries, breweries, creameries, and tanneries discharge considerable quantities of organic wastes into fish habitats. Domestic sewage is also a serious problem. At Lake Tahoe, for example, sewage discharged into the lake has resulted in such an increase in dissolved nutrient salts that phytoplankton blooms have been triggered. As a consequence of the decomposition of this plant growth in late summer, game fish have been adversely influenced by the increased BOD. In order to alleviate this problem a 6-million-gallon sewage disposal plant is being constructed. It is hoped that the incipient lake eutrophication will be checked. (The filtered effluents will be transported over the mountains to provide irrigation water for nearby arid regions.)

Some industrial chemicals may exert an indirect ER on fish populations by destroying preferred fish foods. Spawning beds may be defiled and fish reproduction curtailed. Other chemicals may affect fish more directly. For example, a large discharge of heavy metal salts may be immediately lethal. Crude oil derivatives and ammonium compounds may be absorbed by fish with disastrous results. Strong acids can kill fish by eroding their vital gill membranes. Heavy metal salts may stimulate excessive mucous secretions which eventually interfere with gill function and cause suffocation. Other chemicals may serve as irritants to the skin, facilitating fatal invasion by bacteria and fungi.

Smith et al. report significant mortality in fathead minnows at concentrations above 272 parts per million of ground wood and 738 parts per million of sulfite pulp; and walleye fingerlings succumb at concentrations of only 74 parts per million of both pollutants (36). Because these pollutants commonly occur in pulp mill discharge effluents, it is apparent walleye survival is in jeopardy adjacent to such plants.

Pollution from Detergents. The widespread use of the nondegradable alkyl-benzene-sulfonate (ABS) detergents has had adverse effects on fish in recent years. Cairns et al. report that the pumpkinseed sunfish suffered gill damage at concentrations of only 9.8 parts per million ABS after several months exposure. After twenty-four hours of exposure to 3.48 milligrams per liter of ABS under laboratory conditions, rainbow trout showed increased respiratory rates, loss of balance, erratic movements, lethargy, and death (7). Dugan reports that exposure to ABS may increase fish susceptibility to DDT and dieldrin, both chlorinated hydrocarbon insecticides (11).

Winter Kill Resulting from Oxygen Depletion. During the long winter of the Northern states lakes may be effectively sealed off from their summer source of atmospheric oxygen by an icy barrier. However, as long as the ice remains clear of snow, sufficient sunlight may filter down through the ice to sustain photosynthesis. As a result, oxygen levels remain adequate. Snow, however, forms an opaque barrier preventing sunlight penetration. The resultant cessation of photosynthesis and the concomitant reduction in oxygen levels often result in heavy fish kills, especially if the lake is fertile and shallow. The decay of dead vegetation with its high BOD accentuates the problem. As winter progresses, oxygen levels may drop to 5 parts per million, at which point many of the more sensitive game species succumb; the more resistant rough fish, such as carp and bullheads, capitulate somewhat later when levels drop to about 3 to 4 parts per million.

In a lake supporting a mixed population of game and rough fish, a *complete* winter kill is more desirable than a *partial* kill. A partial kill is selective, eliminating only the preferred game fish, and necessitates costly and time-consuming rough-fish

Figure 11–7   Melting ice cover reveals winter fish kill caused by oxygen depletion in Wisconsin lake. Note large walleye. [Wisconsin Conservation Department]

removal operations (poisoning and seining) before game fish restocking can be initiated. On the other hand if all the fish die, fishery biologists can begin stocking immediately. In their excellent book *Northern Fishes*, Eddy and Surber describe a classic example of winter kill in a shallow southern Minnesota lake which had a dense population of bullheads. Although the ice cover that formed in November ultimately became 20 inches thick, oxygen levels initially were adequate. However, during the second week of January, a storm covered the ice with a 6-inch layer of snow. Only two days later tests revealed that oxygen was severely depleted. After the spring ice melt thousands of dead bullheads littered the shore. Not one fish survived (12).

Summer Kill Resulting from Oxygen Depletion. Beasley reports that dense growth of *Microcystis,* a scum-forming algae, contributed to thermal stratification by heat absorption and

Figure 11–8 White bass killed as a result of algae clogging their gills. High Cliff State Park (Calumet County), Wisconsin. [Wisconsin Conservation Department]

promoted oxygen depletion at the lower levels of five experimental fertilized ponds in Alabama by blocking the incident sunlight. Oxygen depletion frequently may occur in the hypolimnion of thermally stratified lakes in late summer regardless of the development of such dense algal mats. Simco et al. found that growth of channel catfish in 0.1 acre earthen ponds in Kansas was retarded as a result of stress caused by critically low oxygen levels of less than 3 parts per million (35). However, when ponds were aerated, the affected fish resumed rapid growth. Fish mortality from oxygen depletion may be caused inadvertently by the use of formalin in the control of heavy plankton blooms. The sudden death and decay of the plants results in a sharply increased BOD and extensive fish kills. Oxygen depletion is less common in streams than in lakes and ponds. However, in a study of the effect of the spawning bed environment on the reproductive success of the pink salmon and chum salmon in three southeastern Alaska streams, McNeil recorded 60 to 90 per cent mortality associated with low dissolved oxygen levels in late summer during and after the spawning period.

Rough Fish. The most destructive of all *rough fish* (fish undesirable as game or food) is the carp. It was introduced to California from Germany in 1872, and to Washington, D.C., in 1877. As has been the case with many introduced exotics, the carp population increased rapidly, following the characteristic sigmoid growth curve. Although they were not brought to Lake Erie until 1873, only twenty years later fishermen were able to remove 3.6 million pounds from that lake. Carp prefer sluggish waters rich in organic matter. Frequently this organic material is derived from sewage. In other cases it may have its origin in the biological growth stimulated by fertilizer-rich run-off from agricultural lands. Carp may uproot extensive quantities of vegetation during their foraging activies. King et al. report that carp consume *Chara* but merely uproot pondweeds, most damage occurring in the growing season when the plants are young and delicate (20). Such activity may result in the destruction of game-fish spawning grounds, the eradication of fish foods, and the reduction of photosynthetic activity because of muddied waters.

The bowfin and long-nosed gar, which may attain weights of 10 and 50 pounds, respectively, are also extremely destructive. Both species are active carnivores, not only killing large quantities of game fish directly but also reducing forage populations on which game species such as black bass, walleyes, and northern pike depend for sustenance.

Parasites and Disease Organisms. Even if disease organisms and parasites do not cause mortality directly, they may depress growth rates and impair the reproductive function. Certain waters are rendered worthless to anglers as a result of parasitic infestations. Hatchery production may be severely limited by diseases; production cost per fish may become excessive. The fisheries departments of several Southeastern states are currently engaged in a cooperative research project, centered at Auburn University, Alabama, to develop control methods for warm-water fish diseases and parasites. The possibility of employing ultraviolet radiation in disinfecting hatchery water is being investigated by biologists in New Hampshire. New York State fisheries biologists have conducted a fifteen-year selective breeding program to develop strains of brook and brown trout which are resistant to a serious bacterial disease known as *furunculosis.*

A number of protozoans may infect a fish's gills or skin and cause tiny blisters to appear. If extremely widespread, such an infection may prove lethal. Not only that, the parasitic invaders may be transferred from fish to fish and ultimately reach epidemic proportions. Leeches may attach themselves to fish by means of muscular suckers and slice open the skin with sharp horny teeth, ingesting the freely flowing blood of the host. Fish are frequently plagued with intestinal tapeworms which slowly absorb partially digested food. Although tapeworms do not ordinarily kill their host, they may severely weaken fish making them vulnerable to predation and disease organisms. Larval tapeworm infections studied by Becker et al. in Goodwin Lake, Washington, reached an epizootic stage when an average of thirty-eight larvae were recorded per fish in spring-plant coho salmon, seventy-eight per fish in spring-plant rainbows and 140 per fish in fall-plant rainbows (1). The bass tapeworm which parasitizes black bass, rock bass, and sunfish, may cause sterility by destroying ovaries. A recent survey by Larson conducted on twelve species of fish from Itasca State Park, Minnesota, showed that every fish was parasitized. Parasites included thirty-one species of trematodes, tapeworms, and roundworms; the most susceptible species were the yellow perch and the rock bass.

An interesting experiment was conducted by workers at Auburn University, Alabama, which indicated the effectiveness of employing the redear sunfish in controlling an infectious flatworm parasite of the bluegill. The sunfish reduces the parasite population by consuming its intermediate host, an aquatic snail. Thus bluegills stocked in combination with redear sunfish averaged only forty-eight parasites per fish compared to the 114 parasites per individual of the control group, when both groups were exposed to the same number of infected snails.

Many game fish become infested with "black grubs" and "yellow grubs,"—larval forms of the flatworms *Neascus* and *Clinostomum,* respectively. The fish louse may cause mortality among wild fish and pose a severe hatchery problem as well.

The white fungus *Saprolegnia* may find access to the interior of a fish's body by way of a skin injury. More prevalent during the summer, this fungus forms a fuzzy white patch which quickly spreads and may eventually kill the host. The fungus *Dermocystidium* which forms small white cysts on gill tissue, was reported by Pauley as having caused 25 per cent mortality of 5,000 adult prespawning salmon, the primary cause of death being anoxia (lack of oxygen) (32).

Predation. Fish are subjected to intense predatory pressure from members of all vertebrate classes, including other fish, amphibians, reptiles, birds, and mammals. Predation has the greatest impact when fish populations are high. According to Herting and Witt, bluegill and large-mouthed bass show increased vulnerability to predation from the bowfin when starving, parasitized, diseased, or physiologically impaired as a result of stress from seining operations (18). A 6-inch muskellunge will consume fifteen minnows daily. A walleye may consume up to 3,000 fish by the time it is three years old. When other food is scarce, many fish will resort to cannibalism. Smaller species may prey on the eggs of larger species which as adults regularly feed on the smaller forms. Thus, Dreyer et al. report that fish eggs occurred in the guts of 23 per cent of 146 herring examined from Lake Superior (10).

An examination of the diet of thirty water snakes from Virginia showed that 60.9 per cent was composed of fish. Unusually low water levels may render fish expecially vulnerable to predation from osprey, terns, and mink. Brous (1882) reports garter snakes "devouring great numbers of smaller fish" stranded in shallow pools during a period of summer drought (4).

Stomach analyses of 186 Michigan snapping turtles, according to Lagler, revealed that game fishes comprised one third of their food (21). Grebes, loons, and cormorants are superbly adapted for underwater fish pursuit. Egrets, herons, and mergansers consume large numbers of fish. Kingfishers may pose serious problems at hatchery rearing ponds. Kortwright has estimated that a single merganser may consume over 35,000 fish annually. The famous ornithologist, John Audubon, found over 9.5 pounds of fish in the stomach of one American merganser. New Brunswick salmon production increased 500 per cent when American mergansers and kingfishers were restricted to a population density of one per 50 acres of water or 15 miles of stream. Among mammals, the bear, otter, fisher, and mink have exerted considerable ER on fish populations. Of course, the most destructive of all fish predators is man himself.

Barriers to Migration. The salmon is an *anadromous* fish— one that spends most of its growing years in the ocean, and, after attaining sexual maturity, ascends freshwater streams in order to spawn. The chinook or king salmon is a handsome Pacific salmon which may attain a weight up to 100 pounds. On the breeding grounds the female excavates a shallow trough, the *redd,* in the sandy or gravelly bed of some swiftly flowing stream emptying into the Pacific Ocean, such as the Sacramento in California, the Fraser in British Columbia, or the Columbia River bordering Oregon and Washington. The female may deposit several thousand eggs in the redd. After the male has fertilized them they are covered with a protective layer of sand. After a two-month period of incubation, the eggs hatch and the young gradually move downstream, eventually entering the open ocean. (Witty reports the average downstream travel rate for coho salmon in the Wallowa River, Oregon, to be 48.1 miles per day for a distance of 433 miles (42).) Only 10 per cent of the fry ultimately reach the ocean. They incur heavy losses from predation. For example, Meehan et al. found that shortly after hatching an estimated population of 30,000 sculpins in Big Kitoi Creek, Alaska, would, on the basis of stomach analyses, consume 135,000 (12 per cent) of the estimated 847,500 pink salmon fry in the creek (27).

The salmon remain in the Pacific Ocean four to seven years, feeding ravenously on small fishes such as herring and anchovies, many moving hundreds of miles from the mouth of their native stream. Thus, adult salmon tagged off Baranof Island, Alaska, were recovered in the Columbia River of Washington. Upon attaining sexual maturity, the salmon ascend the mouths of their native streams, apparently recognizing them by their distinctive smell, and gradually make their way up to the shallow headwaters near the site of their hatching. This may be accomplished only after they have negotiated all sorts of obstacles, including rushing cataracts, a variety of predators (gulls, ospreys, bears), fishermen, pollution (silt, heated waters, radioactive materials, chemicals), the nets of research biologists and big dams. Once arriving at the headwater, they immediately spawn and die, thus completing their life cycle.

In 1913, railroad builders inadvertently set off an avalanche of rock and rubble which clogged up the narrow channel of the Fraser River at Hell's Gate. As a result, the sockeye salmon run was hopelessly blocked, and countless thousands of fish, loaded with eggs and sperm, died below the rock slide, unable to press on to their spawning grounds.

The erection of numerous power and irrigation dams across the migration path of the Pacific salmon has effectively cut off considerable numbers from their spawning grounds. The 550-foot tall Grand Coulee Dam effectively blocks salmon spawning migrations on the Columbia. High water temperatures may be just as effective as a dam. Thus, Major et al. report that water temperatures of 70 degrees or above barred movement of sockeye salmon (*Oncorhynchus nerka*) from the Columbia River into the tributary Okanogan River (24). However, when temperatures dropped below 70 degrees F., the migration resumed. There has been a marked decline in the once abundant Columbia River salmon harvest, the 1963 yield of 82,000 cases being only 13 per cent of the peak 629,000 case harvest back in 1883. (Of course, other ER factors, such as pollution and overfishing contributed to this decline.)

Figure 11–9 Salmon jumping Brooks Falls (Alaska) during migration to spawning grounds. [Bureau of Commercial Fisheries, U.S. Department of the Interior]

Figure 11–10 Spawning king salmon at the Nimbus hatchery on the American River near Sacramento, California. [California Department of Fish and Game]

Various state and federal agencies are trying to improve artificial spawning and rearing areas and to control disease and predators in order to reduce the 90 per cent salmon mortality from hatching to time of sea entry. The U.S. Corps of Engineers is making studies of turbine blade design and of operating procedures which would be safest for migrating salmon. They are also investigating the feasibility of guiding salmon past dam barriers by means of light stimuli (14).

Big dam barriers have raised havoc with anadromous fish on the Atlantic seaboard, including the Atlantic salmon, the shad, and the herring. Sixty years ago the shad was the third most valuable commercial fish in the United States, rated behind the cod of New England and the Pacific salmon. By 1945, largely because of dam-blocked spawning runs, its rating had dropped from third to thirtieth.

Fishing Pressure. Overfishing undoubtedly has been a major factor in the decline of many of our freshwater commercial and game fishes. The classic example of extreme fishing pressure is afforded by trout fishermen on the opening weekend of the trout season. During their enthusiastic quest for the king of American game fishes, they frequently become crowded shoulder to shoulder along stream margins. Fishing pressure is increasing. The number of licensed anglers has increased from 10 to 30 million within the last three decades. One of every eight Americans is a fisherman, or fisherwoman. And with the nation's increasing population, the increase in leisure hours and mobility, and the desperate need for the release from urban pressures afforded by the wilderness, the pressure of the human predator on fish populations is bound to intensify.

Fish Management

Fish management may be defined as the manipulation of fish populations and their environment to increase sport and commercial fish harvests. In its broadest sense fish management embraces all the laws, policies, research and techniques having as their ultimate objective the enhanced value of the fisheries resource for the greatest number of people over the longest period of time. The sustained-yield concept is implicit in all sound fish management activities.

To manage a fish population effectively the fisheries biologist must understand the dynamics of the fish population. He must be able to predict the over-all effect of a specific level of fishing pressure. He must be prepared to cope with the adverse environmental factors of disease, competition, parasites, pollution, drought, and oxygen depletion. Ordinarily the fisheries biologist draws on knowledge derived from life history studies of the species. From such studies data are secured on food habits, longevity, mortality factors, growth rates, sex and age ratios, breeding behavior, spawning habitat, and so on. We shall briefly discuss the following fish management procedures: restrictive laws, artificial propagation, introduction of exotics, transplantations, habitat improvement, artificial selection and hybridization, and the management of endangered species.

Restrictive Laws. As in the case of wild game, an early step taken in fisheries restoration was the establishment of protective laws. Closed seasons were established during the breeding period of a species. It was apparent that when a female bass or walleye was taken when swollen with eggs, the angler was removing much more than a single adult fish—he was also removing thousands of future young fish as well. Creel limits were imposed. Certain fishing techniques were outlawed, such as seining, poisoning, dynamiting, spearing and using multiple-hook lines for taking game fish. It was felt that if the activities of the human predator were effectively controlled, fish populations inevitably would assume their original abundance.

In certain cases restrictive laws have been successful. A case in point is the sturgeon population of California's Sacramento River. In the late nineteenth century the sturgeon were heavily exploited, up to 5,000 being taken monthly in 1872. Because the catch had been reduced to virtually nothing by 1917, the sturgeon was placed on the protected list. The remnant population thereafter gradually increased to a level which was sufficient in 1954 to permit a limited sport-fishing season (30).

In recent years fisheries biologists have been experimenting with more liberalized regulations on many species of warm-water fish. In many states size limits on panfish (sunfish, blue-gills, rock bass, crappies) have been lifted (6). On the other hand, increased size limits have been imposed on predatory species such as black bass and northern pike. The twin objectives of these regulations are to reduce overpopulation and stuntedness of the panfish and to provide more opportunity for anglers to catch larger bass and pike. The effects of creel limits, varying fishing methods and gear, open and closed seasons, and winter fishing on fish populations are continuously being evaluated by fisheries biologists (6).

Legislation in relation to fish management is discussed by Karl Lagler in his excellent book *Freshwater Fishery Biology* (22). In his view there is a cause for both pessimism and optimism. The negative features of fisheries legislation include: (1) the multiplicity of restrictions, which make it difficult for even the well-informed angler to refrain from committing occasional violations, (2) the setting up of different regulations for two closely related species which are extremely difficult to distinguish in the field, such as the whitefish and cisco, the northern pike and grass pickerel, and the bluegill and green sunfish, (3) the establishment of different regulations for the two margins of the same river serving as a common boundary of two states, e.g., the Mississippi River between Wisconsin and Minnesota.

According to Lagler, however, when properly conceived and administered, laws are effective management tools. Examples of legislation which has had a beneficial effect on our fisheries resources are the following: (1) In 1950 the Dingell-Johnson law was passed by Congress. It has raised money for federally approved fisheries research and habitat acquisition projects by placing an excise tax on fishing tackle. These funds are distributed to the states on the basis of fishing license sales and area. (2) Many states in recent years have learned that effective management of their common water resource demands an integrated effort. For example, in 1955 the Great Lakes Basin Compact was set up by the states bordering the Great Lakes in which cooperation is pledged with regard to both fisheries research and use. (3) The United States has entered into international agreements with Canada which have established the Great Lakes Fishery Commission to implement and coordinate sea lamprey control and the International Pacific Salmon Commission, for the protection and restoration of salmon occurring in international waters (22).

Artificial Propagation. In the early history of fish management it seemed logical to biologists and anglers alike that if man could supplement natural reproduction of a given fish species by artificial methods, and introduce these artificially propagated fish into a given habitat, the fish population of that area would be augmented and the angling success of fishermen virtually assured. Since about 1935, however, on the basis of intensive studies of population dynamics, it has become apparent that this technique frequently results in dismal

Figure 11–11 Wisconsin angler poses with huge sturgeon which he has just speared through the ice. [Wisconsin Conservation Department]

failure, especially if the objective is to increase the numbers of an already well-established species. Moreover, the cost of artificial propagation, in terms of facilities, maintenance, staff, rearing, and eventual distribution of the young fish is almost prohibitive. For these reasons, artificial propagation, generally speaking, is regarded critically by most fisheries biologists. Fish stocking, other than introductions, may have various objectives: It may re-establish a fish population which had been destroyed by predators, drought, pollution, an epizootic disease, or some other environmental factor. A fisheries biologist may wish to stock a Southern farm pond with *Tilapia* in order to get rid of excess aquatic vegetation. He may wish to stock a reservoir which has an overpopulation of stunted bluegill with a predatory species. Impoundments may be stocked with rainbow, brook, or brown trout if the water temperature does not exceed 65 degrees F. Large-mouthed bass or spotted bass may be stocked in reservoirs and farm ponds where water temperatures of 80 degrees F. or higher are recorded. Frequently bass ponds are stocked with forage fishes such as bluegills, crappies, rock bass, catfish, or even golden shiners and fathead minnows (22).

If salmon and trout populations are to be maintained at reasonably high levels, artificial stocking is imperative. The U.S. Fish and Wildlife Service maintains a number of salmon

Figure 11–12 U.S. Fish and Wildlife Service biologist delivers channel catfish to stock flood water retarding structure near Coolidge, Texas. [Soil Conservation Service, U.S. Department of Agriculture]

Figure 11–13 A plastic tag is placed near base of dorsal fin to mark stocked trout. Recapture data on such marked fish give important information regarding movements, growth, longevity, and mortality. [Wisconsin Conservation Department]

hatcheries along the Columbia and Sacramento Rivers. Without the artificial propagation of trout, the thrill of snaring one of these scrappy fish would soon be nothing but a memory for most anglers, despite the most ingeniously tied fly and the most sophisticated arch of bamboo rod. Currently both federal and state fish hatcheries rear brook, brown, cutthroat, rainbow, and lake trout. In mountainous areas of Wyoming and Colorado trout fingerlings may be stocked by means of aerial drops (6). The official policy of the federal hatcheries is to propagate trout to fill the following needs: (1) To stock trout in suitable waters in which they do not occur. Such waters may be newly created reservoirs or may be waters from which competitive rough fish have been eradicated. (2) To stock trout in waters where conditions for growth are good, but where natural spawning sites are inadequate. Growth usually is rapid. Nevertheless, such streams must be restocked at intervals of one to three years. (3) To stock trout in waters where fishing pressure is too great to be sustained by natural reproduction. This is sometimes known as "put-and-take" stocking. The trout planted are catchable size. Most of them are caught the same season they are planted.

Figure 11–14 Fingerling rainbow trout are planted by air in Lake Powell behind Glen Canyon Dam on the Colorado River. [Bureau of Sport Fisheries and Wildlife, U.S. Department of the Interior]

Figure 11–15 Stocking young trout in a Wisconsin lake. [Wisconsin Conservation Department]

Figure 11-16 Opening day of the New Jersey trout season on the Musconetcong River near Hackettstown. These anglers hopefully will catch trout stocked on a "put-and-take" basis. [Soil Conservation Service, U.S. Department of Agriculture]

According to a recent fish distribution report of the Fish and Wildlife Service, our federal hatcheries distributed 227.5 million (eggs, fry, and fingerlings, and fish 6 inches or longer) individuals with an aggregate biomass of 4 million pounds. The most abundantly propagated species were the chinook or king salmon (69.4 million individuals), the bluegill (32.6 million), the rainbow trout (28.2 million), the largemouthed bass (21.5 million), and the northern pike (13.7 million).

Introductions. An *introduction* may be defined as the stocking of an animal in a new geographical region. The introduced species may be native to the United States, or it may be an exotic.

Native Introductions. In 1966 the Conservation Department of Michigan introduced about 800,000 coho salmon from the Pacific Coast into streams tributary to Lake Michigan and Lake Superior. It is hoped that these salmon will not only

399

Figure 11–17 Wisconsin angler with good-sized coho salmon recently stocked in Lake Michigan. [Wisconsin Conservation Department]

provide excellent sport and commercial fishing, but also serve as an effective agent of biological control in curbing the exploding populations of the alewife, a weed species whose activities severely compete with more desirable Great Lakes fishes. Because the coho has a short life-span, an abundant food supply is essential for appreciable growth.

The Minnesota Conservation Department has enjoyed a great deal of success with walleye introductions. For example, only three years after walleye fry were introduced to 4,000-acre Brule Lake (Cook County, Minnesota), it was possible to catch legal limits of walleyes in any part of the lake. Hawaiian fishermen are catching 40-pound channel catfish which were introduced from the contiguous states. Kokanee have been introduced to Maine, New York, Connecticut and Pennsylvania; although growth and yield vary considerably, good results have been achieved, especially in Connecticut. From 1963 to 1966, over 42,000 steelhead trout were stocked in Pennsylvania rivers in an attempt to establish an ocean-run population. During a three-year program, 15,888 Bonneville cisco adults and 205,000 eggs from Bear Lake (Utah–Idaho) were recently stocked in Lake Tahoe (California–Nevada) (15). American smelt were successfully introduced to the Great Lakes region from the Atlantic and Pacific coasts. During the spawning run of the smelt in early April, fishermen come from all over Michigan and Minnesota to net or sein the silvery little fish as they ascend tributary streams. During a good run it is not uncommon for smelt fisherman to catch a tubful of fish in a half hour! During 1957–1962, smelts were introduced into six new environments in Maine. Notable fish introductions which met with failure or at least extremely limited success were those of the American eel to Michigan from the Atlantic Coast and the king salmon from the Pacific Coast to the Great Lakes. The ranges of many native minnows have been accidentally extended by fishermen who dump their surplus bait at the end of a day's fishing.

Figure 11–18 Fisherman nets haul of smelt in river north of Algoma, Wisconsin. [Wisconsin Conservation Department]

EXOTIC INTRODUCTIONS. The introduction of the European brown trout was eminently successful. It has been able to establish itself in waters too warm or too badly polluted for survival of native brook trout. The infamous European carp is a celebrated example of an introduction that has been embarrassingly successful. Although this highly adaptable fish has delighted many a modern Tom Sawyer with canepole and worms, it has been the bane of the sophisticated adult fisherman, as well as most fisheries biologists. Recently the federal Fish Farming Experimental Station at Stuttgart, Arkansas, imported a number of Israeli carp for experimental purposes and found them effective control agents of undesirable pond weeds. At this same station, remarkable growth rates were observed in the grass carp (a species brought over from Malaysia); during their first year, 3-inch fish weighing 4 grams attained a length of 20 inches and a weight of 1,816 grams.

Habitat Improvement. In recent years many fisheries biologists have come to the conclusion that the most effective long-range measure for improving sport and commercial fishing is improving the carrying capacity of fish habitat. Students of fish management have seen fishing in a particular lake and stream deteriorate despite the most stringently enforced restrictive laws (closed seasons, creel limits, and so on) and despite the most intensive and carefully supervised programs of propa-

Figure 11–19 Although considered a rough fish, the European carp has some redeeming qualities. Here it provides sport for Wisconsin spear fishermen. [Wisconsin Conservation Department]

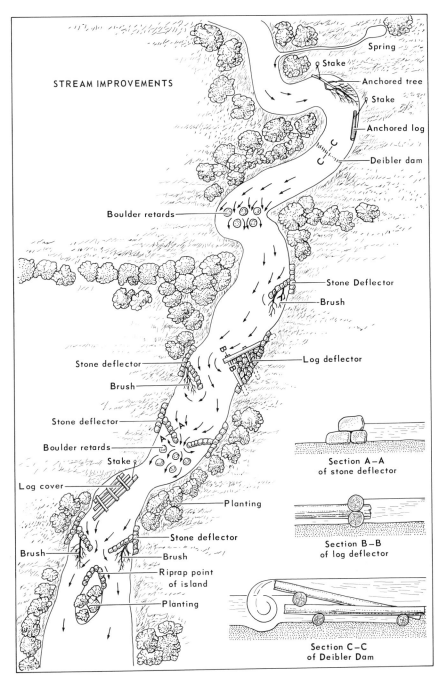

Figure 11–20 Methods of improving stream habitat for fish. On hard bottom streams spawning and refuge pools may be established by erecting low dams constructed of either logs or boulders. In sand-bottom streams use of properly situated deflectors will result in the build-up of a silt bank and weed bed (essential substrates for many fish food organisms) on the downstream side. In shallow streams the shelter area can be enlarged by the introduction of streamside shrubs and trees. Note riprap at point of island to prevent erosion. Shrubs may be planted to intercept sunlight and prevent critical warming of water during midsummer. Note plunge basin and shelter formed by Diebler dam. [Adapted from Karl F. Lagler, *Freshwater Fishery Biology* (Dubuque, Iowa: William C. Brown Company, Publishers, 1956).]

gation and stocking. A feeling persists in many professional circles that if the carrying capacity of the lake or stream is good (in terms of food supply, cover, unpolluted water, abundance of breeding sites, proper oxygen levels, suitable water temperatures, and so on), some of the other fish management measures may be de-emphasized or, in some situations, abandoned completely.

SHELTER AND COVER. Artificial shelters enhance fish survival in a number of ways. They provide cover enabling a forage fish to escape predators. They increase the substratum on which the green plant food base of many fish food chains can become established. They provide shaded areas where fish may retreat during the heat of midday.

A series of brush shelters may be anchored along the inner margin of a lake's littoral zone with great effectiveness. In the winter season brushpiles can be set up on the ice cover in strategic areas and weighted with bags of stones; they will gradually sink to their proper place on the lake bottom as soon as the ice melts in spring (22).

Figure 11–21 Stream improvement on the Plover River in Wisconsin. The deflector will provide a deep pool where game fish can find cover. [Wisconsin Conservation Department]

WEED CONTROL. A certain amount of aquatic vegetation is useful to fish populations as cover, refuge sites, spawning sites, food, and as a source of the oxygen released during photosynthesis. Nevertheless, when vegetation becomes too profuse, it may be more destructive than beneficial, by competing for nutrients with phytoplankton, by utilizing too much water space, and by permitting escape from predators to such an extent that overpopulation and stunting results. Moreover, in late summer the decomposition of the accumulated vegetation on the lake bottom exerts a high BOD which may result in serious oxygen depletion. Under such conditions the weeds must be removed, either by weed-cutting machines, by biological methods, or by species-specific herbicides.

Among the more serious water-weed pests in the United States are the lotus (Texas, Tennessee), water chestnut (New York), and water hyacinth (Texas, Florida, Louisiana). At least twenty-seven major weed control programs have been conducted in fifteen states and Puerto Rico, with the aid of $400,000 in federal funds. The experimental control of algae and submerged plants has been achieved with copper sulfate and sodium arsenite; floating and emergent plants have been destroyed with 2, 4-D amine and fuel oil. However, great caution must be exercised in the selection of herbicides, for they may affect both fish food organisms and fish adversely. Considerable research is currently being conducted to determine the total impact of herbicides on the entire aquatic ecosystem, whether stream, lake, or reservoir.

Because fertilization increases the growth of phytoplankton, the resultant decrease in light intensity may effectively control the reproduction and survival of rooted vegetation. Much interest has been generated in recent years in the possibility of controlling weeds with the fish *Tilapia mossambica,* introduced from abroad. In an experimental study Childers et al. found that a population density of 1,000 tilapias per acre will eliminate rooted submergent vegetation and algae (8). They suggest that *Tilapia* would be useful in artificial lakes and ponds as a weed control agent, and where aesthetic values are of consideration. Its use would be restricted to Southern lakes, because the subtropical tilapias cannot tolerate water temperatures of 55 degrees F. (12.8 degrees C.) and below for extended periods.

ARTIFICIAL SPAWNING SITES. The fish production of a body of water may be increased by providing artificial spawning substrates where suitable natural ones are lacking. Thus, sand or gravel might be introduced on the otherwise muddy bottom of a lake or stream to enhance bass or trout production. The use of commercially available nylon was tested by Chastain et al. as an artificial spawning substratum for large-mouthed bass in five ponds. Spawns were observed on sixty-eight of ninety (75.5 per cent) mats over a two-year period. Of eighty spawns observed in 1965, 71 per cent were located on nylon mats. Transfer of these spawn-laden mats to rearing ponds for incubation and growth was moderately successful, one trial resulting in a per-acre production of 54.3 pounds of biomass made up of 37,600 2-inch fingerlings.

Spawning habitat may be increased or decreased by manipulating water levels of reservoirs. Intensive study of the breeding behavior of the northern pike has revealed that shallow marshy fringes of the littoral zone are the preferred spawning habitat. Flooding of marshes with the aid of low dikes may enhance spawning conditions for this species (22). In recent years suitable spawning sites for the northern pike have been greatly reduced as a result of real estate developments, marina construction, and industrial expansion. State fish and game departments are attempting to rectify the situation. During the period 1950–1965, with the aid of $250,000 in federal funds (derived from a tax on tackle), Wisconsin, Iowa, and Minnesota have acquired an aggregate 3,927 acres of marshes for the development of northern pike breeding and spawning habitat (6).

When overpopulation problems result in stunted fish, the situation may be rectified by destroying nests and spawning grounds, either by water manipulation at impoundments or by depositing unsuitable materials on the substratum.

FERTILIZATION.   Just as the abundance of a farmer's corn crop depends largely on the fertility of his soil, so the black bass or pike crop of a lake or stream depends on the fertility of the water. Water fertility (i.e., the concentration of dissolved salts such as carbonates, nitrates, sulfates and phosphates) in turn ultimately depends on the soil fertility of the watershed. Water fertility determines the abundance of phytoplankton, which in turn forms the base of fish food chains.

Many lakes in central Minnesota, occupying a region of fertile soil, produce up to 80 pounds of animal food (dry weight) per acre; this is 400 times the 0.2 pound of animal food (dry weight) produced per acre by rockbound lakes in the infertile watersheds of northeastern Minnesota. It is apparent, therefore, that the use of artificial fertilizers can increase fish production in a lake or farm pond just as it can on a farmer's fields. It would, of course, be prohibitively expensive in a lake of any considerable area. Lyakhonovich et al. found that pond fertilization with superphosphate, ammonium nitrate, and manure increased production of both phytoplankton and zooplankton, and natural production of fish was increased two to three times (30).

Wild birds, of course, may assist man in fertilizing lakes. Immense quantities of droppings are voided by birds in the vicinity of their nesting areas. Some of this nitrate- and phosphate-rich material falls into the water, heightening its fertility. This may result in increased phytoplankton production, which, in turn, permits higher densities of the small aquatic invertebrates utilized as food by fish. Recently, fish and duck farms have been established in Russia, in which the ducks not only increase fish productivity by fertilizing the water but serve to control excessive aquatic weeds (30)

PREDATOR CONTROL. Just as many deer hunters feel that any deer-eating wolf should be shot on sight, so the angler becomes equally incensed over the depredations of piscivorous herons, egrets, mergansers, pelicans, grebes, loons, eagles, ospreys, kingfishers, mink, otter, and bear. It is true that egrets, kingfishers, and herons may occasionally become destructive at hatchery holding ponds. However, most piscivores may be performing a beneficial population-control function which may minimize stuntedness caused by food shortages, as well as reduce the occurrence of epizotic diseases. The absence of this predatory pressure might leave more fish for the angler, but many would be so small as to be hardly worth catching. In any case, when food analysis studies are made, the accusations of sportsmen frequently appear unfounded. Thus a study of digestive tracts and scat contents of otters from Wisconsin, Michigan, and Minnesota revealed that although fish were indeed the otter's main prey, these predators seldom took game fish.

Sea Lamprey and Its Control. Although most predators and parasites do not affect the fish population appreciably, on occasion a specific predator may cause a drastic population reduction. A classic example is the havoc wrought in the Great Lakes by the sea lamprey on the lake trout population. The lamprey is a primitive jawless vertebrate belonging to the Class Cyclostomata. It has a slender eel-like body. The muscular suctorial funnel around its circular mouth enables it to attach tenaciously to its prey. Its pistonlike tongue, which is armed with numerous horny, rasping teeth, is moved back and forth through the lake trout's tissues, tearing both flesh and blood vessels and opening up profusely bleeding wounds. After gorging itself on a blood and body-fluid meal, the predator may drop off its host and permit it to swim weakly away. However, if the trout does not eventually die from the direct pre-datory attack, it may succumb secondarily to bacterial and fungal parasites which can freely invade the body through the open wound. Even when a lake trout survives, the ugly scar left on its body makes it commercially worthless.

Originally, the lamprey was exclusively an anadromous fish, spending its adult life in marine habitats but ascending fresh-water streams to spawn. Today, the lampreys along our Atlan-tic Coast retain this anadromous behavior. However, the Great Lakes lampreys spend their entire life cycle in fresh water. The fasting adults migrate up tributary streams to mate, spawn, and die. The adults usually build a shallow nest on a gravel or sand bottom into which eggs are deposited. A 15-inch female may produce 60,000 eggs. The larval lampreys, known as am-mocetes, hatch from the eggs and drift downstream until they come to a muddy substratum. They then burrow tail first into the mud, allowing only their heads to remain exposed to the swiftly moving current. Larvae employ a ciliary feeding method, sweeping minute insects, crustaceans, worms, and algae into

Figure 11–22 Stages in the development of the sea lamprey. (*Center*) About one year old and still nonparasitic. Early eyeless state, about 2 inches long. (*Upper*) Three-year-old larva, still nonparasitic. About 4½ inches long. (*Lower*) recently transformed larva almost ready to assume parasitic life. Ventral view showing untransformed mouthparts. [U.S. Fish and Wild-life Service]

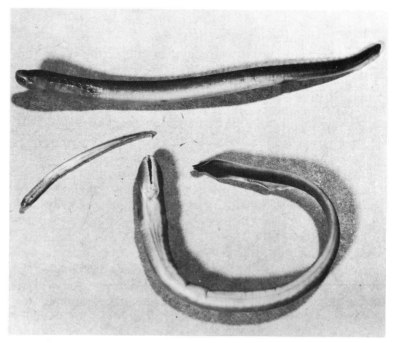

their digestive tract. After several years, they acquire the suctorial funnel and rasping tongue of the adult, emerge from their
burrows, swim into the open waters of the lake, and assume the
predatory behavior of their parents.

The lamprey originally occurred in the shallow waters off
the Atlantic seaboard from Florida to Labrador, in the waters
of the St. Lawrence River, and also in Lake Ontario at the
eastern end of the Great Lakes chain. For many centuries, the
westward extension of the lamprey's range into Lake Erie was
blocked by Niagara Falls. However, in 1833 man unwittingly
provided an invasion pathway by constructing the Welland
Canal to benefit commercial shipping. The spread of the lamprey through Lake Erie was relatively slow. (It was not taken in
the Detroit River until the 1930's, possibly because of a lack of
suitable spawning streams.) However, once it invaded Lake
Huron it spread rapidly through the remainder of the Great
Lakes chain and by the 1950's it had reached western Lake
Superior. Its predatory activity soon threatened the multimillion dollar Great Lakes trout fishing industry with total
collapse. The total annual catch declined from 10 million
pounds in 1940 to one-third million pounds in 1961, a 97 per
cent reduction in twenty-one years. Idle nets rotted along the
waterfront. Veteran fishermen, too old to acquire new skills,
went on relief. Many of the younger men emigrated to Minneapolis, Milwaukee, Chicago, and Detroit to seek employment.

Confronted with the economic and biological dilemma
posed by the sea lamprey, research teams of the Lakes States
fisheries departments and the U.S. Fish and Wildlife Service
collaborated in an intensive effort to eradicate the predator.
Various stratagems were employed. Adults were netted, seined,
and taken in "electric fences" as they attempted to ascend their
spawning streams. These methods, however, met with only
partial success. From 1951 to 1959 over 6,000 chemicals were
tested by biochemists to determine their suitability as agents
of lamprey control. Finally, a selective poison (3,4,6-trichloro-
2-nitrophenol) was developed, known by its trademark *Dow-
lap*. A concentration of 12 parts per million destroyed all
lamprey larvae within sixteen hours. A twenty-four-hour exposure of 36 parts per million had no adverse effect on trout,
sunfish, and rock bass. Moreover, it is harmless to fish food
organisms such as lake chums, creek chubs, and a variety of
aquatic insect larvae (29).

As a result of the encouraging findings, the Great Lakes
Fishery Commission employed Dow-lap and related nitro-
phenols on all lamprey-spawning streams tributary to the Great
Lakes. By 1962 the lamprey had been reduced to 20 per cent of

its peak numbers. In 1960 almost a million lake trout were stocked in Lake Superior; later stockings were made in Lake Huron and Lake Michigan. The combination of restocking and the continued chemical treatment of lamprey-spawning streams hopefully may restore the lake trout fishery (29).

ROUGH FISH REMOVAL. Rough fish like carp, bowfins, and gar, because of their destructiveness to game fishes, either directly or indirectly, are frequently the focus of intensive eradication projects. Even gizzard shad and panfish, ordinarily valuable as forage or game fish, may require control if they become abundant. However, complete eradication of any of these species from a given body of water would be enormously difficult to accomplish. Various control methods under study currently are chemicals, seining, commercial fishing, manipulation of water levels, and fish-spawning control. Carp, for example, probably could not be completely eliminated unless dynamite or a chemical were employed. Before state or federal biologists may employ a specific chemical, it must first be registered with the U.S. Department of Agriculture and approved not only by state health and pollution agencies, but also by the Federal Committee on Pest Control (6). Lemmon reports that a recently developed toxicant, antimycin, was found to kill carp more readily than it does most other fish and does not appear deleterious to invertebrates. The gizzard shad, a forage fish which has become excessive in certain Texas reservoirs, can be eliminated by the precise application of selective chemicals released from low-flying helicopters (6). Rotenone, derived from the roots of an Asiatic legume, will kill fish at a concentration of only 1 part per million within minutes at water temperatures of 70 degrees F. Unfortunately, both dynamiting and massive poisoning with rotenone would be unselective, resulting in the indiscriminate death of many species. Moreover, if some fisherman comes along a few days later and dumps his surplus carp bait minnows into a lake which has just been "decarped," with the aid of its tremendous reproductive capacities, carp will soon be just as numerous as before the eradication project was launched. More acceptable methods would be to keep the carp population down to reasonable levels either by trapping them on their spawning grounds or by periodic seining. Thousands of pounds of carp have been removed from certain shallow lakes in southern Minnesota and Wisconsin in a single day by using these methods.

CONTROL OF OXYGEN DEPLETION IN WINTER. There are various methods of alleviating winter kill of fish from oxygen depletion. If the lake is small, the opaque snow blanket may be

Figure 11–23 Seining carp and other rough fish from Lake Maloney near North Platte, Nebraska. [U.S. Fish and Wildlife Service]

removed with snowplows to permit sunlight to penetrate to the aquatic vegetation. Parts of the frozen lake may be blasted with dynamite to expose surface waters to atmospheric oxygen. Oxygen may be introduced through ice borings by means of motorized aerators, a technique which has proven effective in Lake Upsilon, North Dakota. However, such an operation would require several dozen aerators and would be prohibitively expensive except on a small lake or under special situations where the improved fishing justified the investment. Finally, because winter depletion of oxygen is aggravated by the aerobic decomposition of aquatic vegetation on the lake bottom, removal of excess weedy growth in the littoral zone prior to the freeze might lessen the winter kill. Thus, lake fertilization to increase fish productivity can be self-defeating if the ensuing explosive growth of aquatic plants accentuates the oxygen depletion problem the following winter.

CONTROL OF OXYGEN DEPLETION IN SUMMER. As previously mentioned, midsummer oxygen depletion frequently occurs in the hypolimnion of thermally stratified lakes. Water mixing and hence circulation of dissolved oxygen may be promoted by mechanical pumping. Irwin et al. report success in reducing thermal stratification of four lakes in southern Ohio (which range in volume from 98 to 1,260 acre-feet) by pumping the bottom water to the surface. Oxygen depletion may limit fish distribution. For example, only 15 per cent of the volume of Lake Erdman was habitable by coho salmon during two periods in 1960 as a result of the combination of high surface temperatures and oxygen depletion in the hypolimnion. The introduction of compressed air into the hypolimnion served to mix the water and increased primary productivity. Dissolved nitrate levels resulted in more than a threefold increase in survival rate and the quantity of salmon produced.

CONSTRUCTION OF FARM PONDS AND RESERVOIRS. The construction of farm ponds, artificial lakes, and reservoirs is the most effective means of providing adequate fishing opportunities for the burgeoning recreational needs of our nation's growing population. As of 1967 the United States had 1,062 reservoirs of over 500 acres, embracing 9,133,000 acres (6). The physical, chemical, and biological characteristics of many new impoundments are being scrutinized with respect to their potential as suitable fish habitat. During the period from 1950 to 1965 under the Dingle-Johnson program of federal aid to states for fish habitat acquisition and development, 246 lakes representing 3,000 water acres were constructed or modified in thirty-nine states at a total construction cost of $21 million. They have provided over 2 million fishing days annually. In 1967 farm ponds and reservoirs supported 40 per cent of all fisherman days, but by the year 2000 they must provide 60

Figure 11–24 Fishing on a 20-acre Georgia farm pond. A good program of pond management including regular fertilization (submerged platform in background) has provided excellent fishing. Watershed above pond is fully protected with cover. [Soil Conservation Service, U.S. Department of Agriculture]

per cent of the total fisherman days. Ten million more acres of reservoirs larger than 10 acres will be required to meet the demand (6). Between 1960 and 2000 according to the Senate Select Committee on Water Resources, an estimated 1.462 million acres of ranch and farm pond are to be constructed, providing 707,000 acres of fishing waters (6). By the year 2000 it is expected that a total of 2.885 million farm ponds embracing an area of 2.242 million acres will be contributing 157 million pounds of fish annually (6).

Natural and Artificial Selection of Superior Fish. It is of considerable interest that some fish living in the Mississippi River (which has been heavily contaminated with pesticides borne in agricultural run-off waters) have developed a degree of natural resistance to pollutants. (This is reminiscent of the DDT resistance genetically acquired by house flies and mosquitos.) It is supposed that the selection for resistance-contributing genes probably operates at the highly sensitive embryonic or larval stage. Possibly fisheries biologists will be able to accelerate this process. Scientists at the Federal Fish Genetics Laboratory at Beulah, Wyoming, are exploring the possibility of developing pesticide-resistant strains of trout by selective breeding experiments.

Larger and higher-quality fish for stocking Southern fish ponds are being developed at the federal Fish Farming Experiment Station at Stuttgart, Arkansas. Giudice reports that a rapidly growing hybrid catfish has been produced by crossing a channel catfish with a blue catfish (16). Measurements taken in August after the second season of growth showed the hybrids to have a weight increment 32 per cent greater than that of the blue catfish and 41 per cent larger than the channel catfish. Even more promising, a seven-month-old hybrid buffalo-fish, resulting from crossing a black buffalo-fish female with a bigmouth buffalo-fish male, showed twice the length and fourfold the weight of the nonhybrids. This should be exciting news to our growing legion of farm pond fishermen.

Management of Endangered Species. In July, 1966, the U.S. Fish and Wildlife Service reported that twenty-four species and subspecies of fish in the United States were *endangered.* This classification indicated that their reproduction and survival was in immediate jeopardy, because of one or a combination of factors, such as loss or defilement of suitable habitat, predation, competition, disease, and heavy fishing pressure. Among the endangered species listed were the following: shortnose sturgeon, longjaw cisco, Lahontan cutthroat trout, Piute cutthroat trout, Montana westslope trout, Gila trout, blue pike, and the Big Bend gambusia.

SHORTNOSE STURGEON. This short-snouted sturgeon, which attains a length of three feet, is on the brink of extinction. Formerly widely distributed along the Atlantic coastal rivers from New Brunswick to Florida, its numbers have been drastically reduced in recent years. The most recent records have come from the Hudson River. According to the New York State Conservation Department, the most important reasons for its decline are domestic and industrial pollution combined with overfishing. Large numbers of this edible fish have been taken in shad gill nets. The only protective measure legislated to date apparently is the 20-inch size limit. Location of its spawning grounds and an intensive study of its breeding behavior would appear to be fundamental to perpetuating the species. Fertilized eggs removed from wild specimens may make propagation in captivity possible in the future (5).

ATLANTIC SALMON. Because this species is still widely distributed in Canada, it is only the population occupying United States waters that is actually endangered. Here the fish is restricted to remnant populations in eight coastal streams in Maine. In the 1880's up to 200,000 pounds of this brown-backed, silver-sided salmon were taken yearly. From this original abundance the American population has become drastically depleted within the past seventy-five years, because of pollution and man-made barriers to its spawning runs. The total annual catch in recent years has been only about 450 fish with an aggregate weight of under 1,000 pounds. Although the reproductive potential is high, females averaging 6,000 eggs, only one salmon of every 1,000 eggs produced eventually reaches the sea, because of the intense ER. Survival in American waters currently depends primarily on propagation by state and federal hatcheries. Over 200,000 fish were hatchery-reared in 1962 (5).

BIG BEND GAMBUSIA. The total world population of this brightly colored, orange-and-yellow-finned sprite is under 1,000 and is restricted to a small area in Texas. The extinction of this tiny fish would be most unfortunate, but its perpetuation presents a stern challenge to fisheries biologists. The Texas spring in which the species was originally discovered, known as Boquillas Spring, dried up in 1928. Hearteningly, however, in 1954 a second population was discovered in Graham Ranch Warm Springs. Currently the entire range of this species is represented by two pools in Big Bend National Park, Texas.

Attempts at transplantation to other ponds within the park have been unsuccessful. Protective measures presently being practiced include the removal of *Gambusia affinis*, an aggressive competitor, as well as repeated habitat surveillance to ensure a constant water supply. (5).

BIBLIOGRAPHY

1. Becker, C. Dale, and Wayne D. Brunson. "*Diphylobothrium* (Cestoda) Infections in Salmonids from Three Washington Lakes," *Jour. Wild. Mgt.*, **31** (1967), 813–824.

2. Behmer, David J. "Movement and Angler Harvest in the Des Moines River, Boone County, Iowa," *Proc. Iowa Acad. Sci.*, **71** (1965) 259–263.

3. Bowen, J. T., and R. E. Putz. "Parasites of Freshwater Fish. IV. Miscellaneous. 3. Parasitic Copepod *Argulus*," *Fish Disease Leaflet 3.* Leetown, West Va.: Bureau of Sport Fisheries and Wildlife, Eastern Fish Disease Laboratory, 1966, 4 pp.

4. Brous, Henry. "Observations on Garter Snakes," *Amer. Natur.*, **16** (1882), 564.

5. Bureau of Sports Fisheries and Wildlife. "Rare and Endangered Fish and Wildlife of the United States," *Resource Publication No. 34.* Washington, D.C.: U.S. Fish and Wildlife Service, 1966.

6. _____ *Fifteen Years of Better Fishing.* Washington, D.C.: U.S. Fish and Wildlife Service, 1967, 32 pp.

7. Cairns, John, Jr., Arthur Scheier, and Nancy E. Hess. "The Effects of Alkyl-Benzene-Sulfonate on Aquatic Organisms," *Ind. Water Wastes,* **9** (1964), 22–28.

8. Childers, William F., and George W. Bennett. "Experimental Vegetation Control by Largemouth Bass-*Tilapia* Combinations," *Jour. Wild. Mgt.*, **31** (1967), 401–407.

9. Colby, Peter J., and Lloyd L. Smith, Jr. "Survival of Walleye Eggs and Fry on Paper Fiber Sludge Deposits in Rainy River, Minnesota," *Trans. Amer. Fish. Soc.*, **96** (1967), 278–296.

10. Dreyer, William R., and Joseph Biel. "Life History of Lake Herring in Lake Superior," *Fish. Bull.,* **63** (1964), 493–536.

11. Dugan, Patrick R. "Influence of Chronic Exposure to Anionic Detergents on Toxicity of Pesticides to Goldfish," *Jour. Water Poll. Cont. Fed.,* **39** (1967), 63–71.

12. Eddy, Samuel, and Thaddeus Surber. *Northern Fishes.* Minneapolis, Minn.: University of Minnesota Press, 1947.

13. Edmondson, W. T. "The Relation of Photosynthesis by Phytoplankton to Light in Lakes," *Ecol.,* **37** (1956), 161–174.

14. Fields, Paul E. *Final Report on Migrant Salmon Light-Guiding Studies at Columbia River Dams.* Portland, Oreg.: North Pacific Corps of Engineers, 1966, 266 pp.

15. Frantz, Ted C., and Almo J. Cordone. "Final Introductions of the Bonneville Cisco (*Prosopium gemmiferum* Snyder) into Lake Tahoe, California and Nevada," *Calif. Fish and Game,* **53** (1967), 209–210.

16. Giudice, John J. "Growth of a Blue X Channel Catfish Hybrid as Compared to Its Parent Species," *Prog. Fish-Culturist,* **28** (1966), 142–145.

17. Hassler, Thomas J., John M. Neuhold, and William F. Sigler. "Effects of Alkyl-Benzene-Sulfonate on Rainbow Trout," *Bureau of Sport Fisheries and Wildlife Technical Paper*, Washington, D.C.: U.S. Fish and Wildlife Service, 1967, 15 pp.

18. Herting, Gerald E., and Arthur Witt, Jr. "The Role of Physical Fitness of Forage Fishes in Relation to Their Vulnerability to Predation by Bowfin (*Amia calva*)," *Trans. Amer. Fish. Soc.*, **96** (1967), 427–430.

19. "Keeping Tahoe Alive," *Time*, **88** (1966), 46–47.

20. King, Dennis R., and George S. Hunt. "Effect of Carp on Vegetation in a Lake Erie Marsh," *Jour. Wild. Mgt.*, **31** (1967), 18.

21. Lagler, Karl. "Food Habits and Economic Relations of the Turtles of Michigan with Special Reference to Fish Management," *Amer. Mid. Nat.*, **29** (1943), 257–312.

22. _____ *Freshwater Fishery Biology*. Dubuque, Ia.: William C. Brown Co., 1956, 421 pp.

23. Lauer, Gerald J., H. Page Nicholson, William S. Cox, and John I. Teasley. "Pesticide Contamination of Surface Waters by Sugar Cane Farming in Louisiana," *Trans. Amer. Fish. Soc.*, **95** (1966), 310–316.

24. Major, Richard L., and James L. Mighell. "Influence of Rocky Reach Dam and the Temperature of the Okanogan River on the Upstream Migration of Sockeye Salmon," *U.S. Fish and Wildlife Service Bulletin*, **66** (1947), 131–147.

25. McClane, A. J. "Where East Meets West," *Field and Stream*, **71** (1967), 78–80, 89–90, 92.

26. McFadden, James T., Gaylord R. Alexander, and David S. Shetter. "Numerical Changes and Population Regulation in Brook Trout *Salvelinus fontinalis*," *Fish. Res. Board Can. Jour.*, **24** (1967), 1425–1429.

27. Meehan, William R., and William L. Sheridan. "Investigations in Fish Control, 8: Effects of Toxaphene of Fishes and Bottom Fauna of Big Kitoi Creek, Afognak Island, Alaska," *Resource Publication 12*. La Crosse, Wis.: Bureau of Sport Fisheries and Wildlife, Fish Control Laboratory, 1966, 1–9.

28. Meyer, Fred P. "Parasites of Fresh Water Fish, II. Protozoa. 3. *Ichthyopthirius multifilis*. "*Fish Disease Leaflet 2*. Leetown, West, Va.: Bureau of Sport Fisheries and Wildlife, Eastern Fish Disease Laboratory, 1966, 4 pp.

29. Milne, Lorus J., and Margery Milne. *The Balance of Nature*. New York: Alfred A. Knopf, 1961, 329 pp.

30. Nikolsky, G. V. *The Ecology of Fishes*. New York: Academic Press, 1963, 352 pp.

31. Norden, Carroll R. "Age, Growth and Fecundity of the Alewife, *Alosa pseudoharengus* (Wilson) in Lake Michigan," *Trans. Amer. Fish. Soc.*, **96** (1967), 387–393.

32. Pauley, Gilbert B. "Prespawning Adult Salmon Mortality Associated with a Fungus of the Genus *Dermocystidium*," *Fish. Res. Board Can. Jour.*, **24** (1967), 843–848.

33. Peters, John C. "Effects on a Trout Stream of Sediment from Agricultural Practices," *Jour. Wild. Mgt.*, **31** (1967), 805–812.

34. Schmittou, H. R. "Sex Ratios of Bluegills in Four Populations," *Trans. Amer. Fish. Soc.*, **96** (1967), 420–421.

35. Simco, Bill A., and Frank B. Cross. "Factors Affecting Growth and Production of Channel Catfish, *Ictalurus punctatus.*," *Univ. Kansas Publ. Natur. Hist.*, **17** (1966), 191–256.

36. Smith, L. L., Jr., R. H. Kramer, and J. C. MacLeod. "Effects of Pulp-wood Fibers on Fathead Minnows and Walleye Fingerlings," *Jour. Water Poll. Cont. Fed.,* **37** (1965), 130–140.

37. Smith, Robert L. *Ecology and Field Biology.* New York: Harper & Row, Publishers, 1966, 686 pp.

38. Surber, Eugene W. "Water Quality Criteria for Freshwater Fishes," *Proc. 16th Ann. Conf. Southeast. Assoc. Game and Fish Comm. 1962,* (1965), 435–436.

39. Uhler, F. M., Cottam, C., and T. E. Clark, "Food of the Snakes of the George Washington National Forest, Virginia," *Trans. 4th North Amer. Wild. Conf.,* (1939), 605–622.

40. U.S. Fish and Wildlife Service. "The Effects of Pesticides on Fish and Wildlife," *U.S. Fish and Wildlife Service Circular 226.* Washington, D.C.: U.S. Fish and Wildlife Service, 1965.

41. Werner, Robert G. "Intralacustrine Movements of Bluegill Fry in Crane Lake, Indiana," *Trans. Amer. Fish. Soc.,* **96,** (1967), 416–420.

42. Witty, Kenneth. "Travel Rate of Downstream-Migrant Coho Salmon." *Prog. Fish-Culturist,* **28,** (1967), 174.

43. Yeo, R. R. "Silver Dollar Fish for Biological Control of Submersed Aquatic Weeds," *Weeds,* **15** (1967), 27–31.

12 Marine Fisheries

Value of Our Commercial Fisheries

During 1966 a sizable fleet of vessels, comprised of 12,677 units of 5 tons or above, and of 69,445 smaller craft (many of them motor boats), were operated by 135,636 American fishermen. The total American catch of 4 billion pounds in 1968 was worth 472 million to the fishermen. Of the 4 billion-pound harvest, 2.3 billion pounds were utilized as food, in the form of filets, clam chowder, fried shrimp, and halibut steak, to enable the United States to maintain an 11-pound per capita consumption of marine food. Marine foods represent the most valuable source of protein, after beef, pork, and poultry.

Of the 1967 catch, 1.6 billion pounds were manufactured into meal oil, fish solubles, homogenized condensed fish, and shell products or were utilized as bait and animal food (36). Ranked by states, the most important commercial fisheries in the United States during 1966 were Louisiana, with a 656.8-million-pound harvest (over 15 per cent of the total United States catch); Alaska, with 581.6 million pounds; California, with 460.9 million pounds; and Virginia, with 418.3 million pounds. The three most important categories of fishes taken in 1968, from the standpoint of volume, were menhaden (1.3 billion pounds, representing over 35 per cent of the entire harvest and worth $19 million), salmon (301 million pounds worth $55 million), and tuna (294 million pounds worth $47 million). The menhaden catch was down 36 per cent from 1960, when 2.01 billion pounds were taken. The decline may be due to depleted menhaden populations; there is some concern whether this valuable fish will be able to withstand the intensive fishing pressure.

Marine Sports Fisheries. In 1967, according to the *Saltwater Angling Survey*, 8.2 million Americans caught approximately 737 million fish weighing an aggregate of 1,474 million pounds. The five most important fish, ranked by weight of catch, were bluefish, 93.209 million pounds (mainly north Atlantic); king mackerel 90.678 million (mainly south Atlantic); spotted sea trout 108.046 million pounds (mainly in the Gulf); groupers 70.494 million pounds (mainly south Atlantic); and striped bass 70.991 million pounds (mainly north Atlantic and Pacific).

Figure 12–1 Menhaden fishermen hauling in seine, June, 1968, off Sealevel, North Carolina. [Bureau of Commercial Fisheries, U.S. Department of the Interior]

Major Features of the Marine Ecosystem

Professor Eugene P. Odum, eminent ecologist from the University of Georgia, lists some of the major ecological features of the oceanic environment (22): (1) It covers 70 per cent of the earth's surface. (2) It extends to depths of up to 6.5 miles (Mariana Trench) and hence has a much greater vertical dimension, or "thickness," than the terrestrial or freshwater environment. (3) The ocean is continuously circulating. Oceanic currents such as the Aleutian current, which brings cold water down the Pacific Coast, and the Gulf Stream, which brings warm water upward along the Atlantic Coast, move water masses horizontally and affect temperatures of adjacent coastal regions. As a result, New York City has a relatively moderate climate even in winter and summer evenings in San Francisco may be quite chilly. There are also vertically moving currents; *upwelling*, for example, brings nutrient-rich cold water from the ocean bottom to surface level. (4) The ocean is salty. It has an average salinity of thirty-five parts salts (by weight) per 1,000 parts water; in contrast, fresh water usually has a salinity of less than one-half part per 1,000 parts water. In other words, the ocean is about seventy times as salty as a lake or stream. (5) The sea is relatively infertile compared to fresh water; nitrates and phosphates are extremely scarce. Two exceptions to this statement are the coastal areas where tributary streams discharge massive loads of sediment, and the areas of upwelling just mentioned.

Zonation of the Ocean. The oceanic environment can be divided into five basic ecological regions, as indicated in Figure 12–2. In the context of this book it will be necessary to describe briefly only the *neritic, euphotic,* and *abyssal* zones.

1. NERITIC ZONE. The neritic zone is the marine counterpart of the littoral zone of a lake. It is a relatively warm, nutrient-rich, shallow-water zone overlying the continental shelf. It extends along our Atlantic, Pacific, and Gulf coasts, has an average width of 10 to 200 miles, and extends to depths of 200 to 600 feet. The neritic zone ends where the continental shelf abruptly terminates and the ocean bottom plunges to great depths. The fertility of the neritic zone is supplied primarily by upwelling and the sedimentary discharge of tributary streams. For example, the Mississippi River washes almost 2 million tons of nutrient-rich mud into the Gulf of Mexico daily. Sunlight normally penetrates to the ocean bottom, thus permitting continuous photosynthetic activity and the presence of a vast population of anchored and floating plants. Animal populations

are rich and varied. Oxygen depletion is not a problem because of photosynthetic activity and wave action. The total amount of biomass supported by the neritic zone is greater per unit volume of water than in any other part of the ocean.

2. EUPHOTIC ZONE. The euphotic zone is the open-water zone of the ocean which corresponds to the limnetic zone of a lake. The term *euphotic*, which literally means "abundance of light," is appropriate to this zone, for it has sufficient sunlight to support photosynthesis and a considerable population of phytoplankton. In turn, the phytoplankton support a host of tiny "grazing" herbivores, such as the small crustaceans which form the largest zooplanktonic component. The total energy made available to animal food chains by euphotic phytoplankton is much greater than that made available by plants of the neritic zone; this is largely because of the vast area of the eu-

Figure 12–2 Zonation of the marine ecosystem. The neritic, euphotic, and bathyal zones roughly correspond to the littoral, limnetic, and profundal zones of the lake ecosystem. Because of the high levels of dissolved nutrients and solar radiation, gross production, and hence plant and animal abundance and diversity, is greatest in the neritic zone. [Adapted from Eugene P. Odum, *Fundamentals of Ecology* (Philadelphia: W. B. Saunders Company, 1959). After Joel W. Hedgepeth, "The Classification of Estuarine and Brackish Waters and the Hydrographic Climate" in *Report No. 11 of National Research Council Committee on a Treatise on Marine Ecology and Paleoecology*. National Research Council, Washington, 1951, 49–56 pp.]

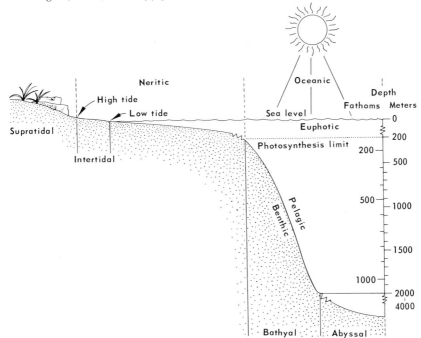

photic zone, which extends for thousands of miles across the open sea. The degree to which light penetrates of course is dependent upon the transparency of the surface waters; usually sunlight cannot penetrate deeper than 200 meters in most marine habitats; hence, this frequently is considered the lower border of the euphotic zone.

3. ABYSSAL ZONE. The abyssal zone is the cold, dark-water zone of the ocean depths which roughly corresponds to the profundal zone of the lake habitat. It lies immediately above the ocean floor. Animal life is extremely sparse. Any animal living in the abyssal zone must be highly specialized to adapt to the extreme conditions. It must adapt to darkness, to intense cold (because the abyssal water frequently approaches the freezing point), to greatly depleted levels of dissolved oxygen (because no photosynthesis can occur here), to water pressures approaching thousands of pounds per square inch, and to considerable scarcity of food. There may be an abundance of nutrient-rich sediments on the ocean floor which may have come from the decaying bodies of marine organisms drifting down from the sunlit waters far above or which may have been derived from the excretions of animals living at upper oceanic levels. For example, in certain areas of the West Atlantic the concentration of phosphates at a depth of 1,000 meters may be ten times the concentration at 100 meters. Because both phytoplankton and herbivorous animals cannot exist in the abyssal zone, most consumers are either predators or scavengers. A number of the deep-sea fishes of the abyss have evolved luminescent organs which may aid them in securing food and mates.

Marine Food Chains and Energy Conversions

Because the ocean covers 70 per cent of the earth's surface it obviously also receives 70 per cent of the earth's solar energy. Except for the anchored green plants of the neritic zone, this solar energy is trapped primarily by the phytoplankton producers swarming in the open waters of the sea. It has been estimated that 19 billion tons of living plant matter (mostly phytoplankton) are produced annually, which in turn supports 5 billion tons of zooplankton biomass. The average number of plankton taken from the upper 50 meters of water in the South Atlantic (away from the continental shelves) at 55 degrees C. was about 100,000 per liter. The zooplankton may be consumed by a variety of filter feeders, including shrimp, herring, anchovy, and blue whale. The terminal link of the marine food chain is frequently represented by predators such as the barracuda, moray eel, shark, cod, bonito, salmon, and killer whale. As in the case of terrestrial food chains, the shorter the chain, the more efficient the production of terminal link biomass. Thus the three-link food chain which occurs off the California coast of phytoplankton–zooplankton–herring is much more efficient in the production of human food than the six-link food chain of phytoplankton–zooplankton–shrimp–lance–small fish–cod which occurs off the Grand Banks of Newfoundland. In the shallow waters of the neritic zone anchored green plants convert much more solar energy into chemical energy than the phytoplankton. However, the efficiency of energy conversion for food chains based on the anchored type of vegetation is not very great. Thus, it has been estimated that 24 million tons of eelgrass (*Zostera*) off the Danish coast is the primary food source of 5 million tons of animals of absolutely no food value to man. It is also the primary food source of 1 million tons of animals, which in turn would be eventually consumed by 10,000 tons of food fishes (plaice and cod), which in turn would be eaten by man. Here, the ratio of *Zostera* crop to the ultimate food crop of plaice and cod usable by man is 2,400 to 1. Obviously this represents a high degree of wasted energy. In contrast, about 0.06 per cent of the annual phytoplankton crop in the English Channel is ultimately harvested as fish fit for human consumption—a somewhat more efficient biomass ratio of 1,666 to 1. Nevertheless, despite this inefficiency in energy transfer (because of the operation of the second law of thermodynamics), the marine ecosystem annually produces 1 to 2 billion tons of biomass usable as food by man, sufficient to supply the protein food requirements of 30 billion people. The current annual fish catch of 50 million metric tons may be only 2.5 per cent of the potential harvest.

Marine Fish

We shall consider the natural history, ecology and economics of three major marine resource categories; *marine fish, shellfish* (shrimp and oysters) and *marine mammals* (seals and whales). Our discussion will begin with marine fishes, not only because their ecology to some degree parallels that of freshwater fishes, but also because they are by far the most abundant source of protein food for mankind.

Fecundity.   Marine fishes on the average are more fecund than freshwater species, possibly because chances of survival are poorer in the oceanic environment. Among marine fishes fecundity is directly proportional to the species's vulnerability to predation, and inversely proportional to the protection given by the parent (35). In the soup-fin shark (*Galeorhinus zyoptarus*), which has relatively few predators and which is ovoviviparous (the embryo developing within the female's body and being "born"), litters range in size from six to fifty-two, with an average of thirty-five. In decided contrast are the fishes which lay buoyant eggs and whose eggs and larvae become part of the plankton, transported by seadrift, tide, and current (21). Thus the moonfish (*Mola mola*) produces 3 billion eggs, the Atlantic cod (*Gadus callarius*) 9 million, the haddock (*Melanogrammus aeglefinus*) 3 million, the Pacific halibut (*Hippoglossus stenolephis*) 2.7 million, the winter flounder (*Pseudopleuronectes americanus*) 1.5 million, the hake (*Merluccius*) 1 million, and the mackerel (*Scomber scombrus*) 0.5 million (15, 19).

Fecundity appears to be inversely proportional to population size. Perhaps the greater productivity of a small population is related to the better breeding condition resulting from more abundant food supplies (21). Fish stocks that have been severely depleted by overfishing often show increased fecundity.

Migrations. According to Nikolsky, fishes conduct three basic types of migration—spawning, feeding, and overwintering (21). A few species, such as gobies and many coral fishes, are essentially nonmigratory. In some species, such as the white fish, the overwintering migration is lacking but feeding and spawning migrations are completed.

1. SPAWNING MIGRATION. The spawning migration ensures favorable physical and biotic conditions for developing eggs and larvae with regard to oxygen, temperature, salinity, currents, food, competitors, and predators. Fishes which live in the ocean for most of their life cycle but ascend freshwater streams to spawn are called *anadromous*. We have described the anadromous migration of the Pacific salmon. Other anadromous species are the American shad (*Alosa sapidissima*) and Atlantic smelt (*Osmerus mordax*), which migrate from the Atlantic into freshwater streams to spawn, and the Pacific herring (*Clupea pallasi*), which moves into shallow bays to deposit its eggs (15). On the other hand, a *catadromous* fish spends most of its life cycle in fresh water but descends to the ocean to spawn. The catadromous American eel (*Anguilla bostoniensis*) descends New England streams when sexually mature, swims hundreds of miles to a site in the Sargasso Sea east of Bermuda, spawns at great depths, and dies. The larvae float to the surface and migrate northward, transported in part by the Gulf Stream, and eventually ascend a freshwater stream, where most of their life cycle is spent. Many North Atlantic fishes—such as mackerel,

silver hake, scup, weakfish, and the winter flounder (*Pseudo-pleuronectes americanus*)—migrate from deeper water to shallow coastal areas to spawn. The North Pacific albacore (*Thunnus alalunga*) moves southward from temperate waters to spawn (15).

2. FEEDING MIGRATION.   Updrafts or convection currents bring nutrients to the upper layers of temperate seas in winter. When light intensities increase in spring, phytoplankton become highly productive. Zooplankton, in turn, increase in response to the superabundant food supply. As waters warm in summer, bluefin tuna, albacore, mako sharks, blue sharks, basking sharks, swordfish, ocean sunfish, and opah migrate into this area of nutritional abundance, where the smaller fish feed on plankton and are in turn consumed by carnivores (19).

Many fishes perform feeding migrations as eggs or larvae. Thus the Atlantic currents transport herring larvae and the eggs and larvae of cod from the Norwegian coast to their Barents Sea feeding grounds (21). Some feeding migrations are vertical rather than horizontal.   Thus the mackerel ascends and descends in rhythm with the movements of the plankton upon which it feeds. Similarly, the swordfish shifts its vertical position in synchrony with that of its sardine prey.

Some vertical migrations are concerned with escape from predation rather than feeding. Thus anchovies in the Black Sea remain at deep levels during the day, where they are unavailable to piscivorous birds; then at night they rise to the surface, after the birds have finished feeding (21).

3. OVERWINTERING MIGRATION.   Nikolsky states that the purpose of the overwintering migrations, conducted by some species, is to provide the most favorable wintering conditions for a fish which will have a reduced metabolism and be relatively inactive (21). Presumably such a wintering area will be relatively free of predators. Marine fish do not begin an overwintering migration until they have accumulated sufficient body fat to sustain them during the winter period of minimal feeding activity. Anchovies of the Black Sea pass the winter in an inactive state at depths of 100 to 150 meters (21).

Water Temperature and Fish Distribution.   Conditioning experiments have shown that both marine and freshwater species are capable of detecting extremely minute changes in the temperature, salinity, and hydrostatic pressure of their environment. Although the salinity-detecting receptors have not as yet been identified, the thermosensors apparently are modified cutaneous nerve endings. Some fishes can detect salinity changes of one-half part per thousand, and water temperature changes of only .03 degrees C. It is not surprising, therefore, that distribution of certain marine fishes may show a high correlation with water temperature patterns. A few examples follow.

1. Although a great abundance of forage organisms exists all along the coast of Baja California, commercial quantities of yellowfin tuna (*Thunnus albacares*) are limited to areas where the water temperature is at least 19 degrees C.; skipjack tuna (*Katsuwonus pelamis*) occur only where the water temperature is a minimum of 17 degrees C. (25).

2. Two thirds of the summer catch of albacore tuna off the Pacific Coast is made in a limited water temperature range of 60 to 66 degrees F. In 1965, just prior to and during the albacore tuna (*Thunnus alalunga*) migration toward the West Coast, water temperatures off central and southern California were much below average and albacore fishing was poor; during that same year water temperatures averaged above normal off Oregon and Washington and resulted in extremely good albacore fishing there in late summer (31).

3. In the oceanic waters of the northwestern Atlantic, the bluefin tuna (*Thunnus thynnus*), which prefers relatively cool water, is dominant in the vicinity of the Gulf Stream during winter and spring; however, as water warms, the bluefin are replaced by the warm-water-loving yellowfin in summer and fall. According to Squire the temperature factor in de-

Figure 12–3 Tuna fishing on the trade wind in the South Pacific. [Bureau of Commercial Fisheries, U.S. Department of the Interior]

termining tuna distribution in this area is brought into sharp focus at the edge of the Gulf Stream, where a sharp temperature gradient permits warm- and cold-water tuna to exist adjacent to each other and yet be distinctly separated (31).

4. A study of cod distribution on the Spitsbergen Shelf in the Northwest Atlantic revealed its confinement to relatively warm waters above 1.5 to 2 degrees C.

5. The seasonal occurrence of fish in a coastal marsh off northwest Florida was correlated with water temperature fluctuations (38).

6. The spawning grounds of many marine species are located within a narrow temperature range, as indicated for several North Atlantic species: cod 0.4–7 degrees C., herring (spring) 3.7–9.3 degrees C., herring (fall) 9.1–13.3 degrees C., pilchard 9–16.5 degrees C., and mackerel 10–15 degrees C. (26).

7. The swordfish prefers to breed in tropical waters with a temperature from 25–29 degrees C. (19).

8. During the 1965 mako shark tournament in the New York–New Jersey region, which previously had resulted in a maximum of forty shark landings, over 900 blue sharks were caught in only two days. This success reflected an unusual temperature pattern during the spring migration from offshore wintering grounds. An unusually warm (60–63 degrees F.) but confined area of surface water occurred off western Long Island and northern New Jersey. The blue sharks were confined within this zone by a barrier of cold water having a temperature of less than 57 degrees F. (7).

9. Research conducted by the Tiburon Marine Laboratory on the basis of bathythermograph data collected by cooperating sport fishing boat operators indicates that predictable relationships between temperature and catch may exist for pelagic migratory species such as bonito (*Sarda chiliensis*), barracuda (*Sphyraena argentea*), and yellowtail (*Seriola dorsalis*) (7).

The U.S. Bureau of Commercial Fisheries systematically takes surface water temperatures over large areas by means of airborne infrared thermometers. From these data it publishes bi-weekly temperature charts. Knowing the temperature preferences of certain species, commercial fishermen would save much time and effort by consulting these charts.

Eggvin has discussed the possibility of utilizing meteorological data and data from weather ships, research ships, liners, and research stations in an attempt to follow the flow of individual water masses (8). In this way localized hydrographic conditions could be forecast for the benefit of commercial fishermen.

In cooperation with the U.S. Coast Guard, airborne surface

temperature surveys of three important fishery areas on the continental shelf of the Pacific Coast (in which infrared detection instruments were employed) were conducted by the Tiburon Marine Laboratory, Bureau of Sports Fisheries and Wildlife, Tiburon, California. It is possible to produce a computer-drawn isotherm chart within ten minutes after transmission of data by telephone circuits to Monterey (Calif.) from any U.S. Navy Weather facility.

The Atlantic Marine Gamefish Research Program has recently published *The Atlas of the Marine Environment,* based on fifty years of temperature records. It shows the average monthly temperatures for the continental shelf from southern Florida to Cape Cod, ranging from ocean surface to bottom. Any pelagic or demersal species of fish, by making the appropriate movements, could remain on this stretch of continental shelf and keep within narrow species-preferred temperature boundaries. Although fish distribution, as in the bluefish, is based on other factors, such as light intensity and day length, the atlas will greatly facilitate the prediction of game and sport fish occurrence.

Environmental Resistance. Among the many destructive agencies which marine fishes encounter we shall briefly describe the biotic factors represented by predators, parasites, red-tide organisms, and competitors, as well as such physical factors as adverse winds and thermal pollution.

PREDATORS. Commercially valuable fish are consumed by a great variety and number of predators, including other fishes, sharks, birds, seals, sea otters, and whales. Belopolsky (4) records the following percentage of fish food in the diet of sea birds in the Barents Sea: guillemot (*Vria lomvia*), 95.6; razorbill (*Alca torda*), 92; puffin (*Fratercula arctica*), 67; tern (*Sterna paradisea*), 55.6; and great blackbacked gull (*Larus marinus*), 40.4. In the Volga Delta cormorants kill 5,000 metric tons of fish annually, equal to 1.5 per cent of the catch in the North Caspian Sea (21). Herring spawn is consumed by haddock in large quantities, and its larvae are eaten by planktonic predators (11). Menhaden (*Brevoortia tyrannus*), which occur along the Atlantic coast of North America, are consumed by whiting, codfish, pollack, dogfish, tuna, flounder, pompano, cavally, bonito, bayonet fish, striped bass, weakfish, sharks, dolphins, and whales (9). It is estimated that natural predators annually destroy 1 million million million menhaden, or 1,000 times the commercial harvest of 1948, a year of record catch (9). Recently, half the dogfish (*Squalus acanthias*) in a mixed dogfish and Pacific hake (*Mer-*

luccius productus) catch in Puget Sound were found to have consumed hake (28).

In some cases one valuable commercial fish may be the predator of another. Thus, the cod is an avid consumer of herring. Studies in Scandinavian waters have shown that a good catch of cod one year is frequently followed by a poor herring catch the next. Conversely, a poor cod harvest may be followed by a sizable herring catch the ensuing year.

PARASITES. In general, parasitic infestations do not contribute to acute fish mortality, but are usually taken in stride by host populations. Fish are parasitized by bacteria, molds, protozoans (flagellates and sporozoans), trematodes, tapeworms, nematodes, crustaceans, and many other organisms. Sixty tapeworms have been found in the gut of a single turbot (11). Trematodes infest kidneys, urinary bladder, cerebral fluid, gall bladder and the circulatory system. The following number of different kinds of trematodes have been found on fish in the Irish Sea: cod, thirteen; flounder, ten; plaice, nine; and haddock, six (11).

Nematodes are common internal parasites that invade the intestines, swim bladder, liver, peritoneum, skin, and muscle. Kabata reports 15 per cent of the North Sea haddock to be infested with growth-retarding copepods (crustaceans) (18). He estimated that if each parasitized haddock lost only 1 ounce in weight, the total loss to the Scottish haddock catch in 1954 would have been 1.96 million pounds.

During the summer of 1963 the *Pasteurella* bacterium contributed importantly to the deaths of many white perch (*Roccus americana*) and striped bass (*Roccus saxatilis*) in American waters.

RED-TIDE ORGANISMS. Under certain conditions of water temperature, salinity, and/or nutrient salts, populations of marine protozoans may rapidly increase. The accumulating metabolic wastes may cause massive fish mortality. Sometimes the ocean water assumes the red-brown color of their densely massed cells, which is the foundation for such expressions as "red sea" or "red tide." Outbreaks of *Gymnodinium* along the Florida coast and of *Gonyalaux* along the southern California coast have caused spectacular fish kills of such proportions that many tons of fish carcasses have littered the beaches. In 1964 a "bloom" of the reddish-brown dinoflagellate *Cochlodinium* in Barnegat Bay, New Jersey, caused the destruction of many marine organisms, including *Menidia*, *Fundulus*, sticklebacks, silver perch, eels, and crabs. An investigation of the outbreak's cause was conducted by the Sandy Hook Marine Laboratory of

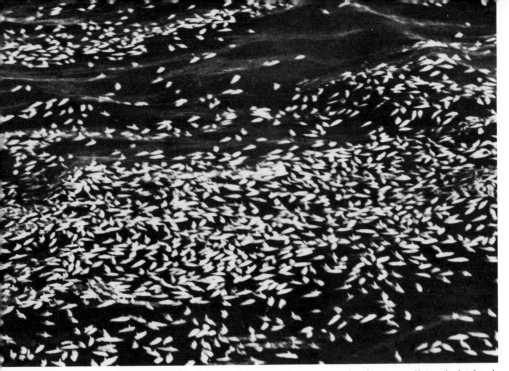

Figure 12–4 Heavy fish mortality in a red tide area off Sanibel Island, Florida. [Bureau of Commercial Fisheries, U.S. Department of the Interior]

Highlands, New Jersey. The predisposing conditions for the outbreak were the combination of the low flushing rate of the Bay in August and the resultant accumulation of domestic and industrial pollutants. The localized abundance of nutrients which resulted in turn made possible a rapid increase in the food organisms of *Cochlodinium*. Apparently, *Cochlodinium* did not kill the fish directly by means of metabolic toxins, but indirectly, through its high biological oxygen demand.

COMPETITION FOR FOOD. Marine fish compete not only with each other for food but also with a diverse assemblage of aquatic mammals, birds, and invertebrates. Among the invertebrates, sea-stars and brittle-stars are especially significant (21). In areas of high density the starfish, which feed primarily on molluscs, may exceed fifteen per square meter, and brittle stars may exceed 400 per square meter of ocean floor (35). Fishes consume only one third to one fourth as much food per unit pound as their echinoderm competitors. Along the Danish coast only 2 to 5 per cent of the potential fish food is actually eaten by fish (33).

Off the California coast sardine and anchovy compete intensively for the same planktonic foods. As might be expected, therefore, when the sardine fishery severely declined in the early 1950's, there was a proportional increase in the anchovy population. It is currently estimated that there is an anchovy stock of 2 to 4 million tons off California and Baja California, partly as a result of the reduced food competition.

ADVERSE WINDS AS A MORTALITY FACTOR. The prevailing winds may have either a beneficial or adverse effect on the reproductive success of a species which produces buoyant eggs. A good example is the poor reproduction of the mackerel (*Scomber scombrus*) along our Atlantic coast during 1932, as reported by Sette (27). The estimated mortality was so severe among eggs and larvae that only one fish survived to an age of thirty-five days out of every 10 million eggs laid. The spawning grounds for this species extends from the coastal waters of Newfoundland south to Chesapeake Bay. Southwest winds are beneficial for young mackerel, for sea drift carries them to food-productive regions, as was demonstrated by the abundant year-classes of 1930–1931. However, in 1932 the prevailing winds were from the northeast and were unusually strong. As a result, it is presumed the larval mackerel were carried away from their nursery grounds along southern New England to the eastern end of Long Island (19).

THERMAL POLLUTION. Most steam-electric generating plants situated near the coast cool their steam condenser systems with seawater. A water-temperature survey conducted by the Tiburon Marine Laboratory (U.S. Fish and Wildlife Service), on the California coast at five plants between Los Angeles and San Diego, showed that the total water output of 1.1874 million gallons per minute was heated about 20 degrees F. above the intake temperature. Similar cases of thermal pollution occur along the Atlantic coast. Fisheries biologists are concerned with the possible effect that this localized water-temperature increase may have not only on fish, but on their plankton and invertebrate food organisms. The Atlantic Marine Gamefish Research Program of the U.S. Fish and Wildlife Service is investigating the effects of thermal pollution by means of simulation studies. Researchers are concerned with the problem anticipated in the Cape Cod Canal as a result of operation of electrical generating plants (31). Warinner et al. report that increased winter water temperatures in the York River of Virginia, (the result of the water passing through a power-plant condenser) caused depressed carbon assimilation by phytoplankton (37). Atomic-powered plants of the future may aggravate the already serious problem. Although warm discharges have been known to attract such game fishes as bonito and barracuda, the long-term effects may be highly deleterious. As Squire has suggested, it may be possible that warm-water discharges interfere with the normal migration of such species as the drums and surf perches.

Marine Fisheries Management. We shall briefly describe the following phase of marine fisheries management: introductions, transplantations, habitat development projects such as the construction of artificial reefs and the artificial induction of upwelling.

INTRODUCTIONS. One aspect of marine fisheries management is the introduction of food and game fishes into new suitable areas for the purpose of establishing or improving the commercial or sport fishing resource. Such introductions began in the late nineteenth century and are continuing today. The commercially profitable striped bass (*Roccus saxatilis*) industry which prevails along the Pacific coast (from Washington to southern California) and Atlantic coast is a notable result of introductions. This species was originally distributed along the Atlantic coast from northern Florida to the Gulf of St. Lawrence. However, in 1879 and 1882 a total of 432 individuals were planted off the California coast near San Francisco (15). Responding to a suitable physical and biotic environment, with abundant food and satisfactory breeding areas, the striped bass population increased so rapidly that commercial harvesting was possible in less than ten years. The striped bass has provided millions of pounds of food fish to commercial fisheries as well as splendid recreation for Pacific coast anglers (6).

Similarly, over 1.5 million young American shad (*Alosa sapidissima*) originally confined to our Atlantic coast and tributary streams were taken from the Hudson River and stocked in the Sacramento River around 1880 (15). The shad catch increased fortyfold within sixty years, from 100,000 to 4 million pounds, and is well established along the Pacific coast from California to Alaska (6). The American smelt (*Osmerus mordax*) has become an important Great Lakes food fish since its introduction in 1912. The Atlantic gizzard shad (*Dorosoma cepedianum*), which attains a length of 20 inches and serves as a forage fish for more valuable game and food fishes, has become widely distributed in freshwater habitats of the central and eastern United States (15). In 1956 two species of excellent food qualities, the red snapper (*Lutjanus vaigiensis*) and the blue-spotted argus (*Cephalopholus argus*), were introduced to the Hawaiian Islands from Tahiti and the Marquesas Islands, respectively (15).

California's inland Salton Sea was recently stocked with several species of croakers (*Sciaenidae*) from the Gulf of California. Subsequently, a few orangemouth, corvina, and sargo were stocked. As a result, sport fishing has been exceedingly good.

Occasionally, of course, a marine fish is transplanted by

natural methods over which man has little control. Thus, fish spawn may be carried on the feet of migratory waterfowl for thousands of miles. In this way the southern stickleback (*Pungitius platygaster*) was probably introduced into enclosed West Siberian lakes from the Aral Sea basin.

TRANSPLANTATION OF PLAICE (*Pleuronectes platessa*). One of the pioneer experiments in fish transplanting was conducted by a British investigator, Garstang, about 1905, in an attempt to increase the plaice harvest in the North Sea fisheries (11). From tag-recapture data it had been determined that growth in this species was correlated with food availability. Unfortunately, young plaice were abundant on the coast of Holland, where food supplies were scarce, but sparse on the food-abundant Dogger Bank, with an area as large as Wales. Thousands of young 8-inch plaice taken from the Dutch coast were measured, weighed, and marked. Half were released immediately at the site of capture; the other half were transported in oxygenated tanks to the Dogger Bank for release. Recapture data indicated that the Dogger Bank transplants grew to nearly three times the length of the controls released off Holland. The International Council for the Exploration of the Sea conservatively estimated that the probable net profit in terms of increased fish yields resulting from a transfer of 1 million plaice from the Dutch coast to Dogger Bank would be about $15,000 (13). However, because a single nation is reluctant to finance a project whose fruits theoretically could be harvested by many countries, the operation has not as yet been undertaken on a commercial basis (15).

CONSTRUCTION OF ARTIFICIAL REEFS. Considerable interest has been shown recently by marine fisheries biologists in the potential of artificial reefs in providing food and cover for game and commercial species. Unger reports that artificial reefs are especially functional in raising the carrying capacity of otherwise flat, sandy coastal plains. As of 1965, nine artificial-reef projects had been launched in the United States; additional reefs had been completed in the Virgin Islands and Japan (34). Venice Pier in Los Angeles County is surrounded by artificial reefs constructed for the benefit of saltwater anglers. In 1962 a reef composed of large boulders and building rubble was started in 70 feet of water off Fire Island, New York. When three years old it was already frequented by large numbers of sea bass, squirrel hake, flounder, cunner, and ocean pout. The Sandy Hook Marine Laboratory constructed an artificial reef of sixteen junk automobile bodies sunk to a depth of 55 feet, two miles off Monmouth Beach, New Jersey. Monthly observations by scuba divers have revealed their attraction for tautog (*Tautoga*), cunner, black sea bass (*Centropristis striatus*), scup (*Stenotomus chrysops*), summer flounder, Atlantic mackerel, pollack, and others. The presence of a number of juvenile fishes generated speculation that such reefs may eventually function as nursery habitats. The laboratory plans to construct several more artificial reefs in the neritic zone along Long Island Sound with the cooperation of the New York State Department of Conservation. It may be that such reefs, much larger than the pilot types described, will not only diminish the municipal junkyard problem, but will provide increased sporting opportunities in an area of heavy recreational angling.

ARTIFICIALLY INDUCED UPWELLING. Upwelling and the resultant mineral enrichment of the important euphotic zone may be induced by artificial methods in the opinion of some authorities. It has been suggested, for example, that compressed air bubbling through perforated pipes laid on the ocean bottom may enhance the vertical movement of water sufficiently to fertilize relatively shallow regions of the ocean. According to Iselin, if the ocean bottom between Cuba and Florida could be adequately roughened (possibly by dumping gravel, rubble, or junk) the resultant turbulence generated by the Gulf Stream might bring cold, nutrient-rich bottom waters to the surface. Such nutrients might ultimately be carried into the Atlantic off the southeast Florida coast and increase fish harvests. Oceanographic experts from the National Academy of Science are of the opinion that nuclear reactors placed on the ocean bottom in areas of deep-lying stagnated waters might produce sufficient heat to cause bottom waters to rise and bring dissolved minerals to upper levels where they might be utilized by phytoplankton, and ultimately by fishes.

FISHING PRESSURE AS RELATED TO OPTIMAL YIELDS. In an attempt to appreciate the various positive and negative factors which determine the optimal yield of a fish stock during a given year, it would be helpful to express the pertinent relationships in the form of an equation first elaborated by Russell and later discussed by Hardy (11):

$$S_2 = S_1 + (A + G) - (C + M)$$

S_1 is the harvestable stock at the beginning of the fishing year. In commercial fisheries it would represent the fish large enough to be taken by certain trawls and nets; they would be too large to slip through the meshes of the nets. In the context of sport fishing we might consider all legal-sized fish as S_1. S_2 signifies the weight of harvestable stock at the termination of the fishing year. *A* represents the addition of young fish to the harvestable stock as a result of the growth during the year. *G* represents the weight increment during the year as a result of the growth of *A* (after entering the harvestable stock) and S_1. *C* is the total weight of fish harvested during the year. *M* represents the weight of catchable stock which died as a result of all causes (both physical and biotic) except those associated with fishing. *A* obvi-

Figure 12–5 Dominance of the 1904 age class in the commercial herring catch of the North Sea, 1907–1919. [Adapted from Eugene P. Odum, *Fundamentals of Ecology* (Philadelphia: W. B. Saunders Company, 1959). After John Hjort, "Fluctuations in the Year Classes of Important Food Fishes." *Jour du Conseil Permanent Internationale pour L'Exploration de la Mer,* **1,** 1–38 pp.]

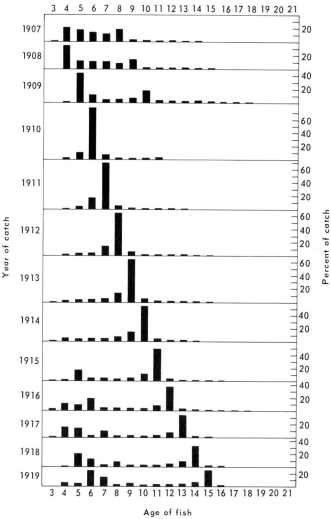

Age of fish

ously depends to some degree on food conditions, spawning success and population density; G depends on the abundance of food and suitable temperatures; C, of course, is variable, depending on fishing pressure and the nature of fishing regulations; and M is based on such factors of the ER as parasites, competitors, disease organisms, predators, pollution, oxygen depletion, adverse winds, and thermal changes. An important point to remember in terms of optimal fishing pressure is that *young fish are more efficient in converting food to biomass than older fish.* Fishing pressure on an old-aged, slow-growing stock may be beneficial up to a critical point, beyond which the stock will be overfished, to permit younger age classes to become established.

With the aid of Table 12–1 (upper) let us examine the theoretical effects of both heavy and light fishing pressure on two different fish stocks, both of which are being recruited at a rate of 1,000 fish annually. (The information for this table, of course, could be secured with the use of the aging techniques described, and of the mark-recapture data obtained by taking samples of the catches of commercial and sport fishermen.) The Roman numerals in the age column represent age classes. The 80 per cent fishing rate on the left is relatively heavy; the 50 per cent rate on the right is rather light. In the columns under fishing rate are listed the number of fish left in each age group from 1,000 fish going into the harvestable stock of age two. (This corresponds to A in our equation.) Assuming a steady addition of 1,000 fish per year, the number of fish in the catchable stock by the time 1,000 fish have been caught is 1,250 at the 80 per cent fishing rate and 2,000 at the 50 per cent rate.

In Table 12–1 (lower) the left-hand column represents the age class. The second column represents the average weight per year class taken in the fishery. The numbers in columns 4 and 5 represent weights of each year class taken (for each rate of fishing pressure) by multiplying the number of fish taken per age class by its average weight. Thus, at the 50 per cent rate of fishing 500 fish of age II class were taken. We multiply 500 by 82 (the average weight per year class) and get 41,000 as the weight of yield from the age class II. Note that the total yield (161,138 grams) at the 50 per cent harvest rate is almost 50 per cent greater than at the 80 per cent rate (106,102 grams), meaning that *a much greater yield can be obtained with much less fishing pressure.* It is apparent that overfishing at the 80 per cent rate when continued will result eventually in diminished yields, even though yearly additions (A) remain constant.

In summary, for optimal sustained fishing harvests fisheries biologists must establish regulations which tend to ensure the most effective fishing pressure (or rates). To this end restric-

Table 12–1*

437

**Marine
Fisheries**

Age	80% fishing rate		50% fishing rate	
	Stock	Withdrawals annually	Stock	Withdrawals annually
I	1,000		1,000	
II	200	800	500	500
III	40	160	250	250
IV	8	32	125	125
V	2	6	62	62
VI		2	31	31
VII			16	16
VIII			8	8
IX			4	4
X			2	2
XI			1	1
	1,250	1,000	2,000	1,000

Age	Weight at end of year	Average weight per year class	Weight of yield	
			per 80% reduction	per 50% reduction
I	40 grams			
II	124	82	65,600	41,000
III	227	175	28,000	43,750
IV	339	283	9,056	35,375
V	460	400	2,400	24,800
VI	586	523	1,046	16,213
			106,102	161,138

* This table originally appeared in E. S. Russell, *The Over-Fishing Problem*. Cambridge: Cambridge University Press.

tions might be made on type of gear, seasons, regions, fish size, and even the number of fishermen.

REGULATIONS. The formulation and enforcement of laws regulating the harvest of the marine fishery is essential to sound management. However, the establishment and enforcement of marine fishing regulations are infinitely more complex than are those for freshwater fish. The trout fisherman more or less expects to observe certain rules imposed by a state or federal agency so as not to undermine the delicate management of a sensitive and vulnerable resource. However, this is not the case for the fisherman of the high seas. As Dr. John Bardach, fisheries biologist at the University of Michigan (2), puts it, "The waters are international territory; they are not the property of a state, a club, or a landlord, and thus are the property of no one until they are captured. There are no international wardens; no fine is to be imposed for taking fish of sublegal size or in excessive numbers; no poachers are put into jail."

State Regulations. The various coastal states have jurisdiction in establishing regulations governing fishing in territorial waters. A great number and variety of state laws have been enacted with respect to the restriction of season, locality, volume of catch, and type of gear. Although formulated with good intentions, both for the resource and the industry, it must be admitted that many of the laws are archaic and, in fact, prevent full realization of the marine fisheries potential. Consider the following examples:

1. Although abalone (a highly edible mollusc) is abundant along California's northern coast, state law forbids commercial harvest.
2. In Washington waters salmon may not be located with electronic devices.
3. In Alaska it is illegal to employ purse seine vessels over 50 feet long in catching salmon.
4. In California fish may not be converted to meal or oil without permission, which is difficult to obtain, from the Fish and Game Commission.
5. Trawl fishing is not permitted in southern California waters, although it is legal off central and northern California. Consequently, the 3 million tons of hake which are found seasonally off southern California cannot be effectively utilized, because they are taken almost exclusively by midwater trawl.
6. It is illegal to harvest anchovy off the coast of southern California despite an abundant stock which would easily yield 500,000 tons annually.
7. There exists a welter of state regulations associated with Atlantic coast fisheries, especially in the Chesapeake Bay area, which are as restrictive as those mentioned above (5).

This is not to say that all state regulations are poorly conceived. Many of them are certainly required and are effective. Nonetheless, many are still in the statute books because of pressure exerted on legislators by fishermen themselves. According to Wilbert Chapman, California Marine Fish Commission, our native fishermen are generally ultraconservative in their harvesting methods (5). They resist using newly developed devices for locating fish schools. They are against the replacement of their obsolescent boats with modern fishing vessels, so that they might favorably compete with more progressive, and aggressive, fishermen. Their resistance to change is based on an understandable effort to keep operating costs to a minimum, although in the long run the cost per ton of fish

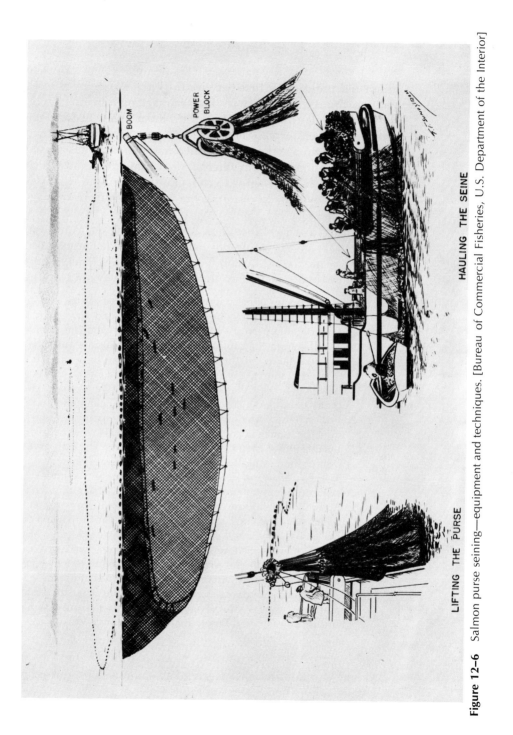

POWER BLOCK

BOOM

LIFTING THE PURSE

HAULING THE SEINE

Figure 12–6 Salmon purse seining—equipment and techniques. [Bureau of Commercial Fisheries, U.S. Department of the Interior]

harvest would be less with the modern techniques and equipment. This attitude is deplorable from the standpoint of maximal sustained yield of a valuable marine resource.

International Regulations. It is simple for nations to adopt the philosophy that because the open sea belongs to all nations, the responsibility for their management belongs to no one in particular. Nevertheless, within the past few decades the phenomenon of decreased harvests of a particular species, such as halibut or tuna, despite intensified fishing effort, has caused interested nations to form international conventions in which the signatory nations agree to cooperate in halting further decline and in eventually restoring the fishery to a basis of maximum sustained yield.

According to Dr. Milner B. Schaefer, even when American biologists are investigating our nation's marine fisheries problems, the work should be conducted not from a restricted provincial view but in a *global* context (26). He lists several reasons.

1. Many species of fish captured by citizens of a coastal state in territorial waters may be highly migratory and may spend a considerable part of their life cycle hundreds or thousands of miles from the capture site. Thus, the albacore and bluefin tuna taken off the California coast may have migrated from the shores of Japan. Similarly, salmon which have hatched in the Columbia or Sacramento rivers may eventually be caught 1,000 miles from the American mainland.

2. Fish stocks on the high seas, far beyond territorial waters, must be managed according to international law as codified by the 1958 Geneva Convention on Fishing and Conservation of the Living Resources of the High Seas.

6. There is an acute need for marine fish protein among the underdeveloped nations of South America, Africa, and Asia. Roughly 500 million people are critically ill from protein deficiency, and their number will increase in proportion to the global population surge in the next few decades.

4. Many marine fisheries products have an international market. For example, Americans may consume tuna caught in the waters of the Atlantic, Pacific, and Indian oceans.

5. American fishing vessels range as far as the coasts of Chile and West Africa. Moreover, the American fish-processing industry is active in Puerto Rico, Samoa, India, West Africa, the Trust Territories of the Pacific, and Central and South America (27).

Among the international marine fish commissions currently involving the United States are the following.

INTERNATIONAL PACIFIC HALIBUT COMMISSION. The International Pacific Halibut Commission was established in 1924; members include the United States and Canada. It manages the halibut resources of the Bering Sea and North Pacific.

Stocks of halibut were obviously on the decline as early as 1916. Largely as a consequence of the commission's efforts the halibut yield has increased greatly. Among provisions directly responsible for the increase were the establishment of catch quotas in four Pacific Coast areas, restricted seasons, and prohibition of fishing operations in areas characterized by runt fish [1, 16]. The fishing fleets of the U.S.S.R. continue to pose a problem for the Commission in the Bering Sea, where the halibut populations have been overfished since 1964 [29]. Even though trawling primarily for bottom fish such as flounder and ocean perch, the Russians incidentally take considerable numbers of juvenile halibut.

From an economic standpoint the fishery is a marginal operation because of the great number of fishermen involved. Roughly one fourth of the men are over sixty years old; over half draw some type of unemployment compensation [20].

INTERNATIONAL COMMISSION FOR THE NORTHWEST ATLANTIC FISHERIES. Established in 1949, members of the International Commission for the Northwest Atlantic Fisheries include Canada, Denmark, France, Germany, Iceland, Italy, Norway, Poland, Spain, the U.S.S.R., the United Kingdom, and the United States. The commission coordinates research programs conducted by member nations. Haddock yields increased after mesh regulations were established by the commission in 1953 for two ocean regions [1, 20].

INTER-AMERICAN TROPICAL TUNA COMMISSION. Unlike most commissions, which are usually set up only after severe resource depletion, the IATTC was established during apparent tuna abundance. Its headquarters are at La Jolla, California, adjacent to the Scripps Oceanographic Institute [1]. The IATTC operates laboratories and field stations in Puerto Rico, Peru, and Ecuador. In 1957, Dr. Milner Schaefer, the commission's first director (who is now director of the University of California's Institute of Marine Resources), predicted the yellowfin tuna's maximum sustainable yield (MSY) would be 194 million pounds annually. This prediction has been borne out. In 1960 the combined tuna fleets harvested some 230 million pounds, but by 1965, with better equipment, the yield had dropped to 180 million pounds [20], The much farther-ranging skipjack tuna is now scheduled for intensive study by the commission [1].

Figure 12–7 A large, yellowfin tuna about to be landed off St. Vincent Island, British West Indies. [Bureau of Commercial Fisheries, U.S. Department of the Interior]

INTERNATIONAL NORTH PACIFIC FISHERIES COMMISSION. The INPFC was established in 1952; its membership includes Canada, Japan, and the United States. The commission provides that a member nation would abstain from exploiting any stock being fully utilized and under conservation management by other nations. This regulation, in practice, is directed toward Japanese inroads on Pacific salmon stocks near the coasts of the United States and Canada (20). The precise definition of areas where salmon stocks of North American and Asiatic origin overlap has been determined only as a consequence of intensive commission-coordinated research (1).

FISH AS A FUTURE FOOD SOURCE. Many authorities regard the ocean (our planet's last frontier), as a potential source of protein food which can be harvested in sufficient quantity to forestall the threat of global famine posed by the human population surge. Because the oceans cover 70% of the earth's surface and receive the same percentage of the earth's incident solar energy,

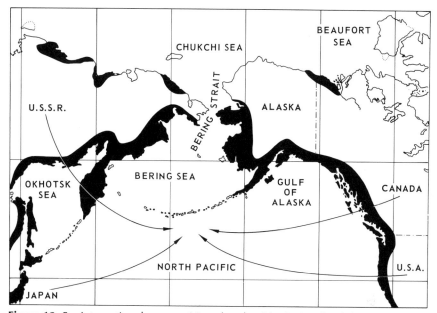

Figure 12–8 International competition for the North Pacific fishery resource. The interest of the United States, Canada, Soviet Union, and Japan conflict in this region. The areas indicated in black include the best salmon rivers in the world. International fishing agreements must be formulated if the resources of the North Pacific are to be most effectively managed and harvested. [Adapted from Guy-Harold Smith, *Conservation of Natural Resources* (New York: John Wiley & Sons, Inc., 1965). After U.S. Fish and Wildlife Service.]

because marine phytoplankton are efficient photosynthesizers, and because the ocean is as yet relatively uncontaminated (although such pollutants as oil, pesticides, sewage, and industrial chemicals are of increasing concern in the neritic zones), there is good reason for this hope. During the decade 1950–1960 the global marine harvest doubled and is continuing to increase vigorously. It is significant that marine food production in 1969 was increasing at a *higher rate than the world population.*

In 1970 the Food and Agricultural Organization (FAO) of the United Nations was working on an Indicative World Plan (IWP) so that accurate predictions can be made relative to world food supply and demand by 1975 and 1985. S. J. Holt, director of FAO's Division of Fishery Resources and Exploitation, believes that the estimated potential catch of 20 million tons in the coastal waters of the United States will easily meet our nation's demands of 10 million tons by 1975 and 20 million tons by 1985. He estimates that the potential global catch is roughly triple the 1969 harvest. His view for global production is equally optimistic: "It would be entirely reasonable to suppose that the maximum sustainable world catch of between 100 million and 200 million tons could be reached by the second IWP target date 1985, or at least by the end of the century."

The realization of these goals, however, will demand much greater efficiency in utilizing the oceanic resources. First, it will require the development of new types of fishing equipment (especially for exploiting deep water stocks), the monitoring of equipment with TV cameras, and the study of behavioral responses of fish to the equipment.

Second, fish detection techniques must be improved. Survey planes of the U.S. Bureau of Commercial Fisheries research base at Pascagoula, Mississippi, flying at night over the Gulf of Mexico, have located schools of thread herring with the aid of an image intensifier. The faint bioluminescence caused by the school's movements is intensified 55,000 times before appearing on a TV screen. More developments of this type are needed.

Third, it will involve the breeding and rearing of marine animals and the upgrading of their food supplies. Some marine forms must be propagated and maintained on a semidomesticated basis, possibly in coastal bays. In Scottish coastal waters the growth rates of plaice, for example, have been greatly increased by adding fertilizer to the water.

Finally, the realization of a maximum sustainable world catch would involve our knowledge of the second law of thermodynamics. We will have to shorten our food chains. Instead of dining on halibut and snapper, we may have to move down the food chain, making greater direct use of crustaceans and perhaps marine algae.

Shellfish

In addition to the true fishes (vertebrates of the class Osteichthyes), our marine fisheries include a great variety of shellfish. Value and poundage of the shellfish landings in 1963 were (1) shrimp, $70 million, 240.3 million pounds; (2) oysters, $25.8 million, 55.6 million pounds; (3) crabs, $23.4 million, 243.8 million pounds; (4) lobsters, $18.3 million, 34.6 million pounds (36). The economic importance of shellfish is apparent in the value ranking of our ten most valuable fisheries: (1) *shrimp*, (2) salmon, (3) tuna, (4) *oysters*, (5) *crabs*, (6) menhaden, (7) *lobsters*, (8) flounders, (9) haddock, (10) *scallops* (23).

Shrimp Fishery. Although shrimp are our most valuable marine fishery, American stocks in 1965 supplied only about 40 per cent of the shrimp consumed by the American people; the remaining 60 per cent was imported. This resulted in a distressing dollar drain on the American economy (4). The annual American shrimp harvest has not been able to meet the enlarged market created by our burgeoning population and an annual per capita consumption which has increased from 0.79 to 1.41 pounds in recent years (4). The United States Bureau of Commercial Fisheries has employed several methods and approaches in an attempt to meet the nation's shrimp demands. For example, they have found dense populations of the large royal red shrimp (*Hymenopenaeus robustus*) off the Atlantic coast of Florida on the mud-and-ooze bottoms of the continental shelf, where water temperatures range from 46 to 52 degrees F. Other populations of this valuable species have been discovered in the Gulf of Mexico 50 to 125 miles from shore at depths of 1,000 to 2,000 feet. Heavier gear, however, must be developed to make catches of these populations commercially feasible (6).

At the bureau's Galveston, Texas, Marine Biology Laboratory researchers are conducting intensive studies on various aspects of shrimp life history, including spawning behavior, feeding habits, migrations, response to temperature fluctuations, growth rates, sex ratios, pollution effects, burrowing and emer-

Figure 12–9 Shrimp trawler cleaning her nets off Sealevel, North Carolina. [Bureau of Commercial Fisheries, U.S. Department of the Interior]

gence behavior of young, predation, metabolism, longevity, and the relation of thermal influences on swimming activity (4). It has been found that most shrimp live only one to two years; this indicates an extremely high mortality rate and a rapid population turnover. Special emphasis is being given to the destructive effects of hydraulic dredging for real estate development in the estuarine marshes used extensively by shrimp as nursery grounds (4). Because adult shrimp occur in deep water and young, rapidly growing shrimp are found inshore (after migrating from open-water spawning grounds), restrictions perhaps should be formulated which would prevent the winter and summer harvesting (and depletion) of young inshore stocks. Finally, improved shrimp trawlers are being developed which operate electrically and which enable shrimp fishermen to catch commercial quantities during daylight hours.

Oyster Fishery. Oysters thrive best in shallow bays or estuaries where temperature, currents, food abundance, salinity, and type of bottom are favorable. Most oysters develop best on rocky or semihard mud bottoms. The American oyster (*Crassostrea virginica*) tolerates salinities ranging from 5 to 30 parts per thousand (10). Occasionally oyster larvae will settle on the partially buried shells of previous generations (30). Oyster colonies or reefs are frequently aligned at right angles to the prevailing water currents so that they can utilize them for the transport of dissolved oxygen and planktonic food organisms. The currents also remove metabolic wastes, sediment, and debris from the colonies (30). Oysters strain out plankton from massive quantities of water swept into their gill cavities by ciliated tracts situated on the gill surface (6). Feeding activity is most intensive during the warm seasons.

ENVIRONMENTAL RESISTANCE. Several biotic factors, including human activities, will be considered in relation to their effect on oyster mortality.

Biotic Factors. Oyster populations may incur sudden depletion as the result of a variety of biotic factors. Extensive oyster beds in the Chesapeake Bay region have been covered with dense blankets of Eurasian water milfoil (*Myriophyllum spicatum*) which has demonstrated explosive growth in the region since 1959. The milfoil's decomposing stems and leaves cause severe oxygen depletion because of the high BOD; in addition, they cause mechanical interference with the oysters' filter-feeding mechanism. The fungus *Dermocystidium marinum,* which is the most destructive oyster disease organism in the

South, has virtually eliminated seed oysters along the Louisiana coast during some summers and can potentially severely curtail oyster production from Delaware to Mexico. During recent years 77 per cent of the oyster populations off the New Jersey coast has been parasitized by the oyster crab, up to 262 parasites having been recorded on a single oyster host. The oyster crabs cause retarded growth and reduced vitality. The Japanese snail, which has been responsible for 15 to 22 per cent oyster mortality in some regions, was accidentally introduced in 1907 along with infected Japanese oyster seed stock. Predatory starfish inflict several million dollars damage to the oyster fisheries annually.

Adverse Effects of Human Activities. Man has destroyed oyster beds by establishing marinas, real estate projects, filling marshes for industrial development, and by using prime oyster habitats as dumping grounds for garbage and sewage. Oil spills may be deleterious not only to oyster vitality but to its commercial value. Thus, in September 16, 1969, 65,000 gallons of fuel oil spilled from a barge which had grounded off West Falmouth, Massachusetts. The high oil content of oysters harvested along the shoreline rendered them unfit for human consumption. The recent expansion of the paper and pulp industry along the Atlantic and Pacific coasts has resulted in toxic discharges which have proven highly deleterious to oyster growth and reproduction. Accelerated erosion due to poor agricultural practices and deforestation has caused the destruction of many once-profitable oyster fisheries along the Atlantic and Gulf coasts by smothering extensive oyster beds with sediment. For example, the neritic zone of Matagorda Bay, Texas, has received an accumulation of up to fourteen feet of sediment, causing the destruction of 6,000 acres of once highly productive oyster reefs.

Intricate chain-reactions may be triggered by the excessive release of nutrients into marine waters, which may have deleterious effects on oysters. For example, several years ago a number of large duck farms on Long Island, New York discharged extensive quantities of duck manure into streams tributary to Great South Bay. The sudden build-up of urea, uric acid and ammonia, in combination with an adverse nitrogen–phosphorus ratio resulted in a rapid population increase of several minute flagellates which ordinarily are quite uncommon. Eventually, they replaced the more common phytoplankton (green flagellates, dinoflagellates and diatoms) which had been the principal oyster food. Unable to digest and assimilate the new type of phytoplankton, many oysters starved even though their digestive tracts were filled.

As in the case of other natural resources, the most serious threat to the perpetuation of America's oyster beds is exploitation by man. For example, over-harvesting reduced the public oyster fisheries of the Delaware and Chesapeake Bay regions to only 25 per cent of their yield in the early 1900's. Such population decrements could be more serious to oyster survival than that of most other organisms. Despite their great fecundity, oysters seem unable to recover their original abundance when reduced below a critical minimal level, even though afforded maximal protection from exploitation. Gross has attributed this phenomenon to the genetic inflexibility of small, isolated oyster populations.

OYSTER CULTURE. The public abuse of the oyster resource, which continued unabated for much of this century, has largely been replaced by the far-sighted responsible programs of private interests. The commercial fishermen, who lease barren, unused areas of the ocean floor, have developed a type of oyster culture in which they provide a suitable substratum upon which the motile oyster larvae can attach themselves and grow into adults. This surface may be in the form of old mollusc shells, gravel, or even slag from blast furnaces. Once the larvae ("spat") have set (by means of a cementing substance produced by the byssus gland), they may be transported by the fishermen to

Figure 12–10 Experimental oyster ponds at the Bureau of Commercial Fisheries Biological Laboratory at Oxford, Maryland. [Bureau of Commercial Fisheries, U.S. Department of the Interior]

food-rich waters which permit a faster growth rate than the nursery grounds. The emphasis is on maximum production per unit of cost, time, and area. These culture methods are practiced primarily in the Chesapeake and Delaware Bays and along the Louisiana coast. Oyster fishermen may harvest a "crop" of 100 bushels per acre under satisfactory conditions.

Since the adult oyster is sessile, and therefore has an extremely limited home range, it is more readily domesticated than forms, such as fish, which are highly motile. Researchers of the U.S. Bureau of Commercial Fisheries have been experimenting with a mode of oyster culture adapted from the Japanese. The Bureau has established a series of artificial, brackish water ponds. Racks placed in the ponds bear thousands of clam shells strung on submerged wires. In this way the researchers utilize the vertical dimension of the habitat as well as merely the two-dimensional ocean floor in providing suitable substratum on which oyster larvae can become established, thereby substantially increasing the carrying capacity of a given volume of oyster habitat. In Japan oyster culturists suspend shells from mobile rafts which can be towed to "plankton

Figure 12–11 Experimental oyster raft. Mollusc shells are attached to the submerged ropes, thus providing an optimal substratum for oyster larvae establishment. Bureau of Commercial Fisheries Biological Laboratory, Oxford, Maryland. [Bureau of Commercial Fisheries, U.S. Department of the Interior]

pastures" of suitable density for maximal oyster growth. Much of the ER which normally confronts oyster populations under natural conditions is reduced by this type of culture. For example, the ravages of bottom-feeding predators, such as starfish, are minimized. By such methods Japanese culturists have been able to secure an annual yield of 13,000 pounds of oyster meat per acre. Such a high meat yield cannot be matched by livestock ranchers on land except under the most optimal conditions.

Marine Mammals

The marine fisheries resource includes whales, porpoises, walruses, sea otters, dugongs, manatees, and fur seals. Through the centuries these sea-going mammals have provided man with a variety of valuable materials—food and furs, bones and tusks for the fashioning of tools, ornaments, and illuminating oil. Here we shall consider the conservation and ecology of two marine mammals, the fur seals and whales.

Alaskan Fur Seal (*Callorhinus ursinus***).** Fur seals may be observed during the winter season about ten to fifty miles off the California coast, feeding primarily on squids and small fish, frequently diving up to 180 feet. After feeding they may float leisurely on the surface of the sea, making "parasols" out of their flippers in order to get some protection from the bright sun. The fur seal annually migrates between its breeding grounds in the Pribilof (300 miles west of Alaska) and Commander Islands in the Bering Sea, and its wintering areas along the Japanese and California coasts. These journeys may be several thousand miles long.

BREEDING. This species shows marked sexual dimorphism; the ponderous bulls attain a weight of 500 to 700 pounds, the relatively puny cows weigh only 50 to 100 pounds. Many bulls may be fully ten times the weight of their cows. The sexually mature bulls (which usually overwinter near the Gulf of Alaska) arrive on the breeding grounds in late May or early June, before the snow has melted (24). They immediately stake out territories up to 40 feet in diameter close to the ocean shore. These territories are vigorously defended throughout the two-month breeding season. During this time the bulls take no nourishment and gradually slim down; some of them lose one third of their original weight. Territorial defense is a vicious business and occasionally results in the death of a badly gored rival. The younger bachelor bulls move somewhat farther inland and generally assume "bachelor societies" sometimes numbering many hundreds of individuals. The cows give birth to a single pup immediately after returning from their wintering grounds off the California coast, and are bred by the harem master within one to two weeks. Each territorial harem master may have from ten to sixty females. Periodically the cow will leave her pup to feed ravenously in the open ocean up to 100 miles from her home territory. Eventually returning, she instinctively seeks out and locates her own pup (from the hundreds of similar pups) and nurses it with her rich milk.

ENVIRONMENTAL RESISTANCE. The fur seal is plagued by a number of large predators such as the sharks and killer whales. A large killer whale may swallow a baby seal whole. Up to twenty-four have been found in the stomach of a single killer whale. A minute parasitic roundworm causes the death of almost one in every five pups on the breeding grounds. In 1964 roughly 22,000 pups died from one cause or another on St. Paul Island alone.

However, the greatest seal killer is man himself. In 1786, when the Russians discovered the Pribilof Island seal herd, seals on the island numbered at least 2.5 million (24). However, early in this century the Pribilof Island fur seal was almost extinct. Much of the decline was due to the environmental resistance exerted by the combined commercial sealeries of Japan, Russia, Canada, and the United States. The technique of pelagic sealing was especially destructive, for the animals were hunted during their migrations through the waters of the open ocean. Sealers would stealthily sneak up on the unsuspecting animals in canoes, a trick learned from the Indians of British Columbia. In the late nineteenth century, pelagic sealing rapidly expanded, and by 1879, 70-ton schooners were transporting hunters and canoes to sealing areas. About half of the kill from pelagic sealing was made up of pregnant cows. Almost 1 million skins were taken in the open ocean between 1868, when Alaska was annexed by the United States, and 1909. Under intense hunting pressure of this type, by 1910 the Pribilof herd decreased from an original 2.5 million to 130,000.

PROTECTION AND MANAGEMENT. The situation was so serious that in 1911 it prompted the formation of the North Pacific Fur Seal Convention, composed of Japan, Russia, Canada, and the United States. This convention prohibited pelagic sealing (except by aborigines using primitive weapons) and instituted other badly needed restrictions on the seal harvest. Studies of the life history and ecology of the fur seal have been pursued by biologists of the U.S. Fish and Wildlife Service and have provided a "shore" of facts upon which a remarkably successful management program has been based. It was learned, for example, that the newborn have a 1 to 1 sex ratio; hence, because these seals are a polygynous species, a number of bulls could be harvested annually with no adverse effect on the herd (24). Currently, the United States has sole responsibility for the administration and harvest of the Pribilof herd. According to international agreement the United States gives 15 per cent of the annual harvest each to Canada and Japan. Although normally only the three-year-old bachelor bulls are taken (at the end of the breeding season), in 1964, in order to reduce slightly the burgeoning herd, all bachelors were taken regardless of age, as well as 16,000 cows. As a result of sound international management of the herd, the Alaskan fur seal herd now represents about 80 per cent of the world's fur seal population.

In 1964 the United States sold 64,206 skins which had an aggregate value of $4.6 million; the average value of a dressed, dyed, and finished bull skin was $105. After the valuable skins had been removed by a highly skilled seventy-one-man crew of Pribilof and Aleutian island natives, the stripped carcasses were processed into frozen ground meat, over 1.6 million pounds of which were sold as mink food to fur farmers (24). Since 1939 the Pribilof herd has sustained an average annual harvest of 69,000 skins (24).

Whales.　Whales range in size from the 3-foot porpoise to the blue whale (*Balaenoptera musculus*), which attains a length of 93 feet and is the largest known animal, including those of prehistory. In 1926 an 89-foot female blue, 10 feet in diameter, was killed in the Antarctic. It was butchered, dismembered, and weighed piece by piece by the Japanese whaling crew and found to have a total weight of 300,707 pounds, or over 150 tons. It yielded over 56 tons of steak.

Whales may be divided into two major groups on the basis of feeding methods—the toothed whales and the baleen whales. The toothed whales include the porpoises, killer whales, and sperm whales, which feed primarily on octopi, squid, fish, and marine mammals. The killer whales (*Grampus sp.*) hunt in packs and may pursue a large baleen whale very much like a pack of timber wolves follow a deer. Aquatic birds and small seals may be swallowed whole. Whales frequently dive to considerable depths in their search for prey; a sperm whale (*Physeter catodon*) was found tangled up in a submarine cable off the northern coast of South America at a depth exceeding 3,700 feet. At least fourteen cases of such sperm whale–submarine cable entanglements have been reported (14). (Some recorded dive durations for several whales are: sperm whale seventy-five minutes, blue whale fifty minutes, bottle-nosed whale 120 minutes (17). Occasionally sperm whales will void a compacted mass of feces known as ambergris, long valued as a perfume base. In 1953 a 926-pound lump washed up on an Australian beach and was sold for $120,000 (6).

The baleen whales include the gray whale (*Eschrichtius gibbosus*), right whale (*Eubalaena sp.*), humpback whale (*Megaptera novae angliae*), and finback (*Balaenoptera physalus*), among others. The baleen whales bear a series of 200 to 300 horny plates which extend downward from the upper jaw and serve as a mechanism for filtering plankton. Investigations over the last thirty-five years have shown that many baleen whales, including the fin and blue whales, feed almost exclusively on *Euphausia superba*, a minute crustacean. Almost a ton of these minute creatures have been found in a blue whale's stomach. Hardy and Gunther (1936) have shown a close correlation between *Euphausia* concentrations and whale abundance as indicated by catches (12). Sverdrup et al. (1946) have shown similar correlations west of Greenland involving sperm, blue, fin, sei, and humpback whales (32).

On the basis of the annually formed laminations in the waxy sound-conducting plug superimposed on the eardrum of whalebone whales, a life span of at least fifty years has been recorded for some individuals. Whale age may also be determined on the basis of seasonal growth variations of the baleen plates, as well as by the number of corpora albicantia in the ovary.

CALIFORNIA GRAY WHALE (*Eschrichtius gibbosus*). The one species that man has a fairly good chance of observing is the far-sojourning California gray whale. At Point Loma, California, where the National Park Service conducts a Public Whale Watch, hundreds are observed during their annual migration. The gray is thirty to fifty feet long, weighs about twenty tons, and is perhaps the best-known whale along the Pacific coast. Its 10,000-mile round-trip migrations are the longest of any mammal in the world. After spending the summer in the North Pacific, Arctic Ocean, and Bering Sea, the grays move southward to their wintering lagoons off the west coast of Baja California. There, in the shallow, warm, placid waters the cow gives birth to a single calf about 15 feet long and weighing half a ton. Mating occurs shortly thereafter and the impregnated cows, along with the bulls and calves, migrate to their Arctic summer home, traveling at an average speed of about seven miles per hour and arriving at their northern destination in April.

Originally occurring all along the Atlantic coast in considerable numbers, the ill-fated gray whale apparently was eradicated in this region because of relentless persecution by the whaling industry in the nineteenth century. Around 1850, observers in the San Diego, California, region, could easily spot 1,000 of these magnificent mammals in a single day as they made their way to the wintering grounds. However, intensive slaughter by overzealous whalers who shamelessly harpooned pregnant female grays right on the calving grounds caused the apparent extinction of the Pacific Coast population as well. Much to the delighted surprise and amazement of marine biologists and naturalists everywhere, the whales suddenly reappeared off the California coast early in the twentieth century. Dr. Carl Hubbs, eminent ichthyologist and marine biologist, estimated the population along our Pacific Coast by 1949 to be in the neighborhood of 3,000 animals. Although the species is certainly no longer in danger of extinction, it is still on the protected list.

WHALING INDUSTRY.   In 1846, when the American whaling industry was at its peak, a fleet of 746 ships, with an aggregate capacity of 233,000 tons and representing a capital investment of roughly $20 million, sailed the seas and netted the industry $7 million annually from the sale of whale oil and whale bone. Whale bone, which once commanded a price of $5,000 a ton, was originally used in the manufacture of everything from brushes to corset stays, from umbrella ribs to hoop skirts and buggy whips. These were the days when a whale had at least a fighting chance of survival, when the major weapon was the harpoon, hurled by the steady, muscular arm of the whaler. However, in the 1860's, when the Norwegians began to employ steamship, winch, and harpoon-cannon, the industry soon made up in efficiency what it lost in color.

The modern whaling industry employs two basic types of vessels, the factory ship and the catcher boat. The factory ship, or "mother" ship, hauls the dead whales aboard and butchers, dismembers and processes them with the aid of highly specialized machinery. The whale products are virtually packaged, frozen, or canned, ready for sale, even before the ship returns to port. The other vessel is the catcher, or "killer," boat. There are about twelve such boats for each mother ship; they are equipped with the harpoon cannon and do the actual pursuit and killing. Helicopters and special sonar facilitate their location. Once a whale is located the catcher ships move out for the kill, sometimes ranging as far as 100 miles from the mother vessel.

Today the whaling fleets of Norway, West Germany, U.S.S.R., Japan, Great Britain, and South Africa are composed of around twenty factory ships and 240 small 900-ton killer boats. The industry employs 15,000 men. Factory ship tonnage increased dramatically from 12,000 tons in 1935 to 586,000 tons in 1960, a forty-sevenfold increase in only twenty-five years.

In 1964 the American whaling industry operated only three shore stations, two at Point San Pablo, California, and one at Warrenton, Oregon. Operating from April to November, these stations took in a total of 274 whales of seven species, including 147 fin whales, sixty-four sperm, twenty-seven humpbacks, twenty grays, thirteen sei, two blues, and one bottlenose. The fin whale harvest was the largest in twenty-five years, largely because of the great abundance of *krill*, composed principally of the minute crustacean *Euphausia pacifica*, which attracted the finbacks to the San Francisco area. Because of obviously depleted stocks, the humpback take in 1964 was only half that of 1963. The twenty grays were taken under a special permit for research purposes. In aggregate these whales were processed into 3.3 million pounds of meal, 3.2 million pounds of oil, and 4.5 million pounds of canned and frozen meat for use as animal food. The total value of these whale-derived products in 1964 was $734,000, a 35 per cent increase over the 1963 take.

The world's whale population has slowly but surely been depleted by man. The blue whale has declined from 76 per cent of the catch in 1930–1931 to less than 6 per cent of the catch in the 1950's. Each year since 1956, despite the most advanced techniques of locating and killing, there has been a steady decline in the whale harvest. This decline has continued despite the protective regulations formulated and accepted by the seventeen nations of the International Whaling Commission that was organized in 1946. The commission made it illegal for factory ships to operate in the calving grounds, and restrictions were put on total annual catch of each species. The commission employs the "whale unit" as the basis for regulating catch. Thus, one unit is equivalent to one blue whale, two finbacks, two and one-half humpbacks, or six sei whales. In addition to these restrictions, the whaling commission has zoned the ocean waters in such a way that the species most endangered secure at least partial sanctuary from the whalers.

Notwithstanding these regulations, the future is grim for these goliaths of the sea. One reason is that the rules of the International Whaling Commission are not always respected. Thus, even though the commission recommended that the take in 1964–1965 be limited to 4,000 units, the fleets of U.S.S.R., Norway, and Japan brashly set up their own combined quota of

8,000 units. Although fifteen of their factory ships operated from December to April, they succeeded in taking only 7,000 units, most of them being sei whales. In 1965, the U.S.S.R. and Japan, which conduct most of the pelagic whaling, were signatories to an agreement to curtail the catch sufficiently to permit replenishment. This might ultimately allow a sustained annual harvest of 20,000 finbacks and 5,000 blues. Whales have been hunted for at least 1,000 years. However, unless Japan and Russia live up to the stringent conservation measures they have formulated, some whale species may well go the way of the dinosaur and saber-toothed cat.

BIBLIOGRAPHY

1. Allen, Shirley W., and Justin W. Leonard. *Conserving Natural Resources.* New York: McGraw-Hill Book Company, 1966, 253 pp.
2. Bardach, John. *Harvest of the Sea.* New York: Harper & Row, Publishers, 1968, 301 pp.
3. Bearden, Charles M. "Salt Water Impoundments for Game Fish in South Carolina," *Prog. Fish-Culturist* **29** (1967), 123–128.
4. Bureau of Commercial Fisheries. *Report of the Bureau of Commercial Fish Biological Laboratory, Galveston, Texas., Fiscal Year 1966. Circular 268.* Washington, D.C.: U.S. Fish and Wildlife Service, 1967.
5. Chapman, Wilbert McLeod. "Politics and the Marine Fisheries," *The Fisheries of North America, Circular No. 250.* Washington, D.C.: U.S. Bureau of Commercial Fisheries, 1966.
6. Cromie, William J. *The Living World of the Sea.* Englewood Cliffs, N.J.: Prentice-Hall, Inc., 1966, 343 pp.
7. Deuel, David G., and John R. Clark. "The 1965 Saltwater Angling Survey," *Resource Publication No. 67.* Washington, D.C.: Bureau of Sport Fisheries and Wildlife, 1968.
8. Eggvin, Jens. "The Possibility of Forecasting Oceanographic Conditions in Northwest European Waters and Their Significance for Fisheries," *International Commission of Northwest Atlantic Fish Special Publication No. 6.* (1965), 903–907.
9. Ellison, W. A. "The Menhaden," in H. F. Taylor (ed.) *Survey of Marine Fisheries of North Carolina.* Chapel Hill, N.C.: The University of North Carolina Press, 1951, pp. 85–107.
10. Galtsoff, Paul S. "The American Oyster," *Fishery Bulletin of the U.S. Fish and Wildlife Service, No. 64.* Washington, D.C.: U.S. Fish and Wildlife Service, 1964.
11. Hardy, Sir Alistair. *Fish and Fisheries.* Boston: Houghton Mifflin Co., 1959, 322 pp.
12. Hardy, A. C., and E. R. Gunther. "Plankton of the South Georgia Whaling Grounds and Adjacent Waters, 1926–1927," *Discovery Reports,* **11** (1936), 1–456.
13. Hardy, A. C. *The Open Sea.* London: Collins, 1957.
14. Heezen, B. C. "Whales Caught in Deep-Sea Cables," *Deep-Sea Research,* **4** (1957), 105–115.
15. Herald, Earl S. *Living Fishes of the World.* Garden City, N.Y.: Doubleday & Co., 1961, 304 pp.

16. Highsmith, Richard M., J. Granville Jensen, and Robert D. Rudd. *Conservation in the United States.* Chicago: Rand McNally and Co., 1962, 322 pp.
17. Irving, L. "Respiration in Diving Mammals," *Physiol. Rev.,* **19** (1939), 112–134.
18. Kabata, Z. "The Scientist, the Fisherman and the Parasite," *Scottish Fisheries Bull.,* 4 (1955).
19. Marshall, N. B. *The Life of Fishes.* Cleveland: The World Publishing Co., 1966, 402 pp.
20. Marx, Wesley. *The Frail Ocean.* New York: Coward McCann, Inc., 1967, 248 pp.
21. Nikolsky, G. V. *The Ecology of Fishes.* New York: Academic Press, 1963, 352 pp.
22. Odum, Eugene P. *Fundamentals of Ecology.* Philadelphia: W. B. Saunders Co., 1959, 546 pp.
23. Power, E. A. *Fisheries of the United States, 1963.* Washington, D.C.: Division of Resource Development, Department of the Interior, 1964.
24. Riley, Francis. "Fur Seal Industry of the Pribilof Islands, 1786–1965," *Bureau of Commercial Fisheries Circular No. 275.* (1967).
25. Schaefer, Milner B. "Oceanography and the Marine Fisheries," *The Fisheries of North America.* Washington, D.C.: Bureau of Commercial Fisheries, 1966.
26. ———. "Problems of Quality and Quantity in the Management of the Living Resources of the Sea," in S. V. Ciriacy-Wantrup and James J. Parsons (eds.), *Natural Resources: Quality and Quantity.* Berkeley: University of California Press, 1967, 87–101.
27. Sette, O. E. "Biology of the Atlantic Mackerel (*Scomber scombrus*) of North America," *Fish. Bull. 50.* Washington, D.C.: U.S. Fish and Wildlife Service, 1943, 149–227.
28. Shippen, Herbert H., and Miles S. Alton. "Predation upon Pacific Hake, *Merluccius productus,* by Pacific Dogfish, *Squalus acanthias,*"
29. Smith, Guy-Harold (ed.). *Conservation of Natural Resources.* New York: John Wiley and Sons, Inc., 1965.
30. Smith, Robert L. *Ecology and Field Biology.* New York: Harper & Row, Publishers, 1966, 686 pp.
31. Squire, James L., Jr. "Progress in Sport Fishery Research," *Resource Publication No. 39.* Washington, D.C.: Bureau of Sport Fisheries and Wildlife, 1967.
32. Sverdrup, H. U., M. W. Johnson, and R. H. Fleming. *The Oceans, Their Physics, Chemistry and General Biology.* New York: Prentice-Hall, Inc., 1942, 1087 pp.
33. Thorson, G. "Marine Level-Bottom Communities of Recent Seas, Their Temperature Adaptation and Their 'Balance' Between Predators and Food Animals," *Trans. N.Y. Acad. Sci.,* Ser. 2, **18,** 8 (1956).
34. Unger, Iris. "Artificial Reefs," *Special Publication, Amer. Litt. Soc., No. 4.* Highlands, N.J.: American Littoral Society, 1966, 74 pp.
35. U.S. Fish and Wildlife Service. *Fishery Statistics of the United States. Annual Report.* Washington, D.C.: Department of Commerce, 1968.
36. ——— *Fishery Statistics of the United States. Annual Report.* Washington, D.C.: Department of Commerce, 1969.
37. Warinner, J. E., and M. L. Brehmer. "The Effects of Thermal Effluents on Marine Organisms," *Inter. Jour. Air and Water Pollution,* **10** (1966), 277–289.
38. Zilberberg, Mark H. "Seasonal Occurrence of Fishes in a Coastal Marsh of Northwest Florida," *Univ. Tex. Inst. Mar. Sci. Publications,* **11** (1966), 126–134.

13 The Pesticide Problem

Causes of Pests

In undisturbed ecosystems there exist naturally occurring regulatory mechanisms (see Chapter 2) which keep population levels of a species at a point of equilibrium. However, whenever the original ecosystem becomes restructured by man, it tends to become simplified, with a resultant disruption of the stabilizing influences of density-dependent regulatory factors. The removal of forests to make way for freeways; the conversion of a swamp into a front lawn or a prairie into a golf course; the establishment of monotypic agriculture—that is, fields composed of a single species where originally their existed a natural ecosystem including several dozen plant species—all are examples of human intervention that tends to simplify the ecosystem. The net result is a man-made ecosystem characterized by high populations of a few species, in marked contrast to the original ecosystem which was characterized by lesser populations of many species. In such biologically simplified ecosystems, a given organism may achieve "pest" status even though in the original diversified ecosystem it was never of economic concern. Let us give an exaggeratedly simple example. In the simplified ecosystem, organism X may be controlled by only one important predator (A). Any environmental change which would depress the population of predator A would, of course, result in a population surge of organism X. In the event that X attains a population level where it becomes detrimental to man—for example, as a transmitter of disease or as a destoryer of crops—it then may be classified as a pest. On the other hand, in the original biologically diversified ecosystem, relatively unaltered by man, organism X might well have been controlled, not only by predator A, but by predators B and C, and a number of parasites and competitors as well.

In the more diversified ecosystem, it is readily apparent that a decrease in predator A might conceivably be countered by a concurrent increase in predator B, especially if they were competitors, so that regulatory pressure on species X would be maintained. As a result of the dynamic interaction of species populations, fluctuations within simplified (disturbed) ecosystems tend to be intensified, whereas those within a diversified ecosystem tend to be dampened.

Secondly, pests may become established in an ecosystem simply because they have been introduced from abroad. In so doing, man unwittingly releases them from their agents of control. Thus, of the 200 weed species regarded by the 1895 *Yearbook of Agriculture* as seriousiy detrimental to crops, 108 (54 per cent) were exotics (17).

Thirdly, an organism may achieve pest status as a result of man's changing cultural patterns. For example, the lygus bug is considered a major pest to the lima bean industry because of the blotches it leaves on an occasional bean; nevertheless, prior to the era of frozen food processing, lygus bugs were considered of minor economic import (20).

Organic Pesticide Industry

Prior to World War II most pesticides were unstable inorganic compounds (such as copper sulfate), which decomposed into their harmless components shortly after application. Organic pesticides were primarily derived from plant tissues. Thus, pyrethrium was obtained from chrysanthemums, nicotine from tobacco, and rotenone from the roots of tropical Asiatic legumes. Since World War II, however, the great majority of pesticides have been organic compounds synthesized in chemical laboratories. Many of these, such as the chlorinated hydrocarbons, are *nonbiodegradable*; they may remain intact for many years in either water or soil (5).

The organic pesticide industry burgeoned at a fantastic rate in the immediate postwar years. Sales mushroomed from $40 million in 1939 to $300 million in 1959 and are expected to reach the $2 billion mark by 1975. By 1963 over 0.25 billion pounds of DDT were produced globally. In 1966 over 8,000 firms were making 60,000 different formulations from 500 basic pesticides. In addition to insecticides, other types such as herbicides, defoliants, fungicides, and miticides have been added. Escalating sales may be attributed to such factors as changing agricultural technology and farm ownership patterns (consolidations) but also to a multimillion dollar advertising assault via all the communications media employed by big business. The use of pesticides will probably continue to expand because of the food requirements of a burgeoning world population and the implementation of insect vector control projects in underdeveloped countries.

Contamination of Ecosystems

Dr. George M. Woodwell, chief ecologist at the Atomic Energy Commission's Brookhaven National Laboratory on Long Island, brands pesticidal contamination as the world's most serious pollution problem. In the United States alone about 400 million acres are treated with pesticides annually. According to Rudd, in merely five control campaigns, against the spruce budworm (United States and Canada), gypsy moth (Northeastern United States), Japanese beetle (Mid-Atlantic, Central United States), Dutch elm disease (Northeastern and Central United States), and the fire ant (Southeastern United States), pesticides were applied to almost 5 *million acres* (18). In addition they are liberally applied to forests, rangeland, residential lawns and gardens, golf links, and parks. Local concentrations of these chemicals in the human environment sometimes approach alarming proportions. For example, a Tennessee farmer reported making sixteen applications of 35 to 40 pounds of pesticides per acre, or an aggregate of 560 to 640 pounds per acre per season (5). These chemicals may gradually seep downward into groundwater aquifers, or they may be washed into streams by run-off. According to the U.S. Public Health Service, all major river basins in North America are polluted with dieldrin, endrin, and DDT. As Dr. Woodward of the U.S. Public Health Service has warned "these chemicals are undesirable additives to water and every effort should be made to keep their concentration not only below the threshold of any toxic effects but also as low as is reasonably possible." Not only have pesticides polluted terrestrial and freshwater ecosystems, but they are being cycled inexorably into the marine environment. Food and Drug Administration chemists have found insecticide

Figure 13–1 Sediment and soil samples are collected in the monitoring area here with a hand-operated corer to help scientists of the Agricultural Research Service, U.S. Department of Agriculture, study the impact of pesticides on the environment. Twenty-five cores are collected in a bucket and mixed together by a sifting process. One gallon of the mixture is then shipped to a laboratory at Gulfport, Mississippi, in a sealed can for analysis. [U.S. Department of Agriculture]

levels of more than 10 parts per million in twelve of thirty-eight marine fish oils. Trace amounts (parts per billion) of DDT have even been detected in the fatty tissues of seals and Adelie penguins from the Antarctic (15).

Classification of Pesticides

The following artificial classification of extensively used pesticides has been adapted from Rudd (18).

ORGANIC PHOSPHATE COMPOUNDS. Examples of organic phosphate compounds are parathion and malathion. These chemicals inhibit the production of cholinesterase at the junctions between adjoining nerve cells. Because cholinesterase normally has the function of breaking down acetylcholine, a substance normally secreted by nerve cell axons when they are "fired," organic phosphate pesticides cause an excessive accumulation of acetylcholine, which tends to interfere with impulse transmission. Extreme muscular weakness, tremors, and dizziness are common symptoms in poisoned mammals. Fish and other aquatic organisms are apparently little affected.

CHLORINATED HYDROCARBONS. Examples of chlorinated hydrocarbons are DDT, dieldrin, and aldrin. The effects of these pesticides on animals are quite varied. However, DDT, the most extensively and abundantly employed, primarily affects the central nervous system. Symptoms in poisoned animals include increased excitability, muscular tremors, and convulsions. DDT residues frequently accumulate in fatty tissues (subcutaneous fat and fatty tissue of the mesenteries, heart, liver, thyroid gland, and gonads). With long-continued ingestion of contaminated foods, the DDT concentration in the fatty depots gradually increases. Residues may be released from these storage areas when stored fat is required as an energy source during periods of stress, as when the animal is engaged in strenuous physical activity (as a migration) or faced with food deprivation. Fish and other aquatic organisms are killed by chlorinated hydrocarbons because of impaired oxygen diffusion through gill membranes. Chlorinated hydrocarbons are quite resistant to biological disintegration by bacteria in either water or soil; in other words they are nonbiodegradable. It has been suggested by some authorities that DDT molecules may remain intact in ecosystems for twenty-five years. In clay-rich soils both DDT and dieldrin are less liable to contaminate food chains because they tend to be fixed by being bound to clay particles (15).

ARSENICAL COMPOUNDS. In poisoned animals arsenical compounds usually cause acute gastric disturbances, diarrhea, convulsions, and death. Malfunctions of both liver and kidneys are common in poisoned animals.

RODENTICIDES. Sodium fluoroacetate is an extremely hazardous pesticide which results in hyperstimulation of the central nervous system (brain and spinal cord) and interferes with heart action. Because it is highly stable in protoplasm, it may be transferred in food chains.

WARFARIN. Rather safe to use, warfarin acts as an anticoagulant, depressing levels of prothrombin, a blood protein essential for blood clotting. Repeated intake of warfarin, therefore, eventually results in death from internal hemorrhaging.

HERBICIDES. The most extensively employed of the herbicides is 2,4-D, which causes plant death by accelerating growth rates. 2,4-D can be quite selective because it is much more effective on broad-leaved weeds (such as plantain) than on narrow-leaved crops (wheat, barley).

FUNGICIDES. Many fungicides, especially those applied to seed grain, contain the element mercury. The accidental ingestion of this mercury (via food chains) may cause brain damage, kidney and liver malfunction, and death. During 1970 the U.S. Public Health Service beçame increasingly concerned with the relatively high concentrations found in the major rivers of at least twenty states. In some states, such as Wisconsin, anglers were warned against the excessive consumption of fish taken in mercury-contaminated waters.

Effect of Pests on Human Welfare

Pests cause irritation, mental anguish, pain, sickness, economic damage, and even death. Consider these items: The annual damage caused by rodents, insects, and weeds in the United States is $2, $4, and $11 billion, respectively (18). Ten per cent of the average annual cotton crop in the United States is destroyed by a single insect species—the cotton boll weevil. From 1940 to 1944 the codling moth caused a 15 per cent annual loss to American apple crops, equivalent to a $25 million setback (10). The U.S. Forest Service reported in 1958 that insects inflicted mortality losses of 5 billion board feet annually as well as growth losses of 3.6 billion board feet. Among serious diseases transmitted to man by insect vectors are sleeping sickness, tularemia, dysentery, bubonic plague, typhus, Chaga's disease, Q fever, and Rocky Mountain spotted fever (17). According to Dr. E. F. Knipling of the U.S. Department of Agriculture mosquito-borne diseases alone are annually responsible for more than 100 million cases of illness throughout the world (17).

Benefits Derived from Insecticides. It is no wonder, therefore, why mankind hailed the insecticidal properties of DDT during the years immediately after World War II. It is an excellent insect killer as are the numerous other insecticides that have been produced by the pesticide industry in the past two decades. There is no doubt that modern insecticides have been a boon to the agriculturist and have sharply decreased mortality caused by insect-transmitted diseases. Thus, Rudd reports that in Texas cotton bollworm control increased yields from 7,203 to 7,860 pounds and yielded a gain of $126.50 per acre (18). Weed control in a North Dakota barley field boosted yield from 45.5 to 49.5 bushels per acre, and resulted in a per acre gain of $5 (18).

According to Dr. A. W. A. Brown, writing in the *World Review of Pest Control*, DDT campaigns in Ceylon reduced human mortality by 34 per cent in a single year (21). They have been instrumental in controlling malaria, which at one time had such a high incidence that in 1938 Dr. Ralph Buchsbaum could state: "At least *half* the people who die, from all causes, are probably killed directly or indirectly by malaria" (3).

Impact of Rachel Carson's "Silent Spring"

During the years just before 1962 a number of scientists became apprehensive about the implications of continued massive release of the nonbiodegradable pesticides into ecosystems of which fish, birds, mammals and man himself were integral components. They advanced the thesis that even though the short-term effects of pesticides were admittedly good, the long-term impact on the flow of nutrients and energy through the ecosystem's well-ordered but sensitive channels might be exceedingly adverse—for both wildlife and man. Most of these people were either ridiculed or ignored, not only by other scientists but by the prospering pesticide manufacturers. As a result, the average citizen was little aware that the wave of pesticide control might carry with it certain subtle effects deleterious to man. Then, in 1962, Rachel Carson, a distinguished marine biologist of the U.S. Fish and Wildlife Service, gave *Silent Spring* to the American public. Widely acclaimed throughout the nation, it precipitated a controversy which raged for years and even now has not completely abated. Miss Carson slashed through the arguments of the propesticide people. She presented the pesticide industry as an industrial colossus inflicting environmental abuse on an unsuspecting society with little regard for future consequences and with primary interest in immediate monetary gains. This was disturbingly reminiscent of the "cut-out-and-get-out" tactics of the early lumber barons at the turn of the century or of the abuse wrought on our prairies by the wheat farmers of the 1930's.

Cycling of Pesticides in the Ecosystem

To elucidate the mechanisms by which pesticide residues may eventually have detrimental effects on other than target organisms, we cite two case histories.

Case History One: Dutch Elm Disease Control. The American elm is a stately tree, providing beauty and shade for countless urban dwellers, gracing parks, boulevards, and college cam-

Figure 13–2 Washington, D.C., near the Jefferson Memorial. The branches of an American elm tree are cut off as the first step in destroying the tree, infected with Dutch elm disease. The tree has witnessed the passing of twelve Presidents and several generations of Washingtonians. It will take eighty years to grow another tree of this size. [U.S. Department of Agriculture]

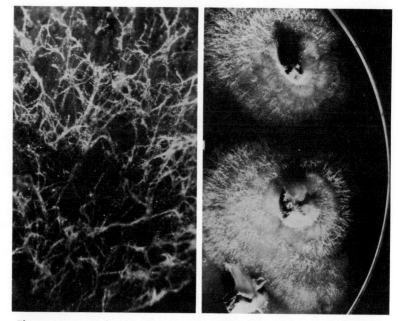

Figure 13–3 (*Left*) Mycelium growing from spores of Dutch elm disease over surface of agar in a Petri plate. (*Right*) Chips of wood infected with Dutch elm disease in agar culture in a Petri plate, with fungus growing on them. [U.S. Department of Agriculture]

puses, and supplying cover, food, and nesting sites for many species of birds. Today, many elms throughout the Midwest and Northeast are either dead or dying because of an exotic fungus accidentally introduced from Europe about 1933. This parasite plugs the tree's phloem tubes, thus interfering with food transport from leaves to roots. The spores of the fungus are effectively dispersed by minute brownish bark beetles, also of European origin. The first indications that elms are afflicted are premature (midsummer) leaf yellowing and defoliation. Although sanitary measures, such as the removal and burning of diseased trees, would be effective in controlling the disease, they are laborious and time consuming.

Under early recommendations from both federal and state agencies, thousands of municipalities initiated intensive DDT spray campaigns to control the elm disease. About 2 to 5 pounds of DDT are employed per tree, usually as a "sherry" (wettable DDT powder suspended in water), by means of spray trucks that project streams of the insecticide into elm canopies. Because DDT is lethal to the elm bark beetles, this method would seem excellent for halting the spread of the disease across mid-America. On the contrary, however, although such control campaigns have been mounted vigorously, by 1970 the disease

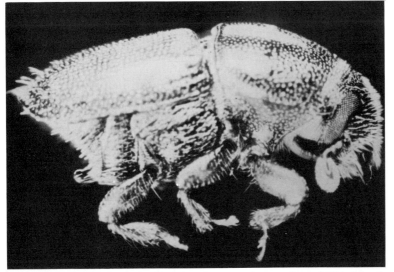

Figure 13-4 European elm bark beetle many times enlarged. This insect may transmit the spores of Dutch elm disease to healthy trees. [U.S. Department of Agriculture]

Figure 13-5 Washington, D. C. The work of the elm bark beetle is visible (short dark veins) where the bark has been cut from this tree. [U.S. Department of Agriculture]

had spread through most of the Northeast from Massachusetts south to Virginia and west to Minnesota.

In the wake of Dutch elm disease control, communities throughout the elm's range are not only experiencing "silent springs" but silent summers, autumns, and winters as well. Although it is extremely difficult if not impossible to prove, (dead animals were rarely observed in nature even before the advent of modern pesticide assaults), several authorities, including Dr. Robert L. Rudd, Professor of Zoology, University of California (Davis), are of the firm opinion that literally *millions* of birds in the United States have succumbed to DDT sprays intended for elm bark beetles.

In 1950 R. J. Barker and his colleagues initiated studies on the University of Illinois campus which revealed how DDT is concentrated as it is transferred from link to link of avian food chains (2). The data from his studies, and from those of George Wallace on the Michigan State University campus, provide insights into the events leading to avian mortality. Firstly, the concentration of the DDT in the home range of a bird may be so high immediately after spraying (remember that 2 to 5 pounds may be used per tree) that the bird dies shortly thereafter from ingesting contaminated foods, such as insects, worms, buds, and so on. Many bird watchers and biologists have observed the tremors and convulsions of dying birds in the wake of control programs.

Secondly, more subtly but perhaps more significantly, mortality results from the delayed expression of the pesticide. DDT remains on the elm leaf surface all summer long despite intermittent showers. After leaf fall in autumn the DDT, which is extremely stable, gradually becomes incorporated into the soil as the leaf fragments are decomposed by soil bacteria and fungi. Earthworms may subsequently become contaminated by ingesting leaf fragments. Tissue analysis of earthworms collected shortly after summer spraying revealed that *all* worms contained residues ranging from 4 parts per million in the nerve cord to 403 parts per million in the crop and gizzard. Of even greater interest, six earthworms secured six months *after* the last application averaged 86 part per million of DDT and 33 parts per million of DDE (a metabolic derivative of DDT).

Shortly after migrant birds return in the spring from their wintering grounds, they begin consuming contaminated worms. It has been estimated that the ingestion of eleven contaminated worms might be fatal to an adult robin—a quantity easily consumed by a hungry bird in less than an hour. The ingested DDT becomes stored and eventually concentrated in the animal's fatty tissues. Up to 120, 252 and 744 parts per million of DDE have been found in the heart, brain, and liver, respectively, of dead robins recovered after spray operations. If stored in the gonads, DDE may interfere with gonadal development and function. The reproductive capacity of the bird may be depressed by impairing fecundity, fertility, hatching success, or the vigor of the nestling. (As of 1970 several alternative methods of Dutch elm disease control were being investigated. One involved the interspersion of elms with other species such as sugar maple and ironwood. Other methods being studied included the development of resistant American-Siberian elm hybrids, the application of beetle-repellents, and the use of parasitic wasps.)

Case History Two: Gnat Control in California. Clear Lake, which is located only 90 miles from San Francisco, has been a favored waterfowl nesting area for many years. In autumn, hunters would converge on the 19-mile-long lake. In 1949 a combined state and federal program was launched to eradicate the tiny gnat which formed dense cloudlike swarms and proved irritating to fishermen and other vacationists. Fourteen thousand gallons of TDE, a chlorinated hydrocarbon, were applied to the lake to destroy the insect's early aquatic stages. The concentration of the insecticide was only 0.02 part per million. By 1957 two additional applications of TDE were made. A few years after the campaign was launched the bodies of dead fish, gulls, ducks, geese, and grebes began to litter the beaches. In particular, the breeding population of the western grebe, a handsome diving bird, was drastically reduced from 800 to only 30 pairs, a decrement of over 98 per cent. Wildlife officials, bird watchers, and hunters became alarmed.

In the ensuing investigation by Eldridge G. Hunt and Arthur I. Bischoff of the California Department of Fish and Game, the bodies of dead grebes were dissected but revealed no internal parasites which might have caused the deaths (13). However, chemical analysis of the gonads revealed high concentrations of TDE. Chemical studies of other organisms in the lake indicated further that the grebes became poisoned by way of the algae-crustacean-fish links in the food chain of which they formed the terminal link. The TDE was originally absorbed by the algae and then transferred with its molecular structure intact to successive links, each functioning as a *biological magnifier* of the pesticide. Thus, although the original concentration of the pesticide was only 0.02 part per million, the crustaceans showed 5 parts per million, the tissues of crustacean-consuming fish revealed several hundred parts per million, and the gonads of fish-eating grebes showed an astounding 1,600 parts per million of TDE, an 80,000-fold increase over the original concentration (13). Apparently the insecticide severely impaired grebe reproduction. One grebe egg finally hatched successfully in 1962 after ten years (1951–1961) of complete nesting failure. The insecticide has shown great persistence, 808 parts per million being found in the fat of grebes in 1963, six years after the last application.

Sublethal Effects of Pesticides on Wildlife

The death of a fish, bird, or mammal is a forthright event, obviously resulting in a population decrement of one. However, of possibly more profound import to a wild animal's population density are the subtle sublethal effects involving reduced vigor, modified behavior, retarded growth, and impaired reproductive function.

There is no evidence available from studies of natural populations that pesticide use has reduced their well-being or vigor. However, there is abundant presumptive evidence from laboratory tests. For example, many hydrocarbons (the chemical group to which DDT and dieldrin belong) are mutagenic in their action; that is, they are capable of inducing mutations in hereditary material. According to Rudd, geneticists employ such hydrocarbons to develop new crop strains. Experimental work by Dewitt has shown that when adult pheasants or quail are given long-sustained diets contaminated with sublethal amounts of chlorinated hydrocarbons, not only do they incur reduced vitality but they *pass this trait along to their progeny* (18).

Field observations reveal that even though wild animals may survive pesticidal exposure, their behavior patterns may be modified in such a way as to increase vulnerability to predators. This phenomenon has been recorded in insects, fish, birds, and meadow mice. Because of their need for increased oxygen, affected fish swim near the water's surface where they become easy prey for herons, egrets, and gulls. Shellhammer has shown a correlation between cholinesterase levels in the brain and learning ability in wild mice (19). By injecting the animals with parathion he was able to depress cholinesterase levels 25 to 50 per cent. Even though cholinesterase levels returned to normal three to four weeks later, the learning ability of the poisoned animals was impaired.

Surprisingly, DDT may actually have a stimulating effect on the reproductive processes of mites. Apparently certain nutrient elements in DDT such as nitrogen and phosphorus are first absorbed from the soil by the plant and metabolized. The mites then secure these nutrients from the plants. The ultimate

Figure 13–6 Newly hatched pheasant chicks. Experiments have shown that the ingestion of DDT-contaminated food greatly reduces the clutch size and hatching success in this species. [Wisconsin Conservation Department]

effect is enhanced reproductive rates in the mites. Thus, despite expensive attempts at chemical control, the result is a population surge of the target organism (18).

Pesticidal Effects on Fish. In recent years laboratory and field studies have been vigorously pursued to determine whether fish accumulate pesticide residues in their tissues, and if so, whether these residues are harmful. In 1961 and 1962 the U.S. Fish and Wildlife Service conducted experiments in artificial fish ponds at Tishomingo, Oklahoma, to determine the effects of aquatic weed control applications of 2,4-D on bluegill sunfish, a favored species for pond stocking in the South. Although 2,4-D was found to be 80 to 100 per cent effective in the control of such aquatic vegetation as potamogeton, cattail, and willow, it adversely affected bluegills inhabiting the ponds. Thus at a concentration of 10 parts per million the herbicide caused 19 per cent bluegill mortality in 1961 and 100 per cent in 1962. Moreover, the spawning of surviving fish was delayed for two weeks. Autopsies revealed damage to liver, blood vessels, and brain.

Researchers of Wisconsin's Department of Natural Resources

conducted a 1965–1967 survey of 2,673 fish of thirty-five species taken from inland lakes and streams as well as from the Mississippi River and Lakes Michigan and Superior (14). *Every fish sample contained DDT or a chemically related pesticide.* Seventy per cent of the fish were contaminated with dieldrin, another nonbiodegradable chlorinated hydrocarbon (14).

Various researchers have found correlations between pesticide residues in fish tissues and impaired fecundity, fertility, and growth rate. Such sublethal effects obviously may have as great significance in depressing fish populations as direct mortality itself. Recently Anderson and Peterson have reported that although DDT did not result in locomotor or visual impairment of experimental brook trout, it reduced their learning ability, that is, their ability to form an association between a connecting doorway and escape from electric shock (1).

Effect of Ingested Pesticides on Human Health

There is no doubt that the persistent pesticides, such as DDT, dieldrin, and endrin, under some conditions, may cause considerable wildlife mortality, especially among fish, waterfowl, gallinaceous birds (pheasants, grouse, and quail), and song birds (thrushes, warblers, and vireos). However, for many people who are not hunters, anglers, bird watchers or nature lovers, such mortality does not cause great concern. But what about man himself? This is the most controversial aspect of the pesticide problem. We shall adopt no affirmative or negative position here but attempt to present both sides of the question.

In 1964 Mississippi's Congressman Jamie L. Whitten participated in a pesticide symposium sponsored by the prestigious National Academy of Sciences-National Research Council. As chairman of the House Appropriations Subcommittee on Agriculture, he asked his investigations staff to collect data relating to pesticide effects on public health. His staff interviewed twenty-three physicians, officials of the American Medical Association, professors at university medical schools, and 185 outstanding scientists, including specialists in the fields of biology, biochemistry, nutrition, pharmacology, toxicology, conservation, agriculture, and public health. We shall list some of the main points elucidated by Congressman Whitten (22):

1. In a test conducted by scientists of the U.S. Public Health Service and the Food and Drug Administration, a dose of 0.027 ounce of DDT was ingested by a human volunteer without adverse effect. However, other volunteers have felt ill after ingesting the equivalent of 0.024 ounce for a 150-pound man. Of course, ingestion of greater doses of DDT

may prove fatal. Thus, four of twenty-three cases of DDT ingestion (fifteen of which involved attempted suicides) listed
in the 1951 Journal of the American Medical Association had
fatal results.

2. Dr. Wayland J. Hayes, Jr., toxicologist for the U.S. Public
   Health Service, stated at a Congressional hearing that the
   death rate from insecticide poisoning in the United States
   remained at one per million people ever since 1939 despite
   the widespread use of organic phosphates and chlorinated
   hydrocarbons since 1946.

3. At the Congress on Environmental Health Problems held by
   the American Medical Association in 1964, Robert Blackwell
   Smith, Jr., president of the Medical College of Virginia
   stated that he knew of "no evidence that the presence of pesticide residues in the human diet at or below tolerance
   levels, set by law on the basis of animal data, has had any
   adverse effect on the health of our citizens."

4. Although the ingestion of increased amounts of DDT results in a gradual increase in the amount stored in body tissues, an equilibrium is eventually reached at around 10 to
   12 parts per million. Reported by Dr. Hayes, these findings
   would appear to allay the apprehension, so eloquently artic-
   ulated by Rachel Carson, that pesticide residue might gradually build up to a threshold in human tissue that would
   result in some insidious malady with perhaps fatal consequences.

5. According to Frederick J. Stare, Harvard nutritionist, "there
   is not one medically documented instance of ill health in
   man, not to mention death, that can be attributed to the
   proper use of pesticides or even to their improper use as far
   as ill health from residues on foods."

6. Will DDT residues in the human body cause cancer? In an
   early study rats developed low-grade malignancies after
   eighteen months of DDT ingestion with food. However,
   because cancers have not subsequently been introduced in
   other test animals when purer forms of DDT were employed,
   it is assumed the cancers may have been induced by im-
   purities taken along with the DDT. Moreover, similar tumors
   can be induced simply by *overfeeding* the animals. One pesticide, DDD, chemically allied to DDT, has actually been
   used to *reduce* tumors of the adrenal cortex. Although liver
   tumors can indeed be induced in mice with the chlorinated
   hydrocarbons aldrin and dieldrin, they are benign. Amino-
   triazole, the herbicide responsible for the cranberry scare in
   1958, does cause thyroid growths in rats, considered to be
   cancerous by some; however, the Food and Drug Administration prohibits any residues of this chemical on foods.

It would appear from the preceding material that the threat of
pesticides to human health is more imagined than real, and that
there is little basis for controversy. Nothing is farther from the

truth. There are many highly regarded medical men, biologists, and ecologists who are definitely concerned despite assurances of the type just presented. Dr. Malcolm M. Hargraves, Senior Consultant of the Mayo Clinic, is of the belief that *more fatalities are caused by pesticides in the United States than by car accidents.* Antipesticide crusaders are apprehensive about the increasing contamination of human diets. It is almost impossible not to ingest pesticide residues today. A recent study by the Food and Drug Administration showed that 50 per cent of many thousands of food samples contained pesticide residues; not only this, but 3 per cent contained residues above the legally accepted levels. It is ironic that the U.S. Department of Agriculture has had to reimburse farmers more than $1 million since 1964 for dumping milk with DDT residues above the legal limits, when this very same department vigorously recommended the use of DDT.

One would suppose that tolerance limits set by the federal government would unquestionably fulfill their objective: the prevention of pesticide poisoning in man. However, Dr. Paul Ehrlich, distinguished Stanford biologist, scoffs at such naivety, "First of all most tolerances are set on the basis of short-term animal experiments and are set one poison at a time. Then, when it proves to be impossible to keep tolerances within limits, pressures are brought on the government, and the tolerances are conveniently raised."

Even though it has been suggested by American toxicologists that DDT residues in human tissues will stabilize at about 10 parts per million, up to 19.2 parts per million have been found in the fatty tissues of Israelis. The American public has been assured that pesticide residues in human tissues should be no cause for concern. Many knowledgeable people, however, are skeptical. Like Rachel Carson, their thoughts go something like this: "But do we really know? Perhaps no dire effects have been recorded to date. But the pesticide program is still in its infancy, and DDT residues have been present in human tissues for twenty-five years at most. How do we know that tissue storage of DDT for thirty or forty years will not ultimately result in serious affliction and death?" Such skepticism is often ridiculed by the propesticide forces as being the product of hysteria and emotionalism. But, as John Kormondy of Oberlin College recently stated, "no self-respecting ecologist can fail to note the high frequency of food sample contamination . . . the accelerating use of DDT (and of other pesticides), and the concentration phenomenon of DDT and other pesticides in the food chain. Not only is continued surveillance of pesticide levels a must as a matter of human health and safety,

Figure 13-7 Two team members study a map of a pesticide-monitoring area where scientists of the Agricultural Research Service, U.S. Department of Agriculture, are studying the impact of pesticides on the environment. In the background, members of a field team are bringing in a fish trap. [U.S. Department of Agriculture]

but investigations are needed of the effects of pesticides in all kinds of populations, even the human one" (15).

Biological Control of Pests

Although chemical control may indeed substantially reduce a pest population, it is frequently only a temporary success, followed by a resurgence of the pest to higher densities than before control was initiated. Moreover, the cost of this short-term success (in addition to the price of the chemicals) frequently is ecosystem contamination, widespread wildlife mortality, and the development of resistance in the target pest. In the view of many ecologists, a preferred alternative would be *biological control*, which may be defined as the conscious intensification of the density-dependent mechanisms (predation, parasitization, and so on) that continuously operate in natural ecosystems. Such control agents may be used in combination. Thus, Gerberich and Laird report that researchers are increasingly exploring ". . . the potentialities of employing combinations of fish that occupy different niches in the same biotope and complement one another as mosquito control agents, e.g., fish that feed on algae and other aquatic vegetation facilitate the access of predaceous species to larvae. This type of biotic activity can be termed "bio-synergistic," the combined effects of different biotic agents greatly exceeding the effect which either is able to produce alone (9)." To elucidate the nature and function of biological control, we shall cite two case histories.

Case History One: Control of a Rangeland Weed. St. John's wort is an *exotic*, which apparently was accidentally introduced from Europe to Washington, Oregon, and California in 1900. Originally established as widely scattered plants, it spread rapidly to form dense stands embracing many millions of acres. Attaining a height of 3 feet, this hardy perennial bears numerous clusters of bright yellow flowers. Because it can reproduce by rhizomes, it is extremely difficult to eradicate from otherwise valuable ranges. Poisonous substances are produced by a series of tiny black glands on the undersurface of the leaves.

The poison when ingested or touched results in sunburn and blistering. In severe cases open sores on the skin and head begin to swell, a condition known as "swellhead." Weight loss accompanied by diarrhea is common. Fatalities, although rare, may occur if the animal consumes 5 per cent of its body weight in plant tissue. Thus, a lethal meal for a 1,000-pound steer would be 50 pounds of St. John's wort.

Figure 13–8 Biological control. The larva of the wasp *Drendrosoter protuberan* feeds on the larva of an elm bark beetle here. Though much smaller than its host, it will suck the body juices of the beetle larva and eventually kill it. [U.S. Department of Agriculture]

Dr. Robert R. Humphrey, Professor of Range Management at the University of Arizona, describes the fascinating method by which this range pest has been brought under control. Although various methods had been attempted since its appearance in the United States, such as grubbing, plowing, burning, and spraying with herbicides, none of these were successful. Finally, in 1944 researchers at the University of California imported a tiny beetle from Australia. The adult and larvae of this beetle were known to feed exclusively on the stem and leaves of St. John's wort. The beetles were released in the Klamath River Valley of California, where St. John's wort (here known as the Klamath weed) had become a serious pest. In a relatively short time the beetle reduced the population of this weed until only a small remnant remained, no longer of any consequence as a range problem. In the case of a flare-up of the pest, the beetle population, responding to the increased food source, would also increase, once more bringing the St. John's wort under control. Of course, were the beetles to move to valuable forage grasses for an alternate food supply, their usefulness as a control agent would terminate. Fortunately, this has not occurred. (12).

Case History Two: Rabbit Control in Australia. The native Australian fauna is unique, being well represented by marsupials but almost completely lacking in placental mammals such as the wolf, fox, coyote, cougar, squirrel, and rabbit. Sheep were introduced to Australia in the nineteenth century. Today they form the basis of a multimillion dollar wool and mutton industry. Many of the flocks graze on semiarid ranges in the continental interior. Early in the twentieth century the European rabbit was introduced to Australia, apparently at the instigation of European immigrants who longed to indulge once again in their favorite sport of hunting the elusive brushland "bounders." Unfortunately, once they were introduced, their numbers sharply increased. Apparently there were no natural predators to serve as limiting factors in controlling their population surge.

As their numbers increased, the rabbits invaded sheep range. In the semiarid grasslands of interior Australia, forage never had been lush. Now, under the combined grazing pressure of both sheep and rabbits, the rangelands rapidly deteriorated. Grasses were clipped to ground level. The denuded earth became vulnerable. Dust clouds and sand dunes were the inevitable result. Faced with impending economic ruin, Australian ranchers banded together in an all-out effort to eradicate the rabbits. They tried all the conventional control methods. They poisoned. They trapped. They staged mammoth round-ups.

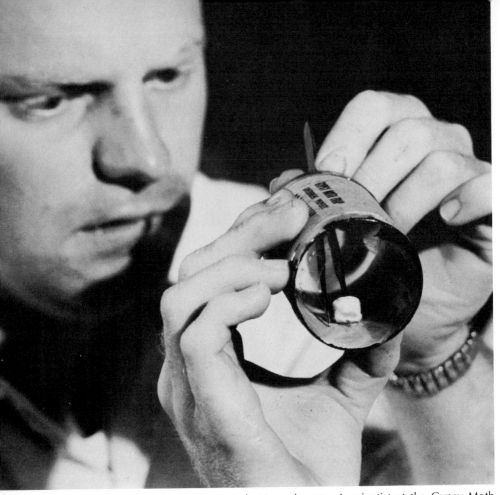

Figure 13–9 Cape Cod, Massachusetts. A scientist at the Gypsy Moth Methods Improvement Laboratory places a small tuft of cotton moistened with gyplure inside a gypsy moth trap. This synthetic attractant is being used to lure male moths to traps and to chemosterilants. It is also being used in a study of a unique method called the *confusion* technique. An area is saturated with the synthetic attractant in the hope of confusing the male moths to the extent that they will not be able to find and mate with the females. [U.S. Department of Agriculture]

They launched huge rabbit-hunting parties, the likes of which Europe had never seen. They even erected a fence several hundred miles long, from Queenland to North Wales, in an attempt to contain the dispersing rabbit hordes. These efforts were all to no avail. Finally, government biologists introduced the myxomatosis virus, lethal to rabbits exclusively, into the target area. A healthy rabbit becomes infected by coming into contact with or by ingesting virus-contaminated forage. In a reasonably short time, the Australian rabbit problem was under control—at least temporarily. Whether the rabbits will ultimately develop immunity to the myxomatosis virus and again disrupt Australia's rangeland economy remains to be seen.

Integrated Control of Pests

Although biological control of pests holds much promise, and was highly successful in the St. John's wort and Australian rabbit problems, many experts believe that for most pest problems the most effective long-term method of control will be an *integrated* one which judiciously employs both biological and chemical control agents either concurrently or sequentially, depending on the problem. Chemicals would not be dispensed in a massive assault on the ecosystem, as was so commonly done in the 1940's and 1950's with disastrous results for wildlife. Instead of overwhelming the ecosystems, the chemicals will be *fitted into* them. A given pesticide would be employed in a highly selective manner, only after an intensive study had been conducted, not only of its immediate effects on target pests but also of its long-term influences on other biotic components of the ecosystem. In most cases, the pesticides would be employed only temporarily, to reduce the target population sufficiently to swing the balance in favor of the pest's predators and parasites. Both native and exotic biological control agents would play significant roles. In an official report of the California Agricultural Experiment Station Stern et al. state that in the approach to integrated control "we must realize that man has developed huge monocultures, he has eliminated forests and grasslands, selected special strains of plants and animals, moved them about, and in other ways altered the natural control that had developed over thousands upon thousands of years. We could not return to those original conditions if it were desirable. We may, however, utilize some of the mechanisms that existed before man's modifications to establish new balances in our favor" (20). There is mounting evidence, from agricultural regions in South Africa to the apple orchards of Nova Scotia and the citrus plots of California, that integrated control can be extremely effective. Integrated control has numerous advantages: First, because it requires use of minimal amounts of chemicals it is relatively inexpensive; second, hazards stemming from food chain contamination are reduced; third, the chance for a build-up of resistant insect strains is restricted; fourth, it permits the gradual restoration of biotic components of the original ecosystem; and fifth, it permits the introduction of exotic agents of control which prior study reveals to be effective against specific target pests (20).

In *Pesticides and the Living Landscape* Robert L. Rudd describes a fascinating example of the use of the integrated method in the control of the hornworm, a serious tobacco pest in the Southeast:

Hornworms on tobacco are usually reduced in numbers by insecticides. Most states in which hornworms occur also recommend cultural control by burning or plowing-under the tobacco stalks that remain after harvest. Handpicking of larvae is sometimes recommended. Generally, there has been little effort to control them with natural antagonists, but any successful means of doing so would bring at once the advantages of lower cost of control and reduced residue problems (a particularly important aspect of insecticide use on tobacco). In recent years Rabb and his colleagues at North Carolina State College have successfully integrated a variety of control techniques against hornworms that are remarkable for their effective simplicity. Paper wasps, known to be effective predators of hornworms, were encouraged to multiply by providing easily constructed artificial shelters around tobacco fields. (Increases in the bird populations of forests in Germany, England and Russia have been achieved in a directly comparable way for similar purposes!) These shelters could be permanently stationed about fields or moved as needed, in the manner that beekeepers move hives for pollination. The predation of wasps alone accounted for a removal of about sixty percent of the total population of hornworms. Under some circumstances reduction was greater. Occasionally, for a variety of cultural and climatic reasons, predator populations were low and insecticides had to be used to effect control. In these instances the chlorinated hydrocarbon insecticides TDE and endrin were used to reduce numbers of hornworms to levels at which wasps could assume control. In contrast to previous insecticide applications, chemicals were applied only to crown portions of plants, and then in lesser amounts, and fewer applications were required. Costs and residue hazards were reduced by this integrated scheme of biological, cultural and insecticidal control [18].

Legal Restrictions on Pesticide Use

For many years, ever since abundant evidence of the devastating effect of pesticide cycling in ecosystems on wildlife populations (in some areas adjacent to massive spraying operations, 98 per cent bird mortality has been recorded), wildlife biologists, ornithologists, bird watchers, nature lovers, and sportsmen have joined forces in an attempt to convince legislative bodies that restrictive regulations must be adopted to prevent further decrements in wildlife populations, as well as mounting deterioration of the human environment. Until recently these antipesticide forces were frustrated in attaining their goals. Then, a series of events, centering around the introduction of coho salmon in the Great Lakes, finally enabled them to make a breakthrough.

As early as 1963 a group of distinguished scientists, forming the President's Science Advisory Committee, declared "elimination of use of persistent toxic pesticides should be the goal." However, despite this highly authoritative high-level prodding, legislators still dragged their feet. As George Laycock, well-known naturalist, so aptly has written in *Audubon Magazine*, "the chemical companies and the agricultural establishment still call most of the shots six years later, arrogantly fighting every effort to halt contamination of the environment with their products."

In the spring of 1966 the Michigan Conservation Department initiated an intensive program of coho salmon propagation and stocking. Many thousands of 5-inch fish were released into Lake Michigan's tributaries. By the spring of 1967 some of these fish, having fed voraciously on the superabundant alewife population, had grown to 4 pounds; some time later salmon up

Figure 13–10 Pesticides are responsible for the drastic decline of the peregrine falcon in the United States. This bird is being studied at the Patuxent Wildlife Research Center, Laurel, Maryland. [Bureau of Sport Fisheries and Wildlife, U.S. Department of the Interior]

to 22 pounds were recorded. It appeared as if the sports and commercial fishermen in that region were in great luck. Anglers flocked to the spawning streams when the coho salmon runs began, usually during later spring or early summer. Along the Manistee River (Michigan) anglers became so excited at seeing the huge silvery fish that a mob scene developed, anglers scooping the fish up in nets or dispatching them with clubs. The Wisconsin Department of Natural Resources also has become interested in the coho. It has started a similar program but on a lesser scale.

However, in the spring of 1969, the Food and Drug Administration found an average of 16 parts per million of DDT in commercially caught cohos which had been transported to Minnesota and Wisconsin markets. Considerably alarmed, the FDA confiscated 14 tons of the salmon. Moreover, the U.S. Bureau of Commercial Fisheries found up to 105 parts per million of DDT in the fatty tissues of Michigan cohos. On April 22, 1969, DDT tolerance levels for fish were set at 5 parts per million by the FDA. The ruling put a damper on the coho boom. Michigan conservation authorities were considerably embarrassed for they had spent several million dollars on facilities for coho propagation and research. The coho-based commercial fisheries in Michigan faced the prospect of an annual $2 million loss in sales.

However, the coho episode, unfortunate as it was, probably served as a catalyst in accelerating legislative action on pesticide control. In the spring of 1969 a notable triumph was achieved by the proponents of environmental quality. The sale of DDT, America's most abundantly used pesticide, was banned in Michigan, and its use was prohibited by the Michigan Agricultural Commission. Soon afterward the use of DDT was either restricted or banned in Arizona, California, Florida, Washington and Wisconsin. Finally, on November 12, 1969, Robert Finch, Secretary of Health, Education and Welfare, announced that the Federal government, at long last, would phase out all except "essential uses" of DDT by 1971. Unfortunately this federal decision came 24 years too late. The human environment has become almost universally contaminated with DDT. As Finch admits "it would take ten years . . . for the environment to purge itself" if all DDT sales were stopped *immediately* rather than in two years. (Finch is being optimistic. An ecosystem like Lake Michigan, over 1000 feet deep, and having only a one per cent annual turnover of water volume, would not be decontaminated in less than a *century*.) Many antipesticide forces decry the government's slow phase-out, and question why the ban cannot be immediately applied. Senator Gaylord Nelson of

Wisconsin declared that the widely publicized ban was "virtually nonexistent" and that 25 million pounds of DDT had been released in the 3½ month period since the ban's announcement. Representative Joseph Karth of Minnesota stated: "We are right where we used to be—no national ban on DDT." A representative of consumer advocate Ralph Nader's legal firm in Washington estimated that by shrewd legal maneuvering the pesticide industry could postpone an *actual* DDT ban until 1975. Five indignant conservation groups (including the Izaak Walton League, National Audubon Society, and the Sierra Club) took legal action against Secretary Hardin and the U.S. Department of Agriculture for its indecisive and ineffective implementation of the ban.

BIBLIOGRAPHY

1. Anderson, John M., and Margaret R. Peterson. "DDT: Sublethal Effects on the Brook Trout's Nervous System," *Science,* **164** (1969), 440–441.
2. Barker, R. J. "Notes on Some Ecological Effects of DDT Sprayed on Elms," *Jour. Wild. Mgt.,* **22,** 3 (1958), 269–274.
3. Buchsbaum, Ralph. *Animals Without Backbones.* Chicago: The University of Chicago Press, 1948, 405 pp.
4. Cairns, John, Jr., Arthur Scheier, and Nancy E. Hess. "The Effects of Alkyl-Benzene-Sulfonate on Aquatic Organisms," *Ind. Water Wastes,* **9** (1964), 22–28.
5. Carson, Rachel. *Silent Spring.* Boston: Houghton Mifflin Co., 1962.
6. DeBach, Paul (ed.). *Biological Control of Insect Pests and Weeds.* New York: Reinhold Publishing Corp., 1964.
7. Dugan, Patrick R. "Influence of Chronic Exposure to Anionic Detergents on Toxicity of Pesticides to Goldfish," *Jour. Water Poll. Cont. Fed.,* **39** (1967), 63–71.
8. Egler, Frank E. "Pesticides—In Our Ecosystem." *Amer. Scientist,* **52,** 1 (1964), 110–136.
9. Gerberich, J. B. and M. Laird. "Bibliography of Papers Relating to the Control of Mosquitoes by the Use of Fish." *FAO Fisheries Technical Paper No. 75.* Rome: U.N. Food and Agricultural Organization, 1968.
10. Haeussler, G. J. "Losses Caused by Insects," *Insects: The Yearbook of Agriculture.* Washington, D.C.: U.S. Department of Agriculture, 1952, 141–146.
11. Holloway, J. K. "Projects in Biological Control of Weeds," in Paul DeBach (ed.), *Biological Control of Insect Pests and Weeds.* New York: Reinhold Publishing Corp., 1964.
12. Humphrey, Robert R. *Range Ecology.* New York: The Ronald Press Co., 1962.

13. Hunt, Eldridge G., and Arthur I. Bischoff. "Inimical Effects on Wildlife of Periodic DDD Applications to Clear Lake," *Calif. Fish and Game,* **46,** 1 (1960), 91–106.

14. Kleinert, Stanton, Paul Degurse, and Thomas Wirth, "Occurrence and Significance of DDT and Dieldrin Residues in Wisconsin Fish," Madison, Wis.: Wisconsin Department of Natural Resources, 1969.

15. Kormondy, Edward J. *Concepts of Ecology,* Englewood Cliffs, N.J.: Prentice-Hall, Inc., 1969, 209 pp.

16. Lauer, Gerald J., H. Page Nicholson, William S. Cox, and John I. Teasley. "Pesticide Contamination of Surface Waters by Sugar Cane Farming in Louisiana," *Trans. Amer. Fish. Soc.,* **95** (1966), 310–316.

17. McMillen, Wheeler. *Bugs or People?* New York: Appleton-Century-Crofts, 1965.

18. Rudd, R. L. *Pesticides and the Living Landscape.* Madison: University of Wisconsin Press, 1964, 320 pp.

19. Shellhammer, H. S. "An Ethological and Neurochemical Analysis of Facilitation in Wild Mice." University of California, Davis. Doctoral thesis.

20. Stern, Vernon M., Ray F. Smith, Robert van den Bosch, and Kenneth S. Hagen. "The Integrated Control Concept," *Hilgardia,* **29,** 2 (1959), 81–101. Calif. Agri. Exp. Sta., University of California, Berkeley, California.

21. Surber, Eugene W. "Water Quality Criteria for Fresh Water Fishes," *Proc. 16th Ann. Conf. Southeast. Assoc. Game and Fish Comm. 1962:* 1965. Pp. 435–436.

22. Whitten, Jamie L. *That We May Live.* Princeton, N.J.: D. Van Nostrand Co., Inc., 1966, 251 pp.

Air Pollution

14

Evolution of the Atmosphere

The air man breathes today is vastly different from that which existed when our planet had its origin 5 billion years ago. According to Paul Weisz (21) the newborn earth probably had an atmosphere composed principally of water vapor (H_2O), ammonia (NH_3), and methane (CH_4). The energy required for the formation of these compounds (from the elements carbon, hydrogen, oxygen, and nitrogen) was probably derived from heat, light, and ultraviolet and X-radiation. Eons later, some of the earliest life forms, such as proto-viruses, possibly secured vital energy from the fermentation of the organic compounds which formed a rich broth in the ancient oceans. Releasing CO_2 as a by-product, such fermentation made possible photosynthesis—the all-important process by which green plants synthesize sugars from CO_2 and H_2O, with the aid of chlorophyll-trapped solar energy. As photosynthetic activity became more extensive, billions of tons of molecular oxygen (O_2) were released into the atmosphere. The stage was now set for the evolution of animals (and ultimately human beings), which utilized the precious gas in respiration. Moreover, with the release of copious quantities of oxygen, the atmosphere underwent an "oxygen revolution;"

485

this extremely active gas combined with methane to form CO_2 and water, and with NH_3 to form N_2 and water. At higher altitudes oxygen molecules combined with other oxygen molecules to form ozone. By some such process of gradual change, operating over millenia of time, the present atmosphere, virtually devoid of NH_3 and CH_4, eventually developed (21).

Composition of the Atmosphere

Today, the dry unpolluted atmosphere has roughly the following composition:

NITROGEN (79 PER CENT).   Despite his inhalation of 11,000 quarts of nitrogen daily, this inert gas in unusable by man. However, in the form of nitrates, it may enter biological food chains and eventually be utilized by man in the synthesis of vital proteins.

OXYGEN (20 PER CENT).   Oxygen is a chemically active gas essential for the respiratory processes of most organisms, including man, by means of which energy is released to power such biological functions as growth, reproduction, hormone synthesis, nerve impulse transmission, muscular contraction, perception of stimuli, and even (in man) thought itself. Fortunately, the world's green plants annually release 400 billion tons of oxygen to the atmosphere in a continuous process of renewal. It has been estimated that were it not for this replenishment, the oxygen supply of the world's atmosphere might become exhausted within 2,000 years.

CARBON DIOXIDE (0.03 PER CENT).   Although not directly utilized by man, carbon dioxide, a colorless, odorless, tasteless gas, is an essential raw material for photosynthesis and hence a *sine qua non* for human survival. It has been estimated by Howard R. Lewis that an acre of deciduous forest removes 2,000 pounds of CO_2 from the atmosphere annually, and the world's green vegetation utilizes an impressive 550 billion tons yearly (10).

INACTIVE GASES (1 PER CENT).   The air also contains negligible quantities of argon, neon, helium, krypton, and xenon, all of which are obviously inactive and of relatively little biological importance.

Value of the Atmosphere

In addition to providing a vital source of oxygen, the earth's atmosphere is of value to man in many other ways. Without the insulation and heat distribution provided by the atmosphere, man would be subjected to drastic day–night temperature changes completely incompatible with survival. Without an atmosphere, sound vibrations could not be transmitted; the earth would be silent. There would be no weather, no spring rains for crops and lawn, no snow, hail, or fog. Without its atmospheric shield, our planet would not only be bombarded with meteorites but exposed to potentially lethal radiations from the sun. In summary, without an atmosphere, life as we know it would be impossible, and the earth's surface would be as desert-like as the moon.

Pollution of the Atmosphere

Natural Pollution. Long before the first white man set foot on American soil, the atmosphere was to some degree polluted, not from man-made sources but from natural causes. Smoke from lightning-triggered forest fires billowed darkly across the land, presumably causing hardship to wildlife. Dust clouds occasionally obscured the sun then as now. A given sample of today's atmosphere may contain a host of natural contaminants, from ragweed pollen to fungal spores, from disease-causing bacteria to minute particles of volcanic ash and salt.

Surprisingly, even extensive forests of spruce, fir, and pine (which otherwise are considered a valuable natural resource) may represent a source of natural air contamination. Thus, according to University of Nevada Professor Frits Went, pine trees and plants like sagebrush may emit terpenes and esters. These chemicals then react with sunlight to form the "smog" or bluish haze which veils many a mountain range and is familiar to every vacationer who has sojourned in the Smoky Mountains. Terpenes may be highly toxic and may actually inhibit the growth of other vegetation. Fortunately, they are washed from the air with rain or snow before attaining levels harmful to man (14).

Pollution Caused by Man. *Homo sapiens* has been fouling his atmosphere ever since Stone Age man first roasted a deer over an open fire, the smoke smudging some of his otherwise magnificent cave wall paintings in southern France—perhaps the first serious property damage caused by air pollution. Even before the Christian era a noted geographer censured the dye pits of Tyre as a source of offensive odors. Queen Elizabeth fled to Nottingham in 1257 to seek haven from dense clouds of coal smoke. In 1306 Parliament passed a law making it illegal to burn coal in a furnace in London; at least one violator was actually tortured for his offense (10). However, it was not until the Industrial Revolution that air pollution reached such massive proportions that it seriously affected the health of large segments of society. In 1909 at least 1,063 deaths in Glasgow, Scotland, were directly attributed to polluted air (10). It was in conjunction with this incident that Dr. H. Des Voeux coined the word *smog* as a contraction of smoke-fog (10). Atmospheric contamination has progressively worsened over the last few decades. Let us examine the major pollutants which concern us today.

MAJOR POLLUTANTS. Major man-generated pollutants in our atmosphere include carbon monoxide, oxides of sulfur, oxides of nitrogen, hydrocarbons, and particulate matter.

Carbon Monoxide. Each passing year, 65 million tons of carbon monoxide (CO) are emitted into the atmosphere of the United States, 1.5 million tons into the skies above New York City alone. This single gas forms 52 per cent by weight of our principal atmospheric pollutants (12). Because this gas combines 210 times more readily with hemoglobin than does oxygen, it tends to replace oxygen in the blood stream. The California Department of Public Health indicated in 1960 that one hour's exposure to 120 parts per million of CO may be a serious health risk to sensitive people (20). At this concentration, CO inactivates about 5 per cent of the body's hemoglobin. Resultant symptoms include headache, dizziness, and lassitude. The presence of CO in the pregnant mother's blood stream has been suggested as a possible cause of stillbirths and deformed offspring. Certain conditions may render some people especially susceptible to CO poisoning. They include heart disease, circulatory impairment, asthma, diseased lungs, high altitudes, and high humidity. CO may be the indirect cause of many fatal traffic accidents in the United States yearly, because the effects of low-level CO poisoning may parallel those of alcohol or fatigue in impairing the motorist's ability to control his vehicle. Exposure to 200 parts per million for a lengthy period of time may cause fainting, coma, convulsions, and death. Concentrations may frequently approach 100 parts per million in garages, tunnels, and even behind automobiles on the open road. On rare occasions, levels as high as *500 parts per million* have been recorded in heavy city traffic.

Oxides of Sulfur. The 23 million tons of oxides of sulfur which are emitted into our atmosphere yearly form roughly 18 per cent (by weight) of our principal atmospheric contaminants (12). Oxides of sulfur form whenever sulfur-containing fuels, such as coal, oil, and gas, are burned. Coal burning yields 48,000 tons of sulfur dioxide (SO_2) in the United States daily and 1.5 million tons annually in New York City alone.

Colorless SO_2 stings the eyes and burns the throat. According to Lewis, about 1 per cent of the population will develop chronic weariness, tortured breathing, sore throat, tonsillitis, coughing, and wheezing when exposed for lengthy periods to the concentrations of SO_2 normally occurring in smog (10). Sulfur dioxide will react with oxygen to form sulfur trioxide (SO_3), which in turn will combine with airborne moisture droplets to form lung-damaging sulfuric acid (H_2SO_4).

Hydrocarbons. The 15 million tons of hydrocarbons emitted yearly in the United States represent 12 per cent of all major atmospheric pollutants. The burning of gasoline in the automobile is by far the major source, 27,000 tons being emitted from auto exhaust daily (8). The hydrocarbons represent a large family of chemicals, most of which are not directly harmful to man at the low concentrations in which they normally occur. Unfortunately some of them may react with nitrogen dioxide (NO_2) in the formation of photochemical smog. Many hydrocarbons at high concentrations may irritate the eyes and respiratory tract. Benzo(a)pyrene and at least eight other hydrocarbons have been implicated as possible causes of cancer (10). Some of these also occur in cigarette smoke. In fact, in terms of

Figure 14–1 Aerial view of smog over New York City over 15 years ago. [U.S. Public Health Service]

these suspected carcinogens, the air breathed in one day by a man living in a badly polluted city would be equivalent to smoking an entire pack of cigarettes.

Particulate Matter. Particulate matter may be defined as solid and liquid particles in the atmosphere, in contrast to gaseous matter. It was estimated that, in November, 1954, a 1,000-foot-thick layer over a 1-square-mile area in downtown Los Angeles contained roughly 870 pounds of particulate matter. Included were at least twenty-one different substances, the most abundant of which were lead, iron, magnesium, sodium, potassium, sulfates, nitrates, organic matter, and hydrocarbons (6). Twelve million tons of particulate matter are injected into our atmosphere yearly (12). According to a survey by the Robert Taft Sanitary Engineering Center of the U.S. Public Health Service, the following particulate matter *tonnage* occurs in an air sample 1 square mile in surface area extending from the ground to an elevation of 100 feet: Salt Lake City, 24; Pittsburgh, 45; San Francisco, 46; Houston, 57; Washington, D.C., 58; Atlanta, 61; Philadelphia, 83; New York, 108; Los Angeles, 118; Chicago, 124; Detroit, 153.

Lead, in the form of antiknock fuels, is added to gasoline to enhance its octane rating. Man takes this lead into his system when inhaling air polluted with motor exhaust. A cumulative poison, it may also be ingested with food or water. It may have an injurious effect on the kidneys, blood, and liver. Moreover, it may damage the brains of youngsters, with ultimate lethal effect. On the basis of lead concentrations in snows at high elevations in the Rockies, Claire C. Patterson, a California Institute of Technology geochemist, suggested in 1965 that lead concentrations in man are 100 times the level of yesteryear. Although his statement has been criticized in some medical circles, the U.S. Public Health Service has been considering setting stiffer lead emission standards (8).

Less common particulates include arsenic, asbestos, beryllium, cadmium, and fluorides. Arsenic, emitted from copper smelters, is suspect as a possible carcinogen. Minute particles from asbestos fibers derived from the wearing away of roofing, shingles, insulation, and brake linings have been associated with lung cancer. Beryllium, used as rocket engine fuel, has induced the formation of cancers in experimental monkeys. Cadmium may adversely affect the heart and increase blood pressure.

Oxides of Nitrogen. The 8 million tons of oxides of nitrogen which are annually spewed into our nation's air form 6 per cent of all the atmospheric pollutants generated by man.

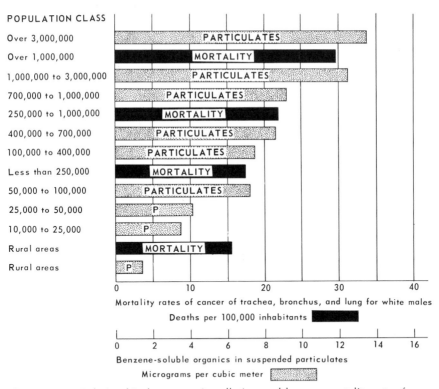

Figure 14–2 Relationship between air pollution and human mortality rates from cancer in white males. [Adapted from Harold Wolozin (ed.), *The Economics of Air Pollution.* By permission of W. W. Norton & Company, Inc. Copyright © 1966 by W. W. Norton & Company, Inc.]

New York City releases 298,000 tons of oxides of nitrogen yearly. Nitric oxide (NO) is relatively harmless at ordinary concentrations. It is formed when atmospheric nitrogen combines with oxygen at the temperatures generated during fuel combustion. At unusually high concentrations, nitric oxide may have lethal effects, causing death by asphyxiation, because it combines 300,000 times more readily with hemoglobin than does oxygen.

Nitric oxide readily combines with atmospheric oxygen to form nitrogen dioxide (NO_2), which, according to Lewis, may cause a variety of human ailments, from gum inflammation and internal bleeding to emphysema and increased susceptibility to pneumonia and lung cancer.

Photochemical Smog and Ozone. The yellow-gray haze known as photochemical smog, which was first recognized in the Los Angeles area, is caused by reactions between precursor hydrocarbons, catalysts, and atmospheric oxygen. The pre-

491

Figure 14–3A Aerial view of Los Angeles on a clear day in 1956. [Los Angeles County Air Pollution Control District]

cursors frequently exist in concentrations of less than 1 part per million. Nitrogen dioxide (NO_2) is the most common catalyst. The energy necessary for triggering these reactions is derived from sunlight; hence, on cloudy days the formation of photochemical smog is somewhat restricted, and at nightfall the process is halted. The products resulting are oxidized hydrocarbons, primarily ozone. These materials (known as *oxidants*) may be severely irritating to human eyes and mucous membranes. This explanation of the nature and origin of photochemical smog was first worked out in 1951 by Dr. Arie Haagen-Smit of the California Institute of Technology.

Ozone occurs naturally in the ozonosphere at an altitude of 20 miles, where it is formed by the action of sunlight on oxygen. Here it provides a shield against potentially lethal ultraviolet rays from the sun and also screens infrared (heat) rays out of the earth's immediate atmospheric envelope, thus ensuring an earthly temperature amenable to life.

Ozone is the principal eye and mucous membrane irritant in photochemical smog. At concentrations frequently found in urban areas, ozone will cause nose and throat discomfort after an exposure of only 10 minutes (20). Experimental subjects exposed for a few hours to 0.8 parts per million of ozone experienced impaired lung function and mental ability. People having

Figure 14–3B Aerial view of Los Angeles under smog in 1956. Smog is trapped by a temperature inversion at about 300 feet above the ground. The upper portion of the Los Angeles City Hall is visible above the base of the temperature inversion. The inversion is present over the Los Angeles Basin approximately 320 days of the year. [Los Angeles County Air Pollution Control District]

prolonged occupational exposure to relatively high levels of ozone have incurred reduced visual acuity, fatigue, recurrent headaches, breathing difficulty, and chest pains (20). It is possible that intermittent exposures over a period of twenty years to only 0.25 parts per million of ozone may induce pulmonary fibrosis (12).

Sources of Pollution

TRANSPORTATION. In 1967 there were 95 million registered motor vehicles in the United States; by 1980 the number is expected to reach 150 million. Because the amount of pollutants discharged in the motor exhaust is related to mileage, it is of interest to note that the total annual motor mileage is expected to leap from 890 billion in 1965 to well over 1 trillion in 1980 (8). Something like 70 billion gallons of fuel are consumed yearly by motor vehicles. From each thousand gallons consumed, 1.5 tons of carbon monoxide, 300 pounds of hydrocarbons, and 100 pounds of nitrogen oxides are released into the atmosphere (3). If a combustion engine were 100 per cent efficient, the only exhaust components would be carbon dioxide and water vapor. However, because combustion is sometimes grossly inefficient, (especially in some of the "rambling wrecks" chugging down our highways trailing plumes of smoke behind them) roughly 200 distinct compounds may be belched from motor exhaust pipes. It was estimated in 1966 that transportation activity (including planes) in the United States annually generates 59.6 million tons of carbon monoxide, 9.7 million tons of hydrocarbons, 3.1 million tons of nitrogen oxides, 1.8 million tons of particulate matter, 0.5 million tons of sulfur oxides, and 0.1 million tons of miscellaneous atmospheric pollutants (12). This represents a total of 74.8 million tons directly attributable to the combustion engine (12).

INDUSTRY. Foremost among the industries which pour out aerial garbage into the skies over the United States are the electrical power plants, which alone emit 15.7 million tons of pollutants yearly, largely from the use of coal. During its consumption, a single ton of coal releases 200 pounds of solids and 48 pounds of sulfur dioxide and nitrogen oxides. The refinery industry is also a prime source. With each passing day 12 million barrels of crude oil are processed by our nation's petroleum refineries, with a concomitant injection of particulates, sulfur oxides, hydrocarbons, ammonia, oxides of nitrogen, organic acids, and aldehydes into the air around us. Large ore smelters

Figure 14–4 Jet plane pollutes the air over Washington, D.C. [U.S. Public Health Service]

and metal industries release sulfur dioxide, carbon monoxide, metallic oxides, as well as lead and arsenic fumes. Ore smelters release 1.7 million tons of sulfur dioxide annually (12). The rubber industry releases vapors from solvents, and chemical industries pollute the air with sulfur dioxide, fluorides, ammonia, hydrogen sulfide, solvents, hydrocarbons and carbon monoxide. Almost 500,000 tons of sulfur dioxide are released from sulfuric acid plants annually. Massive quantities of dust are produced by the glass, asbestos, and cement industries, as well as in the manufacture of stone products, concrete, and abrasives. In aggregate, all industries in the United States other than electrical power plants annually emit 8.7 million tons of sulfur dioxide, 6 million tons of particulates, 3.7 million tons of hydrocarbons, 1.8 million tons of carbon monoxide, 1.6 million tons of nitrogen oxides and 1.6 million tons of other miscellaneous air contaminants.

LEAF-BURNING AND REFUSE DISPOSAL. The burning of leaf piles in late autumn is for many a simple pleasure; moreover, it generates a pungent fragrance which delights thousands of gardeners everywhere. Surprisingly, however, leaf-burning may be a source of profound health problems, having caused allergic reactions in certain sensitive individuals which contribute to a variety of respiratory ills, including asthma, hay fever, and bronchitis. Inhaled leaf smoke has even been directly responsible for mortality in young children.

The great majority of American families burn paper, rags,

Figure 14–5 Air pollution from oil refineries in Baton Rouge, La., over 10 years ago. [National Air Pollution Control Administration]

Figure 14–6 Smoke from the Kenilworth Dump, where the refuse of Washington, D.C., is burned, billows over the Capitol of the United States, in a cloud many times the size of the Capitol, April 18, 1967. [U.S. Department of Agriculture]

Figure 14–7 Smoke from the Redding, California, city dump, December 13, 1965. [National Air Pollution Control Administration]

and other refuse in crude backyard incinerators which frequently are highly inefficient and may be nothing more than converted oil drums. The emission from a single disposal unit is of little consequence, but the aggregate emissions from tens of thousands of such units in a major community can pose a serious health hazard. One ton of incinerated refuse, for example, releases 25 pounds of solids, 5 pounds of sulfur oxides, and 4 pounds of oxides of nitrogen. According to the Committee on Pollution, Waste Management and Control of the National Academy of Sciences, refuse disposal spews 3.3 million tons of contaminants into America's skies annually (12).

CULM AND GOB BANKS. Coal-processing plants dispose of inferior fuel of no commercial value by dumping it onto wasteland sites where it accumulates over the years into hills of culm (anthracite) and gob (bituminous). They blight extensive areas in Alabama, Alaska, Colorado, Illinois, Indiana, Kentucky, Montana, New Mexico, Ohio, Pennsylvania, Tennessee, Utah, Virginia, West Virginia, and Wyoming. A single bank may contain 20 million tons of coal waste. These banks are easily ignited by a carelessly dropped cigarette, by forest fires, or by the insidious process of spontaneous combustion. In 1965 the 450 culm and gob banks burning somewhere in the United States generated 183,000 tons of acrid sulfur dioxide fumes.

Disasters. Polluted atmosphere has caused several episodes within the past few decades that have inflicted widespread misery and taken an appalling toll of human lives.

Meuse River Valley in Belgium. In December, 1930, a stagnant mass of air, accompanied by a dense fog, settled into the highly industrialized Meuse River Valley in Belgium. As glass factories, zinc smelters, blast furnaces, coke ovens, and sulfuric acid plants continued to belch poisonous chemicals into the air, residents along a 15-mile stretch of the valley soon found themselves enveloped in a thick industrial smog, which persisted for a full week. Factory workers stayed home, complaining of headaches and nausea, and school children fell unconscious onto classroom floors. Eventually, a violent rainstorm cleared the air, but only after the pollution episode had brought illness to 6,000 and death to 63 (10).

Monongahela River Valley, Donora, Pennsylvania. Thirty miles south of Pittsburgh, along a U-shaped bend of the Monongahela River, nestle the three industrial communities of Donora, Webster, and Carroll, with an aggregate population of 14,000. Major industrial plants in the area manufacture steel, wire, sulfuric acid, and zinc. On October 26, 1948, a fog closed in on the valley accompanied by a thermal inversion. In a short time the pungent odor of sulfuric dioxide permeated the air. Six thousand people (43 per cent of the total population) became ill, the most prevalent symptoms being nausea, vomiting, headache, nose, eye, and throat irritation, and constriction of the chest. Although the smog persisted only five days, it left twenty deaths in its wake. Autopsies on three of the dead people showed marked changes in the lungs, such as edema, purulent bronchitis, capillary dilatation, and hemorrhage (10).

London. From December 4 to December 9, 1952, the twin weather phenomena of fog and a thermal inversion blanketed a 700 square mile area in London and triggered a major pollution disaster. The accumulating smog caused huge traffic jams, many motorists being forced to abandon their cars. Outdoor shows and concerts had to be terminated because of poor visibility. Only twelve hours after the smog developed, people started to become ill. Hospitals were inundated with patients complaining of respiratory or heart problems. A characteristic symptom was labored breathing and cyanosis. The deaths of at least 4,000 people, primarily from heart disease, bronchitis, and bronchopneumonia, were directly attributed to the smog (10).

New York City. A stagnant mass of air persisted over our nation's largest city from November 12 to November 22, 1953. Soot, dust, and fly ash accumulated to an average concentration of 3.5 tons per cubic mile of air. Sulfur dioxide was five times the normal level. Airports were closed. One could not even take a ferry boat to the Statue of Liberty. Within a few days, untold thousands of inhabitants suffered from burning eyes and uncontrollable bouts of coughing. Although winds and rain finally dissipated the smog on November 22, during its 10-day persistence, it was directly responsible for the deaths of about 200 people (10).

Factors Contributing to Pollution Episodes. When most of the air pollution disasters are studied, a common pattern is revealed. First, they occur in densely populated areas. Second, they occur in heavily industrialized centers where pollution sources are abundant. Third, they occur in valleys, which might serve as topographical "receptacles" for receiving and retaining pollutants. Fourth, they are accompanied by fog. It appears that the minute droplets of moisture absorb pollutant chemicals on their surface. When inhaled, these chemicals result in irritation of the respiratory membranes. Fifth, they are accompanied by a thermal inversion which effectively puts a meteorological lid on the air mass in the valley and contributes to its stagnation (10).

Pollution Effects on Vegetation. Airborne contaminants inflict a $325 million annual loss on our nation's agricultural industry (12). Pollutants damage at least thirty-six important commercial crops (20). Automotive pollution has caused vegetational damage in twenty-two states and, ironically, the District of Columbia. The exhaust emissions from the flood of vehicles rushing along our new interstate highway network seriously hamper commercial crop production on nearby farms. It has been estimated that in southern California automotive pollution causes $10 million worth of crop damage yearly (10) and damage recently has become equally serious along the Atlantic seaboard from Boston to Washington (20).

Flowers and ornamental plants of many varieties have also been injured. Backyard gardeners in the larger cities are noting increasing damage to such favorite flowers as petunias, snapdragons, chrysanthemums, larkspur, carnations, orchids, pansies, zinnias, and roses (20). Symbolically, even the potted plants in New York's City Hall, such as philodendron, pandanus, and podocarnus, in order to survive, must be removed periodically from the contaminated Manhattan atmosphere for a "breather" in a greenhouse at the edge of town.

The specific chemicals inflicting plant injury have been identified to some degree. Among the more serious are ozone, sulfur dioxide, fluorides, ethylene, herbicides, and oxidized hydrocarbons. At least fifty-seven species are susceptible to ozone. Because plants are much more sensitive to this gas than is man himself, it frequently causes widespread destruction before man is even aware of the problem. Ozone diffuses through the stomata of plants and kills the palisade cells. The result is a reddish-brown spotting of the leaf. Ozone has severely curtailed the once prosperous flower-growing industry in the Los Angeles area (10). As little as 8 to 10 parts of ozone in 100 million will cause serious injury to tobacco plants after a brief four-hour exposure (12). Even trees are not immune to ozone. Thus, in West Virginia, large acreages of eastern white pine have succumbed to a disease known as postemergence chronic tip burn. Initially thought to be caused by a parasitic fungus, the Southeastern Forest Experiment Station of the U.S. Department of Agriculture has recently attributed the disease to ozone emanating from motor exhaust.

In the San Bernardino and San Jacinto Mountains of southern California, thousands of ponderosa pines have been killed by wind-borne ozone originating in Los Angeles 60 miles distant. Since the 1950's up to 60 per cent of San Bernardino National Forest's 160,000 pine acres has incurred moderate to severe damage. In early 1970 the smog was destroying about 3 per cent of the ponderosa pines annually. According to U.S. Forest Service pathologist Paul Miller, photosynthesis is inhibited almost immediately. Smog concentrations of .25 ppm will reduce photosynthesis 66 per cent. This in turn reduces the flow of resins under the bark. Since the resins protect the tree to some degree against the ravages of plant diseases and insect pests, the smog-triggered forest destruction may be extensive.

Sulfur dioxide (of which 300 million tons is annually belched into the atmosphere of our nation) is also a threat to plants. Sulfur dioxide reacts with water inside the plant leaf cells to form a lethal sulfite. Some plants succumb to a concentration of one part of sulfur dioxide in 10 billion parts of air (10). Alfalfa is damaged by a 1 part per million concentration (12). In 1910–11, sulfur fumes from an Anaconda (Montana) smelter killed all major tree species within a 5- to 8-mile radius (20). In the late 20's a smelter near Trail, British Columbia, emitted 18,000 tons of sulfur pollution annually, causing plant injury 52 miles distant. Valuable stands of Douglas fir and ponderosa pine sustained 60 to 100 per cent injury. Even in 1936, two years after control devices had been installed, 80 per cent of the surviving pines were coneless (20).

Figure 14–8 Hydrogen fluoride gas injury to peony leaves in southern New Jersey. Note withered, light areas. [U.S. Public Health Service]

Hydrogen fluoride may damage plants at a concentration of only 1 part in 10 billion. Fluorides emitted from Florida phosphate plants have ruined 25,000 acres of citrus groves. In other regions, fluorides have damaged a number of shade and ornamental species including sycamore, silver maple, mountain ash, and mulberry (10).

Nitrogen dioxide has been found recently to restrict growth in certain plants without causing any diagnostic symptoms, thus posing an insidious curtailment of agricultural income the cause of which may not even be suspected (20).

Effects of Pollution on Animals. Livestock may incur lethal dosages of air-borne chemicals, such as fluorides, lead and arsenic, by consuming contaminated pasturage. Thus, the number of cattle in Polk County, Florida, was diminished by 30,000 because of fluorides emanating from the numerous phosphate plants in the region. Seventy-one per cent of 777 cattle surveyed showed the characteristic symptoms of *fluorosis*—from the thickening of bones to the stiffening of joints. The herd value deterioration is pointed up by the predicament of one rancher who was forced to sell a prize $10,000 Brahma bull for a paltry $36. Elsewhere, cattle have been poisoned by eating vegetation contaminated with molybdenum from steel plants or foundry-emitted lead. Near Anaconda, Montana, arsenic from mammoth smelters settled on pasturage; when ingested it caused nose ulcers in horses and mortality among sheep which had been grazing up to fifteen miles from the pollution source (10).

Cost of Air Pollution. According to federal estimates, air pollution may be costing each man, woman, and child in the United States a minimum of $65 annually. The average yearly loss sustained by farmers and ranchers alone may approach $0.5 billion. Air pollution costs the nation as a whole at least $11 billion (3). In 1962 the Civil Aeronautics Board cited air pollution as the direct cause of fifteen to twenty air crashes, involving multi-million-dollar plane damage and loss of human life. Air-borne contaminants tarnish, soil, abrade, corrode, weaken, discolor and erode a variety of materials. Ozone causes textiles to fade. Sulfuric acid mist can reduce an expensive pair of nylon stockings to shreds in the time it takes a woman to walk to lunch and back. Store buildings, archways, and monuments are covered with grime and rendered unsightly. Grim testimony to the rapid rate at which we are degrading our atmospheric resource is demonstrated by the fate of Cleopatra's Needle in New York. Although the famed obelisk was not brought to this country

Figure 14–9A Effects of fluorine on a cow. Note bone damage to skeleton, especially on forelegs. [U.S. Public Health Service]

Figure 14–9B This skin cancer developed on mouse after its skin was painted with pollutants from urban air. [U.S. Public Health Service]

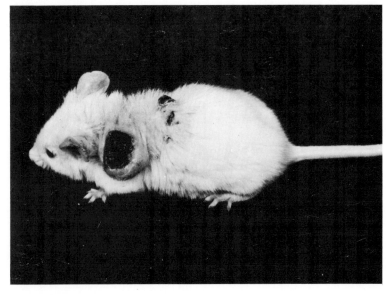

Figure 14–10 Statue of Alexander Hamilton suffers soiling from air pollution at the U.S. Treasury Building, Washington, D.C., April 11, 1966. [National Air Pollution Control Administration]

until 1881, it has deteriorated more since its arrival here than during its entire three thousand year history in Egypt.

Electric light bills for many urban families are substantially higher simply because the available sunlight is reduced 15 to 20 per cent by smoke and dust. Corrosion of industrial equipment, raw materials, and facilities perhaps is the gravest economic blow dealt by air pollutants. Steel surfaces corrode two to four times faster in urban than in nearby agricultural areas because of sulfur pollution. Because palladium and silver are corroded by sulfur, electrical contacts must be made of costly gold by the manufacturers of electrical equipment, thus increasing the cost of the product to the consumer. Add to this the bills for medical treatment and hospitalization incurred by thousands victimized annually by pollution-triggered respiratory diseases, and the total air pollution cost to America becomes substantial indeed.

Air Pollution Abatement and Control

Industry. Well over 50 per cent of all air and water pollution has its source in the operations of the 300,000 industrial organizations of our nation. Regrettably, however, certain segments of industry still resist any concerted attempt at pollution control. According to Stewart Udall, former Secretary of the Interior, one of the biggest roadblocks to atmospheric clean-up is the "attitude" of industry. Typical of this attitude is the 1966 statement of a Detroit industrialist, "People are hysterical about air pollution. There is no proof that it is injurious to public health." In light of published medical data, such a statement is completely ludicrous. However, pressure from an ever more enlightened and indignant public, acting through all levels of government, is mounting. Because the current air pollution crisis represents the cumulative end product of many years of environmental abuse, the U.S. Public Health Service feels that only a massive and sustained control effort will be of any avail.

In his Environmental Message to Congress, Feb. 10, 1970, President Nixon advocated the use of court-imposed fines, up to $10,000 per day, as a deterrent to industrial pollution. There are indications that at least some industrial leaders are finally accepting the principle that pollution control costs are part of the cost of doing business. Indicative of this changing attitude is a statement made at a 1970 meeting of the American Marketing Association by Edward Gelsthorpe Jr., president of Hunt-Wesson Foods: "Beginning right now you are going to see companies making substantial investments to clean up pollution. Companies will be saying to share holders: You don't need a dividend this quarter because we are going to use the money for a chimney in our Ohio plant that's putting sulphur in the air."

POLLUTION CONTROL DEVICES. Although many of the pollution control devices currently available are not 100 per cent efficient in removing industrial contaminants, they often do significantly reduce emission levels. Certainly industry cannot wait another few years for the "perfect" control device to be developed; that day may never come.

Four standard types of equipment for controlling particulates are available (4). In the *electrostatic precipitator*, dust particles, which have been negatively charged, are retained on positively charged plates. Although presently employed to only a limited degree, electrostatic precipitators can remove up to 99 per cent of the cinders, fly ash, and other particulates normally released during coal-burning operations. The *fabric filter bag house* operates like a giant vacuum cleaner which collects particles in huge cloth sacks. The *wet scrubber* removes dust from an incurrent air stream by spraying it with water. Frequently employed in conjunction with other devices, the *cyclone filter* removes heavy dust particles with the aid of gravity and a

Figure 14–11 Effect of air pollution control equipment. Top: Industrial stack emitting contaminants prior to installation of control device. Bottom: Emissions effectively curbed after installation. [U.S. Public Health Service]

downward spiraling air stream. Sales of these four standard pollution control devices are expected to mushroom from $73 million in 1966 to $130 million by 1975.

Other types of control equipment, such as vapor conservators, afterburners, and condensation and absorption devices, are available for noxious gases. Research has recently been conducted on catalytic methods of control; calcium and magnesium oxides, for example, may be employed to convert foul-smelling sulfur dioxide into a harmless or even valuable product.

In many of the larger coal-using industries, the high sulfur content can be reduced before burning. About one third of the sulfur is present as tiny particles of iron disulfide. Much of this inorganic sulfur can be removed by physical methods after the coal has been pulverized. Some authorities feel that industry and government should spend $25 to $50 million annually on research to develop better methods for desulfurizing coal and fuel oil (19). Recently New York City passed an ordinance making it illegal, as of 1971, to consume coal or fuel oil with a sulfur content above 1 per cent. This could result in a substantial reduction of sulfur dioxide emissions, because in 1966 coal sulfur levels went as high as 2.8 per cent (13).

The cost of control methods and equipment may add substantially to the over-all cost of production, although such costs vary widely. It may cost a steel mill 5 per cent more to reduce emissions to acceptable levels; the cleanest cement plant may pay 10 per cent above its base operational cost, and it may cost a foundry melt shop 15 to 20 per cent more to clean up its operation (11).

PROGRESS BY INDUSTRY. Although industry as a whole must be prodded repeatedly, an increasing number of concerned, responsible, far-sighted industrial leaders are showing not only that aerial contaminants can be markedly curtailed but that recovery of some commercially valuable wastes may help to absorb the cost of pollution control equipment. A few examples follow:

1. A major chemical company which installed control equipment for $85,000 is now recovering $50,000 worth of odious benzothiazole annually.
2. The massive St. Clair power plant of Detroit Edison has been experimentally employing a catalytic process that would reduce offensive sulfur dioxide fumes to easily disposable calcium sulfate (plaster of paris), a procedure that would increase utility costs a negligible 3 per cent.
3. American Cyanamid installed a dust-collecting apparatus that annually removes 4,000 tons of high carbon fly ash which is reusable as fuel.

Figure 14–12 Before installation of special cleaning equipment over 150 tons of smoke used to pour daily from these chimneys at U.S. Steel's Duquesne plant. Now, the new equipment wets down the smoke, washes it, and compresses it into disposable briquets. [U.S. Public Health Service]

4. Several large utility companies sell the fly ash recovered from their stack gases for use in the manufacture of cinder blocks, paving materials, abrasives, and portland cement.

5. Tennessee Corporation once decimated large stretches of the Georgia hillsides with its sulfur gases; today these wastes are being converted into the company's major product, sulfuric acid. It is estimated that if other coal-consuming industries did likewise, the 23 million tons of annual sulfur dioxide emissions could be profitably converted into 15 million tons of sulfuric acid—almost equivalent to our country's total yearly consumption (9).

6. With only an $8,000 investment in control devices a mineral-processing firm is recovering high-quality particulates worth more on a tonnage basis than the original product.

The automobile industry once shrugged off its responsibilities in restricting exhaust emissions. For example, a standard Detroit joke in the early 1960's was: "What California needs is filter-tipped people!" That early mood of flippancy has changed to serious concern. The industry realizes that it has to make radical changes in motor design—mounting pressure from both consumers and pollution control agencies will demand nothing less. Car manufacturers now regard the pollution issue even more of a threat to car sales than the safety issue of the mid-1960's. Henry Ford II branded it "by far the most important problem" the industry will encounter in the 1970's.

Transportation vehicles emit 74.8 million tons of atmospheric pollutants yearly (12). This represents 59 per cent of our annual total air pollution tonnage (12). Certain advocates of strong air pollution control measures—such as John W. Gardner, former Secretary of the Department of Health, Education and Welfare, and Frank M. Stead, Chief of Environmental Sanitation for California—believe that the gasoline-powered vehicle sooner or later will have to be removed from the American scene in the interest of health (18). New York City's Task Force in Air Pollution has strenuously urged the development of a mammoth program to develop an efficient alternative to the internal combustion engine to keep America's greatest cities from becoming uninhabitable within a decade (8).

The basis for such apprehension is underscored in a briefing document prepared in August 1969 for Dr. Lee Du Bridge, President Nixon's science advisor: "There is strong evidence that the use of federal standards geared to controlling the internal combustion engine will not result in the drastic inroads on the problem needed to safeguard public health. At best the effect of present federal standards will be to postpone in time the upward growth of pollution levels rather than to reverse the trend. These controls (are) far less than adequate to cope with a problem already well out of hand. . . . There is no guarantee that the degree of control that is possible with the internal combustion engine will be adequate. *The problem is already beyond reasonable bounds. . . .*" In 1970 Senator Gaylord Nelson of Wisconsin introduced legislation (the Low Emission Vehicle Act) which would phase out the internal combustion engine by 1978 unless it can meet national emission standards by that time.

The suitable alternative may be an electric car powered by a fuel cell, a special type of battery that is refuelable, like a gas engine, and that converts the fuel directly into electrical power, with air-contaminating emissions reduced to zero. Although several automobile manufacturers are working on the development of an efficient fuel cell, it may well be 1975 or 1980, if ever, before a reasonably good battery car (of short range and perhaps a top speed of 50 miles per hour) will appear on the highways of America. Some have suggested that private industry and the federal government mount a $100 million-a-year research program to this end, over a five-year period. (A few electric-powered buses are already in operation in certain European cities.)

Until the electric car is mass produced (and it may never fulfill the promise predicted for it), we must reduce emissions from the gasoline-powered motor car to an absolute minimum. In 1968 all new motor cars were required to meet federal control standards patterned after those of California, in which carbon monoxide emissions are limited to 1.5 per cent of the total motor exhaust, and hydrocarbon pollutants are reduced to 275 parts per million (8). In 1970, all new motor cars were required to reduce carbon monoxide to 1 per cent and hydrocarbons to 180 parts per million, standards to be met largely by subtle engine design modifications, such as smoother cylinders, retarded spark timing, and the use of leaner gas mixtures, and adding only $25 to the purchase price of the vehicle (3). By these and other control techniques, such as pumping air into the exhaust manifold to increase hydrocarbon consumption efficiency, motor exhaust pollutants may be reduced by 60 per cent.

Figure 14–13 Traffic congestion in New York City. The exhaust fumes from these cars are contributing to the haze which shrouds the Empire State Building. [U.S. Public Health Service]

Of course, these devices do not reduce nitrogen oxides, evaporative emissions, or heavy particle pollutants

Federal regulations will reduce carbon monoxide and hydrocarbon emissions in 1971 models to roughly 25 per cent of the emissions from the pre-1968 models. Federal restrictions on nitrogen oxide emissions will go into effect initially on the 1973 model cars. By 1975 federal standards will demand that particulate emissions be reduced to one third, and nitrogen oxides to one seventh the levels permitted in 1971 models. Also, by 1975, hydrocarbons must be reduced to less than one fourth, and carbon monoxide emissions to less than one half those permissible in 1971. The federal government's objective by 1980 is to reduce all categories of emissions 50 per cent below the levels permitted in 1975. The modifications required to meet these federal standards will result in a $50 to $200 increase in the car's purchase price.

Control of Pollutants from Refuse-Burning. The vast tonnage of refuse discarded in this country at the rate of 8 pounds per person per day (1) must be disposed of. There is no valid excuse, however, for the open burning of paper, garbage, leaves, junk, and assorted debris by the individual householder, the apartment caretaker, or private industry. A simple, well-enforced city ordinance can solve this problem forthwith. Communities can provide collection and disposal services for a very slight increase in taxes. Refuse may then be consumed in modern municipal incinerators, operating with much greater combustion efficiency than the converted oil drum, that rusty backyard eyesore so extensively used at present. A highly satisfactory alternative, especially for smaller towns, is the landfill method, in which debris is dumped into a low-lying wasteland area, such as a swamp or bog, and later covered with earth. A community of 10,000 people requires 1 acre of land per year to dispose of a 10-foot layer of refuse. The individual family can dispose of garbage by composting, thus accelerating the recycling of nitrogen and enhancing the soil's fertility. Such nitrate-enriched sites can later be used as highly productive garden plots.

Federal Legislation. The first anti-air pollution legislation was passed by Congress in 1955. It authorized a federal program of technical assistance, training, and research. In 1963 the Clean Air Act provided for expansion of the program to include financial support to state, local, and regional control agencies. The act also provided for the curbing of atmospheric pollution emanating from federal facilities (12). The Air Quality Act of

1967, however, superseded all earlier legislation; its main purposes were to authorize financial aid to air pollution control agencies; to intensify and widen the research effort relating to the identification and control of air pollutants emanating from combustion engines, especially the motor car; to provide for the establishment of regional control commissions; and to authorize the establishment of minimal standards of air quality. In the event of air pollution disaster, the Department of Health, Education and Welfare is empowered to request an immediate injunction to check pollutant emissions by summarily closing down industries, halting the flow of traffic, and prohibiting the use of incinerators.

Under the Air Quality Act the air pollution problem is attacked by the Department of Health, Education and Welfare (HEW) primarily on a regional basis. Initially, HEW designates certain pollution-control "regions," defined as meteorological, topographical, and climatic units which affect the diffusion of atmospheric pollution. As of late 1969 eight such regions were set up by HEW's National Air Pollution Control Administration. They include the metropolitan areas of New York, Los Angeles, Philadelphia, Chicago, Denver, and Washington. Federal funds have been utilized to set up interstate planning commissions which have the responsibility of establishing air-quality standards and the most effective means of attaining them. By early 1969 emission standards had been set up in these regions for sulphur oxides and particulates. In 1970 the NAPCA emission criteria were established on motor vehicle contaminants such as nitrogen oxides, hydrocarbons and carbon monoxide. It is expected that standards will be established by HEW for over thirty other atmospheric pollutants including lead, fluorides and pesticides within the near future. The governors of the states involved receive recommendations issued from the commission for pollution control, as well as information from HEW relative to the technology available for implementation of the commission's suggestions. If the states fail to act within a reasonable time, the Department of Health, Education and Welfare has the authority to assume direction, implementation, maintenance, and enforcement of pollution abatement and control for the state. The bill also provides $375 million over three years to support research on control of combustion pollutants. It provides for an advisory board on air quality, appointed by the President, which includes the Secretary of HEW and fifteen other members. It provides for a study of pollution control's effect on the economic health of industry, community, and nation. Under the bill, states may receive funds for setting up motor exhaust emission testing systems.

Even though the Air Quality Act of 1967 is a firm step forward, HEW would be the first to admit that it is just that—a single step in the long march toward full-fledged air pollution control (5).

Detection. Since 1953, when the U.S. Public Health Service established the National Air Sampling Network (NASN), primarily designed to measure smoke and fly ash concentrations, the number of monitoring stations has increased from only seventeen in the dirtiest cities to 200 urban and thirty nonurban stations. The federal government provides the equipment, and manpower is provided by local and state agencies. With increasing indications that gaseous pollutants were potentially more damaging than particulates, the U.S. Public Health Service inaugurated the Continuous Air Monitoring Program (CAMP) in six major cities (15). By means of sophisticated instrumentation (some units cost $2,000 to $7,000), CAMP takes continuous measures of carbon monoxide, nitric oxide, nitrogen dioxide, sulfur dioxide, total hydrocarbons, and total oxidants (15).

CAMP has shown that a city's rating may be good for one contaminant and poor for another. Thus, the air of San Francisco has a minimum of total suspended particulates but a very poor rating for nitrogen dioxide. Data provided by CAMP has shown that some of the major variables affecting the nature and gravity of air pollution problems at any one place and time are types of pollutants, quantity of pollutants, wind speed and direction, topography, sunlight, precipitation, and decrease or increase in temperature (15).

The federal government may relay pollution data to state and local authorities, to give them advance warning of the development of a possible major pollution incident, very much as our weather stations provide forewarning of violent thunderstorms, hurricanes, or tornadoes.

Financial Aid to Education. In 1965 the Division of Air Pollution of the U.S. Public Health Service awarded $1.2 million in training grants and fellowships to a dozen universities, including the University of Cincinnati, Howard University, the University of Michigan, the University of Minnesota, New York University, Oregon State University, Pennsylvania State University, the University of Pittsburgh, the University of Southern California, Yale University, the University of Washington, Texas A and M, and Tulane University. Fellowships support graduate students studying biomedical, biometeorological, socioeconomic, or engineering and physical science aspects of the pollution problem. Moreover, in 1966 the Division of Air Pollution itself was offering twenty-six courses at the Robert A. Taft Sanitary Engineering Center at Cincinnati, which embraced a broad spectrum of subjects, from air pollution data valuation to public information and community relations (16). This program, however, must be expanded. In 1966 only 1,200 professionally qualified people were available to deal with a nationwide pollution problem. According to the U.S. Public Health Service (19), by 1980 we will need 9,000 people, and a $24 million grant and fellowship program for 1967–1977 must be launched to bridge this alarming gap in trained personnel.

Control of Pollution at the Regional Level. Regulation of atmospheric pollution frequently cannot be adequately imposed by a local, county, or even state agency because the pollutants do not recognize political boundaries. For example, a town like Princeton, New Jersey, may do an excellent job of reducing its own emissions and yet have periodic severe pollution problems having their origin in several major sources in proximity to, but outside, the town of Princeton itself. The air pollution created in cities like Detroit and Cincinnati frustrates the control programs of nearby small cities. The unit of regulation should be geographical and meteorological rather than political. This unit has been termed the *problem shed* and is defined as a

Figure 14–14 Localities in which major interstate air pollution problems are expected to develop. [Adapted from Harold Wolozin (ed.), *The Economics of Air Pollution*. By permission of W. W. Norton & Company, Inc. Copyright © 1966 by W. W. Norton & Company, Inc.]

"geographic area that contains a complex of interrelated polluters, the media by which their pollutants are dispersed or collected, and the great majority of the activities and population
that are affected" (12). A good example of a problem shed is the
Bay Area Air Pollution Control District in California, which
embraces six counties in the San Francisco Bay region. Another
is the so-called Penjerdel Region, which includes eleven counties on either side of the Delaware River and embraces Trenton,
New Jersey, Philadelphia, Pennsylvania, and Wilmington, Delaware. It had a population density of roughly 1,100 per square
mile in 1960. It is a highly diversified, industrialized region
characterized by petrochemical, heavy steel, metal-working,
textile, and electronic equipment plants. It is a cohesive meteorological unit, with air pollutants being transported from
south southwest to north northeast by the prevailing wind. It
has a myriad political subdivisions and transcends the borders
of three states, eleven counties, and 377 municipalities (12).

Control of regional pollution problems which embrace more
than a single state become the responsibility of the federal government. Federal abatement action by the end of 1966 had
begun in nine interstate regions. One of these was the Washington, D.C.–suburban Maryland–northern Virginia region;
another embraced seventeen counties in New York and New
Jersey (18).

Control of Pollution at the State Level.   The primary responsibility for the control and abatement of air pollution at its source
has to be shouldered at state and local levels, with the federal
government serving as a source of technical assistance and
financial aid. Certainly a state must ensure protection for its
smaller communities which may be subject to fumes from
nearby towns outside their jurisdiction. A state also has the
responsibility to give financial and technical aid to small industrial towns with grave pollution sources

The scope and number of state air pollution control programs
increased sharply after the passage of the Clean Air Act of 1963.
Prior to the act, seventeen states were spending a minimum of
$5,000; their total budget was $2 million dollars. By the end of
1966, however, at least forty states spent $5,000 on control. Only
nine of the forty states, however—Delaware, Hawaii, Illinois,
Indiana, New Jersey, New York, Oregon, Pennsylvania, and
West Virginia—included regulatory authority (19). State control budgets ranged from zero for twelve states to $2.4 million
for California. The highest annual per capita budgets in 1966
were those of California ($15.20), West Virginia ($13.70), and
Hawaii ($11.70) (17).

Control of Pollution at the Local Level. Los Angeles pioneered in pollution control, developing an effective organization which has served as a prototype for many other communities. Coal combustion is prohibited throughout the year; during peak smog months the burning of oil is similarly banned. Some of our major cities are striving vigorously for effective control and abatement. As of 1966, 1,500 people were employed full-time to cope with air pollution on the local level. Ordinances against excessive smoke and odors exist in almost every community in the United States. Chicago, Detroit, and New York City have recently written tough new control laws (12). In 1967, Chicago had a $1.5 million control budget and maintained a 130-man staff. Violations of Chicago's pollution ordinance are quickly spotted with a zoom-lens-equipped television camera which continuously revolves atop a downtown skyscraper. Police officers in radio-equipped patrol cars have the authority to issue $10 tickets to violators. Total air pollution control budgets for 1966 ranged from zero for Honolulu and New Orleans to $3.6 million for Long Beach–Los Angeles. The number of air pollution programs on the local level budgeting a minimum of $5,000 annually and 0.03¢ per capita increased from forty in 1952 to sixty-one in 1965 (19).

Pollution control in smaller towns is usually inadequate if it exists at all. Funds are frequently lacking for staffing, detection, or enforcement. If local authorities do attempt to enforce a local pollution ordinance, industry may threaten to move elsewhere, crippling the town's economy.

One of the most promising anti-air pollution programs on the community level is Cleaner Air Week, sponsored by the Air Pollution Control Association. Community agencies may use federal grant money to promote Cleaner Air Week (CAW). The major goals of CAW are to enlighten the community concerning the importance of restoring or maintaining a fresh air supply, to make a progress report on local pollution control efforts, and to interest more citizens in assuming responsibility in future abatement projects. Under the aegis and direction of pertinent local governmental agencies, the one-week campaign may be conducted by the local medical association, board of trade, chamber of commerce, women's clubs, Boy Scout troop, or other social, civic and educational unit.

Summary

The increasing public awareness of the medical, ecological, and economic implications of our air pollution problem, as well as the upgrading of federal, state, and local pollution con-

trol programs, is encouraging. Nevertheless, within the remaining years of this century the major emission sources in
this country will increase at an astounding rate as urbanization,
industrialization, the consumption of fuels, and the use of
motor vehicles all increase. Consider the following data: Our
urban population is expected to mushroom from the 144 million
of 1965 to 272 million by 2000; steel production will rise from the
220 million tons of 1960 to 460 million tons by 2000; chemical
production will be 450 per cent greater in 2000 than in 1965;
petroleum production will increase sharply from the 3 billion
barrels of 1960 to almost 7 billion by 2000. By 2000 there will be
240 million privately owned motor cars on our highways, consuming an aggregate 160 billion gallons of gasoline yearly—
roughly four times the figure for 1960. Moreover, it has been
estimated that by the year 2000 the total annual production of
combustible waste will zoom to a staggering 175 million tons,
sufficient to bury all of Washington, D.C., in 30 feet of trash (19).

It is apparent that our recently strengthened pollution control
programs will not even enable us to maintain our present position in the pollution crisis. *We must do much more than we are
now doing, and we must do it quickly.*

BIBLIOGRAPHY

1. Abelson, Philip H. "Waste Management and Control," *Science,*
   152 (1966), 3720.
2. _____ "A Damaging Source of Air Pollution," *Science,* **158** (1967),
   3808.
3. Bregman, J. I., and Sergei Lenormand. *The Pollution Paradox.* New
   York: Spartan Books, Inc., 1966, 191 pp.
4. "Cleaning Up the Nation's Air," *Business Week* (July 23, 1966),
   89–96.
5. "Congress Starts Clearing the Air," *Business Week* (July 24, 1967).
6. Faith, W. L. *Air Pollution Control.* New York: John Wiley and Sons,
   Inc., 1959.
7. Hanks, James J., and Harold D. Kube. "Industry Action to Combat
   Pollution," *Harvard Business Review* (September–October, 1966),
   49–62.
8. Lessing, Lawrence. "The Revolt Against the Internal Combustion
   Engine," *Fortune* (July, 1967), 79–83, 180–184.
9. "Let's Clear the Air!" *The American City* (August, 1967), 1324.
10. Lewis, Howard R. *With Every Breath You Take.* New York: Crown
    Publishers, 1965, 322 pp.
11. Lund, Herbert F. "Industrial Air Pollution," *Factory* (October,
    1965), 11.
12. National Academy of Sciences. *Waste Management and Control.*
    Publication No. 1400. Washington, D.C.: National Research Coun-
    cil, 1966.
13. Ridgeway, James. "Stench from New Jersey," *The New Republic*
    (July 16, 1966), 13–15.
14. "Trees as Source of Pollution," *Time,* **88,** 11 (1966), 57.

15. U.S. Public Health Service. *Air Pollution: A National Sample.* Publication No. 1562. Washington, D.C.: Division of Air Pollution, U.S. Public Health Service, 1966.

16. _____ *Air Pollution Training Programs.* Publication No. 1542. Washington, D.C.: Division of Air Pollution, U.S. Public Health Service, 1966.

17. _____ *State and Local Programs in Air Pollution Control.* Publication No. 1549. Washington, D.C.: Division of Air Pollution, U.S. Public Health Service, 1966.

18. _____ *The Federal Air Pollution Program.* Publication No. 1560. Washington, D.C.: Division of Air Pollution, U.S. Public Health Service, 1966.

19. _____ *Today and Tomorrow in Air Pollution.* Publication No. 1555., Washington, D.C.: Division of Air Pollution., U.S. Public Health Service, 1966.

20. _____ *The Effects of Air Pollution.* Publication No. 1556. Washington, D.C.: U.S. Public Health Service, 1967.

21. Weisz, Paul B. *The Science of Biology.* New York: McGraw-Hill Book Co., 1959, 796 pp.

The Human Population Problem

15

Up to this point we have discussed the nature, utilization, and intelligent conservation of a number of our natural resources, but the most important resource of all we have reserved for this final chapter. This resource is man himself.

Population Increase

Phylogenists place man at the pinnacle of the animal kingdom because of his ability to assess a problem, to devise a solution, and to put that solution into operation. However, at this crucial period in human history, man has as yet not effectively applied his talents to solving the problem of his exploding population. If unresolved, this population increase may bring calamity to the human species.

Man is the most abundant mammalian species on earth. According to Marston Bates, ecologist at the University of Michigan, 187 babies are born each minute. Although 142,000 people die each day, 270,000 are born daily; thus, there is a daily increment of 128,000 to the world population. To give each person in this daily increase a glass of milk would require milk from 9,600 cows; it would take 200 acres of wheat to give each a loaf of bread. Each month the world has to provide the necessary food, water, shel-

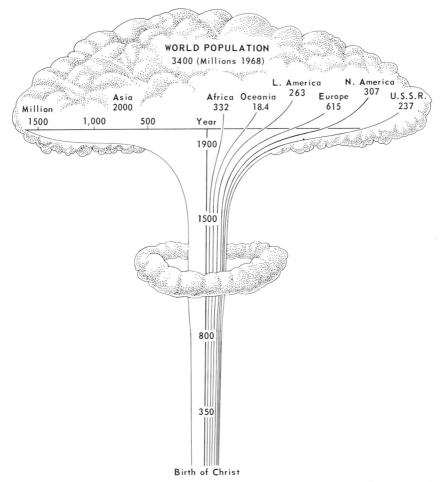

Figure 15–1 The world population "bomb." The number of people increased from 250 million at Christ's birth to over three billion in the late 1960's. The horizontal line indicates numbers of people in millions. The vertical line indicates years and the base line represents date of Christ's birth. Note the accelerated growth during the twentieth century. Asia is becoming populated with an increasing percentage of the world population. [Adapted from Georg Borgstrom, *Too Many* (New York: The Macmillan Company, 1969)]

ter, and living space to sustain 4 million additional people. Four billion pounds of human biomass are synthesized annually, a far greater increase than that for any other mammal.

Dr. Philip Hauser, Director of the Population Research Training Center at the University of Chicago, has pointed out that an initial population of 100 people increasing at a rate of only 1 per cent per year for 5,000 years would produce a population density of 2.7 billion people per square foot of land on earth. But our global rate of annual increase is much greater than 1 per cent. In 1967 it was 2.1 per cent per year and may even soar to 3 per cent soon. In 1968 the United States had a population of 200 million; by the year 2000 it is expected to reach 300 million. It took man 2 million years to attain a population of the present 3.3 billion, but in only thirty-five additional years this figure will be doubled. Using 1957 as a bench mark, the population of Costa Rica will have doubled by 1973; Syria will double its population by 1974, Libya by 1976, Viet Nam by 1978, Mexico, Panama, and the Philippines by 1979, and Brazil by 1980. By the mid 1970's the annual population increase in China will equal the total 1963 population of the United States. Some demographers predict that the world population will reach 12 billion by 2050.

Factors Underlying Reduced Mortality

We regard today's medical technology as a wonder, a boon for man. However, this advanced medical technology is largely responsible for the present surge in human numbers. Prior to the advent of modern medicine human mortality rates were much higher. Aristotle once noted three centuries before Christ that "most babies die before the week is out." Man was at one time extremely vulnerable to the lethal attacks of infectious parasites, such as viruses, bacteria, and protozoa. Medieval Europe was scourged with the horror of plague. It killed over 25 million people in Asia and Europe. Smallpox spread like wildfire and killed one out of every four afflicted until Jenner developed his vaccine at the close of the eighteenth century (1). A child born in 1550 had a life expectancy of only eight and one-half years. In 1900 the prime killer was tuberculosis, with pneumonia running a close second. As late as 1919 the influenza virus took a toll of 25 million people. The mortality picture has drastically changed. Largely because of modern medicine the mortality rate in the United States has been cut from 25 per thousand per year in 1900 to 9.4 in 1967. The world death rate of 25 per thousand in 1935 is expected to fall to 12.7 by 1980. Today, the primary fatal diseases are heart disease and cancer, in that order; both are primarily associated with the aging process.

Early in the twentieth century the mosquito-borne disease of malaria was either directly or indirectly responsible for 50 per cent of all human mortality. Today, thanks to modern insecticides such as DDT and to superior drugs for killing the red-blood-cell-invading *Plasmodium* parasite, the malarial threat has greatly diminished. Consider Ceylon. Because of the intensive malarial control campaign launched there in 1946 the Ceylonese mortality rate was reduced from 22 to 13 per thousand within about six years. The elimination of malaria in many areas of Latin America caused the population growth rate to zoom to 4 per cent per year (4). Advances in medical and para-medical technology, then, have largely contributed to man's "golden" opportunity for growing old. Man is unique in his characteristic type of mortality today. He dies because of senescence. This is of course not the case in nature. There are few senile foxes or quail, very few aged deer or brook trout. Wild animals almost never live out their theoretical life-span. Wild animal mortality invariably results from the pressures of environmental resistance.

The Malthusian Principle and Food Scarcity

This planet's crush of people has caused a hornet's nest of problems. Consider, for example, the problems of pollution, of shrinking space, of big-city noise, of land and water abuse, of maintaining aesthetically satisfying wilderness areas for recreation, and so on. However, the most important of the problems resulting from the population increase is food scarcity. This problem was predicted in 1798 by the British economist Robert Malthus. According to his thesis, because the human population tends to increase in *geometrical* progression and food supplies increase at only an *arithmetical* rate, there would inevitably be more people to feed than food to feed them. Malthus argued that the only way this dilemma could ultimately be resolved was by pestilence, warfare, starvation, or other human calamities, which we would now sum up as "environmental resistance."

Today, two of every three people in the world are suffering from chronic malnutrition. Nutritionists assume that the average person must have a minimum of 2,200 calories daily. Western Europeans and North Americans get 3,200 calories daily. They are among the fortunate. The average Indian or African has only 1,600 calories daily. This 600-calorie deficit undermines strength, causes severe mental and physical lethargy, and weakens resistance to a broad spectrum of diseases.

Indian women have been known to abandon their infants along the roadside, because they no longer have enough milk in their breasts to nourish them. Some years ago an American diplomat visiting in Siberia noticed that the bark of many riverside willows along the Volga appeared to have been stripped away as if by some giant rodent. When he questioned his Russian associates as to what animal was responsible, they replied "the human animal." The natives used willow bark as a basic ingredient in a soup which they regularly prepared in order to survive. Today, 12,000 people will die from hunger throughout the world; tomorrow, 12,000 more will die.

Solving the Food Shortage Problem

There are three basic methods for solving the food shortage problem—by increasing man's environmental resistance, by restricting his ability to reproduce, and by increasing his production of food.

Increasing Man's Environmental Resistance. As we have already learned, the population level of any species is dependent upon the interaction of two antagonistic forces, the positive force of the organism's biotic potential (BP), and the negative force of its environmental resistance (ER). Therefore, any increase in the ER would result in a population decrease and might conceivably bring the species within dynamic balance of its food supplies. Cannibalism, infanticide, and warfare are all examples of environmental resistance used by man against himself, with the result of reduced population.

Decreasing Man's Biotic Potential. A more humane method of alleviating the food crisis is to restrict man's capacity to reproduce. This may be done by various methods, such as sterilization, use of mechanical and chemical contraceptives, exercise of moral restraints, delayed marriage, use of the "rhythm" method, and legalization of abortion.

STERILIZATION. Either the man or the woman may be rendered incapable of procreation by the process of sterilization. However, neither the sexual drive nor the gratification from intercourse is diminished. In the male, sterilization simply involves cutting the muscular sperm duct which transfers the sperm from the testes to the penis during intercourse. This is a simple operation. (A man might walk into a doctor's office at 1:00 P.M. and walk out at 1:30 P.M. completely sterilized.) Sterilization of the female involves opening the abdominal cavity and cutting the oviducts, or egg tubes, which convey the mature eggs from the ovary to the uterus.

There exists today a small but dedicated group of people, known as *eugenicists*, who would like to "improve" the quality of the human species by the simple technique of making sterilization mandatory for "inferior" individuals (cripples, the mentally slow, criminals, the lazy, and so on). The eugenicists believe that by this simple technique the "quality" of human beings would increase in a few generations. This theory seems sound on the surface, and it would aid in restricting the human

BP. However, geneticists inform us that such a program of compulsory sterilization would have to operate for many centuries before any substantial "improvement" in the human species could be discerned. There are obviously powerful ethical, moral, and religious arguments against the establishment of such a program.

To be a successful birth control method, sterilization would require an intensive and extensive education campaign to allay the fears of both sexes concerning reduced abilities during intercourse. Among underdeveloped countries only the governments of Taiwan, Korea, Pakistan, and India have initiated official sterilization programs (17). It is the only method to date which has been effective in India. The State of Madras launched a voluntary sterilization program in 1957 which included incentives for participants, such as a free operation, the equivalent of a $7.50 cash bonus, and a three- to six-day holiday for government employees (17). Other Indian states quickly followed suit. Despite the considerable handicap imposed by the doctor shortage, the New Delhi government achieved about 5 million male sterilizations in 1970.

CHEMICAL CONTRACEPTIVES. Considerable progress has been made by the technologically advanced nations of the West in the use of the chemical contraceptive. The chemical contraceptive most widely employed is taken in pill form and is a steroid similar to the hormone *progesterone* secreted by the ovary's corpus luteum (5). By exerting a negative feedback on the pituitary gland, the latter is prevented from secreting the follicle-stimulating hormone (FSH) necessary for the maturation of the ovum (5). There are certain drawbacks, however, to the use of "the pill." It has some undesirable side effects and the long-term effect on the emotional life of the woman is still unknown. Moreover, it demands a high degree of self-discipline, because a woman must remember to take twenty pills monthly at the right time (5). Moreover, because the pills are expensive, they do not lend themselves to use among the impoverished nations, where the need for them is most acute. Currently, intensive research is being conducted to develop a pill which need be taken only once each month, and a retroactive, "morning-after" pill may even be in the offing (17).

MECHANICAL CONTRACEPTIVES. Some population experts hope that the intrauterine device (IUD) will prove effective in the underdeveloped countries (17). Factories are even being built to produce them cheaply in these nations on a mass basis. The IUD is a plastic or nylon coil that is inserted in the womb to prevent implantation of the embryo.

RHYTHM METHOD. The rhythm method of birth control alone has the full sanction of the Catholic Church. It is, of course, practiced extensively by non-Catholics as well. It is based upon the fact that the viability of egg and sperm extends for only 2 days after they have entered the oviduct and vagina, respectively. After this period the gametes perish and are incapable of reproducing. The average human female has a twenty-eight-day menstrual cycle and ovulates on the fourteenth day. If she abstains from intercourse, therefore, from days 11 through 17, she probably would not be able to conceive. Although this method is not completely reliable from the individual's standpoint, for the population as a whole it may serve to reduce birth rates appreciably. It has been advocated, in conjunction with other methods, for developing nations.

DELAYED MARRIAGE. In Ireland a considerable proportion of engaged couples delay marriage for several years. For example, the average age for Irish brides and bridegrooms is twenty-six and thirty-two, respectively. This is in marked contrast to the average ages of nineteen and twenty-one for their American counterparts. Ireland is not endowed with rich mineral wealth, an abundance of fertile soil, a long growing season, or many other natural prerequisites for a prosperous economy. Thus, because they cannot afford it, many Irish couples postpone marriage. This effectively restricts the ultimate size of their families.

MORAL RESTRAINT. Currently, according to Dr. Bogue of the University of Chicago, there appears to be a trend toward smaller families, not only in America, but in Europe, Canada, Great Britain, Australia, and New Zealand as well (2). Where it was once considered most desirable to have three children, it is now becoming stylish in the United States and Europe to have a two-child family. This permits a higher standard of living in which the color TV or second car takes the place of the third child (2). There are many other families, however, which have restricted their size because of a feeling of moral responsibility to a population-beseiged world.

LEGALIZED ABORTION. The expulsion of the fetus from the uterus before full term is known as an *abortion* if it causes fetal death. Some abortions occur naturally, and fortunately so, for almost 40 per cent of these fetuses would otherwise develop into physically and mentally impaired offspring. Some abortions, on the other hand, are caused by human intervention and result in death of a fetus which probably would have developed into a normal, healthy baby. The legalization of artificial abortions may become an effective method of population control.

After World War II, Japan, with its expansionist dreams shattered and with only 0.166 acre per capita, was faced with the vexing problem of a zooming population. The government acted quickly and boldly. Abortions were legalized in 1948. By 1955 over 1.2 million abortions were being performed annually. In 1949 Japan had a birth rate of 32 per thousand, whereas by 1967 the birth rate had been reduced to a mere 19.4 per thousand. This desperate bid on the part of the Japanese government to restrict its population surge has been celebratedly successful. It had to be. The alternative was certainly a severely depressed economy and grinding poverty for thousands. Contributing to Japan's remarkable success, however, was a low illiteracy rate of only 1.1 per cent and an extensive and sophisticated medical profession. It is quite doubtful that her success with legalized abortion could be duplicated in any of the developing nations.

There are obviously strong ethical, moral, and religious arguments against the legalization of abortions. What right does a man who happens to be living today have to take the life of another human being who, except for the violent act of abortion, would be alive tomorrow? In the eyes of many eminent in law, medicine, or religion, the wilful practice of abortion is murder. This interpretation has made the practice illegal in the United States, except in the case of rape or incest, or where either the health of child or mother would be in severe jeopardy.

However, since 1967, when Colorado led the way, thirteen states have liberalized their abortion laws. (These states include Arkansas, California, Delaware, Georgia, Hawaii, Kansas, Maryland, New Mexico, New York, North Carolina, Oregon and South Carolina). New York's law, passed in April 1970, is the most liberal, permitting abortions for any reason. However, since abortions are relatively expensive (averaging $600 in California), and since psychiatric consultations are often a prerequisite, illegal abortions are still frequent. Thus, in California there were only 14,000 legal abortions in 1969 compared to 80,000 illegal ones. Nevertheless, it would appear that the trend toward more relaxed abortion laws will eventually serve to dampen our nation's population surge.

Increasing Food Production. There are several methods by which food production can be increased in a hungry world. Some of them are still in the experimental stage; some are proved successes.

HYDROPONICS OR NUTRICULTURE. *Hydroponics* is the technique of growing crops in an aqueous nutrient solution without soil. It has certain advantages to more conventional crop production. Food tonnage per acre may be six to eight times higher. Problems of soil sterility and soil-borne pests are obviated. It is economical of water because it can be continuously recirculated as long as it is replenished with appropriate nutrients. It may temporarily alleviate an acute fresh vegetable shortage. It was employed during World War II to feed our military personnel on the volcanic ash of Ascension Island and the wasteland of Labrador. Hydroponics has provided fresh foods for manganese miners isolated in the Amazonian wilderness. It has many disadvantages, however. There are problems attending the air- and water-borne moulds and bacteria. Hydroponics requires a heavy capital investment in tanks, pumps, and other equipment. All nutrients must be supplied, rather expensively, by man, and balanced according to a precise prescription for each type of crop. Although the United States has had at least 100 nutriculture farms in commercial operation, it would appear to be a prohibitively costly operation in less technologically advanced countries.

ALGAL CULTURE. About 0.1 to 0.5 per cent of the solar radiation reaching the earth is converted by crops into chemical energy. Only 1 calorie of human food is derived for every million calories of sunshine received by this planet. It takes roughly

Figure 15–2 Farm consolidation makes practical the use of heavy, expensive equipment such as this modern grain combine moving through a Washington wheat field. Use of such equipment will aid in boosting world food production [U.S. Department of Agriculture]

100,000 pounds of algae to produce 1 pound of fish. These facts are explicable in terms of the second law of thermodynamics, as noted earlier. It would seem, therefore, that if man shortened his food chains and consumed algae directly, a much larger food base would be available to nourish a food-deficit world. Large-scale algal culture has been conducted in the United States, England, Germany, Venezuela, Japan, Israel, and the Netherlands. The alga *Chlorella* can be grown in huge tanks; it is rich in proteins, fats, and vitamins and apparently contains all the essential amino acids. Each acre devoted to algal culture can produce up to 40 tons, dry weight, of algae. This is forty times the protein yield per acre of soybeans and 160 times the per acre yield of beef protein. Algal food may be used as a supplement in soups and meat dishes and as livestock feed. Undoubtedly, algal culture is a technological success. Because of the huge capital investment, however, it is not an economic success. It may not be a feasible food production method for poor nations for at least several decades.

FOOD SYNTHESIS. The technology is available for the laboratory synthesis of the basic sugars, fats, amino acids, vitamins and minerals of the human diet. This is an extremely complicated and expensive process, however. The major attempt so far to synthesize human diet calories was conducted

Figure 15–3 Fish, fish meal, and flour, stages in the production of fish protein concentrate. [Bureau of Commercial Fisheries, U.S. Department of the Interior]

by the Germans during the edible fat scarcity imposed by World War II. By the Fischer-Tropsch process, beginning with the hydrogenation of coal, the Germans managed to produce 2,000 tons of synthetic fats annually, much of which was then converted into margarine. It is probable that the bulk of our food calories will always be produced by conventional agricultural methods. A few of our amino acids and vitamins, on the other hand, may be synthesized. Synthetic sources today may provide all the vitamins necessary for vigorous health at a modest annual cost of 25¢ to $1 to the consumer. The people of the underdeveloped countries, who rely heavily on cereal foods, frequently incur a dietary deficiency of such important amino acids as lysine, tryptophane, and methionine. Although these can all be synthetically produced, a year's requirement of these three amino acids would cost about $40, and hence would be prohibitively expensive. United States food manufacturers have succeeded in producing substitute meats, high-protein breakfast foods and beverages simply by fortifying basic cereals with protein. This process requires an astonishing small amount of protein. For example, the protein content of a ton of wheat can be raised to a level close to that of milk casein with the addition of a few pounds of lysine. Indians by the thousands are now consuming lysine-fortified bread marketed by Indian government bakeries in Bombay and Madras. Looking far into the future, Dr. Harrison Brown of the California Institute of Technology suggests that some day our food technology might be in a position to synthesize some pretty good steaks from vegetables; he even goes so far as to provide them with plastic sinews to make them chewy (4).

YEAST CULTURE. Much interest has been shown recently in the prospects of yeast culture in alleviating protein-deficient diets. Yeast can be grown on organic substrates such as coal, petroleum, citrus-cannery waste, grain hulls and straw, beet and cane sugar molasses, and the black liquor derived from paper-pulp manufacture. One French researcher suggests that yeasts could synthesize the equivalent of all the animal protein consumed globally today by using only 3 per cent of our petroleum output as a yeast substrate (17). Yeast culture provides a method by which the hitherto inedible crop residues such as corn cobs, stalks, stems, and woody fibers can be converted into protein-rich food. In the United States, for example, where a man consumes 0.37 tons of food annually, but where each year 1.75 tons per capita of inedible corn and wheat residues accumulate, it would be theoretically possible to increase food supplies from 50 to 100 per cent. Moreover, yeasts are 65 per cent efficient in the conversion of carbohydrate to protein; this com-

pares with the 4 to 20 per cent efficiency of livestock. Yeast food
has been produced in Africa, Jamaica, Puerto Rico, Australia,
Florida, Hawaii, and Wisconsin. Four thousand tons of yeast
are produced annually in Green Bay, Wisconsin, as a by-
product of the pulp industry. The yeast may be used as a supplement in rice dishes, casseroles, soups, and stews (16). To
date, however, yeast has been cultured on only a limited scale
and is expensive to produce.

EXTENSION OF AGRICULTURE INTO NEW AREAS. According
to the Woytinskys, in order to be productive, land must embrace the proper combination of soil texture, soil chemistry,
temperature, rainfall, growing season and topography (24). Of
the 12.5 acres of the world's land available per capita, only 1.1
are being cultivated. However, according to a United Nations
document *Statistics of Hunger*, a minimum of 2.65 additional
acres per capita have food production potential. A U.S. Department of Agriculture report states that the world's farmers are
now tilling only 30 per cent of the potentially productive land.

There is a vast unexploited acreage in South America's tropical rain forests which might be of considerable agricultural
potential. Its advantages include a long growing season and an
abundance of precipitation. Unfortunately, the iron-rich *later-
itic* soil is quite shallow. When the vegetational cover is removed, the soil bakes brick hard under the equatorial sun.
During the torrential downpours of the wet season it rapidly
becomes leached of nutrients. Moreover, fertilization is both
difficult and expensive. Frequently, after only two years of cropping, the soil becomes impoverished and must be abandoned.
Currently, however, intensive research is being conducted to
develop both fertilizers and crop varieties that will be able to
succeed in this region. In 1967, USDA agronomists aided the
Brazilian government in locating land suitable for development.
Seventy-five million acres are being sought in the western two
thirds of the country. When the survey has been completed,
Brazilians will be translocated from overpopulated regions to
selected sites where they will have a reasonable chance of
agricultural success.

It has been suggested that by subjugating the podzols of the
wet and cold regions, as well as the laterites of the warm and
wet tropics, we could increase cultivated land in North and
South America by 50 to 60 per cent, in Asia by 30 per cent. If
we brought these newly subjugated areas, as well as the currently cultivated regions, to the productive level of Western
Europe today, we could adequately feed 4 to 5 billion additional people. But this increase in food production would be

predicated on a corresponding increase in the development of research, education, fertilizer plants, crop and livestock breeding programs, credit institutions, marketing services, transportation facilities, storage accommodations, and farm extension programs of global scope. Moreover, it would require two to three decades to complete at an estimated over-all cost of $500 billion.

Crop production in the tundra is severely limited by the abbreviated growing season of seventy-five to eighty-five days, the continuous summer sunlight (many crops require a period of darkness), and the scant precipitation of less than 10 inches annually. Perhaps geneticists of the future may develop short-season crops with accelerated growth rates which can mature before the onset of the Arctic frost. Russian scientists have discovered that the growing season can be extended a month by scattering coal dust on the snow to accelerate melt. Moreover, crop growing time can be shortened by *vernalization,* the technique of inducing seed germination artificially and then retaining the seedlings temporarily in cold storage.

Some day agriculture may be possible in the Sahara Desert. In 1960 an area of fertile land was discovered in the central Sahara which was equal to the total area of Great Britain. Water might be secured from underground aquifers. For example, in 1950 the Albienne Nappe, a nodular sandstone aquifer, was found. One thousand feet thick in some places, this aquifer now supplies water for an oil town of 30,000 people, for the extension of oases, and for the survival of 50,000 trees planted in 1960. In 1961 the wells in the area were yielding 90 million cubic meters of water annually.

DRAINAGE. Man has achieved notable success as well as a few infamous failures through drainage schemes. The agriculturally productive Fen land of Britain was once a swamp. Flourishing Israeli settlements now occupy the site of the former waterlogged Huleh marshes. Grain is now abundantly produced in Canada's prairie provinces in areas once dominated by muskeg. Arable land may even be reclaimed to a limited extent from shallow seas; in Holland the ingenious Dutch have increased their agricultural area 1 million acres by draining the Zyder Zee. Many additional millions of acres might be reclaimed by lowering the water table. A considerable area could be brought into cultivation in the marshy lowlands of the Sudan simply by redirecting the wasted waters northward to the Nile.

INCREASED USE OF FERTILIZER. Japan has only 0.166 acre of arable land per capita, only one-thirteenth that of the United

States. Only with the most intensive agricultural methods is Japan able to feed her 100 million people. She has achieved amazing success, producing 13,200 calories per cultivated acre, almost three times the per acre calorie production of American farmers, and 350 per cent higher than the world average of 3,800 calories per acre per day. One key to Japan's agricultural accomplishments is the large amounts of fertilizer applied to her farms. A great variety of fertilizers are employed, from sardine-soybean-cottonseed cakes to compost, and from green manure to human dung; in addition, the standard commercial preparations are used (16). It has been shown that Japan's success with soil enrichment can be repeated in many underdeveloped countries, even though it be on a smaller scale. By adding double superphosphate to the soil the Institute for Soil Research in Indonesia increased rice production 308 pounds per acre; the application of ammonium phosphate resulted in further per acre increments of 1,100 pounds. In northern Nigeria an extra 300 pounds per acre of guinea corn resulted from the per acre use of 50 pounds of superphosphate; and manuring of impoverished farmland in Southern Rhodesia has boosted maize production over 200 per cent (16). FAO-sponsored fertilizer trials in Turkey raised wheat production 52 per cent, the increased harvest value being $2.60 for each fertilizer dollar. In Ghana, groundnut yields were boosted 57 per cent. Fertilizer increased Guatemalan cabbage production 140 per cent, with each fertilizer dollar resulting in a $63.90 increase in harvest value. Even without modifying any farm method 9,500 fertilizer field trials conducted by the FAO in fourteen countries have shown an overall average yield increase of 74 per cent (17).

The preceding data show what can be done in the developing nations on an experimental basis. The sobering truth is that fertilizer application in these countries must be greatly increased to ensure the necessary food increments. Even though hungry nations have 55 per cent of the world's arable land and 70 per cent of the world's population, as recently as 1962 they were utilizing only 10 per cent of the world's fertilizer production (17). Age-old superstitions and social practices may hinder acceptance of fertilizers. For example, in East Africa, the Bantu of North Kavirondo are reluctant to employ cattle dung for manuring because they associate its use with evil magic. The size of the dung heap in the cattle-kraal is also a status symbol and indicates the owner's wealth in numbers of cattle. Although India has twenty-five times the cultivated area of Japan, until very recently she used only 1 per cent as much fertilizer (17). One reason for this disparity is the almost prohibitive cost. Because most fertilizer must be imported from abroad, Indian

Figure 15–4 Modern grain storage in India. During recent years the United States has been sending large quantities of food grains to India under Public Law 480, to help alleviate India's chronic shortage of food. Proper storage of food grains in India is essential for the most efficient use of the available stock. To help India overcome this problem, the U.S. Agency for International Development (AID) assisted in building silos and godowns. This is India's first grain storage elevator situated at Hapur, near India's capital, New Delhi. In addition to the elevators AID has made available the services of U.S. technicians to advise on construction and operation of the facility. [U.S. Department of Agriculture]

rice farmers pay three to four times as much as the Japanese in terms of the price they get for their crops. The problem may not finally be solved until the governments of the developing nations launch an aggressive program of fertilizer plant construction. This will require technical assistance, considerable amounts of raw materials, and capital (4). In addition, it will be necessary to construct an extensive transportation system to get the fertilizer to the farmer. It is a tremendous job and one that has to be done soon.

CONTROL OF AGRICULTURAL PESTS. On a global scale insects alone cause $21 billion of agricultural damage yearly (3). Rats, insects, and fungi annually destroy 33 million tons throughout the world, sufficient to feed all the people in the United States (5). One of every fourteen people in the world will starve because of food deprivation imposed by agricultural pests (5). A fungus disease, which caused 90 per cent rice crop destruction in some areas, contributed significantly to the appalling Indian famine of 1943. In India, where rats may outnumber people ten to one, up to 30 per cent of the crops are ravaged by rodents. Rats destroyed thirty-five to forty per cent of Vietnamese farm produce in 1962. Even in the United States as recently as 1943 the European corn borer (*Pyrausta nubilalis*) chewed its way into 120.648 million bushels of corn. Recently the golden nematode (*Heterodera rostochiensis*) devastated so much of Europe's prime potato country that this basic food crop has been restricted to a four-year rotation. The microscopic malarial parasite *Plasmodium* has been a scourge to the farmers of Southeast Asia. It incapacitates millions of rice farmers at the critical periods of transplanting and harvesting. In an attempt to escape the malarial season in northern Thailand farmers are prevented from raising a second rice crop, one which could be used to great advantage in alleviating hunger elsewhere.

In some areas of Africa commercial hog raising is impossible because of the high incidence of the almost 100 per cent lethal African swine fever. During the period 1961 to 1966 over 300,000 horses, mules, and donkeys, the "farm engines" of developing nations, have succumbed to African horse sickness in eight countries of the Near East and Southeast Asia.

The effective control of agricultural pests in the developing nations would markedly boost food output. The United States and Western Europe have developed sophisticated techniques of pest control. Their control experts now wage war against agricultural pests with a veritable arsenal of weapons, including chemosterilants, gamma radiation, sound waves, sex attractants, resistant mutants, natural predators, and microbial agents in addition to the more conventional pesticides. The USDA's Agency for International Development is currently disseminating some of this know-how to the rural regions of South America, Africa, and Asia. In equatorial Africa, twenty-three varieties of tsetse fly, vector of the trypanosome which causes the dread sleeping sickness in man and an equally serious disease in livestock, have effectively prevented livestock production in an area larger than the entire United States. The AID and the Agricultural Research Council of Central Africa have sponsored a research team of USDA, British, and African scientists which has attempted to eradicate the tsetse fly with the use of chemosterilants. The objective has been to sterilize great numbers of male flies and release them to mate with normal wild females, thus rendering the latter incapable of producing young, a technique which was first employed with dramatic success against the screw worm fly in the southeastern United States.

Another team of USDA and African scientists is taking a stand against contagious bovine pleuropneumonia (CBPP), a lung disease which may destroy between 10 and 70 per cent of an infected cattle herd. When American cattle were plagued with CBPP in the 1890's, it was eradicated by the wholesale slaughter of both diseased animals and healthy "carriers"—a control technique that would be singularly inappropriate in tribal Africa, where food supplies are critical. The research team believes that the development of a suitable vaccine will be the African solution to CBPP control.

By the very extension of his cultivation programs, man has unwittingly improved breeding conditions for locusts. Their migratory hordes have decimated man's grainfields since the time of Moses. Examples of locust "nurseries" provided by man are the alfalfa fields of Libya and the crop "islands" in Saudi Arabia, Yemen, and the plains of the Red Sea. Because of their great mobility, adult locusts may destroy crops over a thousand miles and several nations away from their hatching sites. International cooperation, therefore, is frequently required to control an extensive outbreak. Piecemeal attempts are doomed to fail. Farmers of hungry nations are at a disadvantage because of their lack of pesticides and ignorance concerning their use. Aid may even come half a world away. The USDA sends scientists and technologists to critical areas to collaborate with the Desert Locust Control Organization for East Africa. In the spring of 1951 locusts threatened Persia with the worst plague in eight decades. They were breeding primarily in a remote, inaccessible 2,000-square-mile area. Prompt action by the United States, which rushed spray planes and the most powerful new insecticides to the region, quickly brought the outbreak under control.

AGRICULTURAL BREEDING PROGRAMS. Within the last decade great strides made in the field of agricultural genetics promise at least partially to close the world's food gap. Plant geneticists have been able to develop sugar beets with a higher sugar content, soybeans with greater protein. They have developed insect- and disease-resistant grains. They have produced wheats which will develop in shorter growing seasons and which are hence adaptable to more northern latitudes. They have developed crops with a larger proportion of edible parts or with a greater ability to use fertilizer. At the University of Washington, plant geneticists have developed a wheat variety which yielded 152 bushels per acre on one experiment plot, fully 750 per cent more than the 20-bushels-per-acre yield considered good some years ago. Varieties of corn have been developed which will utilize 200 pounds of nitrogen per acre compared to the 90 pounds utilized per acre only a few years ago. Crops have been developed which are resistant to heat, cold, and drought. A variety of grain has been secured which will tolerate the continuous sunlight of the brief Arctic summer.

The introduction of improved strains of sweet potatoes into China by the Food and Agricultural Organization of the United Nations increased food output 37 per cent. A five-year testing program for hybrid corn, sponsored by the FAO in twenty-one European countries in 1953, showed that the superior North American hybrids yielded 60 per cent more than the best local open-pollinated varieties (17). In 1954 the European planting of hybrid corn resulted in a yield increase of 640,000 tons. Recently an American–African research team crossed an African strain of maize with one from Central America; the resultant hybrid gave 100 per cent greater yields than local African types (21). Although only 3,000 acres were planted in 1963, the year of its introduction, by 1966 farmers were so pleased they increased plantings to 100,000 acres. Edible legumes, such as beans, peas, and soybeans, have great food potential for millions of hungry Asians. It is highly significant, therefore, that USDA and Asian scientists, collaborating in India and Iran, have located a Lebanese cowpea which gives 21 per cent greater yields than local Asian types. Moreover, a chickpea was discovered in Cyprus which produced a 40 per cent greater crop than commonly grown Iranian strains (21). Recently scientists at Purdue University, as a result of the mutant opaque-2 gene, have developed a strain of corn bearing large quantities of lysine and tryptophane (21). Because these amino acids are essential for normal human growth, nutrition experts agree that this mutant corn may represent a practical approach to solving the severe protein deficiencies in the diets of Africa, South America, and Asia, where meat, fish, eggs, and poultry are prohibitively costly or short in supply.

The International Maize and Wheat Improvement Center, sponsored by the Rockefeller and Ford foundations, was established in Mexico in 1943 at a time when that country was experiencing a critical food scarcity (22). After twenty-five years of intensive research a huge "bank" of seed varieties has been established. When aid is sought by a developing nation this bank can provide a seed variety which will be adapted to that nation's particular combination of soil chemistry, soil structure, climate, rainfall, and growing season. The center has developed strains of rust-resistant beans which have increased yield from 150,000 to 600,000 tons annually (22). It has produced blight resistant potatoes which have shown a 500 per cent yield increase. Partly as a result of the Improvement Center's work, grain production in Mexico has soared from 700 pounds to 4,200 pounds per acre. In 1962 the International Rice Institute was set up by the Rockefeller and Ford Foundations in the Philippine Islands. Because rice is a staple in the diet of 60 per cent of mankind, it was of considerable moment when, in 1966, the Institute developed a new rice called IR8 (22). Among its outstanding features was a capacity to respond to high levels of fertilization (whereas other varieties might "burn up") and an insensitivity to day length. As a result, IR8 is adaptable to a wide spectrum of soil and climatic conditions (23). It has already transformed the Philippine Islands from a rice-import to a rice-export nation and has enhanced the economy of southeastern Asia by $300 million (22).

Livestock production among hungry nations could be substantially increased by the adoption of European and American methods of selection and breeding. For several years meat output per capita of cattle population in Europe has been seven times that of Africa and ten times that of the Far East. Periodic progress has been made among underdeveloped nations in recent years. For example, milk production among dairy cattle in the United Provinces of India was increased 400 per cent after twenty-five years of culling and cross-breeding. In Puerto Rico the hybrid cattle from a brown Swiss–native breed cross produced 30 to 40 pounds of milk daily as compared to the 14 to 20 pounds from native breeds. In 1943 hybrid hens developed at Minghsien College in China showed an annual egg production of 118 compared to 62 for common hens.

America has been foremost in the development of superior livestock strains. In the 1920's the King Ranch of Texas crossed the shorthorn with the Brahman to develop the Santa Gertrudis. In the 1930's the Brangus strain was produced by

Oklahoma breeders by crossing the shorthorn with the Black Angus. Both Santa Gertrudis and Brangus are meaty, tick and heat resistant and both form the basis of livestock production in several tropical countries. The recent development of *artificial insemination* has made possible greatly accelerated improvement of livestock. For example, although in natural service a New York bull might inseminate only thirty-five cows in the immediate locality, in artificial insemination stud that same animal may be "mated" to 2,000 cows. Because refrigerated bull sperm may retain viability for at least five years, ranches in Brazil, Southern Rhodesia, Viet Nam, or India may have contemporaneous access to germ plasm of, say, a Black Angus from Oklahoma or a Wisconsin Holstein. In the near future it may even be possible for breeders to predetermine sex of progeny resulting from artificial insemination programs, an obvious advantage to dairy farmers.

Through Western methods of selection and cross-breeding, a rancher can rapidly develop cattle with meatier carcasses or swine with larger litters and faster growing rates. Cows have

Figure 15–5 Research being conducted during 1967 at the University of Wisconsin has made it clear that wood will play an increasingly important dual role for livestock feeding—as roughage and as a source of carbohydrate. [U.S. Forest Products Laboratory, Forest Service, U.S. Department of Agriculture]

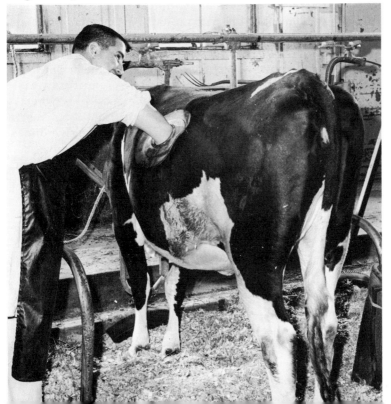

been produced with milk flow vastly superior to dairy cattle of undeveloped nations. For example, American test breeds of Holsteins produce up to 2,000 pounds of milk annually, compared to the 300-pound annual flow from the yellow cattle of China. Chickens with greater egg-laying capacity and more efficient feed-biomass conversions have been developed by American researchers. As late as 1955 the feed–chicken conversion ratio was 3 pounds of feed to 1 pound of chicken. However, University of Georgia breeders recently raised a pen of eight broilers that averaged 4.2 pounds on only 8 pounds of feed; this was roughly a 35 per cent reduction in feed requirements for equivalent weight increments as compared to traditional broiler types. With the assistance of the United Nations' FAO, ranchers from underdeveloped countries will gradually acquire the technical assistance required for greatly improving the quality of their livestock.

Prospects for the Future. In 1966 President Lyndon Johnson proposed that America assume global leadership in a war against hunger. It was a matter of self-interest as well as humanity, for hunger increases the probability of violence. War and revolution may stem from hunger. America would stand ready to send food in emergencies. He intimated, however, that the time is rapidly approaching when the total food output of the technologically advanced nations simply would not be sufficient to meet the requirements of the hungry nations. America would assist with know-how, but the underdeveloped nations ultimately would have to face up to the problem of becoming more agriculturally self-reliant. Some experts were skeptical. The pessimists felt that even with the dissemination of Western technology the have-not countries, because of their high rate of illiteracy, rampant disease, cultural patterns (which may cause fragmentation of farm holdings), and religious mores (which in India result in sacred cows), food production could not be sufficiently increased to forestall a famine of massive dimensions by 1975 or 1980.

However, the mood appears to be gradually changing to one of cautious optimism. Within the last two years a veritable revolution in crop production has occurred. India and Pakistan, for example, have boosted food output by the use of new seed varieties, more intensive application of fertilizer, irrigation, crop rotation, and proper soil conservation techniques. By 1970 Pakistan is expected to be self-sufficient in wheat production. Hampered by drought in recent years, India's 1968 wheat harvest was a record breaker. Iran is already wheat sufficient. Whereas in 1943 Mexico was forced to *import* 10 million bushels of wheat and 160,000 tons of corn, as of 1968 she was *exporting* these grains in substantial quantities. Lester R. Brown, head of the International Agricultural Development Service of the U.S. Department of Agriculture, suggests that the current agricultural revolution in Asia could become the most significant world-wide economic development since the reconstruction of Western Europe following World War II.

Recently a study was conducted by the USDA's Economic Research Service of farm production in twenty-six developing countries. Significantly, twelve of them increased crop output in recent years at a rate of 4 per cent per year during the wartime decade. The significant point is that these increases have been achieved under widely diverse environments. Boosted production has been attained whether climates were temperate or tropical, whether arable land was abundant or scarce, and under highly varying literacy rates, cultural patterns, and governmental systems.

The farmers of the developing countries have been severely hampered in the past because they have lacked certain things that the American farmer has largely taken for granted—price incentives, printed money, credit systems, market news services, storage facilities, transportation systems, county agents, farm extension services, and agricultural colleges. The development of these institutions is the responsibility of governments. The farmers cannot do it all. It is encouraging, therefore, according to Mr. Brown, head of IAD, that "one senses a new political commitment by Asian Governments to respond to the demand by farmers. . . ." In the words of a recent USDA report, the one condition pertaining to all nations increasing their food output is "an aggressive national policy to improve agricultural production and obtain favorable incentives for farmers."

Perhaps, then, man's scientific and technological powers will yet forestall the massive famine that some experts predict will occur by 1975. This would be a *temporary* respite at best. It would permit the survival of more people who would eventually reproduce and contribute to a still greater population whose increased food requirements would precipitate still another food crisis, and so on. You recall that when the Kaibab deer population increased precipitously, the environment eventually deteriorated so severely as to decimate the herd. Men are not deer but they are subject to the same basic ecological laws. It could well be that in man's intensive efforts to save himself, he may destroy himself. Perhaps in the long run, it would be more humanitarian to permit a relatively small-scale starvation now than to ensure an overwhelming. catastrophic food crisis, say, within fifty years. Were you to ask your neighbor this very day what he thought of the possibilities of global famine within a century, he might answer, *"Somehow, science and technology will see to that."* But that is just the point. Despite all the wonders science and technology have wrought for twentieth-century man, "the population problem cannot be solved in a technical way, any more than can the problem of winning the game of tick-tack-toe" (11).

If the world population continues to increase at its present rate, the world's surface will eventually be saturated with people, at which point population increase will end. As Garrett Hardin, eminent professor of biology at the University of California, states, "It is clear that we will greatly increase human misery if we do not, in the immediate future, assume that the world available to the terrestrial human population is finite. Space is no escape" (11).

Is this what man wants? To maximize his population on earth? It took the human population 1 million years before Christ to double from 2.5 to 5 million. Today, we have a global population of 3 billion; at the current rate of increase it will double in thirty-seven years! As Ehrlich states, "If growth continued at that rate for about 900 years there would be some 60,000,000,000,000,000 people on the face of the earth. Sixty million billion people. This is about 100 persons for each square yard of the earth's surface, land and sea . . ." (8).

Family planning will not prevent the ultimate crisis. As Kingsley Davis states, contemporary planning continues "to treat population growth as something to be planned *for*, not something to be *itself planned*" (6). There is a solution to this dilemma. But the solution depends neither on science or technology; it depends on a re-evaluation of values, it involves a new type of *morality*, it is a "simple" matter of the great majority of people reaching a decision either not to procreate or to restrict their families to one or two children, and abiding by that decision.

Population Growth and Urban Expansion

Today, America is building the equivalent of one new city of 250,000 people each month, or a major metropolis of 3 million people each year (18). However, much of this industrial, commercial, and residential construction is added to the original city with very little planning. Much of the construction is haphazardly thrown together, with little, if any, preconceived notion of how effectively the new components are integrated into the operation of the city as a whole. There is minimal consideration for the aesthetic appeal of the urban landscape, or for the importance of architectural diversification. Raw economics frequently determines expansion patterns, regardless of attendant environmental desecration. Gomer speaks of it as "the pressure for doing things most cheaply regardless of ultimate cost to society. . . . If it is a little cheaper to build a steelmill on a lake dune, no matter how unique, chances are the mill will be built there" (10).

This lack of imagination, planning, and appreciation of aesthetic values is nowhere more evident than in the suburbs, where uncontrolled, cancerlike growths have occurred in the past two decades. Historically, the suburbs have developed as a refuge for middle-class Americans who wished to leave behind the pollution, ugliness, and crowding of the aging "central city." With the development of comfortable, high-speed motor cars and of well-constructed highways, it was relatively simple for the suburbanite, initially, to commute between his home and place of work in the commercial or industrial section of the city proper.

However, in spite of its amenities, suburbia has left much to

Figure 15-6 Pennypack Park, part of Philadelphia's Fairmount Park system, leaves a narrow strip of open parkland amid large areas of urban expansion. (Note the sterile sameness of the housing construction at the right of the park.) [Soil Conservation Service, U.S. Department of Agriculture]

be desired. From the aesthetic standpoint alone, it has been a massive failure, with whole blocks of fundamentally identical houses, frequently ornamented with the same kind of shrubbery and basket-weave redwood fences. Even the trees are uniform—in location, age, height, and species. (In many cases the species is American elm, a most unfortunate choice, considering the rapid dispersion of the Dutch elm disease in recent years.)

Population Growth and Pollution.   There are many competent ecologists who believe that in his very attempt to feed the world's burgeoning masses, man may so disrupt the delicate bio-geo-chemical adjustments of his ecosystem as to precipitate disaster. This is the lesson history teaches. It appears that *when man strives to improve his "living standards" he permits his environmental standards to deteriorate.*

Certainly American effluence has increased with her affluence. At a time when America's living standards are the envy of the world, her environmental standards, at least from the standpoint of pollution, are among the most loathsome. America is contaminating her environment at a rate unprecedented in her history. However, America's rapid population increase (from 150 million in 1950 to 200 million in 1968) is also responsible for

Figure 15–7   As human population densities increase, there is a mounting need for periodic relaxation in wilderness areas. These hikers are passing the falls of the Toxaway River in the Pisgah National Forest, North Carolina. [U.S. Department of Agriculture]

Figure 15–8A Phoenix, Arizona, as it appeared in 1907, when it had a population of 10,000. [Bureau of Reclamation, U.S. Department of the Interior]

Figure 15–8B Phoenix, Arizona, as it appeared in 1963, when its population had increased forty-five times to 450,000. (Both photos taken from same point.) [Bureau of Reclamation, U.S. Department of the Interior]

the degradation of her environment. As Paul Ehrlich, an authority in population biology at Stanford, states, "The causal chain of the deterioration is easily followed to its source. Too many cars, too many factories, too much detergent, too much pesticide . . . inadequate sewage treatment plants, too little water, too much carbon dioxide—all can be traced easily to *too many people*" (8). The problem is obvious in the great urban centers of the country.

Population Growth and Solid Wastes. "It must be viewed with bitter irony that the enduring pyramid for our affluent and productive age may prove to be a massive pile of indestructible bottles, cans, and plastic containers paid for by the collective sweat of the public brow." This statement by Senator Gaylord Nelson before Congress on April 1, 1970, was well founded. Each day each American throws twenty pounds of solid wastes away. Each year 20 million Californians alone produce enough trash to form a gigantic mound 100 feet wide and thirty feet high extending from Oregon to Mexico. Each year Americans junk 100 million tires, twenty million tons of paper, forty-eight billion cans, twenty-eight billion bottles, and seven million motor cars. American industrial plants alone produce 165 million tons of solid wastes yearly. As of 1970 our nation junked 360 million tons of solid waste, by 2000 it will dispose of 400 million tons.

It has been customary for municipalities, industries and individuals to incinerate trash, such as garbage, leaves, old newspapers, boxes and broken furniture. However, when air pollution experts pointed out that the atmosphere was being desecrated in the process, alternative methods of disposal were explored. The most extensively employed technique today is the *landfill* method, in which waste is deposited in a trough excavated by bulldozers in a marsh, or in some natural depression at the edge of town, compacted, and then covered with dirt. This technique may serve other functions than mere waste disposal. Thus, in England, at least, the "hills" formed by the soil-and-vegetation-mantled waste add interest to the landscape. By returning garbage, leaves, and other organic materials to the soil, many elements are recycled and later may enter the food-chains of wildlife, domesticated animals, or even man himself. By filling in marshes and other depressions, real estate values may be enhanced. In New York City, sunbathers and swimmers at Jones Beach utilize an area made available by a landfill operation.

Unfortunately, however, the landfill method also has its disadvantages. It may obliterate an area which once served as a

Figure 15–9 Unauthorized dumping of trash at upper end of open ditch. It will later be washed downstream but now affects the beauty of countryside and later will pollute the stream. [Soil Conservation Service, U.S. Department of Agriculture]

Figure 15–10 The city of Newnan, Georgia (population 14,000), maintains a 100-acre sanitary landfill tract. In 1961 over 10,200 tons of garbage and 1,080 truck loads of trash and leaves were buried. The city has employed this method since 1950. [International Harvester Company]

Figure 15–11 Landfill at edge of Cochraneville, Pa. [*Solid Wastes Management*]

wildlife habitat. Thus, a certain sandy region in northwestern Wisconsin, which the nonbiologist might brand wasteland, was nevertheless rich in ecological and faunistic interest. It was populated by jack pines, blue-flowered spider-wort, pocket gophers, badgers, bullsnakes, digger wasps, and tiger beetles. Bird watchers visited this sand "barren" to hear the tinkling song of the horned lark, or the dry "buzz-buzz" of the clay-colored sparrow. Now the barren is barren indeed—buried under countless tons of landfill. In some regions the decomposition of accumulated tons of garbage has resulted in the emission of such quantities of methane gas as to give health and safety officials considerable concern. In San Francisco landfill operations have obliterated a substantial portion of San Francisco Bay. In the process the area's carrying capacity for waterfowl has been destroyed, fishing and other aquatic-based recreations have been curtailed, and the picturesque beauty of the Bay has been greatly diminished.

Another method of solid-waste disposal, which has been used to advantage in New York City, San Francisco, and other coastal cities, is the formation of *artificial reefs* out of assorted

Figure 15–12 All areas appearing white in this aerial photo of New York City have been created by refuse landfill operations. In the process, however, bays and harbors gradually diminish in size, with possible disadvantages to shipping, aesthetics, and marine life. [*Solid Wastes Management*]

junk and debris. The rusting hulks in automobile graveyards have been used in reef construction. Not only does this technique solve the solid-waste disposal problem (at least on a small scale), but it provides cover and breeding sites for various marine fish. Moreover, it has been suggested that when such reefs are strategically located in the paths of ocean currents, they might intensify the upwelling phenomenon and thus increase the fishing potential of the region.

The Experimental City. Professor Athelstan Spilhaus of the University of Minnesota has conceived of a novel solution to the vexing problems which increasingly plague America's urban areas. He proposes the establishment of an "experimental city" (18). This is not just a dream. Spilhaus and two other colleagues have received a federal grant of $250,000 to support the planning of the unique community. It represents a radical departure from the traditional concept of a city. As Spilhaus states, all American cities heretofore have developed by "accidents of history, changing populations, altering economics." His experimental city, on the other hand, would be built from scratch, only after the most intensive planning.

Industrial, transportation, and domestic power requirements would be secured from a centrally located atomic plant. Because all vehicles would be electrically operated there would be no possibility that exhaust pollutants, such as benzopyrenes and carbon monoxide, would foul the air. Noise pollution would be reduced to a minimum. Waste problems would be solved by novel techniques. However, there would be no sewage systems because domestic and industrial wastes would be reprocessed and converted into usable materials. As Spilhaus states, "ways must be found to manage, control and make use of wastes before mankind is buried by his own trash." Solid wastes would not be permitted to accumulate. Containers would be designed so as to be either reusable or decomposable, so that the component elements could be incorporated into the soil. Cardboard materials might be impregnated with nutrient chemicals so that upon disposal they actually would enhance the soil's fertility. Some wastes will be employed as fertilizer to enhance food production at the community's greenhouse. To the greatest extent possible industrial wastes would be processed into usable materials. If this is not feasible, attempts will be made to effect desirable chemical interactions between wastes from neighboring factories. Thus, noxious *acid* wastes from factory A might react with harmful *alkaline* wastes from factory B so as to form *neutral* or even commercially valuable substances, even as sulfur dioxide is converted into plaster of paris or sulfuric acid in some progressive industrial plants today. If such conversion is not possible, the industrial wastes might be effectively removed from the atmosphere by means of a system of "aerial sewers." Some wastes, otherwise resistant to processing or control, could serve as fuel to warm the city in winter, a device which is already employed in primitive form by the Eskimos (18).

Because all buildings would be constructed of structural components which would be easily disassembled and reused in different configurations, the blight of obsolescence and slummy deterioration would be nonexistent. The sterile monotony of architectural patterns, which characterizes the average American suburb, would be conspicuously absent. Flexibility in the use of building materials would make infinite variety possible (18).

The experimental city would be built to accommodate 250,000 people. The population would be made up of volunteer residents selected only after their applications were carefully screened. It would include the same proportion of racial and ethnic groups as exists in America today. However, because there would be no slums, no second-class housing, and no unemployment, the tensions, riots, and exacerbations which characterize the long, hot summers of today's urban society would be minimized, if not absent completely. As Spilhaus admits, such a city would be expensive to construct, but not more so than the New York World's Fair, which catered to pleasure rather than the solution of a major socioecological problem (18).

Today, the Experimental City is on the planning boards; tomorrow, it may be a reality. Spilhaus is the first to admit that the experiment could fail. Failure is possible with any experiment. But if it succeeds it would solve, in a novel and ingenious way, most of the problems besetting urban America today.

BIBLIOGRAPHY

1. Asimov, Isaac. *A Short History of Biology.* Garden City, N. Y.: The Natural History Press, 1964.
2. Bogue, Donald J. "End of Population Explosion?" *U.S. News and World Report* (March 11, 1968), 59–61.
3. Borgstrom, George. *The Hungry Planet.* New York: The Macmillan Company, 1965.
4. Brown, Harrison. "If World Population Doubles by the Year 2000," *U.S. News and World Report* (Jan. 9, 1967), 51–54.
5. Calder, Ritchie. *Common Sense About a Starving World.* New York: The Macmillan Company, 1962, 176 pp.
6. Davis, Kingsley. "The Urbanization of the Human Population," *Sci. Amer.,* **213,** 3 (1965), 53.
7. *Eau Claire Herald-Tribune,* September 29, 1969.
8. Ehrlich, Paul R. *The Population Bomb.* New York: Ballantine Books, 1968.
9. *Encyclopedia Brittanica,* Vol. 5. Chicago: William Benton, Publisher, 1967.
10. Gomer, Robert. "The Tyranny of Progress," *Bulletin of the Atomic Scientists,* **24,** (2) (February, 1968).
11. Hardin, Garrett. "The Tragedy of the Commons," *Science,* **162** (1968), 1243–1248.
12. Higbee, Edward. *Farms and Farmers in an Urban Age.* New York: The Twentieth Century Fund, 1963, 183 pp.
13. Joslyn, Maynard A., and Harold S. Olcott. "Food Consumption and Resources," in Martin R. Huberty and Warren L. Flock (eds.), *Natural Resources.* New York: McGraw-Hill Book Co., 1959, 288–327.
14. Leopold, Aldo. *A Sand County Almanac.* New York: Oxford University Press, 1949.
15. Mosher, Arthur T. *Getting Agriculture Moving.* New York: Frederick A. Praeger, Publishers, 1966, 191 pp.
16. Oser, Jacob. *Must Men Starve?* New York: Abelard-Schuman, Ltd., 1957, 331 pp.
17. Paddock, William, and Paul Paddock. *Famine—1975!* Boston: Little, Brown and Co., 1967, 176 pp.

18. Spilhaus, Athelstan. "The Experimental City," *World Book*. Chicago: Encyclopedia Science Service, Inc., 1967.

19. Sumner, Lowell. Quoted in Paul R. Ehrlich. *The Population Bomb*. New York: Ballantine Books, 1968.

20. Udall, Stewart. *The Quiet Crisis*. New York: Holt, Rinehart and Winston, 1963.

21. U.S. Department of Agriculture. *Annual Summary 1966. International Agricultural Development*. Washington, D.C.: U.S. Department of Agriculture, 1968.

22. *U.S. News and World Report*. "One War U.S. Is Winning—Bigger Crops for a Hungry World" (June 10, 1968), 64–66.

23. Woodham-Smith, Cecil. *The Great Hunger*. New York: Harper & Row, Publishers, 1962, 510 pp.

24. Woytinsky, W. S., and E. S. Woytinsky. *World Population and Production*. New York: Twentieth Century Fund, 1953.

Politics, Education, and Survival

16

The Nixon Program

In his State of the Union message of January 1970, President Nixon proclaimed: "The great question of the 1970's is: Shall we surrender to our surroundings or shall we make our peace with nature and begin to make reparations for the damage we have done to our air, to our land and to our water?" The main features of his message of environmental import were:

1. Recognition that affluence could not necessarily guarantee happiness: "Our recognition of the truth that wealth and happiness are not the same require us to measure success or failure by new criteria."
2. Promise of a new program for buying wilderness and recreation areas.
3. A proposal to assist states set and enforce clean air standards by spending $104 million for this purpose.
4. A promise to establish stricter federal auto emission standards.
5. A five-year $10 billion program to enable all municipalities to have modern municipal waste-treatment plants "in every place in America where they are needed to make our waters clean again" (15).

A few days later Nixon presented a $200.8

551

billion budget for fiscal 1970. It provides that federal spending on recreational resources would be $546 million, almost four-fold the sum spent in 1961; $465 million would be spent during fiscal 1971 on water pollution control, over ten times the $44 million spent in fiscal 1961, and $104 million would be spent on air pollution control almost fifteen times the sum of $7 million spent during fiscal 1961.

On the face of his message and the proposed budget it would appear that the cause of conservation and environmental quality would be well served in 1970 and for the duration of Nixon's term(s) in office. After all, this is the first time in many years that a president has stressed environmental problems and their resolution in a State of the Union address. As *Time* magazine put it: "President Nixon's . . . message illustrated anew how swiftly a once radical idea can become national consensus and good politics. Only a few years ago the thought that the quality of life in America is not good enough, and that the United States is wantonly despoiling its physical environment was the concern mainly of left-wing critics, grumpy academics and dedicated conservationists well out of the mainstream of American politics. Yet . . . the President effectively moved to assume personal command of the gathering battle for a better environment" (13).

However, the consensus of most Democrats in Congress, and more significantly, of most professional ecologists and conservationists was that President Nixon did not go nearly far enough in his proposed financial support of environmental quality and anti-pollution programs. First of all, the federal government would provide only 40 per cent of the $10 billion municipal waste treatment program, the remainder would have to be paid from state and local sources. It might be extremely difficult for communities to raise the necessary monies since their bond markets (as of 1970) are very tight. And even if the $10 billion can be raised from combined federal-state-community sources, this would be "peanuts" compared to the sums really required in serious, wide-sweeping water pollution abatement. Thus University of Wisconsin ecologist David Archbald states: "In view of the federal government's own estimate that it will take $40 billion just to "clean up" Lake Erie, does the President's proposal of only a $10 billion program mean Lake Erie has been written off as a lost cause? . . . What about sources of water pollution other than municipalities, that in industry, mining, agricultural fertilizers, pesticides, erosion and animal wastes? What about solid waste disposal?" (16) Just what *real* impact the Nixon administration will have on upgrading the American environment remains to be seen.

Early in 1970, Dr. Lee A. DuBridge, President Nixon's science advisor, commented on the enormity of the pollution control problem, and the preservation and/or improvement of environmental quality as compared with the Apollo project: "It is unfortunate, but true, that pollution is not just a technical problem, as was the case of putting man on the moon. It is as much sociological as technological. Political personalities, economic interests are involved. There is vast overlapping of authority over environment between government agencies at all levels" (2). Representative of political personality conflicts was the "tug-of-war" between Senators Edmund S. Muskie of Maine and Henry M. Jackson of Washington. In late 1969, each wished to send his own national environmental policy bill to Congress. Muskie, who is chairman of the Public Works Subcommittee on Air and Water Pollution, and Jackson, the Interior Committee chairman, reached such an impasse in an effort to further the jurisdiction of their respective committees, that action on the bill was seriously retarded, even though it was eventually enacted into law (15).

Agency conflicts may become just as intense and deleterious to environmental progress as personality differences. Nowhere are agency antagonisms more apparent than between the Departments of Agriculture and Interior. Thus, the taxpayer discovers to his amazement that his money is being used by the Department of Agriculture to pay farmers for draining wetlands at the same time that the Department of the Interior pays farmers to maintain them. On the pesticide issue these departments again are at odds. The Department of Agriculture strongly supported massive DDT applications in insect control (prior to the DDT "ban" in late 1969), while the Department of Interior favored restricting its employment. The Army Corps of Engineers and the Department of the Interior have frequently been in conflict—the latter criticizing dam and canal construction by the Engineers as being detrimental to wildlife and aesthetics. With such heated bickering occurring at the federal level, there is little wonder that the individual citizen occasionally becomes cynical and apathetic toward environmental issues.

Let's Get Down to Earth

Astronaut Frank Borman has described the moon as a "vast, lonely forbidding type of existence, a great expanse of nothing, that looms rather like clouds and clouds of pumice stone. It certainly would not appear to be a very inviting place to live or work." During his close-up view of the moon Astronaut Jim Lovell commented: "The vast loneliness of the moon . . . makes you realize just what you have back there on earth . . . ."

The federal government spent $21 billion during the decade of the 1960's to put *four* men on the lunar waste land for a few hours. Now it is high time to spend much greater sums to repair an earth on which over *three billion* people exist. Recently Charles A. Lindbergh, the renowned aviator, remarked: "The cost of adequate conservation is small in relation to what we spend on space exploration, aviation, and so forth; yet the natural resources we neglect offer far more to us and to our children, than do all such enterprises combined." Joseph Wood Krutch, one of America's foremost naturalists, has put space exploration and other technological feats in proper perspective: "Science and technology can point to achievements as spectacular as any in their previous history. The physicists and mathematicians have sent men around the moon and brought them back safely to earth. . . . But despite these achievements ours is, even more conspicuously than it was years ago, an age of anxiety. Three of the threats we are most aware of—overpopulation, epidemic crime, and the increasing pollution of our environment—were threats many of us didn't worry about a decade ago. And they are not likely to be solved by the so-called conquest of space . . ." (6).

Nevertheless, in September 1969, President Nixon's Space Task Group recommended that our national space effort be directed toward a manned Mars landing in 1986. The overall cost of such a program, including the development of space stations and vehicles which can be reused, would be more than $100 billion. This would be the *ultimate ecological absurdity*. We certainly are in no position to afford the luxury of sending space ships to the moon, Mars or anywhere. There might be no habitable earth to which the spacemen could return! As Senator Nelson admonished in a message to Congress on January 19, 1970: "Just to control pollution, it will take $275 billion by the year 2000." It would seem much wiser, from the stand point of human well-being (or should I say survival), to cancel the Martian adventure and use the $100 billion to clean up the earth.

This is not to suggest that we abandon all of the sophisticated technology which made our lunar explorations possible, quite the contrary. But we should apply these developments to earthly objectives. Walter Orr Roberts, former president of the American Association for the Advancement of Science, suggested in December 1969 that future space research be earth-oriented. A high-priority future item in space research would be manned space stations with earth directed instrumentation. Roberts visualized the eventual development of a world monitoring network ". . . with teams of skilled observers studying hurricanes, tropical ocean-atmosphere energy transformations, ocean current flow patterns for fish migration analysis, air pollution drift, and spread of insect pests and plant diseases, assessing water reserves in the world's watersheds, and making a host of other terrestrial studies . . ." (10).

Conservation Education

If America is to win her environmental struggle, it is imperative that appreciation, respect and understanding of the delicate sun-soil-water-air-organism complex be fostered already at the *preschool* level. The old aphorism "as the twig is bent the tree is inclined" is pertinent. Sociologists inform us that many adult attitudes were already shaped prior to age six. Many European grade schools are far ahead of their American counterparts in the quality of environmental education accomplished. At the Convocation on Ecology and the Human Environment of the St. Albans School (Washington, D.C.), Admiral H. G. Rickover, U.S. Navy, remarked: "During a visit to Switzerland for the purpose of familiarizing myself with their educational system, I was much impressed by the way ecology was taught in a one-room village school house. It was part of the curriculum through all the primary grades, being presented at first very simply—but always graphically; later, on a more complex level; and always alongside the three R's and history and government, so that the children absorb it as part of their general education. . . . I wonder too, whether ecology, properly presented at the higher secondary school levels, might not help dissipate the tendency in contemporary thinking of regarding technology as an irresistible force with a momentum of its own that puts it beyond human direction and restraint" (9).

Wisconsin's Senator Gaylord Nelson has made strenuous attempts to initiate and/or improve the quality of conservation education at the primary and secondary grade levels. According to Nelson: "Too often elementary and secondary school teachers are uncomfortable with the thought of using the outdoors as a classroom. New techniques are being devised for teacher training to help break down this barrier so the relationships between man and his artificial world and nature can be viewed as a whole" (1). In late 1969 Nelson introduced a bill which would make conservation education a required component of classroom curricula from preschool to postgraduate levels. Through this Environmental Quality Education Act the testing and upgrading of environmental teaching programs would receive federal financial support.

An encouraging example of how concerned citizens can effectively promote environmental education is provided by the Minnesota Environmental Sciences Foundation. A few years ago Minnesota's commissioner of education, Howard B. Casmey, was instrumental in the establishment of an Environmental Science Center. Financed with federal funds, it was concerned with environmental science curricula and teacher training. It was dedicated to the proposition that the development of a proper "land ethic" can be accomplished most effectively by public instruction. When citizens of the Minneapolis-St. Paul area became aware that federal support would be withdrawn in July, 1970, they rallied to the cause, forming a non-profit, tax-exempt corporation known as the Minnesota Environmental Sciences Foundation—the first of its kind in America. It accepts financial contributions from business, industry, individuals, and other foundations to sustain its program. Its board of directors includes a county court judge, professor of wildlife management, radio station personnel, industrialists, and representatives of The League of Women Voters, National Audubon Society, Izaak Walton League, The Conservation Federation, University of Minnesota, St. John's University and the U.S. Fish and Wildlife Service.

Citizen Involvement

Although definitely aware that their environment is deteriorating at an appalling pace, many Americans feel that some how, some way, the government will remedy America's current environmental ills. Unfortunately, more often than not, the wheels of government, at high levels, turn slowly. But our environmental posture demands action soon—or not at all. As Dr. David Archbald, ecologist at the University of Wisconsin, put it, ". . . . those who rely completely on Washington to point the way in environmental matters are abrogating their own responsibilities. Washington certainly has no monopoly on environmental brains. And often it seems doubtful it even has its share. . . . At the community level the citizenry will have to develop a deeper concern for, identify better with, and take a keener interest in programs on local environmental problems than with national programs with Washington calling the shots. In other words a community will be more inclined to do 'its own environmental thing' than to do 'Washington's environmental thing.' Sometimes forthright action by dedicated citizens at the grassroots and community levels can make significant contributions to mending ecosystems and do it quickly" (16).

Archbald describes a novel approach to environmental problems involving a nationally-coordinated action program at the community level, completely emancipated from bureaucratic impedimenta. Named the MEC (Man-Environment Communications) Center, it has been initiated at Madison (Wisconsin) on a trial basis; if successful, other similar community centers will be established. According to Archbald: ". . . the MEC Center will be administered by a board representing all segments of the community. Hence the center will have access to the resources and guidance of the whole community," including university researchers, industrial executives, park and recreations officials, high school teachers, sanitarians, farmers, housewives, sportsmen and conservation groups. All pertinent reliable pollution data will be fed into the center's computer. When other MEC Centers become established they "will exchange information and maintain close communications." Thus, by pooling their pollution data and experiences, recommendations for action can be made which would be much more reliable and authoritative than if each center operated in isolation (16).

Mounting Public Concern

During the spring of 1970 Americans mounted a crescendo of concern over their nation's environmental posture. The attitude of the general public has changed drastically since 1966. As Jim Kimball, conservation writer for the *Minneapolis Tribune*, recently stated: "Only three or four years ago I was reluctant to write because it sounded like a scare campaign, that the future of man is in jeopardy—is doomed—if he does not change his ways. Now, I am reluctant to write it but for a different reason. So many people are saying it that it is repetitious. In the past five years, or even in the past three years, the thinking of a nation has changed. It must be the fastest change in history on a profound issue. Very recently people thought that a conservationist was a bird watcher, a guy who belonged to a sportsmen's club or someone who didn't take more than his limit of fish. These same people have now added entirely new words to their vocabulary—words such as *ecology, environmental science* and, most important of all, *environmental education. . . .* The activities of man have exterminated hundreds of species, but he never cared very much. Now he cares because suddenly he realizes that his number is up. He may be the next to go. . . ." (5).

Growing public anxiety for environmental abuse was indicated in a Gallup Poll taken in 1969 for the National Wildlife Federation. It indicated that 51 per cent of the people interviewed were seriously disturbed by the gravity of pollution. A heartening development is that even Congress, at long last, is showing concern, as is reflected in the fact that the material on environment inserted by senators and congressmen in the *Congressional Record,* January–June 1969, was exceeded only by material dealing with the Viet Nam War (4).

In late 1969 Senator Nelson and California's Congressman McCloskey called for a nationwide "Environmental Teach-In" in an attempt to marshall the energies of America's college youth "to halt the accelerating pollution and destruction of the environment." There were good reasons for focusing the effort at the student level: First, over 50 per cent of our population is under 25 years of age; second, youth are more flexible, more adaptable than their elders, and certainly any significant abatement of our pressing environmental problems will be predicated on substantial social, technological and cultural changes which will place great demands on such adaptability; and third, America's youth can approach the problem with greater objectivity than their parents since they were not the generation directly responsible for the present crisis.

According to Nelson and McCloskey, "the present student generation's commitment will determine whether we reverse the present trends. Hopefully, our young people, in a day of nationwide environmental review, will set specific goals for the 1970's, goals for a decade of national effort which will recognize that environmental quality deserves the same priorities of expenditures as did the moon-shot effort of the 1960's. More than any other issue in this country today, environmental concern cuts across generations, political parties and attitudes" (1).

Can Man Survive?

Will man eventually, because of environmental mismanagement, blunder his way to extinction? Will *Homo sapiens* follow the path of the passenger pigeon and saber-toothed cat? The distinguished ecologist, Barry Commoner, has voiced this opinion:

". . . We are in a crisis of *survival*; for environmental pollution is a signal that the ecological systems on which we depend for our life and our livelihood have begun to break down and are approaching the point of no return. My own estimate is that if we are to avoid environmental catastrophe by the 1980's we will need to begin the vast process of connecting the fundamental incompatabilities of major technologies with the demands of the ecosystem. This means that we will need to put into operation essentially emissionless versions of automotive vehicles, power plants, refineries, steel mills, and chemical plants. Agricultural technology will need to find ways of sustaining productivity without breaking down the natural soil cycle, or disrupting the natural control of destructive insects. Sewage and garbage treatment plants will need to be designed to return organic waste to the soil, where, in nature, it belongs. Vegetation will need to be massively reintroduced into urban areas. Housing and urban sanitary facilities will need to be drastically improved. All of these will demand serious economic adjustments, and our economic and social system will need to be prepared to meet them. . . . I believe that we have, as of now (1970), a single decade in which to design the fundamental changes in technology that we must put into effect in the 1980's—if we are to survive. We will need to seize on the decade of the 1970's as a period of grace—a decade which must be used for a vast pilot program to guide the coming reconstruction of the nation's system of productivity. This, I believe, is the urgency of the environmental crisis—we must determine, now, to develop, in the next decade, the new means of our salvation" (3).

The Washington-based headquarters of the Environmental Teach-In of April 22, 1970, has eloquently described America's plight and the essential commitments which society must make.

> A disease has infected our country. It has brought smog to Yosemite, dumped garbage in the Hudson, sprayed DDT on our food, and left our cities in decay. Its carrier is man.
> The weak are already dying. Trees by the Pacific. Fish in our streams and lakes. Birds and crops and sheep. And people.
> We must act *now* to reclaim the environment we have wrecked.
> Earth Day is a commitment to make life better, not just bigger and faster; to provide real rather than rhetorical solutions.
> It is a day to examine the ethic of individual progress at mankind's expense.
> It is a day to challenge the corporate and governmental leaders who promise change, but who short-change the necessary programs.
> It is a day for looking beyond tomorrow.
> Earth Day seeks a future worth living.
> Earth Day seeks a future period.

Americans must make every day an Earth Day. We must make these commitments and act on them, for every day of our natural lives. In this crucial period it is imperative that we elect responsible leaders in government at all levels who "recognize and act upon the fact that time is running out, that only the resolute rejection of war, profits as usual, procreation as usual, comforts as usual, and politics as usual will prevent our planet from sliding to disaster" (13).

J. Mayone Stycos of Cornell University states that all major social (and environmental) changes are not finally realized until they have passed through four phases:

1. No Talk—No do.
2. Talk—No do.
3. Talk—*Do*.
4. No-talk—*Do*.

America has just entered phase two. Time for phases three and four is limited. Knowledgeable men have made predictions concerning man's fate if the trend of deterioration continues at its present pace. After noting that land and resources are finite, Martin Litton, a director of the Sierra Club, sounds a note of pessimism: "We are prospecting for the very last of our resources and using up the nonrenewable things many times faster than we are finding new ones. . . . We've already run out of earth and nothing we can do will keep mankind in existence for as long as another two centuries" (7).

Slightly more optimistic is Gardner D. Stout, president of the American Museum of Natural History: "That man will survive is likely. When the chips are down he is astonishingly adaptable, cunningly expert. But the concept of survival by itself is a minimal and chilling one. Survival can be appallingly rudimentary . . ." (11).

America is in crisis—and time is running out. Were the rising voice of concern to be muffled, the American Dream may yet turn to a nightmare. As Lowell Sumner has written, ". . . the human population explosion, and its declining spiral of natural resources, is . . . the greatest threat of all. The time is ripe, even dangerously over-ripe, as far as the population control problem is concerned. We shall have to face up or ultimately perish, and what a dreary, *stupid*, unlovely way to perish, on a ruined globe stripped of its primeval beauty" (12).

BIBLIOGRAPHY

1. *Audubon Magazine.* January 1970.
2. *Christian Science Monitor.* January 20, 1970.
3. Commoner, Barry. "Salvation: It's Possible," *The Progressive* (Madison, Wis.), April 1970, 12–18.
4. *Congressional Record.* Proceedings and Debates of the 91st Congress, Second Session. Washington, D.C. January 19, 1970.
5. Kimball, Jim. *Minneapolis Tribune,* January 18, 1970.
6. Krutch, Joseph Wood. "Dropouts, Do-Gooders, and the Two Cultures," *American Forests,* August 1969, 34, 35, 41.
7. Litton, Martin. Quoted in *Time,* February 2, 1970, 62.
8. Mackey, Roberta. "Activists Turn to Pollution Problem." *Detroit Free Press,* January 4, 1970.

9. Rickover, Admiral H. G. "A Humanistic Technology," *American Forests,* August 1969.

10. Roberts, Walter Orr. "After the Moon, the Earth!" *Science,* **167** (January 2, 1970), 11–16.

11. Stout, Gardner D. Quoted in Creighton Peet, "Can Men Survive?," *American Forests,* August 1969, 5–7, 41–42.

12. Sumner, Lowell. Quoted in Paul Ehrlich, *The Population Bomb.* New York: Ballantine Press, 1968.

13. *The Progressive.* "Action for Survival," (Editorial). Madison, Wis. April 1970, 3–6.

14. *Time,* February 2, 1970.

15. Trumbull, Van. "Washington Lookout," *American Forests,* November 1969.

16. *Wisconsin State Journal,* February 1, 1970.

Appendix A

The Tragedy of the Commons

The population problem has no technical solution; it requires a fundamental extension in morality.

GARRETT HARDIN

At the end of a thoughtful article on the future of nuclear war, Wiesner and York (1) concluded that: "Both sides in the arms race are . . . confronted by the dilemma of steadily increasing military power and steadily decreasing national security. *It is our considered professional judgment that this dilemma has no technical solution.* If the great powers continue to look for solutions in the area of science and technology only, the result will be to worsen the situation."

I would like to focus your attention not on the subject of the article (national security in a nuclear world) but on the kind of conclusion they reached, namely that there is no technical solution to the problem. An implicit and almost universal assumption of discussions published in professional and semipopular scientific journals is that the problem under discussion has a technical solution. A technical solution may be defined as one that requires a change only in the techniques of the natural sciences, demanding little or nothing in the way of change in human values or ideas of morality.

In our day (though not in earlier times) technical solutions are always welcome. Because of previous failures in prophecy, it takes cour-

Reprinted from *Science,* **162** (Dec. 13, 1968), 1243–48, by permission of the publisher and the author. Copyright 1968 by the American Association for the Advancement of Science.

age to assert that a desired technical solution is not possible. Wiesner and York exhibited this courage; publishing in a science journal, they insisted that the solution to the problem was not to be found in the natural sciences. They cautiously qualified their statement with the phrase, "It is our considered professional judgment. . . ." Whether they were right or not is not the concern of the present article. Rather, the concern here is with the important concept of a class of human problems which can be called "no technical solution problems," and, more specifically, with the identification and discussion of one of these.

It is easy to show that the class is not a null class. Recall the game of tick-tack-toe. Consider the problem, "How can I win the game of tick-tack-toe?" It is well known that I cannot, if I assume (in keeping with the conventions of game theory) that my opponent understands the game perfectly. Put another way, there is no "technical solution" to the problem. I can win only by giving a radical meaning to the word "win." I can hit my opponent over the head; or I can drug him; or I can falsify the records. Every way in which I "win" involves, in some sense, an abandonment of the game, as we intuitively understand it. (I can also, of course, openly abandon the game—refuse to play it. This is what most adults do.)

The class of "No technical solution problems" has members. My thesis is that the "population problem," as conventionally conceived, is a member of this class. How it is conventionally conceived needs some comment. It is fair to say that most people who anguish over the population problem are trying to find a way to avoid the evils of over-population without relinquishing any of the privileges they now enjoy. They think that farming the seas or developing new strains of wheat will solve the problem—technologically. I try to show here that the solution they seek cannot be found. The population problem cannot be solved in a technical way, any more than can the problem of winning the game of tick-tack-toe.

What Shall We Maximize?

Population, as Malthus said, naturally tends to grow "geometrically," or, as we would now say, exponentially. In a finite world this means that the per capita share of the world's goods must steadily decrease. Is ours a finite world?

A fair defense can be put forward for the view that the world is infinite; or that we do not know that it is not. But, in terms of the practical problems that we must face in the next few generations with the foreseeable technology, it is clear that we will greatly increase human misery if we do not, during the immediate future, assume that the world available to the terrestrial human population is finite. "Space" is no escape (2).

A finite world can support only a finite population; therefore, population growth must eventually equal zero. (The case of perpetual wide fluctuations above and below zero is a trivial variant that need not be discussed.) When this condition is met, what will be the situation of mankind? Specifically, can Bentham's goal of "the greatest good for the greatest number" be realized?

No—for two reasons, each sufficient by itself. The first is a theoretical one. It is not mathematically possible to maximize for two (or more) variables at the same time. This was clearly stated by von Neumann and Morgenstern (3), but the principle is implicit in the theory of partial differential equations, dating back at least to D'Alembert (1717–1783).

The second reason springs directly from biological facts. To live, any organism must have a source of energy (for example, food). This energy is utilized for two purposes: mere maintenance and work. For man, maintenance of life requires about 1600 kilocalories a day ("maintenance calories"). Anything that he does over and above merely staying alive will be defined as work, and is supported by "work calories" which he takes in. Work calories are used not only for what we call work in common speech; they are also required for all forms of enjoyment from swimming and automobile racing to playing music and writing poetry. If our goal is to maximize population it is obvious what we must do: We must make the work calories per person approach as close to zero as possible. No gourmet meals, no vacations, no sports, no music, no literature, no art. . . . I think that everyone will grant, without argument or proof, that maximizing population does not maximize goods. Bentham's goal is impossible.

In reaching this conclusion I have made the usual assumption that it is the acquisition of energy that is the problem. The appearance of atomic energy has led some to question this assumption. However, given an infinite source of energy, population growth still produces an inescapable problem. The problem of the acquisition of energy is replaced by the problem of its dissipation, as J. H. Fremlin has so wittily shown (4). The arithmetic signs in the analysis are, as it were, reversed; but Bentham's goal is still unobtainable.

The optimum population is, then, less than the maximum. The difficulty of defining the optimum is enormous; so far as I know, no one has seriously tackled this problem. Reaching an acceptable and stable solution will surely require more than one generation of hard analytical work—and much persuasion.

We want the maximum good per person; but what is good? To one person it is wilderness, to another it is ski lodges for thousands. To one it is estuaries to nourish ducks for hunters to shoot; to another it is factory land. Comparing one good with another is, we usually say, impossible because goods are incommensurable. Incommensurables cannot be compared.

Theoretically this may be true; but in real life incommensurables *are* commensurable. Only a criterion of judgment and a system of weighting are needed. In nature the criterion is survival. Is it better for a species to be small and hideable, or large and powerful? Natural selection commensurates the incommensurables. The compromise achieved depends on a natural weighting of the values of the variables.

Man must imitate this process. There is no doubt that in fact he already does, but unconsciously. It is when the hidden decisions are made explicit that the arguments begin. The problem for the years ahead is to work out an acceptable theory of weighting. Synergistic effects, nonlinear variation, and difficulties in discounting the future make the intellectual problem difficult, but not (in principle) insoluble.

Has any cultural group solved this practical problem at the present time, even on an intuitive level? One simple fact proves that none has: there is no prosperous population in the world today that has, and has had for some time, a growth rate of zero. Any people that has intuitively identified its optimum point will soon reach it, after which its growth rate becomes and remains zero.

Of course, a positive growth rate might be taken as evidence that a population is below its optimum. However, by any reasonable standards, the most rapidly growing populations on earth today are (in general) the most miserable. This association (which need not be invariable) casts doubt on the optimistic assumption that the positive growth rate of a population is evidence that it has yet to reach its optimum.

We can make little progress in working toward optimum population size until we explicitly exorcize the spirit of Adam Smith in the field of practical demography. In economic affairs, *The Wealth of Nations* (1776) popularized the "invisible hand," the idea that an individual who "intends only his own gain," is, as it were, "led by an invisible hand to promote . . . the public interest" (5). Adam Smith did not assert that this was invariably true, and perhaps neither did any of his followers. But he contributed to a dominant tendency of thought that has ever since interfered with positive action based on rational analysis, namely, the tendency to assume that decisions reached individually will, in fact, be the best decisions for an entire society. If this assumption is correct it justifies the continuance of our present policy of laissez-faire in reproduction. If it is correct we can assume that men will control their individual fecundity so as to produce the optimum population. If the assumption is not correct, we need to reexamine our individual freedoms to see which ones are defensible.

Tragedy of Freedom in a Commons

The rebuttal to the invisible hand in population control is to be found in a scenario first sketched in a little-known pamphlet (6) in 1833 by a mathematical amateur named William Forster Lloyd (1794–1852). We may well call it "the tragedy of the commons," using the word "tragedy" as the philosopher Whitehead used it (7): "The essence of dramatic tragedy is not unhappiness. It resides in the solemnity of the remorseless working of things." He then goes on to say, "This inevitableness of destiny can only be illustrated in terms of human life by incidents which in fact involve unhappiness. For it is only by them that the futility of escape can be made evident in the drama."

The tragedy of the commons develops in this way. Picture a pasture open to all. It is to be expected that each herdsman will try to keep as many cattle as possible on the commons. Such an arrangement may work reasonably satisfactorily for centuries because tribal wars, poaching, and disease keep the numbers of both man and beast well below the carrying capacity of the land. Finally, however, comes the day of reckoning, that is, the day when the long-desired goal of social stability becomes a reality. At this point, the inherent logic of the commons remorselessly generates tragedy.

As a rational being, each herdsman seeks to maximize his gain. Explicitly or implicitly, more or less consciously, he asks, "What is the utility *to me* of adding one more animal to my herd?" This utility has one negative and one positive component.

1) The positive component is a function of the increment of one animal. Since the herdsman receives all the proceeds from the sale of the additional animal, the positive utility is nearly +1.

2) The negative component is a function of the additional overgrazing created by one more animal. Since, however, the effects of

overgrazing are shared by all the herdsmen, the negative utility for any particular decision-making herdsman is only a fraction of −1.

Adding together the component partial utilities, the rational herdsman concludes that the only sensible course for him to pursue is to add another animal to his herd. And another; and another. . . . But this is the conclusion reached by each and every rational herdsman sharing a commons. Therein is the tragedy. Each man is locked into a system that compels him to increase his herd without limit—in a world that is limited. Ruin is the destination toward which all men rush, each pursuing his own best interest in a society that believes in the freedom of the commons. Freedom in a commons brings ruin to all.

Some would say that this is a platitude. Would that it were! In a sense, it was learned thousands of years ago, but natural selection favors the forces of psychological denial (8). The individual benefits as an individual from his ability to deny the truth even though society as a whole, of which he is a part, suffers. Education can counteract the natural tendency to do the wrong thing, but the inexorable succession of generations requires that the basis for this knowledge be constantly refreshed.

A simple incident that occurred a few years ago in Leominster, Massachusetts, shows how perishable the knowledge is. During the Christmas shopping season the parking meters downtown were covered with plastic bags that bore tags reading: "Do not open until after Christmas. Free parking courtesy of the mayor and city council." In other words, facing the prospect of an increased demand for already scarce space, the city fathers reinstituted the system of the commons. (Cynically, we suspect that they gained more votes than they lost by this retrogressive act.)

In an approximate way, the logic of the commons has been understood for a long time, perhaps since the discovery of agriculture or the invention of private property in real estate. But it is understood mostly only in special cases which are not sufficiently generalized. Even at this late date, cattlemen leasing national land on the western ranges demonstrate no more than an ambivalent understanding, in constantly pressuring federal authorities to increase the head count to the point where overgrazing produces erosion and weed-dominance. Likewise, the oceans of the world continue to suffer from the survival of the philosophy of the commons. Maritime nations still respond automatically to the shibboleth of the "freedom of the seas." Professing to believe in the "inexhaustible resources of the oceans," they bring species of fish and whales closer to extinction (9).

The National Parks present another instance of the working out of the tragedy of the commons. At present, they are open to all, without limit. The parks themselves are limited in extent—there is only one Yosemite Valley—whereas population seems to grow without limit. The values that visitors seek in the parks are steadily eroded. Plainly, we must soon cease to treat the parks as commons or they will be of no value to anyone.

What shall we do? We have several options. We might sell them off as private property. We might keep them as public property, but allocate the right to enter them. The allocation might be on the basis of wealth, by the use of an auction system. It might be on the basis of merit, as defined by some agreed-upon standards. It might be by lottery. Or it might be on a first-come, first-served basis, administered to long queues. These, I think, are all the reasonable possibilities. They are all objectionable. But we must choose—or acquiesce in the destruction of the commons that we call our National Parks.

Pollution

In a reverse way, the tragedy of the commons reappears in problems of pollution. Here it is not a question of taking something out of the commons, but of putting something in—sewage, or chemical, radioactive, and heat wastes into water; noxious and dangerous fumes into the air; and distracting and unpleasant advertising signs into the line of sight. The calculations of utility are much the same as before. The rational man finds that his share of the cost of the wastes he discharges into the commons is less than the cost of purifying his wastes before releasing them. Since this is true for everyone, we are locked into a system of "fouling our own nest," so long as we behave only as independent, rational, free-enterprisers.

The tragedy of the commons as a food basket is averted by private property, or something formally like it. But the air and waters surrounding us cannot readily be fenced, and so the tragedy of the commons as a cesspool must be prevented by different means, by coercive laws or taxing devices that make it cheaper for the polluter to treat his pollutants than to discharge them untreated. We have not progressed as far with the solution of this problem as we have with the first. Indeed, our particular concept of private property, which deters us from exhausting the positive resources of the earth, favors pollution. The owner of a factory on the bank of a stream—whose property extends to the middle of the stream—often has difficulty seeing why it is not his natural right to muddy the waters flowing past his door. The law, always behind the times, requires elaborate stitching and fitting to adapt it to this newly perceived aspect of the commons.

The pollution problem is a consequence of population. It did not much matter how a lonely American frontiersman disposed of his waste. "Flowing water purifies itself every 10 miles," my grandfather used to say, and the myth was near enough to the truth when he was a boy, for there were not too many people. But as population became denser, the natural chemical and biological recycling processes became overloaded, calling for a redefinition of property rights.

How To Legislate Temperance?

Analysis of the pollution problem as a function of population density uncovers a not generally recognized principle of morality, namely: *the morality of an act is a function of the state of the system at the time it is performed* (10). Using the commons as a cesspool does not harm the general public under frontier conditions, because there is no public; the same behavior in a metropolis is unbearable. A hundred and fifty years ago a plainsman could kill an American bison, cut out only the tongue for his dinner, and discard the rest of the animal. He was not in any important sense being wasteful. Today, with only a few thousand bison left, we would be appalled at such behavior.

In passing, it is worth noting that the morality of an act cannot be determined from a photograph. One does not know whether a man killing an elephant or setting fire to the grassland is harming others until one knows the total system in which his act appears. "One picture is worth a thousand words," said an ancient Chinese; but it may take 10,000 words to validate it. It is as tempting to ecologists as it is to reformers in general to try to persuade others by way of the photographic shortcut. But the essence of an argument cannot be photographed: it must be presented rationally—in words.

That morality is system-sensitive escaped the attention of most codifiers of ethics in the past. "Thou shalt not . . ." is the form of traditional ethical directives which make no allowance for particular circumstances. The laws of our society follow the pattern of ancient ethics, and therefore are poorly suited to governing a complex, crowded, changeable world. Our epicyclic solution is to augment statutory law with administrative law. Since it is practically impossible to spell out all the conditions under which it is safe to burn trash in the back yard or to run an automobile without smog-control, by law we delegate the details to bureaus. The result is administrative law, which is rightly feared for an ancient reason—*Quis custodiet ipsos custodes?*—"Who shall watch the watchers themselves?" John Adams said that we must have "a government of laws and not men." Bureau administrators, trying to evaluate the morality of acts in the total system, are singularly liable to corruption, producing a government by men, not laws.

Prohibition is easy to legislate (though not necessarily to enforce); but how do we legislate temperance? Experience indicates that it can be accomplished best through the mediation of administrative law. We limit possibilities unnecessarily if we suppose that the sentiment of *Quis custodiet* denies us the use of administrative law. We should rather retain the phrase as a perpetual reminder of fearful dangers we cannot avoid. The great challenge facing us now is to invent the corrective feedbacks that are needed to keep custodians honest. We must find ways to legitimate the needed authority of both the custodians and the corrective feedbacks.

Freedom To Breed Is Intolerable

The tragedy of the commons is involved in population problems in another way. In a world governed solely by the principle of "dog eat dog"—if indeed there ever was such a world—how many children a family had would not be a matter of public concern. Parents who bred too exuberantly would leave fewer descendants, not more, because they would be unable to care adequately for their children. David Lack and others have found that such a negative feedback demonstrably controls the fecundity of birds (11). But men are not birds, and have not acted like them for millenniums, at least.

If each human family were dependent only on its own resources; *if* the children of improvident parents starved to death; *if,* thus, overbreeding brought its own "punishment" to the germ line—*then* there would be no public interest in controlling the breeding of families. But our society is deeply committed to the welfare state (12), and hence is confronted with another aspect of the tragedy of the commons.

In a welfare state, how shall we deal with the family, the religion, the race, or the class (or indeed any distinguishable and cohesive group) that adopts overbreeding as a policy to secure its own aggrandizement (13)? To couple the concept of freedom to breed with the belief that everyone born has an equal right to the commons is to lock the world into a tragic course of action.

Unfortunately this is just the course of action that is being pursued by the United Nations. In late 1967, some 30 nations agreed to the following (14):

> The Universal Declaration of Human Rights describes the family as the natural and fundamental unit of society. It follows that any choice and decision with regard to the size of the family must irrevocably rest with the family itself, and cannot be made by anyone else.

It is painful to have to deny categorically the validity of this right; denying it, one feels as uncomfortable as a resident of Salem, Massachusetts, who denied the reality of witches in the 17th century. At the present time, in liberal quarters, something like a taboo acts to inhibit criticism of the United Nations. There is a feeling that the United Nations is "our last and best hope," that we shouldn't find fault with it; we shouldn't play into the hands of the archconservatives. However, let us not forget what Robert Louis Stevenson said: "The truth that is suppressed by friends is the readiest weapon of the enemy." If we love the truth we must openly deny the validity of the Universal Declaration of Human Rights, even though it is promoted by the United Nations. We should also join with Kingsley Davis (15) in attempting to get Planned Parenthood-World Population to see the error of its ways in embracing the same tragic ideal.

Conscience Is Self-Eliminating

It is a mistake to think that we can control the breeding of mankind in the long run by an appeal to conscience. Charles Galton Darwin made this point when he spoke on the centennial of the publication of his grandfather's great book. The argument is straightforward and Darwinian.

People vary. Confronted with appeals to limit breeding, some people will undoubtedly respond to the plea more than others. Those who have more children will produce a larger fraction of the next generation than those with more susceptible consciences. The difference will be accentuated, generation by generation.

In C. G. Darwin's words: "It may well be that it would take hundreds of generations for the progenitive instinct to develop in this way, but if it should do so, nature would have taken her revenge, and the variety *Homo contracipiens* would become extinct and would be replaced by the variety *Homo progenitivus*" (16).

The argument assumes that conscience or the desire for children (no matter which) is hereditary—but hereditary only in the most general formal sense. The result will be the same whether the attitude is transmitted through germ cells, or exosomatically, to use A. J. Lotka's term. (If one denies the latter possibility as well as the former, then what's the point of education?) The argument has here been stated in the context of the population problem, but it applies equally well to any instance in which society appeals to an individual exploiting a commons to restrain himself for the general good—by means of his conscience. To make such an appeal is to set up a selective system that works toward the elimination of conscience from the race.

Pathogenic Effects of Conscience

The long-term disadvantage of an appeal to conscience should be enough to condemn it; but has serious short-term disadvantages as well. If we ask a man who is exploiting a commons to desist "in the name of conscience," what are we saying to him? What does he hear? —not only at the moment but also in the wee small hours of the night when, half asleep, he remembers not merely the words we used but also the nonverbal communication cues we gave him unawares? Sooner or later, consciously or subconsciously, he senses that he has received two communications, and that they are contradictory: (i) (intended communication) "If you don't do as we ask, we will openly condemn you for not acting like a responsible citizen"; (ii) (the unintended communication) "If you *do* behave as we ask, we will secretly condemn you for a simpleton who can be shamed into standing aside while the rest of us exploit the commons."

Everyman then is caught in what Bateson has called a "double bind." Bateson and his co-workers have made a plausible case for viewing the double bind as an important causative factor in the genesis of schizophrenia (17). The double bind may not always be so damaging, but it always endangers the mental health of anyone to whom it is applied. "A bad conscience," said Nietzsche, "is a kind of illness."

To conjure up a conscience in others is tempting to anyone who wishes to extend his control beyond the legal limits. Leaders at the highest level succumb to this temptation. Has any President during the past generation failed to call on labor unions to moderate voluntarily their demands for higher wages, or to steel companies to honor voluntary guidelines on prices? I can recall none. The rhetoric used on such occasions is designed to produce feelings of guilt in noncooperators.

For centuries it was assumed without proof that guilt was a valuable, perhaps even an indispensable, ingredient of the civilized life. Now, in this post-Freudian world, we doubt it.

Paul Goodman speaks from the modern point of view when he says: "No good has ever come from feeling guilty, neither intelligence, policy, nor compassion. The guilty do not pay attention to the object but only to themselves, and not even to their own interests, which might make sense, but to their anxieties" (18).

One does not have to be a professional psychiatrist to see the consequences of anxiety. We in the Western world are just emerging from a dreadful two-centuries-long Dark Ages of Eros that was sustained partly by prohibition laws, but perhaps more effectively by the anxiety-generating mechanisms of education. Alex Comfort has told the story well in *The Anxiety Makers* (19); it is not a pretty one.

Since proof is difficult, we may even concede that the results of anxiety may sometimes, from certain points of view, be desirable. The larger question we should ask is whether, as a matter of policy, we should ever encourage the use of a technique the tendency (if not the intention) of which is psychologically pathogenic. We hear much talk these days of responsible parenthood; the coupled words are incorporated into the titles of some organizations devoted to birth control. Some people have proposed massive propaganda campaigns to instill responsibility into the nation's (or the world's) breeders. But what is the meaning of the word responsibility in this context? Is it not merely a synonym for the word conscience? When we use the word responsibility in the absence of substantial sanctions are we not trying to browbeat a free man in a commons into acting against his own interest? Responsibility is a verbal counterfeit for a substantial *quid pro quo*. It is an attempt to get something for nothing.

If the word responsibility is to be used at all, I suggest that it be in the sense Charles Frankel uses it (20). "Responsibility," says this philosopher, "is the product of definite social arrangements." Notice that Frankel calls for social arrangements—not propaganda.

Mutual Coercion
Mutually Agreed Upon

The social arrangements that produce responsibility are arrangements that create coercion, of some sort. Consider bank-robbing. The man who takes money from a bank acts as if the bank were a commons. How do we prevent such action? Certainly not by trying to control his behavior solely by a verbal appeal to his sense of responsibility. Rather than rely on propaganda we follow Frankel's lead and insist that a bank is not a commons; we seek the definite social arrangements that will keep it from becoming a commons. That we thereby infringe on the freedom of would-be robbers we neither deny nor regret.

The morality of bank-robbing is particularly easy to understand because we accept complete prohibition of this activity. We are willing to say "Thou shalt not rob banks," without providing for exceptions. But temperance also can be created by coercion. Taxing is a good coercive device. To keep downtown shoppers temperate in their use of parking space we introduce parking meters for short periods, and traffic fines for longer ones. We need not actually forbid a citizen to park as long as he wants to; we need merely make it increasingly expensive for him to do so. Not prohibition, but carefully biased options are what we offer him: A Madison Avenue man might call this persuasion; I prefer the greater candor of the word coercion.

Coercion is a dirty word to most liberals now, but it need not forever be so. As with the four-letter words, its dirtiness can be cleansed away by exposure to the light, by saying it over and over without apology or embarrassment. To many, the word coercion implies arbitrary decisions of distant and irresponsible bureaucrats; but this is not a necessary part of its meaning. The only kind of coercion I recommend is mutual coercion, mutually agreed upon by the majority of the people affected.

To say that we mutually agree to coercion is not to say that we are required to enjoy it, or even to pretend we enjoy it. Who enjoys taxes? We all grumble about them. But we accept compulsory taxes because we recognize that voluntary taxes would favor the conscienceless. We institute and (grumblingly) support taxes and other coercive devices to escape the horror of the commons.

An alternative to the commons need not be perfectly just to be preferable. With real estate and other material goods, the alternative we have chosen is the institution of private property coupled with legal inheritance. Is this system perfectly just? As a genetically trained biologist I deny that it is. It seems to me that, if there are to be differences in individual inheritance, legal possession should be perfectly correlated with biological inheritance—that those who are biologically more fit to be the custodians of property and power should legally inherit more. But genetic recombination continually makes a mockery of the doctrine of "like father, like son" implicit in our laws of legal inheritance. An idiot can inherit millions, and a trust fund can keep his estate intact. We must admit that our legal system of private property plus inheritance is unjust—but we put up with it because we are not convinced, at the moment, that anyone has invented a better system. The alternative of the commons is too horrifying to contemplate. Injustice is preferable to total ruin.

It is one of the peculiarities of the warfare between reform and the status quo that it is thoughtlessly governed by a double standard. Whenever a reform measure is proposed it is often defeated when its opponents triumphantly discover a flaw in it. As Kingsley Davis has pointed out (21), worshippers of the status quo sometimes imply that no reform is possible without unanimous agreement, an implication contrary to historical fact. As nearly as I can make out, automatic rejection of proposed reforms is based on one of two unconscious assumptions: (i) that the status quo is perfect; or (ii) that the choice we face is between reform and no action; if the proposed reform is imperfect, we presumably should take no action at all, while we wait for a perfect proposal.

But we can never do nothing. That which we have done for thousands of years is also action. It also produces evils. Once we are aware that the status quo is action, we can then compare its discoverable advantages and disadvantages with the predicted advantages and disadvantages of the proposed reform, discounting as best we can for our lack of experience. On the basis of such a comparison, we can make a rational decision which will not involve the unworkable assumption that only perfect systems are tolerable.

Recognition of Necessity

Perhaps the simplest summary of this analysis of man's population problems is this: the commons, if justifiable at all, is justifiable only under conditions of low-population density. As the human population has increased, the commons has had to be abandoned in one aspect after another.

First we abandoned the commons in food gathering, enclosing farm land and restricting pastures and hunting and fishing areas. These restrictions are still not complete throughout the world.

Somewhat later we saw that the commons as a place for waste disposal would also have to be abandoned. Restrictions on the disposal of domestic sewage are widely accepted in the Western world; we are still struggling to close the commons to pollution by automobiles, factories, insecticide sprayers, fertilizing operations, and atomic energy installations.

In a still more embryonic state is our recognition of the evils of the commons in matters of pleasure. There is almost no restriction on the propagation of sound waves in the public medium. The shopping public is assaulted with mindless music, without its consent. Our government is paying out billions of dollars to create supersonic transport which will disturb 50,000 people for every one person who is whisked from coast to coast 3 hours faster. Advertisers muddy the airwaves of radio and television and pollute the view of travelers. We are a long way from outlawing the commons in matters of pleasure. Is this because our Puritan inheritance makes us view pleasure as something of a sin, and pain (that is, the pollution of advertising) as the sign of virtue?

Every new enclosure of the commons involves the infringement of somebody's personal liberty. Infringements made in the distant past are accepted because no contemporary complains of a loss. It is the newly proposed infringements that we vigorously oppose; cries of "rights" and "freedom" fill the air. But what does "freedom" mean? When men mutually agreed to pass laws against robbing, mankind became more free, not less so. Individuals locked into the logic of the commons are free only to bring on universal ruin; once they see the necessity of mutual coercion, they become free to pursue other goals. I believe it was Hegel who said, "Freedom is the recognition of necessity."

The most important aspect of necessity that we must now recognize, is the necessity of abandoning the commons in breeding. No technical solution can rescue us from the misery of overpopulation. Freedom to breed will bring ruin to all. At the moment, to avoid hard decisions many of us are tempted to propagandize for conscience and respon-sible parenthood. The temptation must be resisted, because an appeal to independently acting consciences selects for the disappearance of all conscience in the long run, and an increase in anxiety in the short.

The only way we can preserve and nurture other and more precious freedoms is by relinquishing the freedom to breed, and that very soon. "Freedom is the recognition of necessity"—and it is the role of edu-cation to reveal to all the necessity of abandoning the freedom to breed. Only so, can we put an end to this aspect of the tragedy of the commons.

REFERENCES

1. J. B. Wiesner and H. F. York. *Sci. Amer.,* **211,** 4 (1964), 27.
2. G. Hardin. *Jour. Hered.,* **50,** 68 (1959); S. von Hoernor. *Science,* **137** (1962), 18.
3. J. von Neumann and O. Morgenstern. *Theory of Games and Eco-nomic Behavior.* Princeton, N.J.: Princeton University Press, 1947, p. 11.
4. J. H. Fremlin, *New Sci.,* 415 (1964), 285.
5. A. Smith. *The Wealth of Nations.* New York: Modern Library, 1937, p. 423.
6. W. F. Lloyd. *Two Lectures on the Checks to Population.* Oxford: Oxford University Press, 1833. Reprinted (in part) in G. Hardin (ed.), *Population, Evolution, and Birth Control.* San Francisco: W. H. Freeman & Co., 1964, p. 37.
7. A. N. Whitehead. *Science and the Modern World.* New York: Mentor Books, 1948, p. 17.
8. G. Hardin (ed.). *Population, Evolution, and Birth Control.* San Fran-cisco: W. H. Freeman & Co., 1964, p. 56.
9. S. McVay. *Sci. Amer.,* **216,** 8 (1966), 13.
10. J. Fletcher. *Situation Ethics.* Philadelphia: The Westminster Press, 1966.
11. D. Lack. *The National Regulation of Animal Numbers.* Oxford: Oxford University Press, 1954.
12. H. Girvetz. *From Wealth to Welfare.* Stanford: Stanford University Press, 1950.
13. G. Hardin. *Perspec. Biol. Med.,* **6,** 366 (1963).
14. U. Thant. *Int. Planned Parenthood News,* 168 (February 1968), 3.
15. K. Davis. *Science,* **158** (1967), 730.
16. S. Tax (ed.). *Evolution After Darwin,* Vol. 2. Chicago: University of Chicago Press, 1960, p. 469.
17. G. Bateson, D. D. Jackson, J. Haley and J. Weakland. *Behav. Sci.,* **1** (1956), 251.

18. P. Goodman. *New York Rev. Books,* **10,** 8 (May 23, 1968), 22.
19. A. Comfort. *The Anxiety Makers.* London: Nelson, 1967.
20. C. Frankel. *The Case for Modern Man.* New York: Harper & Row, 1955, p. 203.
21. J. D. Roslansky. *Genetics and the Future of Man.* New York: Appleton-Century-Crofts, 1966, p. 177.

Appendix B

Enforcement of the 1899 Refuse Act Through Citizen Action*

Persons who furnish information to the U.S. Attorney leading to the conviction of anyone violating the Refuse Act are entitled to half the fine.

1. What is Prohibited and Where. The 1899 Refuse Act is a powerful, but little used, weapon in our Federal arsenal of water pollution control enforcement legislation. Section 13 of the Act (Title 33, United States Code, section 407) prohibits *anyone,* including any individual, corporation, municipality, or group, from throwing, discharging, or depositing any refuse matter of any kind or any type from a vessel or from a shore-based building, structure, or facility into either (a) the Nation's navigable lakes, rivers, streams, and other navigable bodies of water, or (b) any tributary to such waters, unless he has first obtained a permit to do so. Navigable water includes water sufficient to float a boat or log at high water. This section of the Act applies to inland waters, coastal waters, and waters that flow across the boundaries of the United States and Canada and Mexico.

The term "refuse" has been broadly defined by the Supreme Court to include all foreign substances and pollutants. It includes solids, oils, chemicals, and other liquid pollutants. The only materials excepted from this general prohibition are those flowing from streets, such as from storm sewers, and from municipal sewers, which pass into the waterway in liquid form.

In addition, the section prohibits anyone from placing on the bank of any navigable waterway, or any tributary to such waterway, any material that could be washed into a waterway by ordinary or high water, or by storms or floods, or otherwise and would result in the obstruction of navigation.

* From The Honorable Henry S. Reuss, Chairman, Conservation and Natural Resources Subcommittee of the Committee on Government Operations.

II. Permits to Discharge. Section 13 of the Act authorizes the Secretary of the Army, acting through the Corps of Engineers, to permit the deposit of material into navigable waters under conditions prescribed by him. Regulations governing the issuance of permits are published in title 33 of the Code of Federal Regulations, Part 209.

III. Penalty for Violations. Violations of the Refuse Act are subject to criminal prosecution and penalties of a fine of not more than $2500 nor less than $500 for each day or instance of violation, or imprisonment for not less than 30 days nor more than 1 year, or both a fine and imprisonment (Title 33, United States Code, Section 411). A citizen, who informs the appropriate United States attorney about a violation and gives sufficient information to lead to conviction, is entitled to one-half of the fine set by the court. (See Section V of this outline).

IV. Procedure for Citizen to Seek Enforcement of Refuse Act.

A. The citizen having information about any discharge of refuse into navigable waters should first ascertain whether the discharge is authorized by Corps permit. If a permit is in effect; the citizen should endeavor to ascertain whether the permittee is complying with its terms. This information can be obtained from the appropriate office of the Corps of Engineers with jurisdiction over the particular waters into which the discharge occurs. Such information is available to the public under the Freedom of Information Act (5 U.S. Code 552; Public Law 90–23).

B. The Refuse Act specifically directs that the appropriate United States attorney shall "vigorously prosecute all offenders." (Title 33, United States Code, section 413.) In order to do so he needs adequate information to prove that the discharges were made and that they violated the law or the conditions of the permit. Furthermore, the statute specifies that the citizen's right to one-half of the fine is conditioned on his providing to the U.S. Attorney information sufficient to *lead to a conviction of the violator.*

In providing information to the U.S. Attorney, the citizen should make a detailed statement, sworn to before a notary or other officer authorized to administer oaths, setting forth:

(a) the nature of the refuse material discharged;

(b) the source and method of discharge;

(c) the location, name, and address of the person or persons causing or contributing to the discharge;

(d) the name of the waterway into which the discharge occurred;

(e) each date on which the discharge occurred;

(f) the names and addresses of all persons known to you, including yourself, who saw or knows about the discharges and could testify about them if necessary;

(g) a statement that the discharge is not authorized by Corps permit, or, if a permit was granted, state facts showing that the alleged violator is not complying with any condition of the permit;

(h) if the waterway into which the discharge occurred is not commonly known as navigable, or as a tributary to a navigable waterway, state facts to show such status;

(i) where possible, photographs should be taken, and samples of the pollutant or foreign substance collected in a clean jar which is then sealed. These should be labeled with information showing who took the photograph or sample, where, and when, and how; and who retained custody of the film or jar.

Where the material is liable to be washed into the waterway from its bank, in violation of the Act, similar information should also be provided to the U.S. Attorney in such a statement.

C. When a citizen furnishes information to the U.S. Attorney for the purpose of aiding in the prosecution of violators of the Refuse Act for past discharges, the citizen should also urge the U.S. Attorney to seek injunctions under the same Act to preclude future discharges, or other orders to require the discharges to remove pollutants already discharged. More frequent use of this authority by the government, together with criminal sanctions, will have lasting pollution control results.

V. "Qui Tam" Suits. Where a statute, such as the Refuse Act provides that part of a fine shall be paid to citizens who furnish sufficient information of a violation to lead to a conviction of the violator, and the government fails to prosecute within a reasonable period of time, the informer can bring his own suit, in the name of the government, against the violator to collect his portion of the penalty. This is called a *qui tam* suit. The informer has a financial interest in the fine and therefore can sue to collect it. The Supreme Court has upheld such *qui tam* suits. Some of these decisions are cited in the Report of the House Committee on Government Operations (House Report 91–917, March 18, 1970) entitled "Our Waters and Wetlands: How the Corps of Engineers Can Help Prevent Their Destruction and Pollution."

The United States district courts apparently have exclusive jurisdiction to hear and decide such suits. (Title 28, United States Code, section 1355.) In such a *qui tam* suit, the citizen must prove that the alleged violator did, in fact, violate the Act.

If the citizen should lose his suit, he probably would have to bear the cost of suing, including his lawyer's fees.

Proper Name Index

Subject Index*

* Italic numbers refer to illustrations.